D0583492

Handbook of
Youth and Justice

THE PLENUM SERIES IN CRIME AND JUSTICE

Series Editors:
James Alan Fox, *Northeastern University, Boston, Massachusetts*
Joseph Weis, *University of Washington, Seattle, Washington*

CONTEMPORARY MASTERS IN CRIMINOLOGY
Edited by Joan McCord and John H. Laub

CONTINUITY AND DISCONTINUITY IN CRIMINAL CAREERS
Paul E. Tracy and Kimberly Kempf-Leonard

CRIMINAL INCAPACITATION
William Spelman

DELINQUENCY CAREERS IN TWO BIRTH COHORTS
Paul E. Tracy, Marvin E. Wolfgang, and Robert M. Figlio

HANDBOOK OF PSYCHOLOGICAL APPROACHES WITH VIOLENT OFFENDERS
Contemporary Strategies and Issues
Edited by Vincent B. Van Hasselt and Michel Hersen

HANDBOOK OF YOUTH AND JUSTICE
Edited by Susan O. White

PERSONAL LIBERTY AND COMMUNITY SAFETY
Pretrial Release in the Criminal Court
John S. Goldkamp, Michael R. Gottfriedson, Peter R. Jones, and Doris Weiland

RACE AND THE JURY
Racial Disenfranchisement and the Search for Justice
Hiroshi Fukurai, Edgar W. Butler, and Richard Krooth

RAPE LAW REFORM
A Grassroots Revolution and Its Impact
Cassia Spohn and Julie Horney

A Continuation Order Plan is available for this series. A continuation order will bring delivery of each new volume immediately upon publication. Volumes are billed only upon actual shipment. For further information please contact the publisher.

Handbook of Youth and Justice

Edited by

Susan O. White
University of New Hampshire
Durham, New Hampshire

KLUWER ACADEMIC / PLENUM PUBLISHERS
NEW YORK, BOSTON, DORDRECHT, LONDON, MOSCOW

Library of Congress Cataloging-in-Publication Data

Handbook of youth and justice/edited by Susan O. White.
p. ; cm.
Includes bibliographical references and index.
ISBN 0-306-46339-3
1. Juvenile justice, Administration of. 2. Juvenile courts. 3. Criminal justice, Administration of. 4. Juvenile delinquents—Legal status, laws, etc. 5. Juvenile delinquents—Family relationships. 6. Adolescent psychology. 7. Child welfare—Government policy. 8. Child abuse—Government policy. I. White, Susan O.

HV9069 .H312 2000
364.36'0973—dc21

00-023857

ISBN: 0-306-46339-3

233 Spring Street, New York, N.Y. 10013

http://www.wkap.nl/

10 9 8 7 6 5 4 3 2 1

A C.I.P. record for this book is available from the Library of Congress

Printed in the United States of America

Contributors

Rosemary Barberet, Scarman Centre, University of Leicester, Leicester LE1 7QA, United Kingdom

Monica Bartlett, College of Criminal Justice, Northeastern University, Boston, Massachusetts 02115

Jodi Brown, Bureau of Justice Statistics, US Department of Justice, Washington, DC 20531

Robert J. Bursik, Jr., Department of Criminology and Criminal Justice, University of Missouri at St. Louis, St. Louis, Missouri 63121

Stephen J. Ceci, Department of Human Development, Cornell University, Ithaca, New York 14853

Meda Chesney-Lind, Women's Studies Program, University of Hawaii at Manoa, Honolulu, Hawaii 96822

Angela Crossman, Department of Human Development, Cornell University, Ithaca, New York 14853

James O. Finckenauer, International Center, National Institute of Justice, Washington, DC 20531

David Finkelhor, Crimes against Children Research Center, Family Research Laboratory, Department of Sociology, University of New Hampshire, Durham, New Hampshire 03824

James Alan Fox, College of Criminal Justice, Northeastern University, Boston, Massachusetts 02115

Richard J. Gelles, Center for the Study of Youth Policy, School of Social Work, University of Pennsylvania, Philadelphia, Pennsylvania 19104-6214

Livia Gilstrap, Department of Human Development, Cornell University, Ithaca, New York 14853

Patricia Y. Hashima, Institute on Family and Neighborhood Life, Clemson University, Clemson, South Carolina 29634-0132

Mary Lyn Huffman, Department of Psychology, Rhodes College, Memphis, Tennessee, 38112

Dorothy Imrich, Department of Communication, University of California, Santa Barbara, California 93106

Daniel A. Krauss, Department of Psychology, Claremont McKenna College, Claremont, California 91711-6420

Lauren J. Krivo, Department of Sociology, Ohio State University, Columbus, Ohio 43210

Marvin D. Krohn, Department of Sociology, University at Albany, Albany, New York 12222

Daniel Linz, Law and Society, and Department of Communication, University of California, Santa Barbara, California 93106

Susan Ehrlich Martin, Prevention Research Branch, National Institute on Alcohol Abuse and Alcoholism, Rockville, Maryland 20892

Joan McCord, Criminal Justice Department, Temple University, Philadelphia, Pennsylvania 19104

Mallie J. Paschall, Pacific Institute for Research and Evaluation, Chapel Hill, North Carolina 27514-2866

Ruth D. Peterson, Department of Sociology, Ohio State University, Columbus, Ohio 43210

Bruce D. Sales, Department of Psychology, University of Arizona, Tucson, Arizona 85721

Matthew Scullin, Department of Human Development, Cornell University, Ithaca, New York 14853

James F. Short, Jr., Department of Sociology, Washington State University, Pullman, Washington 99164-4014

Simon I. Singer, Department of Sociology, SUNY at Buffalo, Buffalo, New York 14260

Terence P. Thornberry, School of Criminal Justice, University at Albany, Albany, New York 12222

Maria B. Vélez, Department of Sociology, Ohio State University, Columbus, Ohio 43210

Susan O. White, Department of Political Science, University of New Hampshire, Durham, New Hampshire 03824

Cathy Spatz Widom, Department of Psychiatry, New Jersey Medical School, Newark, New Jersey 07107-3000

Barbara Bennett Woodhouse, University of Pennsylvania Law School, Philadelphia, Pennsylvania 19104

Mary Ann Zager, Division of Criminal Justice, Florida Gulf Coast University, Fort Myers, Florida 33965-6565

Preface

When approached by Plenum to put together a volume of social science research on the topic of "youth and justice," I found the interdisciplinary challenge of such a project intriguing. Having spent 2 years as Director of the Law and Social Science Program at the National Science Foundation, I was well aware of the rich diversity of research that could fit within that topic. I also knew that excellent research on youth and justice was coming from different communities of researchers who often were isolated from each other in their respective disciplines as psychologists, sociologists, criminologists, or policy analysts. I saw this project as an opportunity to break down some of this isolation by introducing these researchers—and their work—to each other and to the broader community of social scientists interested in law and justice.

There was another gap, or set of gaps, to be bridged as well. The juvenile justice system and the criminal justice system differ in significant ways, and the civil justice system, which is a major venue for issues of youth and justice, is yet another separate world. Few researchers are likely to know the whole picture. For example, a focus on juvenile justice often ignores the extent to which civil justice proceedings shape the lives of young people through divorce, custody, adoption, family preservation policies, and other actions (and vice versa). Yet each of these three justice systems can have significant effects on the lives of anyone who is below the age of majority—effects to which adults are not subject.

Young people are treated differently than adults by the law and its enforcers, and their behavior with respect to the law raises different questions. Young people are particularly vulnerable before the power of the law because they have neither the full rights nor the autonomous status that protects and empowers adults. Indeed, they often are dependent on the law for protection even while the law denies them legitimacy as full-fledged claimants. At the same time, young people often are the most difficult for the law to deal with in the exercise of its appropriate authority. It is fitting, therefore, that youth and justice should be treated as a single topic. Since most researchers tend to focus exclusively on juvenile justice or criminal justice or civil justice, this volume is an attempt to bridge these disciplinary gaps by providing a broader picture of the topic youth and justice.

Beyond the specific focus on youth and justice, the diversity of the interdisciplinary field of law and social science encompasses a number of perspectives. At least four can be identified: (1) the scholarly study of law, including jurisprudence; (2) legal practice; (3) the sociology (and anthropology, political science, and psychology) of law; and (4) transformative legal analysis. These perspectives often seem to clash, sometimes deliberately and passionately but seldom with malice aforethought. More problematic is the propensity of each perspective to ignore the others. It is my view that each is the weaker for that propensity, a victim of intellectual isolation and consequent inbreeding. On the premise that each perspective can learn much from the others, and that truth has many parts, it is my inclination to err on the side of inclusivity. Most of the research in this volume represents the perspective of social science, but readers will detect the flavors and some of the passions of all four perspectives. That is my editorial intent.

A major purpose of this volume, therefore, is to bring different perspectives together as a way of breaking down interdisciplinary barriers. It is my hope that the volume will become a catalyst for intellectual exchange across the disciplines that comprise the broad field of law and social science research. Its chapters do not exhaust the many topics that could be included under the rubric "youth and justice," of course. Each chapter was written especially for this volume as a vehicle to encourage further research. They not only are original contributions but also seek to define an important aspect of youth and justice for future research. Perhaps a future volume will expand in directions that are not now obvious but will become apparent to a reader who sees a problem in a new light and recasts a research question in different terms.

Such a result is what Felice Levine and Bruce Sales had in mind when they asked me to edit this volume. I want to thank them for encouraging this undertaking, my Plenum editor Eliot Werner for his support, and the authors for their efforts and their valuable contributions to interdisciplinary research.

Susan O. White

Contents

Part VII. Administration of Justice

Part I

Law and Social Science Perspectives on Youth and Justice

1

Understanding Victimization and Offending

Definitional Issues

SUSAN O. WHITE

YOUTH AND JUSTICE AS INTERDISCIPLINARY RESEARCH

The study of law and society has drawn interest from many different disciplines. Beginning with sometimes awkward discussions between academic lawyers and sociologists of law some 40 years ago, scholars of various stripes have created a broad and lively interdisciplinary field of study. Indeed, the field is now so broad that no single network of scholarly communication currently exists, even when the focus of inquiry is seemingly well defined. "Youth and justice" is an obvious example because it is the focus of specialized inquiry for a number of disciplines: law, sociology, psychology, anthropology, political science, social work, criminology, each of which conforms to its own disciplinary constitution and perspective. A major purpose of this volume is to bring these different perspectives together as a way of breaking down interdisciplinary barriers.

Breaking down the intellectual isolation of these parts will allow each perspective to better understand the kinds of contributions that can flow from the others. The scholarly study of law is different from its practical applications in many respects. While social scientists eschew the doctrinal analysis that is so dear to the scholars of law, they share the goal of understanding the law: that is, what particular laws mean to the actors in the different contexts of legislative intent and judicial enforcement. They also share the legal practitioner's desire to understand how the law works in practice (which is, of course, often quite different from the scholars' vision or legislators' intent). Social science has the further goal of understanding the effects of law on the society and its members. This goal requires taking theoretical positions for the purposes of explanation. These are not legal theories, such as Aquinas' natural law or

---

SUSAN O. WHITE • Department of Political Science, University of New Hampshire, Durham, New Hampshire 03824.

Handbook of Youth and Justice, edited by White. Kluwer Academic / Plenum Publishers, New York, 2001.

Hart's legal positivism, but rather theories that purport to explain human and organizational behavior.

Over all, however, a certain inescapable normative aura persists, which emanates from the subject matter of law itself. Many social scientists would deny any normative aspect to their work, while others would embrace it. The difference between these positions often may be found in the methodology each researcher chooses to employ. But counting or not counting, "hard" or "soft" analysis, are matters of style and not the requisite test of "truth." No methodology is a sufficient—or even necessary—stepping stone to truth (although there certainly are degrees of precision in the statements that can be made on the basis of whichever methodology is employed). On this premise, therefore, I have chosen to present research from a variety of methodologies, illustrating the basic coherence of the interdisciplinary study of law and social science despite its diversities.

This volume contains work by scholars of law as well as by quantitative social scientists; it presents experimental and other statistical studies of behavior as well as descriptive analyses of legal practice and institutions. Underlying all the chapters is that inescapable normative aura, for most law and social science research is activated by an interest in the ways in which the powerful institutions of the law affect our lives. This will be most obvious in the fact that most of the authors designed their research in light of public policy issues and apply their findings accordingly. In short, the volume is clearly about both youth and justice.

DEFINITIONAL ISSUES

Much social science research must contend with a variety of definitional issues. This problem is especially acute for research that relies on official records, but it is a problem that besets all scientific research for the simple reason that science is by definition a cumulative enterprise. In order to build on the work of others, or even to compare data, it is necessary to use the same measures. Data sources do not automatically provide standard measures of events or activities or attitudes or behaviors. Official records vary alarmingly from jurisdiction to jurisdiction, especially across the multitudinous boundary lines that mark off legal jurisdictions in the United States and its states and communities. Standardization of official records is work very much in progress, and then only after much pressure from the federal government. Most assume that full standardization may never occur.

Even if official standardization could come about, variations in reporting will occur because of differences in social attitudes from region to region and across class and gender lines. As socialization varies, so do perceptions about what is serious or dangerous or trivial or private. Such variations create differences in the laws themselves across states and communities. Even when the laws are uniform, the perception of what is clearly a crime in some jurisdictions does not make it to the files in others. In addition, political considerations often cause the official reporters (e.g., police) to exaggerate or minimize the size of a statistic; when next year's budget or election depends on the size of a crime statistic, for example, there are many ways to reduce or inflate the numbers.

Reporting also is problematic for the accuracy of data from official records just because they are official: that is, many events and behaviors are never reported to officials. As will be illustrated in several of the chapters in this volume, the local official records that form the basis of the FBI's Uniform Crime Reports (UCR) show considerably lesser rates of crime than does the National Crime Victimization Survey (NCVS). Although generally considered the most accurate measure of crime rates in the United States, even the NCVS poses problems for researchers. For example, definitions of offenses are so broad and/or ambiguous that some behaviors overlap, making it difficult if not impossible to identify them in the database. Also, the age cutoff in the reporting sample poses special problems for those doing research on children.

In addition to problems with official records and reporting, researchers face definitional issues with respect to categorizing for common use the behaviors they are attempting to study. For example, what qualifies as victimization? The federal government in effect took this issue out of the hands of the larger research community when it established the NCVS in the 1970s. Since the data collection is federally funded and controlled, most researchers rely on the resulting data. While the NCVS has served social science research very well, it does exclude (through omission or ambiguity) kinds of victimization that some researchers on children consider essential. For example, questions about "normal" physical assaults between children or corporal punishment in the family cannot be answered through standard data sources such as the NCVS. Instead, researchers must develop special funding for very expensive new surveys, which funding agencies then hope will prove broadly useful to the research community.

Other examples of definitional problems include what to categorize as gang activity and how to define the standard for "in the best interests of the child" in custody disputes. The gang problem occurs because there are many different views of what is "normal," or "good," or "bad" group behavior among young people. The term itself carries emotional and even ideological baggage, which means that political considerations and even issues about what kinds of research can or cannot be supported by public funding can influence or control the research enterprise. In an entirely different venue, researchers who are interested in child custody issues have found that there is no common operational definition of the "best interests of the child." Indeed, it is difficult to talk about a standard at all, let alone compare cases or the status of custody standards and practices across legal jurisdictions. There are many more such examples in this volume.

YOUTH AND JUSTICE

Finally, we come to the meat of this volume. The volume is divided into six sections, with an introductory chapter by Finkelhor, Paschall, and Hashima that poses a variety of questions about youth and justice. The chapter describes five contexts in which youths encounter the justice system. The authors not only sketch out the wide range of situations that draw children and youth into contact with various authorities but they also convey the complexity of the issues facing the justice system.

The first section of the volume deals with a variety of forms of victimization. While not exhaustive, the section covers a range of topics. In Chapter 3, Cathy Spatz Widom reviews the literature on child abuse and neglect, providing considerable detail about this central problem. Widom notes that existing research suggests the existence of a "cycle of violence" in which victims grow up to become perpetrators. She points out that retrospective research designs are weak not only because of the fallibility of memory but also because they cannot provide valid data to test the cycle of violence hypothesis. Widom asserts that her prospective cohorts design has provided data that suggest there are gender, race, and ethnicity differences in the consequences of child abuse and neglect.

David Finkelhor and his associates are among the most prolific and creative contributors to the child victimization literature. Chapter 4 by Finkelhor and Hashima is a good example of their leadership in this area. They propose a new field of "developmental victimology" to take account of the very different ways that victimization can occur across the life span. They discuss examples of definitional problems in existing data, noting the lack of data on corporal punishment, on the effects of witnessing violence, and on child prostitution. Even so, they argue, existing data sources demonstrate the disproportionate victimization of children. Their chapter provides an excellent statistical profile of youth victimization.

In Chapter 5, Daniel Linz and Dorothy Imrich provide a comprehensive review of the issues and literature concerning child pornography, both criminological and psychological. They discuss the production of child pornography and its effects on the children involved. They also review and assess the evidence of the effects of pornography on behavior. Linz and Imrich then put this social science information into the legal context, discussing the various efforts to regulate pornography including legislation, court decisions, and enforcement. The chapter ends with a provocative and instructive look at child pornography in cyberspace.

The second section of the volume focuses on offending. It begins with a lucid review of demographic data in Chapter 6 by Fox, Brown, Zager, and Bartlett. The chapter reports homicide data based on the age structure of American society and then on age and race. The authors confine their analyses to homicide because it is the only major crime that is not subject (to any significant extent) to reporting error. The chapter draws important conclusions about the importance of demographic change, and of race as well as age. This is a controversial topic today and these authors' argument in support of their conclusions is an important contribution to the public policy debate as well as to social scientific understanding of demographic change.

Chapter 7 looks at gender differences in offending, focusing in particular on the behavior of girls. "Girls, Violence, and Delinquency: Popular Myths and Persistent Problems" by Meda Chesney-Lind provides an extensive review of data on gender differences. It also considers the very different problems faced by girls than those faced by boys in situations ranging from status offenses such as running away and truancy to gangs. Since most studies of delinquency have focused on boys, the chapter sheds welcome new light on issues raised by different treatment based on gender.

Chapter 8 is an extensive review of data on behavior, interventions, and public policy issues. Susan Martin discusses the prevalence of underage drinking, the use and misuse of alcohol by underage youth, and the problems that result. Particularly interesting is her review of various legal changes and their effects, as well as the enforcement issues that these legal strategies pose. Martin concludes with a provocative discussion of different kinds of interventions, their successes and failures, and the need for future research to provide a better knowledge base for success.

The third section presents two chapters illustrating cross-cultural analyses of youth and justice. In Chapter 9, James Finckenauer reports on his ongoing work comparing the attitudes and behaviors of Russian and US youth. Finckenauer uses various measures of legal values to test perceptions of fairness and authority in each population. He also discusses the juvenile justice systems and reviews crime statistics for youths in each country.

Rosemary Barberet presents juvenile crime statistics for a number of European countries in Chapter 10. She notes the lack of common categories or even a central depository for such data as yet in the European Union, making true comparative analyses impossible for now. The potential for meaningful comparisons across different but largely contiguous cultures is an intriguing prospect for the future. Barberet also compares the criminological approaches in Europe with those in the United States, finding some interesting and provocative differences in the kinds of offenses that draw the attention of researchers and policymakers on the two sides of the Atlantic.

In the fourth section, researchers focus on different environmental influences that are commonly thought to be major factors in the production of youth victimization and offending. Joan McCord, in Chapter 11, discusses the debate over heritability versus child rearing, exposing some common misconceptions. She also comments on the various literatures on these topics and briefly reviews the literature on the effects of both physical and economic environments as well. She then focuses on child rearing, describing three ways in which child-rearing practices can influence child development: (1) through conveying values; (2) through supporting (or not) the development of family ties; and (3) through establishing the legitimacy of different kinds of interpersonal relations.

James Short tackles the question of gang influence in Chapter 12. As the title of his chapter suggests, Short raises a number of questions about common perceptions of gangs. He reviews the literature on gangs, noting the variation in the different issues that receive attention: purpose? activities? violence? ethnicity? criminal orientation? He makes clear that definitional problems make it difficult to do quality research in this field. Short argues that there are different types of "gangs" and that researchers should look at both the individual characteristics of members and at group processes. He also suggests that the role of a purported "gang" in the community is a key variable to be explored.

The influence of the community on youth behavior is the focus of Robert Bursik's Chapter 13. Reviewing basic literature, he describes the historical change in the way the concept of community has been understood: from analyzing social organization to studying social disorganization. He discusses the importance of relational networks in understanding how individuals and the community interact. Finally, Bursik focuses in particular on the literature that deals with the effects of economic deprivation on youth development and behavior.

Peterson, Krivo, and Vélez enlarge on Bursik's discussion in Chapter 14. They review and discuss the assumptions that have activated concern over the effects of racial segregation on the part of both policymakers and social scientists. They focus in particular on how social isolation affects attitudes toward community and perceptions of disadvantage and argue that social isolation is a major mechanism leading to high rates of homicide. The authors identify a number of gaps in knowledge that hamper better understanding of the pathologies in social isolation and other effects of racial segregation and provide an extensive and sophisticated agenda for needed research on these complex questions.

The fifth section includes three chapters that look at different ways to explain behavior that affects youth and justice. In Chapter 15, Thornberry and Krohn present their argument for one influential theory of delinquency. They apply interaction theory to the controversial question of continuity versus change in delinquent careers. Why do most juveniles eventually cease their delinquent careers, while others persist in delinquency and then adult crime? The authors discuss the complexity of the problem of explanation and propose interactional theory as a way of making sense of the voluminous data on delinquency. They review the literature in light of the theory, focusing on such issues as the significance of what is called early onset and the effects of social and economic deficits.

Susan White reviews the controversies over the applicability of moral/legal development theory to understanding youthful propensity toward offending or not offending in Chapter 16. White discusses the many critiques of this literature, including design and measurement problems, the rigidity of the theoretical position, and problems in applying the theory across gender, class, and cultural categories. She then proposes a way of looking at reasoning about issues of justice using data from group deliberations. The chapter includes analyses of extensive excerpts from the deliberations to illustrate this methodology. White concludes that the power of social norms, as they are activated through group processes, have an important influence on individual reasoning about issues of justice.

In Chapter 17, Stephen Ceci and his associates present data from a series of experiments designed to determine, progressively, the extent to which children remember sexual abuse accurately. The chapter brilliantly illustrates the use of experimental design to answer certain kinds of questions. The precision of the methodology, as applied to a highly controversial topic, exemplifies one way in which social science can make a telling contribution to the knowledge necessary for making appropriate decisions about public policy. The authors begin and end their chapter by asking the reader to focus on the sometimes controversial role of social scientists in the policy arena.

The last section of this volume presents four chapters on issues concerning the administration of justice. These chapters all view children and youth as objects (and often victims) of the justice system and government policies. In Chapter 18, Simon Singer looks at the organizational aspects of juvenile justice. He first provides a historical review of the various ideological bases for different perspectives in the literature, setting the stage for understanding the conflicting protective versus punitive characteristics of juvenile justice and the current debate over its appropriate direction. He describes variations in actual juvenile justice systems that demonstrate the extent to which local legal culture colors the operation of juvenile justice in reality. Singer also reviews what he calls "soft" and "hard" approaches and their organizational effects, the role of diversion strategies, and the impact of various legal decisions.

Richard Gelles broadens the perspective on the administration of justice to include all contacts between the justice system and children in Chapter 19. He analyzes the goal of family preservation as an official policy of family courts, social welfare agencies, and juvenile justice to determine its effectiveness. Gelles begins with a historical review of family preservation policy, including the effects of the "discovery" of child abuse in the 1960s. He reviews explanations of parenting problems in light of attempts to enforce family preservation even in the face of serious and continuing abuse problems. Finally, Gelles focuses on the dilemma of intervention and underscores the difficulty of choosing whether and how to intervene in situations where children are at serious risk of abuse in alternative care as well as within their families.

Barbara Bennett Woodhouse provides a comprehensive historical review of the legal literature on children's rights in Chapter 20. This highly useful review raises many issues about the legal treatment of children in the past and present and in cases ranging from divorce and custody to juvenile justice. Woodhouse makes clear the legal complexities involved as social attitudes and practices toward children changed. As the legal status of children changed, so eventually did the status of human rights claims. Her analysis poses many questions for social policy, which she discusses in terms of five human rights principles. She finds that these principles often conflict in the case of children, making policy decisions doubly difficult. Her discussion covers current policy arenas including international.

Finally, in Chapter 21, Daniel Krauss and Bruce Sales tackle the issues surrounding child custody decisions. They review the legal history of the "in the best interests of the child" standard (BICS) and its enforcement. The authors then present empirical evidence of its effects, drawing on literature from various fields. They discuss the effects of child characteristics, parental characteristics, and family process on a child's adjustment after divorce. Krauss and Sales argue that the BICS itself is so ill defined that accurate readings of its effects, positive or negative, cannot be determined. They focus on the role of experts in custody decisions, especially in light of the definitional ambiguities in the standard. Their recommendations for future research include a plea to focus on what leads to successful adjustment rather than on the pathologies that dominate current literature.

CONCLUSION

These chapters lay out the core of existing research on key topics concerning youth and justice. They review literature, present data, and illustrate different methodologies used in the field. They are as various as the several disciplines that engage in law and social science research, but together they demonstrate a coherence of intellectual concerns. Each chapter has put forward a rationale and suggestions for a research agenda based on the analysis of the conceptual and design problems and gaps identified in the literature. In these terms, the volume should provide a useful guide for future research.

The volume also should illustrate that different methodologies, and even different perspectives on the scientific enterprise, can coexist productively. In the case of youth and justice, manifest policy concerns provide a natural center around which law and social science research can coalesce. The different contributions to this volume, despite variations in approach, are all clearly about both youth and justice.

2

Juvenile Crime Victims in the Justice System

DAVID FINKELHOR, MALLIE J. PASCHALL, and PATRICIA Y. HASHIMA

The literature on juvenile justice is largely concerned with offenders: topics such as juvenile courts, the rights of juvenile offenders, the adjudication of juveniles as adults, and the effectiveness of delinquency prevention programs. But juveniles have contact with the justice system in another role—in the role of victims—and this is not an intersection that has been addressed nearly so intensively by research or public policy. Child victimization is a social problem of no less importance than child offending. Moreover, child victims occupy as much time and attention and resources within the justice system as offenders. But the matter of child victims in the justice system has not been addressed nearly so systematically.

The purpose of this chapter is to highlight the main contexts in which juvenile victims have contact with the justice system, that is, with the police, the prosecutors, and the juvenile and criminal courts. We assemble some of the data that give some dimensions to the frequency or intensity of this contact. We also highlight some of the major policy questions that are considered or should be considered in trying to improve the quality of justice system response to these juvenile victims.

In considering the contexts in which juvenile victims have contact with the justice system, it may be useful to make two important conceptual distinctions. First, situations where the child's own victimization is the major focus of justice system involvement (e.g., a child abduction) can be distinguished from situations where the child's victimization is not the focus of the involvement even though it may be closely or even causally related to that involvement. Thus, for example, a large proportion of runaways and other status offenders picked up by police are victims of abuse or neglect (which may be why they have run away), but this is not the initial focus for justice system involvement. We might call this difference primary versus

DAVID FINKELHOR • Crimes against Children Research Center, Family Research Laboratory, Department of Sociology, University of New Hampshire, Durham, New Hampshire 03824. **MALLIE J. PASCHALL** • Pacific Institute for Research and Evaluation, Chapel Hill, North Carolina 27514-2866. **PATRICIA Y. HASHIMA** • Institute on Family and Neighborhood Life, Clemson University, Clemson, South Carolina 29634-0132.

Handbook of Youth and Justice, edited by White. Kluwer Academic / Plenum Publishers, New York, 2001.

secondary focus justice system contexts. Second, child victims, of both the primary focus and secondary focus types just described, get involved in the justice system at two levels: the criminal and noncriminal level. There are different issues raised by each of these two levels.

Although these two dimensions might suggest a fourfold typology, in reality we would propose distinguishing the following five justice contexts in which juvenile victims appear:

1. *Juvenile victims involved in criminal investigations and prosecutions.* These would include abducted children and sexually assaulted children. It also would include children victimized by other children, if these acts are the subjects of police intervention. We also would include in this category child witnesses to crimes (such as an unharmed companion in a drive-by shooting), what might be called vicarious victims. All such children go through investigations and perhaps may be called on to provide testimony or be exposed to publicity or stigma as a result of their involvement.
2. *Juvenile victims involved in child protection actions.* These would include abused and neglected children, but of course there is some overlap with the victims involved in the criminal justice system. In addition to the investigatory component, the justice system plays a big role in determining the living and family situation of such children.
3. *Children victimized by domestic violence and custodial abductions.* Children enter the penumbra of the justice system when it adjudicates domestic violence and custody offenses. Children in homes with domestic violence generally have witnessed violence or themselves been victimized. Children who have been subject to abductions often have been victimized through deprivation of contact with family, friends, and neighbors. Such cases appear in both the civil and criminal side of the justice system, and although there is some overlap here with issues of child maltreatment and criminal victimization, frequently for these children the justice context is one where it is not their own victimization that is the initial focus of justice activity but the grievance or victimization of a parent. This puts the problem for child victims on somewhat different footing.
4. *Child victims involved in criminal offenses.* Large percentages of children arrested and adjudicated for criminal delinquent behavior also have histories of victimization that play a part in the trajectory that leads to their offenses. It is not clear to what extent the justice system is aware of this victimization history or takes it into account in its deliberation and adjudication.
5. *Child victims involved in status offenses.* Children get picked up by police and adjudicated by courts for running away, truancy, disobedience, and curfew violations. As with criminal offenders, large percentages of these children are victims of family and community violence. The victimization frequently becomes an important issue in the resolution of the case, even if it was not the initial focus of the justice system contact.

In the following sections of this chapter, we will take up each of these justice system contexts and try to describe what is known and what may need to be known about the dimensions of the problem and the important justice system issues.

JUVENILE VICTIMS INVOLVED IN CRIMINAL INVESTIGATIONS AND PROSECUTIONS

Juveniles are among the most criminally victimized segments of the population. The National Crime Victimization Survey (NCVS) shows that 12- to 17-year-olds have rates two to three times higher than adults for rape, robbery, and simple and aggravated assaults (Table 1)

Table 1. Violent Crime Victimizations of Juveniles and Adults: Population Estimates and Ratios, 1994[a]

	Number of victimizations		Rate of victimizations (per 1000)		
Type of crime	Juveniles aged 12–17	Adults	Juveniles aged 12–17	Adults	Juvenile–adult rate ratio
Violent crimes	2,625,600	8,235,100	116	43	2.7**
Rape/sexual assault	76,500	356,300	3	2	1.5
Rape/attempted rape	43,300	248,700	2	1	2.0
Sexual assault[b]	19,300[c]	54,200	1	0.3	3.3
Verbal threat of rape/sexual assault	6,900[c]	35,800	0.3	0.2	1.5
Unwanted sexual contact without force	7,000[c]	17,600[c]	0.3	0.1	3.0
Robbery	263,900	1,034,900	12	5	2.4
Complete robbery	160,900	634,200	7	3	2.3
With injury	50,300	237,400	2	1	2.0
Without injury	110,600	396,900	5	2	2.5
Attempted robbery	103,000	400,600	5	2	2.5
With injury	12,000[c]	109,800	1[c]	1	1.0
Without injury	91,000	290,900	4	2	2.0
Assault	2,285,200	6,843,900	101	36	2.8**
Aggravated	594,600	1,883,600	26	10	2.6
Completed with injury	165,800	512,700	7	3	2.3
Attempted with weapon	184,200	538,400	8	3	2.7
Threatened with weapon	244,500	832,500	11	4	2.8
Simple	1,690,600	4,960,300	75	26	2.9**
With injury	418,100	1,047,900	19	5	3.8*
Without injury	667,700	1,678,700	30	9	3.3*
Verbal threat of assault	604,700	2,233,700	27	12	2.3

[a]From Hashima and Finkelhor (1999).
[b]Includes sexual attack with minor or serious assault and sexual assault wihtout injury.
[c]Estimate is based on fewer than 10 cases.
$*P < .05$
$**P < .01$

(Hashima & Finkelhor, 1999). The rates of victimizations involving injuries and weapons also are substantially higher for juveniles compared to adults taken as a group. Juveniles also have disproportionately high rates of property crime victimization (Finkelhor & Ormrod, in press).

Unlike delinquency, vulnerability to crime victimization precedes the adolescent period and encompasses early childhood. Substantial numbers of assaults and sexual assaults occur to preadolescent children, and many of the acts of child abuse (discussed below), which occur to even very young children at the hands of family members and caretakers, are nominally criminal acts as well. Unfortunately, however, data from the NCVS do not cover crimes occurring to children younger than age 12. Nor does the current Uniform Crime Report data from local police agencies break down crime reports according to victim age. However, the new National Incidence-Based Reporting System (NIBRS) being implemented in a variety of states soon may provide the basis for some estimates. Preliminary estimates from twelve states suggest that, by virtue of not counting victims under 12, NCVS estimates of crime victimization may be missing over half the sexual assaults and a quarter of the other assaults (Finkelhor & Ormrod, 2000).

Like delinquency, only a fraction of juvenile victimization comes to the attention of the police (Table 2), but juvenile victims are still overrepresented in police reports. Twenty-nine

Table 2. Police-Reported Violent Crime Victimizations of Juveniles and Adults[a]

Type of violent crime	Juveniles (12–17) Total number of crimes	Juveniles (12–17) % reported	Juveniles (12–17) % of all juvenile reports to police	Adults (18+) Total number of crimes	Adults (18+) % reported	Adults (18+) % of all adult reports to police
All violent crimes	2,625,600	28.9	—	8,235,100	45.6	—
Rape/sexual assault	76,500	46.4	4.7	356,300	28.5	2.7
Rape/attempted	43,300	39.5	2.2	248,700	28.2	1.9
Sexual assault	19,300	48.0	1.2	54,200	41.5	0.6
Verbal threat or unwanted contact	13,900	65.5	1.2	53,400	16.9	0.2
Robbery	263,900	38.8	13.5	1,034,900	59.6	16.4
Completed	160,900	48.4	10.2	634,200	68.5	11.6
Attempted	103,000	23.9	3.2	400,600	45.5	4.8
Assault	2,285,200	27.2	81.8	6,843,900	44.4	80.9
Aggravated	594,600	38.9	51.3	1,883,600	55.6	27.9
Simple	1,690,600	23.0	30.5	4,960,300	40.1	53.0

[a]From 1994 NCVS and Hashima and Finkelhor (1999).

percent of NCVS-reported crime victimizations for 12- to 17-year-olds are reported to the police, a substantially lower rate than the 46% of adult reported victimizations (Finkelhor & Ormrod, 2000). Moreover, it is recognized that much violent victimization, especially among youth, is not even reported in the NCVS because it may not be perceived as qualifying among the crime type events asked about in that survey. Even with underreporting, the estimated 750,000 crimes reported to the police by youth (a rate of about 34 per 1000 teens each year) represent about 17% of all crimes reported to the police, this from a group that makes up only 10.6% of the population over 12.

Crimes against children do occupy a significant portion of the energy and resources of the criminal justice system, especially as many states have developed routine practices of referring all child abuse cases to justice authorities. Unfortunately, relatively few data are systematically collected to track the handling of such cases. No national data exist on the percentages of arrests or prosecutions that involve child victims. However, some data are available on the portion of the prison population serving time for crimes against children. According to a 1991 survey of inmates in state prisons, one in five violent incarcerated offenders were serving time for a crime against a juvenile. The percentage of child victimizers was higher among the older prisoners (35% for those age 45 or older) compared to younger prisoners (15% for those age 25 or less) (Beck et al., 1993).

One thing that is quite clear about the justice system's handling of crimes against juveniles is that of all the victimizations coming to its attention, sex crimes receive special priority. First, they are the only violent crimes reported to the police at a higher rate for youth than for adults (Table 2). Thus, of NCVS-reported sexual assaults on youth, 46% were reported to the police, higher than the 28% of the NCVS-reported sexual assaults on adults and higher than the 29% reporting rate for all youth violent victimization.

As another indication of the special attention sexual assaults receive, even though according to the NCVS they constitute just under 5% of all youth victimizations coming to the attention of the police, they are clearly the crimes that receive the largest amount of criminal justice activity. This is apparent in the literature on crimes against children and on child victims as witnesses, which deals almost exclusively with sexual abuse and sexual assault (Whitcomb, Goodman, Runyan, & Hoak, 1994; Whitcomb et al., 1991). In a 1993 American

Bar Association national survey of 600 prosecutors, 80% reported that they prosecute substantially more sexual abuse than physical abuse (Smith & Goretsky, 1992). The disproportionate focus on sexual assault is apparent in figures on incarcerated offenders. Seventy-one percent of those incarcerated for violent crimes against children are in jail for committing a sexual assault (Beck et al., 1993). This contrasts with the fact that only 10% of all juvenile reports to police for violent crimes perpetrated by adults (and thus vulnerable to prison time) are for sexual assaults. It also contrasts with the fact that among those who offend violently against adults, only 17% are incarcerated for sexual assaults.

This raises a key policy issue concerning crimes against children: whether the justice system's special focus on sexual assault—an overall small proportion of the child victimization picture—is a rational emphasis or a distortion of priorities in some larger context. It is clear that there is substantial public anxiety about the sexual exploitation of children, which provides popular support for aggressive criminal justice action in this area. Sexual assaults are believed to be particularly frightening and damaging kinds of victimizations for children. The evidence is not so clear, however, that sexual assaults are substantially and uniformly more traumatic than other kinds of violent victimization (Boney McCoy & Finkelhor, 1995). There is reason to believe that in spite of their seriousness, physical assaults without a sexual component and even aggravated assaults by adults against children do not receive a great deal of police and prosecutorial priority. Part of the problem may be the reluctance of youth and their families to report physical assaults. Another part of the problem may be the degree to which physical assaults by other youth, because they come within the purview of the juvenile justice system, are not taken as seriously. Finally, a third part of the problem may be that adult physical assaults against children, especially because so many of them occur in a caretaking relationship, are difficult to prosecute given the legal protection most states provide to acts claimed to be disciplinary in nature. However, a National Institute of Justice study has demonstrated that some select prosecutors, when they give it equal emphasis, can achieve rates of prosecution for physical abuse that actually exceed that of sexual abuse (Smith, 1995). An overall evaluation of justice activity in response to physical assaults and abuse against children is an important policy need (Smith & Goretsky, 1992).

A variety of related public policy issues concern how the criminal justice system operates differently in cases involving child as compared to adult victims. A spectrum of concerns has been raised. At one end are arguments that child victims are badly mistreated by the criminal justice system, that their reports are not taken seriously, that their cases are not prosecuted out of fear that they will make unreliable or easily impeached witnesses, and that they will be easy targets for defense attorneys. At the other end are arguments that child victims are privileged in ways that trample on the rights of the accused, including claims that police investigators have been taught to always believe children and that juries are overly swayed by images of child victims. A large number of reforms have been proposed and implemented (and then subjected to legal challenge) in recent years, such as the use of closed circuit video transmissions of children's testimony, out of concern that the criminal justice system was not sensitive to children and contained obstacles to their involvement (Myers, 1994).

Despite this controversy, relatively little research has examined the operation of the criminal justice system in relation to child victims or evaluated the reforms that have been implemented to help them. Most of what has been done concerns cases of sexually abused children exclusively. On the whole, the research shows a complex and possibly reassuring picture.

Like much of the criminal justice system, a large portion of victimizations that get reported to the police do not go much further. Statistics do not appear to be available on what proportion of child victimizations are cleared by arrest. In terms of arrests that are referred for prosecution, estimates from various sources suggest that 60–75% go on to prosecution (Whitcomb et al., 1991). Most prosecuted cases involving children (80–90%) are settled by a guilty plea, and 50–70% of convicted offenders against children end up serving some jail time (American Bar Association, 1987; Finkelhor & Williams, 1988). These overall statistics do not differ that much from those associated with the processing of comparable crimes against adults.

It also does not appear that sentences for offenders against children are systematically either lower or higher than sentences for offenders against adults, given equivalent crimes. According to the 1997 Survey of Inmates, those convicted of murdering a juvenile and currently in prison had the same median sentence length (300 months) as those convicted of murdering an adult (Finkelhor & Ormrod, 2000). For the crimes of negligent manslaughter, robbery, and assault, sentences were somewhat higher when the victim was a child. For crimes of rape and sexual assault, sentences were substantially lower, but a variety of factors probably account for this disparity including the larger number of family and acquaintances among the child victimizers, the lesser use of firearms and other weapons, and the less frequent presence of victim injury in sex crimes against children.

Overall, the picture of the criminal justice system suggests that juvenile victims of sexual crimes are treated in a way that may be distinct from juvenile victims of other violent crimes. But there is relatively little evidence that the system is biased for or against such victims in comparison to adult sexual assault victims.

Given the importance of these issues, it is disappointing that there is so little statistical information available to evaluate the operation of the criminal justice system in regard to child victims. For example, there is little information on whether reforms result in more prosecutions, more convictions or acquittals, more plea bargains, or fewer cases being dropped because of victim unavailability or noncooperation. Two particularly important priorities would seem to be gathering justice system data on the full spectrum of child victims, not just those reporting a sex crime, and collecting data in a way that allows a better comparison to the processing of crimes against adults.

A variety of other issues regarding criminally victimized children have received little or no attention in the literature. One issue concerns the use of crime victim services and compensation plans by juvenile crime victims. One of the important purposes in establishing crime victim services and compensation plans was to help vulnerable groups such as children. Anecdotal evidence suggests that children do use such services and apply for compensation more regularly than other crime victims. Little good documentation exists, however, about the pattern of usage of these services. Among service providers, there is an often-repeated concern that child victims and families do not follow through with treatment services and that there are enormous variability in services and substantial barriers to service provision and receipt (Finkelhor & Berliner, 1995).

Another important victim rights issue that has received some policy attention in recent years concerns the right of victims to receive information about the disposition of offenders and changes in offender status, such as when the offender is paroled or returned to the community. Because a large proportion of offenders against children are themselves juveniles, an important policy question concerns the degree to which concern about victim rights can be integrated into the operation of the juvenile justice system. Some questions are: (1) Are victims entitled to compensation when offenders are juveniles? (2) Are they informed of disposition of offenders and change in status? (3) Are there avenues for being heard as part of sentencing?

JUVENILE VICTIMS INVOLVED IN CHILD PROTECTION ACTIONS

The number of children referred for child protection investigations rose dramatically in the 1970s and 1980s, but then leveled off and even declined somewhat by the late 1990s (Jones

& Finkelhor, 2000). It was estimated that almost 3 million children in the United States were targets of child maltreatment reports in 1998, for which nearly 1.8 million investigations were conducted. About 29% of the investigations resulted in a disposition of substantiated or indicated child maltreatment. This translates into over 900,000 children whose maltreatment was substantiated, a rate of 12.9 victims per 1000 children under 18 in the United States (US Department of Health and Human Services, 2000).

Neglect was the predominant form of maltreatment among substantiated victims, accounting for 53% of the children whose maltreatment was substantiated (Table 3). Physical abuse occurred to 23% of the children and sexual abuse to 11%.

A key problem in regard to this population of child victims is that relatively few data are available about what happens to them after the investigatory process, what services are provided, what court actions are taken, whether criminal cases are filed and what their outcomes are, and how often such children reappear in the child welfare and justice system. Even basic statistics on the number of abused children reported and substantiated nationally are still not adequate for many policy analysis purposes.

Criminal court involvement is one justice system outcome that occurs to about 13% of all children whose maltreatment is substantiated (Whitcomb et al., 1994). As indicated earlier, this outcome is much more common for cases of sexual abuse than other kinds of maltreatment. The simultaneous occurrence of criminal prosecution and child protection actions is something that has created a number of policy dilemmas, including concerns that it may stall treatment and placement plans and increase the adversariality of the protection process. A variety of recommendations have been made for coordinating criminal prosecutions and child protection proceedings, but research suggests that half of all jurisdictions have little such coordination (Whitcomb et al., 1994).

Removal from the home (temporarily or permanently) is another dramatic justice system outcome in child maltreatment cases that is tracked at least partially. Despite the large number of substantiated maltreatment cases, removal from the home is relatively uncommon, occurring for only 15% of the victims, somewhere in the vicinity of 150,000 children. This is approximately the same percentage of cases for whom dependency court actions were initiated. Relatively little information is available about what ultimately happens to these children taken into custody or subjected to court action.

There has been substantial debate about the consequences of out-of-home placement of maltreated children and the conditions under which it is warranted. Some research shows that such children do at least as well, or sometimes better, than children left in the home (Widom, 1991). However, such placement is not inexpensive for states. Concerted efforts to reduce

Table 3. Child Victims of Abuse and Neglect, 1998[a]

Reports of maltreatment	2,806,000	
Substantiated or indicated[b]	1,048,062	100%
Physical abuse	195,891	23%
Neglect	461,274	54%
Medical neglect	20,338	2%
Sexual abuse	99,278	12%
Emotional abuse	51,618	6%
Other	217,640	25%

[a]From US Department of Health and Human Services (2000).
[b]Percentages total more than 100% because children may have been victims of more than one type of maltreatment.

placement in the 1980s through intensive family support services did not result in a clear-cut success. A majority of studies failed to find that intensive interventions reduced placement rates, but agencies also had a difficult time targeting the intervention services to the families at imminent risk of losing a child to placement (Gelles, 1996).

It is well recognized that children identified by the child protective services (CPS) system are at high likelihood to be re-reported to that system, as well to other justice-related systems, at a later time. Data from Massachusetts, for example, show that 37% of new substantiated reports concern children with an already substantiated prior report of maltreatment (Felix, Berman, & Carlisle, 1995). (Contact of maltreated children with other portions of the justice system will be discussed later.) This confirms the potential utility of the CPS system as a context for identifying children at high risk for future involvement with the justice system.

In spite of this, however, there is a widespread acknowledgment that relatively limited services are provided to these children and their families (Kolko, 1998). Given that child abuse is recognized as a risk factor for later delinquency (Widom & Ames, 1994) as well as other negative life outcomes, it would seem that interventions for maltreated children should be a high policy priority. A large national study (the National Longitudinal Study of Child Welfare) to track the experiences of children as they pass through the child welfare system is currently under way.

One possible barrier to the provision of more services is the absence of research demonstrating what services work best. There is a substantial and somewhat encouraging literature on services to abusing families, but much of it has been focused on what services reduce parents' propensity to abuse and neglect, rather than what results in positive social and psychological outcomes for the children. Daro et al. (1992) found that parental child abuse potential was most likely to decline with the delivery of multiple interventions (play groups, support groups, education classes) delivered intensively (multiple times per week), including aggressive outreach to high-risk families.

Services targeted directly at ameliorating the short-term and long-term effects of maltreatment to children themselves have developed more in the domain of sexual abuse (Kolko, 1998). In this domain, a professional consensus has developed that "abuse-focused treatment" is a preferred intervention. Such treatment is structured and tries to address the specific fears and misconceptions that are typically engendered by abuse and to empower victims to resist and report future abuse (Finkelhor & Berliner, 1995). Such approaches have proven superior to general supportive therapies in experimentally designed studies (Cohen & Mannarino, 1997).

Some prospective longitudinal studies currently are underway to examine the life course of abused children (Kelley, Thornberry, & Smith, 1997; Widom & Ames, 1994), but what are less common are studies designed to track the impact of justice system-related interventions and innovations to help lessen the trauma for these child victims and decrease the likelihood of their returning to the justice system sometime later in their lives.

CHILDREN VICTIMIZED BY DOMESTIC VIOLENCE AND CUSTODIAL ABDUCTIONS

It has been estimated that 11–20% of children witness acts of violence between parents (Wolak & Finkelhor, 1998). But the number of children who end up involved in the justice system as a result of such violence is more difficult to estimate.

One major form of justice system involvement is when police are called or make an arrest for domestic assault. There are an estimated 490,000 police reports of domestic violence annually based on the NCVS data (Greenfeld et al., 1998). According to an analysis of police experience in five urban areas, there were children in 74–81% of households where the police substantiated an incident of domestic violence, and 40–48% of these households had at least one child under the age of 5. In fact, in 11–12% of the episodes the child placed the call to the police, and in 16–27% the child was a factor in the eruption of the violent dispute (Fantuzzo, Boruch, Beriama, Atkins, & Marcus, 1997).

Child witnesses to domestic violence also come into contact with the civil courts. Each year about half a million couples with children file for divorce and the rate of violence between divorcing couples has been estimated at above 50% (Kurz, 1996). Hundreds of thousands of parents with children seek restraining orders against their partners every year for protection against domestic violence.

Although this group of child witnesses is a conceptually distinct population from those children who are themselves victims, in practice the distinction is difficult to maintain. It is estimated that 30–60% of those who have witnessed parental violence also have been victimized by the parental violence themselves. Moreover, in studies looking at the long-term consequences of witnessing parental violence, it is difficult to differentiate such children from direct victims (Durant, Cadenhead, Pendergrast, Slavens, & Linder, 1994; Wolak & Finkelhor, 1998). Part of the problem is that even children who have not been directly victimized may have suffered from various kinds of nonreported parental neglect or emotional maltreatment.

Child victims of custodial interference and abduction are another facet of this picture. An estimated 354,000 family abductions occurred in 1988, and in 44% the police were involved to try to recover the child or adjudicate the dispute (Finkelhor, Hotaling, & Sedlak, 1990). (The number of prosecutions for family abduction is currently unknown.) Domestic violence is a common feature in family abduction situations (Plass, Finkelhor, & Hotaling, 1997), and physical and sexual abuse less so (Finkelhor et al., 1990); but even in the absence of violence exposure children are victimized by the loss of contact with family and friends and the disruption of their routines and living arrangements.

These are categories of child victims about whom good statistics are particularly scarce. In the case of domestic violence, since the primary victims or complainants are seen as adults, the involvement of children is not systematically recorded. In the case of family abductions, the relatively recent explosion of this kind of crime has not been accommodated by categories in justice-related record systems. A very high priority is for better and more comprehensive statistics on justice system contacts with families where domestic violence or criminal custodial interference has impinged on the lives of children.

The absence of good statistics is indicative of a more general policy question about the extent to which the justice system is aware of these child victims and their potential needs. When intervening in domestic violence, police and criminal courts in most jurisdictions do not take specific actions with regard to children, unless a caretaker initiates something on their behalf. No formal mechanisms exist for inquiry about the situation of children in situations where restraining orders are requested and granted. Judges and social agencies are perhaps more focused on children who have been abducted than those who are simply witnesses to parental violence.

In some communities, cooperative arrangements exist to involve child protection workers in order to ensure the safety and interests of children in cases where domestic or custodial violence has been identified. But these policies have engendered substantial controversy (Edelson, 1997). Advocates for battered women have pointed out that child protective investigations focused narrowly on children's safety can further victimize abused women, who now face, in addition to a violent partner, a hostile state investigation into their capacities as parents at a time when they may be ill-prepared to defend themselves. A very high priority for public policy is to find out more about the variety of mechanisms that exist in communities for providing assistance, support, representation, and protection for children in situations of domestic and custodial violence and the comparative effectiveness of these mechanisms, both at protecting children and the interests of victimized adults.

An additional general priority in this area should be to add a concern about the child victims to all policy research on domestic violence. Although there has been an increasing expansion of policy research in recent years on justice system interventions in marital violence, such as mandatory arrest and prosecution policies, none of that literature to our knowledge has focused on the impact on children. It is unclear whether and under what circumstances children are relieved, upset, or embarrassed and effectively protected from physical and emotional harm when the justice system intervenes to arrest or prosecute their parents and how their interests converge or diverge with those of the abused parent.

CHILD VICTIMS INVOLVED IN CRIMINAL OFFENSES

Over 2.7 million juvenile arrests occurred in 1994; of these, an estimated 150,200 were for violent index crimes (homicide, forcible rape, robbery, aggravated assault) and 748,100 were for property index crimes (burglary, larceny-theft, motor vehicle theft, arson) (Table 4) (Snyder, Sickmund, & Poe-Yamagata, 1996). The majority of these arrestees were formally processed by juvenile courts (i.e., they were petitioned to the court), but relatively few resulted in detention and out-of-home placement.

Juvenile victims of crime and child maltreatment are overrepresented in this population of juvenile offenders, a fact not monitored by national statistics but revealed in small-scale studies. In one study of 226 incarcerated juvenile offenders in New Jersey, 66% of the youth reported that they had been beaten with a belt or extension cord, 32% reported that they had been beaten repeatedly, and 20% reported that they had been threatened with a knife or a gun (Geller & Ford-Somma, 1984). This study also found that a subsample of juveniles incarcerated for violent offenses were significantly more likely to report routine family violence than youth incarcerated for other kinds of offenses. A study of 213 incarcerated male adolescents in Arizona revealed that 49% of the youth had been physically abused by family members (Spaccarelli, Coatsworth, & Bowden, 1995). Similar to the study by Geller and Ford-Somma (1984), this study found that violent offenders were two to three times as likely as nonviolent offenders to report either being victims or witnesses of family violence.

Studies based on official reports of child abuse and crime records also consistently show

Table 4. How Violent and Property Offense Cases Were Processed by the Juvenile Justice System in 1994

Type of offense	Number of arrests	Number (%) of arrestees going to court	Number (%) of court cases	Number (%) of court cases placed out-of-home[a]
Violent index crimes[b]	150,200	130,600 (87)	93,400 (71)	33,300 (36)
Property index crimes[c]	748,100	566,700 (76)	301,000 (53)	61,600 (20)

[a]These figures are based on all person and property crimes and are therefore approximations.
[b]Violent crimes include criminal homicide, forcible rape, robbery, and aggravated assault.
[c]Property crimes include burglary, larceny theft, motor vehicle theft, and arson.

Table 5. Comparison of the Delinquency Rates Found in Abused and Nonabused Children: Findings from Longitudinal Studies

Study	Delinquency rate in the abused group (%)	Delinquency rate in the control group (%)	Risk ratio[a]	Sample size (*N*)	Follow-up period
McCord (1983)	20.0	11.0	1.82	232	40 years
Zingraff et al. (1993)	13.7	9.0	1.52	810	3–4 years
Widom & Ames (1994)	26.0[b]	16.8[b]	1.55	1575	30 years
	28.6[c]	21.1[c]	1.35		
Kakar (1996)	10.0	6.4	1.56	440	2–5 years
Kelley, Thornberry, & Smith (1997)	45.0	32.0	1.40	1000	3 years

[a]All differences in delinquency rates between abused and control groups were significant at the .05 level.
[b]Percent arrested for juvenile offenses.
[c]Percent arrested for adult offenses.

that youth with a history of maltreatment are more likely to come into contact with the juvenile or adult court for delinquent or criminal acts (Table 5). Risk ratios in Table 5 indicate only a modest effect of child maltreatment on subsequent delinquency and crime. However, the strength of the relationship between child maltreatment and juvenile delinquency or adult crime actually may be underestimated by these studies as they relied only on official records of abuse and delinquency. It is commonly known that many episodes of child abuse and juvenile delinquency go unreported, and thus do not appear in court records.

In addition to histories of child maltreatment, a number of studies also show that juvenile offenders have high rates of current criminal victimization. For example, a study with data from the National Youth Survey found that 45% of youth who reported delinquent acts in the previous year had been physically assaulted or threatened with a weapon during the same period, compared to only 12% of nondelinquent youth (Lauritsen, Sampson, & Laub, 1991). While delinquency may increase a juvenile's risk for victimization, a growing number of studies suggest that living in a violent home or community and fear of victimization also lead to delinquent and criminal behavior among juveniles (Durant et al., 1994; Jenkins & Bell, 1994). In either case, the population of juvenile delinquents includes a disproportionate number of victims.

The strong evidence that (1) child maltreatment is causally related to juvenile delinquency and adult crime, and (2) juvenile offenders are disproportionate as victims of violent crimes raises important policy questions. First, are the child maltreatment and victimization histories of juvenile offenders being adequately assessed? Given current knowledge about the psychological and social impact of child maltreatment and victimization, such information would be important for courts and others to take into account in trying to develop the best strategy for adjudicating and rehabilitating juvenile offenders. There may be treatment needs that are revealed by such an assessment. For example, many juvenile victims are at high risk for adverse but potentially treatable psychological outcomes such as posttraumatic stress disorder and depression (e.g., Boney-McCoy & Finkelhor, 1995). This assessment also may reveal protection needs, such as protection from abusive family members, violent gangs, or generally unsafe neighborhoods.

Second, awareness of juvenile offenders' victimization histories could influence their disposition by courts. According to Feld (1993, p. 262), juvenile courts have moved away from examining juvenile offenders' "best interests" and toward "proportional and determinate sentences based on the present offense and prior record." This shift in the court's treatment of juvenile offenders is reflected in the fact that from 1988 to 1992, the number of juvenile offense cases transferred to adult criminal court increased by 68%, from 7,000 to 11,700 (Butts, Snyder, Finnegan, Aughenbaugh, & Poole, 1996). Treating more juvenile offenders as adult criminals in all likelihood will lead to increases in victimization as they are incarcerated in adult prisons.

More knowledge of juvenile offenders' victimization histories and research on the effects of victimization also could help to inform judgments about dangerousness and likelihood of recidivism. Few studies have investigated the links between different types of victimization and subsequent delinquency (e.g., Widom & Ames, 1994). A comprehensive system for tracking child victims who enter the justice system would provide an excellent means of filling this important research gap. An important question that could be answered through such a data system is whether the likelihood of recidivism by juvenile offenders is affected by victimization history and/or victimization subsequent to placement by the juvenile or adult courts. If victimization were an important determinant of recidivism, then it would seem to be in the court's best interest to factor both the history and probability of future victimization into its disposition of juvenile offenders.

Such assessment could be facilitated by better instruments for ascertaining offenders' victimization history. These instruments could be developed from a growing number of models that already have been tested with samples of youth in a variety of settings, including low-income communities and juvenile detention facilities (e.g., Durant et al., 1994; Geller & Ford-Somma, 1984; Spaccarelli et al., 1995). Coupled with other diagnostic tools, such as instruments to assess psychological disorders, victimization assessments could provide important information regarding the types of treatment and protection most appropriate for juvenile offenders.

In addition to victimization histories based on self-reported information, there is a need for better cross-referencing between child protection, police, and delinquency records. Availability of such data across agencies would help social workers, law enforcement officials, and other service providers to conduct a more comprehensive assessment of the needs of juvenile victims and appropriate strategies for their treatment and rehabilitation.

Finally, assessment of victimization should be systematically reported in statistics gathered on delinquency. Although juvenile victimization is prominently featured in recent reports from the Office of Juvenile Justice and Delinquency Prevention (OJJDP) (Snyder et al., 1996) and in a recent review of the juvenile court system (Lewit & Schuurmann Baker, 1996), there has been no systematic attempt to examine the victimization histories of juvenile offenders themselves. Statistics on victimization in these reports are derived primarily from the National Crime Victimization Survey, and thus are not associated with the population of juvenile offenders being processed by the juvenile court system. Therefore, a key issue for OJJDP, the juvenile courts, and other referring agencies is how a system for documenting the victimization histories of juvenile offenders could be put into place as a means of (1) more accurately characterizing juvenile offenders and (2) informing intervention strategies such as counseling of youth and their families and out-of-home placement.

In summary, research indicates that juvenile offenders are overrepresented as victims and witnesses of crimes. Unfortunately, no systems are in place at the federal or state levels to (1) track child victims who enter the justice system, (2) assess and document the victimization histories of juvenile offenders, or (3) monitor the effectiveness of interventions implemented on behalf of child victims, such as out-of-home placement (Barth, 1996). Although the majority of first-time juvenile offenders do not return to juvenile court, it is entirely possible that court dispositions are placing many juvenile offenders in situations in which they are at high risk for further victimization. Only through a more comprehensive system of assessing and documenting the careers of child victims will we be able to help juvenile offenders and assess the outcomes of victimization services provided by child protection agencies and the juvenile courts.

CHILD VICTIMS INVOLVED IN STATUS OFFENSES

In 1994, nearly 500,000 juvenile arrests were for status offenses, about half of them runaways (Table 6) (Snyder et al., 1996). Most status offenses are handled by police without further court involvement, but the exact number referred to the court is not known (Butts et al., 1996). Only 20% of court referrals resulted in formally petitioned cases in 1994 (Steinhart, 1996) and even fewer resulted in out-of-home placement.

Like juveniles who have committed violent and property crimes, juvenile status offenders include a disproportionate number of child abuse and crime victims. A national study of 587 runaway and homeless adolescents revealed that 46% of youth interviewed in shelters and 39% of youth interviewed on the street had been victims of physical abuse in their homes (Greene, Ringwalt, & Kelly, 1995). At least 60% of the youth had suffered emotional abuse and about half were classified as thrownaway youth. Unfortunately, the victimization experiences of these runaway, thrownaway, and homeless youth do not end in their homes. At least 7% of the youth living in shelters and 11% of the street youth had suffered from some type of violent victimization (robbery, physical assault, sexual assault) after leaving their homes. Not surprisingly, these victimization percentages were substantially higher among youth who had not returned to their homes for an extended period of time. Compared to the general population of adolescents, these runaway, thrownaway, and homeless youth also were at high risk for a variety of problem behaviors including substance abuse, suicide attempts, unsafe sexual behavior, and criminal activities. Many of these illegal activities were commonly referred to as survival tactics (e.g., exchanging sex for money, food, subsistence, or drugs).

Research and policy issues that arise for status offenders are similar to those discussed in the previous section on juvenile delinquency and crime. In general, little is known about the victimization histories and futures of status offenders, particularly runaway or thrownaway youth who make up the largest proportion of status offenders. This lack of information has resulted in part from inadequate assessment, documentation, and reporting by agencies

Table 6. How Status Offense Cases Were Processed by the Juvenile Justice System in 1994

Type of offense	Number of arrests	Number of arrestees going to court	Number of court cases	Number (%) of court cases placed out-of-home
Runaway	248,800	?	21,500	6,200 (29)
Liquor law violation[a]	120,000	?	33,600	2,000 (6)
Curfew/loitering	128,400	?	?	?
Truancy	?	?	36,400	4,000 (11)
Ungovernable	?	?	15,700	4,400 (28)

[a]Liquor law violation arrests include public drunkeness as well as underage drinking.

providing services (e.g., shelters) for runaway and homeless youth. Although arrest statistics are available from police departments, these data do not provide information on the circumstances surrounding the arrests nor do they tell us why the vast majority of status offenders never appear in juvenile court. Similarly, juvenile court statistics tell us little about the importance of prior and future victimization in the adjudication of status offenders. Thus it is impossible to determine whether only a small percentage of status offenders are victims of maltreatment or whether a large number of status offenders are being returned to homes and communities where they will be revictimized. A better system for documenting and tracking status offenders who enter the broadly defined justice system would help us to know more about these youth and better serve their needs.

Despite the recent movement to deinstitutionalize status offenders, juvenile courts may be in the best position to provide leadership in (1) establishing a better system for documenting the intake and assessing victimization histories of status offenders and (2) ensuring that adequate services are available for these youth (Steinhart, 1996). While some researchers and policymakers have argued that the juvenile courts should not have jurisdiction over status offenders (e.g., Ketcham, 1977; Schwartz, 1989), others have argued that juvenile courts should take an active role in helping communities develop adequate service options for these youth (Edwards, 1992). Although this may be a nontraditional role for the juvenile court, it could in the long run serve to reduce the court's burden of status offender cases that is likely to increase with the growing adolescent population (Steinhart, 1996).

CONCLUSION

It is impossible on the basis of current knowledge to estimate the aggregate number of juvenile victims who come within the purview of the justice system, broadly speaking. Estimates developed in this chapter suggest that each year about 750,000 teen victims of violent crime are reported to police, 1.1 million substantiated or indicated victims of child abuse and neglect are known to child protection authorities, and 360,000–400,000 children reside in a home where police are called for spousal violence. Of the 900,000 youth arrested for serious violent or property offenses or the 500,000 arrested for status offenses, some significant proportion (ranging from 20 to 50%) are victims of child maltreatment and a similar proportion victims of other recent kinds of crimes and assaults. Such figures cannot be aggregated, of course, since many of them count the same children through the lens of different justice system processes. However, the numbers clearly portray a justice system with access to a large number of childhood victims of crime, violence, and abuse.

The relative proportions also are difficult to compare. It may not be coincidental that the largest figure—the one for substantiated and indicated child abuse and neglect—is also the only one based on a large formal data system established specifically to count victims coming to the attention of authorities.

Based on the data available, some crude sketch can also be made of the mixture of children of different ages being identified by the various systems (Fig. 1). The child protection system tends to identify somewhat more younger than older children. Juveniles being arrested and detained for criminal and status offenses tend to be almost exclusively teenagers. Close to half of all children in families with spousal assault arrests appear to be under 6 years, with less than a quarter older than 12 years. Crime victims reported to the police tend to be primarily teens with fewer school-age children and very few preschoolers.

Thus, the overall developmental picture appears to be as follows: Preschool victims

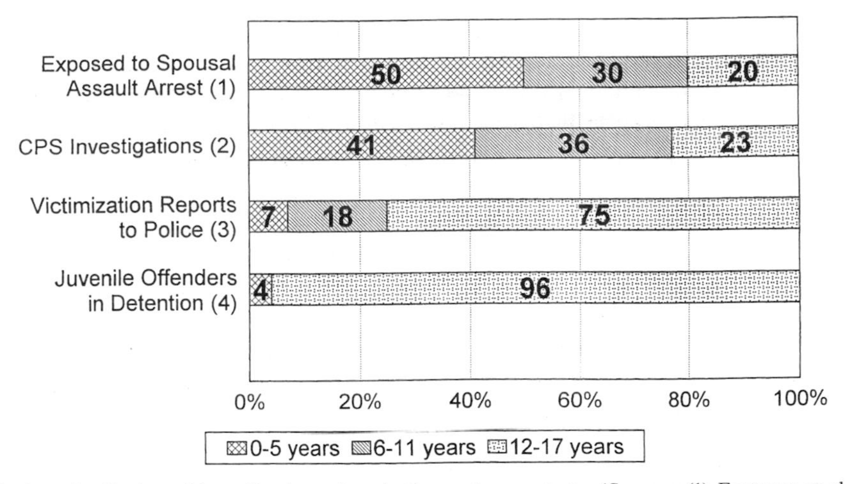

Figure 1. Age distribution of juveniles in various justice system contexts. (*Sources*: (1) Fantuzzo et al. [1997]; (2) National Center on Child Abuse and Neglect [1997]; (3) Snyder and Sickmund [1995]; (4) Butts et al. [1996].)

primarily come into the justice system via reports of child abuse and in conjunction with spousal assaults. School-age children come to attention via these same two routes, plus a certain amount of direct police reported crime victimization. Teenagers come into justice system contact through all five avenues, with the delinquency and status offense route being one they exclusively monopolize.

This review has attempted to make clear that the problem of child victims in the justice system is indeed complex and multifaceted and can be looked at from many angles. It can be looked at from the angle of the type of victimization experienced, from the angle of the ages of the children victimized, or from the angle of the justice system process in which the children are involved. The policy issues are numerous and wide-ranging and vary according to many of these dimensions. It is clear that considerable debate has occurred about these issues in recent years and much progress been made.

But it also is true that this agenda is to some extent hampered by the absence of a clear sponsor. That is to say, in this policy domain, unlike some others, there is no single or primary lobbying group, profession, or government agency whose major objective is to foster progress in regard to child victims in the criminal justice system. Government agencies like the Office of Juvenile Justice and Delinquency Prevention and the National Center on Child Abuse and Neglect occupy themselves with only a part of problem. Organizations like American Professional Society on the Abuse of Children likewise are only partially involved.

A comprehensive approach to dealing with child victims within the justice system should perhaps focus on four primary goals, abbreviated by the words recognition, protection, rehabilitation, and accountability:

1. Recognition. It should be a goal of the justice system to recognize more fully the presence and extent of victimization among the children who come within its purview by better history taking and assessment and by improved record-keeping and exchange of information among components of the system.
2. Protection. It should be a goal of the justice system to protect child victims of crimes from both continued victimization by their perpetrators and from unnecessary trauma and discomfort associated with the processes and procedures of a system not designed

with the needs of children in mind. Child victims should have all the safeguards and opportunities afforded adults in protecting them from further victimization. They also should have special mechanisms and services, to the extent consistent with the constitution, to help mitigate the experience of justice system contact.

3. Rehabilitation. It should be a goal of the justice system to help child victims recover from the effects of victimization. Services and programs should be available so that victimization is less likely to have continuing effects on children's development and less likely to result in further involvement with the justice system.
4. Accountability. It should be a goal of the justice system to have information systems that allow it to fully evaluate its impact on children and the impact of new policies and programs. This should mean being able to track adequately the length of time children are involved in the justice system, the reasons for their involvement, and the kinds of interventions and outcomes that result.

A justice system able to implement such goals would certainly be one that brought a much larger measure of justice to the lives of children and youth.

ACKNOWLEDGMENT

The authors would like to thank the Family Violence Research Seminar for comments on a draft of this chapter.

REFERENCES

American Bar Association. (1987). *Child sexual abuse: An analysis of case processing.* (NIJ Grant 84-IJ-CX-0074).

Barth, R. P. (1996). The juvenile court and dependency cases. *The Future of Children, 6*(3), 100–110.

Beck, A., Gilliard, D., Greenfeld, L., Harlow, C., Hester, T., Jankowski, L., Snell, T., Stephen, J., & Morton, D. (1993). *Survey of state prison inmates, 1991.* Washington, DC: Bureau of Justice Statistics.

Boney-McCoy, S., & Finkelhor, D. (1995). The psychosocial impact of violent victimization on a national youth sample. *Journal of Consulting and Clinical Psychology, 63*, 726–736.

Butts, J. A., Snyder, H. N., Finnegan, T. A., Aughenbaugh, A. L., & Poole, R. S. (1996). *Juvenile court statistics 1994.* (Statistics Report). Washington, DC: Office of Juvenile Justice and Delinquency Prevention.

Cohen, J. A., & Mannarino, A. P. (1997). A treatment study for sexually abused preschool children: Outcome during a one-year follow-up. *Journal of the American Academy of Child and Adolescent Psychiatry, 36*, 1228–1235.

Daro, D., Jones, E., McCurdy, K., George, S., Keeton, K., Downs, B., & Thelen, J. (1992). *Evaluation of the William Penn Foundation child abuse and prevention initiative.* (Final Report). Chicago, IL: Center on Child Abuse Prevention Research—National Committee for the Prevention of Child Abuse.

Durant, R. H., Cadenhead, C., Pendergrast, R. A., Slavens, G., & Linder, C. W. (1994). Factors associated with the use of violence among urban black adolescents. *American Journal of Public Health, 84*, 612–617.

Edelson, J. L. (1997). Charging battered mothers with "Failure to Protect" is often wrong. *APSAC Advisor, 10*(2), 2–3.

Edwards, L. P. (1992). The juvenile court and the role of the juvenile judge. *Juvenile and Family Court Journal, 43*(2), 29.

Fantuzzo, J., Boruch, R., Beriama, A., Atkins, M., & Marcus, S. (1997). Domestic violence and children: Prevalence and risk in five major US cities. *Journal of the American Academy of Child and Adolescent Psychiatry, 36*, 116–122.

Feld, B. C. (1993). *Justice for children: The right to counsel and the juvenile courts.* Boston: Northeastern University Press.

Felix III, A. C., Berman, R. A., & Carlisle, L. K. (1995). *Massachusetts Department of Social Services: 1994 child maltreatment statistics.* Boston: Department of Social Services.

Finkelhor, D., & Ormrod, R. (2000). *Characteristics of crimes against juveniles.* (Juvenile Justice Bulletin—NCJ 179034). Washington, DC: US Government Printing Office.

Finkelhor, D., & Ormrod, R. (in press). *Juvenile victims of property crimes.* (Juvenile Justice Bulletin). Washington, DC: Office of Juvenile Justice and Delinquency Prevention.

Finkelhor, D., & Berliner, L. (1995). Research on the treatment of sexually abused children: A review and recommendations. *Journal of the American Academy of Child and Adolescent Psychiatry, 34*(11), 1408–1423.

Finkelhor, D., & Williams, L. M. (1988). *Nursery crimes: Sexual abuse in day care.* Newbury Park, CA: Sage.

Finkelhor, D., Hotaling, G. T., & Sedlak, A. (1990). *Missing, abducted, runaway and thrownaway children in America: First report.* Washington, DC: Juvenile Justice Clearinghouse.

Geller, M., & Ford-Somma, L. (1984). *Violent homes, violent children: A study of violence in the families of juvenile offenders* (prepared for the National Center on Child Abuse and Neglect). Trenton, NJ: New Jersey State Department of Corrections, Division of Juvenile Services.

Gelles, R. J. (1996). *The book of David.* New York: Basic Books.

Greene, J. M., Ringwalt, C. L., & Kelly, J. E. (1995). *Youth with runaway, thrownaway and homeless experience: Prevalence, drug use and other at-risk behaviors,* Volume I: *Final report.* Washington, DC: U.S. Department of Health and Human Services, Administration on Children, Youth and Families.

Greenfeld, L. A., Rand, M. R., Craven, D., Klaus, P. A., Perkins, C. A., Ringel, C., Warchol, G., Maston, C., & Fox, J. A. (1998). *Violence by intimates: Analysis of data on crimes by current or former spouses, boyfriends, and girlfriends* (Bureau of Justice Statistics Factbook NCJ-167237). Washington, DC: US Department of Justice.

Hashima, P. Y., & Finkelhor, D. (1999). Violent victimization of youth versus adults in the National Crime Victimization Survey. *Journal of Interpersonal Violence, 14*(8), 799–820.

Jenkins, E. J., & Bell, C. G. (1994). Violence among inner-city high school students and post-traumatic stress disorder. In S. Friedman (Ed.), *Anxiety disorders in African Americans* (pp. 76–88). New York: Springer.

Jones, L., & Finkelhor, D. (2000). *The decline in sexual abuse cases: Exploring the causes.* (Juvenile Justice Bulletin). Washington, DC: Office of Juvenile Justice and Delinquency Prevention.

Kakar, S. (1996). *Child abuse and delinquency.* Lanham, MA: University Press of America.

Kelley, B. T., Thornberry, T. P., & Smith, C. A. (1997). *In the wake of childhood maltreatment.* (Juvenile Justice Bulletin). Washington, DC: Office of Juvenile Justice and Delinquency Prevention.

Ketcham, O. W. (1977). Jurisdiction over status offenders should be eliminated from juvenile courts. *Boston University Law Review, 57,* 645–662.

Kolko, D. (1998). Treatment and intervention for child victims of violence. In P. K. Trickett & C. J. Schellenbach (Eds.), *Violence against children in the family and the community* (pp. 213–249). Washington, DC: American Psychological Association.

Kurz, D. (1996). Separation, divorce, and woman abuse. *Violence Against Women, 2*(1), 63–81.

Lauritsen, J. L., Sampson, R. J., & Laub, J. H. (1991). The link between offending and victimization among adolescents. *Criminology, 29,* 265–292.

Lewit, E. M., & Schuurmann Baker, L. (1996). Child indicators: Children as victims of violence. *The Future of Children, 6*(3), 147–156.

McCord, J. (1983). A forty year perspective of effects of child abuse and neglect. *Child Abuse and Neglect, 7,* 265–270.

Myers, J. E. B. (1994). Adjudication of child sexual abuse cases. *The Future of Children, 4*(2), 84–101.

Plass, P. S., Finkelhor, D., & Hotaling, G. T. (1997). Risk factors for family abduction: Demographic and family interaction characteristics. *Journal of Family Violence, 12*(3), 333–348.

Schwartz, I. (1989). *Justice for juveniles: Rethinking the best interests of the child.* Lexington, MA: D.C. Heath.

Smith, B., & Goretsky, S. R. (1992). The prosecution of child sexual abuse cases. *Juvenile and Child Welfare Law Reporter, 11*(5&6), 78–96.

Smith, B. E. (1995). *Prosecuting child physical abuse cases: A case study in San Diego.* Washington, DC: National Institute of Justice.

Snyder, H. N., & Sickmund, M. (1995). *Juvenile offenders and victims: A national report.* Washington, DC: Office of Juvenile Justice and Delinquency Prevention.

Snyder, H. N., Sickmund, M., & Poe-Yamagata, E. (1996). *Juvenile offenders and victims: 1996 update on violence.* (Statistics Summary). Washington, DC: Office of Juvenile Justice and Delinquency Prevention.

Spaccarelli, S., Coatsworth, J. D., & Bowden, B. S. (1995). Exposure to serious family violence: Among incarcerated boys: Its association with violent offending and potential mediating variables. *Violence and Victims, 10*(3), 163–182.

Steinhart, D. J. (1996). Status offenses. *The Future of Children, 6*(3), 86–99.

US Department of Health and Human Services, Administration on Children, Youth, and Families. (2000). *Child maltreatment 1998: Reports from the states to the National Child Abuse and Neglect Data System*. Washington, DC: US Government Printing Office.

Whitcomb, D., Goodman, G. S., Runyan, D. K., & Hoak, S. (1994). *The emotional effects of testifying on sexually abused children.* (Research in Brief). Washington, DC: National Institute of Justice.

Whitcomb, D., Runyan, D. K., De Vos, E., Hunter, W. M., Cross, T., Everson, M. D., Peeler, N. A., Porter, C. Q., Toth, P. A., & Cropper, C. (1991). *Final report: Child victim as witness research and development program.* (Grant Proposal 87-MC CX 0026). The University of North Carolina at Chapel Hill: Education Development Center Inc.

Widom, C. S. (1991). The role of placement experiences in mediating the criminal consequences of early childhood victimization. *American Journal of Orthopsychiatry, 61*, 195–209.

Widom, C. S., & Ames, M. A. (1994). Criminal consequences of childhood sexual victimization. *Child Abuse and Neglect, 18*, 303–318.

Wolak, J., & Finkelhor, D. (1998). Children exposed to partner violence. In J. L. Jasinski & L. M. Williams (Eds.), *Partner violence: A comprehensive review of 20 years of research* (pp. 73–111). Thousand Oaks, CA: Sage Publications.

Zingraff, T. M., Jeffrey, L., Kristen, A. M., & Matthew, C. J. (1993). Child maltreatment and youthful problem behavior. *Criminology, 31*, 172–202.

Part II

Victimization

3

Child Abuse and Neglect

CATHY SPATZ WIDOM

INTRODUCTION

Child abuse and neglect represent complex social problems confronting our society today. From 1976, when the first national figures for child maltreatment were generated, to the most recent period, child maltreatment reports have been increasing steadily. In 1992, child protective service agencies received an estimated 1.9 million reports of child abuse and neglect involving an estimated 2.9 million children. Maltreatment was substantiated or indicated in 41% of these reports. Each year, including 1992, approximately 1100 children die as a result of abuse and neglect. In 1992, this translated into more than 1 death per 1000 substantiated victims (Sedlak & Broadhurst, 1996).

The alarming number of reported and substantiated cases of child abuse and neglect has prompted some observers to refer to this problem as reaching "epidemic" proportions in the United States. At the same time, a recent National Research Council (1993) report concluded that research in the field of child maltreatment is relatively undeveloped when compared with fields such as child development, social welfare, and criminology. The limited knowledge base in the field of child abuse and neglect is in part a function of the methodological and definitional issues that challenge researchers in the field, in addition to insufficient research funds.

The goal of this chapter is to offer suggestions for direction to guide future research in the area of child abuse and neglect over the course of the next decade. However, the chapter is limited in its scope, since it focuses on the connections between the experiences of early childhood abuse (physical and sexual abuse) and childhood neglect and delinquency and youth violence. The first part of this chapter describes some of the background literature on this topic and more recent findings from my own research as well as that of others on the relationship between child abuse and neglect and delinquency and youth violence. The second part of the chapter highlights six research needs that I believe warrant more attention: (1) examine the consequences of child abuse and neglect by gender and race–ethnicity; (2) pay more attention to neglected children; (3) examine the role of the juvenile justice system in the processing and handling of child abuse and neglect cases; (4) examine the role of criminal sanctions in cases

CATHY SPATZ WIDOM • Department of Psychiatry, New Jersey Medical School, Newark, New Jersey 07107-3000.

Handbook of Youth and Justice, edited by White. Kluwer Academic / Plenum Publishers, New York, 2001.

of child abuse and neglect; (5) consider the effects on children of witnessing violence in the home and community; and (6) identify protective factors or intervention experiences.

THE CONNECTION BETWEEN CHILD ABUSE AND NEGLECT AND DELINQUENCY AND YOUTH VIOLENCE

Early Work

One of the frequent observations in the criminology literature has been the association between child abuse and neglect and delinquency and violent criminal behavior. A number of studies examined the relationship between child abuse and neglect and delinquency (for reviews, see Garbarino & Plantz, 1986; Gray, 1986; Widom, 1989b). However, as late as 1984, a national conference was held to examine whether child abuse represented a prelude to delinquency (Gray, 1986). That 1984 conference ended with a call for research that clarified the link between child abuse and neglect and later delinquency.

Early prospective studies that followed up abused or neglected children found that the incidence of later delinquency was between 10 and 17% (Alfaro, 1981; Bolton, Reich, & Gutierres, 1979; McCord, 1983). In retrospective studies (in which a sample of delinquent youths is asked about or official records are checked to determine the extent of abuse or neglect in their backgrounds) estimates of abuse generally ranged from 9 to 29%. Interestingly, in both types of studies, the majority of delinquents were not abused or neglected as children and the majority of abused and neglected children did not appear to become delinquent, despite the fact that abused and neglected children were at increased risk for delinquency.

Several further studies (Alfaro, 1981; Fagan, Hansen, & Jang, 1983; Geller & Ford-Somma, 1984; Gutierres & Reich, 1981; Hartstone & Hansen, 1984; Jenkins, 1968; Kratcoski, 1982; Kruttschnitt, Heath, & Ward, 1986; Lewis et al., 1985; Lewis, Shanok, Pincus, & Glaser, 1979; McCord, 1983) examined the link between child abuse and neglect and *violent* criminal behavior. However, these findings were contradictory. Some provided support for the relationship. In some, abused and nonabused delinquents did not differ (Kratcoski, 1982). In at least one study, abused delinquents were less likely to engage in later aggressive crimes (Gutierres & Reich, 1981). Fagan et al. (1983) found low incidences of both child abuse and parental violence among violent juvenile offenders compared with nationwide rates.

In an earlier review of the cycle of violence literature, Widom (1989a) concluded that "methodological problems play a major role in restricting our knowledge of the long-term consequences" of childhood victimization, particularly in regard to delinquency and violent criminal behavior. With few exceptions, studies relied on retrospective, unsubstantiated reports of abuse and neglect and most did not incorporate control groups in their designs. Since many of the same family and demographic characteristics found in abusive home environments also relate to delinquency and adult criminality, appropriate control groups are necessary to assess the independent effects of childhood victimization. Without control groups to prove rough estimates of such base rates, it has been difficult to assess the magnitude of these relationships. As Monahan (1981) argued, the most important piece of information we can have in the prediction of violence is the base rate of violent behavior in the population with which we are dealing.

The second generation of research on the child abuse and neglect and delinquency connection was designed to avoid a number of the methodological problems identified in the earlier research. In the next section, some of the more recent research linking childhood victimization to delinquency and youth violence is described.

Recent Work

My research involves a prospective cohorts design study in which a large group of children who were abused and/or neglected between 25 and 30 years ago were followed up through an examination of official criminal records and compared with a matched control group of children of the same age, sex, race, and approximate social class. These were court-substantiated cases of physical and sexual abuse and neglect that were processed during the years 1967 through 1971 in a metropolitan county area in the Midwest. Cases were restricted to children who were 11 years of age or younger at the time of the abuse, to avoid ambiguities in the temporal ordering of childhood victimization and offending (for details of the design and subject selection criterion, see Widom, 1989a).

Information on delinquency and juvenile arrests was gathered from juvenile and criminal court files. Records of local, state, and federal law enforcement agencies were searched for adult arrests. Initial criminal history searches were conducted in 1987 and 1988 and earlier publications (e.g., Rivera & Widom, 1990; Widom, 1989b) reflect that information. Since previously published findings may have represented underestimates of the relationship between early childhood victimization and subsequent crime and violence, updated criminal history searches were conducted and completed in June 1994 (Maxfield & Widom, 1996).

Early child abuse and neglect increased a person's risk of arrest as a juvenile by 59% (see Table 1) and their risk of arrest for a violent crime as a juvenile by 67% (see Table 2). Specifically, more abused and neglected children were arrested as a juvenile (27% vs. 17%) and for a violent crime as a juvenile (5% vs. 3%) than controls. These findings demonstrated that childhood victimization was associated with an increased risk of arrest as a youth. However, these findings also indicated that the linkage between childhood victimization and later antisocial and criminal behavior is far from inevitable. Early abuse and neglect may predispose children toward a negative life trajectory, but the relationship is by no means deterministic.

My research was conducted in a metropolitan county area in the Midwest, using cases of abuse and neglect that came to the attention of the courts during the years 1967 through 1971. One question about those findings concerns the extent to which they are unique to that part of the country and to that time period. As part of the Rochester Youth Development Study (RYDS), Thornberry and his colleagues collected information on child abuse and neglect from the Department of Social Services in Rochester, New York, for the children they had been studying as part of their longitudinal study. They examined the relationship between child abuse and later delinquency, using self-report as well as official arrest information, and found relationships between child abuse and neglect and later delinquency similar to Widom's (1989b).

Specifically, Thornberry (1994) reported that 69% of the youths who had been maltreated as children reported involvement in violence as compared to 56% of those not maltreated

Table 1. Childhood Victimization and Juvenile Arrests

Juvenile arrests (%)	*n*	Abuse/control	Control	Odds ratio
Overall	1575	27.4	17.2	1.81**
Male	776	35.3	23.1	1.82**
Female	799	20.0	11.4	1.94**
Black	515	40.6	20.9	2.58**
White	1053	21.8	15.2	1.55*

*$P < .01$; **$P < .001$.

Table 2. Childhood Victimization and Youth Violence

Juvenile arrests (%)	*n*	Abuse/control	Control	Odds ratio
Overall	1575	5.3	2.7	2.01**
Male	776	8.6	5.1	1.75
Female	799	2.2	0.3	7.28*
Black	515	12.1	5.1	2.55**
White	1053	2.3	1.4	1.64

*$P < .05$; **$P < .01$.

(maltreatment includes substantiated cases of physical or sexual abuse or neglect that occurred before age 12). Other analyses indicated that child maltreatment also was a significant risk factor for the prevalence and frequency of delinquency, even when gender, race–ethnicity, family structure, and social class were controlled (Smith & Thornberry, 1995).

Using maltreated children and two court-aged, nonmaltreated comparison samples from another geographic area of the country (Mecklenburg County, North Carolina), Zingraff, Leiter, Myers, and Johnsen (1993) also found that maltreated children had higher rates of delinquency complaints than nonmaltreated school and impoverished children. The effects were diminished when the authors controlled for demographic and family structure variables.

Thus, in these recent prospective studies in different parts of the country and using cases from different time periods, childhood abuse and neglect have been found to increase a person's risk of arrest as a delinquent. Together, these studies are beginning to disentangle the connections between childhood victimization and subsequent delinquency and violence. Nonetheless, there remain many important gaps in our knowledge about the consequences of childhood victimization. The next section calls attention to six critical research needs.

FUTURE RESEARCH NEEDS

Examine the Consequences of Child Abuse and Neglect by Gender and Race–Ethnicity

Research in the field of child abuse and neglect has demonstrated that abusive early childhood experiences are a major component of many child and adult mental and behavioral disorders, ranging from relatively short-term to longer-term consequences. For example, physical consequences range from minor injuries to severe brain damage and even death. Psychological consequences are believed to include chronic low self-esteem, depression, and higher suicide attempt rates. Cognitive effects of abuse and neglect have included attentional problems and learning disorders as well as severe organic brain syndromes and limited intellectual development. The behavioral consequences range from poor peer relations to extraordinarily violent behaviors. Thus, the consequences of child abuse and neglect not only affect the victims themselves but the larger society in which they live (Widom, 2000).

Gender Differences in Consequences of Child Abuse and Neglect

Surprisingly little research has compared the consequences of child abuse and neglect for males and females separately. While some studies have reported gender differences in response to abuse (Dodge, Bates, & Pettit, 1990; Friedrich, Urquiza, & Beilke, 1986; Harrison, Hoffmann, & Edwall, 1989; Ireland & Widom, 1994; Livingston, 1987; Toray, Coughlin, Vuchinich, & Patricelli, 1991; Widom, 1989b, 1994; Widom, Ireland, & Glynn, 1995), others have not found such differences (Dembo et al., 1989, 1990).

Early clinical reports on the connections between childhood abuse and neglect and violence primarily described violent *male* adolescents. Studies of childhood victimization and sexual promiscuity and teenage pregnancy have focused on samples of *females* and primarily females who were sexually abused. For each of these sex-linked outcomes (violence:male and sexuality:female), studying the nonstereotypic sex may yield important insights. Finkelhor (1990) has called attention to the need to study males who have been sexually abused in childhood at the same time that we continue to attend to the research and treatment needs of female childhood sexual abuse. It also may be instructive to examine the extent to which sexually abused males are sexually promiscuous and involved in paternity as a teenager (even if they are not responsible for the care of the child).

Although gender differences in the consequences of child abuse and neglect have not received much attention, some writers have discussed differences in the manifestations of distress, suggesting some conformity to gender roles (Dohrenwend & Dohrenwend, 1976; Downey, Feldman, Khuri, & Friedman, 1994; Horwitz & White, 1987; Widom, 1984). Downey et al. (1994) have suggested that gender differences in the consequences of abuse may parallel the gender differences in expressions of psychopathology, and that aggression and depression may be different expressions of the same underlying distress, perhaps reflecting different strategies for maintaining self-esteem in the face of perceived rejection. For example, one might expect males to direct their suffering in an outward (externalizing) direction, as in aggression, and females to direct their pain inwardly (internalizing), with self-destructive behaviors and depression.

Some gender differences in the consequences of early childhood victimization have been reported recently. For example, using two different alcohol-related outcomes, Ireland and Widom (1994) and Widom, Ireland, and Glynn (1995) found that abused and neglected females were at increased risk for alcohol problems (arrests for alcohol and/or drugs and alcohol abuse/dependence diagnoses), whereas males were not. Luntz and Widom (1994) reported that abused and neglected males were at increased risk of diagnosis of antisocial personality disorder (ASPD) in young adulthood, whereas females were not. However, the Luntz and Widom (1994) findings were based on a subset of the larger sample in the follow-up study ($N = 699$). In subsequent analyses with the completed follow-up sample ($N = 1196$), abused and neglected males and females were at increased risk for being diagnosed as ASPD, findings that persisted despite controls for age, race, and criminal history (Widom, 1998).

Looking back at Table 1, it is clear that both male and female abused and neglected children are at increased risk of being arrested as a juvenile. Looking at Table 2, it also is clear that abused and neglected males and females have higher rates of arrest for violence as juveniles than controls. The odds of abused and neglected females being arrested for a violent crime as a juvenile are 7.3 times higher than for controls; for males, the odds are 1.7 times higher (by conventional standards, not quite a significant difference for males). For males, the dichotomous indicator of arrest for violent crime does not differentiate the abused and neglected males from control males. However, abused and neglected males have significantly higher numbers of arrests for violence throughout their life course than control males.

For females, the pattern observed in Table 2 (arrests for violence as a juvenile) was found to continue into adulthood (Maxfield & Widom, 1996). One might speculate that the increase in risk of arrest for violence among the abused and neglected females into young adulthood would be associated with a different kind of violence (domestic violence, as in child and spouse abuse) that might develop later and also is less likely to come to the attention of criminal justice officials. On the other hand, what some might have considered a weak finding in earlier reports (that is, that abused and neglected females were significantly more likely to be arrested as a *juvenile* for a violent crime than control females) might have presaged a more enduring pattern of behavior that is more accurately depicted when subjects are traced through early adulthood. These relationships are missed when studies focus exclusively on youths and do not follow individuals into adulthood and peak years of risk for violent offending.

Our general expectation that abused and neglected females should manifest the consequences of their early childhood experiences in internalizing directions (such as suicide attempts) has received some support (Widom, 1998). However, for this sample, our findings suggest that abused and neglected females are at increased risk for externalizing (being arrested for a violent crime and being diagnosed with ASPD) as well as internalizing. Based on these findings, one might conclude that the sex-role-stereotyped expectations of males to externalize and females to internalize do not represent an adequate picture of these abused and neglected children in young adulthood. For this sample, at least, the evidence suggests that the consequences of childhood victimization may be more complex than previously envisioned.

Other factors also introduce complexity into the study of gender differences in consequences of childhood victimization. First, some of the lack of attention to gender differences in consequences may result from the small number of male victims of sexual abuse in most studies and the lower rates of reporting childhood sexual abuse in males (Finkelhor, 1990). Second, males and females are not necessarily subject to the same forms of maltreatment (Adams-Tucker, 1982; Gutierres & Reich, 1981). Since males and females may experience different types of abuse or neglect, any differences in their responses to maltreatment may be a function of the type of maltreatment rather than gender differences. Thus, type of childhood abuse or neglect might be the critical variable in determining the person's risk for subsequent problem behaviors. Finally, there are differences in the prevalence of certain forms of psychopathology and psychiatric diagnoses by gender (Robins & Regier, 1991), which at a minimum suggest interactions in outcome patterns by gender. Studies are needed with sample sizes large enough to provide systematic examination of some of the issues raised here.

Race–Ethnicity Differences in Consequences of Child Abuse and Neglect

Korbin (1980) has called attention to the importance of culture in defining and understanding child abuse. For example, at least one report comparing the profiles of Chinese-American, Native Indian, and Anglo-Canadian children and abusers has suggested that there may be important cultural differences in the role of substance abuse (Leung & Carter, 1983). In our work on the cycle of violence (Maxfield & Widom, 1996; Widom, 1989a), black abused and neglected children (as compared to black nonabused and nonneglected children) were at increased risk of arrest for a violent crime, whereas this pattern of increased risk of arrest associated with childhood victimization was not found for the white children in the sample.

Societal practices can lead to unequal distribution of resources and educational and employment opportunities. Wyatt (1990) has called attention to the ways in which racial and ethnic minority children may encounter discrimination against their race, color, language, life, and family styles that affect their self-esteem and exacerbate the initial and lasting effects of earlier childhood victimization. In a paper on the epidemiology of trauma, Norris (1992) reported complex findings regarding race, which she felt "highlighted the importance of specifying the cultural context in which traumatic events occur." There is a need to examine differences in consequences of childhood victimization associated with race–ethnicity as well as the role of family and community factors, especially since poor and ethnic minority children are more likely to be identified as maltreated than children from more affluent white families (Newberger, Reed, Daniel, Hyde, & Kotelchuck, 1977).

If there are differences in the community or system's response to abused and neglected children as a function of differences in ethnic or racial backgrounds, then it is important to identify these differences, particularly if they relate to subsequent levels of violence in these children. Lewis, Shanok, Cohen, Kligfield, and Frisone (1980) compared two samples of adolescents—one sent to a correctional facility and the other admitted to a state psychiatric hospital—in one urban area during a 1-year time period. The most powerful distinguishing factor between the two groups was race: 71% of the hospitalized adolescents were white, whereas 67% of the incarcerated adolescents were black: "Our clinical and epidemiological findings indicate clearly that many seriously psychiatrically disturbed, aggressive black adolescents are being channeled to correctional facilities while their equally aggressive white counterparts are directed toward psychiatric treatment facilities" (p. 1216). Not only would this practice "reinforce the stereotypes instead of demolishing them" (Comer, 1972), but it would perpetuate the segregation of white and black violently disturbed adolescents.

In a more recent examination of the role of clinical and institutional interventions in children's recovery from sexual abuse, Newberger and Gremy (1995) found that children of color received later and less outpatient therapy than white children and were more likely to be placed outside the home and to be hospitalized for psychiatric diagnoses. If the abuse or neglect experiences of some children are being identified at a later point in the process, then there is less opportunity to intervene positively in these children's lives and more time for dysfunctional behaviors to become firmly entrenched. If earlier identification of abuse and neglect leads to positive interventions, then this should minimize negative outcomes. The longer society waits to intervene, the more difficult the change process becomes and the less time positive influences have to affect the developing child. Abused and neglected children may become angry and hostile in response, adopting what has been called a "hostile world-view" (Crittendon & Ainsworth, 1989). In turn, these angry and hostile feelings may give way to antisocial and violent behavior patterns.

Furthermore, access to therapeutic care is often determined by social service or law enforcement personnel, and availability of medical or psychological services is vastly uneven in different social contexts. As a result, in some communities, only a small portion of victims have access to services they need. Given the apparent race-specific nature of the relationship between childhood victimization and violent offending (Maxfield & Widom, 1996; Rivera & Widom, 1990) and the fact that other researchers have found background experiences associated with violent crimes to vary depending on the person's race (Kruttschnitt et al., 1986), it seems critical to attempt to examine these relationships more closely.

Surveillance bias further complicates the issue. Poor and ethnic minority children are more likely to be identified as maltreated than more affluent white families (e.g., Newberger et al., 1977). A reanalysis of the first National Incidence Study (National Center for Child Abuse and Neglect, 1981) found that class and race were the best predictors of whether an incident was reported by hospitals, with impoverished black families more likely to be reported than affluent white families, regardless of the severity of the incident (Newberger, Newberger, & Hampton, 1983). Service availability and severity of worker caseloads also may affect reporting by ethnicity (Light, 1974; Wolock & Horowitz, 1985).

Maxfield and Widom (1996) suggested that childhood victimization is best viewed as one among a constellation of risk factors. This observation takes on added meaning when considering the overall levels of arrests among abused or neglected individuals and controls, especially for specific subgroups. Forty percent of black victims of child abuse and neglect (compared to 21% of black controls) were arrested as juveniles (Table 1); 11% were arrested as a juvenile for a violent offense (Table 2) compared to 5% of black controls. The already higher risk of arrest for blacks compared to whites is exacerbated by childhood victimization. As one of a constellation of risk factors, abuse or neglect magnifies preexisting disparities between blacks and whites. This perspective is particularly important when administrative data from agency records are used to identify cases, as they are in many contemporary studies, since it is known that agency records overrepresent low-income families (Sedlak, 1990). Similarly, arrests for violent and nonviolent offenses are inversely associated with income (Weis, 1986). However, the findings shown in Table 2 indicate that childhood abuse and neglect increment the risk of arrest for violence among a group of people already at higher risk. We lack systematic knowledge about the ways in which the juvenile justice and social service systems respond to children of different ethnic backgrounds and the ways in which those responses influence the subsequent development of these children.

Pay More Attention to Neglected Children

Widom (1989b) reported that childhood victims of physical abuse and neglect were significantly more likely to be arrested for a violent offense. Six years later, after updating criminal histories, Maxfield and Widom (1996) reported that the effects of physical abuse and neglect persisted into young adulthood. Although physically abused children had the highest rate of arrest for any violent crime (21% arrested as a juvenile or as an adult), neglected children had arrest rates for violence almost as high (20%). While these findings support the notion of a cycle of violence, they also reinforce the need to recognize the consequences of neglect. This is especially important given that neglect is far more common in nationwide estimates of abuse and neglect. The 1993 incidence rates have been estimated to be 13.1 per 1000 children for neglect compared to 5.7 and 3.2 for physical and sexual abuse, respectively (Sedlak & Broadhurst, 1996).

The long-term effects of neglect may be at least partly related to the fact that neglect is defined by public officials as a more chronic condition compared to physical or sexual violence inflicted on a child. Research has shown that family violence, including child abuse, is more likely to involve repeat attacks than stranger violence (Moore, Prothrow-Stith, Guyer, & Spivak, 1994). But neglect is by definition a persistent failure to provide proper care, nutrition, hygiene, and living environment. At least one study has claimed that parents who are neglectful expose their children to more negative behavior over a longer period of time than abusive parents (Burgess & Conger, 1978). Other researchers have suggested that neglect by itself might be more harmful, having serious long-term negative consequences (Bousha & Twentyman, 1984; McCord, 1983). While researchers have begun to pay more attention to neglect, there is a critical need for research on this topic.

Examine the Role of the Juvenile Justice System in the Processing and Handling of Child Abuse and Neglect Cases

The next two sections rely heavily on recommendations of the National Research Council (1993) report on *Understanding Child Abuse and Neglect*. (I want to acknowledge my debt to the National Research Council panel report. I was a member of that panel and believe these recommendations are particularly relevant to the concerns of this chapter.)

Much has been written about the short- and long-term consequences of childhood victimization experiences (e.g., Widom, 2000). However, rather than the victimization experience per se, problem behaviors in abused and neglected children may result from the chain of events occurring subsequent to the victimization. For example, being separated from one's biological parents, subsequent to the abuse and neglect incident(s), and placed in foster care can be associated with deleterious effects (Bohman & Sigvardsson, 1980; Bryce & Ehlert, 1977; Canning, 1974; Frank, 1980; Littner, 1974).

The observed relationship between early childhood victimization and later problem behaviors, such as delinquency or violence, also may be affected by practices of the juvenile justice system, which may disproportionately label and adjudicate maltreatment victims as juvenile offenders. Indeed, Garbarino and Plantz (1986) suggested that the behavioral responses to maltreatment ultimately may lead to delinquency as a consequence of maltreatment. A child who becomes estranged from his or her parents or from prosocial peers may develop friendships with antisocial friends. In turn, this association with delinquent friends leads to the adoption of a highly visible delinquent lifestyle.

Although some child abuse and neglect cases substantiated by child protection agencies are dealt with by juvenile, family, and criminal courts, there is no standard policy that provides a framework or guide for the justice system's response to these cases. Juvenile courts handle dependency proceedings, including adoption and foster care placements. Family courts may become involved in child abuse and neglect cases when one parent seeks action against another in a custody case or when evidence of abuse is considered in visitation or family custody decisions. Criminal courts respond to charges against adults who have abused or molested a child.

After completing its review, the National Research Council (1993) panel concluded that research directed at understanding the factors that influence methods used to investigate allegations of maltreatment was needed. For example, the panel cited the work of Thoenes and Tjaden (1990), which indicated that factors that appear to be correlated with the substantiation of a report include the beliefs or assumptions of child protection services workers, the victim's age, and reports of multiple or recent indictments. However, the panel noted that relatively little empirical evidence exists about the progression of these cases over time. State agencies typically lack reliable criteria to assist their staff in making informed judgments in their investigations of reported or suspected child abuse or neglect.

Similarly, research on the operation of the child protection system, including an evaluation of the sequential stages by which children receive treatment following reports of child abuse or neglect, is needed. The factors that influence different aspects of case handling decisions, factors that improve the delivery of case services, and alternatives to existing arrangements for providing services to children and families in distress need to be described and evaluated. Research also is needed on the interactions (or lack of interactions) of the different agencies involved in intervention and treatment programs for abused and neglected children and their families and the extent to which decisions made by one agency affect outcomes made by others.

> Legal interventions in child abuse and neglect cases are often complicated by many factors, including the lack of physical evidence, difficulties in obtaining consistent and reliable testimony from children, and the emotional traumas that might be associated with the testimony itself. (National Research Council, 1993, p. 273)

Despite the fact that relatively few cases of sexual abuse are processed through the criminal courts, the treatment of child sexual abuse cases has received substantial research attention

(Goodman, Bottoms, Herscovici, & Shaver, 1989; King, Hunger, & Runyan, 1988; Runyan, Everson, Edelsohn, Hunter, & Coulter, 1988; Whitcomb, 1992). In contrast, little is known about the impact and quality of court experiences for cases of childhood physical abuse or neglect. Similarly, there is a need to know more about the impact of guardian ad litem and volunteer court-appointed special advocates (CASA) programs on the outcome of court cases and on the children involved.

Examine the Role of Criminal Sanctions in Cases of Child Abuse and Neglect

The use of criminal sanctions is an important part of the prevention of child abuse and neglect because of the belief that strict legal standards and punishment will reduce the incidence of child maltreatment. Nevertheless, the National Research Council (1993) concluded that

> the use of criminal penalties to deter offenders and the development of judicial and administrative procedures to remove children from abusing parents may be counterproductive in some cases, particularly in situations involving parental offenders and mild to moderate forms of child abuse or neglect. (p. 190)

They pointed out that reliance on criminal penalties does not address issues of improving parenting skills for abusive and neglectful parents.

Research is needed to determine whether criminal penalties deter child abuse or neglect. In considering the effectiveness of criminal sanctions in cases of child abuse and neglect, however, the often present multiple problems of abusive and neglectful families need to be recognized. Many of these families are already involved with the legal system as a result of other behaviors, such as substance abuse, spouse abuse, or other crimes. Since perpetrators of child abuse may have been removed from the home for a variety of reasons or may not be living in the home, assessment of the impact of criminal sanctions in cases of child abuse and neglect is complex.

Research also is needed to determine whether and to what degree removal of offenders or children from the home protects the child from further abuse. Ideally, research involving case–control designs, similar to those used to assess alternative intervention strategies in cases of spouse abuse (Sherman, 1992) would be undertaken. The work of Sherman (1992), for example, suggests that field experiments can be conducted in an ethical and sensitive manner. Since the effectiveness of treatment versus punishment might vary depending on the type of abuse or neglect involved, future research needs to consider the effectiveness of these interventions in cases involving different types of childhood maltreatment.

Consider the Effects on Children of Witnessing Violence in the Home or Community

A new area of research recently has begun to focus on the effects of witnessing violence in the home or community. Studies differ in regard to methodological rigor and not surprisingly findings are not consistent. For example, some studies have reported that the effect of a child's witnessing violence toward parents may be as harmful as the experience of direct victimization (Rosenbaum & O'Leary, 1981), while other studies have not found this to be the case (Christopoulos et al., 1987; Hughes, 1988; Wolfe, Zak, Wilson, & Jaffe, 1986). Children from violent homes have shown more externalizing behavior problems than comparison group children (Jaffe, Wolfe, Wilson, & Zak, 1986; Wolfe et al., 1986), whereas other studies have found that exposure to marital violence was associated with increased levels of aggression in females only (Forsstrom-Cohen & Rosenbaum, 1985) or in school-age boys (Hughes & Barad, 1983). Hershorn and Rosenbaum (1985) found no differences between violent and nonviolent groups if the families displayed about the same amount of marital discord. Wolfe, Jaffe, Wilson, and Zak (1985) found that if concurrent maternal psychological adjustment and family stress and crises were factored in, the differences in the magnitude of externalizing problems between children from violent and nonviolent homes were eliminated.

Studies have examined the effects of witnessing verbal hostility and physical violence between parents on children compared to witnessing verbal hostility alone (Fantuzzo et al., 1991). However, Sternberg et al. (1993) found that witnessing spouse abuse did not affect children's evaluations of their adjustment as much as did being a victim of physical abuse or being a victim and witness of spousal abuse. Given the differences in methodologies and design, it is not surprising that different findings emerged. But, given the widespread nature of these childhood experiences, it seems imperative to understand their impact on children.

A second type of research is represented by studies that focus on the effects of witnessing violence in the community. Initially, clinical reports described the aftermath of witnessing traumatic events, such as sniper attacks (Pynoos & Nader, 1989) or the experiences of a group of children who had been kidnapped from their school bus and buried alive (Terr, 1990). Frederick (1985) characterized children traumatized by catastrophic situations as having fears of recurrence, continuing concerns about security, anger, and preoccupations about revenge, among other problems. In play, these children have been found to repeat the traumatic themes they have witnessed, particularly those of fear and/or aggression (Terr, 1990). Osofsky, Wewers, Hann, and Fick (1993) described symptoms of "reduced involvement with the external world resulting in constricted affect, fewer interests, and feelings of estrangement." Some of these children developed posttraumatic stress disorder (PTSD), whereas others became angry and violent. As a group, these children became more aggressive in their play and imitated behaviors they had seen. Their behavior was interpreted as a desperate effort to protect themselves and to "act tough" to deal with their fear; as a result, these children developed counterphobic reactions and acted uncaring because of having to deal with so much hurt and loss. Reaching a similar conclusion, based on a study of low-income African-American youth (ages 7–18), Fitzpatrick (1993) found that "youths chronically exposed to violence experienced a desensitization process."

It is too early to draw firm conclusions from this new area of research on the effects of witnessing violence, especially about the relationship between these childhood experiences and adult antisocial behavior. However, given the level of violence in some communities around the country, research examining the effects on children of growing up in these neighborhoods and families clearly is needed.

Identify Protective Factors or Intervention Experiences

Not all abused and neglected children succumb to the kinds of negative outcomes that are the focus of this chapter—delinquency and violent offending. Studies of the impact of childhood abuse and neglect find substantial groups of individuals who appear to have little or no symptomatology (Caffaro-Rouget, Lang, & Van Santen, 1989; Conte & Schuerman, 1987; Kaufman & Zigler, 1987; Kendall-Tackett, Williams, & Finkelhor, 1993; Mannarino & Cohen, 1987; McCord, 1983; Sirles, Smith, & Kusama, 1989; Tong, Oates, & McDowell, 1987; Widom, 1989a, 1994). A number of explanations for these findings can be offered, including inadequate measurement techniques or denial on the part of the victims. However, it also is possible that some characteristics of the child (good coping skills) or the child's environment (a relationship with a significant and supportive person) may have acted to buffer the individual from long-term negative consequences. Garmezy (1981) has called these protective factors—those dispositional attributes, environmental conditions, biological predispositions, and positive events that can act to mitigate against early negative experiences.

What are some of the possible mediating variables (attributes and experiences) that may act to buffer abused and neglected children from the negative outcomes? High (or above average) intelligence and good scholastic attainment may exert a protective effect in the context of an abusive environment. Intelligence may play a direct role or it may operate as a protective influence mediating such other factors as school performance, problem-solving skills, or levels of self-esteem. Frodi and Smetana (1984) found that, if one controls for IQ, differences between maltreated and nonmaltreated children in their ability to discriminate emotions disappeared. High-IQ children maintained good achievement test performance at both low and high levels of stress, whereas low-IQ children showed a drop in performance under high stress (Garmezy, Masten, & Tellegen, 1984).

Empirical findings suggest that a person's cognitive appraisal of life events strongly influences his or her response (Lazarus & Launier, 1978). The same event may be perceived by different individuals as irrelevant, benign, positive, or threatening and harmful. In thinking about the effects of abuse and neglect, it is likely that the child's cognitive appraisal of these events will determine at least in part whether they are experienced as neutral, negative, or harmful. In part, this might reflect the system's response to the abusive or neglectful experience or the individual child's perception of the experience. Cognitive appraisal may be particularly important in abuse involving older children who have the cognitive skills necessary to process the event (Maccoby, 1983).

As part of a larger 14-year longitudinal study of 2000 families, Zimrin (1986) identified 35 families with abused children. Abused children ($N = 9$) who survived the trauma of their childhood and grew up to be well-adjusted individuals were compared with the nonsurvivor children, who showed a high degree of psychosocial pathology. A number of variables distinguished the two groups of children, including fatalism, self-esteem, cognitive abilities, self-destructiveness, hope and fantasy, behavior patterns, and external support. Zimrin's interpretation was that the perception of the survivor group of their good personal resources, intellectual potential, good self-image, and hope, coupled with relatively sound external resources, tipped the scale in their favor.

For some children, having a difficult temperament may place a child at risk by virtue of its negative effects on parent–child interactions (Patterson, DeBaryshe, & Ramsey, 1989). Although there is some indication that children with difficult temperaments are singled out for abuse (Herrenkohl & Herrenkohl, 1981), other researchers have not found this to be the case (Friedrich & Boriskin, 1976), and the issue remains open for further investigation. It is likely that temperament interacts with early childhood experiences to exacerbate in some cases or to minimize in other cases a child's level of risk for the development of subsequent problem behaviors.

Clinicians and child protection service workers also have stressed the importance of a significant person in the lives of abused and neglected children as a protective factor, although relatively little systematic evidence of their role as buffers for victimized children exists. Garmezy (1981) identified the presence of a supportive family member as one of the important themes in the lives of children who overcame adversity. In a follow-up study by Lynch and Roberts (1982), children who had recovered from their childhood maltreatment had the support of an adult. Farber and Egeland (1987) found few competent "survivors" among physically or emotionally neglected children. Children who were more likely to be competent were those children whose mothers showed some interest in them and were able to respond to them emotionally. For sexually abused children, one positive mediating variable appears to be the presence of a supportive, positive relationship with a nonabusive parent or sibling (Conte & Schuerman, 1988).

Finally, although out-of-home placements and foster care are conceptualized as interventions designed to positively affect the development of abused and neglected children, the role of these experiences remains controversial and ethically complex (Runyan, Gould, Trost, & Loda, 1982). While critics have argued against foster care and out-of-home placement experiences, some evidence suggests that out-of-home placement for some abused and neglected children may not be detrimental to their long-term development and that early stable placements may be associated with better outcomes (Widom, 1991). When a foster parent becomes a "significant person" for an abused or neglected child, this may represent a turning point in that child's life and serve in a protective manner.

Despite promising leads, it is clear that more research is needed on protective characteristics of the child or his or her life experiences that positively influence development away from delinquency and violent criminal behavior and toward more positive behavioral outcomes. Research also is needed to examine the role of placements as buffers in the lives of abused and neglected children. For example, it is unknown whether there are critical time periods after which interventions become substantially less effective. Research on behavior change suggests that interventions may be more effective in the early stages of development than at later stages. It is not surprising that once problem behaviors have occurred, later interventions become more labor intensive and face more entrenched behavior patterns than when efforts are targeted at younger children.

CONCLUSION

While research in the field of child abuse and neglect has made substantial methodological and theoretical progress over the last 20 years, the field remains in the early stages of development. There is a critical need for an influx of research input and resources from scholars and funding agencies. Child abuse and neglect represent major social problems and the incidence of cases of child abuse and neglect keeps increasing. While the consequences of child abuse and neglect have a potentially broad reach to affect many domains of a child's functioning, the spillover from direct consequences to the child to the child's family, future family, neighborhood, and community are enormous.

ACKNOWLEDGMENTS

This research was supported by grants from the National Institute of Mental Health (MH49467), National Institute of Alcohol Abuse and Alcoholism (AA09238), National Institute on Drug Abuse (DA10060), and the National Institute of Justice (86-IJ-CX-0033, 89-IJ-CX-0007, and 93-IJ-CX-0031). Points of view are those of the author and do not necessarily represent the position of the United States Department of Justice.

REFERENCES

Adams-Tucker, C. (1982). Proximate effects of sexual abuse in childhood: A report on 28 children. *American Journal of Psychiatry*, *139*, 1252–1256.

Alfaro, J. D. (1981). Report on the relationship between child abuse and neglect and later socially deviant behavior. In R. J. Hunner & Y. B. Walker (Eds.), *Exploring the relationship between child abuse and delinquency* (pp. 175–219). Montclair, NJ: Allanheld, Osmun.

Bohman, M., & Sigvardsson, S. (1980). Negative social heritage. *Adoption and Fostering*, *3*, 25–34.

Bolton, F. G., Reich, J., & Gutierres, S. E. (1979). Delinquency patterns in maltreated children and siblings. *Victimology*, *2*, 349–359.

Bousha, D. M., & Twentyman, C. T. (1984). Mother–child interactional style in abuse, neglect and control groups: Naturalistic observations in the home. *Journal of Abnormal Psychology*, *93*, 106–114.

Bryce, M. E., & Ehlert, R. C. (1977). 144 foster children. *Child Welfare*, *50*, 499–503.

Burgess, R. L., & Conger, R. D. (1978). Family interaction in abusive, neglectful, and normal families. *Child Development*, *49*, 1163–1173.

Caffaro-Rouget, A., Lang, R. A., & Van Santen, V. (1989). The impact of child sexual abuse on victims' adjustment. *Annals of Sex Research*, *2*(1), 29–47.

Canning, R. (1974). School experiences of foster children. *Child Welfare*, *53*, 582–587.

Christopoulos, C., Cohn, D. A., Shaw, D. S., Joyce, S., Sullivan-Hanson, J., Kraft, S. P., & Emery, R. E. (1987). Children of abused women: I. Adjustment at time of shelter residence. *Journal of Marriage and the Family*, *49*, 611–619.

Comer, J. (1972). *Beyond black and white*. New York: Quadrangle.

Conte, J. R., & Schuerman, J. R. (1987). Factors associated with an increased impact of child sexual abuse. *Child Abuse and Neglect*, *11*, 201–211.

Conte, J. R., & Schuerman, J. R. (1988). The effects of sexual abuse on children: A multidimensional view. *Journal of Interpersonal Violence*, *2*, 380–390.

Crittendon, P. M., & Ainsworth, M. D. S. (1989). Child maltreatment and attachment theory. In D. Cicchetti & V. Carlson (Eds.), *Child maltreatment* (pp. 432–463). New York: Cambridge University Press.

Dembo, R., Williams, L., La Voie, L., Berry, E., Getreu, A., Wish, E., Schmeidler, J., & Washburn, M. (1989). Physical abuse, sexual victimization, and illicit drug use: Replication of a structural analysis among a new sample of high-risk youths. *Violence and Victims*, *4*, 121–137.

Dembo, R., Williams, L., La Voie, L., Schmeidler, J., Kern, J., Getreu, A., Barry, E., Genung, L., & Wish, E. (1990). A longitudinal study of the relationship among alcohol use, marijuana/hashish use, cocaine use, and emotional/psychological functioning problems in a cohort of high risk youths. *International Journal of the Addictions*, *25*, 1341–1382.

Dodge, K. A., Bates, J. E., & Pettit, G. S. (1990). Mechanisms in the cycle of violence. *Science*, *250*, 1678–1683.

Dohrenwend, B. P., & Dohrenwend, B. S. (1976). Sex differences in psychiatric disorders. *American Journal of Sociology*, *81*, 1447–1459.

Downey, G., Feldman, S., Khuri, J., & Friedman, S. (1994). Maltreatment and childhood depression. In W. M. Reynolds & H. F. Johnson (Eds.), *Handbook of depression in children and adolescents* (pp. 481–508). New York: Plenum Press.

Fagan, J., Hansen, K. V., & Jang, M. (1983). Profiles of chronically violent delinquents: Empirical test of an integrated theory. In J. Kleugel (Ed.), *Evaluating juvenile justice* (pp. 91–119). Beverly Hills, CA: Sage Publications.

Fantuzzo, J. W., DePaola, L. M., Lambert, L., Martino, T., Anderson, G., & Sutton, S. (1991). Effects of interparental violence on the psychological adjustment and competencies of young children. *Journal of Consulting and Clinical Psychology*, *59*, 258–265.

Farber, E. A., & Egeland, B. (1987). Invulnerability among abused and neglected children. In E. J. Anthony & B. Cohler (Eds.), *The invulnerable child* (pp. 253–288). New York: Guilford Press.

Finkelhor, D. (1990). Early and long-term effects of child sexual abuse: An update. *Professional Psychology: Research and Practice*, *21*, 325–330.

Fitzpatrick, K. M. (1993). Exposure to violence and presence of depression among low-income, African-American youth. *Journal of Consulting and Clinical Psychology*, *61*(3), 528–531.

Forsstrom-Cohen, B., & Rosenbaum, A. (1985). The effects of parental marital violence on young adults: An exploratory investigation. *Journal of Marriage and the Family*, *47*, 467–472.

Frank, G. L. (1980). Treatment needs of children in foster care. *American Journal of Orthopsychiatry*, *50*, 256–263.

Frederick, C. (1985). Children traumatized by catastrophic situations. In J. Laube & S. A. Murphy (Eds.), *Perspectives on disaster recovery* (pp. 10–30). East Norwalk, CT: Appleton-Century-Crofts.

Friedrich, W., & Boriskin, J. A. (1976). The role of the child in abuse: A review of the literature. *American Journal of Orthopsychiatry*, *46*, 580–590.

Friedrich, W. H., Urquiza, A. J., & Beilke, R. L. (1986). Behavior problems in sexually abused young children. *Journal of Pediatric Psychology, 11*, 47–57.

Frodi, A., & Smetana, J. (1984). Abused, neglected, and nonmaltreated preschoolers' ability to discriminate emotions in others: The effects of IQ. *Child Abuse and Neglect, 8*, 459–465.

Garbarino, J., & Plantz, M. (1986). Part I Review of the literature. (Findings of a research conference conducted by the National Committee for Prevention of Child Abuse, April 7-10, 1984). In E. Gray, J. Garbarino, & M. Plantz (Eds.), *Child abuse: Prelude to delinquency?* (pp. 5–18). Washington, DC: US Department of Justice, Office of Juvenile Justice and Delinquency Prevention.

Garmezy, N. (1981). Children under stress: Perspectives on antecedents and correlates of vulnerability and resistance to psychopathology. In A. I. Rabin, J. Arnoff, A. M. Barclay, & R. A. Zucker (Eds.), *Further explorations in personality* (pp. 196–269). New York: Wiley.

Garmezy, N., Masten, A., & Tellegen, A. (1984). The study of stress and competence in children: A building block for developmental psychopathology. *Child Development, 55*, 97–111.

Geller, M., & Ford-Somma, L. (1984). *Violent homes, violent children: A study of violence in the families of juvenile offenders*. (Prepared for the National Center on Child Abuse and Neglect). Trenton, NJ: New Jersey State Department of Corrections, Division of Juvenile Services.

Goodman, G. S., Bottoms, B. L., Herscovici, B. B., & Shaver, P. (1989). Determinants of the child victim's perceived credibility. In S. J. Ceci, D. F. Ross, & M. P. Toglia (Eds.), *Perspectives on children's testimony* (pp. 1–22). New York: Springer Verlag.

Gray, A. H. (1986). *Child abuse: Prelude to delinquency?* Paper presented at the research conference conducted by the National Committee for Prevention of Child Abuse.

Gutierres, S. E., & Reich, J. W. (1981). A developmental perspective on runaway behavior: Its relationship to child abuse. *Child Welfare, 60*, 89–94.

Harrison, P. A., Hoffmann, N. G., & Edwall, G. E. (1989). Sexual abuse correlates: Similarities between male and female adolescents in chemical dependency treatment. *Journal of Adolescent Research, 4*, 385–399.

Hartstone, E., & Hansen, K. V. (1984). The violent juvenile offender: An empirical portrait. In R. A. Mathias, P. DeMuro, & R. S. Allinson (Eds.), *Violent juvenile offenders: An anthology* (pp. 83–112). San Francisco: National Council on Crime and Delinquency.

Herrenkohl, R. C., & Herrenkohl, E. C. (1981). Some antecedents and developmental consequences of child maltreatment. In R. Rizley & D. Cicchetti (Eds.), *New directions for child development, developmental perspectives on child maltreatment* (Vol. 11, pp. 57–76). San Francisco: Jossey-Bass.

Hershorn, M., & Rosenbaum, A. (1985). Children of marital violence: A closer look at the unintended victims. *American Journal of Orthopsychiatry, 55*, 260–266.

Horwitz, A. V., & White, H. R. (1987). Gender role orientations and styles of pathology among adolescents. *Journal of Health and Social Behavior, 28*, 158–170.

Hughes, H. M. (1988). Psychological and behavioral correlates of family violence in child witnesses and victims. *American Journal of Orthopsychiatry, 58*, 77–90.

Hughes, H. M., & Barad, S. J. (1983). Psychological functioning of children in a battered women's shelter: A preliminary investigation. *American Journal of Orthopsychiatry, 53*, 525–531.

Ireland, T., & Widom, C. S. (1994). Childhood victimization and risk for alcohol and drug arrests. *International Journal of the Addictions, 29*, 235–274.

Jaffe, P., Wolfe, D., Wilson, S., & Zak, L. (1986). Similarities in behavioral and social maladjustment among child victims and witnesses to family violence. *American Journal of Orthopsychiatry, 56*, 142–146.

Jenkins, R. L. (1968). The varieties of children's behavioral problems and family dynamics. *American Journal of Psychiatry, 124*, 1440–1445.

Kaufman, J., & Zigler, E. (1987). Do abused children become abusive parents? *American Journal of Orthopsychiatry, 57*, 186–192.

Kendall-Tackett, K. A., Williams, L. M., & Finkelhor, D. J. (1993). The impact of sexual abuse on children: A review and synthesis of recent empirical studies. *Psychological Bulletin, 113*, 164–180.

King, N. M. P., Hunger, W. M., & Runyan, D. K. (1988). Going to court: The experience of child victims of intrafamilial sexual abuse. *Journal of Health Politics, Policy, and Law, 13*(Winter), 1–17.

Korbin, J. E. (1980). The cross-cultural context of child abuse and neglect. In C. H. Kempe & R. E. Helfer (Eds.), *The battered child* (3rd ed., pp. 21–35). Chicago: University of Chicago Press.

Kratcoski, P. C. (1982). Child abuse and violence against the family. *Child Welfare, 61*, 435–444.

Kruttschnitt, C., Heath, L., & Ward, D. (1986). Family violence, television viewing habits, and other adolescent experiences related to violent criminal behavior. *Criminology, 24*, 235–267.

Lazarus, R. S., & Launier, R. (1978). Stress-related transactions between person and environment. In L. A. Pervin & M. Lewis (Eds.), *Perspectives in interactional psychology* (pp. 287–327). New York: Plenum Press.

Leung, S. M. R., & Carter, J. E. (1983). Cross-cultural study of child abuse among Chinese, Native Indians, and Anglo-Canadian children. *Journal of Psychiatric Treatment and Evaluation, 5*, 37–44.

Lewis, D. O., Shanok, S. S., Pincus, J. H., & Glaser, G. H. (1979). Violent juvenile delinquents: Psychiatric, neurological, psychological, and abuse factors. *Journal of the American Academy of Child Psychiatry, 18*, 1161–1167.

Lewis, D. O., Shanok, S. S., Cohen, R. J., Kligfield, M., & Frisone, G. (1980). Race bias in the diagnosis and disposition of violent adolescents. *American Journal of Psychiatry, 137*, 1211–1216.

Lewis, D. O., Moy, E., Jackson, L. D., Aaronson, R., Restifo, N., Serra, S., & Simos, A. (1985). Biopsychological characteristics of children who later murder: A prospective study. *American Journal of Psychiatry, 142*, 1161–1167.

Light, R. J. (1974). Abused and neglected children in America: A study of alternative policies. *Harvard Educational Review, 43*, 556–598.

Littner, N. (1974). *Some traumatic effects of separation and placement*. New York: Child Welfare League of America.

Livingston, R. (1987). Sexually and physically abused children. *Journal of the American Academy of Child and Adolescent Psychiatry, 26*, 413–415.

Luntz, B. K., & Widom, C. S. (1994). Antisocial personality disorder in abused and neglected children grown up. *American Journal of Psychiatry, 151*, 670–674.

Lynch, M. A., & Roberts, J. (1982). *Consequences of child abuse*. New York: Academic Press.

Maccoby, E. E. (1983). Social–emotional development and response to stressors. In M. Rutter & N. Garmezy (Eds.), *Stress, coping, and development in children* (pp. 217–234). New York: McGraw-Hill.

Mannarino, A. P., & Cohen, J. A. (1987). A clinical–demographic study of sexually abused children. *Child Abuse and Neglect, 10*, 17–23.

Maxfield, M. G., & Widom, C. S. (1996). The cycle of violence: Revisited six years later. *Archives of Pediatrics and Adolescent Medicine, 150*, 390–395.

McCord, J. (1983). A forty-year perspective on effects of child abuse and neglect. *Child Abuse and Neglect, 7*, 265–270.

Monahan, J. (1981). *Predicting violent behavior: An assessment of clinical techniques*. Beverly Hills, CA: Sage Publications.

Moore, M. H., Prothrow-Stith, D., Guyer, B., & Spivak, H. (1994). Violence and intentional injuries: Criminal justice and public health perspectives on an urgent national problem. In A. J. Reiss, Jr., & J. A. Roth (Eds.), *Understanding and preventing violence* (Vol. 4, pp. 167–216). Washington, DC: National Academy Press.

National Center for Child Abuse and Neglect. (1981). *National Study of the Incidence and Severity of Child Abuse and Neglect* (81-30325). Washington, DC: US Department of Health and Human Services.

National Research Council. (1993). *Understanding child abuse and neglect*. Washington, DC: National Academy Press.

Newberger, C. M., & Gremy, I. M. (1995, July 21–24). *The role of clinical and institutional interventions in children's recovery from sexual abuse*. Paper presented at the Fourth International Family Violence Research Conference, Durham, NH.

Newberger, E. H., Reed, R. B., Daniel, J. H., Hyde, J. N., & Kotelchuck, M. (1977). Pediatric social illness: Toward an etiological classification. *Pediatrics, 50*, 178–185.

Newberger, E. H., Newberger, C. M., & Hampton, R. L. (1983). Child abuse: The current theory base and future research needs. *Journal of the American Academy of Child Psychiatry, 22*, 262–268.

Norris, F. H. (1992). Epidemiology of trauma: Frequency and impact of different potentially traumatic events on different demographic groups. *Journal of Consulting and Clinical Psychology, 60*, 409–418.

Osofsky, J. D., Wewers, S., Hann, D. M., & Fick, A. C. (1993). Chronic community violence: What is happening to our children? *Psychiatry Interpersonal and Biological Processes, 56*(1), 36–45.

Patterson, G. R., DeBaryshe, B. D., & Ramsey, E. (1989). A developmental perspective on antisocial behavior. *American Psychologist, 44*, 329–335.

Pynoos, R. S., & Nader, K. (1989). Case study: Children's memory and proximity to violence. *American Academy of Child and Adolescent Psychiatry, 28*(2), 236–241.

Rivera, B., & Widom, C. S. (1990). Childhood victimization and violent offending. *Violence and Victims, 5*, 19–34.

Robins, L. N., & Regier, D. A. (1991). *Psychiatric disorders in America: The epidemiologic catchment area study*. New York: The Free Press.

Rosenbaum, A., & O'Leary, K. D. (1981). Marital violence: Characteristics of abusive couples. *Journal of Consulting and Clinical Psychology, 49*, 63–71.

Runyan, D. K., Gould, C. L., Trost, D. C., & Loda, F. A. (1982). Determinants of foster care placement for the maltreated child. *Child Abuse and Neglect, 6*, 343–350.

Runyan, D. K., Everson, M. D., Edelsohn, G. A., Hunter, W. M., & Coulter, M. L. (1988, October). Impact of legal intervention on sexually abused children. *Journal of Pediatrics*, 647–653.

Sedlak, A. J. (1990). *Technical amendments to the study findings—National incidence and prevalence of child abuse and neglect [NISZ] 1988.* Washington, DC: US Department of Health and Human Services.

Sedlak, A. J., & Broadhurst, D. D. (1996). *Third National Incidence Study of Child Abuse and Neglect, final report.* Washington, DC: US Department of Health and Human Services, Administration for Children and Families, Administration on Children, Youth and Families, National Center on Child Abuse and Neglect.

Sherman, L. W. (1992). *Policing domestic violence.* New York: Free Press.

Sirles, E. A., Smith, J. A., & Kusama, H. (1989). Psychiatric status of intrafamilial child sexual abuse victims. *Journal of the American Academy of Child and Adolescent Psychiatry, 28*, 225–229.

Smith, C., & Thornberry, T. P. (1995). The relationship between childhood maltreatment and adolescent involvement in delinquency. *Criminology, 33*, 451–481.

Sternberg, K. J., Lamb, M. E., Greenbaum, C., Cicchetti, D., Dawud, S., Cortes, R. M., Krispin, O., & Lorey, F. (1993). Effects of domestic violence on children's behavior problems and depression. *Developmental Psychology, 29*(1), 44–52.

Terr, L. A. (1990). *Too scared to cry: Psychic trauma in childhood.* Grand Rapids, MI: Harper & Row

Thoennes, N., & Tjaden, P. G. (1990). The extent, nature, and validity of sexual abuse allegations in custody/visitations disputes. *Child Abuse and Neglect, 14*(2), 151–163.

Thornberry, T. P. (1994). Violent families and youth violence. Fact Sheet #21: Office of Juvenile Justice and Delinquency Prevention, US Department of Justice.

Tong, L., Oates, K., & McDowell, M. (1987). Personality development following sexual abuse. *Child Abuse and Neglect, 11*, 371–383.

Toray, T., Coughlin, C., Vuchinich, S., & Patricelli, P. (1991). Gender differences associated with adolescent substance abuse: Comparisons and implications for treatment. *Family Relations, 40*, 338–344.

Weis, J. G. (1986). Issues in the measurement of criminal careers. In A. Blumstein, J. Cohen, J. A. Roth, & C. A. Visher (Eds.), *Criminal careers and "career criminals"* (Vol. 2, pp. 1–51). Washington, DC: National Academy Press.

Whitcomb, D. (1992). *When the victim is a child* (2nd ed.). Washington, DC: US Department of Justice, Office of Justice Programs. National Institute of Justice.

Widom, C. S. (1984). *Sex roles and psychopathology.* New York: Plenum Press.

Widom, C. S. (1989a). The cycle of violence. *Science, 244*, 160–166.

Widom, C. S. (1989b). Does violence beget violence? A critical examination of the literature. *Psychological Bulletin, 106*(1), 3–28.

Widom, C. S. (1991). The role of placement experiences in mediating the criminal consequences of early childhood victimization. *American Journal of Orthopsychiatry, 6*, 195–209.

Widom, C. S. (1994). Childhood victimization and risk for adolescent problem behaviors. In M. E. Lamb & R. Ketterlinus (Eds.), *Adolescent problem behaviors* (pp. 127–164). New York: Erlbaum.

Widom, C. S. (1998). Childhood victimization: Early adversity and subsequent psychopathology. In B. P. Dohrenwend (Ed.), *Adversity, stress, and psychopathology* (pp. 81–95). New York: Oxford University Press.

Widom, C. S. (2000). Understanding the consequences of childhood victimization. In R. M. Reece (Ed.), *The treatment of child abuse* (pp. 339–370). Baltimore: Johns Hopkins University Press.

Widom, C. S., Ireland, T., & Glynn, P. J. (1995). Alcohol abuse in abused and neglected children followed-up: Are they at increased risk? *Journal of Studies on Alcohol, 56*, 207–217.

Wolfe, D. A., Jaffe, P., Wilson, S. K., & Zak, L. (1985). Children of battered women: The relation of child behavior to family violence and maternal stress. *Journal of Consulting and Clinical Psychology, 53*, 657–665.

Wolfe, D. A., Zak, L., Wilson, S., & Jaffe, P. (1986). Child witnesses to violence between parents: Critical issues in behavioral and social adjustment. *Journal of Abnormal Child Psychology, 14*, 95–104.

Wolock, I., & Horowitz, B. (1985). Child maltreatment and material deprivation among AFDC-recipient families. *Social Service Review, 53*, 175–194.

Wyatt, G. E. (1990). Sexual abuse of ethnic minority children: Identifying dimensions of victimization. *Professional Psychology: Research and Practice, 21*, 338– 343.

Zimrin, H. (1986). A profile of survival. *Child Abuse and Neglect, 10*, 339–349.

Zingraff, M. T., Leiter, J., Myers, K. A., & Johnsen, M. C. (1993). Child maltreatment and youthful problem behavior. *Criminology, 31*, 173–202.

4

The Victimization of Children and Youth

A Comprehensive Overview

DAVID FINKELHOR and PATRICIA Y. HASHIMA

THE VICTIMIZATION OF CHILDREN

While the field of juvenile delinquency stands as a monument to social science, one of its most mature, theoretically and empirically developed domains, the topic of juvenile victimization—the opposite pole of the offender–victim equation—has been comparatively neglected. It is true that one can find substantial research on specific child victimization topics like child abuse or child sexual assault, but there is nothing like the integrated and theoretically articulated interest that characterizes the field of juvenile delinquency.

This neglect is ironic for a variety of reasons. For one thing, as we will demonstrate below, children are among the most highly victimized segments of the population. They suffer from high rates of the same crimes and violence adults do, and then they suffer from many victimizations relatively particular to childhood. Second, victimization has enormous consequences for children, derailing normal and healthy development trajectories. It can affect personality formation, have major mental health consequences, impact on academic performance, and also is strongly implicated in the development of delinquent and antisocial behavior. It is clear that because of several factors such as children's special developmental vulnerability to victimization, its differential character during childhood, and the presence of specialized institutions to deal with it (like child protection agencies) the victimization of children and youth deserves both more attention and specialized attention within the larger fields of criminology, justice studies, and even developmental psychology. Elsewhere we have proposed that this field be called developmental victimology (Finkelhor & Kendall-Tackett, 1997).

DAVID FINKELHOR • Crimes against Children Research Center, Family Research Laboratory, Department of Sociology, University of New Hampshire, Durham, New Hampshire 03824. **PATRICIA Y. HASHIMA** • Institute on Family and Neighborhood Life, Clemson University, Clemson, South Carolina 29634-0132.

Handbook of Youth and Justice, edited by White. Kluwer Academic / Plenum Publishers, New York, 2001.

Definitional Issues

One reason why traditional criminology may not have fully explored this area is that child victimizations do not map neatly onto conventional crime categories. While children do suffer from all the crimes that adults do, many violent and deviant behaviors that harm children are ambiguous in their status as crimes. The physical abuse of children, although technically criminal, is not frequently prosecuted and generally is handled by a different set of social control agencies from the police and criminal courts. Peer assaults, unless very serious or occurring among older children, are generally ignored by the official criminal justice system.

To encompass these complexities, we have proposed that the victimization of children in the justice area be defined as including three categories: (1) conventional crimes in which children are victims (rape, robbery, assault), which we will call "crimes"; (2) acts that violate child welfare statutes, including some of the most serious and dangerous acts committed against children like abuse and neglect, but also some less frequently discussed topics like child labor, which we will call "child maltreatment"; and (3) acts that would clearly be crimes if committed by adults against adults, but by convention are not generally of concern to the criminal justice system when they occur among or against children. These would include sibling violence and assaults between pre-adolescent peers, and these "noncriminal juvenile crime equivalents" we will call "noncrimes" for short.

Each category is a complex domain, but each has its ideal type or stereotype. When the public thinks of crimes against children, what stands out are stranger abductions and extra-family child molestations; situations of adults threatening children, in which the proper domain of protective and retributive action is clearly the police, courts, and criminal justice system. When the public thinks of child maltreatment, they tend to think of parents abusing or neglecting parental responsibilities and the appropriate domain of intervention being family courts, social work, and mental health remedies. The public also is aware that there is noncriminal violence against children and they think of peer assaults, offenses that would be handled by parents or school authorities.

Different as their stereotypes may be, however, these are not neat and distinct categories; there is substantial overlap. Child maltreatment is sometimes treated as criminal, sometimes not (see Fig. 1). Child molesting, for example, is often considered both as a crime and as a child welfare violation. Moreover, there are normative shifts that are in progress (illustrated by arrows in Fig. 1). Sibling sexual assaults once may have been viewed as neither crimes nor child maltreatment, but increasingly they are being handled by criminal justice and child welfare authorities. The abduction of children by family members is increasingly being viewed as both a crime and child maltreatment.

The noncrime category is one that often draws objections. It is seen as a watering down of the concept of victim or crime to include acts like peer or sibling assault among children.[1] But it is difficult to deny the functional equivalence, for example, between one adult hitting another, say, in a bar, and one child hitting another, say, on a playground. The fact of the young age of the victim does not remove and may in fact increase the pain, sense of violation, or risk for harm (Greenbaum, 1989). Some sibling and peer assaults are rather minor in their impact, but because even minor assaults are technically crimes among adults, the issue is really whether minor assaults, not whether child assaults, fall within the purview of victimology. This question seems to have been clearly answered in the affirmative by the design and definitions used in the National Crime Victimization Survey.

An even more problematic type of juvenile crime equivalent, however, is spanking and corporal punishment, which is a form of violence and would be considered an assault among

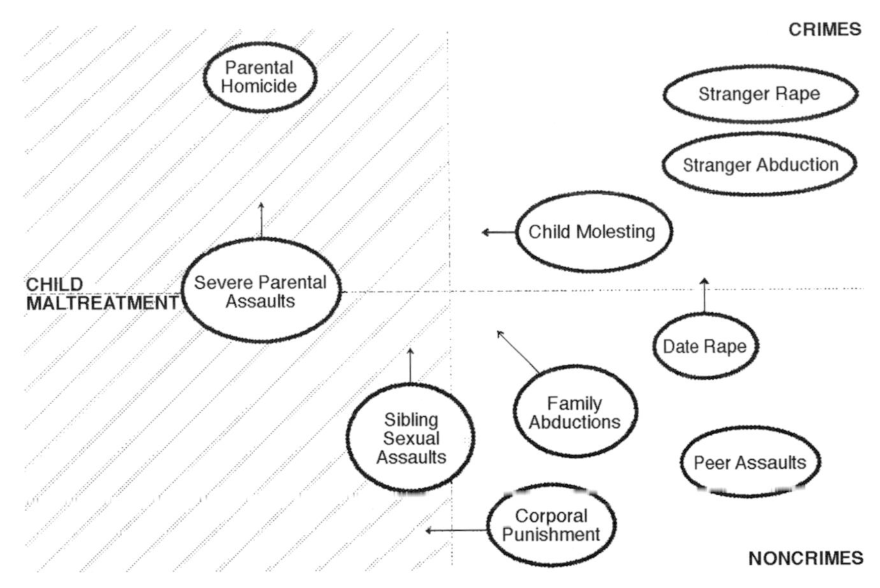

Figure 1. Child victimizations: Crimes, noncrimes, and child maltreatment.

adults. But corporal punishment is not just typically viewed as minor victimization; it is actually viewed as salutory and educational by many segments of society. However, there are signs that a normative transformation is in progress regarding corporal punishment (Greven, 1990). A majority of states have banned it in schools, several Scandinavian countries have outlawed its use even by parents, and the American Academy of Pediatrics has officially opposed its use. Social scientists have begun to study it as a form of victimization with short- and long-term negative consequences (Strassberg, Dodge, Pettit, & Bates, 1994; Straus, 1994). Some have argued that it is the template on which other violent behavior gets built. Clearly, a developmental victimology needs to take account of corporal punishment, although it may deserve individualized theoretical and empirical treatment.

Another somewhat problematic category in juvenile or developmental victimology concerns indirect victimizations, situations where children witness or are closely affected by the crime victimization of a family member or friend. These include children who are first-hand witnesses to wife abuse (Jaffe, Wolfe, & Wilson, 1990; Wolak & Finkelhor, 1998), who are deprived of a parent or sibling as a result of a homicide (Kilpatrick, Amick, & Resnick, 1990), or who are present but not injured in playground massacres or the public killing of a teacher (Nader, Pynoos, Fairbanks, & Frederick, 1990), all situations that have been studied by researchers. While indirect victimization affects adults as well as children, the latter are particularly vulnerable to effects due to their dependency on those being victimized. Since most of the acts creating indirect victimizations are crimes, these situations could be readily categorized in the "crime" category, but some, such as the witnessing of marital assault, also are treated as child welfare violations in which the child is seen as a direct, not indirect, victim.

An additional complexity in the domain of developmental victimology is that, unlike in the domain of adult victimization, specific victimization categories have been much less clearly drawn. Thus, for example, child sexual assault, child sexual abuse, and child molestation are often thought of interchangeably, but these terms also can refer to very different portions of the problem of sexual offenses involving children. Thus child sexual abuse, when discussed in child welfare contexts, often means sexual offenses committed against children by *caretakers*, and thus might not include sexual assaults by strangers or peers. Child molestation in colloquial terms is thought of as sexual offenses committed against children by adults, and thus might exclude date rapes and sexual assaults by other juveniles. Child sexual assault is sometimes taken in its literal meaning to refer to violent and forceful sexual crimes against children, and thus excludes nonassaultive sexual crimes against children. All this suggests that the field could benefit from a great deal of definitional refinement and organization.

Methodological Limitations

Another obvious barrier that has limited the development of a field of developmental victimology is the lack of good data about such victimization. Until recently and still in the case of most states, crimes reported to the FBI with the exception of homicide were not tabulated according to the age of victim, so that crimes against children were difficult to single out. The National Crime Victimization Survey (NCVS) obtained information only on children aged 12 and older. Many special forms of crime victimization involving children, such as involvement in child prostitution, have not been systematically counted at all and others, like stranger abductions, were counted only periodically using methodologies that have not been tested and refined. It is interesting to note that the statistical picture is much more comprehensive and systematic in regard to the medical and health conditions of children, including even very rare conditions, than in regard to their criminal and violent victimization, even though the latter has been a major public policy preoccupation.

Children Are More Victimized Than Adults

One reality, not widely recognized about child victimization and obscured in part because of the lack of comprehensive statistics, is that children are more prone to victimization than adults. This is difficult to establish unambiguously because of the lack of comprehensive data particularly about younger children. But the proposition is clearly true for teenagers. According to NCVS, the overall violent crime victimization rate for ages 12–17 in 1994 was 2.8 higher than the rate for adults (Hashima & Finkelhor, 1999). It was three times as high for assault and twice as high for rape and robbery (Table 1). Teenagers as a group are murdered at about the same rate as adults, but the rate for 16- to 17-year-olds is 50% higher than the adult average.

Unfortunately, however, with the exception of homicide, the picture for children younger than 12 is more difficult to assess. Studies do suggest that assaults and sexual assaults are very common below age 12 (Finkelhor, 1994; Kilpatrick, 1992). Kilpatrick found that 29% of all forcible rapes occurred to females under age 11, although this age group makes up only 17% of the population. Other studies show assault rates for youth aged 10 and 11 that are just as high as for older youth (Finkelhor & Dziuba-Leatherman, 1994a), and school observation studies show a great deal of assault throughout grade school (Olweus, 1991). However, for homicide, rates for those under 12 are quite low, running about a quarter of the adult rate. The only exception is for infants, whose intentional deaths are often masked as accidents, and whose homicide rate, according to some estimates, may reach or exceed the level of the adult population (McClain, Sacks, Froehlke, & Ewigman, 1993).

It is unfortunate that few comparative statistics exist for younger children. But the rates for 12- to 17-year-olds in the NCVS are so much higher than the rate for adults that the overall

Table 1. Crime Victimization Ratio in Youth and Adults, 1994

	Rate per 1000		Risk ratio
	Youth 12–17	Adult 18+	youth ÷ adult
All violent crime[a]	116	43	2.7
Assault[a]	101	36	2.8
Simple[a]	75	26	2.9
Aggravated[a]	26	10	2.6
Rape and sexual assault[a]	3	2	1.5
Robbery[a]	12	5	2.4
Homicide[b]	0.07	0.10	0.7
Theft[a]	173	114	1.5

[a]From Hashima & Finkelhor, 1999. Analysis based on US Department of Justice, Bureau of Justice Statistics. *National Crime Victimization Survey*, 1994 [Computer file]. Conducted by US Department of Commerce, Bureau of the Census. 7th ICPSR ed. Ann Arbor, MI: Inter-university Consortium for Political and Social Research [producer and distributor], 1996. Data table.

[b]US Department of Justice, Federal Bureau of Investigation. *Uniform Crime Reporting Program Data*: [United States] [Supplementary Homicide Reports, 1994] [Computer file]. Compiled by the US Department of Justice, Federal Department of Investigation. ICPSR ed. Ann Arbor, MI: Inter-university Consortium for Political and Social Research [producer and distributor], 1996. Data table.

crime victimization rate for all children 0–17 would still be higher than the overall rate for adults (Moone, 1994), even under the limiting (and absurd) assumption of no victimizations at all for children under 12.

Once we go beyond the national crime victimization survey definitions and methodology, the disproportionate victimization of children becomes clearer still. One major well-known weakness of the NCVS is in its counting of family violence (Garbarino, 1989). Children are enormously more vulnerable than adults to intrafamily victimization over the whole of childhood. For example, in the National Family Violence Survey, adults report that they inflict over twice as much severe violence (which includes beating up, kicking, hitting with a fist or object) against a child in their household than they do against their adult partner (Straus & Gelles, 1990). If we include less severe acts of violence like slapping, the differential is even greater. Moreover, younger children experience more family violence than older children, so this differential holds over the entire span of childhood.

Then, there are the forms of victimization in childhood that do not have direct equivalents in adulthood. These include things like neglect and family abductions, which particularly affect very young children. These forms of victimization add to the picture of a very highly victimized youth population.

One objection sometimes made to the portrait of youth as highly victimized is the idea that, on the whole, youth victimizations, even if numerous, are of a minor nature and are *less serious* (Garofalo, Siegel, & Laub, 1987). Youth victimizations, particularly as captured in the NCVS, have been characterized as school-yard fighting and the like. However, examination of the NCVS data do not bear out this benign stereotype. Youth are almost three times more likely than adults to have a crime-related injury (Table 2), and although the numbers for specific injuries are small and possibly unreliable, they suggest that youth are considerably more likely to sustain a knife, gunshot, or bullet wound or other weapon injury. Their rate of hospitalization for crime injuries is about the same as adults, possibly an indication that victimized youth avoid medical care when injured. In some other indicators of crime seriousness (Table 3),

Table 2. Crime Victimization Injuries for Youth and Adults, 1994[a]

Episode characteristic	Rate per 1000	Population estimate	Percent of violent crime victims
Injury (all)			
12–17	30.2	681,160	25.9
18+	11.1	2,124,798	25.8
Bruises, cuts			
12–17	23.0	519,825	19.8
18+	8.7	1,662,030	20.2
Knife, stab wound			
12–17	0.6[b]	14,654	0.6
18+	0.2	44,182	0.5
Gun shot, bullet wound[b]			
12–17	0.5[b]	11,576	0.4
18+	0.1[b]	27,820	0.3
Other weapon injury			
12–17	3.1	69,437	2.6
18+	1.3	239,017	2.9
Broken bones or teeth			
12–17	1.0[b]	21,628	0.8
18+	0.6	115,276	1.4
Internal injuries, knocked unconscious			
12–17	0.6[b]	12,868	0.5
18+	0.7	125,410	1.5
Other injuries			
12–17	5.5	123,646	4.7
18+	2.1	406,025	4.9
Hospitalization			
12–17	0.7[b]	14,999	0.6
18+	0.4	67,222	0.8

[a]From US Department of Justice, Bureau of Justice Statistics, 1994, data file. See Table 1a for complete reference.
[b]Based on fewer than 10 sample cases.

youth also are much more likely to face multiple assailants (36.1 vs. 12.1 per 1000) or to face armed assailants (9.9 vs. 5.5). The only indicator of less serious victimization for youth is that, in the case of theft, fewer of their stolen objects are worth more than $250, partly reflecting the fact that youth tend not to own expensive things. But overall there is little support for the idea that their victimizations are less serious than those of adults.

Statistics on Child Victimization

There is no single source for statistics on child victimizations. But the public policy interest in specific kinds of victimizations has resulted in national estimates for some of them, although they are far from methodologically rigorous. The national statistics about child victimization gleaned from more than a dozen sources are arrayed in Table 4 in rough order of magnitude. The categories by which they are listed are certainly not distinct and mutually exclusive. For example, rape estimates include some sexual abuse and vice versa; assault includes some physical abuse and nonfamily abduction.

Under some victimization categories, the estimates of several different studies have been listed, sometimes showing widely divergent numbers. These differences stem from two factors

Table 3. Crime Victimization Seriousness for Youth and Adults, 1994[a]

Episode characteristic	Rate per 1000	Population estimate	Percent of violent crime victims
Multiple perpetrators			
12–17	36.1	815,813	31.1
18+	12.1	2,320,576	28.2
Use, presence of firearm			
12–17	9.9	224,473	8.5
18+	5.5	1,056,088	12.8
Object stolen worth $250+			
12–17	9.0	204,226	7.8
18+	24.2	4,629,654	56.2

[a]From National Crime Victimization Survey, 1994. Data file.
[b]Percent victims of completed theft.

in particular: the source of the report and the definition of the activity. Of the three main sources of reports—children themselves, caretakers knowledgeable about children's experiences, and agencies such as the police and child protection services—children and caretakers are likely to provide many more accounts than are available from agencies alone. This in part explains, for example, why the estimate of physical abuse from the National Family Violence Survey (a caretaker study) is more than double that of the 50 State Survey (agency statistics). Estimates also diverge because some studies used more careful or restrictive definitions.

This is far from an exhaustive inventory of all the victimizations children could be said to suffer. There are many types of even criminal victimizations for which we could identify no reliable national statistics, such as involvement in child prostitution. It also does not provide any estimates of children as secondary or indirect victims, that is, when crimes are committed against the households in which they live or other members of their household (Morgan & Zedner, 1992).

What follows are some specific notes and observations about the statistics in Table 4:

1. Sibling assaults. Sibling assaults appear to be the most common kind of violent victimization for children, affecting 80% of all children in some form and over half of all children in its more severe form (which includes hitting with an object, kicking, biting or punching, beating up, or threatening with a knife or gun).[2] These rates are confirmed in other smaller-scale self-report studies of children (Goodwin & Roscoe, 1990; Roscoe, Goodwin, & Kennedy, 1987). Serious sibling assaults are highest for children age 3–4, and decline with age (592 per 1000 down to 309 per 1000 for age 15–17).
2. Corporal punishment. Corporal punishment has its highest frequency for children under age 8 and declines thereafter, but a fifth of all teenagers are still being physically punished by parents (Moore, Gallup, & Schussel, 1995). Annual parent surveys have shown a steady decline over the last decade in the numbers saying that they use it on young children, with rates down about 25% since 1988 (Daro, 1995).
3. Theft, assault, robbery, and rape. These are all crimes measured by the National Crime Victimization Survey but that also have been subject to other national surveys. The NCVS estimates tend to be substantially lower than other self-report estimates. This may be in part a result of the NCVS method whose context has in the past especially emphasized people's stereotypical ideas about crime.

Table 4. Rates and Incidence of Various Childhood Victimizations

Type	Age	Rate/1000[a]	No. victimized[b]	Year	Source[c]	Report type[d]	Notes
Sibling assault	3–17	800.0	50,400,000*	1975	NFVS-1	C	*Any violence
	3–17	530.0	33,300,000†	1975	NFVS-1	C	†Severe violence
Corporal punishment	0–17	(570.0)	(35,910,000)	1995	Gallup	C	
Theft	11–17	(497.0)	+++	1978	NYS	S	
	12–15	95.3	+++	1993	NCS93	S	
Assault	11–17	(310.6)	+++	1978	NYS	S	
	Gr. 8	(172.0)	+++	1988	NASHS	S	
	12–17	101.2	+++	1994	NCVS94	S	
Robbery	11–17	(245.8)	+++	1978	NYS	S	
	Gr. 8	(160.9)	+++	1988	NASHS	S	
	12–17	11.7	+++	1994	NCVS94	S	
Rape/sexual assault	Gr. 8	(118.0)	+++	1988	NASHS	S	
	11–17	(78.0)	+++*	1978	NYS78	S	*Girls only
	12–17	3.4	+++	1994	NCVS94	S	
Physical abuse	0–17	(49.0)	(3,087,000)	1995	Gallup	C	
	0–17	9.1	614,108	1993	NIS-3	A	
	0–17	(3.5)	(252,900)	1993	NCCAN93	A	
Neglect	0–17	(19.9)	(1,355,100)*	1993	NIS-3	A	*Physical and emotional neglect
	0–17	(7.3)	(510,980)	1993	NCCAN93	A	
Sexual abuse	0–17	19.0	1,197,000	1995	Gallup	C	
	0–17	(2.2)	(151,611)	1993	NCCAN93	A	
	0–17	4.5	300,200	1993	NIS-3	A	
Emotional abuse	0–17	7.9	532,200	1993	NIS-3	A	
Family abductions	0–17	5.6	354,100	1988	NISMART	C	
Nonfamily abductions	0–17	0.05–0.07	3200–4600*	1988	NISMART	A	*Legal definition
	0–17	0.003–0.005	200–300†	1988	NISMART	A	†Stereotypical kidnapping
Homicide	0–17	(0.039)	2,697	1993	UCR93	A	

[a]Numbers given in parentheses did not appear in original source, but were derived from data presented therein.
[b]+++, Numbers were only computed for complete populations (i.e., age 0–17).
[c]Source acronyms: NCVS94, National Crime Victimization Survey, 1994 (Data analyzed by authors); NASHS, National Adolescent Student Health Survey (American School Health Association, 1989); NCCAN93, National Center on Child Abuse and Neglect (1995); Gallup, Disciplining Children in America (Moore et al., 1996); NFVS-1, National Family Violence Survey, 1975 (Straus & Gelles, 1990); NIS-3, Third National Incidence Study of Child Abuse and Neglect, 1993 (Sedlak & Broadhurst, 1996); NISMART, National Incidence Study of Missing, Abducted, Runaway and Thrownaway Children, 1988 (Finkelhor, Hotaling, & Sedlak, 1990); NYS, National Youth Survey (Lauritsen, Sampson, & Laub, 1991); NYS78, National Youth Survey, 1978 (Ageton, 1983); and UCR93, Uniform Crime Reports, 1993 (FBI, 1995).
[d]Report types: A = agency reports, C = caretaker reports, S = self-reports.

It must be kept in mind that these assault figures (as well as theft, robbery, vandalism, and rape) pertain only to older children (12 and older). However, it should not be assumed that they would necessarily be lower if younger children were included. Some smaller studies suggest that nonfamily peer assaults are as high or higher for primary school age children than for teens.

4. Physical abuse, neglect, sexual abuse, and emotional abuse. The child abuse and neglect figures are relatively crude. One source (NCCANDS) is based on compilations of official reports substantiated by state child welfare authorities but subject to great variations in state definitions and local practices. Another source, the National Incidence Study (NIS), is from a survey that attempts to include cases known to other professionals, but possibly unknown to official reporting agencies. Much child abuse, however, is not identified by professionals at all (Garbarino, 1989). Attempts have been made to estimate physical and sexual abuse from parent self-reports (Finkelhor, Moore, Hamby, & Straus, 1997; Moore et al., 1995), but in this methodology the physical abuse measure does not include a harm component that is part of the definition in the National Incidence Studies, and the sexual abuse measure includes noncaretaker abusers that would not be counted in the other methodologies.
5. Family abductions. Estimates come from a national study that interviewed caretakers (Finkelhor, Hotaling, & Sedlak, 1990) and may be biased, since only the aggrieved parent was consulted. The definition of family abduction is fairly broad and includes relatively minor events, since a child needed to have been kept or taken in violation of a custody arrangement only for a relatively short period of time. Family abductions occur most commonly to children under the age of 10.
6. Nonfamily abductions. Nonfamily abductions that meet the public stereotype of a true kidnapping (that is where the child is taken a great distance or to another state or held overnight or killed) are relatively rare. But less serious abductions occur in the course of other crimes, such as rapes and assaults, that meet the legal criteria for abductions (forcible removal into a car or building or over a short distance or forcible detention for a period as short as a half hour). These were not well estimated because the NISMART methodology relied on police records and many of these crimes are not reported to police or the abduction component is not recorded in police records. Because nonfamily abductions primarily occur in conjunction with sexual assaults, the most frequent victims, contrary to public stereotype, tend to be teenage girls.
7. Homicide. Homicides are generally considered among the most accurately counted crimes, but the homicides of particularly young children may be underestimated by 50%, according to one study (McClain et al., 1993), because of the difficulty of distinguishing them from accidents and sudden infant death syndrome. Homicide rates are highest for very young children and teenagers.

An effort to pull together the information from these and some other sources (Vital Statistics, National Fire Incident Reporting System) as part of a National Institute of Justice study (Miller, Cohen, & Wiersema, 1996) concluded that the total number of all crime victimizations to children was between 3.36 and 4.95 million per year (Table 5). Many of the component figures for this estimate are crude extrapolations, but do provide guesses for aspects of the victimization picture that have not yet been directly surveyed. For example, the analysts derived estimates for assaults to children under 12 by taking the number of assaults to youth 12–17 from the NCVS and multiplying it by a ratio. The ratio came from a comparison of 0- to 11-year-olds versus 12- to 17-year-olds treated in hospitals or emergency rooms as a

Table 5. National Institute of Justice Study Rough Estimates of Child and Youth Victimizations

	Victimizations estimate or range	
	Ages 0–11	Ages 12–17
Homicide, excl. arson/DWI/abuse and neglect	265–1,991	265–1,991
Child abuse and neglect	397,000–487,000	482,000–562,000
Fatal	1,180	75
Sexual abuse	97,000–187,000	88,000–168,000
Physical abuse	194,000+	161,000+
Emotional abuse	105,000	233,000+
Rape, omitting sex abuse	250,000–315,000	204,000–257,000
Other assault or attempt	289,000–450,000	1,167,000–2,261,000
With injury	116,000–139,000	468,000–698,000
No injury	173,000–311,000	699,000–1,563,000
Robbery or attempt	UNK	219,000–261,000
Drunk driving	125,000	224,000
Arson with injury	2,000	1,000
Total	1,060,000–1,380,000	2,300,000–3,570,000

[a]From Miller et al. (1996).

result of nondomestic assaults in several states. The range of the estimates in Table 5 is due primarily to different ways of counting so-called "series" victimizations, crimes in which the same thing happened to a person on multiple occasions, which tend to be difficult for survey respondents to count accurately. These researchers also tried to make the categories as mutually exclusive as possible. But the source data for these estimates and extrapolations often are very crude themselves and are based on many assumptions that are impossible to verify.

A Typology of Child Victimization by Incidence

The figures in Table 4, in spite of their methodological limitations, definitional imprecision, and variability, nonetheless can be broken into three rough and broad categories according to their order of magnitude. First there are the *pandemic* victimizations that occur to a majority of children at some time in the course of growing up. These include at a minimum assault by siblings, physical punishment by parents, and theft, and probably also peer assault, vandalism, and robbery. Second, there are what might be called *acute* victimizations. These are less frequent and occur to a minority, although perhaps sizeable minority, of children, but may be on average of a generally greater severity. Among these we would include physical abuse, neglect, and family abduction. Finally, there are the *extraordinary* victimizations that occur to only a very small number of children but that attract a great deal of attention. These include homicide, including gang homicide, child abuse homicide, and nonfamily abduction.

Several observations follow from this typology. First, there has been much more public and professional attention paid to the extraordinary and acute victimizations compared to the pandemic ones. For example, sibling violence, the most frequent victimization, is conspicuous for how little it has been studied in proportion to how often it occurs. This neglect of pandemic victimizations needs to be rectified. For one thing, it fails to reflect the concerns of children themselves. In a recent survey of 2000 children aged 10–16, three times as many were concerned about the likelihood of their being beaten up by peers as were concerned about being sexually abused (Finkelhor & Dziuba-Leatherman, 1995). The pandemic victimizations deserve greater attention, if only for the alarming frequency with which they occur and the influence they have on children's everyday existence.

Second, this typology can be useful in developing theory and methodology concerning child victimization. For example, different types of victimization may require different conceptual frameworks. Because they are nearly normative occurrences, the impact of pandemic victimizations may be very different from the extraordinary ones that children experience in relative isolation.

Finally, the typology helps illustrate the diversity and frequency of children's victimization. Although homicide and child abuse have been widely studied, they are notable for how inadequately they convey the variety and true extent of the other victimizations that children suffer. Almost all the figures in Table 4 have been promoted in isolation at one time or another. When we view them together, we note that they are just part of a total environment of various victimization dangers in which children live.

Why is the Victimization of Children So Common?

When the victimization of children is considered as a whole and its scope and variety are more fully appreciated, it prompts a number of interesting and important theoretical questions. The first concerns why the victimization of children is so common. Obviously this is a complex question; a complete answer will undoubtedly require the explanation of elevated risks for different categories of children for different kinds of victimization. However, some generalizations may apply. Certainly the weakness and small physical stature of many children and their dependency status put them at greater risk. They can be victimized because they cannot retaliate or deter it as effectively as those with more strength and power. The social toleration of child victimization also plays a role. Society has an influential set of institutions—the police and criminal justice system—to enforce its relatively strong prohibitions against many kinds of crime, but much of the victimization of children is considered outside the purview of this system.

Another important generalization about why children are at high risk for victimization concerns the relationship between choice and vulnerability (Lynch, 1991). *Children have comparatively little choice over whom they associate with, less choice perhaps than any segment of the population besides prisoners.* This can put them into more involuntary contact with high-risk offenders, and thus at greater jeopardy for victimization. For example, when children live in families that mistreat them, they are not free or able to leave. When they live in dangerous neighborhoods, they cannot choose on their own to move. If they attend a school with many hostile and delinquent peers, they cannot simply change schools or quit. The absence of choice over people and environments affects children's vulnerability to both intimate victimization and street crime. Some adults, like battered women and the poor, suffer similar limitations, but still many adults are able to seek divorces or change their residences in reaction to dangerous conditions. Adults also have more ready access to cars and sometimes have the option to live and work alone. Children are obliged to live with other people, to travel collectively, and to work in high-density, heterogeneous environments, which is what schools are. To put it in more abstract language, children have difficulty gaining access to the structures and mechanisms in society that help segregate people from dangerous associates and environments. This makes them more vulnerable.

Differential Character of Child Victimization

A second interesting theoretical question concerns how the victimization of children differs from the victimization of adults. Children, of course, suffer from all the victimizations that adults do (including economic crimes like extortion and fraud), but they also suffer from some that are particular to their status. The main status characteristic of childhood is its condition of dependency, which is a function, at least in part, of social and psychological immaturity. The violation of this dependency status results in forms of victimization, like physical neglect, that are not suffered by most adults (with the exception of those, like the elderly and sick, who also become dependent).

The dependency of children creates a spectrum of vulnerability. Interestingly, the victimization categories that we identified in Table 4 can be arrayed on a continuum, according to the degree to which they involve violations of children's dependency status (Figure 2). At the one extreme is physical neglect, which has practically no meaning as a victimization, except in the case of a person who is dependent and needs to be cared for by others. Similarly, family abduction is a dependency-specific victimization, because it is the unlawful removal of a child from the person who is supposed to be caring for him or her. Emotional abuse happens to both adults and children, but the sensitive psychological vulnerability of children in their dependent relationship to their caretakers is what makes society consider emotional abuse of children a form of victimization that warrants an institutional response.

At the other end of the continuum are forms of victimization that are defined without reference to dependency and that exist in very similar forms for both children and adults. Stranger abduction is prototypical in this instance, since both children and adults are taken against their will and imprisoned for ransom or sexual purposes. Homicide is similar; the dependency status of the victim does little to define the victimization. In some cases, to be sure, children's deaths result from extreme and willful cases of neglect, but there are parallel instances of adult deaths resulting from extreme and willful negligence.

Finally, there are forms of child victimization that should be located along the midsection of the dependency continuum. Sexual abuse falls here, for example, because it encompasses at least two different situations, one dependency related and one not. Some sexual abuse entails activities, ordinarily acceptable between adults, that are deemed victimizing in the case of children because of their immaturity and dependency. But other sexual abuse involves violence and coercion that would be victimizing even with a nondependent adult.

In the case of physical abuse, there also is some mixture. While most of the violent acts in

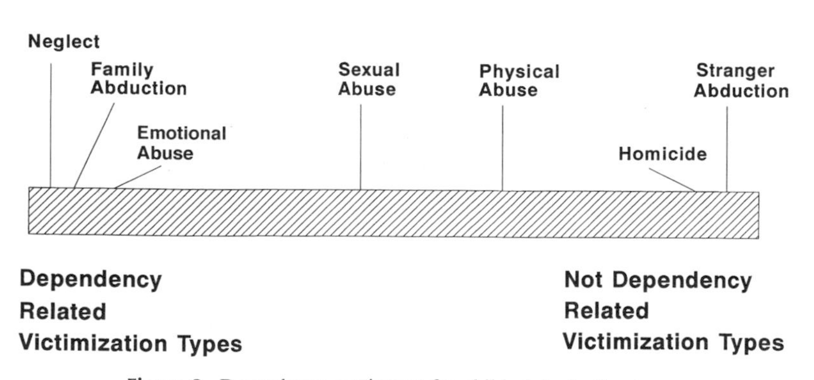

Figure 2. Dependence continuum for child victimization types.

this category would be considered victimizing even between adults, some of them, like the shaken baby syndrome, develop almost exclusively in a caretaking relationship where there is an enormous differential in size and physical control.

The dependency continuum is a useful concept in thinking about some of the unique features of children's victimizations. It also is helpful in generating some hypotheses about the expected correlates of different types of victimization at different ages.

DEVELOPMENTAL PROPOSITIONS

Childhood is such an extremely heterogenous category—4-year-olds and 17-year-olds having little in common—that it is inherently misleading to discuss child victimization in general without reference to age. We would expect the nature, quantity, and impact of victimization to vary across childhood with the different capabilities, activities, and environments that are characteristic of different stages of development. This is the key principle of developmental victimology. Unfortunately, we do not have good studies of the different types of victimization across all the ages of childhood with which to examine such changes.

There are two plausible propositions about age and child victimization that could be a starting place for developmental victimology. One is that victimizations stemming from the dependent status of children should be most common among the most dependent, hence, the youngest children. A corollary is that as children get older, their victimization profile should come more and more to resemble that of adults.

We can examine such propositions in a crude way with the data that are available. In fact, we do see (Table 6) that the types of victimization that are most concentrated in the under-12 age group are the dependency-related ones (see the Dependency Continuum in Fig. 2), particularly family abduction and physical neglect. Victimizations like homicide and stranger abduction, which we grouped at the nondependency end of the continuum, involve a greater percentage of teenagers. However, not everything falls neatly into place; sexual abuse seems anomalously concentrated among teenagers, too. We believe this to be an artifact of the NIS data on sexual abuse, which was based on reported cases only, and thus undercounted sexual abuse of young children.[3] When we look at sexual abuse, based on data from retrospective self-reports, we find that 64% of victimizations occur before age 12 (Finkelhor et al., 1990), a pattern more consistent with the hypothesis and the place of sexual abuse on the dependency continuum.

Table 6. Victimizations of Younger Children

Type of victimization	Percent under 12 of all juvenile victims	Source[a]
Family abduction	81	NISMART
Physical neglect	70	NIS-2
Emotional abuse	58[b]	NIS-2
Physical abuse	56	NIS-2
Homicide	43[c]	UCR
Sexual abuse	40	NIS-2
Stranger abduction	27	NISMART

[a]NIS-2, National Study of the Incidence and Severity of Child Abuse and Neglect, 1986 (Sedlak, 1991). See Table 4 for other source acronyms.
[b]Reflects the midpoint of two divergent estimates.
[c]Age group for this category is under 10.

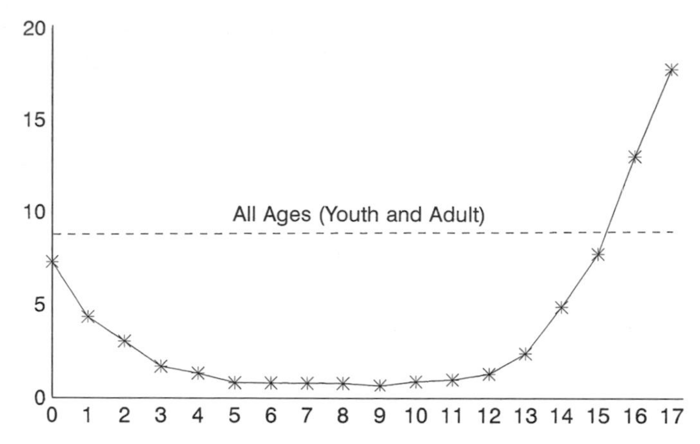

Figure 3. Homicide rates for youth aged 0 to 17, per 100,000 US children. *Source*: Supplemental Homicide Reports (1991–1992), Federal Bureau of Investigation, analysis by author.

For additional insights about development and victimization, we also can look at child homicide, the type of victimization to which a developmental analysis has been most extensively applied (Christoffel, 1990; Christoffel et al., 1983; Crittenden & Craig, 1990; Jason, 1983; Jason, Carpenter, & Tyler, 1983). Child homicide has a conspicuous bimodal frequency, with high rates for the very youngest and the oldest children (Fig. 3). But the two peaks represent very different phenomena. The homicides of young children are primarily committed by parents, by choking, smothering, and battering. In contrast, the homicides of older children are committed mostly by peers and acquaintances, most often with the use of firearms (Figs. 4 and 5).

Although the analysts do not agree entirely on the number and age span of the specific developmental categories for child homicides, a number of propositions are clear. There is a distinct group of neonaticides: children killed in the first day or few weeks of life. The proportion of female and rural perpetrators is unusually high in this group (Jason et al., 1983).

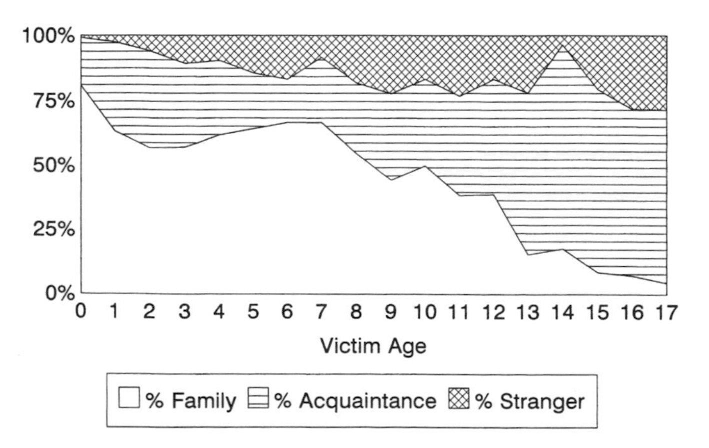

Figure 4. Relationship of child homicide victims to perpetrators. *Source*: See Figure 3.

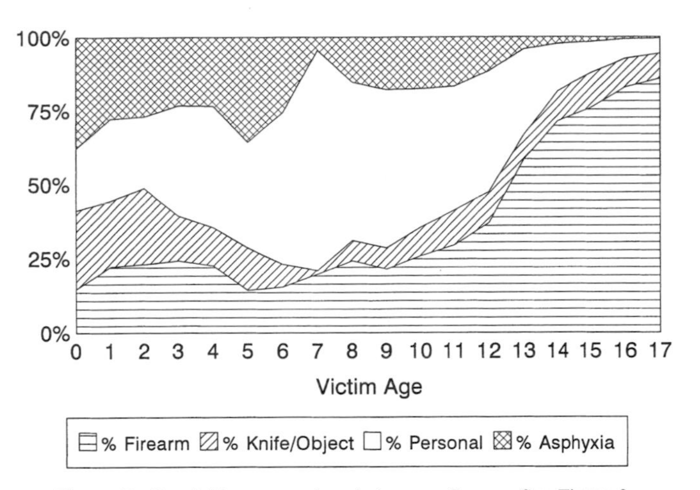

Figure 5. Homicide weapon by victim age. *Source.* See Figure 3.

Homicide at this age is generally considered to include many isolated parents dealing with unwanted children.

After the neonatal period, there follows a period through about age 5 in which homicides are still primarily committed by caretakers using "personal weapons," but the motives and circumstances are thought to be somewhat different. These appear to be mostly cases of fatal child abuse that occur as a result of parents' attempts to control child behavior or reactions to some of its aversive qualities (Christoffel, 1990; Crittenden & Craig, 1990). Because of their small size and physical vulnerability, many children at this age die from acts of violence and force by adults that would not be fatal to an older child.

As children become of school age, the rate of child homicide declines and the nature of child homicide becomes somewhat different. Among school-age children, killings by parents and caretakers gradually decline and those by peers and acquaintances rises. There are more firearm deaths. Children are targeted by suicidal parents killing their whole families. Children are killed in sexual assaults and as innocent victims in robberies and arsons.

Then at age 13, the homicide picture changes again and rapidly. The rate for boys diverges sharply from that for girls. Acquaintances become the predominant killers. Gangs and drugs are heavily involved, and the rate for minority groups—African Americans, Hispanic Americans, and Asian Americans—soars.

These trends clearly suggest that the types of homicide suffered by children are related to the nature of their dependency and to the level of their integration into the adult world. They provide a good case for the importance and utility of a developmental perspective on child victimizations and a model of how such an approach could be applied to other types of victimization.

Intrafamily Victimization

Unlike many adults, children do not live alone; they live mostly in families, so another plausible principle of developmental victimology is that more of the victimization of children occurs at the hands of relatives. The findings on homicide suggest this as a developmental trend: that younger children have a greater proportion of their victimizations at the hands of intimates and correspondingly fewer at the hands of strangers. This is because they live more sheltered lives, spend more time in the home and around family, and have fewer of the characteristics that might make them suitable targets for strangers, such as money and valuable possessions.

An additional possible principle is that the identity of perpetrators may vary according to the type of victimization and its place on the dependency continuum (Fig. 2). Victimizations that are more dependency related should involve more perpetrators who are parents and family members. As shown in Table 7, parents are 100% of the perpetrators of neglect (Sedlak, 1991)—the most dependency-related victimization—but only 28% of the perpetrators of homicide (Federal Bureau of Investigations, 1992). This pattern occurs because the responsibilities created by children's dependency status fall primarily on parents and family members. They are the main individuals in a position to violate those responsibilities in a way that would create victimization. Thus, when a sick child fails to get available medical attention, it is the parents who are charged with neglecting the child, even if the neighbors also did nothing.

Gender and Victimization

Developmental victimology needs to take account of gender as well. On the basis of the conventional crime statistics available from the NCVS and Uniform Crime Report, boys would appear to suffer more homicide (2.3 to 1), more assault (1.7 to 1), and more robbery (2 to 1) than girls, while girls suffer vastly more rape (8.1 to 1) (Bureau of Justice Statistics, 1992; Federal Bureau of Investigations, 1992). But this primarily pertains to the experience of adolescents and does not consider age variations.

Because gender differentiation increases as children get older, a developmental hypothesis might predict that the pattern of victimization would be less gender specific for younger children. That is, because younger boys and girls are more similar in their activities and physical characteristics, there might be less difference between gender in the rate of victimization.

This pattern does indeed appear to be the case at least for homicide, the type of victimization for which we have the best data. Rates of homicide are quite similar for younger boys and girls, even up to age 13, after which point the vulnerability of boys increases dramatically (Fig. 6).

This increased differentiation with age also is apparent for physical abuse, at least based on one data set. Caretaker reports from the National Family Violence Survey show more abuse of boys after age 5, rising particularly high in later adolescence. But data from another source, the NIS, based on reported cases, do not support this conclusion, showing girls to be the

Table 7. Childhood Victimizations Perpetrated by Parents

Type of victimization	Percent victimized by parent	Source[a]
Physical neglect	100	NIS-2
Emotional abuse	100	NIS-2
Physical abuse	90	NIS-2
Abductions	80	NISMART
Sexual abuse	51	NIS-2
Homicide	28	UCR

[a]See Tables 4 and 6 for source acronyms.

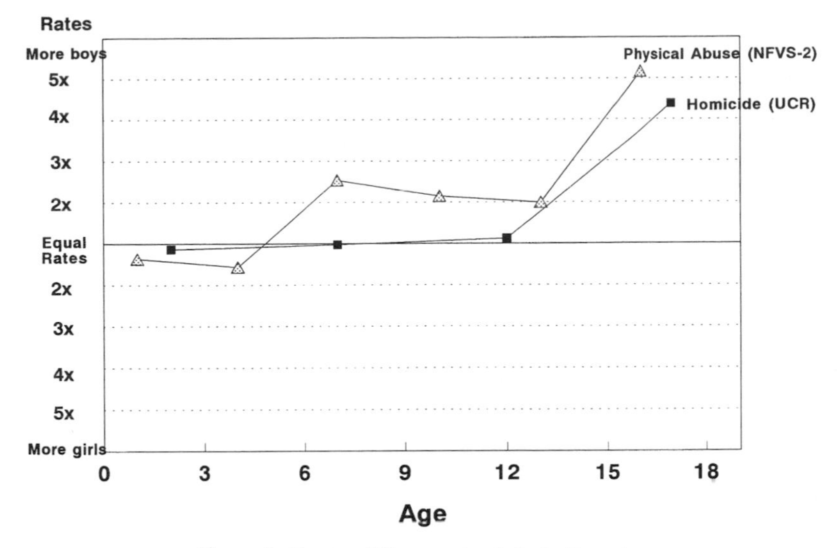

Figure 6. Gender differences in victimization rates.

predominant victims of physical abuse during adolescence. It could be that the physical abuse of adolescent boys is particularly underdetected by professionals (on whose observations the NIS is based).

The developmental pattern in gender differentiation may apply to some forms of victimization but not others. Some victimization types may have unique gender patterns reflecting their particular dynamics. Issues of reporting and disclosure also may influence gender patterns. More research on this issue is needed.

ROUTINE ACTIVITIES THEORY AND CHILDREN

Routine activities theory (RAT), a popular conceptual framework in the victimology field, has been applied to the analysis of youth victimization as it has to other issues. The theory predicts that victimization risk will be governed by lifestyle and routine activities that in particular increase proximity and exposure to crime (e.g., living in a high-crime neighborhood, being out at night), reduce guardianship (e.g., the protective presence of others), and enhance target attractiveness (e.g., owning expensive appliances). The application to youth has tended to focus on how increased *exposure* and decreased *guardianship* heighten youth vulnerability. Young people are viewed as engaging in risky behaviors, such as staying out late, going to parties, and drinking, that compromise the guardianship provided by parents and adults and expose them to more possibilities for victimization (Jensen & Brownfield, 1986). Much of the RAT approach to youth victimization has stressed particularly its connection to delinquent activities (Lauritsen, Laub, & Sampson, 1992; Lauritsen, Sampson, & Laub, 1991). Delinquency is seen as a lifestyle that puts a person in close proximity to other offenders—aggressive or delinquent companions or rival gang members—and also greatly reduces guardianship because delinquents tend to avoid conventional social environments and through their activities also largely forfeit their claims on the protection of police and other authorities

(Sparks, 1982). Empirical research has confirmed that delinquents are indeed more prone to victimization than other youth (Lauritsen et al., 1991, 1992).

However, this perspective on youth victimization has some obvious limitations. For one thing, many youth who get victimized have no involvement in delinquency. Delinquent activities primarily are the domain of adolescents, particularly adolescent boys. But even young children get assaulted, kidnapped, and sexually abused (Finkelhor & Dziuba-Leatherman, 1994b) without any connection to delinquent behavior. Moreover, the lifestyle and routine activities theories were designed for and always have been best at explaining variations in stereotypical street crime like stranger assaults and robberies. But much of youth victimization occurs at the hands of acquaintances and family members. This is particularly true for younger children (Finkelhor & Dziuba-Leatherman, 1994b).

These acquaintance and intrafamily victimization are not well suited to the RAT concepts. For example, routine activities studies often operationalize guardianship as the amount of time routinely spent within the family household on the assumption that this activity is protective. However, for a child at risk of parental violence, time spent in the family household is not protective. Nor does being out at night, another popular lifestyle variable, increase exposure to parental violence. In fact, for intrafamily victimization it is not entirely clear that time "exposed" outside or inside the family makes much difference at all.

Thus, it is not surprising that theories developed to explain many specific forms of acquaintance and family victimization among youth have virtually ignored routine activities theory and have relied on other concepts besides exposure and guardianship. For example, in trying to account for who becomes the target of bullying, observers have noted that these tend to be children with avoidant–insecure attachment relationships with primary caregivers, who lack trust, have low self-confidence, expect hostility from others, and are socially isolated (Smith, Bowers, Binney, & Cowie, 1993). Bullied boys tend to be physically weaker and may be more likely to have physical impairments (Olweus, 1993). Something about the behavior of these children, both their physical and psychological vulnerability and perhaps a relational style irritating to other children, seems to attract victimization. Interestingly, as opposed to lacking guardianship, this literature suggests that some victims of bullies if anything tend to be overprotected by parents and bullied in part because of it (Smith et al., 1993).

The literature on parental assault on children also takes a very different tack from the lifestyles approach. This literature tends to equate victimization risk primarily with family and parental attributes, like family stress, isolation, alcoholic and violence-prone caretakers, and parents who have victimization histories and unrealistic expectations of their children (National Research Council, 1993). To the extent that victim factors play a role, particularly in the case of adolescents, the parental assault literature notes that such youth may be more at risk if they are disobedient, uncooperative, or temperamental or have problems or impairments that are a burden or source of disappointment for caregivers (Berdie, Berdie, Wexler, & Fisher, 1983; Garbarino, 1989; Libby & Bybee, 1979; Schellenbach & Guerney, 1987).

A still different victimization literature, the one on child sexual assault, notes even some other risk factors. For this form of victimization, girls are at substantially greater risk than boys (Finkelhor, 1994). Also at risk are children from stepparent families and children whose parents fight or are distant and punitive (Finkelhor, 1993). Finkelhor (1984) has hypothesized that risk for sexual abuse is increased by factors that reduce parental supervision as well as those that create emotional deprivation. Emotional deprivation makes children and youth vulnerable to the offers of attention and affection that sexual predatory offenders sometimes use to draw children into sexual activities.

A challenge for the field of developmental victimology is to find ways to blend the theoretical approaches relevant to specific forms of child victimization together with the insights of routine activities theory, to the extent that they apply. Elsewhere, Finkelhor, and Asdigian (1996) have proposed a framework for beginning this task.

EFFECTS OF CHILD VICTIMIZATION

Inflicted injuries, neglect, and criminal acts are responsible for the deaths of more than 2000 children per year, and homicide is currently one of the five leading causes of child mortality in the United States (Goetting, 1990; Martinez-Schnell & Waxweiler, 1989). Victimization also results in a substantial toll of nonfatal injuries that are more difficult to count accurately. The NIS estimated that, as a result of abuse or neglect over the course of one year, 565,000 children suffered serious injuries (i.e., life-threatening conditions, long-term physical, mental or emotional impairment) and 822,000 others suffered moderate injuries (i.e., observable injuries or impairments that lasted for at least 49 hours)(Sedlak & Broadhurst, 1996). From the NCVS, one can estimate that approximately 700,000 teenagers aged 12 to 17 sustained physical injury due to an assault in a single year (Table 2). Another national survey of 10- to 16-year-olds suggests that the annual number of injured youth is on the order of 2.8 million, with 250,000 needing medical attention (Finkelhor & Dziuba-Leatherman, 1994a). A Massachusetts study suggests that each year 1 in every 42 teenage boys receives hospital treatment for an assault-related injury (Guyer, Lescohier, Gallagher, Hausman, & Azzara, 1989).

Children's level of development undoubtedly influences the nature and severity of injuries resulting from victimization, although few analyses have taken such a developmental approach. An obvious example is the greater vulnerability of small children to death and serious harm as a result of blows inflicted by hands and other so-called "personal objects." Another obvious example is the higher likelihood of older children exposed to sexual abuse-related HIV infection, because older children suffer more penetrative abuse (Kerns & Ritter, 1992).

In addition to physical injury, there is a growing literature documenting that victimization has grave short- and long-term effects on children's mental health as well. For example, sexually victimized children appear to be at substantially increased lifetime risk for virtually all categories of psychiatric disorder (Table 8), a finding supported by Saunders, Villeponteaux, Lipovsky, Kilpatrick, and Veronen (1992). Scott (1992) estimates that about 8% of all psychiatric cases within the population at large can be attributed to childhood sexual assault.

Although they do not involve such specific epidemiological assessments, other studies

Table 8. Increased Risk for Psychiatric Disorders among Victims of Child Sexual Abuse[a]

Disorder	Risk ratio[b]	Disorder	Risk ratio
Any disorder	3.8	Alcohol abuse or dependence	2.1
Any affective disorder	2.4	Phobia	3.4
Drug abuse or dependence	5.2	Depression	3.4

[a]From Scott (1992).
[b]Only risks significantly different from risk for nonvictims are included.

also have demonstrated increased rates of mental health morbidity for other types of childhood victimization including physical abuse (Kolko, 1992), emotional abuse (Briere & Runtz, 1990), and physical punishment (Straus & Gelles, 1992). A national survey has demonstrated that victimized youth have higher levels of posttraumatic stress disorder and depression, that a wide variety of specific forms of victimization result in such effects, and that such effects are independent of prior levels of symptoms (Boney-McCoy & Finkelhor, 1995, 1996). A number of other studies also show the traumatic impact of violence exposure and in particular its serious effects on those from ethnic minority communities and communities with higher violence rates (DuRant, Getts, Cadenhead, Emans, & Woods, 1995; Martinez & Richters, 1993; Singer, Anglin, Song, & Lunghofer, 1995).

In addition to general mental health impairments, a proposition that has been established across various types of victimization is that a history of such victimization increases the likelihood that someone will become a perpetrator of crime, violence, or abuse. Although this popular shibboleth has been criticized and qualified (Kaufman & Ziegler, 1987), evidence to support it comes from a wide variety of methodologies—longitudinal follow-ups (McCord, 1983; Widom, 1989a), studies of offender populations (Hanson & Slater, 1988; Lewis, Shanok, Pincus, & Glaser, 1979), and surveys of the general population (Straus, Gelles, & Steinmetz, 1980)—and concerns a wide variety of perpetrations, including violent crime, property crime, child abuse, wife abuse, and sexual assaults (for review, see Widom, 1989b). An important qualification is that victims are not necessarily most prone to repeat their own form of victimization. But the proposition that childhood victims are more likely to grow up to victimize others is firmly established.

Theory about post-traumatic stress disorder (PTSD) is being applied to and may be a unifying concept for understanding common psychological effects of a wide variety of child victimizations (Eth & Pynoos, 1985). Terr (1990) has made some effort to cast PTSD in a more developmental framework, but its application is mostly anecdotal.

Sexual abuse is the only area in which a developmental approach to the psychological impact of victimization has advanced on the basis of empirical studies (Kendall-Tackett, Williams, & Finkelhor, 1993). For example, in reaction to sexual abuse, symptoms of sexualization seem to appear more frequently among preschool than among school-age girls who seem more aware of appropriate and inappropriate sexual conduct (Friedrich et al., 1992). This is the direction the entire area of child victimization needs to take.

One of the challenges for a field of developmental victimology is to document how victimization at different stages of development can have different kinds of effects (Trickett & Putnam, 1993). Such developmentally specific effects can be related to four different aspects of development, according to a formulation Shirk (1988) made in regard to physical abuse and elaborated by Finkelhor and Kendall-Tackett (1997): (1) differences in the developmental tasks children are facing at the time of victimization; (2) differences in cognitive abilities affecting the appraisals children make about the victimizations; (3) differences in the forms of symptom expression available to the child at that stage of development; and (4) differences in the social context for children of different stages, which affects how their environment and social network may respond to the victimization. In the following, we elaborate briefly on these dimensions.

A number of models in the developmental literature point to pivotal tasks that children need to accomplish at various ages (Egeland & Sroufe, 1981; Erikson, 1968) and the related idea that there are sensitive periods during which developmental tasks or processes are particularly vulnerable to disturbance (MacDonald, 1985). Several specific examples exist in the research literature of attempts to document how victimization can interfere with such stage-specific processes. For example, young children victimized at an early age by their primary caretakers seem to suffer a big developmental impact in the form of insecure attachments to caregivers (Carlson, Cicchetti, Barnett, & Braunwald, 1989; Crittenden, 1988; Egeland & Sroufe, 1981). Children victimized during preschool years, when children experiment with normal dissociative skills, may be those who become most likely to use dissociation as a defense mechanism and to develop a pattern of dissociation that becomes chronic (Kirby, Chu, & Dill, 1993). Sexual abuse and other trauma can hasten the onset of puberty (Herman-Giddens, Sandler, & Friedman, 1988; Putnam & Trickett, 1993).

A second developmental component to the impact of victimization concerns how children's beliefs about what happened may mediate the experience of victimization (Rutter, 1989). It has been found that victims seem to be more affected by crime in which they believed they were going to die or be seriously injured, or in which they felt helpless and out of control (Kilpatrick et al., 1989; Resnick, 1993). But this cognitive appraisal process works very differently among children, who know much less about the world or make assumptions different from those of adults (Dalenberg, Bierman, & Furman, 1984), and these cognitive appraisal skills, including those that apportion responsibility and blame for bad events, change over the course of development.

Third, in addition to stage-specific vulnerabilities and cognitive appraisals, another domain highlighted by Shirk (1988) is developmental differences in symptom expression. Whatever the stage at which a child may have been victimized or whatever appraisals a child may make, the subjective distress from that victimization will usually be expressed within a vocabulary of behaviors or symptoms specific to the current stage of development. Thus, distress expressed by preschool age children in the form of disruptive behavior in preschool may take the form of self-blame or depression at a later stage. Shirk labels this process "developmental symptom substitution."

Finally, reactions to victimization are affected by developmental differences in the environments children inhabit. For example, a young child who suffers a sexual assault is much less likely to be blamed by friends and family than a teenage victim. This can increase the impact and make recovery more difficult. In understanding how children respond to victimization over the course of development, these processes need to be better described, documented, and related to the child victimization literature.

Economic Costs of Juvenile Victimization

In a recent effort to estimate the economic effects of victimization on individuals and households (Miller et al., 1996), child and youth victimizations were estimated to cost about $164 billion per year, about 36% of the $450 billion national total. This estimate did not include costs for collective criminal justice and crime prevention efforts (police, courts, etc.), but it did include a monetary estimate for an individual's quality of life losses. Medical expenses related to children's victimization were estimated to be about $8.7 billion, about half the national total, and more than 1% of all US medical spending. Other tangible victimization-related losses like property damage and mental health and social service care for juveniles came to about $15.3 billion. Crimes against children were among the most costly of all crimes. For example, child sexual abuse incurred an average cost of $5800 in mental health care (the highest of any crime) and $1100 in social services. The study estimated that as much as 5–10% of the mental health care expenditures in the United States may be attributable to child abuse. Child abuse also entailed very major quality of life costs, estimated at $52,000 per victimization, compared to other victimizations.

Legal Issues

Legal interventions vary considerably for different types of juvenile victimizations. Some are crimes and some are not; some are subject to civil interventions, and in many cases the relation to the law is very complex. The reasons for these variations are not always entirely straightforward, nor have they received much consideration in the literature on jurisprudence. (Black's [1976] propositions on the behavior of law appear to apply only marginally to juvenile victimizations.) Although practices are changing, to some extent the variations do correspond to the distinctions made out at the outset of this chapter among the categories of crimes, juvenile noncrime equivalents, and child welfare violations.

Crime

Certain stereotypical crimes against children (in particular, stranger abductions, sexual molestation, and nonfamily homicides) are readily incorporated within conventional operation of the criminal justice system and are taken very seriously by its major players. Public and political concern about these kinds of crimes has led in recent years to efforts to try to increase the aggressiveness and punitiveness of the criminal justice system in regard to such crimes.

However, when violence against children contain elements that shade away from these stereotypes, it quickly raises problems for criminal justice system. Some of the main factors that raise difficulties include: (1) when the perpetrator (assailant, molester or abductor) is a family member or member of child's social network; (2) when the perpetrator is not an adult; or (3) when a child's abilities or characteristics interfere with their credibility or testimonial capacities.

This has led to charges that crimes against children are both too aggressively or too passively handled within the criminal justice system. Some have argued that public hysteria over a crime against children makes it difficult for offenders to be treated fairly (Nathan & Snedeker, 1995). Others have argued that the immaturity of children, their difficulties in providing credible testimony, or their low social status means that police and prosecutors ignore or do not fully pursue such cases (Armstrong, 1994). However, studies that have compared the adjudication of crimes against children, particularly sexual abuse cases, with those against adults, have found few dramatic differences. The prosecution rates for crimes against children, the level of guilty verdicts, and the severity of sentences overall do not appear to be out of line with those for adult crimes (Boston Globe Spotlight Team, 1987; Bureau of Justice Statistics, 1989; Chapman & Smith, 1987; Cross, 1995). This topic is in need of much more thorough research, but currently available evidence suggests that although the concerns of critics may apply in particular cases, crimes against children taken as a whole do not seem to receive especially severe or lenient handling.

Juvenile Crime Equivalents

In contrast to clear-cut crimes, there is a class of violent acts and victimizations, as we indicated earlier, that tend to be frankly noncriminal when they involve child actors. These particularly involve violence involving child assailants: peer assaults, sibling assaults, and to some extent, sexual victimizations perpetrated by other children. Although children suffer from high rates of victimization by other children, the major overt reason for the noncriminalization of such juvenile crime hinges on the different legal framework that has historically surrounded juvenile offenders. Modern jurisprudence holds that juvenile offenders, in contrast to adult offenders, are developmentally immature, and thus (1) not (or less) accountable for criminal acts, and (2) more amenable to rehabilitation (Melton, 1989; Mnookin & Weisberg, 1989; Snyder & Sickmund, 1995). Based on this logic, the justice system has removed the adjudication of violence involving juvenile perpetrators from the criminal law and placed it into a special system.

While this logic explains why juvenile and family courts have been given jurisdiction over juvenile perpetrators, it does not fully explain why so much child-on-child violence is completely ignored by police and other agents of social control. There appear to be other less clearly formulated social assumptions that help explain the exclusion of child-on-child violence from formal systems of social control. These assumptions may include, for example: (1) that these forms of victimization are an unavoidable part of childhood, not particularly harmful to child victims, or that child victims are more resilient than adult victims; (2) that culpability in these events is more shared between the offender and the victim (they are fights rather than assaults); (3) that the problem is so pervasive that it would be overwhelming for any portion of the legal system to regulate; (4) that formal methods of sanctioning or intervening in juvenile violence would not be understood by those involved or would cause more harm than good; (5) that violence by children against other children rarely threatens the adult community; and (6) that children need to learn to be independent and protect and defend themselves without outside, adult intervention, a notion highly valued in independence-oriented American culture.

Interestingly, the management of and research on child-on-child violence usually focuses on issues concerning the juvenile offenders, generally ignoring the implications for juvenile victims. This is regrettable because there are many important victimology issues. There is the question, for example, of whether it matters to a child victim's sense of justice whether his or her assailant is adjudicated in criminal court, juvenile court, or simply sanctioned informally.

In part because of the possibly increasing frequency and severity of some child-on-child violence, there has been a trend to bring more formal sanctions to bear. One avenue that has been tried is through suits brought against school systems asking that they use their power of *in loco parentis* to more reliably ensure students' safety (Davis, 1994; Greenfield, 1993; Milani, 1995). Another avenue, specifically for student-inflicted sexual harassment, has been to bring suits against schools for violating nondiscrimination statutes (Savage, 1996). These approaches have had a mixed record of success in state and federal courts (Stein, 1999). Still a third avenue has been the growing trend toward allowing prosecution of juveniles in criminal court. Many states have enacted laws that sentence juvenile offenders to penalties similar to those for adults who are convicted of the same offense and make transfer of juveniles to criminal court easier or even automatic (Grisso, 1996).

Child Maltreatment

Much of what is considered child maltreatment is covered under criminal codes but not frequently investigated or prosecuted by the criminal justice system (Tjaden & Thoennes, 1992). Those most frequently investigated by police or filed for criminal proceedings tend to be sexual abuse cases. Physical abuse is much less prosecuted than sexual abuse and neglect is rarely prosecuted at all (Smith, 1995; Tjaden & Thoennes, 1992).

The noncriminalization or nonprosecution of child maltreatment seems to be related in part to the sanctity of parental and family relationships, a widely held distaste for government intruding on family matters, a belief that priority should be given to the preservation of the family unit, and the presumption that criminal justice intervention will do more harm than good. Of course, these arguments do not fully explain why sexual abuse involving family perpetrators gets prosecuted more than physical abuse. One factor may be that sexually abusive parents tend to be more exclusively men, and the legal system may not view the child's relation to the father equivalent to the child's relation to her or his mother. But perhaps another reason why sexual abuse is prosecuted more than physical abuse is because sexual behavior toward children is not acceptable in any circumstance, whereas the use of physical force is viewed as acceptable or even salutory in some instances. For example, in the state of New Hampshire, the law specifically states:

> A parent, guardian or other person responsible for the general care and welfare of a minor is justified in using force against such minor when and to the extent that he reasonably believes it necessary to prevent or punish such minor's misconduct. (Criminal Code Section 627: 6, I)

In fact, all 50 states permit corporal punishment as a method for parents to discipline their children (Edwards, 1996). Thus, adults charged with physically assaulting children have a large gray area for defending their actions as falling within the reasonable right to discipline a child. Although there was some movement to deprive nonparental adults of such rights through anticorporal punishment laws, in response to the rise in school violence a number of states, like Michigan, have reinstituted the permission for school personnel (Papakirk, 1993).

Nonetheless, the assumption that criminal prosecution of caregivers is detrimental to the family bond or to the welfare of the child has been increasingly challenged. In many parts of the country, advocates for sexual abuse victims have argued that prosecution of parental perpetrators actually enhances both the protection of the child and willingness of the parent to change (Harshbarger, 1987; Myers, 1985–1986). There also may be a national trend toward more termination of parental rights (Bross, 1995). The Violent Crime Control and Law Enforcement Act of 1994 (Public Law 103-322) allowed for more prosecution of noncustodial family abductors (Title 18, Section 1201). Finally, in some states the felony murder statutes have been amended to permit child abuse homicide as a basis for first-degree felony murder convictions (McMillen, 1995; Rainey & Greer, 1995). This all suggests that family relationship is becoming less of a barrier to full criminal prosecution.

As can be seen from this brief review, the legal policies affecting the criminal justice system's relationship to child victims are based on many untested and in some cases poorly articulated assumptions about children, their development, and their relationships with family and social institutions. If we want to institute effective procedures to facilitate justice for children, the topic of juvenile victims and the criminal justice system deserves more empirical and theoretical research.

RESEARCH NEEDS

The research needs in this field of child victimization are vast and urgent, given the size of the problem and the seriousness of its impact, and they range from studies of risk factors to studies of treatment efficacy to studies of criminal justice policy. But in the limited space of this review, we will mention only three important points.

First, if we are to take it seriously, we need much better statistics to document and analyze the scope, nature and trends of child victimization. The National Crime Survey records crime victimizations only from age 12 and older. The Uniform Crime Reports in the past has made no age information available about crimes, with the exception of homicide (something that is changing under a new system, but the full national implementation of this system is still a long way off). The national data collection system about child abuse fails to include all states and has severe methodological limitations, which means that the information cannot be aggregated nationally or compared across states (National Center on Child Abuse and Neglect, 1992). We need comprehensive yearly national and state figures on all officially reported crimes and forms of child abuse committed against children. These need to be supplemented by regular national studies to assess the vast quantity of unreported victimization, including family violence, child-to-child, and indirect victimization. While there are methodological challenges in such efforts, studies like the ones referenced in this chapter demonstrate that this is feasible.

Second, we need theory and research that cuts across and integrates the various forms of child victimization. A good example is the work on posttraumatic stress disorder in children, which has been applied to the effects of various victimizations: sexual abuse, stranger abduction, and the witnessing of homicide (Boney-McCoy & Finkelhor, 1995, 1996; Eth & Pynoos, 1985; Terr, 1990). Similar cross-cutting research could be done on other subjects, such as what makes children vulnerable to victimization or how responses by family members buffer or exacerbate the impact of victimization. To be truly synthesizing, this research needs to study the pandemic victimizations, not just the acute and extraordinary victimizations, which have been the main focus in the past.

Finally, the field needs a more developmental perspective on child victimization. This would begin with an understanding of the mix of victimization threats that face children of different ages. It would include the kind of factors that place children at risk and the strategies for victimization avoidance that are appropriate at different stages of development. It also would differentiate how children at different stages react and cope with the challenges posed by victimization.

CONCLUSION

It is ironic that until recently the problem of children as aggressors has had more attention in social science than children as victims, reflecting perhaps the priorities of the adult world. It is encouraging that as the needs of children are more fully recognized, this balance is finally changing.

ACKNOWLEDGMENTS

The authors would like to gratefully acknowledge the Boy Scouts of America for financial support, the Franklin Pierce Law Center of Concord, New Hampshire, for assistance in legal research and Kelly Foster for help in preparing the manuscript.

APPENDIX

Sources of Data

Acronym	Survey
NCS90	National Crime Survey (Bureau of Justice Statistics, 1992)
NCS93	National Crime Survey (Bureau of Justice Statistics, 1995)
UCR	Uniform Crime Reports (Federal Bureau of Investigations, 1992)
UCR93	Uniform Crime Reports (Federal Bureau of Investigations, 1995)

NFVS-1	National Family Violence Survey, 1975 (Straus & Gelles, 1990)
NFVS-2	National Family Violence Resurvey, 1985 (Straus & Gelles, 1990)
NIS-2	National Study of the Incidence and Severity of Child Abuse and Neglect, 1986 (Sedlak, 1991)
NIS-3	Third National Incidence Study of Child Abuse and Neglect, 1993 (Sedlak & Broadhurst, 1996)
NYS	National Youth Survey (Lauritsen, Sampson, & Laub, 1991)
NYS78	National Youth Survey 1978 (Ageton, 1983)
NASHS	National Adolescent Student Health Survey (American School Health Association, 1989)
OJJDP 92	Office of Juvenile Justice and Delinquency Prevention (Moone, 1994)
NCCAN 93	National Center on Child Abuse and Neglect (National Center on Child Abuse and Neglect, 1995)
NISMART	National Incidence Study of Missing, Abducted, Runaway and Thrownaway Children, 1988 (Finkelhor, Hotaling, & Sedlak, 1990)

ENDNOTES

1. For example, in an effort to understand more about school-related victimizations, Garofalo, Siegel, and Laub (1987) obtained and read the narrative descriptions of the episodes occurring to youth aged 12 to 17 years recorded by National Crime Survey interviewers. The descriptions of many of the episodes sounded to these authors less serious than what is usually thought of as crime and they concluded that the victimizations of juveniles tended to be less serious than victimizations of adults:

   > The average person might not view the incidents as "real crimes." Scuffles, threats, arguments can end up being designated as assaults ... 72% of the narratives contained additional information about injury and most served to confirm its minor nature. For example, "while on school grounds respondent accidently spilled milk on another student who turned on the respondent with great anger and hit her on the head with clenched fist. Offender's ring caused pain and a lump to form." (p. 332)

   It is interesting how the fact that these were children and that the issue was spilled milk can contribute to the diminution of the sense of seriousness of an act of violence. I think it unlikely that a scenario of an adult customer accidentally spilling beer on another customer in a bar, which was responded to by a clenched fist punch on the head resulting in a lump, would move most observers to comment on the minor nature of the injury and the inappropriateness of designating this a crime.
2. The 1975 Family Violence Survey actually gathered its information about sibling assault *perpetrations* rather than victimizations. This means the figures may be underestimates, since for every sibling perpetrator there was at least one, but possibly several, sibling victims.
3. The undercount stems from two problems: (1) Most sexual abuse reports, unlike other forms of child maltreatment, start from children's own disclosures, which are more difficult for younger children to make. (2) Much sexual abuse goes on for extended periods of time before being disclosed and the age data in the NIS is based on age at the time of report, not age at onset.

REFERENCES

Ageton, S. S. (1983). *Sexual assault among adolescents.* Lexington, MA: Lexington Books.

American School Health Association. (1989). *The national adolescent student health survey: A report on the health of America's youth.* Kent, OH: Author.

Armstrong, L. (1994). *Rocking the cradle of sexual politics: What happened when women said incest.* Reading, MA: Addison-Wesley.

Berdie, J., Berdie, M., Wexler, S., & Fisher, B. (1983). *An empirical study of families involved in adolescent maltreatment*. San Francisco, CA: URSA Institute.

Black, D. (1976). *The behavior of law*. New York: Academic Press.

Boney-McCoy, S., & Finkelhor, D. (1995). The psychosocial impact of violent victimization on a national youth sample. *Journal of Consulting and Clinical Psychology*, *63*, 726–736.

Boney-McCoy, S., & Finkelhor, D. (1996). Is youth victimization related to PTSD and depression after controlling for prior symptoms and family relationships? A longitudinal study. *Journal of Consulting and Clinical Psychology*, *64*, 1406–1416.

Boston Globe Spotlight Team. (1987, November 8–11). Child sexual abuse: The crime of the 80's. *Boston Globe*, p. 7.

Briere, J., & Runtz, M. (1990). Differential adult symptomatology associated with three types of child abuse histories. *Child Abuse and Neglect*, *14*, 357–364.

Bross, D. C. (1995). Terminating the parent–child legal relationship as a response to child sexual abuse. *Loyola University Chicago Law Journal*, *26*, 287–319.

Bureau of Justice Statistics. (1989). *Redesign of the national crime survey*. Washington, DC: US Department of Justice.

Bureau of Justice Statistics. (1992). *National crime survey*. Washington, DC: US Department of Justice.

Bureau of Justice Statistics. (1995). *Criminal victimization in the United States, 1993: A national crime victimization survey report (NCJ-134126)*. Washington, DC: US Department of Justice.

Carlson, V., Cicchetti, D., Barnett, D., & Braunwald, K. (1989). Disorganized/disoriented attachment relationships in maltreated infants. *Developmental Psychopathology*, *25*, 525–531.

Chapman, J. R., & Smith, B. E. (1987). *Child sexual abuse: An analysis of case processing*. Washington, DC: American Bar Association.

Christoffel, K. K. (1990). Violent death and injury in US children and adolescents. *American Journal of Diseases of Children*, *144*, 697–706.

Christoffel, K. K., Anzinger, N. K., & Amari, M. (1983). Homicide in childhood: Distinguishable pattern of risk related to developmental levels of victims. *The American Journal of Forensic Medicine and Pathology*, *4*(2), 129–137.

Crittenden, P. A., & Craig, S. E. (1990). Developmental trends in the nature of child homicide. *Journal of Interpersonal Violence*, *5*, 202–216.

Crittenden, P. M. (1988). Distorted patterns of relationship in maltreating families: The role of internal representational models. *Journal of Reproductive & Infant Psychology*, *6*, 183–199.

Cross, T. P. (1995). Criminal justice outcomes of prosecution of child sexual abuse: A case flow analysis. *Child Abuse and Neglect*, *19*, 1431–1442.

Dalenberg, C., Bierman, K., & Furman, W. (1984). A re-examination of developmental changes in causal attributions. *Developmental Psychology*, *20*, 575–583.

Daro, D. (1995). *Public opinion and behaviors regarding child abuse prevention: The results of NCPCA's 1995 Public Opinion Poll (Working Paper 840)*. Chicago: The National Center on Child Abuse Prevention Research: The National Committee to Prevent Child Abuse.

Davis, K. M. (1994). Reading, writing, and sexual harassment: Finding a constitutional remedy when school fail to address peer abuse. *Indiana Law Journal*, *69*, 1123–1163.

DuRant, R. H., Getts, A., Cadenhead, C., Emans, S. J., & Woods, E. R. (1995). Exposure to violence and victimization and depression, hopelessness, and purpose in life among adolescents living in and around public housing. *Developmental and Behavioral Pediatrics*, *16*(4), 233–237.

Edwards, I. P. (1996). Corporal punishment and the legal system. *Santa Clara Law Review*, *36*, 983–1001.

Egeland, B., & Sroufe, L. A. (1981). Developmental sequelae of maltreatment in infancy. *New Directions for Child Development*, *11*, 77–92.

Erikson, E. (1968). *Identity, youth and crisis*. New York: Norton.

Eth, S., & Pynoos, R. S. (1985). *Post-traumatic stress disorder in children: Progress in psychiatry*. Washington, DC: American Psychiatric Press.

Federal Bureau of Investigations. (1992). *Crime in the United States, 1991: Uniform Crime Reports*. Washington, DC: US Department of Justice.

Federal Bureau of Investigations. (1995). *Crime in the United States, 1993: Uniform Crime Reports*. Washington, DC: US Department of Justice.

Finkelhor, D. (1984). *Child sexual abuse: New theory and research*. New York: Free Press.

Finkelhor, D. (1993). Epidemiological factors in the clinical identification of child sexual abuse. *Child Abuse and Neglect*, *17*, 67–70.

Finkelhor, D. (1994). Current information on the scope and nature of child sexual abuse. *The Future of Children*, *4*(2), 31–53.

Finkelhor, D., & Asdigian, N. L. (1996). Risk factors for youth victimization: Beyond a lifestyles theoretical approach. *Violence and Victims, 11*, 3–20.

Finkelhor, D., & Dziuba-Leatherman, J. (1994a). Children as victims of violence: A national survey. *Pediatrics, 94*, 413–420.

Finkelhor, D., & Dziuba-Leatherman, J. (1994b). Victimization of children. *American Psychologist, 49*, 173–183.

Finkelhor, D., & Dziuba-Leatherman, J. (1995). Victimization prevention programs: A national survey of children's exposure and reactions. *Child Abuse and Neglect, 19*, 125–135.

Finkelhor, D., & Kendall-Tackett, K. (1997). A developmental perspective on the childhood impact of crime, abuse and violent victimization. In D. Cicchetti & S. Toth (Eds.), *Developmental perspectives on trauma: Theory, research, and intervention* (pp. 1–32). New York: Plenum Press.

Finkelhor, D., Hotaling, G. T., & Sedlak, A. (1990). *Missing, abducted, runaway and thrownaway children in America: First report.* Washington, DC: Juvenile Justice Clearinghouse.

Finkelhor, D., Moore, D., Hamby, S., & Straus, M. (1997). Sexually abused children in a national survey of parents: Methodological issues. *Child Abuse and Neglect, 21*, 1–9.

Friedrich, W. N., Grambasch, P., Damon, L., Hewitt, S. K., Koverola, C., Lang, R., & Wolfe, V. (1992). Child Sexual Behavior Inventory: Normative and clinical comparisons. *Psychological Assessment, 4*, 303–311.

Garbarino, J. (1989). Troubled youth, troubled families: The dynamics of adolescent maltreatment. In D. Cicchetti & V. Carlson (Eds.), *Child maltreatment: Theory and research of the causes and consequences of child abuse and neglect* (pp. 685–706). New York: Cambridge University Press.

Garofalo, J., Siegel, L., & Laub, J. (1987). School-related victimizations among adolescents: An analysis of National Crime Survey (NCS) narratives. *Journal of Quantitative Criminology, 3*, 321–338.

Goetting, A. (1990). Child victims of homicide: A portrait of their killers and the circumstances of their deaths. *Violence and Victims, 5*, 287–296.

Goodwin, M. P., & Roscoe, B. (1990). Sibling violence and agnostic interactions among middle adolescence. *Adolescence, 98*, 451–467.

Greenbaum, S. (1989). *School bullying and victimization NSSC resource paper.* Malibu, CA: National School Safety Center.

Greenfield, A. M. (1993). Annie get your gun 'cause help ain't comin': The need for constitutional protection from peer abuse in public schools. *Duke Law Journal, 43*, 588–624.

Greven, P. (1990). *Spare the child: The religious roots of punishment and the psychological impact of physical abuse.* New York: Alfred A. Knopf.

Grisso, T. (1996). Society's retributive response to juvenile violence: A developmental perspective. *Law and Human Behavior, 20*, 229–247.

Guyer, B., Lescohier, I., Gallagher, S. S., Hausman, A., & Azzara, C. V. (1989). Intentional injuries among children and adolescents in Massachusetts. *New England Journal of Medicine, 321*, 1584–1589.

Hanson, R. L., & Slater, S. (1988). Sexual victimization in the history of sexual abusers: A review. *Annals of Sex Research, 4*, 485–499.

Harshbarger, S. (1987). Prosecution is an appropriate response in child sexual abuse cases. *Journal of Interpersonal Violence, 2*, 108–112.

Hashima, P. Y., & Finkelhor, D. (1999). Violent victimization of youth versus adults in the National Crime Victimization Survey. *Journal of Interpersonal Violence, 14*(8), 799–819.

Herman-Giddens, M. E., Sandler, A. D., & Friedman, N. E. (1988). Sexual precocity in girls: An association with sexual abuse? *American Journal of Diseases of the Child, 142*, 431–433.

Jaffe, P. G., Wolfe, D. A., & Wilson, S. K. (1990). *Children of battered women.* Newbury Park: Sage.

Jason, J. (1983). Child homicide spectrum. *American Journal of Diseases of Children, 137*, 578–581.

Jason, J., Carpenter, M. M., & Tyler, C. W. J. (1983). Underrecording of infant homicide in the United States. *American Journal of Public Health, 73*, 195–197.

Jensen, G. F., & Brownfield, D. (1986). Gender, lifestyles, and victimization: Beyond routine activity theory. *Violence and Victims, 1*, 85–99.

Kaufman, J., & Ziegler, E. (1987). Do abused children become abusive parents? *American Journal of Orthopsychiatry, 57*, 186–192.

Kendall-Tackett, K. A., Williams, L. M., & Finkelhor, D. (1993). Impact of sexual abuse on children: A review and synthesis of recent empirical studies. *Psychological Bulletin, 113*, 164–180.

Kerns, D. L., & Ritter, M. L. (1992). Medical findings in child sexual abuse cases with perpetrator confessions (Abstract). *American Journal of Diseases of Children, 146*, 494.

Kilpatrick, D. (1992). *Rape in America: A report to the nation.* Charleston, SC: Crime Victims Research and Treatment Center.

Kilpatrick, D. G., Saunders, B. E., Amick-McMullan, A., Best, C. L., Veronen, L. J., & Resnick, H. S. (1989). Victim and crime factors associated with the development of crime-related post-traumatic stress disorder. *Behavior Therapy*, *20*, 199–214.

Kilpatrick, D. G., Amick, A. A., & Resnick, H. S. (1990). *The impact of homicide on surviving family members: Final report* (Grant No: 87-IJ-CX-0017). Washington, DC: National Institute of Justice.

Kirby, J. S., Chu, J., & Dill, D. L. (1993). Correlates of dissociative symptomatology in patients with physical and sexual abuse histories. *Comprehensive Psychiatry*, *34*(4), 258–263.

Kolko, D. J. (1992). Characteristics of child victims of physical violence: Research findings and clinical implications. *Journal of Interpersonal Violence*, *7*, 244–276.

Lauritsen, J. L., Sampson, R. J., & Laub, J. H. (1991). The link between offending and victimization among adolescents. *Criminology*, *29*, 265–292.

Lauritsen, J. L., Laub, J. H., & Sampson, R. J. (1992). Conventional and delinquent activities: Implications for the prevention of violent victimization among adolescents. *Violence and Victims*, *7*, 91–108.

Lewis, D. O., Shanok, S. S., Pincus, J. H., & Glaser, G. H. (1979). Violent juvenile delinquents: Psychiatric, neurological, psychological and abuse factors. *Journal of the American Academy of Child Psychiatry*, *18*, 307–319.

Libby, P., & Bybee, R. (1979). The physical abuse of adolescents. *Journal of Social Issues*, *35*, 101–126.

Lynch, J. P. (1991). Victim behavior and the risk of victimization: Implications of activity-specific victimization rates. In G. Kaiser, H. Kury, & H. J. Albrect (Eds.), *Victims and criminal violence* (pp. 543–566). Freiburg, Germany: Eigenverlag Max-Planck-Institute.

MacDonald, K. (1985). Early experience, relative plasticity, and social development. *Developmental Review*, *5*, 99–121.

Martinez, P., & Richters, J. E. (1993). The NIMH community violence project: II. Children's distress symptoms associated with violence exposure. In D. Reiss, J. E. Richters, M. Radke-Yarrow, & D. Scharff (Eds.), *Children and violence* (pp. 22–35). New York: Guilford Press.

Martinez-Schnell, B., & Waxweiler, R. J. (1989). Increases in premature mortality due to homicide—United States, 1968–1985. *Violence and Victims*, *4*, 287–293.

McClain, P. W., Sacks, J. J., Froehlke, R. G., & Ewigman, B. G. (1993). Estimates of fatal child abuse and neglect, United States, 1979 through 1988. *Pediatrics*, *91*, 338–343.

McCord, J. (1983). A forty year perspective of effects of child abuse and neglect. *Child Abuse and Neglect*, *7*, 265–270.

McMillen, J. P. (1995). Prosecuting child abuse homicides in Iowa: A proposal for change. *Drake Law Review*, *43*, 129–151.

Melton, G. B. (1989). Taking Gault seriously: Toward a new juvenile court. *Nebraska Law Review*, *68*, 146–181.

Milani, A. A. (1995). Harassing speech in the public schools: The validity of schools' regulation of fighting words and the consequences if they do not. *Akron Law Review*, *28*, 187–235.

Miller, T. R., Cohen, M. A., & Wiersema, B. (1996). *Victim costs and consequences* (Research report 90-IJ-CX-0050): Washington, DC: National Institute of Justice.

Mnookin, R. H., & Weisberg, D. K. (1989). *Child, family and state: Problems and materials on children and the law* (2nd ed.). Boston: Little, Brown and Company.

Moone, J. (1994). *Juvenile victimization: 1987–1992* (Fact Sheet 17). Washington, DC: Office of Juvenile Justice and Delinquency Prevention, US Department of Justice.

Moore, D. W., Gallup, G. H., & Schussel, R. (1995). *Disciplining children in America: A Gallup poll report.* Princeton, NJ: The Gallup Organization.

Morgan, J., & Zedner, L. (1992). *Child victims: Crime, impact, and criminal justice.* Oxford, England: Clarendon Press.

Myers, J. (1985–1986). The legal response to child abuse. In the best interest of children? *Journal of Family Law*, *24*(149), 179–181.

Nader, K., Pynoos, R., Fairbanks, L., & Frederick, C. (1990). Children's PTSD reactions one year after a sniper attack at their school. *American Journal of Psychiatry*, *147*, 1526–1530.

Nathan, D., & Snedeker, M. (1995). *Satan's silence: Ritual abuse and the making of a modern American witch hunt.* New York: Basic Books.

National Center on Child Abuse and Neglect. (1992). *National child abuse and neglect data system (Working Paper No. 1): 1990 summary data component* (DHHS Publication No. (ACF) 92-30361): Washington, DC: Department of Health and Human Services.

National Center on Child Abuse and Neglect. (1995). *Child maltreatment 1993: Reports from the states to the National Center on Child Abuse and Neglect.* Washington, DC: US Government Printing Office.

National Research Council. (1993). *Understanding child abuse and neglect.* Washington, DC: National Academy Press.

Olweus, D. (1991). Bully/victim problems among schoolchildren: Basic facts and effects of a school based intervention program. In D. J. Pepler & K. H. Rubin (Eds.), *The development and treatment of childhood aggression* (Vol. xvii, pp. 411–448). Hillsdale, NJ: Lawrence Erlbaum.

Olweus, D. (1993). Bullies on the playground: The role of victimization. In C. H. Hart (Ed.), *Children of playgrounds: Research perspectives and applications* (pp. 85–128). Albany: State University of New York Press.

Papakirk, J. (1993). Michigan's new corporal punishment amendment: Where the good act giveth, did the amendment taketh away? *Thomas M. Cooley Law Review, 10*, 383–407.

Putnam, F. W., & Trickett, P. K. (1993). Child sexual abuse: A model of chronic trauma. In D. Reiss, J. E. Richters, & M. Radke-Yarrow (Eds.), *Children and violence* (pp. 82–95). New York: Guilford Press.

Rainey, R. H., & Greer, D. C. (1995, January/February). Criminal charging alternatives in child fatality cases. *The Prosecutor*, 16–18.

Resnick, P. A. (1993). The psychological impact of rape. *Journal of Interpersonal Violence, 8*(2), 223–255.

Roscoe, B., Goodwin, M., & Kennedy, D. (1987). Sibling violence and agonistic interactions experienced by early adolescents. *Journal of Family Violence, 2*(2), 121–137.

Rutter, M. (1989). The role of cognition in child development and disorder. In S. Chess, A. Thomas, & M. E. Hertzig (Eds.), *Annual progress in child psychiatry and child development: 1988* (pp. 77–101). New York: Brunner/Mazel.

Saunders, B. E., Villeponteaux, L. A., Lipovsky, J. A., Kilpatrick, D. G., & Veronen, L. J. (1992). Child sexual assault as a risk factor for mental disorders among women: A community survey. *Journal of Interpersonal Violence, 7*, 189–204.

Savage, D. G. (1996, October 8). High court lets stand harassment suit barrier. *Los Angeles Times*, pp. A1,A23.

Schellenbach, C. J., & Guerney, L. F. (1987). Identification of adolescent abuse and future intervention prospects. *Journal of Adolescence, 10*(1), 1–12.

Scott, K. D. (1992). Childhood sexual abuse: Impact on a community's mental health status. *Child Abuse and Neglect, 16*, 285–295.

Sedlak, A. J. (1991). *National incidence and prevalence of child abuse and neglect: 1988—Revised report*. Rockville, MD: Westat.

Sedlak, A. J., & Broadhurst, D. D. (1996). *Third national incidence study of child abuse and neglect*. Washington, DC: US Department of Health and Human Services.

Shirk, S. R. (1988). The interpersonal legacy of physical abuse of children. In M. B. Straus (Ed.), *Abuse and victimization across the life span* (pp. 57–81). Baltimore, MD: The Johns Hopkins University Press.

Singer, M. I., Anglin, T. M., Song, L. Y., & Lunghofer, L. (1995). Adolescents' exposure to violence and associated symptoms of psychological trauma. *Journal of the American Medical Association, 273*(6), 477–482.

Smith, B. E. (1995). *Prosecuting child physical abuse cases: A case study in San Diego*. Washington, DC: National Institute of Justice.

Smith, P. K., Bowers, L., Binney, V., & Cowie, H. (1993). Relationships of children involved in bully/victim problems at school. In S. Duck (Ed.), *Learning about relationships* (pp. 184–205). Newbury Park, CA: Sage.

Snyder, H. N., & Sickmund, M. (1995). *Juvenile offenders and victims: A national report*. Washington, DC: Office of Juvenile Justice and Delinquency Prevention.

Sparks, R. F. (1982). *Research on victims of crime*. Washington, DC: Government Printing Office.

Stein, N. (1999). *Classrooms and courtrooms: Facing sexual harassment in K-12*. New York: Teachers College Press.

Strassberg, Z., Dodge, K. A., Pettit, G. S., & Bates, J. E. (1994). Spanking in the home and children's subsequent aggression toward kindergarten peers. *Development and Psychopathology, 6*, 445–461.

Straus, M. A. (1994). *Beating the devil out of them: Corporal punishment in American families*. New York: Lexington Books.

Straus, M. A., & Gelles, R. J. (1990). *Physical violence in American families: Risk factors and adaptations to violence in 8,145 families*. New Brunswick, NJ: Transaction Press.

Straus, M. A., & Gelles, R. J. (1992). *Physical violence in American families: Risk factors and adaptations to violence in 8,145 families*. New Brunswick, NJ: Transaction Press.

Straus, M. A., Gelles, J., & Steinmetz, S. K. (1980). *Behind closed doors*. Newbury Park, CA: Sage.

Terr, L. (1990). *Too scared to cry*. New York: Harper/Collins.

Tjaden, P. G., & Thoennes, N. (1992). Predictors of legal intervention in child maltreatment cases. *Child Abuse and Neglect, 16*, 807–821.

Trickett, P. K., & Putnam, F. W. (1993). Impact of child sexual abuse on females: Toward a developmental psychobiological integration. *Psychological Science, 4*, 81–87.

Widom, C. S. (1989a). The cycle of violence. *Science, 244*, 160–166.

Widom, C. S. (1989b). Does violence beget violence? A critical examination of the literature. *Psychological Bulletin, 106*, 3–28.

Wolak, J., & Finkelhor, D. (1998). Children exposed to partner violence. In J. L. Jasinski & L. M. Williams (Eds.), *Partner violence: A comprehensive review of 20 years of research* (pp. 73–111). Thousand Oaks, CA: Sage.

5

Child Pornography

DANIEL LINZ and DOROTHY IMRICH

INTRODUCTION

Health professionals attending the 1993 UNESCO Conference in Brussels, Belgium, have asserted that child prostitution and child pornography are highly organized industries that operate on a national and international scale. At the conference, officials from Asia, Europe, and North and South America reported on what they saw as a dramatic increase over the last 10 years in the number of children being treated for sexually transmitted diseases. Experts at the conference speculated that one factor contributing to what they claimed was an increase in the use of children in pornography is the financial lure of a multimillion-dollar international sex industry featuring children in pornography, peep shows, and on "sex tours" (Simons, 1993).

In this chapter we ask: what is child pornography, who is attracted to it, who produces it, what harms befall its child victims, and what does the law say about controlling these materials, producers, and users, In order to establish a social–historical context for asking these questions we begin with a brief review of the history of human adult–child sexual behavior. We then describe the psychological disorder of pedophilia, the sexual attraction to children. A distinction is made between pedophiles (adults sexually attracted primarily to children) and child molesters (adults who act on this attraction as well as other adults who sexually abuse children for more opportunistic reasons).

We then describe pedophiles' and child molesters' use of child pornography, including materials "homemade" by pedophiles for their own use and professional publication of child pornography.

We then list the large number of effects the production and circulation of child pornography is presumed to have on children by lawmakers. As we note below the harms of child pornography are usually treated as self-evident and empirical research is limited on the effects of these materials on victims. Most often, the primary sources of information of victim effects come from clinicians who have treated victims. Few studies employing other methods exist on the effects of these materials on adult viewers.

DANIEL LINZ • Law and Society, and Department of Communication, University of California, Santa Barbara, California 93106. **DOROTHY IMRICH** • Department of Communication, University of California, Santa Barbara, California 93106.

Handbook of Youth and Justice, edited by White. Kluwer Academic/Plenum Publishers, New York, 2001.

We then ask: what have the courts said about laws banning this material? We describe the Protection of Children Against Sexual Exploitation Act of 1977 and Child Pornography Prevention Act of 1996, as well as the most important court cases concerning child pornography including the most important of these, *New York v. Ferber* (1982), which established that a state may regulate child pornography even if the material is not legally obscene. Within the context of these laws and court decisions we raise the question of the constitutional dilemma of differentiating legitimate art from child exploitation.

In the last section we discuss the problem of child pornography and "cyberspace." We review the concerns of parents and policymakers concerning child pornography on the Internet and the possibility that adult predators will contact children through this medium for the purposes of sexual abuse.

WHAT IS CHILD PORNOGRAPHY AND WHO IS ATTRACTED TO IT?

Defining Child Pornography

Child pornography has become a social problem only relatively recently, primarily as a result of still photography, film making, and lately, with the advent of the videocassette recorder. Not until the early 1980s was child pornography legally distinguished from other forms of pornography and obscenity and defined according to a stricter standard.

Most recently, with the Child Pornography Prevention Act of 1996, the US Congress has attempted to define child pornography as "... any visual depiction, including any photograph, film, video, picture, or computer or computer-generated image or picture, whether made or produced by electronic, mechanical, or other means, of sexually explicit conduct, where the production of such visual depiction involves the use of a minor engaging in sexually explicit conduct" ("New digital child porn law," 1996). Lately, controversy has arisen over this latest attempt by Congress to regulate images of children because for the first time the law now refers to computer-generated images and raises the possibility that materials can be prosecuted despite the fact that an actual child is not used in their production.

A History of Human Adult–Child Sexual Behavior

The legal prohibition of minors used as sexual objects or portrayed in a sexual manner such as the restrictions laid out in the Child Pornography Prevention Act of 1996 is a late 20th-century idea. Contrary to the contemporary tendency to protect children from sexual exploitation from adults, the historical and cross-cultural record clearly reflects a long-standing acceptance of the use of children in sexual practices.

Worldwide, there has never been a universal consensus on the appropriateness of adult–child sex outside the nuclear family. While little recorded history exists pertaining exclusively to children, the evidence that does exist indicates that the sexual use of children has a long history (Aimes & Houston, 1990). Bullough's (1964) historical review of human adult–child sexual behavior suggests that sexual behavior between adults and children was much more prevalent in previous time than today. Adult–child sexual relations have occurred throughout history with varying degrees of acceptability.

Most well known is the sexual use of young boys in Ancient Greece where pubescent males were taken by warriors as lovers (Vanggaard, 1972). These boys always took the passive role, since adult males who allowed themselves to be sodomized were held in lowest contempt by members of Greek society (Ungaretti, 1978).

The growth of Christianity led to the condemnation of these practices, though apparently not to protect the young males as much as to prevent masturbation or sexual relations that did not lead to procreation (Goodrich, 1976). According to Goodrich, these condemnations served to protect male children somewhat, but no such protection was afforded female children. Medieval religious law *officially* forbade the marriage of girls less than 12 years old, but it was not uncommon to find girls of 10 married to very old men (Nobile, 1976). The streets of 14th-century Florence were filled with male and female children acting as prostitutes (Goodrich, 1976).

Accounts from the 18th century indicate that adult–child sex (particularly same-sex pairings) was an accepted practice in China, Turkey, Arabia, Egypt, and the Islamic areas of India (Trumbach, 1977). Acceptance also was apparently widespread in Western societies. Bullough (1964) reports that in 19th-century London the going price for a 12-year-old girl was reported to be 400 pounds. Nineteenth-century writers such as Lord Byron, Lewis Carroll, and Horatio Alger all appear to have had significant sexual interest in children or adolescents.

Adult–child sex continues to proliferate today in Western societies. Two relatively recent "travel guides for gentlemen" show that the desire for sexual interaction with children still is apparent in the Western world. The *Discreet Gentleman's Guide to the Pleasures of Europe* (1975) advises the male traveler on where he can find "Lolita-eyed nymphettes who make pocket money with every orifice but the natural one" (p. 916).

Adult sexual interest in children is not confined to the contemporary Western world. Ritualized homosexuality involving young boys is still practiced in 10 to 20% of Melanesian societies (Herdt, 1984). Variations of the manner in which sex is allowed are found from one tribe to another with some using fellatio, others anal intercourse, and still others masturbation. In these societies, girls as young as 8 years old also are used for special ceremonies that involve making medicine from seminal fluids gathered from the child after intercourse. Young brides of the Kimam Papuan tribe are "tested" by many men prior to the wedding ceremony to ensure their fitness for marriage (Serpenti, 1984).

Despite the recent concerns of UNESCO officials an others, the problem of child sexual exploitation is an old one with a long history. As with adult pornography, the possibility of wide distribution and the relative permanency of images of children as sex objects preserved in child pornography has served to continually keep the problem in the forefront of legal concern in contemporary society. Today, it is nearly universally presumed that sexual relations with children is deviant and reprehensible and that those attracted to such relations are mentally ill.

Pedophilia as a Psychological Disorder

Those people sexually attracted to children in contemporary Western society, most notably, in the United States and Europe, are generally described as "pedophiles" and are considered to be suffering from a serious mental health disorder by psychiatrists, psychologists, and other mental health workers. According to the *Diagnostic and Statistical Manual of Mental Disorders*, 4th edition (DSM-IV) of the American Psychiatric Association (1994) the essential feature of this disorder is recurrent, intense, sexual urges and sexually arousing fantasies, of at least 6 months' duration, involving sexual activity with a prepubescent child (13 or younger). The age of the person is arbitrarily set at age 16 years or older and at least 5 years older than the child. A person will be diagnosed as a pedophile if over a period of at least 6 months the person has had recurrent intense sexual urges and sexually arousing fantasies involving sexual activity with a prepubescent child or children, or the person has acted on these urges, or is markedly distressed by them.

Pedophiles generally report an attraction to children of a particular age range, which may be as specific as within a range of only 1 or 2 years. Those attracted to girls usually prefer 8- to 10-year-olds, whereas those attracted to boys usually prefer slightly older children. Attraction to girls is apparently twice as common as attraction to boys. Many people with pedophilia are sexually aroused by both young boys and young girls.

People with this disorder who act on their urges with children may limit their activity to undressing the child and looking, exposing themselves, masturbating in the presence of the child, or gentle touching and fondling of the child. Others, however, perform fellatio or cunnilingus on the child or penetrate the child's vagina, mouth, or anus with their fingers, foreign objects, or penis, and use varying degrees of force to achieve these ends. These activities are commonly explained with excuses or rationalizations such as they have "educational value" for the child, that the child "derives asexual pleasure" from them, or that the child was "sexually provocative."

According to the DSM-IV, the person may limit his activities to his own children, stepchildren, or relatives or may victimize children outside his family. Some people with the disorder threaten the child to prevent disclosure. Others, particularly those who frequently victimize children, develop complicated techniques for obtaining children, which may include gaining the trust of a child's mother, marrying a woman with an attractive child, "trading" children with others with the disorder, or, in rare instances, bringing foster children from nonindustrialized countries or abducting children from strangers.

Except in cases in which the disorder is associated with the psychological disorder of sexual sadism, the adult may be generous and very attentive to the child's needs in all respects other than the sexual victimization in order to gain the child's affection, interest, and loyalty and to prevent the child from reporting the sexual activity.

Behavioral scientists have devised subtypologies in an attempt to refine the DSM-IV category of pedophilia. For example, the presence of antisocial tendencies and the degree of entrenchment or fixation of the behavior (Groth, 1979; Knight, Carter, & Prentky, 1989), degree of force used (Groth, 1979), and social inadequacies of the offender (Fitch, 1962; Gebhard, Gagnon, Pomeroy, & Christenson, 1964; Knight et al., 1989; Mohr, 1964) have been suggested as helpful distinctions to be made in predicting which pedophiles pose a risk to children. Most often, however, the distinction between pedophile and child molester has been employed by both legal and mental health officials.

Distinguishing Pedophiles and Child Molesters

All pedophiles are not child molesters, nor are all child molesters pedophiles. According to McCary and McCary (1984), approximately 30% of sex offenders are classified as pedophiles. The profile of a pedophile is an individual who is for the most part male, over 25 years of age, single and never married who lives alone or with parents, has an excessive interest in and associates mainly with children, and has increased access to children (Lanning, 1992; Hanson, Steffy, & Gaulthier, 1993). A study by Abel, Lawry, Karlstrom, Oebom, and Gillespie (1994) determined that offenders' awareness of their pedophilia occurred at an early age.

A pedophile is an individual who fantasizes about sexual contact with children, while a child molester actually commits that act in some form. Therefore, although it is possible to be labeled a pedophile, unless one acts on an urge, he or she is not a child molester.

Child molesters most commonly are divided into two categories: "fixated" and "regressive" groups. A fixated child molester is an individual who exhibits a persistent pattern of primary interest in children. A regressive child molester's sexual interest in children is a departure from a primary sexual orientation toward adults.

A further categorization, developed by Dietz (1983), divides child molesters into either situational or preferential offenders. Situational child molesters are defined as individuals who do not have a preference for children but engage in molestation due to low self-esteem or poor coping skills. They may be sexually indiscriminate and may exhibit a life pattern of using and abusing others including children or those suffering from psychological disorders including mental retardation or senility. Preferential child molesters are pedophiles who manifest fantasies and active sexual behavior targeted solely toward children. The four major characteristics of the preferential child molester are: (1) long-term and persistent pattern of behavior; (2) children as preferred sex objects; (3) sexual fantasies focusing on children; and 4), well-developed techniques in obtaining victims (Lanning, 1992, p. 15).

Several specific patterns of behavior and offender characteristics are present in most preferential child molesters. Extroverted offenders will use seduction to entice victims, while introverted offenders, lacking the interpersonal skills necessary to attract victims, will employ covert methods such as obscene phone calls, exhibitionism, or the molesting of very young children. Characteristics of preferential child molesters include frequent changes in employment or residence, prior arrests, and multiple victims. Preferential molesters also exhibit high levels of predictable sexual behavior known as sexual rituals and may have specific victim age and gender preferences (Lanning, 1992). Finally, even though the typical pedophile is a young adult, Becket and Kaplan (1989) found that 58% of adult offenders admitted to sex crimes committed as adolescents.

Studies of child victimization based on arrest statistics indicate that preferential child molesters have a much higher probability of molesting a large number of victims per offender than do situational offenders (Lanning, 1992). However, ascertaining a definitive estimate of the prevalence of adult–child sexual victimization is difficult. Estimates derived from crime statistics involve only reported cases and are likely to be an underrepresentation.

Little is known about these repeat offenders. Recidivism rates for same sex versus opposite sex offenders are mixed, with the best risk predictor appearing to be a history of prior convictions (Hanson et al., 1993). Other research indicates that pedophiles who join organizations looking for victims usually are exclusively male and target male victims (Abel et al., 1994). According to McCary and McCary (1984), the rate of recidivism for homosexual pedophiles is approximately 15 to 30%. The rate of recidivism among heterosexual child molesters is approximately one-half that of homosexual child molesters. Finally, Hanson et al. (1993) noted that the risk factor for reoffending also is much higher for molesters who select extrafamiliar victims.

Retrospective reports carry their own inherent problems but are perhaps the best source of knowledge at this time concerning the frequency of molestation. From these reports researchers have ascertained that a sizable portion of the US population may have experienced some form of unwanted sexual contact or abuse. Finkelhor (1979) conducted a survey of 530 female and 266 male college students questioning them about their sexual experiences in childhood. Results revealed that 11% of the females and 4% of the males reported having had an unwanted sexual experience with an adult before the age of 12. Females reported that 46% of such encounters involved a relative, 33% an acquaintance, and 24% a stranger. Males were less often abused by a relative and more often abused by acquaintances (53%) and strangers (30%).

Self-report data on the differential incidence of offending across perpetrators indicates that a relatively small number of preferential child molesters are responsible for a large number of offenses. Reports obtained from a sample of approximately 250 child molesters, who were guaranteed confidentiality, revealed that on average they had victimized about 80 children (Able, Mittelman & Becker, 1987). Incarcerated molesters also report a high incidence of encounters and, on average, report having 11 more victims than those for which they were prosecuted (Groth, Longo & McFadin, 1982). A completely accurate estimate of the number of child molesters is probably impossible to obtain with the current data. What can be said is that child molesters commit many offenses across a lifetime of offending and are not always prosecuted for many of the offenses they commit.

Preferential Child Molesters Use of Child Pornography

Lawmakers and law enforcement officials have focused on the preferential child molester as most dangerous to children, and according to the FBI most preferential child molesters collect some form of child pornography or erotica (Abel et al., 1994). FBI Behavioral Sciences Unit Supervisory Special Agent Kenneth Lanning (1992) notes that the size of the pornography collection appears to be based on the offender's socioeconomic status, living arrangements, and age. The older the child molester, the larger the collection is likely to be. The material often is kept in a highly organized, ritualistic fashion.

Child molesters also may produce homemade pornographic, erotic, or nonpornographic matter that relates to children such as diaries, fantasy writings, personal letters, and telephone and address books. This material can be obtained in a number of ways including newsletters through pedophile support groups, detective magazines, and most recently computers and CD-ROM disks (Lanning, 1992).

Although no survey data on law enforcement beliefs currently are available, many law enforcement officials appear to believe that there is a reasonably stable connection between being a child molester and collecting child pornography. According to Lanning (1992) "... if there is probable cause to believe that an offender is a preferential child molester, then it is also likely that the offender has some form of child pornography or erotica" (p. 31).

The presence of child pornography among molesters does not, of course, imply that all consumers of child pornography will sexually molest children. Research that moves beyond the often anecdotal reports by police is needed to determine to what extent pedophiles and child molesters collect such materials.

THE PRODUCTION OF CHILD PORNOGRAPHY

There are three primary sources of child pornography production. The first is "homemade" production of materials by pedophiles for themselves. These materials are shared, sold, or traded with other pedophiles. The second source may be professional publishers or large-scale producers of child pornography. However, as will be noted below, it is difficult to establish the magnitude of such publishing and distribution enterprises. The third category is pornography that is "technically" child pornography produced by commercial producers of adult pornography who have employed (possibly inadvertently) actors or actresses under 18. This category is thought to be increasingly rare due to mandatory age reporting laws imposed on professional producers of adult pornography in the United States (described below), and thus will not be described in this chapter.

Homemade Production by Pedophiles

How much of what we term child pornography is made by nonprofessionals for personal use? How much of this is shared with others? There are no reliable data available on the number of pedophiles across the country who have collections of child pornography. An understanding of the types of materials most likely to be found comes in the form of case studies usually reported by the police.

The following three case studies are compiled from police reports of sting operations by the US Post Office that involve searches of the home of persons arrested after receiving a controlled delivery of pornographic materials (United States Sentencing Commission, 1996). In the course of these operations police may uncover videotapes and photographs taken by the defendant for his own use:

- *Case 1*: Records from a mail-order pornography operation indicated the defendant had ordered 22 pornographic items involving juveniles. Defendant was sent a solicitation from a Postal Inspection Service undercover operation, from which he then ordered a videotape and a magazine containing explicit sexual contact between minors, some of which were under age 12. After a controlled delivery, a search of the defendant's home uncovered these materials as well as five Polaroid photographs of a partially clothed 15-year-old male. The defendant was convicted of receiving child pornography.
- *Case 2*: The defendant responded to an advertisement placed in the *Kinky Market Place* by a US Postal inspector. The defendant requested a tape depicting 1 hour of incest. The undercover inspector sent a return letter asking for verification that the defendant was not an undercover officer as well as the type of "action" in which he was interested. The defendant said he was interested in family incest between parents and their children. A controlled delivery was made to the defendant's home. After the defendant removed the package from his mail box and carried it inside, the US postal inspectors executed a search warrant at the residence. Inspectors found the tape in addition to literature and photographs of bestiality and literature on incest.
- *Case 3*: An informant in a child prostitution case revealed to the police that he knew of a man in another state who claimed he could procure child pornography. This information was passed on by the local police to a US postal inspector. The postal inspector began corresponding with the suspect under the guise of being a collector of youthful erotic art. The suspect subsequently advised that he might be able to provide both photographs and videotapes of children and teens performing sexual acts. The postal inspector sent the title pages of several archived, commercially produced child pornography magazines. Also provided were the titles of archived, commercially produced, child pornography 8-mm film transferred to videotape. The suspect then wrote the postal inspector and specifically requested several of these items. He further offered not only to provide the inspector with original child pornography, but also to introduce the inspector to young children whom the inspector could photograph. This search revealed a large collection of foreign-produced child pornography, plus an extensive collection of correspondence with other men sharing a sexual interest in young children. The suspect's collection also included Polaroid photographs of very young children in sexually explicit poses with adults.

As is evident by these cases, often a police sting operation will yield materials nonprofessionally produced. These operations sometimes lead to large caches of materials and correspondence with other pedophiles. How typical the features presented above are of all collectors of homemade materials is unknown.

Professional Publication

Generally, state and federal law makes no distinction between production for commercial purposes and production for personal, noncommercial use. Thus, cases are not classified according to the type of material (homemade vs. commercial). Little is actually known about the amount of commercially produced material available. In 1977, it was reported to the US Congressional Committee Investigating Sexual Exploitation of Children that there was in existence over 260 different magazines that depict children engaging in sexually explicit conduct: "Such magazines depict children, some as young as three to five years of age.... The activities featured range from lewd poses to intercourse, fellatio, cunnilingus, masturbation, rape, incest and sadomasochism" (p. 92). In Los Angeles alone, police reported at the hearings that "30,000 children have been sexually exploited through child pornography" (p. 3).

The veracity of these claims is unknown. It is difficult to establish how many professionally produced materials exist. Materials that have been confiscated include that produced in the United states several decades ago or in many cases materials of foreign origin. In fact, according to the United States Sentencing Commission (1996) there were no production cases that reach the scale of commercial adult pornography. Only a minority of cases sentenced under this guideline in 1995 and 1996 involve the production of pornography for commercial distribution. The following is the most extreme example reported by the US Sentencing Commission of a defendant attempting and possessing professional publication.

- *Case 4*: Defendant met young boys through the Big Brother organization and through trips to Mexico and Thailand. Numerous photographs were taken and developed by the defendant of at least 14 boys, appearing to be between the ages of 10 to 18. The photos depicted the boys posing nude, engaged in masturbation, or in mutual masturbation or oral sex with the defendant. Defendant also possessed commercially made child pornography from the 1960s, 1970s and early 1980s. Two letters dated from early 1980, one from a pornography publisher in Sweden and the other in Denmark, indicate that the defendant had tried to get some of his photographs published in these countries.

In 1980, the report to the General Assembly by the Illinois Legislative Investigating Committee called *Sexual Exploitation of Children* dismissed the claim of 30,000 children involved in multimillion dollar child pornography rings. The report did discover that child pornography in the United States was primarily made for private use or circulation by "individual child molesters" (Illinois Legislative Investigating Commission, 1980, p. 27).

According to the Illinois report the longest-lasting, biggest-selling underground child porn magazine of the 1970s, the *Broad Street Magazine* (of which one out of 12 pages in a typical issue included images of children) never sold to more than 800 individuals or grossed more than $30,000 a year. A spokesman for the National Law Center for Children and Families, a conservative children's advocacy group, said to the *New York Times* in February 1995: "There's really no commercial child pornography in the United States" (Carvajal, 1995, p. 17).

There are several vociferous critics of what has been called the "child abuse industry"—organizations and individuals who make their living arousing public concern about the problem of child pornography and professionals who have steadily continued their call for more legislation through the use of exaggerated statistics (see Desen-Gerber & Hutchinson, 1979; Gentile, 1982; Jones, 1991). These authors point out that the act of photographing minors in sexually explicit poses has been illegal in the United States for many years, but it is not uncommon to hear testimony in legislative hearings claiming that there is a "growing 'kiddie' porn subculture'' catered to by underground dealers filming ''sex acts on infants as young as eight months'' and that child pornography creates more victims every time it is used by its customers (''News in Brief,'' 1984, p. 2; Tyler & Stone, 1985). However, valid documentation of these claims is not often provided. According to Jones (1991), the vast majority of such claims, in the literature and elsewhere, are not founded on rigorous research.

To date, no empirical studies have been done to estimate the amount of professionally produced or personally made materials. Most materials become known as a result of attention from law enforcement officials, often through sting operations where materials are solicited from child pornography collectors by government officials. More research is needed on the extent of professional publication in the United States and abroad. More recently, researchers have turned their attention to these materials on the Internet, a subject we will return to later in this chapter.

EFFECTS ON CHILDREN

Regardless of the level of distribution of these materials, the use of children as subjects of pornographic material is assumed to be harmful to the physiological, emotional, and mental health of the child. The materials themselves also are assumed to be a stimulus for sexual arousal and sexual molestation by pedophiles. The 1977 Senate Judiciary Committee found that subjects of child pornography tended to be vulnerable children who were easily victimized and who became deeply scarred by their ordeals (S. Rep. No. 438, 95th Cong., 2nd Sess. 5, 1977).

The Attorney General's Commission on Pornography (1986) recounted what it described as the devastating effects of pornography on its victims:

> In the short term the effects of such involvement include depression, suicidal thoughts, feelings of shame, guilt, alienation from family and peers, and massive acute anxiety. Victims in the longer term may successfully ''integrate'' the event, particularly with psychiatric help, but many will likely suffer a repetition of the abuse cycle (this time as the abuser), chronic low self-esteem, depression, anxiety regarding sexuality, role confusion, a fragmented sense of self, and possible entry into delinquency or prostitution. All, of course, will suffer the agony of knowing the record of their sexual abuse is in circulation, its effects on their future lives unknowable and beyond their control. (pp. 613–614)

Most recently, nearly all of the possible harmful effects of child pornography on children and society have been enumerated in the Child Pornography Prevention Act of 1996. In the preamble to this Act, Congress found:

> (1) the use of children in the production of sexually explicit material, including photographs, films, videos, computer images, and other visual depictions, is a form of sexual abuse which can result in physical or psychological harm, or both, to the children involved;
>
> (2) where children are used in its production, child pornography permanently records the victim's abuse, and its continued existence causes the child victims of sexual abuse continuing harm by haunting those children in future years;
>
> (3) child pornography is often used as part of a method of seducing other children into sexual activity; a child who is reluctant to engage in sexual activity with an adult, or to pose for sexually explicit photographs, can sometimes be convinced by viewing depictions of other children ''having fun'' participating in such activity;
>
> (4) child pornography is often used by pedophiles and child sexual abusers to stimulate

and whet their own sexual appetites, and as a model for sexual acting out with children; such use of child pornography can desensitize the viewer to the pathology of sexual abuse or exploitation of children, so that it can become acceptable to and even preferred by the viewer;

(5) new photographic and computer imaging technologies make it possible to produce by electronic, mechanical, or other means, visual depictions of what appear to be children engaging in sexually explicit conduct that are virtually indistinguishable to the unsuspecting viewer from unretouched photographic images of actual children engaging in sexually explicit conduct;

(6) computers and computer imaging technology can be used to—(A) alter sexually explicit photographs, films, and videos in such a way as to make it virtually impossible for unsuspecting viewers to identify individuals, or to determine if the offending material was produced using children; (B) produce visual depictions of child sexual activity designed to satisfy the preferences of individual child molesters, pedophiles, and pornography collectors; and (C) alter innocent pictures of children to create visual depictions of those children engaging in sexual conduct;

(7) The creation or distribution of child pornography which includes an image of a recognizable minor invades the child's privacy and reputational interests, since images that are created showing a child's face or other identifiable feature on a body engaging in sexually explicit conduct can haunt the minor for years to come;

(8) the effect of visual depictions of child sexual activity on a child molester or pedophile using that material to stimulate or whet his own sexual appetites, or on a child where the material is being used as a means of seducing or breaking down the child's inhibitions to sexual abuse or exploitation, is the same whether the child pornography consists of photographic depictions of actual children or visual depictions produced wholly or in part by electronic, mechanical, or other means, including by computer, which are virtually indistinguishable to the unsuspecting viewer from photographic images of actual children;

(9) the danger to children who are seduced and molested with the aid of child sex pictures is just as great when the child pornographer or child molester uses visual depictions of child sexual activity produced wholly or in part by electronic, mechanical, or other means, including by computer, as when the material consists of unretouched photographic images of actual children engaging in sexually explicit conduct;

(10) (A) the existence of and traffic in child pornographic images creates the potential for many types of harm in the community and presents a clear and present danger to all children; and (B) it inflames the desires of child molesters, pedophiles, and child pornographers who prey on children, thereby increasing the creation and distribution of child pornography and the sexual abuse and exploitation of actual children who are victimized as a result of the existence and use of these materials;

(11) (A) the sexualization and eroticization of minors through any form of child pornographic images has a deleterious effect on all children by encouraging a societal perception of children as sexual objects and leading to further sexual abuse and exploitation of them; and (B) this sexualization of minors creates an unwholesome environment which affects the psychological, mental and emotional development of children and undermines the efforts of parents and families to encourage the sound mental, moral and emotional development of children;

(12) prohibiting the possession and viewing of child pornography will encourage the possessors of such material to rid themselves of or destroy the material, thereby helping to protect the victims of child pornography and to eliminate the market for the sexual exploitative use of children; and

(13) the elimination of child pornography and the protection of children from sexual exploitation provide a compelling governmental interest for prohibiting the production,

> distribution, possession, sale, or viewing of visual depictions of children engaging in sexually explicit conduct, including both photographic images of actual children engaging in such conduct and depictions produced by computer or other means which are virtually indistinguishable to the unsuspecting viewer from photographic images of actual children engaging in such conduct. (18 U.S.C.A. S 2256 [8] [3] [West Supp. 1999])

Evaluation of the Evidence for Harm Effects

Three primary types of harm effects can be gleaned from the Attorney General's Commission on Pornography and the Child Pornography Prevention Act of 1996: (1) sexually exploited children are unable to develop healthy affectionate relationships in later life, have sexual dysfunctions, and have a tendency to become sexual abusers as adults; (2) child pornography is often used by pedophiles and child sexual abusers to stimulate and whet their own sexual appetites, and as a model for sexual acting out with children; and (3) exposure to child pornography can desensitize the viewer to the pathology of sexual abuse or exploitation of children, so that it can become acceptable to and even preferred by the viewer. Below, we evaluate the social science evidence for these harm claims.

Sexually Exploited Children Are Unable to Develop Healthy Affectionate Relationships

Much of the evidence for the harms done to children consists of clinical reports from therapists who have treated victims of sexual abuse or from studies of child molesters who report sexual abuse in their own childhoods. For example, as Monahan and Walker (1998) note, one study often used to substantiate the finding that sexually exploited children are unable to develop healthy affectionate relationships in later life, have sexual dysfunctions, and have a tendency to become sexual abusers as adults was done by Schoettle (1980a). This research is a brief case study of "Kathy," a 12-year-old girl who, along with her siblings, engaged in photographed sexual acts with adults and with each other. The principal findings of this report are that after police investigation of a child pornography ring, Kathy and her family were referred to our sex abuse clinic for psychiatric evaluation and weekly therapy. At the first session Kathy's complaints related to feeling guilty about being accused of involving her younger siblings in the sexual exploitation schemes. Kathy's history and presentation were consistent with a diagnosis of sexual deviation with associated depression. Nearly all other research used to substantiate these harms also are primarily clinical in nature. The methodology for these studies consist of either case studies of children who have been used in child pornography (see Burgess & Holmstrom, 1978; Densen-Gerner, 1980; Ellerstein & Canavan, 1980; Finch, 1973; Schoettle, 1980b).

Other forms of research consist of interviews with adults who had become sex offenders to determine whether abuse in their own childhoods was related to subsequent child molestation. In one of the most frequently cited studies, Groth (1979) examined sexual trauma in rapists and child molesters who were interviewed and asked to report on their life histories. The subjects for this study consisted of 348 men convicted of sexual assault and referred to a security treatment center for diagnostic observation. These data were supplemented with a study of their clinical records. Sexual trauma was operationally defined as any sexual activity witnessed or experienced that was emotionally upsetting or disturbing to the subject. As a comparison group, 62 male law enforcement officers were administered an anonymous questionnaire in regard to sexual trauma experienced during their development. This police sample was roughly comparable to the offender sample in regard to age and socioeconomic background. Evidence of some form of sexual trauma during their developmental years (ages 1 to 15) was found in the life histories of 106 (31%) of the subjects. No evidence of any sexual trauma was found for 203 (58%) of the subjects, and no data were available for 39 (11%) of the subjects in this study. In comparison, only two (3%) of the sample of law enforcement officers reported any history of sexual trauma during their formative years.

Other studies employing a similar methodology have revealed a possible connection between abuse in childhood and later tendencies to become an abuser. Earls, Bouchard, and Laberge (1984) obtained a sample of 34 child molesters incarcerated in Canada. They found 53% of this sample claimed to have been victims of sexual abuse themselves. These findings have been replicated in a US sample of 68 pedophiles incarcerated in Massachusetts for sexual abuse of children. Of these men, 57% reported having been victims of sexual abuse in childhood. This finding compared to 23% of 107 rapists in the same institution (Bard et al., 1987). An explorative investigation was carried out by Freund, Watson, and Dickey (1990). The results of this investigation indicated that sexual abuse in childhood by an adult female or male was significantly more often reported by pedophilic sex offenders against children than by controls who erotically prefer physically mature females.

The notion that adults who had become sex offenders did so because of abuse in their own childhoods (including being victimized in child pornography) is substantiated to some degree by research evidence. Some psychotherapists who treat sex offenders against children appear to adhere to the theory that pedophilia, or at least an individual's proness to sexually offend in adulthood, is caused by the offender's having himself been sexually abused in childhood. Garland and Dougher (1990) coined for this notion the term "abused abuser hypothesis." The psychotherapists best known among the proponents of this theory are Groth and Burgess (1977). The theory rests on the observation that a larger proportion of pedophiles, and of sex offenders in general, claim sexual abuse in childhood than of men who have not committed a sex offense. Evidence for this theory is mixed.

Many of the studies that have attempted to find causal variables have either not used control groups or have attempted such controls based solely on the type of offense. Furthermore, the existing data are almost exclusively obtained from incarcerated pedophiles, thus limiting the generalizability of the findings. In their review of the scientific literature, Garland and Dougher fail to confirm that adult–child sexual contact is either a necessary or a sufficient cause for the child later becoming a pedophile. Condy, Templer, Brown, and Veaco (1987) found that when an appropriate control group of nonsexual offenders are compared with sex offenders, the incidence of adult–child sexual contact is actually higher in the control group than in the sex offender group.

One of the main problems with the hypothesis that abuse in childhood leads to adults becoming abusers is that proof of its validity rests on retrospective self-reports, and in particular on such reports of accused or charged sex offenders against children. In this situation self-reports are not very dependable (see Hindman, 1988). It also has been pointed out by Finkelhor (1984) that a large majority of sex offenders against children do not claim they were sexually seduced in childhood.

In conclusion, the commonsense assumption is that child victims portrayed in child pornography are psychologically and physiologically harmed by these portrayals generally is supported by the available clinical research, but this evidence is not without its problems. Nearly all the investigations are case studies of individuals who have come to the attention of clinicians and who report being traumatized by their victimization. Obviously, those children who were used by adults in the production of pornography but who have not sought the help of a mental health expert are not included in these studies. Consequently, what is not known is the degree to which involvement in child pornography affects all victims. Most is known about those who, for whatever reason, have reported their experiences to clinicians.

Exposure to Child Pornography, Sexual Arousal, and Sexual Acting Out with Children

The assumption that exposure to child pornography by adults leads to child molestation is far more questionable. In fact, the question of whether or not exposure to child pornography causes pedophiles to become either situational of preferential molesters is largely unanswered at this time. There are no experimental studies that have isolated a cause-and-effect relationship between exposure to pornography and molestation behavior or increases in sexual arousal, attitudes, or beliefs that may facilitate molestation of children. Such studies, wherein adults are exposed to child pornography and then tested for heightened sexual arousal to children or other propensities to molest children are difficult to undertake for ethical and practical reasons.

Previous research on the effects of exposure to certain forms of adult pornography (see Linz & Malamuth, 1993; Donnerstein, Linz, & Penrod, 1987) offer suggestions as to the possible effects of exposure to child pornography among pedophiles. In the past we have argued that violent pornography that appears to justify rape or assault against women may inspire or incite an imitation effect among certain viewers (Linz, Turner, Hesse, & Penrod, 1984b). This effect may be most pronounced among men already predisposed to violence against women (see Malamuth, Linz, Heavy, Barnes, & Acker, 1995, and Linz & Malamuth, 1993, for a discussion of the individual differences among men that may predispose them to sexual violence). A similar set of processes may be invoked with regard to pedophile exposure to child pornography.

By analogy we may speculate that among potential molesters, some forms of child pornography may serve to both incite the act of child molestation and provide specific instructions as to how to undertake it. For example, research that has examined the effects of adult female victims response in a rape depiction and males' sexual arousal, acceptance of violence against women, and actual violent behavior. Malamuth, Heim, and Feshbach (1980) have found that if the victim was portrayed as becoming involuntarily sexually aroused by the assault, male subjects' own sexual arousal, as indexed by both self-reports and penile tumescence measures, becomes as high as, and sometimes higher than, sexual arousal resulting from mutually consenting depictions. In other studies (Malamuth, Haber, & Feshbach, 1980; Malamuth & Check, 1980a,b; Malamuth & Check, 1981), males who watched or listened to rape depictions that supposedly had positive consequences for the victim thought the victim had suffered less and they believed that a larger percentage of women in general would find forced sex or rape pleasurable compared to males who were exposed to materials depicting a negative consequence for the victim.

From these research findings we can begin to construct a profile of what may constitute the most "risky" set of materials for child molestation, that is, the type of film or magazine portrayal that may inspire or instigate an imitation effect among potential child molesters. The materials that are most likely to pose a risk for an incitement effect are portrayals that show child victims becoming involuntarily sexually aroused or otherwise responding positively to sexual aggression. Potential molesters who watch child sex depictions that supposedly had positive consequences for the victim may come to think that the victim does not suffer and may believe that a larger percentage of children would find forced sex pleasurable. Other messages that may pose a risk for molestation are that the adult–child sex interaction is "educational" or that the child was being sexually provocative.

The messages that children experience positive consequences from sexual contact with adults and the notion that they become involuntarily sexually aroused may be more routinely available. One source of messages such as these may be publications of the North American Man Boy Love Association (NAMBLA). NAMBLA is allegedly the largest organization of pedophiles in the United States, with an estimated membership of 4000 in 1994 (Echols, 1997). All NAMBLA members receive the *NAMBLA Bulletin*, which features testimonials from adults and boys concerning the pleasures and benefits of child–adult sex. The publication also includes semiclad photos of boys.

Further, this publication and others of similar content may provide information on how to undertake sex with an underage victim. According to law enforcement officials, the bulletin has step-by-step "how to" instructions for locating, seducing, sexually assaulting, and preventing the disclosure of their crimes by their child victims (Echols, 1997). During a 3-year period in the early 1990s, police in Vancouver, Canada, reported that 53% of the more than 100 men they arrested for sexually assaulting boys were members of NAMBLA and/or possessed copies of NAMBLA publications (Echols, 1997).

The contrary argument could be made that there is much more social support for rape and certain forms of violence against women in US society than sex with children. Many authors have written about a culture of male violence that legitimates rape and sexual assault of women (see Linz & Malamuth, 1993, for a review). Myths about rape and sexual assault portrayed in pornography and other mass media depictions serve to perpetuate beliefs supportive of sexual assault against women. This level of social support obviously does not exist in our society for adult–child sexual abuse. However, many preferential child molesters may have their predilections validated by organizations like NAMBLA or even by the presence of child molesters on public forums such as computer bulletin boards that afford social support for deviant activities. The reader must be cautioned that the effects of these materials may apply only to those men who would be classified as situational or preferential child molesters. It is doubtful that individuals merely classified as pedophiles without the predisposition to molest are likely to engage in such activity following exposure to child pornography.

Much more research is needed on the possible incitement and instructional effects of child pornography. Laboratory and field experimental studies which manipulate exposure to child pornography to determine if there is a causal link between exposure to these materials and attitudes that may facilitate molestation would be welcome, but are probably impossible to conduct for ethical reasons. In the absence of true experiments, researchers should continue to conduct quasi-experimental studies. Persons naturally exposed to these materials should be identified and compared with "control" groups of individuals matched for all characteristics save exposure to child pornography. Finally, longitudinal studies examining the relationship between early exposure to child pornography and later molestation behavior would be useful.

Exposure to Child Pornography Can Desensitize the Viewer to the Pathology of Sexual Abuse

There are virtually no scientific studies available on the tendency for viewers of child pornography to become desensitized to the seriousness of child abuse. However, it may be reasonable to apply findings from research on affective reactions to violent messages that has been concerned with the possibility that continued exposure to violence in the mass media will undermine feelings of concern, empathy, or sympathy viewers might have toward victims of actual violence. The early research on desensitization to media violence involved exposure to rather mild forms of television violence for relatively short periods of time (Cline, Croft, &

Courrier, 1973; Thomas, 1982; Thomas, Horton, Lippencott, & Drabman, 1977). These studies indicated that heavy viewers of media violence showed less physiological reactivity to violent film clips compared to light viewers; that general physiological arousal decreases as viewers watched more violent media; and that children as well as adults are susceptible to this effect.

Research on longer-term exposure and more graphic forms of sexual violence has shown further desensitization effects. For example, Linz, Donnerstein, and Penrod (1984a, 1987) measured the reactions of college-age men to films portraying violence against women (mostly in a sexual context) viewed across a 5-day period. Comparisons of first and last day reactions to the films showed that, with repeated exposure, initial levels of self-reported anxiety decreased substantially. Furthermore, subjects' perceptions of the films also changed from the first day to the last day. Material that was previously judged to be violent and degrading to women was seen as significantly less so by the end of the exposure period. Subjects also indicated that they were less depressed and that they enjoyed the material more with repeated exposure. Most importantly, these effects generalized to a victim of sexual assault presented in a videotaped reenactment of a rape trial. Subjects who were exposed to the violent films rated the victim as less severely injured compared to a no-exposure control group. In a similar study (Linz, Donnerstein, & Penrod, 1988), subjects also were less sympathetic to the rape victim portrayed in the trial and less able to empathize with rape victims in general, compared to no-exposure control subjects and to subjects who viewed non-violent films.

Linz et al. (1984a, 1988) suggested that the viewers in these studies become increasingly comfortable, or desensitized, to what are initially anxiety-provoking situations. Further, it was suggested that self-awareness of reductions in anxiety and emotional arousal may be instrumental in the formation of new perceptions and attitudes about the violence portrayed in the films. These views then may be carried over to other contexts. This position is similar to that offered in the behavioral treatment of pathological fears from exposure therapy.

In therapy, simply exposing a patient to the situations or objects he or she is frightened of diminishes the anxiety or negative affect that was once evoked by the problem stimulus. Foa and Kozak (1986) have speculated that a patient's perception of his or her own habituation in the presence of a feared stimulus plays an important role in helping the patient become comfortable with that stimulus. Self-awareness of reduced anxiety may provide the patient with information that helps to facilitate a reduction in fear. That awareness might also facilitate changes in the negative valence associated with the feared stimulus. Patients then may begin to evaluate the "badness" of the feared stimuli in a less exaggerated manner.

Similar processes may operate when subjects are exposed repeatedly to graphic media depictions of children in sexual poses or engaged in sexual conduct. Once viewers are emotionally "comfortable" with the content of child pornography, they also may evaluate these materials more favorably in other domains. Material originally believed to be morally offensive or degrading to the victims of child sexual abuse may be evaluated as less so with continued exposure. A reduction in the level of anxiety also may blunt viewers' awareness of the frequency and intensity of child abuse in the films. Reductions in anxiety may serve to decrease sensitivity to emotional cues associated with each child sex episode and thereby reduce viewers' perceptions of the amount of violence in the films. Consequently, by the end of an extensive exposure period, viewers may perceive aggressive films as less abusive to children than they had initially. These altered perceptual and affective reactions then may be carried over into judgments made about victims of child sexual abuse in other more realistic settings.

As with the possibilities discussed in the prior sections more research is needed to substantiate whether a desensitization effect similar to that observed for violent and sexually violent materials also would be obtained with depictions of children engaged in sex. One likely source of desensitization to the degrading and abusive aspects of child pornography may be repeated exposure to "adult" pornography wherein the models, although over the age of 18, are described and depicted as underage. It is possible that exposure to these materials may lessen viewer anxiety to materials depicting illegal images of children engaged in sexual behavior.

WHAT DO THE COURTS SAY ABOUT CHILD PORNOGRAPHY LAWS?

In the late 1970s, concern about child pornography percolated to the top of the social agenda and laws were passed making it illegal to produce child pornography. The Supreme Court ruled on the first of these laws in the early 1980s. Later cases fine-tuned this ruling by concentrating on issues such as the illegality of private possession of these materials and strengthening reporting laws to ensure only adult models are employed in the production of pornography.

The Protection of Children Against Sexual Exploitation Act of 1977

Congress began dealing in earnest with child pornography in 1977. Law enforcement officials, social welfare advocates, and others came to the conclusion that child pornography was a particularly widespread and abhorrent form of child abuse. Theses concerns were consolidated in the Protection of Children Against Sexual Exploitation Act of 1977, which prohibited knowingly transporting, shipping, receiving, distributing, or reproducing a visual depiction, if such depiction involves the use of a minor engaging in sexually explicit conduct. States around the country adopted similar laws. Constitutional challenges to these laws were undertaken in the early 1980s and continued into the 1990s.

New York v. Ferber (1982)

This landmark case decided by Supreme Court established that child pornography was "a category of material outside the protection of the First Amendment." In *Ferber*, the court broadened the potential scope of child pornography legislation when it upheld a New York statute similar to the Protection of Children Act of 1977 that banned material depicting sexual conduct by children. The New York statute (many other states had similar laws) prohibits persons from knowingly promoting a sexual performance by a child under the age of 16 by distributing material that depicts such a performance. The statute defines "sexual performance" as any performance that includes sexual conduct by a child, and "sexual conduct" defined as actual or simulated sexual intercourse, deviate sexual intercourse, sexual bestiality, masturbation, sadomasochistic abuse, or lewd exhibition of the genitals.

The defendant in the case was a bookstore proprietor who was convicted under the statute for selling films depicting young boys masturbating. The New York Court of Appeals reversed, holding that the statute violated the First Amendment as being both underinclusive and overbroad. The court reasoned that the statute did not include the traditional elements of an obscenity standard, and therefore would prohibit the promotion of materials traditionally entitled to protection under the First Amendment.

The Supreme Court ruled that states are entitled to greater leeway in the regulation of pornographic depictions of children for the following reasons: (1) the legislative judgment that the use of children as subjects of pornographic materials is harmful to the physiological, emotional, and mental health of the child easily passes muster under the First Amendment; (2) the standard of *Miller v. California* (1973) for determining what is legally obscene is not a satisfactory solution to the child pornography problem; (3) the advertising and selling of child pornography provide an economic motive for and thus are an integral part of the production of such materials, an activity illegal throughout the nation; (4) the value of permitting live performances and photographic reproductions of children engaged in lewd exhibitions is exceedingly modest, if not *de minimis*; and (5) recognizing and classifying child pornography as a category of material outside the First Amendment's protection is not incompatible with this court's decisions dealing with what speech is protected. The court (*New York v. Ferber*, 1982) ruled that when a definable class of material, such as that covered by the New York statute, "bears so heavily and pervasively on the welfare of children engaged in its production, the balance of competing interests is clearly struck, and it is permissible to consider these materials as without the First Amendment's protection" (pp. 756–764).

After *New York v. Ferber*, many cases of child pornography were brought to the attention of the law either by photodeveloping businesses that receive film for processing and finding questionable pictures of minors, informants, or special sting operations (e.g., *US v. Koelling*, 1993, wherein postal inspectors learned from a mail-order photofinishing business in Missouri that the company had received film for processing that it suspected was child pornography; and *US v. Brown*, 1989, concerning the United States Postal Inspection service sting operation named "Project Looking Glass," in which letters soliciting child pornography were sent to certain individuals identified by local law enforcement as being interested in these materials).

Osborne v. Ohio (1990)

Until 1990, the Supreme Court had held that the federal statute that made it criminal to produce child exploitative films or receive them in relation to the mails or commerce subject to federal law was constitutionally permissible. The statute did not criminalize mere possession of child pornography. *Osborne v. Ohio* (1990) made it illegal to possess and view child pornography. The court, ruling on a Ohio statute, reasoned that criminalizing possession of child pornography, unlike adult pornography, which is legal to possess (*Stanley v. Georgia*, 1969), removed a danger from society. According to the court,

> Ohio does not rely on the paternalistic interest in regulating Osborne's mind, but has enacted its law on the basis of its compelling interests in protecting the physical and psychological well-being of minors in destroying the market for the exploitative use of children by penalizing those who possess and view the offending materials. (*Osborne v. Ohio*, 1990, p. 1)

Moreover, the Court maintained, the ban may encourage possessors to destroy such materials. This is beneficial because child pornography permanently records the victim's abuse, and thus may haunt him or her for years to come, and the available evidence suggests these materials are used by pedophiles to seduce other children.

US v. X-Citement Video Inc. et al. (1994)

Finally, the 1988 Child Protection and Obscenity Enforcement Act as amended by the 1990 Child Protection Restoration and Penalties Enhancement Act imposes record keeping and disclosure requirements on the production of certain sexually explicit materials. The Attorney General's Commission on Pornography found that because producers tended to use performers who could pass for minors, distributors were able to avoid prosecution on a claim of ignorance of a child performer's true age, while producers could assert that they had been deceived. To address this problem the amended statute provides that any producer of books, magazines, films, or videotapes that contain visual depictions of actual sexually explicit conduct shall create and maintain individually identifiable records pertaining to every performer, most importantly the date of birth of each performer.

Current Child Pornography Laws

As a result of court rulings on the constitutional issues in the previously discussed cases most states now have laws prohibiting production and distribution of child pornography. Many also place restrictions on the possession of such materials. While there are differences among the many state and federal statutes, five categories of conduct (and attempted conduct) are regulated: (1) production: employment or use of a minor to engage in, or assist any other person to engage in, any sexually explicit conduct for the purpose of producing a depiction of such conduct; (2) trafficking: importation, distribution, sale, loan, gift, exchange, receipt, or transportation of material with knowledge that it depicts minors engaged in sexually explicit conduct; (3) advertisement: advertisement or notice seeking or offering material depicting minors engaged in sexually explicit conduct or seeking or offering a minor to engage in sexually explicit conduct; (4) possession: possession of material with knowledge that it depicts minors engaged in sexually explicit conduct; and (5) procurement: procurement, buying or selling, coercion, persuasion, inducement, enticement, transportation, or kidnapping of a minor, to engage in, or assist any person to engage in, any sexually explicit conduct for the purpose of producing any depiction of such conduct.

Following *New York v. Ferber*, the child pornography laws of the majority of states and the federal government do not require obscenity as an element of the offense. However, all these laws define the sexual content of the prohibited child pornography. Most define child pornography as visual depictions of a minor engaged in "sexual conduct" or "sexually explicit conduct" and then define those terms more specifically. A few states leave such terms undefined.

Most child pornography statutes prohibit a wide variety of visual depictions of sexual conduct involving children and youth, including books, magazines, newspapers, photographs, pictures, motion pictures, electronic reproductions, and other materials or reproductions. A number expressly include film, negatives, mechanical or chemical reproductions, and audio recordings. Most also proscribe live performances.

Attempts to Broaden the Definition of Child Pornography: The Child Pornography Prevention Act of 1996

More recently, the Child Pornography Prevention Act of 1996 has been introduced into the US Congress. It has defined child pornography as:

> ... any visual depiction, including any photograph, film, video, picture, or computer or computer-generated image or picture, whether made or produced by electronic, mechanical, or other means, of sexually explicit conduct, where—(A) the production of such visual depiction involves the use of a minor engaging in sexually explicit conduct; (B) such visual depiction is, or appears to be, of a minor engaging in sexually explicit conduct; or (C) such visual depiction conveys the impression that the material is or contains a visual depiction of a minor engaging in sexually explicit conduct. (18 U.S.C.A. S 2256 [8] [3] [West Supp. 1999])

The reader will note that the new bill, sponsored by Senator Orrin Hatch (R-Utah), bans the production and sale of sexually explicit material depicting people who "appear to be" children and refers to visual depictions that convey "the impression" of a minor engaging in sexually explicit conduct. Many policymakers worry that these two elements significantly broaden the definition of child pornography beyond that previously approved by the Supreme Court (Hernandez, 1996).

The proposed expansion to include drawings or computer-generated images of nonrecognizable children is keyed to no justification that is recognized in existing law. This may be unconstitutional given the existing state of the law.

Bruce A. Taylor, president and chief counsel of the National Law Center for Children and Families has articulated the arguments in support of the expanded definition. He notes that child pornography is illegal and it is not protected speech according to the Supreme Court. The proposed restrictions on images that "appear to be children" merely allows child pornography laws to be current with relevant contemporary technological advances. Taylor testified before the US Congress during hearings involving the Child Pornography Prevention Act of 1996 and told the committee that he believes the bill "is and would be found valid and constitutionally enforceable and that it is an essential and necessary modernization of the federal child exploitation law" ("New digital child porn law," 1996). In his testimony, Taylor pointed out that both "real and apparent [child pornography] become and are equally dangerous because both have the same incitement effect on the pedophile and the same seductive effect on a child victim" ("New digital child porn law," 1996).

With regard to the second element in the law, First Amendment attorney Michael Bamberger asserts that the bill's amendments would establish an entirely subjective test "based on the impression received by a viewer." In a memo outlining the threatening implications of the Child Pornography Prevention Act, Bamberger wrote: "One can hardly think of a more chilling prospect for publishers, producers, and retailers, who will have to guess how random members of the public may react. As a result, it is likely they will simply self-censor protected materials" ("New digital child porn law," 1996). Among the constitutionally protected material that could fall prey to such an expanded definition of pornography are works ranging from the current biography of Lewis Carroll (Random House) to movies like "Romeo and Juliet," "The Last Picture Show," and "Midnight Cowboy."

Krug ("New digital child porn law," 1996), who also is executive director of the Freedom to Read Foundation and chair of the Media Coalition, has expressed concern that the new legislation creates three new categories of prohibited material that do not involve the depiction of real minors who are being sexually abused and that taken together these provisions create a new definition of child pornography that is so broad that it will exert a chilling effect on an array of constitutionally protected material. Krug maintains that while the suppression of child pornography is an important social goal, it will only be realized by focusing on depictions of real minors being sexually exploited and abused. According to Krug, defining child pornography more broadly would dilute the effort to protect children, while exerting a chilling effect on the dissemination of books, magazines, movies, and videos that are protected by the First Amendment.

In an attempt to modify the bill so that it will pass constitutional muster, Senator Joseph Biden (D-Delaware) has introduced an amendment that would ban only material produced with the likeness of an "identifiable" minor. This would limit the government's ability to prosecute wholly fictitious images generated by computer. Biden's provision is meant to address the harm caused by using computer software to graft the likeness of a real minor's face on the body of an adult engaged in sexual conduct. The Biden amendment would require the prosecution to produce expert evidence that the depiction was an actual photograph and not a computer-generated image. The Child Pornography Prevention Act of 1996 awaits court review.

Differentiating Legitimate Art from Child Exploitation

Concerns about broadening the definition of child pornography would appear to be justified in light of past prosecutions. So far we have discussed the legal restrictions placed on material that is evidence of victimization or used to victimize children in the future. Often, law enforcement officials have not limited arrest and prosecution to only those materials clearly used in such victimization. As noted above, in an effort to curb criminal activities involving children, child pornography laws in the United States of America were revised and vigorously enforced. By 1989, several artists and art professionals were indicted on child pornography charges.

The most well publicized of these prosecutions involved the exhibit featuring artist Robert Mapplethorpe who worked in several genres including still life who had produced photographs of two children with exposed genitals. When the traveling retrospective exhibition, "Robert Mapplethorpe; the Perfect Moment," opened at the Contemporary Art Center of Cincinnati, the director, Dennis Barrie, was charged with two counts of child pornography. Neither of the photographs of children depicted or suggested sexual acts. The children face the camera, genitals exposed.

The Institute of Contemporary Art in Philadelphia, which organized the Mapplethorpe retrospective, had received a $30,000 grant from the National Endowment for the Arts (NEA). The exhibition appeared without incident at three major art institutions between December 1988 and the Spring of 1989, and the Corcoran Gallery of Art, in Washington, DC canceled the exhibition 2½ weeks before it was to open there in June. In July, the Senate passed its appropriations bill with the Helms amendment forbidding the disbursement of federal funds, through the NEA (H.R. 2788 as passed by the Senate in 1989) "to promote, disseminate or produce" obscene or indecent materials depicting "sadomasochism, homo-eroticism, the exploitation of children or individuals engaged in sex acts."

In another controversial case in 1990, FBI agents and local police entered the studio of San Francisco photographer, Jock Sturges, and confiscated files, photographs, negatives, and studio and darkroom equipment on the grounds that Sturges was producing child pornography. Sturges is best known for his black and white images of women and young girls, many of whom are posed nude. Similar photographs, taken of their own children nude by contemporary photographers Ellen Brooks, Cynthia MacAdams, Sally Mann, Starr Ockenaga, and Alice Sims have sparked legal responses. (For related reading on the legal underpinnings surrounding censorship debates involving images of children, see Stanely, 1989, Vance, 1990).

Finally, there are two cases involving films generally considered to be legitimate works of art that have engendered legal controversy. The Video Software Dealers Association (VSDA) has filed a federal class-action suit against the Oklahoma Police Department, which raided six video stores in 1997, seizing copies of the Oscar-winning movie, "The Tin Drum," which a judge had declared to be obscene. The film, based on the Gunter Grass novel, includes a scene suggesting that a boy of about 7 has oral sex with a teen-age girl. Oklahoma law bars depiction of a person under 18 engaging in a sex act.

Most recently a new controversy has arisen over the film that first became a test of both artistic license and freedom, "Lolita," the film remake that opened across Europe but not in the United States. Major distributors have so far shunned Vladimir Nabokov's disturbing story of an older man's passion for a prepubescent girl (Bohlen, 1997). According to the director there are very few sex scenes in "Lolita." The director took the unusual step of consulting a lawyer specializing in First Amendment cases and spent 5 to 6 weeks making cuts to bring the film into conformity with the Child Pornography Prevention Act of 1996.

These cases illustrate the possibility of the chilling effects on speech of laws designed to restrict child pornography. In the future, artists, writers, and film makers may be reluctant to create and disseminate material that involves children shown nude or portrayed in situations that involve sex in any manner. This may or may not be an appropriate price for society to pay to prevent the victimization of children in child pornography. To date, the debate has not been settled.

CHILD PORNOGRAPHY AND CYBERSPACE

Some jurisdictions specifically prohibit the use of computers in connection with the distribution of child pornography. Computers can be used to store pornographic images and information on young victims, sexual experiences, and the offenders' collecting activities. Computers also can be used to transmit or receive pornographic images, modify these images, and contact adults or youngsters for the purposes of producing or distributing child pornography.

To combat the use of computers to facilitate crimes involving child pornography, federal law specifies that it applies to persons who knowingly transport visual depictions or advertisements "by any means, including by computer." Some states have enacted similar provisions. The federal prohibitions on child pornography arise primarily from Congress's authority to regulate commerce, including the mail. Consequently, in federal cases there must be some connection to interstate or foreign commerce or use of the mail. This element may be satisfied if the material originated abroad or in another state, or was made using materials that traveled through the mail (inter- or intrastate) or foreign commerce. In some cases, both federal and state charges may be brought against the same defendant. Consecutive or concurrent prosecutions for the same conduct would violate federal policy.

Child Pornography on the Internet

There is a plethora of pornographic material including photographs, pictures, bulletin boards, referrals, and networks on the Internet. However, erotic photographs of juveniles themselves are relatively rare on the Internet. More common are pedophilic stories. These have been estimated to constitute about 10% of the content of one of the major erotica user groups (Williams & McShane, 1995).

Child Pornographers Operating on the Internet

Law enforcement efforts recently have been devoted to the arrest of individuals who exchange in computer images of children on the Internet. In September 1995, the FBI announced the results of an investigation into the viewing habits of 3.5 million America Online subscribers. The agency claimed to have located 125 potential child pornography offenders. This investigation yielded persons soliciting sex acts with children as well as persons trafficking in images (Johnston, 1995).

One of the more infamous cases involves Robert Thomas, owner of the Amateur Action Bulletin Board in Milpitas, California. The online pornography market dealer in nude prepubescent children advertised his collection as having more than 1200 pictures depicting sex scenes between family members (even though there was no evidence that any of the participants were actually related). These "incest" images were among his biggest sellers, accounting for 10% of downloads (Sussman, 1995).

Law enforcement efforts are concentrated primarily on "sting operations" (Kaplan, 1997). Officers of the law will exchange e-mail messages with potential child pornographers who promise photographs of underage models. The officers will ask the suspect to send pictures of children having sex. US Customs agents have even secretly set up a child pornography website to entrap suppliers from Northern Europe and Japan, as well as the United States. To trap them, customs offers photos from its own library of child pornography. In Internet chat rooms law enforcement officials often pose as young girls, hoping to lure suspects into sending material.

Computerized "bulletin boards," according to the US Customs Service, are becoming increasingly popular conduits for child pornographers, who use them to acquire subscribers to a worldwide pornographic picture ring. In what authorities dubbed "Operation Long-arm," federal Customs agents carried out raids in 18 different states on suspects whose names were taken from one of these bulletin boards. Approximately 40 people in 14 states were arrested 2 years ago for exchanging child pornography online (Elmer-Dewitt, 1995). The ring, based in Denmark, used computers and telephone lines to transmit explicit photos of children ages 5 to 12.

US police captured 13 pedophiles who were videotaping the sexual abuse of young girls and broadcasting it live on the Internet. The case emerged as a result of a routine allegation of child abuse against Ronald Riva, 38, an unemployed truck driver, former prison officer, and father of four young children, by the mother of a 10-year-old girl in a southern California farming community in June. The girl, who told her parents that she had been abused, had stayed overnight in Riva's house at a slumber party for his 8-year-old daughter. Local detectives discovered that Riva's house contained equipment capable of staging live "photo-shoots" on the Internet. Computer files containing pedophile pornography also were recovered. Shortly afterward, police arrested another southern Californian, Melton Lee Myers, 55, who also had equipment capable of broadcasting digital video pictures of children on the Internet. The FBI and US Customs authorities were called in. It emerged that the two were part of a group, including other members from the United States, Finland, Australia, and Canada, who were abusing children as young as 5 and broadcasting pictures live on the Internet. The process this group used is similar to video conferencing.

The 16 members of the ring called themselves the Orchid Club. According to the California state indictment, the Orchid Club's activities included the videotaping of a 5-year-old girl somewhere in the Midwest. At least 11 men had watched the child being abused live on the Internet. During the session they had sent requests to the man abusing the child detailing what form of abuse they wished to see.

How many child pornographers are operating on the internet? There is very little reliable evidence. Primarily through sting operations a few pornographers have been located. The number appears to be a very small proportion of the population of Internet users.

Online Child Molesters

When children are online, will they fall prey to child molesters hanging out in electronic chat rooms? It is estimated that 10 million children now surf the net. Children's facility with this form of electronic communication exacerbates the problem. It often children who are the computer experts in our nation's families. Evidence of online victimization is scattered and primarily consists of individual and often sensational cases reported in the popular press.

One such case was reported in 1997 by the Massachusetts Child Exploitation Network. A police precinct received a call from a woman who found that her 12-year-old son had been receiving sexually explicit messages via a sports-oriented computer bulletin board. The messages, purportedly received from another 12-year-old boy, included graphic descriptions of sexual experiences, offers to send pornographic pictures via electronic mail, and suggestions that the two boys meet for some "fun." The messages also urged her son not to reveal this correspondence to his parents or anyone else, as they would "not understand" the friendship.

The investigating officer contacted a state police expert in computer crime, who in turn contacted the field office of the FBI. A check with the telephone company revealed that the number of the computer bulletin board was registered to a 28-year-old man whose past offenses included several convictions for indecent exposure. A search of the suspect's home revealed a small collection of child pornography, along with a number of nonpornographic photographs of boys, including some picturing the boys with the suspect. The archived messages in the suspect's computer revealed that he was corresponding with a number of young boys he had met through the bulletin board. Material contained in a database in the suspect's computer led to the identification of some of the boys in the photographs. Questioning by a child abuse unit revealed that at least two of these boys had engaged in sexual activities with the suspect. The suspect ultimately pled guilty to several counts of statutory rape and agreed to cooperate with the police in identifying all of his victims as well as the sources of his child pornography.

Children and youth who become the victims of computer-initiated crimes often have similar characteristics to those who become the victims of other forms of sexual exploitation. They tend to be emotionally vulnerable, withdrawn from their peers, and often the children of parents who do not have the desire or capacity to spend much time with them.

While groups like the Family Research Council insist that online child molesters represent a clear and present danger, there is no evidence that it is any greater than the thousand other threats children face every day. The National Center for Missing and Exploited Children acknowledges that there have been 10 or 12 fairly high-profile cases in the past year of children being seduced or lured online into situations where they are victimized. Children who are not online also are at risk, however; more than 800,000 children are reported missing every year in the United States.

Virtual Communities: Encouraging Sexual Deviance or Promoting Socially Positive Attitudes?

While using computers specifically to lure children into sexual exploitation may be relatively rare, discussions of sexual activity including adult sex with children is ubiquitous on the Internet. Online discussion is not limited to comments or critiques about commercial pornography or personal stories. In fact, much of what is "sexual" on the networks consists of diverse lines of discussion as well as real-time conversations often far removed from the visual or textual types of pornography, particularly industry-produced forms, that have typically concerned the courts.

Indeed, Ball-Rokeach and Reardon (1988) argue that what they call "telelogic" communication, or participation in talking or writing at a distance (i.e., via computer), is a unique form of communication that should be distinguished from "monologic" (traditional mass media) and "dialogic" (interpersonal) forms. They propose that telelogic systems provide the functions of "exchange" (i.e., of goods and services), "association" (establishing and maintaining personal relationships), and "debate" (expression of opinions on certain topics), all within the same electronic community. However, despite the abundance of sex-related telelogic communication (compared to traditional online pornography), little research attention has been given to the potential functions (harmful or beneficial) of such interaction common to online newsgroups and bulletin boards.

Nevertheless, a growing body of research has examined newsgroup or bulletin board use in *nonsexual* contexts, the findings of which may have implications for sex-related communication online. A number of researchers have found support for Ball-Rokeach and Reardon's concepts of association, debate, and exchange. Newsgroups and bulletin boards have been found to bring like-minded people together and create "communities" based solely on their shared interests (Baym, 1995; James, Wotring, & Forrest, 1995; Ogan, 1993; Rafaeli, 1988). Despite geographic or social barriers, meaningful relationships and companionship can develop (Baym, 1995; James et al., 1995), valuable information can be exchanged (Baym, 1995; Garramone, Harris, & Anderson, 1986; James et al., 1995; Ogan, 1993), and political or social issues can be debated (Garramone et al., 1986; Ogan, 1993). Indeed, topics that would fail to obtain the critical mass of interest necessary to sustain a club in one's local environs (such as homosexuality in a small town) can thrive in one of the over 12,000 newsgroups available on the Internet where the critical mass derives from the international community (Rheingold, 1993).

The ability of the Internet to construct communities based solely on shared interests is a feature of the new technology that often is hailed as a virtue (e.g., Rheingold, 1993). Whether the shared interest is politics or pet care, the Internet has been seen as contributing to a type of communicative revolution (Hiltz & Turoff, 1978/1992), opening up opportunities for extending and equalizing information exchange, and cultivating diversity and democracy in collective activities and decision making (Sproull & Kiesler, 1991; see also Spears & Lea, 1994). Indeed, most studies on newsgroup or bulletin board use have primarily sought to identify these potential social and personal benefits for users and society (e.g., James et al., 1995).

However, when the shared interest centers around issues of sexuality, such as the advocacy of sex with children, the value of functions like community, information exchange, and debate becomes controversial. Of course, whether community and information exchange among sexually deviant individuals is good or bad depends on who you are talking to and the types of sexual deviance you are talking about. For example, bringing together geographically distant homosexuals or advocates of group sex may be considered harmless and even useful by those who regard each of those behaviors as a lifestyle alternative (Meyer, 1995). Conversely, those who consider such behaviors immoral or otherwise distasteful or harmful may consider their advocacy dangerous. The occurrence of "burn in Hell" or "you perverts" posts among the enthusiastic posts of sexual experiences reflects this value judgment controversy. Furthermore, even sexual newsgroup users whose own practices are considered "perverted" by mainstream standards (e.g., bondage, bestiality) often have voiced opposition to pedophilia and "man–boy love" (Furniss, 1993).

Pedophilia, or recurrent fantasies, urges, or behaviors involving sexual activity with children have served as a lightning rod for cyberpornography opponents. Durkin and Bryant (1995) propose that the "carnal computer" may serve several functions, some similar to those of Ball-Rokeach and Reardon (1988), that may encourage such reviled and potentially dangerous forms of sexual deviance, such as pedophilia. One of these functions, akin to Ball-Rokeach and Reardon's concept of "association," is "social consolidation," or bringing together large numbers of individuals of "similar sexually deviant persuasion" (Durkin & Bryant, 1995, p. 195) to form a newsgroup or bulletin board. Once enough individuals post consistently to the group, ideas and practices can be disseminated rapidly and widely, and a social context is created for people's deviant inclinations.

In this social context, Durkin and Bryant argue, newsgroups then may serve as an arena for posting "intellectual graffiti" (somewhat comparable to Ball-Rokeach and Reardon's concept of "exchange"). Users may post questions, advice, opinions, and fantasies that may violate social norms outside of the group, but which would not receive social sanctions from within (see also Bryant, 1982). Durkin and Bryant argue that the virtual anonymity (or pseudonymity) that computer networks provide may even further encourage such expression, and otherwise private (perhaps withering?) fantasies can become externalized, reinforced, and fed through interaction. Ultimately, networks may serve as a means of "metamorphosis," with the creation of an opportunity structure for transforming these reinforced and extended fantasies into actualized behavior.

A growing body of research that has addressed anonymity and interpersonal behavior in nonsexual computer-mediated communication (see Spears & Lea, 1994; Walther, Anderson, & Park, 1994, for recent reviews) may have implications for effects of sexual newsgroup discussions. For example, recent research on computer-mediated communication and social identity (e.g., Lea & Spears, 1991; Spears, Lea, & Lee, 1990) provides some support for Durkin and Bryant's reasoning on newsgroups encouraging sexual deviance.

According to Reicher's (1984) conceptualization of social identity theory (see also Turner, Hogg, Oakes, Reicher, & Wetherell, 1987), "if people identify with a group, and that group membership is made salient to them, then they will be more likely to be influenced by the group under de-individuating conditions" (Lea & Spears, 1991, p. 288). In other words, under conditions of anonymity within a group, because intragroup differences are minimized, an individual's social or group identity can become more salient and influential than his or her own individual identity (Reicher, 1984).

Tested in online group decision-making experiments (Lea & Spears, 1991; Spears et al., 1990), deindividuation (operationalized as visual anonymity, or communication via computer in separate rooms) and group salience (placing subjects' focus on how groups use computers versus how individuals do) are typically manipulated. Results indicate that indeed greater social influence and polarization toward a preestablished group norm occur among deindividuated members of a salient group (Lea & Spears, 1991). By contrast, when individuality is made salient, even under conditions of anonymity, groups become more "depolarized," or shifted away from group norms.

Applied to Durkin and Bryant's concerns about sexual deviance, the research of Lea and Spears suggests that people who identify with a sexually deviant group (such as pedophilia), under conditions of anonymity and consequent deindividuation (such as in this case in network newsgroups) may indeed become more extreme in their advocacy of deviant behavior. It is important to note, however, that because polarization occurs in the direction of the group's norms, a group can become more "extreme" in favor of caution as well as in favor of risk or action, depending on the initial group trend (Lea & Spears, 1991). In other words, if the deviant group is tending toward the actualization of fantasized behavior, then members may become more likely to encourage setting up opportunities to fulfill those fantasies. Similarly, if the group tends toward the importance of fantasy over behavior, then advocacy of potential criminal behavior is not likely to be the extreme position.

However, this application of social identity in computer-mediated communication studies to network newsgroups is limited, as it greatly simplifies the newsgroup or bulletin board discussion process. Unlike the experimental situations in which groups discuss prearranged topics in real time, newsgroup discussions proceed by members reading only those posts of interest and then responding. As a result of this selection and respond process, several group "trends" or norms may be going on simultaneously, with some members participating in only one line of discussion and others participating in many.

Furthermore, because many newsgroup members only post occasionally and most do not post at all, researchers need to investigate to what extent group identity is salient among users of varying levels of participation. For the small group of members who regularly post, group identity is likely to be strong, and thus, the encouragement of extreme group trends, such as toward setting up opportunities for actualizing pedophilic fantasies, may present a real danger of facilitating criminal behavior. In contrast, members who merely "lurk" may, despite anonymity, retain an individual sense of identity as they watch their group "from afar." Some lurkers may not even consider themselves part of the group at all, but instead just drop in, as one user put it, "to stare at the pervs" (Furniss, 1993, p. 27). From this reasoning, Durkin and Bryant's notion of newsgroup influence and widespread diffusion of sexually deviant practices may be overstated.

Research on social community and information exchange supports the argument that online newsgroups and bulletin boards provide people with deviant or marginalized sexual interests a means of consolidation and a social context for expression. Studies on social identity in computer-mediated decision-making groups support, for some users, Durkin and Bryant's (1995) argument that such consolidation and expression may encourage even more extreme antisocial preferences. However, others also have argued that these same consolidation and expression functions actually may have socially positive rather than negative consequences.

Law professor Carlin Meyer (1995), for example, argues that open access to discussion on the Internet actually may prevent both adults and children from becoming future pedophiles or sex criminals. She argues that individuals who seem propelled by a biological or psychological predisposition toward an abusive sexual lifestyle may find support and understanding online. There is some evidence that perpetrators of sexual aggression or sex abuse of children frequently come from sexually repressive households, often in which even signs of sexuality were rebuked (see Popkin & Simons, 1994). Thus, Meyer argues that a strategy that attempts to combat sexual deviance with additional repression may not prove to be the most successful course.

Indeed, for those who feel disconnected from society because of their sexual proclivities or problems, "sexually oriented boards act as a kind of support group" (Furniss, 1993, p. 20), helping people to "feel better about themselves" (p. 25) by realizing that they are neither alone nor inevitably headed down an abusive or criminal path (Meyer, 1995). Even in the real-time sexual encounters of "compu-sex," Branwyn (1993) found evidence of such informal counseling.

Furthermore, encouraging people to express their fantasies, however deviant, may not necessarily encourage actualizing such behavior in the "real world." Meyer (1995), in fact, argues the opposite:

> It is not clear that pedophiles ... who indulge their tastes on the Internet, or those who merely indulge their curiosity or sexual pleasure in viewing such taboo imagery, thereby become more harmful to society: The opposite conclusion is more logical. Easy access to private viewing [or reading or talking] in circumstances in which masturbatory fantasy can be indulged is as likely to alleviate the need or desire to pursue actual children as it is to encourage taking action in real space rather than cyberspace. (pp. 1999–2000)

In other words, the online sexual experience may in some circumstances be cathartic, not in the vicarious sense unsupported in the media violence literature (see, e.g., Eron, Gentry, & Schlegel, 1994), but in the literal sense, through the physical release of sexual arousal.

In fact, Branwyn (1993) and others (see Levy, 1995) argue that online sexual interaction (deviant or mainstream) in newsgroups and chat rooms may act as the ultimate "safe sex" for the 1990s. Meyer (1995) maintains that this is especially important for adolescents, who can explore "in the privacy of their rooms and in the anonymity of conversation in which they are both invisible and unknown, what other children and adolescents are feeling and thinking about their bodies and sexuality" (p. 2007). Preliminary findings of Sherry Turkle's work on adolescents' experiences on the Internet (see Levy, 1995) provides support for this argument.

Finally, although newsgroups bring together people with shared sexual interests, the discussion that emerges between these people is not necessarily characterized by a unified encouragement of like-minded deviant preferences or behaviors. On the contrary, newsgroup discussion (sexual or otherwise) is notorious for its open, uninhibited, and even hostile conflict (Chapman, 1995; Dery, 1995). As mentioned earlier, Tamosaitis (1995) found that disputing factions (e.g., pro- versus anti-gay male marriage) commonly appear in the sex-related newsgroups, and although not always intelligent dialogues [many erupt into personal "flame wars," with increasingly snide insults and lengthy diatribes (Dery, 1995)], such debate could be an important mediator of the influence of online sexual images and fantasies. Durkin and Bryant (1995) do not allow for this "debate" function (Ball-Rokeach & Reardon, 1988) in their discussion of online sexual deviance.

The Online Industry Policing Themselves

There is growing concern over police tactics and the civil rights problems presented in the use of sting operations to capture pedophiles operating on the Internet. David Sobel, legal counsel for the Electronic Privacy Information Center, a civil liberties organization in Washington, DC, has remarked: "It chills the environment to know that an online service is patrolled by FBI agents who are pretending to be 14-year-old girls" (D. Sobel, personal communication). Further, there have been attempts by Congress to criminalize purveyors of indecent materials on the Internet. So far, the courts have thwarted these efforts. In 1997, the Supreme Court struck down a law designed to keep these materials from children. It said the 1996 Communications Decency Act, in attempting to protect children from indecent material on the Internet, improperly restricted the free-speech rights of adults.

Internet online service providers are beginning to fear that if there is not an effective industry-led solution, there will be a massive, nationwide backlash that will stunt the growth of the Internet. In response to police tactics and threats of criminalization of online users, the online industry has announced it will develop ways to report child pornography to law enforcement officials. These reporting responsibilities were urged on the industry by Vice President Al Gore who held a White House conference in 1997 on ways to make the Internet a safer place for America's children. At these meetings industry groups covering 95% of home Internet users have pledged their efforts to help enforce existing laws against child pornography. Under the policy, Internet providers would remove child pornography from their own bulletin boards and services. The National Center for Missing and Exploited Children's also will establish a toll-free hot line to report incidents of child sexual exploitation, including child pornography online. These two initiatives, according to the Vice President, are a warning to criminals and a promise to parents that there are Internet police for those activities that are illegal and that they will capture and punish those who abuse the Internet to harm and hurt children.

Finally, some civil liberties groups oppose the government's attempts to persuade the Internet industries to voluntarily report child pornography and other potentially harmful materials on the grounds that this requirement restricts free speech. Instead, they recommend that parents and guardians block children's access to objectionable Internet content by use of one of the many commercially available screening devices such as "Surfwatch" and "Net-nanny."

SUMMARY

Child pornography is legally defined as

> ... any visual depiction, including any photograph, film, video, picture, or computer or computer-generated image or picture, whether made or produced by electronic, mechanical, or other means, of sexually explicit conduct, where the production of such visual depiction involves the use of a minor engaging in sexually explicit conduct. (18 U.S.C. S 2256 [8] [3])

Despite the recent concerns of policymakers, the problem of child sexual exploitation has a long history. Those people sexually attracted to children in contemporary society are generally described as "pedophiles" and are considered to be suffering from a serious mental health disorder by psychiatrists, psychologists, and other mental health workers.

A distinction may be made between pedophiles (adults sexually attracted primarily to children) and child molesters (adults who act on this attraction as well as other adults who sexually abuse children for more opportunistic reasons). A pedophile is an individual who fantasizes about sexual contact with children, while a child molester actually commits that act in some form. Therefore, although it is possible to be labeled a pedophile, unless one acts on an urge, he or she is not a child molester. Many law enforcement officials appear to believe that there is a reasonably stable connection between being a child molester and collecting child pornography.

The first source of child pornography production is "homemade" production of materials by pedophiles for themselves. These materials are shared, sold, or traded with other pedophiles. The second source may be professional publishers or large-scale producers of child pornography. However, it is difficult to establish the magnitude of such publishing and distribution enterprises.

The harms of child pornography are usually treated as self-evident and empirical research is limited on the effects of these materials on victims. Most often, the primary sources of information of victim effects come from clinicians who have treated victims. Few studies employing other methods exist on the effects of these materials on adult viewers. Three primary types of harm effects have been asserted by law and policymakers: (1) sexually exploited children are unable to develop healthy affectionate relationships in later life, have sexual dysfunctions, and have a tendency to become sexual abusers as adults; (2) child pornography often is used by pedophiles and child sexual abusers to stimulate and whet their own sexual appetites and as a model for sexual acting out with children; and (3) exposure to child pornography can desensitize the viewer to the pathology of sexual abuse or exploitation of children, so that it can become acceptable to and even preferred by the viewer. The social science evidence for these harm claims primarily is indirect evidence collected on the effects of exposure to adult pornography and violent materials. This research suggests that exposure to child pornography may have similar antisocial effects.

The Protection of Children Against Sexual Exploitation Act of 1977 and Child Pornography Prevention Act of 1996 represent the most important pieces of legislation concerning child pornography. The Supreme Court in *New York v. Ferber* (1982) established that a state may regulate child pornography even if the material is not legally obscene. A new bill, sponsored by Senator Orrin Hatch (R-Utah), bans the production and sale of sexually explicit material depicting people who "appear to be" children and refers to visual depictions that convey "the impression" of a minor engaging in sexually explicit conduct. Many policymakers worry that these two elements significantly broaden the definition of child pornography beyond that previously approved by the Supreme Court.

We raised the question of the constitutional dilemma of differentiating legitimate art from child exploitation. Several cases of prosecution involving legitimate photographers and art galleries illustrate the possibility of the chilling effects on speech of laws designed to restrict child pornography. In the future, artists, writers, and film makers may be reluctant to create and disseminate material that involves children shown nude or portrayed in situations that involve sex in any manner.

Finally, we reviewed the concerns of parents and policymakers concerning child pornography on the Internet and the possibility that adult predators will contact children through this medium for sexual abuse. Research on social community and information exchange supports the argument that online newsgroups and bulletin boards provide people with deviant or marginalized sexual interests a means of consolidation and a social context for expression.

REFERENCES

Able, G., Mittelman, M., & Becker, J. (1987). Sexual offenders: Results of assessment and recommendations for treatment. In M. H. Ben-Aron, S. J. Hucker, & C. D. Webster (Eds.), *Clinical criminology: The assessment and treatment of criminal behavior*. Toronto, Canada: Butterworth.

Abel, G. G., Lawry, S. S., Karlstrom, E., Oebom, C. J. L., & Gillespie, C. F. (1994). Screening tests for pedophilia. *Criminal Justice and Behavior, 21*(1), 115–131.

American Psychiatric Association. (1994). *Diagnostic and statistical manual of mental disorders*, 4th ed. Washington, DC: Author.

Ames, A., & Houston, D. (1990). Legal, social, and biological definition of pedophilia. *Archives of Sexual Behavior, 19*, 333–342.

Attorney General's Commission on Pornography. (1986). *Final report*. Washington, DC: US Department of Justice.

Ball-Rokeach, S. J., & Reardon, K. (1988). Monologue, dialogue, and telelog. In R. P. Hawkins, J. M. Wiemann, & S. Pingree (Eds.), *Advancing communication science: Merging mass and interpersonal processes* (pp. 135–161). Newbury Park, CA: Sage.

Bard, L., Caster, D., Cerce, D., Knight, R., Rosenberg, R., & Schneider, B. (1987). A descriptive study of rapists and child molesters: Developmental, clinical and criminal characteristics. *Behavioral Science and Law, 5*, 203–220.

Baym, N. K. (1995). The emergence of community in computer-mediated communication. In S. G. Jones (Ed.), *Cybersociety: Computer-mediated communication and community* (pp. 138–163). Thousand Oaks, CA: Sage.

Becket, J., & Kaplan, M. (1989). The assessment of adolescent sex offenders. In R. Prinz (Ed.), *Advance in behavioral assessment of children and families* (pp. 97–118). Greenwich, CT: JAI Press.

Bohlen, C. (1997, September 23). New "Lolita" is snubbed by US distributors. *The New York Times*. New York, http://www.nytimes.com.

Bryant, D. (1982). *Sexual deviancy and social proscription*. New York: Human Science Press.

Branwyn, G. (1993). Compu-sex: Erotica for cybernauts. *South Atlantic Quarterly, 92*, 779–791.

Bullough, V. (1964). *The history of prostitution*. New Hyde Park, NY: University Books.

Burgess, A., & Holmstrom, L. (1978). *Accessory-to-sex: Pressure, sex and secrecy*. In A. Burgess, A. Groth, L. Holmstrom, & S. Sgroi, *Sexual assault of children and adolescents* (pp. 85–94). New York: Garland.

Carvajal, D. (1995, February 19). Pornography meets paranoia. *The New York Times*. New York, http://www.nytimes.com.

Chapman, G. (1995, April 10). Flamers: Cranks, fetishists and monomaniacs. *New Republic*, *212*(15), 13–15.

Child Pornography Prevention Act. (1996). 18 U.S.C.A. S 2256 (8) (3) (West Supp. 1999).

Cline, V. B., Croft, R. G., & Courrier, S. (1973). Desensitization of children to television violence. *Journal of Personality and Social Psychology*, *27*, 360–365.

Condy, R. C., Templer, D. I., Brown, R., & Veaco, L. (1987). Parameters of sexual contact of boys with women. *Archives of Sexual Behavior*, *16*, 379–394.

Densen-Gerner, J. (1980). Child prostitution and child pornography: Medical, legal and societal aspects of the commercial exploitation of children. Reprinted in *Sexual abuse of children: Selected readings*. Washington, DC: US Department of Health and Human Services.

Densen-Gerber, J., & Hutchinson, S. F. (1979). Sexual and commercial exploitation of children: Legislative responses and treatment challenges. *Child Abuse and Neglect*, *3*, 61–66.

Dery, M. (1995). *Flame wars*. Durham, NC: Duke University Press.

Dietz, P. E. (1983). Sex offenses: Behavioral aspects. In S. Kadish (Ed.), *Encyclopedia of crime and justice*. (Vol. 4, pp. 1485–1493). New York: Free Press.

The Discreet Gentleman's Guide to the Pleasures of Europe. (1975). New York: Bantam Books.

Donnerstein, E., Linz, D., & Penrod, S. (1987). *The question of pornography: Research findings and policy implications*. New York: Free Press.

Durkin, D. F., & Bryant, C. D. (1995). "Log on to sex": Some notes on the carnal computer and erotic cyberspace as emerging research frontier. *Deviant Behavior*, *16*, 179–200.

Dworin, W. (1984). Testimony before the Permanent Subcommittee on Investigations of the Committee on Governmental Affairs, United States Senate, November 30. Child Pornography and Pedophilia, Part 1. Washington, DC: Superintendent of Documents, US Government Printing Office (S. Hrg. 98-1277).

Earls, C., Bouchard, L., & Laberge, J. (1984). Etude descriptive des delinquents sexual incarceres dans les penitencier Quebicios, Cashier de Recherce No. &, Institute Philippe Pinel de Montreal, Montreal, Canada.

Echols, M. (1997). *Brother Tony's boys: The largest case of child prostitution in US history, the true story*. Amherst, MA: Prometheus Books.

Ellerstein, & Canavan. (1980). Sexual abuse of boys. *American Journal of Diseases of Children*, *255*, 256–257.

Elmer-Dewitt, P. (1995, July 3). On a screen near you: Cyberporn. *Time Magazine*.

Eron, L. D., Gentry, J. H., & Schlegel, P. (1994). *Reason to hope: A psychosocial perspective on violence and youth*. Washington, DC: American Psychological Association.

Finch, (1973, March). Adult seduction of the child: Effects on the child. *Medical Aspects of Human Sexuality*, *170*, 185–192.

Finkelhor, D. (1979). Psychological, cultural and family factors in incest and family sexual abuse. *Journal of Marriage and Family Counseling*, *4*, 41–49.

Finkelhor, D. (1984). *Child sexual abuse: New theory and research*. New York: Free Press.

Foa, E. B., & Kozak, M. J. (1986). Emotional processing of fear: Exposure to corrective information. *Psychological Bulletin*, *99*, 20–35.

Freund, K., Watson, R., & Dickey, R. (1990). Does sexual abuse in childhood cause pedophilia: An exploratory study. *Archives of Sexual Behavior*, *19*, 557–568.

Furniss, M. (1993). Sex with a hard (disk) on: Computer bulletin boards and pornography. *Wide Angle*, *15*(2), 19–37.

Garland, R., & Dougher, M. (1990). The abused/abuser hypothesis of child abuse: A critical review of theory and research. In J. R. Feierman (Ed.), *Pedophilia: Biosocial dimensions* (pp. 488–509). New York: Springer-Verlag.

Garramone, G. M., Harris, A. C., & Anderson, R. (1986). Uses of political computer bulletin boards. *Journal of Broadcasting and Electronic Media*, *30*, 325–339.

Gebhard, P., Gagnon, J., Pomeroy, W., & Christenson, C. (1964). *Sex offenders*. New York: Harper & Row.

Gentile, D. (1982, July 28). Tells of babies in porn. (Report of testimony before the New York State Senate Select Committee on Crime.) *New York Post*.

Goodrich, M. (1976). Sodomy in medieval secular law. *Journal of Homosexuality*, *1*, 295–302.

Groth, N., Longo, R., & McFadin, J. (1982). Undetected recidivism among rapists and child molesters. *Crime and Delinquency*, *28*, 450–458.

Groth, A. N., & Burgess, A. W. (1977). Motivational intent in the sexual assault on children. *Criminal Justice Behavior*, *4*, 253–264.

Groth, N. (1979). Sexual trauma in the life histories of rapists and child molesters. *Victimology*, *4*, 450–458.

Hanson, R. K., Steffy, R. A., & Gauthier, R. (1993). Long-term recidivism of child molesters. *Journal of Consulting and Clinical Psychology, 61*, 646–652.
Herdt, G. (1984). *Ritualized homosexuality in Melanesia*. Berkeley: University of California Press.
Hernandez, D. G. (1996). Papers threatened with "porn" purge. (Child pornography legislation). *Editor & Publisher, 129*(28), 22.
Higonnet, A. (1996). Conclusions based on observation. *The Yale Journal of Criticism, 9*(1), 1–18.
Hiltz, S. R., & Turoff, M. (1978/1992). *The network nation: Human communication via computer*. Reading, MA: Addison-Wesley.
Hindman, J. (1988). Research disputes assumptions about child molesters. *NDAA Bulletin, 7*, 1–3.
Illinois Legislative Investigating Commission. (1980). Sexual exploitation of children. A report to the Illinois General Assembly, p. 27.
James, M. L., Wotring, C. E., & Forrest, E. J. (1995). An exploratory study of the perceived benefits of electronic bulletin board use and their impact on other communication activities. *Journal of Broadcasting and Electronic Media, 39*, 30–50.
Johnston, D. (1995, September 14). Use of computer network for child sex sets off raids. *New York Times*, pp. A1, A18.
Jones, G. P. (1991). Sexual abuse of children. *American Journal of the Diseases of Children, 136*, 142–146.
Kaplan, D. E. (1997, May 26). New cybercop tricks to fight child porn: Police struggle against an online onslaught. *U.S. News & World Report, 122*(20), 29.
Knight, R. A., Carter, D. L., & Prentky, R. A. (1989). A system for the classification of child molesters: Reliability and application. *Journal of Interpersonal Violence, 4*, 3–23.
Lanning, K. V. (1992). *Child molesters: A behavioral analysis*, 3rd ed. Quantico, VA: Federal Bureau of Investigation.
Lea, M., & Spears, R. (1991). Computer-mediated communication, de-individuation and group decision-making. *International Journal of Man–Machine Studies, 34*, 283–301.
Levy, S. (1995, July 3). No place for kids? A parents' guide to sex on the net. *Newsweek, 126*(1), 46–50.
Linz, D., Donnerstein, E., & Penrod, S. (1984a). The effects of long-term exposure to filmed violence against women. *Journal of Communication, 34*, 130–147.
Linz, D., Donnerstein, E., & Penrod, S. (1987). *The question of pornography*. New York: Free Press.
Linz, D., Donnerstein, E., & Penrod, S. (1988). Effects of long-term exposure to violent and sexually degrading depictions of women. *Journal of Personality and Social Psychology, 55*, 758–768.
Linz, D., & Malamuth, N. M. (1993). Communication Concepts 5: Pornography. In S. Chaffee (Ed.), *Communication concepts series* (pp.). Newbury Park, CA: Sage.
Linz, D., Turner, C., Hesse, B., & Penrod, S. (1984b). *Pornography and sexual aggression*. Academic Press, Inc.
McCary, S. R., & McCary, J. L. (1984). *Human sexuality*. Belmont, CA: Wadsworth.
The news in brief. (1984, July 24). *Los Angeles Times*, p. 2.
Malamuth, N. M., & Check, J. V. P. (1980a). Penile tumescence and perceptual responses to rape as a function of victim's perceived reactions. *Journal of Applied Social Psychology, 10*, 528–547.
Malamuth, N. M., & Check, J. V. P. (1980b). Sexual arousal to rape and consenting depictions: The importance of the woman's arousal. *Journal of Abnormal Psychology, 89*, 763–766.
Malamuth, N., & Check, J. V. P. (1981). The effects of mass media exposure on acceptance of violence against women: A field experiment. *Journal of Research in Personality, 15*, 436–446.
Malamuth, N. M., Haber, S., & Feshbach, S. (1980). Testing hypotheses regarding rape: Exposure to sexual violence, sex differences, and the "normality" of rape. *Journal of Research in Personality, 14*, 121–137.
Malamuth, N. M., Heim, M., & Feshbach, S. (1980). Inhibitory and disinhibitory effects. *Journal of Personality and Social Psychology, 38*, 399–408.
Malamuth, N., Linz, D., & Heavy, C., Barnes, G., & Acker, M. (1995). Using the confluence model of sexual aggression to predict men's conflict with women: A ten year follow-up study. *Journal of Personality and Social Psychology, 69*, 353–369.
Marshall, W. L., & Pithers, W. D. (1994). A reconsideration of treatment outcomes with sex offenders. *Criminal Justice and Behavior, 21*(1), 10–27.
Meyer, C. (1995). Cybersexual possibilities. *Georgetown Law Journal, 83*, 1969–2008.
Miller v. California 413 US 15, 93 (1973).
Mohr, J. W. (1964). A child has been molested. *Medical Aspects of Human Sexuality, 2*(11), 43–50.
Monahan, J., & Walker, L. (1998). *Social science in law: Cases and materials* (4th ed.). Westbury, NY: Foundations Press.
New digital child porn law in budget bill. (1996, October 3). *New York Times*, New York, http://www.nytimes.com.
New York v. Ferber, 458 US 747, 73 L Ed 2d 1113, 102 S Ct 3348. (1982).

Nobile, P. (1976). Introduction. In W. Kramer (Ed.), *The normal and abnormal love of children* (pp. 1–8). Kansas City, MO: Sheed, Andrews & McMeel.
Ogan, C. (1993). Listserver communication during the gulf war: What kind of medium is the electronic bulletin board? *Journal of Broadcasting and Electronic Media, 37*, 177–196.
Osborne v. Ohio, 495 US 103 (1990).
Paterson C., & Pettijohn, T. (1982). Age and human mate selection. *Psychological Reports, 51*, 70.
Popkin, J., & Simons, J. (1994, September 19). Natural born predators. *US News & World Report*, p. 64.
Radbill, S. (1980). Children in the world of violence: A history of child abuse. In C. H. Kempe & R. E. Helfer (Eds.), *The battered child* (pp. 44–97). Chicago: University of Chicago Press.
Penal Code Handbook of California. (1994). Altamonte Springs, FL: Gould Publications.
Radovitch, J. (1984, August 9). Pornography called trigger for child molesting. (Report of U.S. Senate testimony of Special Agent Kenneth Lanning, the FBI's expert on sexual victimization of children). *The Los Angeles Times*, p. B3.
Rafaeli, S. (1988). Interactivity: From new media to communication. In R. P. Hawkins, J. M. Wiemann, & S. Pingree (Eds.), *Advancing communication science: Merging mass and interpersonal processes* (pp. 110–134). Newbury Park, CA: Sage.
Rheingold, H. (1993). *The virtual community: Homesteading on the electronic frontier*. Reading, MA: Addison-Wesley.
Reicher, S. D. (1984). Social influence in the crowd: Attitudinal and behavioural effects of de-individuation in conditions of high and low group salience. *British Journal of Social Psychology, 23*, 341–350.
Rosenbaum, J. L., & Prinsky, L. (1991). The presumption of influence: Recent responses to popular music subcultures. *Crime and Delinquency, 37*(4), 528–535.
Schoettle, P. (1980a). Treatment of the child pornography patient. *American Journal of Psychiatry, 137*, 1109.
Schoettle, P. (1980b). Child exploitation: A study of child pornography. *Child Psychology, 51*, 27–34.
Serpenti, L. (1984). The ritual meaning of homosexuality and pedophilia among the Kimam-Papuans of South Irian Jaya. In G. H. Herdt (Ed.), *Ritualized homosexuality in Melanesia* (pp. 318–335). Berkeley: University of California Press.
Simons, M. (1993, April 9). The sex market: Scourge on the world's children. *The New York Times*, p. A3.
Sproull, L., & Kiesler, S. (1991). *Connections: New ways of working in the networked organization*. Cambridge, MA: MIT Press.
Spears, R., & Lea, M. (1994). Panacea or panopticon? The hidden power in computer-mediated communication. *Communication Research, 21*, 427–459.
Spears, R., Lea, M., & Lee, S. (1990). De-individuation and group polarization in computer-mediated communication. *British Journal of Social Psychology, 29*, 121–134.
Stanely, L. A. (1989). The child porn myth. *Cardozo Arts & Entertainment Journal, 7*(20), 295–358.
Stanley v. Georgia 394 US, 557 (1969).
Sussman, V. (1995, January 23). Policing cyberspace. *US News and World Report*, 54.
Tamosaitis, N. (1995). *net.sex*. Emeryville, CA: Ziff-Davis Press.
Thomas, M. H. (1982). Physiological arousal, exposure to a relatively lengthy aggressive film, and aggressive behavior. *Journal of Research in Personality, 16*, 72–81.
Thomas, M. H., Horton, R. W., Lippencott, E. C., & Drabman, R. S. (1977). Desensitization to portrayals of real-life aggression as a function of exposure to television violence. *Journal of Personality and Social Psychology, 35*, 450–458.
Trumbach, R. (1977). London's sodomites: Homosexual behavior in Western culture in the eighteenth century. *Journal of Social History, 11*, 1–33.
Turner, J. C., Hogg, M. A., Oakes, P. J., Reicher, S. D., & Wetherell, M. S. (1987). *Rediscovering the social group: A self-categorization theory*. Oxford, England: Blackwell.
Tyler, R. P., & Stone, L. E. (1985). Child pornography: Perpetuating the sexual victimization of children. *Child Abuse and Neglect, 9*, 313–318.
Ungaretti, J. (1978). Pederasty, heroism and the family in classical Greece. *Journal of Homosexuality, 3*, 291–300.
S. Res. No. 438, 95th Cong., 2nd Sess. 5 (1977).
United States Sentencing Commission (1996). Report to Congress: Sex offenses against children; Findings and recommendations regarding federal penalties. United States Sentencing Commission, Washington, DC.
US v. Brown. (1989). 862 F 2d 1033 (3rd cir., 1988).
US v. DePugh, 993 F 2d 1362 (8th cir, 1993).
US v. Koelling, 992 F 2d 817 (8th cir., 1993).
US v. Wiegand, 812 F 2d 1239 (9th cir., 1987).

US v. X-Citement Video Inc. et al., 130 L Ed 2d (1994).
Vanggaard, T. (1972). Phallos: A symbol and its history in the male world. London: Cape.
Van Curen, E. (1995, January 24). Travelling the information superhighway. *Journal of Justice Science*, *25*, 222–223.
Vance, C. S. (1990, November). Reagan's revenge: Restructuring the NEA. *Art in America*, *49*, 17–19.
Walther, J. B., Anderson, J. F., & Park, D. W. (1994). Interpersonal effects in computer-mediated communication: A meta analysis of social and anti-social communication. *Communication Research*, *21*, 460–487.
Williams, W., & McShane, L. (1995). Senate approves measure making obscenity on the internet a crime. *The Chronicle of Higher Education*, *27*, A19.
Zipperer, J. (1994, September 12). The naked city: "Cyberporn" invades the American home. *Christianity Today*, *38*(10), 42–49.

Part III

Offending

6

Demography and Death by Violence

A Demographic Analysis of US Homicide Offending Trends

JAMES ALAN FOX, JODI BROWN, MARY ANN ZAGER, and MONICA BARTLETT

INTRODUCTION

For several years, the United States has been enjoying a strong downward trend in the rate of homicide. As shown in Fig. 1, homicide rates of the mid-1990s dropped to levels not seen in this country since the late 1960s, before the double-digit inflation in killings grabbed the attention of the press and politicians alike. Before celebrating this substantial decline, however, we need to examine and account for patterns and trends within subgroups of the population that may underlie these aggregate rates.

Criminologists have long recognized the importance of demographic analysis in understanding patterns of offending, however they are measured (see Barnett & Goranson, 1996; Cohen & Land, 1987; Farrington & Langan, 1992; Markides & Tracy, 1977; Marvell & Moody, 1991). Demographic change has been shown to affect reported crime and arrest rates (Blumstein & Nagin, 1975; Chilton, 1986, 1987, 1991; Chilton & Speilberger, 1971; Cohen & Land, 1987; Farrington & Langan, 1992; Ferdinand, 1970; Johnson & Lazarus, 1989; Laub, 1983; Markides & Tracy, 1977; President's Commission on Law Enforcement and the Administration of Justice, 1967; Sagi & Wellford, 1968; Schwartz & Exter, 1990; Steffensmeier & Harrer, 1987, 1991; Wellford, 1973), conviction rates (Lee, 1984; Maxim & Jocklin, 1980), as well as prison populations (Blumstein, Cohen, & Miller, 1981; Langan, 1991; MacKenzie, Tracy, & Williams, 1988).

JAMES ALAN FOX and MONICA BARTLETT • College of Criminal Justice, Northeastern University, Boston, Massachusetts 02115. **JODI BROWN** • Bureau of Justice Statistics, US Department of Justice, Washington, DC 20531. **MARY ANN ZAGER** • Division of Criminal Justice, Florida Gulf Coast University, Fort Myers, Florida 33965-6565.

Handbook of Youth and Justice, edited by White. Kluwer Academic / Plenum Publishers, New York, 2001.

Figure 1. US homicide rate, 1950–1996.

The focus of this chapter is the role of demographics in producing homicide rate changes over the past few decades. The "demographic change hypothesis" (MacKenzie et al., 1988) can be described as follows: The general population is thought to consist of different demographic segments, some of which have a propensity to commit crimes (and homicides in particular) at relatively high rates. In periods when such crime-prone segments are a growing percentage of the overall population (assuming all other things are equal), the aggregate offense rate will increase. Similarly (assuming all other things are equal), the aggregate rate will decrease during times when crime-prone segments are a declining percentage of the total population.

Prior Research on Effects of Demographic Change

The demographic change hypothesis frequently has been used to explain fluctuations in crime rates. Research has illustrated that much of the increase in crime over the past three decades has been due to shifts in the demographic mix of the population (Blumstein & Nagin, 1975; Chilton, 1986, 1987, 1991; Chilton & Speilberger, 1971; Cohen & Land, 1987; Farrington & Langan, 1992; Ferdinand, 1970; Fox, 1978; Laub, 1983; Lee, 1984; President's Commission, 1967; Sagi & Wellford, 1968; Steffensmeier & Harer, 1987, 1991; Wellford, 1973). These studies demonstrated how the large number of children born in the post-World War II baby boom (which began in 1946 and lasted until 1964) were moving into the high-crime-prone ages (15–24 years old) during the 1960s and 1970s, thus contributing to a sharp rise in crime.

As a result of the baby boom, the US population in the 1960s experienced a rapid increase in the proportion of young people. In the 1950s and early 1960s, approximately 15% of the population was between ages 15 and 24. By 1970, 15- to 24-year-olds were nearly 20% of the population.

Much of the social unrest and increases in crime in the 1960s and 1970s has been attributed to the increase in the proportion of young adults in the population as a result of the baby boom (Wilson & Dupont, 1973; Moynihan, 1973). Because the young crime-prone group in the 1960s and 1970s was increasing much faster than other groups in the population, the crime rate for the nation as a whole could have been expected to grow, whether the rate for any given age increased or not.

Criminologists conducting demographic analyses typically define demographics solely in terms of the age structure of the population (Chilton & Speilberger, 1971; Cohen & Land, 1987; Markides & Tracy, 1977; Sagi & Wellford, 1968; Steffensmeier & Harer, 1987, 1991; Wellford, 1973). Most researchers of the age–crime relationship assume that age structure affects crime rates through the supply of potential offenders (Marvell & Moody, 1991). Sometimes, in addition to age, researchers attempt to attribute changes in the crime rate to changes in the sex distribution of the population (Barnett & Goranson, 1996; Blumstein & Nagin, 1975; Chilton, 1986, 1991; Laub, 1983; Lee, 1984; Maxim & Jocklin, 1980; President's Commission, 1967). While cross-sectional differences exist, trend data have shown repeatedly that the sex distribution of the general population does not significantly change over time. Therefore, no portion of the change in crime rate can possibly be attributable to shifts in the sex distribution of the general population.

Although urbanization also is a correlate of crime (Chilton, 1982; Hindelang, 1978; Quinney, 1964; Silberman, 1978), research has demonstrated that race is the key variable (Farrington & Langan, 1992; Laub, 1983). In other words, changes in the racial structure of the general population account for variation in urban and rural crime rates better than changes in the urban and rural distribution of the population account for variation in crime rates across racial lines. Relatively few demographic analyses exist in which demographics is defined in terms of both age and race (Chilton, 1987; Farrington & Langan, 1992).

The President's Commission on Law Enforcement and Administration of Justice (1967) assessed how accurately known changes in the size of the general population in the age structure and in the rural–urban, sex, and racial composition of the population predicted the change in the volume of crime from 1960 to 1965. Commission researchers applied 1960 (base-year) arrest rates for age, sex, race, and place of residence to the 1965 population in these groups to "predict" what the volume of crime would have been in 1965 if arrest rates for these groups had remained constant. Their analysis indicated that population growth and changes in the age structure accounted for almost half (49%) of the total increase in the reported number of arrests.

Just after the President's Commission (1967), Sagi and Wellford (1968) estimated that between 30% and 50% of the increase in the absolute volume of crime in the United States over the years 1958 to 1964 could be attributed to changes in the age structure of the general population. Increases in population size and fluctuations in the relative proportion of individuals in crime-prone age categories accounted for almost half the increase. In a follow-up study, Wellford (1973) indicated that when the time series was expanded to cover the period 1958 to 1969, the volume of crime increased by 175%, but the offense rate increased by only 97%. He confirmed that age composition effects alone could be said to account for about 45% of the increase in the volume of crime over the 1958 to 1969 period.

In his study of demographic shifts and criminality, Ferdinand (1970) measured the effects of urbanization and age structure on the volume of index crimes in the United States for the 1950 to 1965 period. He attributed approximately 19% of the increase in the volume of index offenses to urbanization, ranging from 8.5% in the case of murder and non-negligent manslaughter to 25.7% in the case of motor vehicle theft. When controlling for urbanization, Ferdinand reported that the volume of manslaughters revealed a negative effect and suggested that this was a result of high manslaughter-prone places, such as rural and suburban areas, that declined in size. He attributed 11.6% of the increase in the volume of index offenses to shifts in the age structure over the 1950 to 1965 period, ranging from 5.5% in the case of homicide to 47.1% in the case of rape. Ferdinand detected that the combined effect of urbanization and age structure on changing crime levels between 1950 and 1965 could account for about 30% of the overall increase in Index crimes.

Although based on different methods and different time periods, most estimates of the effect of demographics on changing crime rates generally show the same effect (Marvell & Moody, 1991). They each assume a positive relationship between crime rates and the size of the crime-prone age and racial groups. Chilton (1987) assessed the extent to which age and race helped to explain trends in homicide and robbery arrests in Chicago from 1962 to 1980. His results implied that Chicago's changing racial composition contributed to changes in the age structure and to the homicide rate. He attributed as much as 24% of the increase in homicide arrests and 45% of the increase in robbery arrests over the 1962 to 1980 period to an increase in the number of nonwhite males in the population. He pointed out that the changing age structure alone explained little of the observed homicide and robbery trends in Chicago. Examining combined changes in age and racial composition better explained the impact of demographic changes on urban homicide and robbery rates than age alone.

In an attempt to explain the increase in crime from 1967 to 1972, Blumstein and Nagin (1975) explored age, sex, and race-specific arrest rates for Pittsburgh residents. They detected that the demographic factors (age, sex, and race) accounted for over 99% of the variance. Blumstein and Nagin concluded that crime rates were almost entirely a function of demographics and that the time factor was relatively insignificant. They determined that the increase in arrest rates in Pittsburgh was due to changes in the relative size of the different demographic groups.

Cohen and Land (1987) investigated the prevalence of teenagers (15- to 19-year-olds) and young adults (20- to 29-year-olds) in the population as it related to murder and motor vehicle theft rates from 1946 to 1984. They revealed that the proportion of 15- to 29-year-olds accounted for 58% of the change in the murder rate and the proportion of 15- to 24 year-olds accounted for about 26% of the change in the motor vehicle theft rate. Their analysis was based exclusively on the relative number of adolescents and young adults in the population.

Steffensmeier and Harer (1987) attempted to determine whether the 1980 to 1984 drop (of 15%) in the nation's index crime rate was due to changes in the age structure of the US population. Steffensmeier and Harer revealed that age effects explained about 40% of the drop in reported crimes (43% for the property index only). Change in age structure had little to no effect on homicide, rape, and assault. The major impacts were on robbery (36% of reported crime and 57% of victimizations), burglary (31% and 39%), larceny (53% and 42%), and motor vehicle theft (70% and 100%). In a follow-up study, Steffensmeier and Harer (1991) expanded their analysis of the effect of shifts in age structure on the index crime rate to the 1980 to 1988 period (during the Reagan Presidency). Overall, they found that the age adjustment explained the entire drop in the reported index rate in the Uniform Crime Reports (UCR).

While Steffensmeier and Harer (1991) examined the declining crime rate solely in terms of the age composition of the population, Farrington and Langan (1992) assessed changes in the crime rate in terms of both the age and racial composition of the population during about the same time period. Contrary to what Steffensmeier and Harer (1991) reported, Farrington and Langan (1992) found that demographics explained little of the decreases in the index crime rates (except for motor vehicle theft) between 1981 and 1986. One possible reason for the difference in findings is that Steffensmeier and Harer attempted to explain the crime rate's decline in terms of age structure changes only, while Farrington and Langan used both age and race.

Similar to Farrington and Langan (1992), Barnett and Goranson (1996) revealed that the changing age structure in the early 1980s hardly explained the contemporaneous drop in murder. In an attempt to answer the question, "why has murder declined among adult black males," Barnett and Goranson noted that the murder arrest rate for black males 25 and older declined steadily between 1976 and 1991. In addition, the drop occurred at a time when the national arrest rate for murder did not fall at all (8.3 per 100,000 in 1973, and 8.5 per 100,000 in 1992). Moreover, they pointed out that the age shifts between 1985 and 1992 demographically predicted a decline in murder, rather than the increase that actually took place.

DECOMPOSING MURDER TRENDS

The purpose of this chapter is to examine the role of demographics in explaining murder rate changes over the past few decades. We focus exclusively on homicide, rather than the other major crimes, not just because of its particularly serious nature, but more so because of the reliability of the reported data. Unlike rates of forcible rape, aggravated assault, and other crime types that are greatly impacted by measurement error as well as changes in police recording practices, homicide has a relatively high level of clearance (permitting the analysis of offender data) and a nearly unambiguous definition.

We approach the demographic analysis of homicide trends through two alternative strategies. First, similar to the tradition of President's Commission on Law Enforcement (1967) and others, we establish over various time periods the extent to which actual crime trends mimic those that could have been expected based only on demographic change. The second approach looks at demographic subgroups of the population and examines differential change over time in homicide offending rates.

Demographic Decomposition

This section examines homicide rate fluctuation from 1964 to 1996 using the UCR and specifying two definitions of demographics: age alone and age and race together. The demographic analyses were conducted using annual UCR data on homicide arrests by age and by age and race and annual Census Bureau demographically disaggregated population data.

The FBI annually publishes offense-specific counts of the number of persons arrested for homicide nationwide for 21 age categories: under 12, 13–14, single age categories from 15 to 24 (15, 16, 17, and so on), 5-year age categories from 25 to 64 (25–29, 30–34, 35–39, and so on), and 65 and over. But the only published offense-specific counts by age and race are for two age categories (under 18 and 18 and over). For analyzing the effect on homicide rates of demographic change in the age–race composition of the population, two age categories are far less than desirable because important changes in age structure are not captured with the simple distinction between "under 18" versus "18 and over." To conduct a more refined demographic analysis, for each racial category arrests for 21 age categories were estimated.

This analysis is not a study of fluctuations in arrest trends; rather, it is a study of crime rate fluctuations. The UCR does not report demographic characteristics of persons who commit crime, but it does report demographic characteristics of persons arrested. For this reason, the demographic characteristics of persons arrested is assumed to mirror the demographic characteristics of persons who commit crime.

The UCR reports the number of persons arrested for murder for 21 separate age categories and the total number of reported murders. The number of reported murders is the number of times that a murder was reported to and recorded by police departments nationally. The proportion of persons arrested for murder in each age group applied to the total number of reported murder forms an estimate of the number of murders attributable to each age group. For example, in 1996 there were 14,447 arrests for murder reported to the UCR and 359 of them were of 15-year-olds. Thus, 15-year-olds represented 2.5% of the 14,447 known murder arrests. According to the UCR, there were an estimated 19,650 murders in the nation in 1996. Assuming that age characteristics of persons arrested mirror age characteristics of persons committing crimes, 15-year-olds then accounted for 2.5% of the 19,650 reported murders. Therefore, we can estimate that 491 15-year-olds committed murder in 1996. This procedure is completed for each of the 33 years and 21 age categories.

The UCR reports, by offense, the number of persons arrested who were under 18 and 18 and over for each race. The proportion of each race that is under 18 or 18 and over and arrested for murder is applied to the total number of reported crimes for each age group for murder to form an estimate of the number of murders attributable to each age and racial group. For example, in 1996 there were 2171 arrests of persons under 18 for murder reported to the UCR and 849 of them were white. Therefore, whites are estimated to represent 39% of the 2171 known murder arrests of persons under 18. Using the method detailed above, we estimated that there were 491 15-year-olds who committed murder in 1996. Since whites were 39% of persons under age 18 who were arrested for murder, 39% of the 491 15-year-olds who committed murder were estimated to be white. Thus, we estimated that 191 white 15-year-olds committed murder. This procedure is performed for each of the 33 years, 21 age, and 3 race groups (white, black, and other).

The following steps were then followed to assess the extent to which change in the murder rate between a given base year (e.g., 1964) and a given target year (e.g., 1996) can be attributed to demographic (age and race) shifts:

1. We divide the base-year (1964) population into 63 categories (21 age categories for each of the 3 race categories) and calculate the percentage that each of the 63 categories is of the total population in the base year.
2. Next, we apply the 63 percentages to the target year (e.g., 1996) population to form 1996 population counts standardized to the 1964 (base year) population distribution.
3. We next calculate 63 age- and race-specific crime commission rates by dividing the estimated number of murders attributable to each age–race category by that category's actual (or observed) 1996 population.
4. To obtain an expected murder volume, we apply the 63 age- and race-specific murder commission rates to the 1996 standardized population. That is, we multiply each of the 63 observed age- and race-specific murder commission rates by the size of its 1996 standardized population.
5. We use the same procedure for each of the 63 age–race groups, then sum the expected murder counts across the 63 age- and race-specific categories and divide by the total 1996 population.
6. Next, we calculate three murder rates: the 1996 expected rate, the 1996 observed rate, and the 1964 observed rate. The expected murder rate is calculated by dividing the expected number of murders in 1996 by the 1996 total population.
7. To calculate how much of the change in the murder rate is attributable to demographic shifts, we calculate the observed and expected changes in the murder rates.
8. Finally, the percentage of the change in the murder rate attributable to demographic shifts is calculated by taking the difference between the observed and the expected changes, then dividing by the observed change.

We applied this eight-step procedure to estimate the effects of demographic shifts (age only and then age and race combined) on homicide rate changes from 1964 to 1980, from 1980 to 1985, and from 1985 to 1996. The actual and expected rates are shown in Figs. 2 through 4, and the overall extent to which demographics accounts for the homicide rate change between the base and target years in summarized in Table 1.

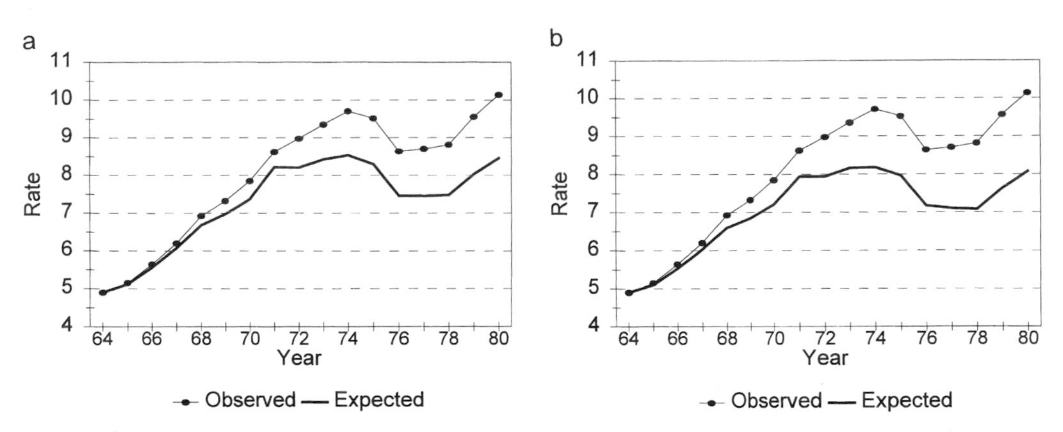

Figure 2. (a) Homicide 1964–1980 (age only). (b) Homicide 1964–1980 (age and race combined).

The homicide rate increased by 107% between 1964 and 1980. As expected, combined changes in the age and racial composition of the US population explained more of the increasing homicide rate than age structure changes alone. Forty percent of the increase in the homicide rate between 1964 and 1980 could be explained by age and racial changes in the population, but age alone could only explain 32% of the change. That is, if the age structure of the population in 1980 was exactly as it was in 1964 (in terms of age *and* race), the homicide rate would have increased about half as much as was observed during the same time period.

The observed homicide rate decreased 22% between 1980 and 1985. When demographic factors (age alone, or age and race combined) are controlled, the expectation is that by 1985 the homicide rate would have decreased more than it did. Therefore, demographic factors artificially increased the crime rate in 1985. Demographic changes in the population were responsible for none of the decreased homicide rate between 1980 and 1985.

The homicide rate decreased 6% between 1985 and 1996. When demographic factors (age alone, or age and race combined) are controlled, the expectation is that the homicide rate will increase to more than what it was in 1985 (observed). Therefore, demographic factors artificially decreased the homicide rate in 1996. Demographics are responsible for all of the decrease between 1985 and 1996.

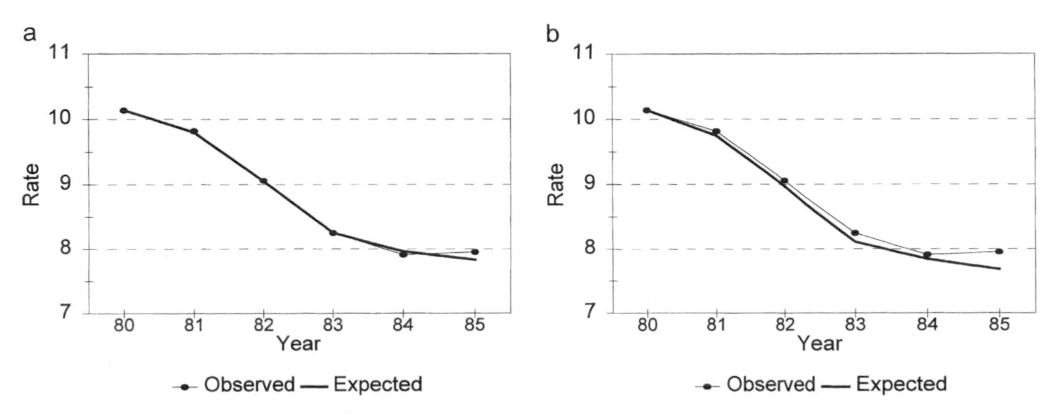

Figure 3. (a) Homicide 1980–1985 (age only). (b) Homicide 1980–1985 (age and race combined).

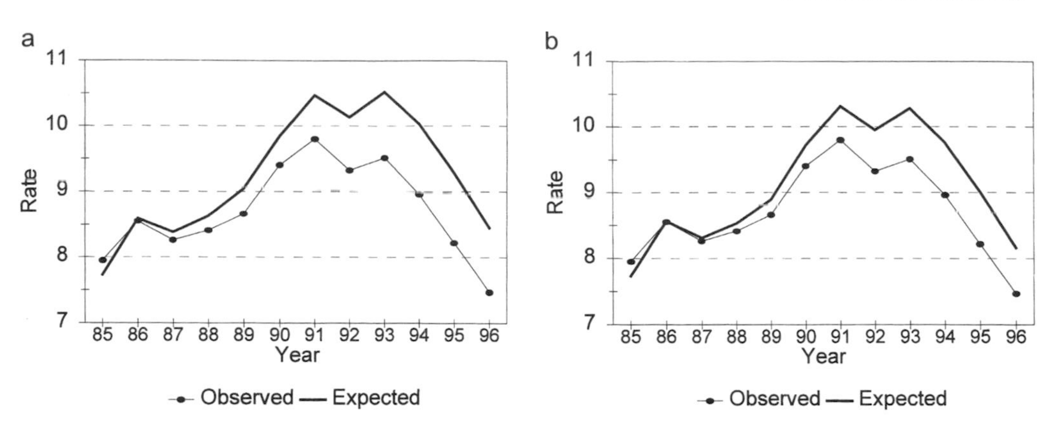

Figure 4. (a) Homicide 1985–1996 (age only). (b) Homicide 1985–1996 (age and race combined).

During periods when the population is aging and becoming more nonwhite and the crime rate is falling, a demographic model controlling only for age attributes a greater portion of the crime rate decline to demographic changes than does a model controlling for age and race. In effect, the model with just age depicts the population as becoming less crime prone, which is reflected in the expected crime rate generated by the model. But by ignoring the racial trend, the model overstates the degree to which the population has become less crime prone. In other words, the age-only model exaggerates the effects of demographic changes on the falling crime rate. The model that accounts for both age and race structure eliminates this distinction. (In general, older people are less crime prone than younger people and nonwhites are more crime prone than whites. Consequently, during periods when the population is aging and becoming more nonwhite, these demographic changes have predictable effects on the crime rate.)

During periods when the population is aging and becoming more nonwhite and the crime rate is rising, a greater portion of the crime rate increase is attributed to age and race combined than to age structure alone. For example, age and race combined accounted for more of the increased homicide rate between 1964 and 1980 than age alone. There is a reason that the model with age and race attributes a greater portion of the increase to demographics than the model with age. The model with both age and race produces an expected crime rate that reflects two opposing forces on the crime rate: the upward effect of race and the downward effect of aging. The model with just age produces an expected rate that fails to reflect the

Table 1. Demographic Decomposition of Homicide Rate Changes

Years	Actual change in homicide rate	Demographic factor(s)	Change controlling for demographic factor(s)	Percent of change due to demographic factor(s)
1964–1980	107%	Age only	72%	32
		Age and race	65%	40
1980–1985	−22%	Age only	−23%	0
		Age and race	−24%	0
1985–1996	−6%	Age only	6%	100
		Age and race	3%	100

upward effect of race. Consequently, the model with age and race attributes more of the crime rate increase to demographics than does the model with age alone. The model that accounts for both age and race structure corrects the underestimate of the age-only model.

Regardless of which model (age alone or age and race combined) explains more of a change in the crime rate, when the demographic characteristics of a population are changing, conceptually it is more accurate to base findings on a model that includes all the changing demographics. To illustrate, say that the age and racial structure of the population changed between the base year and the comparison year. Further, say that age alone explains 25% of a crime rate decrease over that period, while age and race combined explains 10%. Then 10% is actually the more accurate (although not the higher) of the two because it is based on two changing demographic crime correlates rather than just one.

In the example above, the 15% difference between age alone (25%) and age and race combined (10%) is not race structure alone. Rather, the 15% difference is a result of the opposing force of race alone. Ten percent of the crime rate decrease can be explained by the changes that occurred in the age and racial structure of the population between the base year and comparison year. The remaining 90% of the crime rate decrease is due to factors other than age or race.

Demographic Comparisons of Homicide Trends

Another approach to analyzing demographic components of homicide trends is to measure and compare homicide rates for various age–race–sex groups. The most expansive data on murder and nonnegligent manslaughter are provided by the Supplementary Homicide Reports (SHR), which are part of the FBI's Uniform Crime Reporting Program. The SHR is an incident-based reporting mechanism that includes information on victim and offender age, race, and sex, victim–offender relationship, weapon, and circumstances, as well as month, year, and reporting jurisdiction, for the overwhelming majority of homicides known to the police. Although the level of compliance by local agencies varies from year to year, on average over 92% of homicides in America are reflected in these data.

For the purpose of this analysis, a cumulative offender file spanning 21 years, from 1976 to 1996, was employed. To adjust for nonreporting agencies, estimated crime counts by states and year were used to adjust upward the available incident reports. This small and reasonable adjustment ensures that annual counts and rates agree with the national estimates published annually by the FBI.

In comparing different age groups of offenders, another source of missing information is far more problematic. Specifically, the characteristics of more than a quarter of the offenders are unknown, mostly because the offenses remain unsolved. Thus, if using only known offenders, offending rates by age group would be seriously attenuated because of missing age information.

To correct this serious problem, an algorithm has been developed to adjust for unsolved cases (see Fox 1997a; Fox & Zawitz, 1998). In essence, solved and unsolved homicides are matched on victim, time, and place characteristics, and the distribution of known offender characteristics is then replicated for unsolved homicides. In particular, unsolved cases are discarded from an offender-based analysis and solved cases are weighted upward to represent matched solved cases. Thus, all offending rates are understood to be estimates, based on solved cases plus unsolved cases with imputed offender characteristics.

Figure 5 illustrates changes in the age distribution of homicide offenders from the mid-1980s to the mid-1990s, reflecting a marked shift toward younger perpetrators. Not only

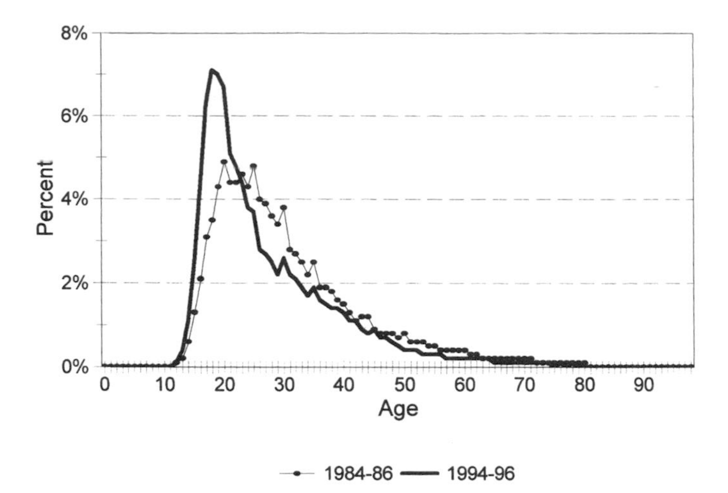

Figure 5. Change in age distribution of homicide offenders.

has the modal age of offenders dropped below 20 years old, but the mean similarly has declined from 34 to 31.

To understand fully the increase in the number of juvenile homicide offenders, we should compare juvenile and adult offenders and account for changes in the age of the population at large. The estimated homicide offending rates and ages of homicide offenders from 1976 to 1996 are presented in Table 2 and illustrated in Fig. 6. The first decade of data indicates an overall decrease in the homicide rate after some fluctuation in the late 1970s and early 1980s; overall, the US homicide rate was lower in 1985 than in 1976. Unfortunately, this trend did not persist, as the country experienced a 32% increase in the total homicide rate from 1985 to 1991. The largest increase in homicide offending during this period was among 14- to 17-year-olds whose rate nearly tripled, from 9.8 offenders per 100,000 population in 1985 to 26.6 per 100,000 in 1991. This represented a 171% increase (an average annual rise of 18.1%) during this time period. The average annual percentage increase for young adults (18- to 24-year-olds) was 11.4%, offending rates for this age group increased 91% from 1985 to 1991.

This dramatic increase was not evident for older offenders. While the rate for those aged 25 to 34 increased slightly, rates for offenders aged 35 and over decreased. Thus, the entire growth in the aggregate homicide rate during the late 1980s was attributable to youthful offenders, including an unprecedented surge in teenage killing.

Homicide rates have generally declined since 1991. From 1991 to 1996, the overall offending rate showed a 25% downturn. The decrease was greater than 20% for all age groups with the exception of the young adult population, 18- to 24-year-olds, whose offending rate decreased only 13% during this time period. After unprecedented high levels for teenagers and young adults in 1993, rates have dropped substantially: by a third among 14- to 17-year-olds (from 30.2 to 19.6) and by more than 10% among 18- to 24-year-olds (from 41.3 down to 35.7). Even after these healthy declines, however, the rate of offending among teens and young adults remained considerably higher than in the mid-1980s.

The analysis of homicide data by age, sex, and race from 1976 to 1996 presented in Table 3 further identifies trends in the homicide offending rate. Generally, the largest increases were for black males, followed by white males and black females. Two time periods are of particular

Table 2. Estimated Homicide Offending Rates per 100,000 Population

Year	Total	Under 14	14–17	18–24	25–34	35–49	50–64	65+
1976	9.5	0.2	10.6	22.4	19.4	11.1	5.2	2.3
1977	9.4	0.2	10.0	22.1	18.7	11.4	5.2	2.2
1978	9.6	0.3	10.1	23.1	19.0	11.4	4.9	2.2
1979	10.5	0.2	11.7	26.2	20.3	11.6	5.5	2.2
1980	11.6	0.2	12.9	29.5	22.2	13.3	5.1	2.0
1981	10.7	0.2	11.2	25.7	20.3	12.8	5.2	2.1
1982	9.9	0.2	10.4	24.2	19.0	11.3	4.8	1.8
1983	9.0	0.2	9.4	22.1	17.5	10.2	4.2	1.5
1984	8.6	0.2	8.5	21.5	16.9	9.5	4.0	1.7
1985	8.5	0.2	9.8	21.4	16.0	9.4	4.3	1.6
1986	9.2	0.2	11.7	23.4	17.6	9.9	4.1	1.6
1987	8.9	0.2	12.3	24.1	16.2	9.2	3.9	1.8
1988	9.3	0.2	15.5	26.9	16.5	8.9	3.6	1.7
1989	9.5	0.3	18.1	30.2	16.4	8.4	3.5	1.4
1990	10.6	0.2	23.7	34.4	17.6	9.5	3.5	1.4
1991	11.2	0.3	26.6	40.8	18.6	8.2	3.3	1.3
1992	10.4	0.3	26.3	38.4	16.8	7.7	3.3	1.3
1993	10.7	0.3	30.2	41.3	15.9	7.4	3.5	1.2
1994	10.2	0.3	29.3	39.6	15.2	7.4	2.9	1.0
1995	9.2	0.3	23.6	36.7	14.4	6.7	2.9	1.1
1996	8.4	0.2	19.6	35.7	13.4	6.2	2.6	0.9
Average change								
1985–91	4.7%	7.0%	18.1%	11.4%	2.5%	−2.3%	−4.3%	−3.4%
1991–96	−5.6%	−7.8%	−5.9%	−2.7%	−6.3%	−5.4%	−4.7%	−7.1%
1993–96	−7.8%	−12.6%	−13.4%	−4.8%	−5.5%	−5.7%	−9.4%	−9.1%

interest: 1985 to 1991 and 1991 to 1996. As previously noted, homicide rates increased 32% overall from 1985 to 1991. The rate for black males between the ages of 14 to 17 increased an average of 21.2% annually during this period, the largest increase in homicide offending rates of any group. Over these 7 years, the rate among black male teenagers increased a total of 218%, from 62.7 to 199.1 per 100,000. During the same time period, the rate for white male teens increased an average of 14.5% per year with an overall increase of 126% (from 9.7 in 1985 to 21.9 in 1991); although not quite comparable to that for their black counterparts, this boost in crime involvement for white male teenagers nonetheless was substantial. The rates for female teens also increased during the late 1980s, with a 4.5% annual increase for whites and a 10.6% annual increase for blacks. Among all combinations of race and sex, the increases for teens from 1985 to 1991 were consistently higher than for older offenders.

The patterns of change in offending for young adults (18- to 24-year-olds) were roughly similar to those of their teenage counterparts. The overall increase from 1985 to 1991 for black males aged 18 to 24 was nearly four times greater than that for white males in the same age group (152% vs. 43%, respectively). The average annual percentage increase for young adult black males was 16.7%, surpassed only by the rate of increase for black male teenagers. Among young adult females, the offending rate for blacks increased 25% overall from 1985 to 1991 compared to 13% overall for whites.

Patterns for older adults were significantly different from those for younger age groups. From 1985 to 1991, while the youth rates soared, homicide offending decreased or remained relatively stable for all race–sex subgroups of adults ages 25 and over.

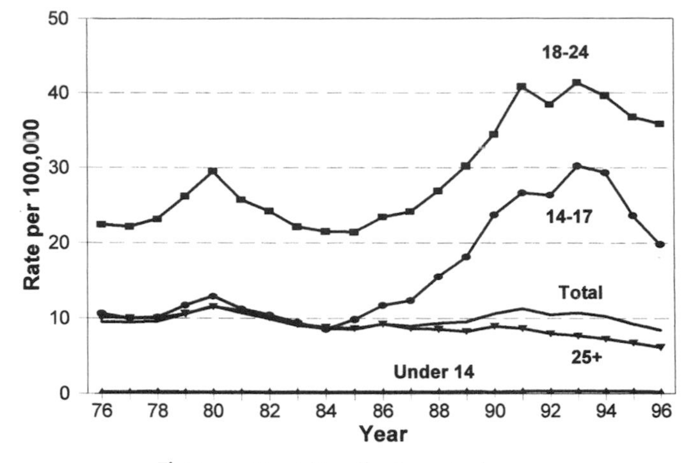

Figure 6. Homicide offending rates by age.

The decreases seen in overall offending rates since 1991 were not universal across race and sex. Homicide offending rates decreased for every age, sex, and race group with the exception of young white females (14- to 17-year-olds and 18- to 24-year-olds). Despite this countervailing trend, white females maintained the lowest homicide offending rates throughout the 21-year period.

The most prominent changes in homicide offending are displayed in Figs. 7 and 8. While the scale for black males is ten times that for white males, the general patterns of change are remarkably similar across racial lines. For younger blacks and whites, rates of male offending rose sharply in the late 1980s before falling recently. The rate among adults (25 and over) declined steadily for males of both races throughout the two decades.

By far the most noteworthy shift during the past two decades occurred among teenage boys. Prior to the mid-1980s, teenage boys of both races committed homicide at the same low level as their parents' generation. Since 1985, however, teens have participated in homicide at a much higher level, more akin to that of their older brothers' generation.

For another perspective of change over time, Table 4 shows the age, sex, and race distribution of homicide victims and offenders in comparison to their respective shares of the US population. This table generally confirms our previous observation that teenagers and young adults are overrepresented as offenders throughout the period from 1976 to 1996. By contrast, children 13 and under are underrepresented as victims and especially as offenders.

Teenagers have been overrepresented as offenders and, until recently, underrepresented as victims. Young adults are consistently overrepresented as offenders and to a lesser extent as victims throughout the time period. Adults over 25 also had been overrepresented as victims and offenders until the late 1980s. Since 1986, as the typical age of offenders shifted downward, adults have been underrepresented as offenders; after 1991, adults have been underrepresented as victims as well.

The representation of different age groups in homicide victimization and offending varies considerably by race and sex. As Fig. 9 shows in detail, since 1976, teenage white males have declined as a percentage of the population yet their representation among victims and offenders has increased. Compared to their share of the population, teenage white males were proportionately represented as offenders until the mid-1980s (when their involvement in-

Table 3. Estimated Homicide Offending Rates per 100,000 Population by Age, Sex, and Race

	14–17 years				18–24 years				25+ years			
	Male		Female		Male		Female		Male		Female	
Year	White	Black	White	Black	White	Black	White	Black	White	Black	White	Black
1976	10.4	72.4	1.3	10.3	21.3	166.4	2.6	30.0	9.4	98.3	1.6	22.3
1977	10.6	66.6	1.3	6.2	21.7	155.4	2.7	29.0	9.8	93.3	1.6	21.2
1978	10.7	64.5	1.2	7.9	23.7	161.2	2.6	26.6	10.0	93.1	1.5	19.3
1979	13.3	70.0	1.2	8.3	26.8	181.5	2.8	27.1	10.8	97.7	1.6	18.6
1980	13.6	85.2	1.1	8.0	30.2	207.9	2.9	30.6	12.1	104.1	1.7	19.2
1981	10.9	73.1	1.3	8.6	26.9	173.1	2.5	24.5	11.4	97.1	1.6	18.1
1982	11.3	61.6	1.2	5.9	24.3	160.2	2.8	25.5	10.9	83.6	1.6	15.8
1983	10.3	50.5	1.6	7.0	23.5	137.7	2.4	23.1	9.7	76.9	1.5	14.2
1984	9.4	47.6	1.2	6.2	24.5	124.2	2.7	19.6	9.8	71.6	1.3	13.1
1985	9.7	62.7	1.0	6.6	22.8	133.7	2.3	18.7	9.7	68.6	1.2	12.9
1986	12.3	72.2	1.1	5.6	24.3	149.9	2.4	20.8	9.9	76.5	1.2	13.2
1987	11.4	81.7	1.4	7.3	23.8	163.0	2.8	17.5	9.7	69.3	1.2	11.6
1988	13.9	111.9	1.0	7.4	23.0	204.0	2.6	22.6	9.1	72.7	1.1	11.5
1989	14.9	141.0	1.0	7.7	25.8	236.9	2.7	19.0	8.8	68.7	1.1	11.7
1990	20.6	175.3	1.5	7.5	30.2	266.7	2.9	20.9	9.3	78.4	1.1	11.0
1991	21.9	199.1	1.3	12.1	32.6	337.5	2.6	23.4	9.4	71.7	1.1	11.2
1992	21.8	195.2	1.4	11.1	31.3	312.0	2.3	19.2	8.2	67.9	1.0	10.1
1993	21.8	244.1	1.5	9.3	31.5	347.6	2.2	21.3	8.0	63.8	1.1	9.4
1994	22.4	226.7	1.4	9.7	31.1	329.8	2.1	20.1	7.7	58.5	1.0	9.6
1995	20.8	165.7	1.4	8.1	31.6	288.1	2.0	15.3	7.5	53.6	0.9	7.2
1996	17.2	133.5	1.7	7.6	30.9	268.0	2.7	18.1	6.6	49.9	0.9	7.2
Average change												
1985–91	14.5%	21.2%	4.5%	10.6%	6.1%	16.7%	2.1%	3.8%	−0.5%	0.7%	−1.4%	−2.3%
1991–96	−4.7%	−7.7%	5.5%	−8.9%	−1.1%	−4.5%	0.8%	−5.1%	−6.8%	−7.0%	−3.9%	−8.5%
1993–96	−7.6%	−18.2%	4.3%	−6.5%	−0.6%	−8.3%	7.1%	−5.5%	−6.2%	−7.9%	−6.5%	−8.5%

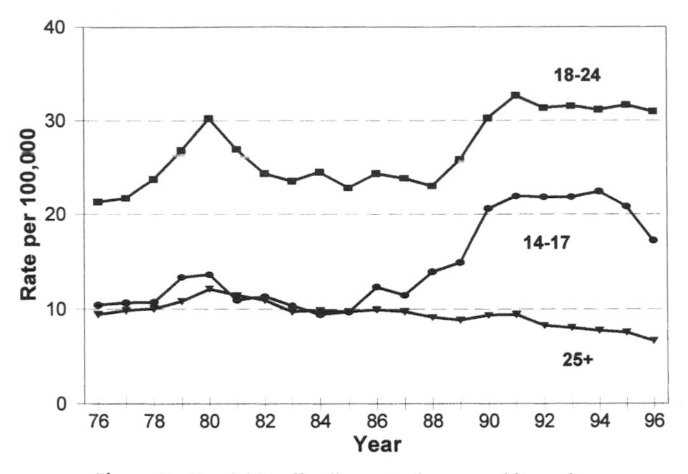

Figure 7. Homicide offending rates by age, white males.

creased) and were disproportionately represented as victims until an increase occurred in the mid-1990s.

The pattern for black male teens is quite different (see Figure 10). Black male teens have remained approximately 0.5% of the population, yet since the mid-1980s have grown rapidly in terms of their share of both victims and offenders. By the 1990s, black male teens were overrepresented as victims by nearly a factor of 10 and as offenders by almost a factor of 20.

Returning to Table 4, the pattern for female offending and victimization appears to be different than that for males. Throughout the period from 1976 to 1996, teenage black females were victims and offenders in almost equal proportions to their share of the population. While this may seem at first to be encouraging, black females were still at a significant disadvantage compared to their white counterparts. During this period, teenage white females were consistently underrepresented as victims and especially as offenders.

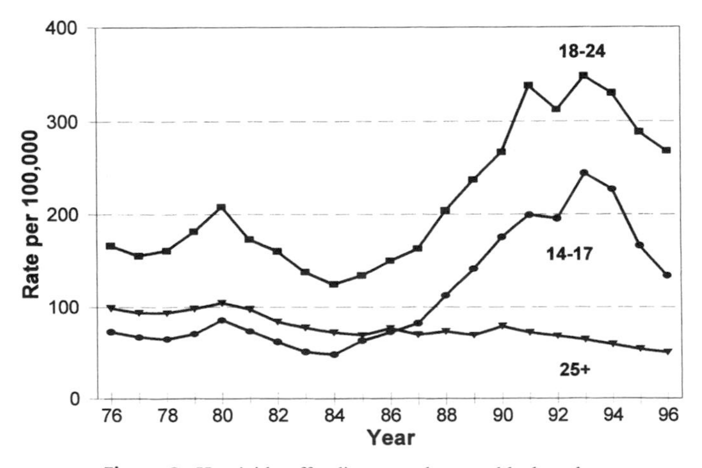

Figure 8. Homicide offending rates by age, black males.

Table 4. Population, Victims, and Offenders by Age, Race, and Sex

	Under 14				14–17 years				18–24 years				25+ years			
	Male		Female		Male		Female		Male		Female		Male		Female	
	White	Black	White	Black	White	Black	White	Black	White	Black	White	Black	White	Black	White	Black
1976–1980																
Population	9.4%	1.6%	9.0%	1.6%	3.3%	0.5%	3.2%	0.5%	5.8%	0.8%	5.7%	0.9%	24.8%	2.5%	27.5%	3.1%
Victims	1.4%	1.0%	1.2%	0.8%	1.6%	1.3%	0.8%	0.4%	8.7%	8.0%	2.9%	2.3%	28.4%	25.8%	9.5%	5.9%
Offenders	0.2%	0.2%	0.0%	0.0%	3.7%	3.6%	0.4%	0.4%	14.0%	13.9%	1.5%	2.4%	25.3%	23.9%	4.3%	6.0%
1981–1985																
Population	8.8%	1.6%	8.4%	1.6%	2.8%	0.5%	2.7%	0.5%	5.5%	0.9%	5.3%	0.9%	25.7%	2.8%	28.5%	3.5%
Victims	1.4%	1.0%	1.3%	0.8%	1.3%	1.3%	0.7%	0.4%	8.5%	7.3%	3.0%	2.0%	29.7%	24.7%	10.7%	5.7%
Offenders	0.2%	0.1%	0.0%	0.0%	3.1%	3.1%	0.4%	0.4%	14.2%	13.2%	1.4%	2.1%	28.0%	23.9%	4.3%	5.5%
1986–1990																
Population	8.6%	1.6%	8.2%	1.6%	2.5%	0.5%	2.4%	0.4%	4.8%	0.8%	4.6%	0.8%	26.8%	3.1%	29.5%	3.8%
Victims	1.4%	1.0%	1.2%	0.9%	1.4%	2.3%	0.6%	0.4%	7.6%	10.6%	2.4%	1.9%	26.4%	25.0%	10.3%	6.3%
Offenders	0.2%	0.2%	0.0%	0.0%	3.7%	5.5%	0.3%	0.3%	12.7%	16.8%	1.3%	1.7%	25.8%	23.3%	3.5%	4.6%
1991–1996																
Population	8.8%	1.7%	8.3%	1.7%	2.3%	0.4%	2.2%	0.4%	4.3%	0.8%	4.1%	0.8%	27.3%	3.3%	29.7%	4.0%
Victims	1.4%	1.2%	1.2%	0.9%	2.3%	3.4%	0.6%	0.5%	8.3%	14.1%	1.9%	1.8%	23.8%	23.4%	9.1%	6.1%
Offenders	0.2%	0.3%	0.0%	0.0%	4.8%	8.5%	0.3%	0.4%	13.2%	23.1%	0.9%	1.5%	21.0%	19.5%	2.9%	3.6%

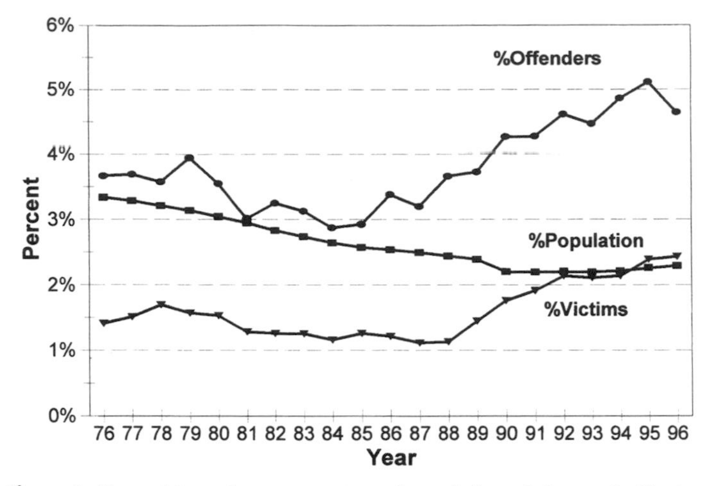

Figure 9. Teen white males as percentage of population, victims, and offenders.

FUTURE DEMOGRAPHIC CHANGE

The findings from this analysis confirm that the level of serious crime is indeed influenced greatly by age and race characteristics of the population, and that age- and race-specific rates reveal very different patterns of change over time. Moreover, even with the downturn since 1993, the rate of youth violence remains considerably above that of previous eras. This phenomenon is confirmed by both official and victim survey data, dispelling the assertion that the increase in youth violence is a myth created by increased police attention to these crimes (see Zimring, 1998). What makes the recent surge in the volume of youth crime particularly noteworthy is that it occurred while the population of teens was on the decline. The volume of youth violence rose during the late 1980s, despite a declining population in the 14- to 17-year-old age group.

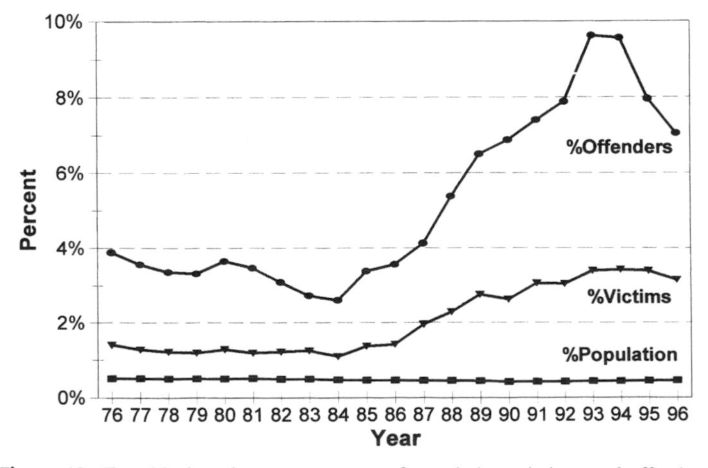

Figure 10. Teen black males as percentage of population, victims, and offenders.

The demographic shrinkage in the size of the adolescent population is now over, however, and the number of teenagers is beginning to rebound. In fact, the population of 14- to 17-year-olds is expected to rise over the next decade, as the offspring of the baby-boomers mature into their adolescence. Specifically, the number of teens aged 14 to 17 should increase by about 15% by the year 2005, or about 2% annually.

This demographic turnaround is precisely what prompted several observers to predict a future wave of youth violence (DiIulio, 1995; Fox, 1995, 1996a,b, 1997b; Snyder & Sickmund, 1995; Bennett, DiIulio, & Walters, 1996). In reaction to these bleak and worrisome projections, critics have questioned the size and significance of the expected demographic shift (see Austin & Cohen, 1996; Murphy, 1996; Blumstein & Rosenfeld 1998). Murphy (1996, p. 4), for example, argued:

> The male "at risk" population is expected to increase over the next decade, and this trend has led some to conclude that we need to brace ourselves for a new crime wave of juvenile violent crime that may well negate recent declines in violent crime rates. *However, a closer look at population projections shows that while the numbers of youth age 15–24 will increase, this increase will not exceed that for the 1980s.* (Emphasis in the original)

In an overall sense, Murphy and other critics are quite correct. The population count of teens and young adults, though expected to increase, will not even achieve levels that existed in the late 1970s, prior to the 1980s shrinkage in the at-risk population.

What Murphy and others overlook, however, is that the race-specific age curves, although similar, differ in rather important ways. Figure 11 displays the teen population projections separately for white and black youth (with the black population count magnified by a factor of 7 to aid in the comparison). While the overall pattern of a downturn during the 1980s, a trough at 1990, and an increase thereafter are alike, the slopes for the black population are greater. The projected rise in the white teen population is modest and the numbers are expected to plateau at a level below that of the mid-1970s. For black youth, however, the population already has exceeded that of the mid-1970s and will continue to rise sharply for decades to come. Given the higher rates of violence perpetrated by black youth as compared with white youth, the disproportionate increase in the number of black teenagers could have a significant impact on

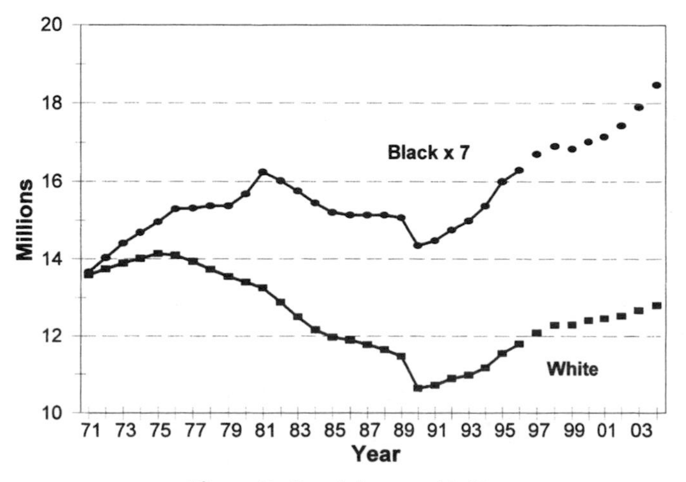

Figure 11. Population ages 14–17.

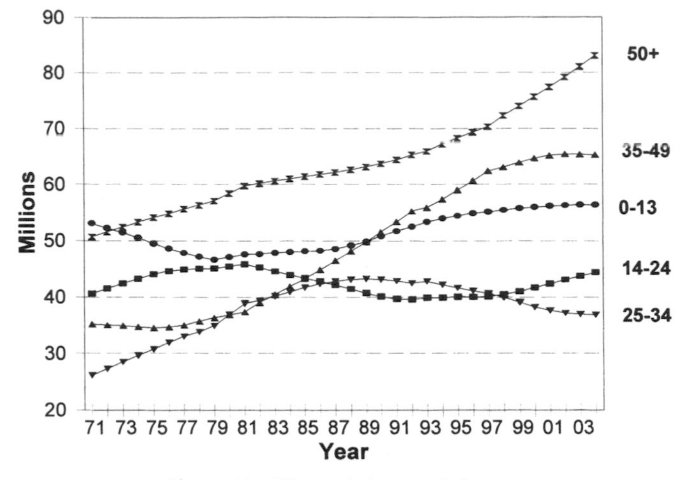

Figure 12. US population trends by age.

the level of youth violence in the years ahead. Even if the rate of teen murder returns to the lower level of the mid-1980s (before the sharp rise in teen violence reported here), the number of teen killings could once again surge as a result of an increase in the population at risk.

It is critically important to place these grim projections into a larger demographic setting. Figure 12 displays population projections for five different age groups: the "high-risk" group of 14- to 24-year-olds along with children under 14 and various subpopulations of adults. The younger age groups will expand, while the number of 25- to 34-year-olds will decline. For older groups, the population 35 to 49 will increase and then level, while the population 50 and over—the aging baby boom cohort—will surge more than any other group. In fact, by the middle of the next decade, the population 50 and over will constitute nearly a third of the US population. Given the rather low proclivity of this group toward violence, the overall rate of violent crime in America will likely continue to fall. That is, the declining level of violence perpetrated by a greatly expanded elder population will more than balance the possible increasing level of violence from a modestly growing teen population.

It is also important, however, not to be misled by aggregates. Even if the FBI announces further declines in violent crime in the years ahead (as they are likely to do), we must look closely within the totals to track the trends in youth violence. The long-term future and health of our nation depends on our ability to control youthful offending, even if it is overshadowed by the "graying" of America.

Even with recent sharp declines in crime, we must resist the sense of complacency that now seems to be settling in over America. Youth crime may be down, but it is far from out. Not only will there be a turnaround in the size of the at-risk population, but the teenage population is regenerated every 5 years. Without continued efforts, we run the risk of having history repeat itself. Now that crime is down, if anything, we should increase our investment in children.

ACKNOWLEDGMENTS

This research was supported by grants from the Bureau of Justice Statistics of the United State Department of Justice and the Charles Stewart Mott Foundation. The views expressed do not necessarily reflect the official position of either organization.

REFERENCES

Austin, J., & Cohen, R. L. (1996). *Why are crime rates declining: An NCCD briefing report*. San Francisco: National Council on Crime and Delinquency.

Barnett, A., & Goranson, J. (1996). Misapplications reviews: Good news is no news? *Interfaces*, *26*, 35–39.

Bennett, W. J., DiIulio, J. J., & Walters, J. P. (1996). *Body count: Moral poverty and how to win America's war against crime and drugs*. New York: Simon and Schuster.

Blumstein, A., & Nagin, D. S. (1975). Analysis of arrest rates for trends in criminality. *Socio-Economic Planning Sciences*, *9*, 221–227.

Blumstein, A., & Rosenfeld, R. (1998). Explaining recent trends in U.S. homicide rates. *Journal of Criminal Law and Criminology*, *88*, 1175–1216.

Blumstein, A., Cohen, J., & Miller, H. D. (1981). Demographically disaggregated projections of prison populations. *Research in Public Policy Analysis and Management*, *1*, 3–37.

Chilton, R. (1982). Analyzing urban crime data: Deterrence and the limitations of arrest offense ratios. *Criminology*, *19*, 590–607.

Chilton, R. (1986). Age, sex, race, and arrest trends for 12 of the nation's largest central cities. In J. M. Byrne & R, J, Sampson (Eds.), *The Social Ecology of Crime* (pp. 102–115). New York: Springer-Verlag.

Chilton, R. (1987). Twenty years of homicide and robbery in Chicago: The impact of the city's changing racial and age composition. *Journal of Quantitative Criminology*, *3*,195–214.

Chilton, R. (1991). Urban crime trends and criminological theory. *Criminal Justice Research Bulletin*, *6*, 3–12.

Chilton, R., & Spielberger, A. (1971). Is delinquency increasing? Age structure and the crime rate. *Social Forces*, *49*, 487–493.

Cohen, L. E., & Land, K. C. (1987). Age structure and crime: Symmetry versus asymmetry and the projection of crime rates through the 1990s. *American Sociological Review*, *52*, 170–183.

DiIulio, J. (1995, November 27). The coming of the super-predators. *Weekly Standard*, p. 23.

Farrington, D., & Langan, P. (1992). Changes in crime and punishment in England and America in the 1980s. *Justice Quarterly*, *9*(1), 5–46.

Ferdinand, T.N. (1970). Demographic shifts and criminality: An inquiry. *British Journal of Criminology*, *10*, 169–175.

Fox, J. A (1978). *Forecasting crime data*. Lexington, MA: Lexington Books.

Fox, J. A. (1995). *Homicide offending patterns, 1976–1993*. Paper read at the Annual Meeting of the American Academy for the Advancement of Science, Atlanta, GA, February 18, 1995.

Fox, J. A. (1996a, March). *Trends in juvenile violence: A report to the United States Attorney General on current and future rates of juvenile offending*. Washington, DC: US Department of Justice, Bureau of Justice Statistics.

Fox, J. A. (1996b, September). The calm before the juvenile crime storm. *Population Today*, pp. 4–5.

Fox J. A. (1997a, April). Missing data problems in the supplementary homicide reports: An offender imputation strategy based on victim characteristics. Bureau of Justice Statistics Workshop of Crime Imputation.

Fox, J.A. (1997b, November). *Trends in juvenile homicide, 1976–1996: An update of the March 1996 report to the U.S. Attorney General on current and future rates of juvenile violence*. Washington, DC: US Department of Justice, Bureau of Justice Statistics.

Fox, J. A., & Zawitz, M. W. (1998, December 4). Homicide trends in the United States. [Online]; http://www.ojp.usdoj.gov/bjs/homicide/homtrnd.htm. Washington, DC: US Department of Justice, Bureau of Justice Statistics.

Hindelang, M.J. (1978). Race and involvement in common law personal crimes. *American Sociological Review*, *43*, 93–109.

Johnson, H., & Lazarus, G. (1989). The impact of age on crime victimization rates. *Canadian Journal of Criminology*, *31*, 309–317.

Langan, P. A. (1991). America's soaring prison population. *Science*, *251*, 1568–1573.

Laub, J. H. (1983). Urbanism, race, and crime. *Journal of Research in Crime and Delinquency*, *20*, 183–198.

Lee, G. W. (1984). Are crime rates increasing? A study of the impact of demographic shifts on crime rates in Canada. *Canadian Journal of Criminology*, *26*, 29–41.

MacKenzie, D. L., Tracy, G. S., & Williams, G. (1988). Incarceration rates and demographic changes: A test of the demographic change hypothesis. *Journal of Criminal Justice*, *16*, 241–253.

Markides, K. S., & Tracy, G. S. (1977). The effect of the age structure of a stationary population on crime rates. *Journal of Criminal Law and Criminology*, *67*, 351–355.

Marvell, T. B., & Moody, C. E. Jr. (1991). Age structure and crime rates: The conflicting evidence. *Journal of Quantitative Criminology*, *7*, 237–273.

Maxim, P. S., & Jocklin, A. (1980). Population size, age structure, and sex composition effects on official crime in Canada. *International Journal of Comparative and Applied Criminal Justice*, *4*, 147–163.

Moynihan, D. P. (1973). Peace: Some thought on the 1960s and 1970s. *The Public Interest*, *32*(Summer), 3–12.

Murphy, L. (1996, May 14). Statement before the congressional black caucus brain trust on juvenile justice. Washington, DC.
President's Commission on Law Enforcement and the Administration of Justice. (1967). *Task force report: Crime and its impact—an assessment*. Washington DC: US Government Printing Office.
Quinney, R. (1964). Crime, delinquency, and social areas. *Journal of Research in Crime and Delinquency, 1*, 149–154.
Sagi, P. C., & Wellford, C. F. (1968). Age composition and patterns of change in criminal statistics. *Journal of Criminal Law, Criminology and Police Science, 59*, 29–36.
Schwartz, J., & Exter, T. (1990). Crime stoppers. *American Demographics, 12*, 24–30.
Silberman, C. E. (1978). *Criminal violence, criminal justice*. New York: Random House.
Snyder, H., & Sickmund, M. (1995). *Juvenile offenders and victims: A national report*. Washington, DC: US Department of Justice.
Steffensmeier, D. J., & Harer, M.D. (1987). Is the crime rate really falling? An "aging" U.S. population and its impact on the nation's crime rate, 1980–1984. *Journal of Research In Crime and Delinquency, 24*, 23–48.
Steffensmeier, D. J., & Harer, M. D. (1991). Did crime rise or fall during the Reagan presidency? The effects of an "aging" U.S. population on the nation's crime rate. *Journal of Research in Crime and Delinquency, 28*, 330–359.
Wellford, C. F. (1973). Age composition and the increase in recorded crime. *Criminology, 11*, 61–70.
Wilson, J. Q., & Dupont, R. C. (1973). The sick sixties. *Atlantic, 232*.
Zimring, F. E. (1998). *American youth violence*. New York: Oxford University Press.

7

Girls, Violence, and Delinquency

Popular Myths and Persistent Problems

MEDA CHESNEY-LIND

Every year, girls account for one out of four arrests of young people in America (Federal Bureau of Investigation, 1995, p. 226). Despite this, the young women who find themselves in the juvenile justice system either by formal arrest or by referral[1] are almost completely invisible. Our stereotype of the juvenile delinquent is so indisputably male that the general public, those experts whose careers in criminology have been built studying "delinquency," and those practitioners working with delinquent youth rarely if ever consider girls and their problems.

This invisibility has worked against young women in several distinct ways. Despite the fact that a considerable number of girls are arrested, the theories of delinquency either explicitly or implicitly avoided them. The academic neglect of girls' lives left undocumented the serious problems, particularly sexual and physical abuse, that sometimes propel girls into behavior that is labeled as delinquent. The lack of solid information on girls also facilitates the periodic "discovery" and demonization of girls' delinquency, particularly girls' violence. Finally, the silence at the academic and policy levels meant that those who worked with girls had virtually no guidance in shaping programs or developing resources that would respond to the problems many girls, particularly girls on the economic margins, experienced.

TRENDS IN GIRLS' ARRESTS

Why are the girls we arrest so invisible, when in 1994 they accounted for 24% of all juvenile arrests (Federal Bureau of Investigation, 1995, p. 226)? Much of this has to do with the sorts of delinquent acts that girls commit. Though many may not realize it, youth can be taken into custody for *both* criminal acts and a wide variety of what are often called "status offenses."

Status offenses, in contrast to criminal violations, permit the arrest of youth for a wide range of behaviors that are violations of parental authority: "running away from home,"

MEDA CHESNEY-LIND • Women's Studies Program, University of Hawaii at Manoa, Honolulu, Hawaii 96822.

Handbook of Youth and Justice, edited by White. Kluwer Academic / Plenum Publishers, New York, 2001.

"being a person in need of supervision," "minor in need of supervision," being "incorrigible," "beyond control," truant, in need of "care and protection." While not technically crimes, these offenses can result in a youth's arrest and involvement in the criminal justice system. Juvenile delinquents, as a category, includes youths arrested for either criminal or noncriminal status offenses. Finally, as this chapter will show, status offenses play a major role in girls' delinquency.

Examining the types of offenses for which youth are actually arrested, it is clear that most youths are arrested for the less serious criminal acts and status offenses. Of the 2 million youth arrested in 1994, for example, only 5.8% of these arrests were for such serious violent offenses as murder, rape, robbery, or aggravated assault (Federal Bureau of Investigation, 1995, p. 226). In contrast, about one fifth (19%) were arrested for a single offense (larceny theft), much of which, particularly for girls, is shoplifting (Shelden & Horvath, 1986).

Table 1 presents the five most frequent offenses for which male and female youth were arrested in 1985 and 1994. From this it can be seen that while less serious offenses dominate both male and female delinquency, trivial offenses, particularly status offenses and larceny theft (shoplifting), are more significant in the case of girls' arrests. For example, the five offenses listed in Table 1 accounted for nearly three quarters of female arrests (72%) during the two periods reviewed and only slightly more than half of male offenses (55%).

Looking at Table 1, it is clear that status offenses play a significant role in girls' official delinquency. Status offenses accounted for about 23% of all girls' arrests in 1994, but only about 8.6% of boys' arrests, figures that remained relatively stable during the last decade (and over previous decades) (see Chesney-Lind & Shelden 1992).

This stability is somewhat surprising since dramatic declines in arrests of youth for these offenses might have been expected as a result of the passage of the Juvenile Justice and Delinquency Prevention Act in 1974. This act, among other things, encouraged jurisdictions to divert and deinstitutionalize youth charged with noncriminal offenses. While the number of youth arrested for status offenses did drop considerably in the 1970s (arrests of girls for these offenses fell by 24%, and arrests of boys fell by an even greater amount—66%) (Federal Bureau of Investigation, 1980, p. 191), this trend was reversed in the 1980s. Between 1985 and 1994, for example, girls' runaway arrests increased by 18.0%, and arrests of girls for curfew violations increased by 83.1%. (Federal Bureau of Investigation, 1995, p. 222).

For many years statistics showing large numbers of girls arrested for status offenses were taken to be representative of the different types of male and female delinquency. However, self-report studies of male and female delinquency (which ask school age youth if they have committed delinquent acts) do not reflect the dramatic differences in misbehavior found in official statistics. Specifically, it appears that girls charged with these noncriminal status offenses have been and continue to be significantly overrepresented in court populations. As an example, Canter (1982) found in a National Youth Survey that there was no evidence of greater female involvement, compared to males, in any category of delinquent behavior. Indeed, in this sample, males were significantly more likely than females to report status offenses (see Chesney-Lind & Shelden, 1992, for a summary of other studies).

GIRLS AND VIOLENCE: IS GIRL'S DELINQUENCY CHANGING?

Discussions of youthful violence, particularly those appearing in the popular media, have increasingly featured assertions that girls as well as boys are acting out violent ways. This has been particularly true of media characterizations of girls in gangs. On August 2, 1993, for

Table 1. Rank Order of Adolescent Male and Female Arrests for Specific Offenses, 1985 and 1994[a]

Male				Female			
Arrests 1985	% of total	Arrests 1994	% of total	Arrests 1985	% of total	Arrests 1994	% of total
(1) Larceny-theft	20.2	(1) Larceny-theft	17.2	(1) Larceny-theft	26.4	(1) Larcency-theft	25.6
(2) Other offenses	16.8	(2) Other offenses	16.4	(2) Runaway	20.2	(2) Runaway	17.1
(3) Burglary	10.0	(3) Other assaults	7.7	(3) Other offenses	15.4	(3) Other offenses	14.4
(4) Vandalism	6.6	(4) Drug abuse	7.1	(4) Liquor laws	7.3	(4) Other assaults	8.6
(5) Liquor laws	5.8	(5) Vandalism	6.7	(5) Other assaults	4.9	(5) Disorderly conduct	6.0

Male	1985	1994	Female	1985	1994
Arrests for serious violent offenses[b]	4.9	6.6	Arrests for serious violent offenses[b]	2.1	3.4
Arrests for all violent offenses[c]	9.6	14.3	Arrests for all violent offenses[c]	7.0	12.0
Arrests for status offenses[d]	8.2	8.6	Arrests for status offenses[d]	24.6	22.9

[a]Compiled from Federal Bureau of Investigation (1994, p. 222).
[b]Arrests for murder and nonnegligent manslaughter, robbery, forcible rape, and aggravated assault.
[c]Also includes arrests for other assaults.
[d]Arrests for curfew and loitering law violation and runaway.

example, in a feature spread on teen violence, *Newsweek* had a box entitled "Girls Will Be Girls," which noted that "some girls now carry guns. Others hide razor blades in their mouths" (Leslie, Biddle, Rosenberg, & Wayne, 1993, p. 44). Explaining this trend, the article notes that, "The plague of teen violence is an equal-opportunity scourge. Crime by girls is on the rise, or so various jurisdictions report" (Leslie et al., 1993, p. 44) (see Chesney-Lind, 1997, for a review of these representations).

A review of girls' arrests for violent crime for the last decade (1985–1994) (see Table 2) initially seems to provide support for the notion that girls are engaged in dramatically more violent crime than a decade earlier. Arrests of girls for murder were up 64.2%, robbery arrests were up 114%, and aggravated assault was up 136.8%. Indeed, arrests of girls for all part 1 offenses[2] were up 42% (Federal Bureau of Investigation, 1995, p. 222). Changes in arrest rates,

Table 2. Trends in Arrest of Girls and Boys, 1985–1994[a]

Offense	Percent change	
	Male	Female
Total	25.1	39.5
Murder and nonnegligent manslaughter	158.3	64.2
Forcible rape	5.5	7.6
Robbery	52.9	114.5
Aggravated assault	89.8	136.8
Burglary	−20.8	6.1
Larceny theft	6.5	35.2
Motor vehicle theft	68.6	113.1
Arson	34.0	82.4
Violent crime	68.6	128.3
Property crime	4.1	36.2
Crime index total	12.4	42.0
Other assaults	105.0	143.1
Forgery and counterfeiting	−11.0	10.9
Fraud	0.3	22.3
Embezzlement	14.1	46.5
Stolen property; buy, receive, possess	29.9	55.9
Vandalism	26.5	54.2
Weapons; carrying, possessing, etc.	101.0	137.3
Prostitution and commercialized vice	−28.3	−71.6
Sex offenses (except forcible rape and prostitution)	−0.9	−3.4
Drug abuse violations	72.0	31.4
Gambling	95.6	144.8
Offenses against family and children	72.1	71.7
Driving under the influence	−42.8	−38.1
Liquor laws	−13.9	−5.3
Drunkenness	−36.9	−37.4
Disorderly conduct	63.8	110.1
Vagrancy	37.7	46.3
All other offenses (except traffic)	21.5	30.3
Suspicion (not included in totals)	−33.5	−37.9
Curfew and loitering law violations	44.7	83.1
Runaways	19.4	18.0

[a]From Federal Bureau of Investigation (1994, p. 222).

which adjust for changes in the population of girls in certain time periods, show much the same pattern (see Table 2).

These increases certainly sound substantial, but they actually are considerably less dramatic on closer inspection. First, the numbers of boys arrested for these offenses have increased during the last decade, so the increase in girls' arrests more or less parallels increases in the arrests of male youth. This pattern, then, reflects overall changes in youth behavior rather than dramatic changes and shifts in the character of girls' behavior.

Serious crimes of violence also are a very small proportion of all girls' delinquency, and that figure has remained essentially unchanged. Only 2.1% of girls' arrests in 1985 were for serious crimes of violence. By 1994, this figure had climbed to 3.4% (16,426 arrests out of a total of 483,578 arrests). Moreover, girls' share of serious crimes of violence (i.e., the sex ratio for these offenses) has changed very little during the two time periods. In 1985, for example, arrests of girls accounted for 11% of all arrests of youth for serious crimes of violence; in 1994, the comparable figure was 14% (Federal Bureau of Investigation, 1995, p. 222).

Relabeling of behaviors that were once categorized as status offenses into violent offenses cannot be ruled out in explanations of arrest rates. A review of the over 2000 cases of girls referred to Maryland's juvenile justice system for "person-to-person" offenses revealed that virtually all these offenses (97.9%) involved "assault." A further examination of these records revealed that about half were "family centered" and involved such activities as "a girl hitting her mother and her mother subsequently pressing charges" (Mayer, 1994). Other mechanisms for relabeling status offenses into criminal offenses include police officers advising parents to block the doorways when their children threaten to run away and then charging the youth with "assault" when they shove their way past their parents (R. Shelden, personal communication, 1995). Such relabeling, which is also called bootstrapping, has been particularly pronounced in the official delinquency of African-American girls (Robinson, 1990; Bartollas, 1993); this practice also facilitates the incarceration of girls in detention facilities and training schools, something that would not be possible if the girl were arrested for noncriminal status offenses.

When exploring the dramatic increases in the arrests of girls for "other assaults" (which increased by 126.2% in the last decade), it also is likely that enforcement practices have dramatically narrowed the gender gap. Minor or "other" assaults can range from schoolyard tussles to relatively serious but not life-threatening assaults (Steffensmeier & Steffensmeier, 1980). These authors first noted a increasing tendency to arrest girls for these offenses in the 1970s and commented that "evidence suggests that female arrests for 'other assaults' are relatively non-serious in nature and tend to consist of being bystanders or companions to males involved in skirmishes, fights, and so on" (Steffensmeier & Steffensmeier, 1980, p. 70).

Detailed comparisons drawn from supplemental homicide reports from unpublished FBI data also hint at the central rather than peripheral way in which gender colored and differentiated girls' and boys' violence. A study of these FBI data on the characteristics of girls' and boys' homicides, between 1984 and 1993, found that girls accounted for "proportionately fewer homicides in 1993 (6%) than in 1984 (14%)" (Loper & Cornell, 1996, p. 324). Their work shows that girls' choice of weapons differed from boys so that in comparison to boys' homicides, girls who killed were more likely to use a knife than a gun and to murder someone as a result of conflict (rather than in the commission of a crime). Girls also were more likely than boys to murder family members (32%) and very young victims (24% of their victims were under the age of 3 compared to 1% of the boy's victims) (Loper & Cornell, 1996, p. 328). When involved in a peer homicide, girls were more likely than boys to have killed "as a result of an interpersonal conflict"; in addition, girls were more likely to kill alone, while boys were more likely to kill with an accomplice (Loper and Cornell, 1996, p. 328). The authors concluded that "the stereotype of girls becoming gun-toting robbers was not supported. The dramatic increase in gun-related homicides ... applies to boys but not girls" (Loper & Cornell, 1996, p. 332).

Trends in self-report data of youthful involvement in violent offenses also fail to show the dramatic changes found in official statistics. Specifically, a matched sample of "high-risk" youth (aged 13–17) surveyed in the 1977 National Youth Study and the more recent 1989 Denver Youth Survey revealed significant *decreases* in girls' involvement in felony assaults, minor assaults, and hard drugs, and no change in a wide range of other delinquent behaviors, including felony theft, minor theft, and index delinquency (Huizinga, personal communication, 1994).

A summary of two recent studies on self-reported aggression (see Table 3) also reflects that while about a third of girls reported having been in a physical fight in the last year, this was true of over half of the boys in both samples (Girls Incorporated, 1996, p. 13). Girls are far more likely to fight with a parent or sibling (34% compared to 9%) whereas boys are more likely to fight with friends or strangers. Finally, boys are two to three times more likely to report carrying a weapon in the past month (Girls Incorporated, 1996, p. 13).

AGGRESSION AND VIOLENCE: THE PSYCHOLOGICAL PERSPECTIVE

The psychological literature on aggression, which considers forms of aggression other than physical aggression (or violence), is also relevant here. Taken together, this literature generally reflects that while boys and men are more likely to be physically aggressive (though some contend this is due to boy's higher activity level) (Bjorkqvist & Niemela, 1992, p. 9), differences begin to even out when verbal aggression is considered (yelling, insulting, teasing). Further, girls in adolescence may be more likely than boys to use "indirect aggression" (such as gossip, telling bad or false stories, telling secrets) (Bjorkqvist, Osterman, & Kaukiai-

Table 3. Actual and Potential Involvement in Physical Violence

	Females (%)	Males (%)	Source[a]
Involved in			
Physical fight in the past year	34	51	Adams et al.
	32	51	Kann et al.
Four or more physical fights in the past year	9	15	Adams et al.
Fought with			
Stranger	7	15	Adams et al.
Friend	24	46	Adams et al.
Date/romantic partner	8	2	Adams et al.
Parent/sibling	34	9	Adams et al.
Other	4	6	Adams et al.
Several of the above	24	26	Adams et al.
Carried a weapon			
In the past month	7	17	Adams et al.
	9	34	Kann et al.

[a]Adams et al. (1995): ages 14–17, 1992 data; Kann et al. (1995): grades 9–12, 1993 data, in Girls, Inc. 1996.

nen, 1992, p. 55). When this broad definition of "aggression" is utilized, only about 5% of the variance in aggression is explained by gender (Bjorkqvist & Niemela, 1992).

Those who study aggression in young children and young adults also note that girls' aggression is usually within the home or "intrafemale," and thus, is likely to be less often reported to authorities (Bjorkqvist & Niemela, 1992, p. 7). The fact that these forms of aggression largely have been ignored by scholars as well as the general public also means that there is substantial room for girls' aggression to be "discovered" at a time where concern about youthful violence is heightened.

VIOLENCE, VICTIMIZATION, AND FEMALE DELINQUENCY

Estimates are that 34% of all girls will suffer some form of abuse before they reach adulthood (Benson, 1990). As just one example of this, girls under 18, who make up only 25% of the female population, were half of those who reported rapes in 1992 in states where such data are kept (Washington Post, 1994, p. A10). In states where information was kept on the perpetrator, it was found that these rapes often are perpetrated by family members and friends. As an example, of girls under 12 who reported rapes, 20% had been raped by their fathers, 46% had been assaulted by relatives, and 50% had been attacked by friends and acquaintances (Washington Post, 1994, p. A10). Given the amount of violence in girl's lives, the core question is not why are some girls violent, but why, in the face of such severe victimization, girls do not turn to violence more frequently.

Studies suggest that status offenses and other problems like early pregnancy and marriage are strongly related to the victimization of female children and adolescents by adults. Girls are roughly three quarters of those who are victimized by child sexual abuse. Beyond this, child sexual abuse begins earlier in the lives of girls compared to boys and persists longer, resulting in severe emotional and psychological dysfunction (Finkelhor & Baron, 1986; DeJong, Hervada, & Emmett, 1983; Browne & Finkelhor, 1986; Chesney-Lind & Sheldon, 1992).

The impact of childhood abuse on females shows up in studies of women incarcerated for crimes. Snell and Morton (1994) surveyed a random sample of women and men ($N = 13{,}986$) in prisons around the country during 1991 for the Bureau of Justice Statistics. For the first time, a government study asked questions about women's *and* men's experiences of sexual and physical violence as children. They found, when they asked these questions, that women in prisons have far higher rates of physical and sexual abuse than their male counterparts. Forty-three percent of the women surveyed "reported they had been abused at least once" before their current admission to prison, while the comparable figure for men was 12.2% (Snell & Morton, 1994, p. 5).

For about a third of all women in prison (31.7%), these authors found the abuse started when they were girls and continued into their adulthood. A key gender difference emerges here, since a number of young men who are in prison (10.7%) also report abuse as boys. Their abuse, however, does not continue to adulthood; about one in four women reporting that their abuse started as adults compared to only 3% of male offenders. Fully 33.5% of the women surveyed reported physical abuse and a slightly higher number (33.9%) had been sexually abused either as girls or young women compared to relatively small percentages of men (10% of boys and 5.3% of adult men in prison).

This research also queried women on their relationship with those who abused them. Predictably, both women and men report that parents and relatives contributed to the abuse they suffered as children, but women prisoners are far more likely than their male counterparts to say that domestic violence was a theme in their adult abuse; fully half of the women said they had been abused by a spouse/ex-spouse compared to only 3% of male inmates.

Sexual and physical abuse is highly implicated in mental illness, alcoholism, and addiction among adult women (Hamilton, 1989). Given these figures, status offending, particularly running away, figures as an adaptive response by girls to conditions of abuse and risk in the home (Chesney-Lind & Shelden, 1992). Yet, it is during those occasions when girls are attempting to evade abuse that they place themselves in other forms of jeopardy.

Adolescent girls experience violence in a variety of settings. While they experience some of the same patterns of violence and victimization perpetrated on adult women, there are important areas of difference. Research comparing female adolescent sexual assault victims with adult female victims indicates that adolescent females were more likely to be under the influence of alcohol or drugs at the time of the assault and to be more at risk for acquaintance rape compared to adult women (Muram, Hostetler, Jones, & Speck, 1995).

CRIMINALIZING GIRLS' SURVIVAL: ABUSE, VICTIMIZATION, AND GIRLS' OFFICIAL DELINQUENCY

Girls and their problems have long been ignored. When gender was considered in criminological theory, it was often as a "variable" in the testing of theories devised to explain boys' behavior and delinquency. As a result, few have considered the possibility that some if not many of the girls who are arrested and referred to court have unique and different sets of problems compared to the boys. Hints of these differences, though, abound.

As an example, it has been long understood that a major reason for the presence of many girls in the juvenile justice system was the fact that their parents insisted on their arrest. After all, who else would report a youth as having "run away" from home? In the early years, conflicts with parents were by far the most significant referral source; in Honolulu, 44% of the girls who appeared in court in 1929–1930 were referred by parents (Chesney-Lind, 1971).

Recent national data, while slightly less explicit, also show that girls are more likely to be referred to court by sources other than law enforcement agencies (which would include parents). In 1991, only 15% of youth referred for delinquency offenses but 58% of youth referred for status offenses were referred to court by non-law enforcement sources. The pattern among youth referred for status offenses, for which girls are overrepresented, also is clear. Well over half of the youth referred for running away from home (two thirds of whom were girls) and 92% of the youth charged with ungovernability (over half of whom were girls) were referred by non-law enforcement sources compared to only 9% of youth charged with liquor offenses (which was 72% male) (Butts et al., 1994; see also Pope & Feyerherm, 1982).

The fact that parents are often committed to two standards of adolescent behavior is one explanation for such a disparity, and one that should not be discounted as a major source of tension even in modern families. Despite expectations to the contrary, gender-specific socialization patterns have not changed very much, and this is especially true for parents' relationships with their daughters (Katz, 1979; Ianni, 1989; Thorne, 1993; Orenstein, 1994). It appears that even parents who oppose sexism in general, feel "uncomfortable tampering with existing traditions" and "do not want to risk their children becoming misfits" (Katz, 1979, p. 24).

Thorne, in her ethnography of gender in grade school, found that girls were still using "cosmetics, discussions of boyfriends, dressing sexually, and other forms of exaggerated 'teen' femininity to challenge adult, and class and race-based authority in schools" (Thorne,

1993, p. 156). She also found that "the double standard persists, and girls who are overtly sexual run the risk of being labeled sluts" (Thorne, 1993, p. 156).

Contemporary ethnographies of school life echo the validity of these parental perceptions. Orenstein's observations also point to the durability of the sexual double standard; at the schools she observed "sex 'ruins' girls; it enhanced boys" (Orenstein, 1994, p. 57). Parents, too, according to Thorne, have new reasons to enforce the time-honored sexual double standard. Perhaps correctly concerned about sexual harassment and rape, to say nothing of HIV/AIDS if their daughters are heterosexually active, "parents in gestures that mix protection with punishment, often tighten control of girls when they become adolescents, and sexuality becomes a terrain of struggle between the generations" (Thorne, 1993, p. 156). Finally, Thorne notes that as girls use sexuality as a proxy for independence; they sadly and ironically reinforce their status as sexual objects seeking male approval, ultimately ratifying their status as the subordinate sex.

Whatever the reason, parental attempts to adhere to and enforce the sexual double standard will continue to be a source of conflict between them and their daughters. Another important explanation for girls' problems with their parents that has received attention only in more recent years is the problem of physical and sexual abuse. Looking specifically at the problem of childhood sexual abuse, it is increasingly clear that this form of abuse is a particular problem for girls.

Girls, as noted above, are much more likely to be the victims of child sexual abuse than are boys. From a review of community studies, Finkelhor estimates that roughly 70% of the victims of sexual abuse are female (Finkelhor & Baron, 1986, p. 45). Girls' sexual abuse also tends to start earlier than boys (Finkelhor & Baron, 1986, p. 48), they are more likely than boys to be assaulted by a family member (often a stepfather) (DeJong et al., 1983; Russell, 1986), and as a consequence their abuse tends to last longer than male sexual abuse (DeJong et al., 1983). All these factors are associated with more severe trauma, causing dramatic short- and long-term effects in victims (Adams-Tucker, 1982). The effects noted by researchers in this area move from the more well-known "fear, anxiety, depression, anger and hostility, and inappropriate sexual behavior" (Browne & Finkelhor, 1986, p. 69) to behaviors of greater familiarity to criminologists, including running away from home, difficulties in school, truancy, and early marriage (Browne & Finkelhor, 1986).

Herman's (1981) study of incest survivors in therapy found that they were more likely to have run away from home than a matched sample of women whose fathers were "seductive" (33% compared to 5%). Another study of women patients found that 50% of the victims of child sexual abuse but only 20% of the nonvictim group had left home before the age of 18 (Meiselman, 1978).

National research on the characteristics of girls in the juvenile justice system clearly shows the role played by physical and sexual abuse in girls' delinquency. According to a study of girls in juvenile correctional settings conducted by the American Correctional Association (1990), a very large proportion of these girls—about half of whom were of minority backgrounds—had experienced physical abuse (61.2%), with nearly half saying that they had experienced this 11 or more times. Many had reported the abuse, but the results of this reporting were sobering, with the majority saying that either nothing changed (29.9%) or that the reporting just made things worse (25.3%). More than half of these girls (54.3%) had experienced sexual abuse, and for most this was not an isolated incident; a third reported that it happened 3–10 times and 27.4% reported that it happened 11 times or more. Most were 9 years of age or younger when the abuse began. Again, while most reported the abuse (68.1%), reporting the abuse tended to result in no change or in making things worse (American Correctional Association, 1990, pp. 56–58).

Given this history, it should be no surprise that the vast majority had run away from home (80.7%), and of those who had run, 39% had run 10 or more times. Over half (53.8%) said they had attempted suicide, and when asked the reason for this they said it was because they "felt no one cared" (American Correctional Association, 1990, p. 55). Finally, what might be called a survival or coping strategy is criminalized; girls in correctional establishments reported that their first arrests were typically for running away from home (20.5%) or for larceny theft (25.0%) (American Correctional Association, 1990, pp. 46–71).

Detailed studies of youth entering the juvenile justice system in Florida have compared the "constellations of problems" presented by girls and boys entering detention (Dembo, Williams, & Schmeidler, 1993; Dembo, Sue, Borden, & Manning, 1995). These researchers have found that female youth were more likely than male youth to have abuse histories and contact with the juvenile justice system for status offenses, while male youth had higher rates of involvement with various delinquent offenses. Further research on a larger cohort of youth ($N = 2104$) admitted to an assessment center in Tampa concluded that "girls' problem behavior commonly relates to an abusive and traumatizing home life, whereas boys' law violating behavior reflects their involvement in a delinquent life style" (Dembo et al., 1995, p. 21).

This portrait suggests that many young women are running away from profound sexual victimization at home, and once on the streets they are forced further into crime in order to survive. Interviews with girls who have run away from home show very clearly that they do not have a lot of attachment to their delinquent activities. In fact, they are angry about being labeled as delinquent, yet all engaged in illegal acts (Chesney-Lind & Shelden, 1992). A Wisconsin study found that 54% of the girls who ran away found it necessary to steal money, food, and clothing in order to survive. A few exchanged sexual contact for money, food, and/or shelter (Phelps, McIntosh, Jesudason, Warner, & Pohlkamp, 1982, p. 67). In their study of runaway youth, McCormack, Janus, and Burgess (1986, pp. 392–393) found that sexually abused female runaways were significantly more likely than their nonabused counterparts to engage in delinquent or criminal activities such as substance abuse, petty theft, and prostitution. No such pattern was found among male runaways.

Finally, as noted earlier, the backgrounds of adult women in prison underscores the important links between women's childhood victimizations and their later criminal careers (Snell & Morton, 1994). The interviews revealed that many of the women in this national sample were the victims of physical and/or sexual abuse (43%).

Confirmation of the consequences of childhood sexual and physical abuse on adult female criminal behavior also has recently come from a large quantitative study of 908 individuals with substantiated and validated histories of these victimizations. Widom (1988) found that abused or neglected females were twice as likely as a matched group of controls to have an adult record (16% compared to 7.5%). The difference also was found among men, but it was not as dramatic (42% compared to 33%). Men with abuse backgrounds also were more likely to contribute to the "cycle of violence" with more arrests for violent offenses as adult offenders than the control group. In contrast, when women with abuse backgrounds did become involved with the criminal justice system, their arrests tended to involve property and order offenses (such as disorderly conduct, curfew, and loitering violations) (Widom, 1988, p. 17).

Given this information, a feminist perspective on the causes of female delinquency seems an appropriate next step. First, like young men, girls are frequently the recipients of violence and sexual abuse. But unlike boys, girls' victimization and their response to that victimization is specifically shaped by their status as young women. Perhaps because of the gender and sexual scripts found in patriarchal families, girls are much more likely than boys to be the victim of family-related sexual abuse. Men, particularly men with traditional attitudes toward women, are likely to define their daughters or stepdaughters as their sexual property (Finkelhor, 1982). In a society that idealizes inequality in male–female relationships and venerates youth in women, girls are easily defined as sexually attractive by older men (Bell, 1984). In addition, girls' vulnerability to both physical and sexual abuse is heightened by norms that require that they stay at home where their victimizers have access to them.

Moreover, girls' victimizers (usually males) have the ability to invoke official agencies of social control in their efforts to keep young women at home and vulnerable. That is to say, abusers traditionally have been able to utilize the uncritical commitment of the juvenile justice system toward parental authority to force girls to obey them. Until recently, girls' complaints about abuse were routinely ignored. For this reason, statutes that were originally placed into law to "protect" young people, in the case of some girls' delinquency, have criminalized their survival strategies. As they run away from abusive homes, parents have been able to employ agencies to enforce their return. If they persisted in their refusal to stay in that home, however intolerable, they were incarcerated.

Young women, a large number of whom are on the run from homes characterized by sexual abuse and parental neglect, are forced by the very statutes designed to protect them into the lives of escaped convicts. Unable to enroll in school or take a job to support themselves because they fear detection, young female runaways are forced into the streets. Here they engage in panhandling, petty theft, and occasional prostitution in order to survive. Young women in conflict with their parents (often for very legitimate reasons) may actually be forced by present laws into petty criminal activity, prostitution, and drug use.

In addition, the fact that young girls (but not necessarily young boys) are defined as sexually desirable and in fact more desirable than their older sisters due to the double standard of aging means that their lives on the streets (and their survival strategies) take on a unique shape, again one shaped by patriarchal values. It is no accident that girls on the run from abusive homes or on the streets because of profound poverty get involved in criminal activities that exploit their sexual object status. American society has defined youthful, physically perfect woman as desirable. This means that girls on the streets, who have little else of value to trade, are encouraged to utilize this "resource" (Campagna & Poffenberger, 1988). It also means that the criminal subculture views them from this perspective (Miller, 1986).

The above model is clearly not the "entire" story on female delinquency, but it is a theory that starts with the assumption that experiences that *differentiate* male and female youth might illuminate perplexing, but persistent facts, such as the fact that more female than male status offenders find their way into the juvenile justice system. Clearly, theories that are sensitive to those aspects of girls' and boys' lives that they share with each other should not be entirely neglected in an attempt to understand delinquency (see Chesney-Lind & Shelden, 1992, for a discussion of how these theories might shed light on female delinquency). These, though, were crafted without any thought to the ways in which gender shapes both boys' and girls' realities, and they need to be rethought with gender in mind.

Two additional comments seem important here. First, a recent attempt to salvage the theories crafted to explain boys' behavior argues essentially that the theories are correct; it is simply that girls and boys are raised very differently, but that *if* girls were raised like boys and found themselves in the same situations as boys, then they would be as delinquent as boys (Rowe, Vazsonyi, & Flannery, 1995). This seems to be a step backward. Girls and boys inhabit a gendered universe and find themselves in systems (especially families and schools) that regulate their behavior in radically different ways. These, in turn, have significant consequences for the lives of girls (and boys). We need to think about these differences and what they mean, not only for crime, but more broadly, what they mean about the life chances of girls and boys.

In the main, the socialization experiences of boys, especially of white privileged boys, prepare them for lives of power (Connell, 1987). The experiences of girls, particularly during adolescence, are very different. Even for girls of privilege, there are dramatic and negative changes in their self-perception, which in turn are reflected in lowered achievement in girls (particularly in math and science) (Orenstein, 1994; AAUW, 1992). Sexual abuse and harassment are just being understood as major rather than minor themes in the lives of all girls. The lives of girls of color, as we shall see in the next section on girls in gangs, show the additional burdens that these young women face as they attempt to contend with high levels of sexual and physical victimization in the home, as well as other forms of neighborhood violence and institutional neglect (Joe & Chesney-Lind, 1995; Orenstein, 1994).

AGGRESSIVE BEHAVIOR, CRIME, AND GIRLS' PARTICIPATION IN YOUTH GANGS[3]

Despite media assertions, crime trend data suggest that the level of violence committed by female youth has not increased significantly over the past decade. But while girls' involvement in serious crimes of violence does not seem to be on the rise, girls' participation in gangs (or our recognition of the presence of girls in the gangs) does appear to have increased over the last decade (Curry, 1995; Chesney-Lind et al., 1996). Because the gang looms largest in economically marginalized communities, the discussion of girls in gangs also further illuminates the lives of girls, particularly girls of color, who grow up in these communities.

Female gangs are still the exception rather than the rule in American cities. A national study of the scope of gang activity from a law enforcement perspective notes that 40 cities reported some 7,205 female gang members (Curry, Fox, Ball, & Stone, 1992). While this number sounds large, girls account for a very small percentage (3.6%) of all youth identified as gang members, since police estimates now put the number of gangs at 4,881 and the number of gang members at approximately 249,324 (Curry et al., 1992). Curry and associates note, though, that some jurisdictions have "law enforcement policies that officially exclude female gangs members" (1992, p. 8). If only those jurisdictions that include girls and women are examined, the proportion climbs to 5.7%.

While Curry and associates' (1992) analysis of official police estimates indicated an extremely small proportion of girls involved in gang activity, other estimates are higher. Miller's (1980) nationwide study of gangs, in the mid-1970s, found the existence of fully independent girl gangs to be quite rare, constituting less than 10% of all gangs, although about half the male gangs in the New York area had female auxiliary groups. By contrast, Moore's important ethnographic work on gang activity in Los Angeles' barrios estimated that fully one third of the youth involved in the gangs she studied were female (Moore, 1991, p. 8).

Given the range of estimates, one might wonder whether girls and their involvement with gang life resembles the involvement of girls in other youth subcultures, where they have been described as "present but invisible" (McRobbie & Garber, 1975). Certainly, Moore's higher estimate indicates that she and her associates saw girls that others had missed. Indeed, Moore's work is noteworthy in its departure from the androcentric norm in gang research. The longstanding "gendered habits" of researchers has meant that girls' involvement with gangs have been neglected, sexualized, and oversimplified.[4] So, while there have been a growing number of studies investigating the connections between male gangs, violence, and other criminal activities, there has been no parallel development in research on female involvement in gang activity. As with all young women who find their way into the juvenile justice system, girls in gangs have been invisible.

As noted earlier, this pattern of invisibility was undoubtedly set by initial efforts to understand visible lower-class male delinquency in Chicago over half a century ago. As an example, Jankowski's (1991) highly regarded *Islands in the Streets* implicitly conceptualizes gangs as a distinctly male phenomena, and females are discussed, as noted earlier, in the context of male property:

> In every gang I studied, women were considered a form of property. Interestingly, the women I observed and interviewed told me they felt completely comfortable with certain aspects of this relationship and simply resigned themselves to accepting those aspects they dislike. The one aspect they felt most comfortable with was being treated like servants, charged with the duty of providing men with whatever they wanted. (p. 146)

Taylor's (1993) work, *Girls, Gangs, Women and Drugs*, marks a complete reversal in themes where girls are the central focus, but from a male-centered perspective. His work, like Thrasher's (1963) and Jankowski's, is a reflection of a general tendency to minimize and distort the motivations and roles of female gang members. These researchers adopted the biased viewpoint or stance of the typical male gang member and reported these observations of the female experience in an unreflexive way (Campbell, 1990). Typically, male gang researchers have characterized female members as maladjusted tomboys or sexual chattel, who in either case are no more than mere appendages to male members of the gang.

Taylor's (1993) study provides a veneer of academic support for the media's definition of the girl gang member as a junior version of the liberated female crook of the 1970s. It is not clear exactly how many girls and women he interviewed for his book, but the introduction clearly sets the tone for his work: "We have found that females are just as capable as males of being ruthless in so far as their life opportunities are presented. This study indicates that females have moved beyond the status quo of gender repression" (Taylor, 1993, p. 8). His work then stresses the similarities between boys' and girls' involvement in gangs, despite the fact that when the girls and women he interviews speak, it becomes clear that such a view is oversimplified. Listen, for example, to Pat in response to a question about "problems facing girls in gangs":

> If you got a all girls crew, um, they think you're "soft" and in the streets if you soft, it's all over. Fellas think girls is soft, like Rob, he think he got it better in his shit 'cause he's a fella, a man. It's wild, but fellas really hate seeing girls getting off. Now, some fellas respect the power of girls, but most just want us in the sack. (Taylor, 1993, p. 118)

Other studies of female gang delinquency stress the image of girls as having auxiliary roles to boys' gangs (see Miller, 1975, 1980; Rice, 1963; Brown, 1977; Flowers, 1987; Bowker, 1978; Hanson, 1964). Overall, these studies portray girls who are part of gangs as either the girlfriends of the male members or "little sister" subgroups of the male gang (see Bowker, 1978, p. 184; Hanson, 1964). Further, they suggest that the role for girls in gangs is "to conceal and carry weapons for the boys, to provide sexual favors, and sometimes to fight against girls who were connected with enemy boys' gangs" (Mann, 1984, p. 45).

Some firsthand accounts of girl gangs, while not completely challenging this image, focus more directly on the race and class issues confronting these girls. Quicker's (1983) study of female Chicana gang members in East Los Angeles found evidence that these girls, although still somewhat dependent on their male counterparts, were becoming more independent. These girls identified themselves as "homegirls" and their male counterparts as "homeboys," a common reference to relationships in the "barrio." In an obvious reference to "strain theory," Quicker notes that there are few economic opportunities within the barrio to meet the needs of the family unit. As a result, families are disintegrating and do not have the capability of providing access to culturally emphasized success goals for young people about to enter adulthood. Not surprisingly, almost all their activities occur within the context of gang life, where they learn how to get along in the world and are insulated within the harsh environment of the barrio (Quicker, 1983).

Moore's (1991) ethnography of two Chicano gangs in East Los Angeles, initiated during the same period as Quicker's, brought the work forward to the present day. Her interviews clearly establish both the multifaceted nature of girls' experiences with gangs in the barrio as well as the variations in male gang members' perceptions of the girls in gangs. Importantly, her study establishes that there is no one type of gang girl, with some of the girls in gangs, even in the 1940s, "not tightly bound to boy's cliques" and also "much less bound to particular barrios than boys" (Moore, 1991, p. 27). Other girls' gangs did bear out the stereotype; but all the girls in gangs tended to come from "more troubled background than those of the boys" (Moore, 1991, p. 30). Significant problems with sexual victimization haunt girls, but not so in boys' lives. Moore also documents that the sexual double standard also characterized male gang members' as well as the neighborhood's more negative view of girls in gangs (see also Moore & Hagedorn, 1996). Girl gang members were labeled as "tramps" and "no good" despite the girls' vigorous rejection of these labels. Further, some male gang members, even those who had relationships with girl gang members, felt that "square girls were their future" (Moore, 1991, p. 75).

Harris' (1988) study of the Cholas, a Latina gang in the San Fernando Valley echoes this theme. While in many respects the Cholas resemble male gangs, the gang did challenge the girls' traditional destiny within the barrio in two direct ways. First, the girls rejected the traditional image of the Latina woman as "wife and mother," supporting instead a more "macho" homegirl role. Second, the gang supported the girls in their estrangement from organized religion, substituting instead a form of familialism that "provides a strong substitute for weak family and conventional school ties" (Harris, 1988, p. 172).

The same "macho themes" emerged in a study of the female "age sets" found in a large gang in Phoenix, Arizona (Moore, Vigil, & Levy, 1995). In these groups, fighting is used by the girls, as well as the boys, to achieve status and recognition. Even here, though, the violence is mediated by gender and culture. One girl recounts that she established her reputation by "protecting one of my girls. He [a male acquaintance] was slapping her around and he was hitting her and kicking her, and I went and jumped him and started hitting him" (Moore et al., 1995, p. 39). Once respect is achieved, these researchers found girls relied on their reputations and fought less often.

Girls in these sets also had to negotiate within a Mexican-American culture that is "particularly conservative with regard to female sexuality" (Moore et al., 1995, p. 29). In their neighborhoods and in their relations with the boys in the gang, the persistence of the double standard places the more assertive and sexually active girls in an anomalous position. Essentially, they must contend with a culture that venerates "pure girls," while also setting the groundwork for the sexual exploitation by gang boys of other girls. One of their respondents reports that the boys sometimes try to get girls high and "pull a train" (where a number of males have sex with one girl), something she clearly rejects for herself, even though she admits to having had sex with a boy she did not like after the male gang members "got me drunk" (Moore et al., 1995, p. 32).

Further explication of the sexual victimization of girls and women involved in Chicano gangs is supplied by Portillos and Zatz (1995) in their ethnography of Phoenix gangs. They noted that girls can enter gangs either by being "jumped in" or "trained in," the former involving being beaten into the gang and the later involving having sex with a string of male gang members. Often, those who are "trained in" are later regarded as "loose" and "not really" a gang member. Portillos and Zatz also found extremely high levels of some type of family abuse among the girls they interviewed, which caused them to conclude that "her treatment by male gang members may simply replicate how she is typically treated by males" (Portillos & Zatz, 1995, p. 24).

Fishman (1995) studied the Vice Queens, who were an African American female auxiliary gang to a boys' gang, the Vice Kings, that existed in Chicago during the early 1960s. Living in a mostly black community characterized by poverty, unemployment, deterioration, and a high crime rate, the gang of about 30 teenage girls was loosely knit (unlike the male gang) and provided the girls with companionship and friends. Failing in school and unable to find work, the bulk of their time was spent "hanging out" on the streets with the Vice Kings, which usually included the consumption of alcohol, sexual activities, and occasional delinquency. Most of their delinquency was "traditionally female" like prostitution, shoplifting, and running away, but some was more serious (e.g., auto theft). They also engaged in fights with other groups of girls, largely to protect their gang's reputation for toughness.

Growing up in rough neighborhoods provided the Vice Queens "with opportunities to learn such traditional male skills as fighting and taking care of themselves on the streets" (Fishman, 1995, p. 87). It generally was expected that the girls had to learn to defend themselves against "abusive men" and "attacks on their integrity" (p. 87). Their relationship with the Vice Kings was primarily sexual, having sexual relations and bearing their children, but with no hope of marriage. Fishman perceptively points out that the Vice Queens were

> socialized to be independent, assertive and to take risks with the expectations that these are characteristics that they will need to function effectively within the black low income community.... As a consequence, black girls demonstrate, out of necessity, a greater flexibility in roles. (Fishman, 1995, p. 90)

There has been little improvement in the economic situation of the African-American community since the 1960s and undoubtedly, today's young women face an even bleaker future than the Vice Queens. In this context, she speculates that "black female gangs today have become more entrenched, more violent, and more oriented to 'male' crime (Fishman, 1995, p. 90). These changes, she adds, are unrelated to the women's movement, but are instead the "forced 'emancipation' which stems from the economic crisis within the black community" (Fishman, 1995, p. 90).

Fishman's bleak speculation about these girls' lives in contemporary poverty-stricken neighborhoods has been largely confirmed by more contemporary research by Lauderback, Hansen, and Waldorf (1992) on an African-American female gang in San Francisco. Disputing the traditional notions of female gang members in which they are portrayed as "maladjusted, violent tomboys" and sex objects completely dependent on the favor of male gang members (Lauderback et al., 1992, p. 57), these interviewers found an independent girl gang who engaged in crack sales and organized "boosting" to support themselves and their young children. Looking past the gang's economic role in their lives, Lauderback and associates noted that the gang fills a void in the lives of its members, since their own family ties were weak at best prior to their involvement in the group. All under 25, abandoned by the fathers of their children, abused and controlled by other men, these young women wished to be "doing something other than selling drugs and to leave the neighborhood," but "many felt that the circumstances that led them to sell drugs were not going to change" (Lauderback et al., 1992, p. 69).

These findings are amplified by Moore and Hagedorn (1996) in their exploration of ethnic differences between African-American and Hispanic female gang members in Milwaukee. Specifically, they found that when asked to respond to the statement, "The way men are today, I'd rather raise my kids myself," 75% of the African-American female gang members agreed, compared to only 43% of the Latina gang members. By contrast, 29% of Latinas but none of the African-American women agreed that "all a woman needs to straighten out her life is to find a good man" (Moore & Hagedorn, 1996, p. 217).

Campbell's (1984, 1990) work on Hispanic gangs in the New York area further explores the role of the gang for girls in this culture. The girls in her study joined gangs for reasons that are largely explained by their situation in a society that has little to offer young women of color (Campbell, 1990). First, the possibility of a decent career, outside of domestic servant, is practically nonexistent. Many have come from female-headed families subsisting on welfare and most have dropped out of school and have no marketable skills. Their aspirations for the future were both sex-typed and unrealistic, with the girls expressing a desire to be rock stars or professional models. Second, they find themselves in a highly gendered community where the men in their lives, while not traditional breadwinners, still make many decisions that circumscribe the possibilities open to young women. Third, the responsibilities that young Hispanic women will have as mothers further restrict the options available to her. Campbell (1990) cites recent data revealing a very bleak future, as 94% will have children and 84% will have to raise their children without a husband. Most will be dependent on some form of welfare. Fourth, these young women face a future of isolation as a housewife in the projects. Finally, they share with their male counterparts a future of powerlessness as members of the urban underclass. Their lives, in effect, reflect all the burdens of their triple handicaps of race, class, and gender.

For these girls, Campbell (1990, p. 173) observes, the gang represents "an idealized collective solution to the bleak future that awaits" them. The girls have a tendency to portray to themselves and the outside world a very idealized and romantic life, while developing an exaggerated sense of belonging to the gang. Many were loners prior to joining the gang, having been only loosely connected to schoolmates and neighborhood peer groups. Even the gangs' closeness, as well as the excitement of gang life, is more fiction than reality. Their daily "street talk" is filled with exaggerated stories of parties, drugs, alcohol, and other varieties of "fun." However, as Campbell (1990) notes:

> These events stand as a bulwark against the loneliness and drudgery of their future lives. They also belie the day-to-day reality of gang life. The lack of recreational opportunities, the long days unfilled by work or school and the absence of money mean that the hours and days are whiled away on street corners. "Doing nothing" means hang out on the stoop; the hours of "bullshit" punctuated by trips to the store to buy one can of beer at a time. When an expected windfall arrives, marijuana and rum are purchased in bulk and the partying begins. The next day, life returns to normal. (p. 176)

Joe and Chesney-Lind's (1995) interviews with youth gang members in Hawaii provides further evidence of the social role of the gang. Everyday life in marginalized and chaotic neighborhoods set the stage for group solidarity in two distinct ways. First, the boredom, lack of resources, and high visibility of crime in their neglected communities create the conditions for turning to others who are similarly situated; consequently, it is the group that realistically offers a social outlet. At another level, the stress on the family from living in marginalized areas combined with financial struggles creates heated tension and in many cases violence in the home. They found, like Moore, high levels of sexual and physical abuse in the girls' lives: 62% of the girls had been either sexually abused or assaulted. Three fourths of the girls and over half the boys reported physical abuse.

It is the group, then, that provides both the girls and the boys with a safe refuge and a surrogate family. While the theme of marginality cuts across gender and ethnicity, there were critical differences in how girls and boys, and Samoans, Filipinos, and Hawaiians, express and respond to the problems of everyday life. For example, let us look at the differences in boys' and girls' strategies for coping with these pressures, particularly the boredom of poverty. For boys, fighting, even looking for fights, is a major activity within the gang. If anything, the presence of girls around gang members depresses violence. As one 14-year-old Filipino put it, "If we not with the girls, we fighting. If we not fighting, we with the girls" (Joe & Chesney-Lind, 1995, p. 424). Many of the boys' activities involved drinking, cruising, and looking for trouble. This "looking for trouble" also meant being prepared for trouble. Although guns are somewhat available, most of the boys interviewed used bats or their hands to fight, largely but not exclusively because of cultural norms that suggest that fighting with guns is for the weak.

For girls, fighting and violence is a part of their life in the gang, but not something they necessarily seek out. Instead, protection from neighborhood and family violence was a consistent and major theme in the girls' interviews. One girl simply stated that she belongs to the gang to provide "some protection from her father" (quoted in Joe & Chesney-Lind, 1995, p. 425). Through the group she has learned ways to defend herself physically and emotionally: "He used to beat me up, but now I hit back and he doesn't beat me much now." Another 14-year-old Samoan girl put it, "You gotta be part of the gang or else you're the one who's gonna get beat up." Although this young woman said that members of her gang had to "have total attitude and can fight," she went on to say, "We want to be a friendly gang. I don't know why people are afraid of us. We're not that violent." Fights do come up in these girls' lives: "We only wen mob this girl 'cause she was getting wise, she was saying 'what, slut' so I wen crack her and all my friends wen jump in" (Joe & Chesney-Lind, 1995, pp. 425–426).

They also found that gangs produce opportunities for involvement in criminal activity, but these are impacted by gender as well. Especially for boys from poor families, stealing and small-time drug dealing make up for a lack of money. These activities are not nearly so common among the female respondents. Instead, their problems with the law originate with more traditional forms of female delinquency, such as running away from home. Their families still attempt to hold them to a double standard that results in tensions and disputes with parents that have no parallel among the boys.

These ethnographic studies challenge the assumption that girls' and boys' aggression can be understood without any understanding of gender. Instead, they provide evidence that girls' aggression can only be fully understood once it is located "within the interpersonal and institutionalized patterns of patriarchal society" (White & Kowalski, 1994, p. 502). Such an understanding will prevent the more typical approaches to girl's and women's aggression, which alternately deny and demonize female aggression.

Violence clearly permeates the social milieu of adolescents who grow up in marginalized neighborhoods. Being a girl, though, is to be subject to certain constraints and risk factors that distinguish her experience of violence in important ways from that of boys in her neighborhood. Girls born into economically and politically marginalized families, particularly girls of color, also experience and cope with violence in ways that are distinct from white girls.

Policies that seek to address girl's involvements in gang life and violence, then, need to be informed by the differential role of the gang in the lives of girls and boys and the ways in which even girls' violence (which is the most serious form of delinquency) differs from that of boys. Policy implications for dealing with both the problems of girls in gangs, as well as the situation of girls involved in more traditional forms of female delinquency, are discussed below.

INSTEAD OF INCARCERATION: WHAT COULD BE DONE TO MEET THE NEEDS OF GIRLS

Girls on the economic and political margins, particularly those who find their way into the juvenile justice system, share many problems with their male counterparts. They are likely to be poor, from disrupted and violent families, and having trouble in school. In addition, though, girls also confront problems unique to their sex: notably sexual abuse, sexual assault, dating violence, depression, unplanned pregnancy, and adolescent motherhood. Both their experience of the problems they share with boys and the additional special problems that they face, then, are conditioned by their gender as well as their class and race. Specifically, since families are the source of many of the serious problems that girls face, solutions must take into account that some girls may not be able to stay safely at home.

Programming for girls clearly needs to be shaped by girls' unique situations, as well as addressing the special problems girls have in a gendered society. Unfortunately, traditional delinquency treatment strategies, employed in both prevention and intervention programs, have been shaped largely by commonsense assumptions about what youth, generally boys, need. Sometimes girls will benefit from these notions and sometimes they will not address girls' problems at all.

There is a tremendous shortage of information on programs that have proved effective in work with girls (see Chesney-Lind & Shelden, 1992). Indeed, many studies that have evaluated particular approaches do not deal with special gender issues and frequently programs do not even serve girls. In addition, programs that have been carefully evaluated often are set in training schools (clearly not the ideal place to try any particular strategy). Finally, careful evaluation of most programs tends to show that even the most determined efforts to intervene and help often show very poor results. Of course, the last two points may well be related; programs set in closed, institutional settings are clearly at a disadvantage, and as a consequence tend to be less effective (Lipsey, 1992). Readers also might want a more extensive consideration of promising, community-based programs for girls, but unfortunately these have been few and far between.

Because of this, it might be fruitful to briefly review the general problems associated with the establishment of programs for girls. Prior to the 1970s (and the second wave of feminism), there was little specific concern over uniquely female problems like wife battering and sexual assault, and even less concern about girls' problems (Gordon, 1988). Instead of girls' victimization, it was girls' sexuality that was perceived as the problem. The typical response to girls' sexuality was to first insist that they return to their dysfunctional families. If they ran from these settings, they were to be placed in a foster home (if they where lucky) and ultimately institutions "for their own protection."

After two decades of "deinstitutionalization efforts," girls remain in the words of one researcher "all but invisible in programs for youth and in the literature available to those who work with youth" (Davidson, 1983, p. viii). Further, programs for young women in general (and delinquents, in particular) have been of low priority in our society as far as funding is concerned. For instance, a report done in 1975 by the Law Enforcement Assistance Administration revealed that only 5% of federally funded juvenile delinquency projects were specifically directed at girls, and that only 6% of all local monies for juvenile justice were spent on girls (Female Offender Resource Center, 1977, p. 34). A much more recent review of 75 private foundations in 1989 revealed that funding "targeted specifically for girls and women hovered around 3.4%" (Valentine Foundation, 1990, p. 5).

An exhaustive study of virtually all program evaluation studies done since 1950 (Lipsey 1992) located reports on some 443 delinquency programs; of these, 34.8% were exclusively male and an additional 42.4% served "mostly males." Lipsey found that only 2.3% of the surveyed programs explicitly served only girls, and only 5.9% of the programs served "some males," meaning that most of the programs' participants were girls (Lipsey, 1992, p. 58).

Finally, a 1993 study of the San Francisco Chapter of the National Organization for Women found that only 8.7% of the programs funded by the major city organization funding children and youth programs "specifically addressed the needs of girls" (Siegal, 1995, p. 18). Not surprisingly, then, a 1995 study of youth participation in San Francisco afterschool or summer sports programs found only 26% of the participants were girls (Siegal, 1995, p. 20).

What are the specific needs of young women in general, and in particular those who come into contact with the juvenile justice system, either as victims or offenders? Davidson (1983) argues that:

> The most desperate need of many young women is to find the economic means of survival. While females today are still being socialized to believe that their security lies in marriage and motherhood, surveys of teenage mothers indicate that approximately 90% receive no financial aid from the fathers of their children. (p. ix)

Likewise, a study of homeless youths in Waikiki, about half of whom were girls, revealed that their most urgent needs are housing, jobs, and medical services (Iwamoto, Kameoka, & Brasseur, 1990). Finally, a survey conducted in a very poor community in Hawaii (Waianae) revealed that pregnant and parenting teens saw medical care for their children, financial assistance, and child care as their major needs. By contrast, social workers in the same community saw parenting classes as the girls' most important need, followed by child care, educational and vocational training, and family planning (Yumori & Loos, 1985, pp. 16–17). These findings suggest that while youth understand that economic survival is their most critical need, such is not always the case among those working with them.

The Minnesota Women's Fund noted that the most frequent risk factors for girls and boys differ, and that for girls the list includes emotional stress, physical and sexual abuse, negative body image, disordered eating, suicide, and pregnancy. For boys the list included alcohol, polydrug use, accidental injury, and delinquency (cited in Adolescent Female Subcommittee, 1994). While clearly not all girls at risk will end up in the juvenile justice system, this gendered examination of youth problems sets a standard for examination of delinquency prevention and intervention programs.

Among other needs that girls' programs should address include the following: dealing with the physical and sexual violence in their lives (from parents, boyfriends, pimps, and others), confronting the risk of AIDS, dealing with pregnancy and motherhood, drug and alcohol dependency, facing family problems, vocational and career counseling, managing stress, and developing a sense of efficacy and empowerment. Many of these needs are universal and should be part of programs for all youth (Schwartz & Orlando 1991). However, most of these are particularly important for young women.

Alder (1986, 1995) points out that serving girls effectively will require different and innovative strategies, since "young men tend to be more noticeable and noticed than young women" (Alder, 1995, p. 3). When girls go out, they tend to move in smaller groups, there are greater proscriptions against girls "hanging out," and they may be justly fearful of being on the streets at night. Finally, girls have many more domestic expectations than their boy counterparts, and these may keep them confined to their homes. Alder notes that this may be a particular issue for immigrant girls.

There is some encouraging news as organizations serving girls (like the YWCA, Girls Incorporated, etc.) begin to realize their responsibility for girls who are in the juvenile justice system. Recent reviews of promising programs for girls (Schwartz & Orlando, 1991; Girls Incorporated, 1996) indicate that programs that specifically target the housing and employment needs of youth, while also providing them with the specific skills they will need to survive on their own, are emerging. These often include a built-in caseworker/service broker, as well as counseling components. Clearly, many girls will require specialized counseling to recover from the ravages of sexual and physical victimization, but the research cautions that approaches that rely simply on the provision of counseling services are not likely to succeed (see Chesney-Lind & Shelden, 1992).

Programs also must be scrutinized to assure that they are culturally specific as well as gender specific. As increasing numbers of girls of color are drawn into the juvenile justice system (and bootstrapped into correctional settings), while their white counterparts are deinstitutionalized, there is a need for programs to be rooted in specific cultures. Since it is clear that girls of color have different experiences of their gender, as well as different experiences with the dominant institutions in the society (Amaro & Agular, 1994; Amaro, 1995; Orenstein, 1994; LaFromboise & Howard-Pitney, 1995), programs to divert and deinstitutionalize *must* be shaped by the unique developmental issues confronting minority girls, as well as building in the specific cultural resources available in ethnic communities.

This review also indicates, though, that innovative programs must receive the same sort of stable funding generally accorded their more traditional/institutional counterparts (which are generally far less innovative and flexible). A careful reading of the descriptions of novel programs reveals that many relied on federal funds or private foundation grants; the same reading reveals how pitifully few survive for any length of time. To survive and thrive, they must be able to count on stable funding. In 1992, Congress asked states to conduct an inventory of programs that are specifically focused on girls. This promising beginning, though, is being deeply challenged by recent Republican efforts in Congress to refocus national attention on youth violence and the imposition of punishments for such offenses (Howard, 1996, p. 22).

Programs also must be continually scrutinized so as to guarantee that they are serving as genuine alternatives to girls' incarceration, rather than simply functioning to extend the social control of girls. There is a tendency for programs serving girls to become more "security" oriented in response to girls' propensity to run away. Indeed, a component of successful programming for girls must be advocacy and continuous monitoring of the closed institutions. If nothing else can be learned from a careful reading of the rocky history of nearly two decades of efforts to decarcerate youth, it is an appreciation of how fraught these efforts are with difficulty and how easily their gains can be eroded.

Finally, much more work needs to be done to support the fundamental needs of girls on the margin. We must do a better job of recognizing that they need less "programming" and more support to live on their own, since many cannot or will not be able go back home again.

ENDNOTES

1. Children, unlike adults, can be "referred" to the juvenile justice system by a variety of sources, including teachers, social workers, or even parents. As this and subsequent chapters will show, these other sources of entry are particularly significant in the case of girls' entry into the juvenile justice system.

2. Part 1 offenses are defined by the FBI as murder, forcible rape, robbery, burglary, aggravated assault, larceny theft, auto theft, and arson.
3. This section of the chapter is drawn from a longer discussion of gender and gang membership in Chesney-Lind et al. (1996).
4. For exceptions, see Brown (1977), Bowker and Klein (1983), Campbell (1984, 1990), Ostner (1986), Fishman (1995), Moore (1991), Harris (1988), Quicker (1983), and Giordano et al. (1978).

REFERENCES

Adams, P. F., Schoenborn, C. A., Moss, A. J., Warren, C. W., & Kann, L. (1995). *Health-risk behaviors among our nation's youth: United States, 1992* (Vital and Health Statistics Series 10, No. 192; DHHS Publication No. (PHS) 95-1520). Hyattsville, MD: US Department of Health and Human Services, Public Health Services, Centers for Disease Control and Prevention, National Center for Health Statistics.

Adams-Tucker, C. (1982). Proximate effects of sexual abuse in childhood. *American Journal of Psychiatry, 193*, 1252–1256.

Adler, F. (1975). *Sisters in crime*. New York: McGraw-Hill

Adolescent Female Subcommittee. (1994). *Needs assessment and recommendations for adolescent females in Minnesota*. St. Paul: Minnesota Department of Corrections.

Alder, C. (1986). "Unemployed women have got it heaps worse": Exploring the implications of female youth unemployment. *Australian and New Zealand Society of Criminology, 19*, 210–224.

Alder, C. (1995). *Delinquency prevention with young women*. Paper presented at the Delinquency Prevention Conference, Terrigal, New South Wales, Australia.

Amaro, H., & Agular, M. (1994). "Programa mama: Mom's project." *A Hispanic/Latino family approach to substance abuse prevention*. Washington, DC: Center for Substance Abuse Prevention, Mental Health Services Administration.

Amaro, H. (1995). Love, sex, and power: Considering women's realities in HIV prevention. *American Psychologist, 50*, 437–447.

American Association for University Women (AAUW). (1992). *How schools are shortchanging girls*. Washington, DC: AAUW Educational Foundation.

American Correctional Association. (1990). *The female offender: What does the future hold?* Washington, DC: St. Mary's Press.

American Psychological Association. (1993). *Violence and youth: Psychology's response*, Vol. I. Washington, DC: Author.

Bartollas, C. (1993). Little girls grown up: The perils of institutionalization. In C. Culliver (Ed.), *Female criminality: The state of the art* (pp. 469–482). New York: Garland Press.

Bell, I. P. (1984). The double standard: Age. In J. Freeman (Ed.), *Women: A feminist perspective* (pp. 256–263). Palo Alto, CA: Mayfield.

Benson, P. L. (1990). *The troubled journey: A portrait of 6th to 12th grade youth*. Minneapolis, MN: Seach Institute.

Bjorkqvist, K., & Niemela, P. (1992). New trends in the study of female aggression. In K. Bjorkqvist & P. Niemela (Eds.), *Of mice and women: Aspects of female aggression* (pp. 1– 16). San Diego, CA: Academic Press.

Bjorkqvist, K., Osterman, K., & Kaukiainen, A. (1992). The development of direct and indirect aggressive strategies in males and females. In K. Bjorkqvist & P. Niemela (Eds.), *Of mice and women: Aspects of female aggression* (pp. 51–64). San Diego, CA: Academic Press.

Bowker, L. (1978). *Women, crime and the criminal justice system*. Lexington, MA: Lexington Books.

Bowker, L., & Klein, M. (Eds.). (1983). The etiology of female juvenile delinquency and gang membership: A test of psychological and social structural explanations. *Adolescence, 13*, 739–751.

Brown, W. K. (1977). Black female gangs in Philadelphia. *International Journal of Offender Therapy and Comparative Criminology, 21*, 221–228.

Browne, A., & Finkelhor, D. (1986). Impact of child sexual abuse: A review of research. *Psychological Bulletin, 99*, 66–77.

Butts, J. A., Snyder, H. N., Finnegan, T. A., Aughenbaugh, A. L., Tierney, N. J., Sullivan, D. P., Poole, R. S., Sickmund, M. H., & Poe, E. C. (1994). *Juvenile court statistics 1991*. Pittsburgh: National Center for Juvenile Justice, Office of Juvenile Justice and Delinquency Prevention Juvenile.

Cain, M. (1989). *Growing up good: Policing the behavior of girls in Europe*. London: Sage.

Callaghan, C. M., & Rivara, F. P. (1992). Urban high school youth and hand-guns. *Journal of the American Medical Association, 267*, 3038–3042.

Campagna, D. S., & Poffenberger, D. L. (1988). *The sexual trafficking in children.* Dover, MA: Auburn House.
Campbell, A. (1990). Female participation in gangs. In C. R. Huff (Ed.), *Gangs in America* (pp. 163–182). Newbury Park, CA: Sage.
Campbell, A. (1995). Female participation in gangs. In M. W. Klein, C. L. Maxon, & J. Miller (Eds.), *The modern gang reader* (pp. 70–77). Los Angeles: Roxbury.
Campbell, A. (1984). *The girls in the gang.* Oxford, England: Basil Blackwell.
Canter, R. J. (1982). Sex differences in self-report delinquency. *Criminology, 20,* 373–393.
Chesney-Lind, M. (1971). *Female juvenile delinquency in Hawaii.* Masters thesis. University of Hawaii at Manoa.
Chesney-Lind, M. (1997). *The female offender: Girls, women and crime.* Thousand Oaks, CA: Sage.
Chesney-Lind, M., & Shelden, R. G. (1992). *Girls, delinquency, and juvenile justice.* Pacific Grove, CA: Brooks/Cole.
Chesney-Lind, M., Brown, M., Leisen, M. B., Perrone, P., Kwack, D., Marker, N., & Kato, D. (1996). *Perspectives on juvenile delinquency and gangs: An interim report to Hawaii's state legislature.* Honolulu: Center for Youth Research, Social Science Research Institute, University of Hawaii at Manoa.
Chesney-Lind, M., Shelden, R., & Joe Laider, K. (1996). Girls, delinquency, and gang membership. In C. R. Huff (Ed.), *Gangs in America* (2nd ed., pp. 185–204). Newbury Park, CA: Sage.
Cloward, R. A., & Ohlin, L. E. (1960). *Delinquency and opportunity.* New York: Free Press.
Cohen, A. (1955). *Delinquent boys: The culture of the gang.* New York: Free Press.
Connell, R. W. (1987). *Gender and power.* Stanford, CA: Stanford University Press.
Curry, G. D. (1995). *Responding to female gang involvement.* Paper presented at the American Society of Criminology Meeting, Boston, MA.
Curry, G. D., Fox, R. J., Ball, R. A., & Stone, D. (1992). *National assessment of law enforcement anti-gang information resources: Draft 1992 final report.* Morgantown, WV: West Virginia University: National Assessment Survey 1992.
Curry, G. D., Ball, R. A., & Fox, R. J. (1994). *Gang crime and law enforcement recordkeeping.* Washington DC: National Institute of Justice.
Davidson, S. (Ed.). (1983). *The second mile: Contemporary approaches in counseling young women.* Tucson, AZ: New Directions for Young Women.
DeJong, A. R., Hervada, A. R., & Emmett, G. A. (1983). Epidemiologic variations in childhood sexual abuse. *Child Abuse and Neglect, 7,* 155–162.
Dembo, R., Williams, L., & Schmeidler, J. (1993). Gender differences in mental health service needs among youths entering a juvenile detention center. *Journal of Prison and Jail Health, 12,* 73–101.
Dembo, R., Sue, S. C., Borden, P., & Manning, D. (1995). *Gender differences in service needs among youths entering a juvenile assessment center: A replication study.* Paper presented at the Annual Meeting of The Society of Social Problems. Washington, DC, August 1995.
Durant, R. H., Getts, A. G., Cadenhead, C., & Woods, E. R. (1995). The association between weapon carrying and the use of violence among adolescents living in and around public housing. *Journal of Adolescent Health, 17,* 376–380.
Federal Bureau of Investigation. (1980). *Crime in the United States 1979: Uniform crime reports.* Washington, DC: US Department of Justice.
Federal Bureau of Investigation. (1994). *Crime in the United States 1993.* Washington, DC: US Department of Justice.
Federal Bureau of Investigation. (1995). *Crime in the United States 1994.* Washington, DC: US Department of Justice.
Female Offender Resource Center. (1977). *Little sisters and the law.* Washington, DC: American Bar Association.
Finkelhor, D. (1982). Sexual abuse: A sociological perspective. *Child Abuse and Neglect, 6,* 95–102.
Finkelhor, D., & Baron, L. (1986). Risk factors for child sexual abuse. *Journal of Interpersonal Violence, 1,* 43–71.
Fishman, L. T. (1995). The vice queens. An ethnographic study of black female gang behavior. In M. W. Klein, C. L. Maxon, & J. Miller (Eds.), *The modern gang reader* (pp. 83–92). Los Angeles: Roxbury.
Flowers, R. B. (1987). *Women and criminality.* New York: Greenwood Press.
Giordano, P., Cernkovich, S., & Pugh, M. (1978). Girls, guys and gangs: The changing social context of female delinquency. *Journal of Criminal Law and Criminology, 69,* 126–132.
Girls Incorporated. (1996). *Prevention and parity: Girls in juvenile justice.* Indianapolis, IN: Girls Incorporated National Resource Center.
Gordon, L. (1988). *Heroes in their own lives.* New York: Viking Press.
Hamilton, J. A. (1989). Emotional consequences of victimization and discrimination in special populations of women. In B. L. Parry (Ed.), *The Psychiatric Clinics of North America* (pp. 35–52). Philadelphia: WB Saunders.
Hanson, K. (1964). *Rebels in the streets: The story of New York's girl gangs.* Englewood Cliffs, NJ: Prentice-Hall.
Harris, M. G. (1988). *Cholas: Latino girls and gangs.* New York: AMS Press.

Hawaii Department of Business and Economic Development and Tourism. (1993). *Hawaii state databook*. Honolulu: Author.

Herman, J. L. (1981). *Father–daughter incest*. Cambridge, MA: Harvard University Press.

Howard, B. (1996). Juvenile justice act's mandates: To stay or go? *Youth Today*, July/August.

Ianni, F. A. J. (1989). *The search for structure: A report on American youth today*. New York: Free Press.

Iwamoto, J. J., Kameoka, K., & Brasseur, Y. C. (1990). *Waikiki homeless youth project: A report*. Honolulu: Catholic Services to Families.

Jankowski, M. S. (1991). *Islands in the street: Gangs and American urban society*. Berkeley: University of California Press.

Joe, K., & Chesney-Lind, M. (1995). Just every mother's angel: An analysis of gender and ethnic variations in youth gang membership. *Gender and Society*, *9*, 408–430.

Kagan, J. (1992). Etiologies of adolescents at risk. In D. E. Rogers & E. Ginzberg (Eds.), *Adolescents at risk: Medical and social perspectives* (pp. 8–18). San Francisco: Westview Press.

Kann, L., Warren, C. W., Harris, W. A., Collins, J. L., Douglas, K. A., Collins, M. E., Williams, B. I., Ross, J. G., & Kolbe, L. J. (1995, March 24). Youth risk behavior surveillance—United States, 1993. *Morbidity and Mortality Weekly Report*, *44*(No. ss-1), 2–55.

Katz, P. A. (1979). The development of female identity. In C. B. Kopp (Ed.), *Becoming female: Perspectives on development* (pp. 3–28). New York: Plenum Press.

Kruttschnitt, C. (1995). Violence by and against women: A comparative and cross-national analysis. In R. B. Ruback & N. A. Weiner (Eds.), *Interpersonal violent behaviors: Social and cultural aspects* (pp. 253–270). New York: Springer.

LaFromboise, T. D., & Howard-Pitney, B. (1995). Suicidal behavior in American Indian female adolescents. In S. Canetto & D. Lester (Eds.), *Woman and suicidal behavior* (pp. 157–173). New York: Springer.

Lauderback, D., Hansen, J., & Waldorf, D. (1992). Sisters are doin' it for themselves: A black female gang in San Francisco. *The Gang Journal*, *1*, 57–72.

Leslie, C., Biddle, N., Rosenberg, D., & Wayne, J. (1993). Girls will be girls. *Newsweek*, August 2, p 44.

Lipsey, M. (1992). Juvenile delinquency treatment: A meta-analytic inquiry in the variability of effects. In T. A. Cook, et al. (Eds.), *Meta-analysis for explanation: A casebook* (pp. 83–136). New York: Russell Sage.

Litt, I. F. (1995). Violence among adolescents: Don't overlook the girls (editorial). *Journal of Adolescent Health*, *17*, 333.

Loper, A. B., & Cornell, D. G. (1996). Homicide by girls. *Journal of Child and Family Studies*, *5*, 321–333.

Mann, C. (1984). *Female crime and delinquency*. Tuscaloosa, AL: University of Alabama Press.

Marker, N., & Brown, M. (1996). *Pu'u honua (places of refuge): Risk among youth in gang prevention programs in Hawaii*. Paper presented at the Annual Meetings of the Western Society of Criminology, Rohnert Park, CA.

Mayer, J. (1994). *Girls in the Maryland juvenile justice system: Findings of the female population taskforce*. Presentation to the Gender Specifics Services Training. Minneapolis, Minnesota.

McCormack, A., Janus, M.-D., & Burgess, A. W. (1986). Runaway youths and sexual victimization: Gender differences in an adolescent runaway population. *Child Abuse and Neglect*, *10*, 387–395.

McRobbie, A., & Garber, J. (1975). Girls and subcultures. In S. Hall & T. Jefferson (Eds.), In *Resistance through rituals: Youth subculture in post-war Britain* (pp. 209–222). New York: Holmes and Meier.

Meiselman, K. (1978). *Incest*. San Francisco: Jossey-Bass.

Miller, E. (1986). *Street woman*. Philadelphia: Temple University Press.

Miller, W. B. (1975). *Violence by youth gangs and youth groups as a crime problem in major American Cities*. Washington, DC: US Government Printing Office.

Miller, W. B. (1980). The molls. In S. K. Datesman & F. R. Scarpitti (Eds.), *Women, crime and justice* (pp. 238–248). New York: Oxford University Press.

Moore, J., & Hagedorn, J. (1996). What happens to the girls in the gang? In R. Huff (Ed.), *Gangs in America* (2nd ed., pp. 205–220). Thousand Oaks, CA: Sage.

Moore, J., Vigil, D., & Levy, J. (1995). Huisas of the street: Chicana gang members. *Latino Studies Journal*, *6*, 27–48.

Moore, J. (1991). *Going down to the barrio: Homeboys and homegirls in change*. Philadelphia: Temple University Press.

Morris, R. E., Harrison, E. A., Knox, G. W., Tromanhauser, E., Marques, D. K., & Watts, L. L. (1995). Health risk behavioral survey from 39 juvenile correctional facilities in the United States. *Journal of Adolescent Health*, *117*, 334–344.

Muram, D. B., Hostetler, R., Jones, C. E., & Speck, P. M. (1995). Adolescent victims of sexual assault. *Journal of Adolescent Health*, *117*, 372–375.

Orenstein, P. (1994). *Schoolgirls*. New York: Doubleday.

Ostner, I. (1986). Die Entdeckung der Mädchen. Neue Perspecktiven für die. Kolner-Zeitschrift-für. *Soziologie und Sozial Psychologie, 38*, 352–371.
Phelps, R. J., McIntosh, M., Jseudason, V., Warner, P., & Pohlkamp, J. (1982). *Wisconsin juvenile female offender project*. Madison, WI: Youth Policy and Law Center, Wisconsin Council on Juvenile Justice.
Pope, C., & Feyerherm, W. H. (1982). Gender bias in juvenile court dispositions. *Social Service Research, 6*, 1–17.
Portillos, E., & Zatz, M. S. (1995). *Not to die for: Positive and negative aspects of Chicano youth gangs*. Paper presented at the annual meeting of the American Society of Criminology, Boston.
Presser, H. (1980). Sally's corner: Coping with unmarried motherhood. *Journal of Social Issues, 36*, 107–129.
Quicker, J. C. (1983). *Homegirls: Characterizing Chicano gangs*. San Pedro, CA: International University Press.
Rice, R. (1963). A reporter at large: The Persian queens. *New Yorker*, October 19, 153–187.
Robinson, R. (1990). *Violations of girlhood: A qualitative study of female delinquents and children in need of services in Massachusetts*. Unpublished Ph.D. dissertation, Brandeis University.
Rowe, D. C., Vazsonyi, A. T., & Flannery, D J. (1995). Sex differences in crime: Do means and within-sex variation have similar causes? *Journal of Research in Crime and Delinquency, 31*(1), 84–100.
Russell, D. E. (1986). *The secret trauma: Incest in the lives of girls and women*. New York: Basic Books.
Schwartz, I. M., & Orlando, F. (1991). *Programming for young women in the juvenile justice system*. Ann Arbor, MI: Center for the Study of Youth Policy, University of Michigan.
Shaw, C., & McKay, H. (1931). *Social factors in juvenile delinquency*. Chicago: University of Chicago Press.
Shelden, R. G., & Horvath, J. (1986). *Processing offenders in a juvenile court: A comparison of males and females*. Paper presented at the annual meeting of the Western Society of Criminology, Newport Beach, CA. February 27–March 2.
Siegal, N. (1995). Where the girls are. *San Francisco Bay Guardian*, October 4, pp. 19–20.
Snell, T. L., & Morton, D. C. (1994). *Women in prison*. Washington, DC: Bureau of Justice Statistics, Special Report.
Steffensmeier, D., & Steffensmeier, R. H. (1980). Trends in female delinquency: An examination of arrest, juvenile court, self-report, and field data. *Criminology, 18*, 62–85.
Strauss, M. (1994). *Violence in the lives of adolescents*. New York: Norton.
Swart, W. J. (Eds.) (1995). Female gang delinquency: A search for "acceptably deviant behavior." In M. W. Klein, C. L. Maxon, & J. Miller (Eds.), *The modern gang reader* (pp. 78–82). Los Angeles: Roxbury.
Taylor, C. (1993). *Girls, gangs, women and drugs*. East Lansing: Michigan State University Press.
Thorne, B. (1993). *Gender play: Girls and boys in school*. New Brunswick, NJ: Rutgers University Press.
Thrasher, F. M. (1963). *The gang: A study of 1,313 gangs in Chicago*. Chicago: University of Chicago Press.
Valentine Foundation and Women's Way. (1990). *A conversation about girls*. Bryn Mawr, PA: Valentine Foundation.
Washington Post. (1994). Study: Many under 18 raped. *Honolulu Advertiser*, June 23, p. A10.
Webster, D. W., Gainer, P. S., & Champion, H. R. (1993). Weapon carrying among inner-city junior high school students: Defensive behavior vs aggressive delinquency. *American Journal of Public Health, 83*, 1604–1608.
White, J. W., & Kowalski, R. M. (1994). Deconstructing the myth of the nonaggressive woman: A feminist analysis. *Psychology of Women Quarterly, 18*, 487–508.
Widom, C. S. (1988). *Child abuse, neglect, and violent criminal behavior*. Unpublished manuscript.
Yumori, W. C., & Loos, G. P. (1985). *The perceived service needs of pregnant and parenting teens and adults on the Waianae coast*. Working Paper. Kamehameha Schools/Bishop Estate.

8

Alcohol, Youth, and the Justice System

Underage Drinking as Normative Behavior, a Status Offense, and a Risk Factor for Delinquency

SUSAN EHRLICH MARTIN

INTRODUCTION

Alcohol clearly is the drug of choice among youth. The vast majority of persons under 21 have consumed it, a significant minority drink heavily, and few youth have difficulty obtaining it. Although in all states the minimum legal drinking age now is 21, and most states prohibit sales to or possession by minors, alcohol misuse and attendant problems are commonplace among adolescents. The most serious of these problems, the three leading causes of death among adolescents—unintentional injuries, homicide, and suicide—also are correlated with alcohol use (US Department of Health and Human Services, 1991). Alcohol-related traffic crashes account for 20% of all deaths of youth between 15 and 20 (Snyder & Sickmund, 1995). Alcohol abuse also is frequently associated with adolescent criminal or delinquent behavior, particularly violent offenses against persons (e.g., Elliott, Huizinga, & Menard, 1989). Nevertheless, scholarly examination of underage drinking as a criminal justice rather than health and safety problem has rarely captured much criminological attention, while drunk driving has been considered a "junk crime" (Ross, 1984).

Despite widespread toleration of underage drinking and weak enforcement of the laws against it, youthful alcohol use has a substantial impact on the juvenile and criminal justice

---

SUSAN EHRLICH MARTIN • Prevention Research Branch, National Institute on Alcohol Abuse and Alcoholism, Rockville, Maryland 20892.

Handbook of Youth and Justice, edited by White. Kluwer Academic/Plenum Publishers, New York, 2001.

systems. In 1997, nearly 14% of all arrests of persons under 18 and 26% of arrests of youth from 18 to 20 were for the alcohol-related offenses of driving under the influence (DUI), drunkenness, liquor law violations, and disorderly conduct (Federal Bureau of Investigation, 1998, pp. 227–228). In addition, an unknown but substantial fraction of the approximately 76,000 arrests of minors for murder and nonnegligent manslaughter, rape, and aggravated assault in 1997 involved alcohol (Federal Bureau of Investigation, 1998, pp. 227–228). Nor does the burden for the criminal justice system stop here: Many studies suggest that the early onset of alcohol use and its misuse by adolescents are major risk factors for and associated with a broader pattern of problem behavior that includes delinquency (e.g., Jessor & Jessor, 1977; Donovan & Jessor, 1985; Elliott et al., 1989) and other drug use (Kandel & Yamaguchi, 1985). Given this correlation of alcohol use and delinquency, finding effective approaches to delaying the onset of drinking and reducing adolescent alcohol abuse may have a broader "ripple" effect on a range of problem behaviors that are dealt with by the juvenile justice system.

The goals of this chapter are to provide an overview of underage drinking as both normative and illegal behavior; to examine the laws related to the minimum legal drinking age, their enforcement, and implications for the justice system; and, given the association between the risk factors for alcohol abuse and delinquency, to examine intervention strategies and programs that reduce youth alcohol consumption, since they also may be effective in reducing delinquent behaviors. The first section examines the prevalence and nature of underage drinking as well as the frequency of alcohol-related offenses including liquor law violations, drinking and driving (DUI), and other delinquent behavior. The second section reviews the history and enforcement of the minimum legal drinking age as well as related "zero tolerance" drinking and driving laws and other liquor law violations. It also addresses the manner in which these offenses are handled by law enforcement, Alcohol Beverage Control (ABC) agencies, and the courts. The third section examines the evidence that youthful alcohol use and abuse is related to other delinquent and criminal behaviors. The fourth section considers alternative approaches to prevention and intervention with underage drinking and possible impacts on delinquent behaviors. The final section identifies unanswered questions and directions for additional research. Thus, in exploring the ramifications of the association of youthful alcohol use and abuse for the juvenile justice system, this chapter will address the direct effects of underage drinking and enforcement of the minimum legal drinking age laws; the association of the early onset, current drinking, and alcohol problems with other offenses including drinking, DUI, and delinquent behavior; and promising interventions to reduce alcohol abuse which also may impact on other delinquent behavior.

Before proceeding, it is necessary to define several terms. The meanings attributed to the terms "minor" and "juvenile" vary. All states have juvenile or family courts that have original jurisdiction over persons defined as "juveniles." Although they vary in their definitions, the oldest age for original juvenile court jurisdiction in delinquency matters is 17. At the same time, all states now have laws that establish 21 as the minimum legal drinking age and an increasing number have lower blood alcohol concentration (BAC) levels for DUI offenses for drivers under 21. While the focus of this chapter is on juveniles, defined as persons 17 years of age or less, it also will include data on minors, defined as persons under 21.

Alcohol use frequently is a predecessor to the use of other illegal drugs (Welte & Barnes, 1985; Yamaguchi & Kandel, 1984a,b; Yu & Williford, 1992). Because use of any nonprescription drug is illegal for minors, researchers often address use of alcohol and other drugs together as "substance abuse." In this chapter, substance abuse refers to findings that do not distinguish between the use or abuse of alcohol and other drugs.

THE PREVALENCE AND NATURE OF UNDERAGE DRINKING AND RELATED PROBLEMS

Prevalence of Underage Alcohol Use

Despite laws in every state establishing the minimum legal drinking age as 21, survey data consistently show that alcohol consumption often begins prior to entering the teenage years and is both widespread and heavy among American youth. Moreover, as Jessor (1982, p. 296) observed, "coming to terms with alcohol, drugs, and sex has emerged as a new developmental task that all adolescents face as part of the normal process of growing up in contemporary American society." For that reason, Tobler (1992) makes a distinction between the "normative" adolescent behaviors that involve "experimental" use, and the "abusive use" of alcohol and drugs. However, there is little agreement on the definition or measurement of alcohol abuse among adolescents.

There are a variety of ways to measure alcohol use and misuse and to define what is normal and what is abusive drinking. The most widely used measures of the frequency of alcohol consumption include lifetime, annual, 30-day, and daily use. Quantity of consumption is measured in standard drinks and often examined in combination with frequency measures to distinguish patterns of consumption. One pattern often identified in studies of adolescent drinking is "binge" drinking, usually characterized as consuming five or more drinks at one sitting (also labeled "heavy" drinking by some authors). While some studies of youth focus on identifying the legal, social, and health problems arising from drinking (e.g., Windle, 1994; Ellickson, McGuigan, Adams, Bell, & Hayes, 1996), far fewer seek to determine whether an individual is alcohol dependent or alcoholic by applying diagnostic criteria.

The lack of consensus about what constitutes misuse among youth reflects developmental differences between adults and adolescents as well as between younger and older adolescents. Because adolescence is a time of rapid change, what is deviant or abusive alcohol use in an 11-year-old may be regarded as normal or normative in one who is 18. Similarly, drinking levels that may cause little or no problems in adults may be dangerous for adolescents who typically differ from adults in body weight, drinking experience, and judgment. Their coordination and reflexes may be negatively affected by only one or two drinks (Ellickson et al., 1996).

In addition, adolescent patterns of alcohol consumption differ markedly from those of adults. Addiction is rare among adolescents and measures of dependency typically used for adults (e.g., craving, inability to control drinking) do not capture the drinking problems found in early and middle adolescence (White & Labouvie, 1989; Martin, Kaczynski, Maisto, Bukstein, & Moss, 1995). Adolescents typically drink less often than adults but consume larger amounts when they drink (Harford & Mills, 1978).

The most consistent data on underage drinking come from the Monitoring the Future (MTF) study conducted annually by the University of Michigan Survey Research Center. Since 1975, self-report data have been collected on a nationally representative sample of approximately 17,000 high school seniors (who also have been followed through young adult years), and since 1991, data also are collected from samples of 8th and 10th grade students.

For every senior class from 1975 through 1999, MTF data show that alcohol use—whether measured as lifetime use, annual use, or 30-day prevalence—is far more widespread than use of any illicit drug, as shown in Fig. 1. The figure also indicates that senior high school students' use of both alcohol and other drugs increased during the late 1970s, peaked in 1979, and declined during the 1980s and into the early 1990s. After 1993 marijuana use again rose while alcohol use remained constant. Nevertheless, in 1999 high school seniors were still about

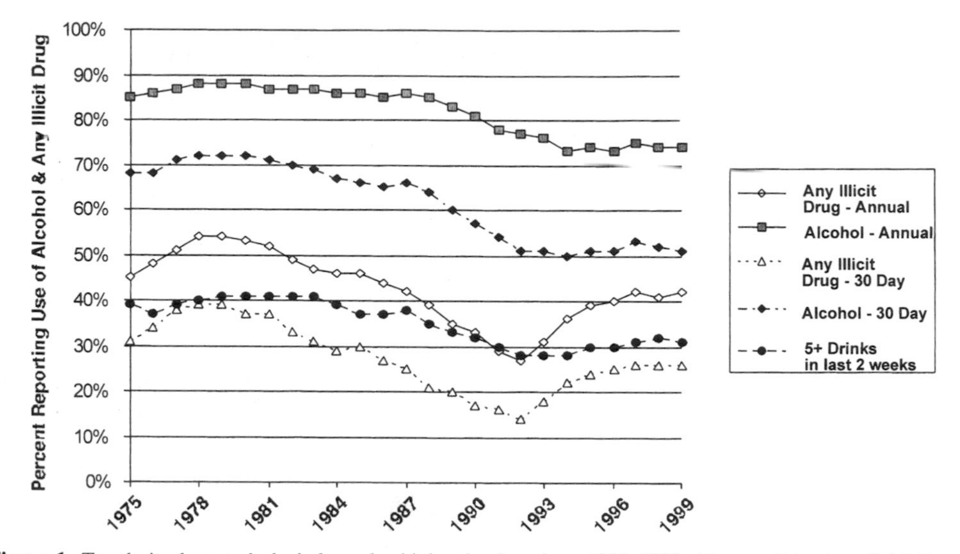

Figure 1. Trends in drug and alcohol use by high school seniors: 1975–1999. (*Source*: Johnston, O'Malley, & Bachman, 1999a, 2000.)

twice as likely to have consumed alcohol than to have used any illicit drug. For example, 85% of the class of 1975, 88% of the class of 1979, and 74% of the seniors in 1999 had used alcohol in the past 12 months (Johnston, O'Malley, & Bachman, 1999a, 2000). In comparison, in 1975, less than half (45%) of high school seniors had used any illicit drug in the past 12 months; in 1979, that figure reached 54%, fell to a low of 27% in 1992, and had risen to 42% in 1999. Trends in 30-day alcohol use prevalence and daily drinking show similar patterns of an increase during the 1970s and gradual declines since that time.

Recent MTF data collected from 8th and 10th graders indicate the pattern of initiation across age/grade as well as indicate age-related increases in use and problem-use measures. As shown in Fig. 2, in 1999, nearly half of all 8th graders (44%), 64% of 10th graders, and 74% of seniors had consumed alcohol in the previous year. In addition, 9% of the eighth graders, 23% of 10th graders, and 33% of seniors had been drunk in the previous 30 days, while 15% of 8th graders, 26% of 10th graders, and 31% of the seniors had binged in the previous 2 weeks (Johnston et al., 2000). These data suggest that both drinking and problem drinking start early and increase in prevalence across the grades of secondary school.

MTF data also indicate that alcohol use varies by both gender and ethnic group. Boys start drinking earlier than girls, but gender differences in annual prevalence of alcohol use diminish through high school (Johnston et al., 1999a). Other studies indicate that boys have higher prevalence rates than girls when heavy or problem use is considered (Ellickson et al., 1996; Windle, 1994). Both MTF and several large probability samples report that both lifetime and annual use of alcohol is highest among white youth, followed by American Indians and Hispanics; lifetime prevalence of drinking is lower among African Americans and Asian-American youth, and in each of these groups males are substantially more likely than females to have consumed alcohol (Johnston et al., 1999a; Barnes & Welte, 1986a).

Both MTF and other data not based on a nationally representative sample indicate that drinking begins even before entry into middle school for many youth. For example, MTF findings indicate that in 1998, among the 48% of 8th graders who had consumed alcohol, 10%

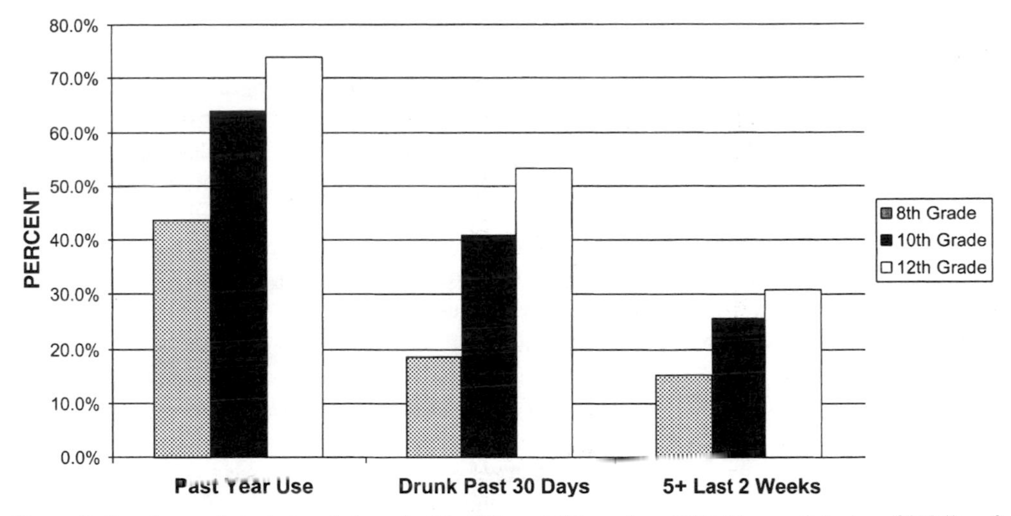

Figure 2. Prevalence of alcohol use/misuse by 8th, 10th, and 12th graders: 1999. (*Source*: Johnston, O'Malley, & Bachman, 2000.)

began using it in 4th grade, 8% began in 5th grade, and 12% began in 6th grade (Johnston et al., 1999a). Based on a different sample, Windle (1991) found that by the end of 6th grade, more than 30% of the males who were heavy drinkers in 10th grade and a quarter of those who were non-heavy drinkers had initiated alcohol use; another 40% began drinking in 7th and 8th grade.

Prevalence of Alcohol Misuse and Alcohol-Related Problems

Alcohol-related problems among youth, including adverse social and legal consequences, have not been a major focus of large-scale national surveys of substance use nor is there agreement on what constitutes misuse or the full range of problem drinking in adolescence. Nevertheless, several large but not nationally representative adolescent sample surveys have included a variety of alcohol-related problem and alcohol risk measures. They have found that misuse and alcohol-related problems are widespread during adolescence, although dependence and medical consequences are infrequent (Windle, Shope, & Bukstein, 1996; Ellickson et al., 1996).

White (1997) identified four dimensions for classifying adolescents' drinking problems: heavy and frequent alcohol use; frequent intoxication; escapist coping by drinking; and specific negative consequences (e.g., blackouts and adverse social consequences). Bailey and Rachal (1993) suggest three problem dimensions including level or frequency of drinking, adverse social consequences, and dependency symptoms.

Based on a sample of 1100 high school juniors and seniors, Windle (1994) found that high proportions of the students that drink also endorsed one or more of 13 items indicating various alcohol-related problems. For example, 29% (33% of the boys and 26% of the girls) had passed out from drinking; 47% (50% of the boys and 45% of the girls) did things while drinking that they regretted the next day; and 6% (including 11% of the boys and 2% of the girls) got into trouble with the law for other than driving-related behaviors while drinking. On all but one measure (i.e., escapist drinking), the proportion of boys reporting the problem was higher than that of the girls. The study also indicated that 17% of the boys and 8% of the girls in the sample were problem drinkers. Such individuals were defined as youth who had consumed either 45 or more alcoholic beverages in the previous 30 days or had six or more drinks on at least three occasions in the last 30 days and who also reported five or more alcohol problems in the last 6 months. Many of those problem drinkers also had high rates of delinquent activity and depressed affect (Windle, 1994).

Ellickson et al. (1996) explored three dimensions of adolescent alcohol misuse: high-risk drinking, drinking that results in negative consequences, and quantity/frequency indices. While each dimension yielded different prevalence estimates, all measures indicated that alcohol misuse was widespread among the nearly 4400 West Coast high school seniors and their former classmates who had dropped out of the same schools. Four different progressively inclusive definitions for each of the three dimensions of misuse in the past year were constructed, based on expert opinions about what constitutes adolescent misuse. The definitions combined two different quantity/frequency cutoff points with measures including daily drinking or binge drinking. The most inclusive indicators reflected the opinion that any high-risk drinking or drinking-related problems in the past year constitutes alcohol misuse. The fourth, most restricted definition combines variety and persistence criteria that required that subjects engage in two or more types of high-risk behavior.

Behaviors defined as high-risk drinking included binging, drinking before or during school, getting drunk, driving after drinking, and mixing alcohol with depressants, stimulants, and marijuana. Problems from drinking included missing school or work, regretting doing something while drinking, feeling sick, engaging in a physical fight, having trouble in school, being arrested, passing out, or having an accident after drinking.

By any of the measures, a substantial proportion of teenagers misuse alcohol. Using the most inclusive definition, nearly 70% of the sample displayed some form of alcohol misuse within the past year, with 74% of this group meeting at least two of the three criteria for misuse. About two thirds of the sample engaged in high-risk drinking; more than half suffered one or more alcohol-related problems; and a third consumed an average of 2.1 drinks per week. Even using the most restricted definition, nearly 40% of the youth had misused alcohol in the past year.

Nearly all (86%) of the teenagers that had consumed alcohol in the previous year also had engaged in some form of misuse; and 80% of those misusers also qualified as high-risk drinkers, while 75% had suffered one or more negative consequences. The most frequent forms of risky drinking included getting drunk (64%), binge drinking (49%), using marijuana with alcohol (36%), and drinking and driving (32%). The alcohol-related problems most commonly encountered were feeling sick (52%) and regretting an action (38%). Adolescents who had used alcohol were less likely to have gotten into a physical fight (17%), been arrested (7%), or had an accident after drinking (7%) (Ellickson et al., 1996).

While teenage girls are nearly as likely as the boys to be high-risk drinkers and to have suffered one or more alcohol-related problem, a gender gap appears as the severity of misuse increases. Teenage girls are substantially less likely than teenage males to experience the same negative consequences repeatedly or persistently; they also exhibit fewer different problems or high-risk behaviors. Boys are more likely than girls to binge drink (56 vs. 43%) and to drive after drinking (39 vs. 25%); they also are twice as likely as girls to get into fights or be arrested because of drinking (Ellickson et al., 1996).

Several studies consistently report ethnic differences in the prevalence of alcohol use as well as alcohol-related problems. White and Hispanic teenagers are far more likely than

African-American and Asian teenagers to ever have used alcohol (Johnston et al., 1999a; Barnes & Welte, 1986a) or to have misused it (Barnes & Welte, 1986b; Ellickson et al., 1996). Nevertheless, Ellickson and colleagues (1996) found that African-American and Hispanic youth encounter more serious alcohol-related problems including being arrested, having an accident, and getting into a fight, although they are substantially less likely to be high-risk drinkers than white teenagers.

Prevalence of Alcohol Use and Misuse among Minors after High School

Data on the prevalence and patterns of drinking of persons between 18 and 20 years old tend to focus on college students (e.g., Berkowitz & Perkins, 1986; Saltz & Elandt, 1986; Haworth-Hoeppner, Globetti, Stern, & Morasco, 1989; Presley, Meilman, & Lyerla, 1993; Wechsler, Davenport, Dowdell, Moeykens, & Castillo, 1994) and to report widespread use and frequent negative consequences of heavy episodic alcohol consumption. For example, a recent study based on a representative national sample of students at 140 American 4-year colleges ($N = 17{,}592$) found that both binge drinking (measured as consumption of five or more drinks in a row for men but as four or more drinks in a row for women during the 2 weeks prior to the survey) and associated alcohol-related problems are widespread (Wechsler et al., 1994). Among the student sample, 16% were nondrinkers, 41% drank but did not binge (35% of the men, and 45% of the women), and nearly half (50% of the men and 39% of the women) were binge drinkers. Moreover, nearly half of those who binged were frequent bingers (i.e., three or more times in the prior 2 weeks, including 23% of the males and 17% of the females). The bingers were far more likely than other students to experience serious health and other consequences of their behavior including injuries, damaging property, and academic problems. For example, 23% of frequent bingers and 9% of bingers reported injuring themselves compared to 2% of the nonbingers; the proportion of students reporting having gotten into trouble with campus or local police were 11%, 4%, and 1%, respectively. A review of other published studies concluded that alcohol was involved in 90% of campus rapes and 95% of violent crime on campus (CASA Commission on Substance Abuse at Colleges and Universities, 1994).

Monitoring the Future also has conducted follow-up surveys of representative samples of previous participants from each high school senior class since the class of 1976, including those who are full-time college students. In 1998, while 32% of high school seniors had binged in the previous 2 weeks, the proportion of binge drinking among college students (most of whom are minors) was 41% (including 51% of college males and 31% of college females [Johnston, O'Malley, & Bachman, 1999b]). This rate is similar to that found by Wechsler and colleagues (1994), although the latter used a four-drink measure for women. MTF also reported overall prevalence rates of binge drinking for 19- and 20-year-olds of 35% and for 21- to 22-year-olds of 40%. Binge drinking rates for persons 23 and older gradually declines with age. Since college-bound high school seniors are less likely to report binge drinking than non-college-bound, it appears that the former catch up with and surpass their non-college-bound peers after high school (Johnston, O'Malley, & Bachman, 1999b). While binge drinking among non-college students declined since 1980, the MTF data indicate little reduction in the prevalence of binge drinking between 1980 (i.e., 44%) and 1998 (39%) among college students (Johnston et al., 1999b).

In sum, American youth start drinking early and use alcohol frequently throughout their teenage years. Alcohol misuse, including binge drinking and alcohol-related problems, also are characteristics of a substantial proportion of adolescents and a major problem by a variety of definitions. As will be shown in the next section, these often are associated with other high-risk behaviors and have long-term negative consequences.

Prevalence of DUI, Alcohol-Related Crashes, and Alcohol-Related Crimes

Adolescent alcohol use and misuse are associated with a number of negative outcomes including drinking and driving, auto crash fatalities and injuries, and violence. Data collected during the 1980s indicate that as many as 40% of young adults have driven after drinking and that 60% have ridden with an intoxicated driver (e.g., Elliott, 1987; Hingson, Heeren, Mangione, Morelock, & Mucatel, 1982; Klitzner, Vegega, & Gruenewald, 1988a; Mayhew, Donaldson, Beirness, & Simpson, 1986). Newer survey data indicate a decrease in frequency for both of these behaviors but continued high rates. For example, Klepp, Perry, and Jacobs (1991) reported that in their sample of Minnesota 10th and 11th graders (mean age 16.7), 33% of the male and 22% of the female students who had driven a motor vehicle in the past 3 months reported driving at least once after drinking two or more drinks on a single occasion during that period. Ellickson and colleagues (1996) found that among high school seniors or their former classmates, 39% of the male and 25% of the female drinkers had driven after drinking in the past year. In Wechsler and colleagues' (1994) national survey of college students, drinking and driving was reported by 50% of the females and 62% of the males who were frequent bingers, 47% of the male and 33% of the female infrequent bingers, and even 13% of the female and 20% of the male nonbinging drinkers.

Motor vehicle crashes are the leading cause of death for youth between the ages of 15 and 20 (Baker, O'Neill, Ginsburg, & Li, 1992). The proportion of fatal crashes in which alcohol is involved has decreased from 63% in 1982 to 38% in 1994, as has the proportion of crashes with blood alcohol concentrations (BACs) at or above 0.10 (Snyder & Sickmund, 1995, p. 62). Despite these positive changes following vigorous anti-DUI campaigns and adoption of laws raising the minimum legal drinking age to 21 nationwide, young drivers continue to be overrepresented among traffic fatalities. At all levels of BAC, they are at greater risk for a fatal crash than older drinking drivers (Zador, 1991), and are involved in fatal accidents at lower levels of BAC than are older drivers (Campbell, Zobeck, & Bertollucci, 1995). At the same time, young drivers are arrested for driving under the influence at rates far below their incidence of alcohol-related crashes. For example, drivers below 21 years of age account for 14% of all fatally injured drivers with a BAC at or above the 0.10% level but make up only 1% of all arrests for DUI (Snyder & Sickmund, 1995). Moreover, there are about three times the number of arrests for every fatally injured drinking driver age 25 and older as there are for every fatally injured drinking driver ages 16 and 17 (Preusser, Preusser, & Ulmer, 1992).

There also is ample evidence that suggests that youth who misuse alcohol are at increased risk of criminal offending (Donovan & Jessor, 1985; Elliott et al., 1989; Fergusson, Lynskey, & Horwood, 1995, 1996; Jessor & Jessor, 1977; Newcomb, Maddahian, & Bentler, 1986). For example, in one birth cohort study of New Zealand youth, those who at age 15 drank frequently, heavily, or abusively had rates of officially recorded offending that were between 2.3 and 4.2 times higher than teens who did not engage in such drinking (Fergusson et al., 1995). At age 16, the same alcohol-misusing youth had 3.2 times the odds of committing violent offenses when compared to young people who did not misuse alcohol, even after adjusting for covariate risk factors (Fergusson et al., 1996).

Given the health-related, legal, and social risks associated with underage alcohol use and abuse, a variety of interventions designed to delay initiation, reduce use, and decrease alcohol-related problems have been implemented. However, far fewer of these have been evaluated and an even smaller proportion of these studies have considered their outcomes for other problem behaviors than alcohol use or related problems. While this chapter cannot review all these interventions, it will next examine one particular environmental prevention approach and its consequences, namely, the use of laws and public policies to reduce underage alcohol consumption and drinking after driving. A later section reviews a wide array of other alcohol intervention approaches in more cursory fashion.

MINIMUM LEGAL DRINKING AGE: HISTORY, INCONSISTENCIES IN THE LAW, AND ENFORCEMENT ISSUES

Changes in the Minimum Legal Drinking Age Since 1970 and the Current Legal Patchwork

Since the adoption of Article XXI of the Constitution (repealing Prohibition), regulation of the sale and distribution of alcohol has been left to the states. Every state has established a minimum legal drinking age (MLDA), which has varied over time and across jurisdictions. Between 1970 and 1975, 29 states lowered their minimum legal age for alcohol consumption to be consistent with the lowering of the voting age from 21 to 18 in 1970. In 1976, however, concerns about the consequences of youth drinking, including increases in alcohol-related motor vehicle crashes, began a reversal of this downward trend in the MDLA. Congress accelerated that change with passage of the National Minimum Drinking Age Act of 1984. That law threatened states with loss of federal highway funds if they failed to raise the MLDA to 21 by October 1, 1986. By 1987, all states had complied. Despite this uniform minimum drinking age brought about by a federal law, there are wide variations among the states with respect to other aspects of drinking age laws and penalties for MLDA violations and large "legal loopholes" that permit widespread underage drinking (Office of the Inspector General, 1991).

Responsibility for enforcing liquor laws in all but two states rests with state administrative agencies, usually called Alcohol Beverage Control (ABC) agencies, and with local law enforcement (i.e., police and sheriffs). Because ABC agencies have limited enforcement staff and lack the authority to cite or arrest minors, however, much of the MLDA enforcement burden actually falls on local law enforcement (Office of the Inspector General, 1991).

Those violations that are detected may be pursued either through criminal prosection of violators or referral to an ABC agency for administrative penalties against the holder of a liquor license. In taking criminal action, the law enforcement officer may cite or arrest the minor, the seller, or the person who purchases alcohol and furnishes it to minors. These offenses may result in misdemeanor or felony convictions and in penalties including fines, jail, community service, and/or driver's license revocation for minors (Office of the Inspector General, 1991). ABC's administrative enforcement of liquor laws may occur concurrently with criminal prosecution or as an independent process.

Enforcement efforts are complicated by the fact that many states permit minors to obtain and possess alcohol under certain circumstances. For example, 35 states allow youth to possess alcohol, including 26 that allow it with parental consent, 11 states that have religious exceptions, and 10 with medical exceptions; 6 states permit minors to actually purchase alcohol; and 42 states do not prohibit minors from entering drinking establishments. Twenty-one states lack specific statutory language prohibiting the consumption of alcohol by minors, although they may be forbidden to possess it. There is no statutory language explicitly prohibiting the deliberate misrepresentation of age by youth to obtain alcohol in 16 states and no specific prohibition of use of a false identification to obtain alcohol in 19 states (Office of the Inspector General, 1991).

Criminal penalties for violation of drinking age laws also vary widely. Youthful violators may face a fine ranging from $15 to $5000, 1 year in jail, or both; someone who supplies alcohol to a minor faces criminal penalties ranging from $50 to $10,000, 5 years in jail, or both (Office of the Inspector General, 1991). Administrative penalties imposed on a licensee range from nothing to $5000 or a 6-month license suspension.

Sources of Alcohol Obtained by Youth

Minors have little difficulty obtaining alcohol. In 1998, 73% of 8th graders and 88% of 10th graders report that alcohol is "fairly easy" or "very easy" to obtain (Johnston et al., 1999a). Their principal sources initially are their homes, siblings, and friends. By midteens they acquire alcohol (usually beer) at parties where it usually has been obtained by older adolescents or other individuals over 21, and they begin to purchase it at commercial outlets, primarily convenience stores (Wagenaar et al., 1993).

Several studies have tested the commercial availability of alcohol to minors through stings or purchase attempts by persons who were or were judged to appear younger than 21. Preusser and Williams (1992) found that underage males were successful in buying beer from stores in 97 out of 100 purchase attempts in Washington, DC; 82% of attempts made in Westchester County, NY; and 44% of attempts made in Albany and Schenectady Counties, NY. In a testing effort initiated by a New Jersey County Prosecutor's office, male minors successfully purchased alcohol in 59% of the 46 establishments visited, including 11 off-sale outlets and 16 bars (O'Leary, Gorman, & Speer, 1994). Forster, Murray, Wolfson, and Wagenaar (1995) used female buyers who were 21 but appeared younger to attempt to purchase beer without an identification at both off-sale and on-sale outlets in 24 small and medium-sized communities in Minnesota and Wisconsin. The buyers purchased beer without an identification card in 50% of their approximately 800 attempts in on-sale outlets and 52% of nearly 1000 off-sale attempts.

Enforcement of MLDA

Enforcement of the MLDA is hampered by a number of obstacles. These include limited resources and staff (which have been cut in recent years), low priority on youth alcohol enforcement, the lack of ABC jurisdiction over minors, and limited communication and cooperation among ABCs and state and local law enforcement agencies (Office of the Inspector General, 1991). Even when agencies take enforcement actions, nominal penalties against vendors and minors limit their effectiveness. Vendors' licenses rarely are suspended following a first offense and even repeat offenders rarely have their licenses revoked. Courts are lenient, in part due to overload and higher priorities given to drug cases (Office of the Inspector General, 1991).

Several studies by Wagenaar and associates (Wagenaar & Wolfson, 1994, 1995; Wolfson, Wagenaar, & Hornseth, 1995; Wolfson et al., 1996a) detail the variations in patterns of criminal and administrative enforcement of MLDA laws across states and among counties in four of the states. They also address the factors contributing to these differences and the barriers to more vigorous enforcement. Using FBI data to calculate each state's average annualized arrest rates for various liquor law offenses for 1988 through 1990, Wagenaar and Wolfson (1994) found that arrest rates of minors for liquor law violations varied from a low of 12 arrests per 100,000 eligible population in Louisiana to a high of 561 in South Dakota. They also documented the disparity between enforcement actions targeting youthful drinkers and those directed at adult or commercial providers. Based on reported consumption rates in MTF, they estimated that only 2 of every 1000 occasions of youth drinking result in an arrest, and 5 of every 100,000 youth drinking occasions result in an ABC action against an alcohol outlet (Wagenaar & Wolfson, 1994, p. 41). In addition, the occasional penalties imposed by ABCs against outlets found to have violated the MLDA are lenient. The median fine is $300, and suspensions average just 7 days (Wagenaar & Wolfson, 1994, pp. 45–46).

Variations in enforcement of the MLDA were found to be related to patterns of enforcement of other laws. States that have higher rates of arrests for minor crimes and higher rates of narcotics enforcement tend to have lower rates of arrests for underage drinking; those states with vigorous enforcement of liquor laws against adults also tend to have higher rates of arrests for underage liquor law violations. Thus attention to liquor law enforcement, rather than a focus on underage drinking per se, is the underlying dimension on which states vary (Wagenaar & Wolfson, 1994).

An examination of MLDA enforcement at the county level (n = 295) in four states (Kentucky, Michigan, Montana, and Oregon) indicated that in general the levels of enforcement actions on underage drinking are very low. The median county had no liquor license suspensions or revocations, one ABC action against an alcohol outlet, one arrest for furnishing to minors, eight arrests of minors for possession, and a total of 26 liquor law arrests (excluding DUI and public drunkenness) of 16- to 20-year-olds annually (Wagenaar & Wolfson, 1995, p. 423). In 12% of the counties there were no arrests of underage youth for illegal possession of alcoholic beverages. Several socioecological variables (e.g., county population, land area, and percent unoccupied housing) accounted for much of the variance in arrest rates. After these variables were controlled, county-level analyses indicated that the higher the level of arrests for all types of minor crime in a county, the higher the arrest level for liquor law violations.

In-depth interviews with law enforcement officers from 15 of the study jurisdictions indicated that the officers are aware of the extent of underage drinking in their communities but are discouraged from taking more vigorous enforcement action by several obstacles (Wolfson et al., 1995). First, citizens put little pressure on law enforcement agencies to increase enforcement of underage drinking laws, while parents tend to regard drinking as "an understandable rite of passage." Second, the absence of juvenile detention facilities in some communities depresses the level of enforcement of MLDA laws, since juveniles must be held in an area separate from adult detainees by police. In agencies without a separate juvenile detention facility, the officer either must constantly supervise the juvenile until he or she is released to a parent or guardian or transport the youth to the nearest juvenile detention facility with available space. This may involve a round-trip of more than 100 miles (Wolfson et al., 1995).

In states that do not permit officers to treat consumption of alcohol as possession, evidentiary obstacles arise because the officer must see actual physical possession in order to cite a minor. This becomes a problem particularly at large parties when drinkers drop their beverages when police arrive. Finally, officers' perceptions that the courts are unwilling or unable to mete out appropriate sanctions for liquor offenses increase their reluctance to cite or arrest underage drinkers for liquor offenses (Wolfson et al., 1995).

Weak ABC enforcement of MLDA also contributes to the failure of alcohol outlet owners and operators to implement consistent policies and practices that may reduce the likelihood of sales to youth. For example, a survey of Wisconsin and Minnesota alcohol outlet owners and managers indicated that fewer than half of all outlets have employee-monitoring systems and that the training of managers and employees is spotty (Wolfson et al., 1996a).

In sum, laws regulating purchase, possession, and consumption of alcohol by minors have limited deterrent effects. This is because they are inconsistent; viewed with some ambivalence by the public; and weakly enforced by law enforcement, ABCs, and the courts.

Arrests and Case Processing of Juvenile Alcohol Offenses

Despite inconsistent laws and weak enforcement efforts, the liquor law violations of minors impose a substantial burden on the justice system. In 1998, fully 15% of the more than 2.6 million arrests of persons under 18 years of age were for alcohol-related offenses. This included about 21,000 arrests for DUI; 157,000 for liquor law violations; 24,600 for drunkenness; and 183,000 for disorderly conduct (Snyder, 1999). In contrast with arrest rates for drug abuse violations, which have increased by 86% between 1989 and 1998, arrests rates for DUI, liquor law, and drunkenness offenses fell by more than 30% between 1980 and 1995. They have risen in the past 3 years, though they are still 10% below the 1990 level, as shown in Fig. 3. Since 1980, only disorderly conduct arrests of juveniles have increased. Their more than 50% climb may represent a shifting of arrest charges so that the officer did not have to prove possession or consumption (Snyder, 1996).

Young people between 18 and 20 also are arrested for the same offenses in even larger numbers than juveniles. In 1997, there were more than 70,000 arrests of youth between 18 and 20 for DUI; just over 180,000 arrests for liquor law offenses; 40,000 arrests for drunkenness; and 75,000 for disorderly conduct (Federal Bureau of Investigation, 1998). Since studies of alcohol-related violence generally have found that alcohol is present in between one half and two thirds of all homicides and serious assaults (Pernanen, 1991; Murdoch, Pihl, & Ross, 1990), perhaps as many as half of the approximately 66,000 arrests of minors for murder and nonnegligent manslaughter, rape, robbery, and aggravated assault in 1997 involved alcohol

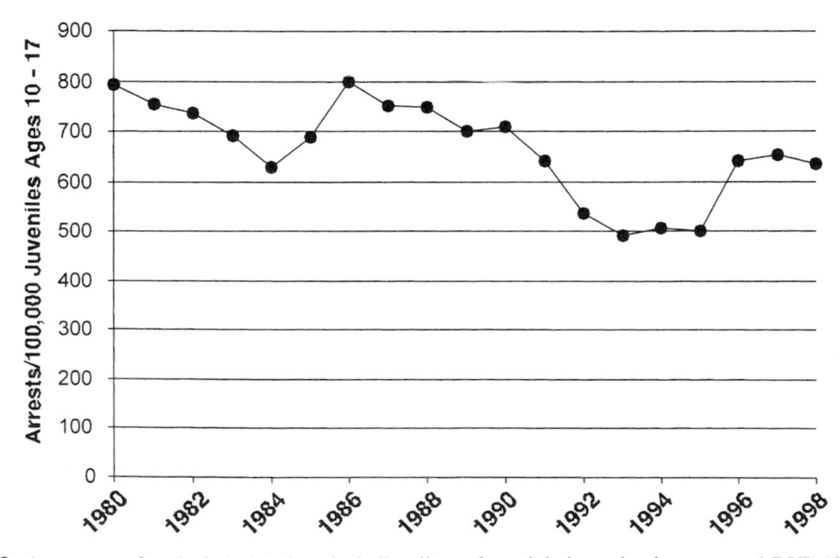

Figure 3. Arrest rates for alcohol violations including liquor law violations, drunkenness, and DUI: 1980–1998. (*Sources*: Snyder, 1997, 1998, 1999.)

(US Department of Justice, 1998). These data suggest that the burden of minors' alcohol-related crime on the criminal justice system is considerable.

Data on case outcomes of juveniles arrested for liquor law and for DUI violations are very limited and inconsistent. Jurisdictions handle youthful liquor law violation cases in divergent ways and provide inconsistent and incomplete case reports to the National Center for Juvenile Justice (NCJJ) for analysis. An earlier NCJJ report tracked all liquor offenses through the juvenile justice system (Sickmund, 1991), but two recent reports (Butts, Snyder, Finnegan, Aughenbaugh, & Poole, 1995, 1996) provide disposition data only for cases that are handled formally by juvenile intake (i.e., petitioned or given an adjudication hearing before a judge or master), and even these dispositions are reported separately for status offenses (i.e., underage purchase or possession) and delinquent acts (i.e., public drunkenness).

The earlier analysis looked at all case records in which an alcohol or drug offense was the most serious charge from 1985 through 1988 drawn from 841 courts in 17 states (Sickmund, 1991). It found that there was little change in case processing over the 4 years and that only about a quarter of the alcohol cases were petitioned in each year while three quarters were handled informally. In contrast, drug cases were increasingly likely to be handled formally so that by 1988, 66% were petitioned. It also found distinct racial differences in youth involvement in drug and alcohol cases and the manner in which cases were handled. For example, in 1988, for every 1000 youth at risk in the jurisdictions in the study, the juvenile courts processed 4.12 drug cases and 3.84 alcohol cases. However, in alcohol cases, the case rate for whites (4.58) was nearly four times the rate for nonwhites (1.16). In contrast, the 1988 rate of drug cases for nonwhites (8.17) was more than 2.5 times the rate for whites (3.0) (Sickmund, 1991).

Looking at the 1988 alcohol case dispositions, of those handled informally, about 45% were dismissed, 30% resulted in a probation sentence, and the rest resulted in another sanction. Among petitioned alcohol cases, 20% were dismissed, 50% resulted in placement on probation, 8% in residential placement, and the rest in another sanction.

DUI cases were more likely to be handled formally and to result in probation than liquor law violation cases. For example, in 1988, 22% of the DUI cases but 43% of the drinking cases were dismissed either with or without a petition (Sickmund, 1991).

Focusing on 1993 status liquor law offense case dispositions, among those that were petitioned (i.e., handled formally), 55% were adjudicated and more then half resulted in a probation sentence (52%) while only 2% were dismissed. Among the remaining 45% that were nonadjudicated, 47% were dismissed, a quarter given probation, and the remainder given another sanction (Butts et al., 1996). A racial breakdown of the dispositions of status liquor law violation cases for which data were available ($n = 16{,}888$) suggests possible bias in the system that merits further examination. African Americans made up only 5% of the offenders, but their cases were substantially more likely than those of whites to be petitioned (52 vs. 34%, respectively), to lead to adjudication (26 vs. 22%), and to result in probation or out-of-home placement (21 vs. 13%, respectively) (Butts et al., 1995). The reasons for these racial differences in sentence are unknown.

Impact of MLDA on DUI and Other Youth Crime

The minimum legal drinking age of 21 was adopted as a highway safety measure, based on earlier findings of its effectiveness in saving lives (Saffer & Grossman, 1987; Wagenaar, 1983). A subsequent study also found that despite weak enforcement, raising the MLDA reduced both underage drinking and several of its negative consequences (O'Malley & Wagenaar, 1991). Self-reported drinking was consistently higher in those states that had 18 as the MLDA at some time between 1976 and 1987 than in states that had an MLDA of 21 throughout that period, after controlling for potential individual-level confounds. In addition, time series analyses indicated that alcohol-involved crashes and single-vehicle nighttime fatalities (a frequent surrogate for DUI) among 18- to 20-year-olds declined as a direct result of the lower levels of consumption following increases in the MLDA.

There also is some evidence that raising the legal drinking age has affected youth violence, particularly homicide rates (Parker & Rehbum, 1995). This analysis focused on the impact of changes in the MLDA on youth homicide by looking at changes in the rates of primary (i.e., between acquaintances) and nonprimary (stranger) homicide for victims aged 15–18, 19–20, and 21–24, per 100,000 population. They used a pooled cross-sectional time series analysis on data for each of the 50 states and the District of Columbia for each year from 1976 through 1983, using dummy codes to identify the year in which drinking age was raised by at least one year. Other variables in the model included alcohol consumption, measured as beer consumption per capita, infant mortality (a poverty index), racial composition, and total state population.

The results suggested that increasing the minimum purchase age had a negative impact on youth homicide net of the principal factors associated with homicide (i.e., beer consumption, poverty, and percentage nonwhite in the population), and that the effect was stronger for those homicides occurring among acquaintances than for stranger homicides that often take place in the context of another serious crime. Given this finding for homicide, it would not be surprising to find that the higher MLDA also is associated with reductions in other violent crimes that frequently are preceded by heavy alcohol consumption, although this has not been studied to date.

DRINKING AND DRIVING LAWS FOR MINORS AND THEIR ENFORCEMENT

Encouraged by the effectiveness of raising the MLDA and getting states to adopt the change by tying it to highway funds, Congress recently included in the National Highway Systems Act of 1995 a provision that mandates a "zero tolerance" law for youthful drivers. Such a provision makes it illegal for young persons to drive after any drinking by setting the legal BAC limit at 0.02 or less. States that had not adopted such a law by the beginning of fiscal year 1999 would have suffered a 5% loss in highway construction funding. By June 1998, all states and the District of Columbia had acceptable zero tolerance laws.

As with MLDA, the zero tolerance policy is supported by research (Hingson, Heeren, Howland, & Winter, 1991; Hingson, Heeren, & Winter, 1994; Blomberg, 1992; Martin & Andreasson, 1996). The positive findings from a comparative analysis of the first four states to reduce legal BAC limits for young drivers (Hingson et al., 1991) were strengthened when that earlier analysis was expanded to the first 12 states to set lower legal blood alcohol limits for drivers under 21. These states were matched with nearby comparison states that did not lower the legal blood alcohol limit. As Hingson and colleagues (1994) reported, the states with lowered BAC levels for young drivers experienced a 20% relative decline in the proportion of single-vehicle nighttime fatal crashes among drivers under 21, a difference that was statistically significant. Moreover, an additional analysis indicated that the greatest declines in adolescent fatal crashes occurred in states where BAC limits were 0.02 or less (i.e., zero-tolerance states); there was little effect on youth crash rates in states that had lowered BACs for youth to 0.04 to 0.06.

A study of a high-visibility experimental media and educational program implemented in six counties in Maryland after that state adopted a 0.02 law for minors also found it to be effective under certain conditions. The program significantly increased knowledge about the law among teenagers in the experimental counties but not in the rest of the counties. Police also perceived a greater decrease in alcohol-related crashes involving drivers under 21 in the experimental counties (i.e., 50%) than the rest of the state (11%) (Blomberg, 1992).

Preliminary findings from an ongoing study of California's Zero Tolerance Law suggest that it too is altering youth attitudes and behavior. The law has several unique provisions designed to increase its deterrent effect. It allows a police officer to immediately seize the license of a youth who refuses to be tested or has a roadside BAC test over 0.01 percent and authorizes administrative license action by the motor vehicle department without the need for a criminal charge and trial, thus increasing swiftness and certainty of sanctioning. It also lengthens from 4 months to 1 year the period of loss of the driver's license for first-offense drunk driving, thereby increasing severity. Surveys of young California drivers conducted shortly before and 18 months after the law took effect indicate that beliefs about peers' attitudes toward driving after drinking have become more negative, and that an increased proportion of youth believe that if they are stopped and tested for drinking and driving, they will lose their license. However, there has been no change in the perceived likelihood of being stopped and breath tested by the police and no increase in the actual number of citations of underage drivers (Martin & Andreasson, 1996). These findings suggest that the norms related to drinking and driving have made it a morally disapproved behavior among a growing proportion of youth, and thus support the observation of Grasmick, Bursik, and Arneklev (1993) that the moral factor (i.e., embarrassment and shame) as distinct from the threat of legal sanctions also is effective in deterring DUI.

There are several reasons that the police tend to underenforce DUI laws against youth in California and elsewhere (Preusser et al., 1992). Because drinking is illegal, youth tend to drink in parks and other locales where patrol officers are less likely to look for or find them. Youthful drivers also are more likely than older drivers to drink on weekend evenings, which also are peak periods for the demand for police services. Youth often do not display the cues of psychomotor impairment (e.g., weaving, inability to walk a straight line) that officers are trained to look for. This absence of familiar cues of intoxication poses an even greater problem for police in deciding which youth to stop and test for zero tolerance offenses. Because police often lack "probable cause" for DUI stops, prosecutors tend to be reluctant to bring low BAC cases, further discouraging police from making such arrests.

ALCOHOL MISUSE AS A RISK FACTOR IN DELINQUENCY AND VIOLENCE

Alcohol use among minors not only is both normative and illegal behavior, it has frequently been associated with crime or delinquency. Although some studies explore the association between alcohol consumption and crime in general, most focus on the association between alcohol use and aggressive or violent behaviors. Despite the voluminous literature on alcohol and violence (for reviews, see Fagan, 1990; Murdoch et al., 1990; Roizen, 1993; Miczek, Weerts, & DeBold, 1993; Collins, 1989; Lipsey, Wilson, Cohen, & Derzon, 1997), most empirical studies focus on adults rather than adolescents, and even fewer of these empirical studies of adolescents provide clear models of the dynamics of the alcohol–delinquency association through the teenage years. In this section, the primary explanatory models linking alcohol use or misuse and delinquent behavior are briefly presented and empirical findings from cross-sectional and longitudinal studies summarized.

Explanatory Models

Three theoretical explanatory frameworks have been proposed to account for the nature and direction of the association of alcohol and other drug use with aggressive or violent behavior as well as with other problem behaviors including drinking and driving (White, 1997). The first model postulates that alcohol use causes aggressive behavior, primarily as a result of psychopharmacological effects of the drug (e.g., through disinhibition or perceptual distortions) that cause aggressive behavior (Fagan, 1990).

A second model postulates that aggressive behavior leads to heavy alcohol use. The model is based on the assumption that aggressive individuals are more likely than nonaggressive individuals to choose or be pressed into social situations or subcultures in which heavy drinking is encouraged (e.g., the professional criminal lifestyle) (Collins & Messerschmidt, 1993), or to use alcohol to self-medicate. According to this model, individuals also may hold expectations that alcohol causes aggression and believe that if they are aggressive when drunk, they will be held less accountable for their behavior (Collins, 1989; Fagan, 1990).

The third model postulates that the link between alcohol and aggression is either coincidental or arises because they share common risk factors. In other words, the association is spurious rather than being a direct causal one, and similar factors promote both alcohol use and aggression (White, Brick, & Hansell, 1993a). The empirical support for each model will be briefly examined below. It should be noted, however, that it is unlikely that any single model can account for all individuals or all types of aggression. Rather, each model may account for different subgroups of the population or different incidents of alcohol-related aggression (Elliott, 1993).

The Association between Alcohol Use and Aggression in Adolescence

Acute Incidents of Alcohol-Related Aggression

Only a few studies have directly assessed acute incidents of alcohol-related violence in adolescence. One of these is the Rutgers Health and Human Development Project (HHDP), a prospective longitudinal study of adolescent development that used a community sample of mostly white, working- and middle-class adolescents. Self-report data were obtained from subjects who indicated the number of times they engaged in several aggressive behaviors including fighting or acting mean, vandalism, fire setting, forcing sex, and hurting someone badly while they were drinking or because of their drinking (White, Hansell, & Brick, 1993b).

While few females in the HHDP sample engaged in any type of alcohol-related aggression, rates for fighting while intoxicated were very high for males and increased with age from about 30% of the 15-year-olds who drink alcohol to about 40% of alcohol users at age 21. Rates for alcohol-related vandalism among males also were relatively high in late adolescence and early adulthood (about 20% of the drinkers) then decreased. Other offenses occurred less frequently (White et al., 1993a).

Mitic (1989) found that about 6% of junior high and 15% of high school students reported engaging in vandalism or violence against others while drinking. Elliott and colleagues (1989) found that when the National Youth Survey (NYS) subjects were between 11 and 17 years old, 23% of the self-reported aggravated assaults (including participating in a gang fight) as well as 14% of the burglaries and 20% of the motor vehicle thefts were committed under the influence of alcohol only. In follow-up data 4 years later, as these subjects entered young adulthood, alcohol use was more likely to precede a violent offense (particularly a sexual assault) than a property offense, suggesting that the relationship between alcohol use and violent offenses changed over the life course. Cumulatively, however, these studies do not suggest that rates of alcohol-related aggressive behaviors are particularly high during adolescence.

Studies of adolescent offenders also indicate relatively low rates of alcohol use at the time of violent crimes (Collins & Messerschmidt, 1993). For example, only 8% of all youth in custody in state institutions reported that they were under the influence of only alcohol when they committed a violent offense, while 24% had committed violent crimes while under the influence of both alcohol and other drugs. This suggests that alcohol does not have a unique effect on violent crime.

Findings from self-report studies regarding the contribution of alcohol intoxication to the respondent's own aggression were mixed. One community sample of youth indicated that they attribute other people's crimes but not their own to their drug use, suggesting that substance use was incidental to crime (Carpenter, Glassner, Johnson, & Loughlin, 1988). In contrast, in another study of adolescents adjudicated for a violent crime, more than half the youths said that using alcohol (29%) or drugs (33%) contributed to their acting violently, and nearly half had used either alcohol (17%) or drugs (34%) immediately before their adjudicated violent crime (Hartstone & Hansen, 1984).

Cross-Sectional and Longitudinal Data on Patterns of Alcohol Use and Aggression

Other studies have examined patterns of alcohol and aggression through correlations or typologies. For example, using the HHDP data, White (1997) found that the average cross-sectional correlation between composite measures of boys' alcohol use and aggression at ages 12, 15, and 18 was significant ($r = .23$), but so was the average correlation of alcohol use and property crime ($r = .30$), suggesting little support for a unique relationship between alcohol and aggression. Likewise, in an inner city sample, Fagan, Weis, and Cheng (1988) found that correlations between alcohol and violent crimes generally were lower than those between alcohol and property crime.

A meta-analysis of cross-sectional studies of alcohol and aggression that did not distinguish studies of adolescents from those of adults concluded that greater alcohol use is associated with higher levels of violent behavior, but that this association does not support a causal connection. In fact, the mean correlation for alcohol–nonviolent crimes was higher than the mean correlation for alcohol–violent crimes using studies that were based primarily on adolescent samples, suggesting that alcohol's association with delinquent behavior is not limited to violence. In 6 of the 14 studies included in this analysis, after statistically controlling for other variables that accounted for a significant portion of the variance in violence independent of the effect of alcohol, the relationship between alcohol use and criminal violence was no longer significant (Lipsey et al., 1997).

While correlation studies suggest that the association between alcohol use and aggression is similar to or weaker than the association between alcohol use and other forms of delinquency, the data also suggest that alcohol and drug users as opposed to nonusers are more likely to be delinquent and more likely to be involved in aggression (Carpenter et al., 1988; Fagan et al., 1987). In the NYS data, for example, Elliott and colleagues (1989) found that level of violence increased across groups from nonusers to alcohol users to marijuana users to polydrug users. Thus, there were greater levels of violence among polydrug users and marijuana users who also used alcohol than among those who only consumed alcohol. Similarly, the level of alcohol use increased from nondelinquents to exploratory delinquents to nonserious delinquents to serious delinquents. After reviewing the literature on the relationship between alcohol use and crime during adolescence, Collins (1986) concluded that alcohol use by itself is not important to the occurrence of serious criminal involvement. Although those who drink and drink heavily are more likely to be involved in other forms of deviance, the association is probably spurious and due to common etiologies. Similarly, Lipsey and colleagues' (1997) meta-analysis concluded that while the individual level correlational data consistently show a statistical association between alcohol use and violent behavior that is positive and nontrivial, that these correlations may represent relationships confounded by other variables rather than a causal relationship.

Using longitudinal data to examine the sequencing of alcohol use/misuse and other deviant behavior, Elliott and colleagues (1989) found that initial involvement in delinquency occurs simultaneous with or prior to the initiation of alcohol consumption, and that minor delinquency almost always precedes drug use. While there are variations in the sequential patterns of behaviors, a substantial percentage of subjects committed minor offenses before initiating alcohol use, but marijuana use usually followed alcohol use, then index offending, and finally polydrug use. They concluded, therefore, that the onset of minor delinquency leads to the onset of drug use and not vice versa; that for a substantial number of adolescents, minor delinquency and alcohol use occur simultaneously; and that these behaviors are the precursors to more serious forms of both substance use and offending behavior.

Other longitudinal studies of high-risk populations looking at developmental patterns suggest that aggressive behavior begins early, is stable over the life course, occurs prior to alcohol use, and is a better predictor of alcohol use than alcohol use is of aggression (White, 1997); nevertheless, others (Virkkunen, 1977; Dembo, Williams, Getreu, Schmeidler, & Wish, 1991) have found that early alcohol use is an important predictor of later violent behavior among arrestees.

Support for a Spurious or Common Cause Model

The most frequently cited and tested explanation for the association between adolescent substance use and juvenile delinquency is that they both are manifestations of a single underlying general propensity to deviance or a predisposition to unconventionality that is expressed in different ways in different individuals. This approach is most fully developed in problem behavior theory (Jessor & Jessor, 1977; Donovan & Jessor, 1985). Other studies have found evidence that drinking and driving also are part of the larger pattern of adolescent involvement in behaviors that violate normative standards (e.g., Elliott, 1987; Donovan, 1993). Other behaviors included in the problem behavior syndrome are cigarette use, precocious sexual behavior, problem drinking, use of marijuana and other drugs, theft, and aggression, all of which clustered together. This cluster of behaviors was explained by the same group of variables and was negatively related to conventional behavior.

While there is substantial support for this theory, there also are a number of unresolved issues such as the nature of changes in the strength of covariation at different stages of the life span (e.g., early onset of alcohol consumption is strongly correlated with delinquency, but the association weakens substantially by midadolescence) and the contribution of unique causal variables in the explanation of specific types of problem behavior (Elliott, 1992). Thus, while adolescents may share a similar set of risk factors and experiment with a variety of deviant behaviors, not all adolescents who engage in one behavior engage in the others. Nor do the risk factors have equal effects on each behavior. Thus, while there is some generality in the set of explanatory factors that may account for a substantial portion of the variance in each of a strongly related subset of problem behaviors, there also are important unique features of each behavior that need separate explanations. These include life experience and opportunities as well as protective factors that mediate the relationship between risk factors and problem outcomes (Hawkins, Catalano, & Miller, 1992).

The most frequently cited predictors of violence and alcohol use reveal substantial overlap. For example, some of the risk factors for violence identified in the National Research Council's Violence report (Reiss & Roth, 1993) were hyperactivity, impulsivity, risk taking, low empathy and low IQ, childhood bullying, harsh and erratic discipline, parental abuse or neglect, low income, familial criminal behavior, early school failure, peer rejection, and growing up in a high-crime neighborhood. All but low income and low IQ also have been found to be risk factors for adolescent alcohol use or adult substance abuse problems (Hawkins et al., 1992; Kandel, 1980).

In addition to common risk factors, the same theories have been applied to explain delinquency or teenage violence and substance abuse. The most frequently tested theories include control theory (Hirschi, 1969), differential association theory (Sutherland & Cressey, 1978), their integration (Elliott, Huizinga, & Ageton, 1985), and social learning models (Bandura, 1977). Many of the theoretical models commonly used include individual characteristics and behavioral tendencies, interpersonal (e.g., family and peer group) factors, and macrolevel situational and environmental factors to account for a clustering of risk factors for both alcohol use/misuse and juvenile offending.

From the perspective of the prevention of both alcohol abuse and delinquency, an important issue is how to identify the conditions and variables that differentiate among those youth likely to progress beyond experimentation with minor forms of delinquency and substance use and those who do not in order to intervene early in the developmental process. Since there appears to be a sequential pattern of drug involvement, with the earliest stages involving use of alcohol before subsequent use of marijuana and other illicit drugs, but no necessary progression to the next stage, effective prevention efforts to delay the initiation of alcohol use may have a profound "ripple" effect that may impact on other forms of problem behaviors. Indeed, according to one study (Elliott et al., 1989), the probability of using illicit drugs and the risk of serious delinquency is reduced by a factor of four if an individual has never used alcohol.

INTERVENTIONS TO REDUCE OR PREVENT UNDERAGE DRINKING

Given the overlap of risk factors for delinquency and substance abuse, a number of prevention programs have been implemented simultaneously to reduce each; others have been designed to address one or the other problem behavior, although they often use similar approaches (for reviews of youth violence prevention programs, see Tolan & Guerra, 1994; Reiss & Roth, 1993; for reviews of substance abuse intervention programs, see Botvin, 1990; Hawkins et al., 1992; Gorman & Speer, 1995; Hawkins, Arthur, & Catalano, 1995). There also are a variety of alcohol-specific programs designed to delay initiation of alcohol use, reduce youth consumption, and/or prevent alcohol abuse and related problems (for reviews, see Windle et al., 1996; Howard, 1993; Klitzner, Stewart, & Fisher, 1993; Wagenaar & Perry, 1994), but their broader impact on delinquency and other problem behaviors has been largely ignored. Nevertheless, because they may affect delinquent behaviors including violence and aggression, they will be summarized in this section. While this section will note findings from a wide variety of programs, the emphasis is on contextual approaches focused on altering laws and changing norms favorable to alcohol consumption and their outcomes.

In general, the most successful approaches are theoretically grounded and integrate the elements from theories of adolescent development, social influence, and deviant behavior. They also take into consideration alcohol's uniqueness as a drug: It appears to have health benefits when used in moderation, is legally available to persons 21 and older, and is widely advertised. This legal status presents complexities in targeting consistent and credible alcohol use prevention messages to youth, since the risk factors associated with alcohol use and abuse include the cultural norms favorable to drinking, its promotion in the mass media, and the widespread availability of alcohol to minors (Windle et al., 1996).

The factors contributing to drinking are not independent. Rather, they interact in a "web of social influences" that vary in causal distance from drinking behavior and operate at both macro- or microlevels. Taking elements from the aforementioned theories of the etiology of problem behaviors, Wagenaar and Perry (1994) present a dynamic "integrated theory of drinking" that combines individual (e.g., alcohol cognitions and expectancies), interpersonal (e.g., peer group and family influences), community, and sociocultural level (e.g., physical, economic, and legal availability of alcohol) variables. The model also simultaneously addresses the supply (i.e., the economic, social, and physical availability of alcohol) and the demand for alcohol and points to potentially fruitful avenues for intervention (Wagenaar & Perry, 1994).

The authors observe, for example, that drinking is directly affected by individual cognitions and perceptions regarding alcohol. Perceptions, in turn, are a result of social interaction with significant others, observation of parents and peers, and formal social controls. In addition to the mediating influence of cognitive variables, other factors (i.e., social and physical availability of alcohol) have a direct effect on drinking behavior as well as operating indirectly by creating perceptions. Thus, programs that change perceptions or beliefs about alcohol are unlikely to have a lasting effect unless they are accompanied by reductions in socioenvironmental conditions that encourage alcohol use (e.g., by altering the community norms and public policies). In addition, since varied macrolevel factors affect the individual drinking behaviors, the more youth encounter simultaneous, consistent messages and actions at multiple levels in the society, the greater the potential for long-term success.

In light of the easy availability of alcohol to youth as well as the negative findings regarding the outcomes of prevention strategies designed to change knowledge and attitudes (Moskowitz, 1989), increasingly programs are based on a public health model that regards alcohol-related problems as the result of three factors and their interaction. These factors are the individual or host (which used to be the whole focus of prevention efforts), the agent or beverage, and the environment (both social and physical), all of which must be considered. Similarly, the focus of prevention has expanded from a concentration on avoiding alcohol dependence to reducing other adverse consequences (e.g., traffic crashes and violence) and delaying the onset of drinking. Increasingly, alcohol intervention programs are multilevel and directed at the drug, alcohol, and environment that encourages drinking, as well as at the individual drinker. Alcohol-focused interventions address pricing, labeling, and packaging; environmental interventions are directed toward altering advertising, availability, legal sanctions, and the sociocultural context. Furthermore, many intervention programs blend various techniques including training and education, media advocacy, policy measures, and law enforcement to meet their goals (Giesbrecht, Krempulec, & West, 1993). In characterizing underage drinking interventions, they have been grouped in terms of their primary setting, namely the family, the school or combined school and family, community, and societal level. The latter may focus on the media or on public policy approaches to reduce access to or the availability of alcohol.

Family-Based Interventions

A number of alcohol intervention programs are designed to address and expand parents' communication with their children regarding alcohol use and drinking and driving, since parental lack of awareness of the true extent of teen drinking hampers their ability to intervene (Beck & Lockhart, 1992). One illustrative program, Preparing for the Drug (Free) Years, is a four-session parent training program that includes alcohol prevention. It has resulted in positive changes in parents' attitudes, motivations, and intentions to use the program strategies but has not reported long-term follow-up (Hawkins, Catalano, & Kent, 1991). Other parent programs focus specifically on improving communication regarding drinking and driving (Turrisi, Jaccard, Valera, & Kelly, 1994).

Concerned parents have formed groups to try to prevent youth alcohol and drug use (Klitzner, Bamberger, & Gruenewald, 1990a). These groups usually try to assert parental control, reduce peer influence, manipulate peer group and community norms, and affect schools' and community agencies' policies (Klitzner, Bamberger, & Gruenewald, 1990b). Their evaluation indicated positive changes in family communication and discipline but weak evidence of impact on adolescent alcohol use.

Promising results were obtained from parental participation in a component of the Midwestern Prevention Program (MPP), a trial of a multicomponent intervention designed to prevent both drug and alcohol abuse among adolescents (Pentz et al., 1989). The MPP parental education program implemented in the Indianapolis site consisted of parent–child homework exercises, parent organization at school sites, parenting skills training workshops, and parent participation in community activities. Participation in the parent program was negatively associated with student use of alcohol and cigarettes at follow-up, after controlling for potentially confounding variables. These findings suggest the value of programmatic efforts to involve parents in substance abuse education as part of a comprehensive, integrated approach with multiple strategies.

School-Based Interventions

The school is the most active site of prevention programs for adolescents. The earliest interventions increased students' knowledge but failed to affect their behavior (Moskowitz, 1989). Programs in the past decade have been more theory-based and effective (Hansen, 1993; Hawkins et al., 1992; Tobler, 1992). For example, Hansen (1992) found that 14 of the 35 programs he reviewed reduced students' alcohol use. He classified programs by their conceptual basis and found that two types of programs were most successful: those that were comprehensive (i.e., included a broad spectrum of prevention strategies) and those that included the social influence approaches (i.e., some combination of normative beliefs, personal commitment, and resistance skills) as part of the package of strategies. Affective approaches, such as those focused on raising self-esteem and goal setting, were less closely correlated with alcohol use, and thus least likely to be effective.

One such combined program [the Alcohol Misuse Prevention Study (AMPS)] taught middle school students about short-term effects of alcohol use and misuse and gave them ample practice in developing skills to resist peer research (Dielman, Klosta, Leech, Schulenberg, & Shope, 1992; Shope, Dielman, Butchart, Campanelli, & Klosta, 1992). The intervention had a modest but enduring statistically significant effect of slowing increased alcohol misuse through grade 8 and into grade 12 (Dielman, 1995). Another, the life skills training

(LST) program, teaches 7th to 9th graders skills to help them resist social influences to use alcohol and other drugs and to enhance general competence and self-esteem (Botvin, Baker, Dusenburg, Tortu, & Botvin, 1990).

A third program, "Project Northland," is a multicomponent, school- and community-based intervention to delay, prevent, and reduce alcohol use and related problems among adolescents. It includes social–behavioral curricula, peer leadership, parental involvement, and communitywide task force activities (Perry et al., 1993). The first 3 years of intervention, conducted in grades six through eight, resulted in significantly lower prevalence of past-month and past-week alcohol use among students in intervention communities compared with controls (Perry et al., 1996). The differences were especially notable among those who were nonusers of alcohol at baseline (Perry et al., 1996).

Other school-based approaches involve extracurricular activities such as establishing Students Against Drunk Driving (SADD) clubs that attempt to alter school and community norms with regard to drinking and driving. While many states encourage development of such clubs and a powerful relationship between norms and DUI has been demonstrated (Klitzner et al., 1988a), there is little research showing that student safety clubs are effective in changing norms or reducing underage drinking or DUI, although the null finding may be due to weak implementation of the clubs (Klitzner, Gruenewald, Bamberger, & Rossiter, 1994).

Community-Based Strategies

Environmental strategies to reduce underage drinking may be implemented at the local community, state, or societal level. Such strategies may involve efforts to reduce alcohol availability through altering laws and public policies and increasing their enforcement or may focus on altering norms related to drinking and to drinking and driving. Such changes are essential for achieving long-term reductions in underage drinking and associated problems because they reinforce the individual changes produced by family and school programs. Without such reinforcement, individual-level changes are likely to fade in the face of constant exposure to prodrinking messages and socioenvironmental conditions that encourage use (Wagenaar & Perry, 1994).

Community activism has been directed to preventing adolescent alcohol use and abuse in a number of ways. Citizen coalitions have strengthened community norms by pressuring retail sellers and servers to obey the law, encouraging zoning ordinances and conditional use permits that restrict the growth of the number or density of sales outlets, supporting server training programs to aid service personnel in age identification and handling underage purchase attempts, and undertaking a variety of prevention initiatives. Other community-based groups have focused specifically on drinking and driving. Some of these communitywide initiatives have been evaluated and their findings recently reported. In addition to the Midwestern Prevention Program, which involved mass media, school-based education, parent education, community organization, and health policy components (Pentz et al., 1989), four recently completed large-scale community-based prevention trials provide encouraging indications of the effectiveness of communitywide efforts to reduce underage drinking (for a summary, see Howard & Boyd, 1996).

The Communities Mobilizing for Change on Alcohol assessed the impact of a theory-based community-organizing effort focusing on access to and consumption of alcohol by underage youth (see Wagenaar & Perry, 1994, for details). After collecting baseline data, the 15 Minnesota and Wisconsin communities participating in the study were randomized to experimental and control conditions and the former given a list of potential interventions from which to select community actions. Most chose to focus on constraining outlet sales of alcohol to minors and provision of alcohol to youth by noncommercial sources. Process evaluation data show that the community organizing efforts affected the accessibility of alcohol to minors. Postintervention comparisons of experimental and control communities indicate that the experimental communities had greater improvement in consistency of on- and off-sale outlets checking the age identifications of youth, more citations for underage sales, and more reported difficulties in alcohol purchases by 12th graders than did the control communities (Howard & Boyd, 1996).

The Community Trial to Reduce Alcohol-Involved Trauma involved a quasi-experimental, nonrandomized design that used three matched pairs of ethnically diverse intervention and control communities (two pairs in California and one in South Carolina). Intervention communities were strongly encouraged to implement a predetermined package of multifaceted environmental interventions designed to reduce alcohol-related trauma among both youth and adults. One of the five intervention components was designed to reduce underage drinking by reducing the availability of alcohol to youth through mass media education, parent training, implementing policies and training in off-premise outlets, and increasing law enforcement; another component focused on drinking and driving through enhanced law enforcement across the age spectrum.

Pre- and postintervention purchase survey data obtained in each of the six study communities indicate that sales of alcoholic beverages to purchasers who looked like minors were significantly reduced in the intervention sites (Grube & Voas, 1996). There also were greater postintervention reductions in single-vehicle nighttime crashes (a frequent surrogate measure for DUI) in the two California intervention communities than in their controls, but no significant change occurred in the South Carolina sites (Howard & Boyd, 1996).

Findings from the Saving Lives Program in Massachusetts, which focused on reducing drinking and driving, also indicate that community initiatives involving enhanced law enforcement, media and educational campaigns, and public–private collaboration can significantly reduce drinking and driving, related driving risks, and traffic deaths and injuries (Hingson et al., 1996). A quasi-experimental evaluation compared the six Savings Lives cities with the rest of Massachusetts and with five control communities. Business, educational, police, and citizens' advocacy groups implemented activities such as high school peer-led education, college prevention programs, alcohol-free prom nights, beer keg registration, increased alcohol outlet surveillance, media campaigns, police training and checkpoints, and speed watch hot lines.

The program was associated with a 39% relative reduction in fatal crashes among drivers aged 15–25 compared with young people in the rest of Massachusetts (Hingson et al., 1996). In addition, the proportion of 16- to 19-year-olds who reported driving after drinking in the month before being interviewed declined 40% relative to teens in the rest of the state. There also was an increase in the proportion of teens in the Saving Lives communities who believed that the license of a person apprehended for driving after drinking could be suspended before trial. But no such change in perception occurred among teens in the rest of the state.

Societywide Context

Laws and Policies

Environmental approaches that alter the legal system have been effectively targeted at both alcohol use and alcohol-related problems, principally drinking and driving. The minimum legal drinking age now is 21, and the effects of this change are more thoroughly discussed above. Beyond the MLDA, other legal interventions to reduce underage drinking focus on driver licensing, since it seems to be the strongest deterrent available. These have included lower BAC levels (e.g., zero tolerance), graduated licensing procedures, nighttime curfews, safe ride programs, and administrative license revocation and suspension that allows the arresting officer to confiscate the license of drivers who test over the legal BAC limit or refuse to take the test (Office of the Inspector General, 1991).

Other efforts to reduce alcohol availability to youth may focus on the holder of a liquor license. The most common type of enforcement technique is a "decoy" or sting operation in which underage purchasers attempt to buy alcohol. This may result in either criminal prosecution or administrative penalties against violators. In one experimental sting program implemented by the Denver Police, cadets purchased beer on 59% of their purchase attempts at baseline. One month later, following extensive media coverage and letters to licensees about the enforcement program, the same stores sold beer to only 32% of the underage cadets attempting to buy. The purchase rate in both a second and third round of purchase attempts (3 and 9 months after the initial buys) was 26%, suggesting both the feasibility and continued benefits from the operation (Preusser, Williams, & Weinstein, 1993). Given the evidence of weak enforcement of the MLDA (Wagenaar & Wolfson, 1995; Wolfson et al., 1995), another legal approach might emphasize eliminating the legal loopholes that make enforcement complex.

Most states now provide for mandatory or voluntary server training programs that educate vendors about the state's alcohol control laws, regulations, and penalties as well as their liability for selling to a minor and how to identify an underage drinker (Office of the Inspector General, 1991). These programs appear to improve server knowledge and attitudes (Glicksman et al., 1993; McKnight, 1993; Russ & Geller, 1987). However, their effects on reducing the likelihood of alcohol sales to underage persons are mixed (Wolfson et al., 1996a,b) and there are no available data on their effectiveness in reducing DUI or alcohol-related violence by youth. Other policy-related approaches to reducing underage drinking include civil liability or "dram shop" laws that are in place in about half the states and specifically permit lawsuits against persons who provide alcohol to minors; beer keg registration laws that are being adopted by a growing number of states; and such innovations as New Jersey's drivers' licenses with profile photos for minors and Alabama's press releases listing the names of minors arrested for alcohol violations (Office of the Inspector General, 1991).

Taxes

Studies have shown that the price of alcoholic beverages influences consumption levels (Chaloupka, 1993; Klitzner, Stewart, & Fisher, 1993), and that taxation is the most efficient means of increasing the price of alcohol (Cook, 1981; Saffer & Grossman, 1987). Because federal and state excise taxes rose very little between 1951 and 1990, the real prices of alcoholic beverages decreased. Simulation studies of the effects of raising excise taxes on beer or all beverage alcohol suggest that this causes some youth to abstain and others to drink less (Chaloupka, 1993; Cook & Moore, 1994); in fact, higher taxes may be an even more effective means of deterring youthful drinking than the MLDA (Laixuthai & Chaloupka, 1993).

Cultural Norms and Media Interventions

Alcohol and its consumption frequently appear in media programming and advertising, yet the influence of these portrayals on the alcohol-related beliefs and behavior of youth still is unclear (Grube, 1995; Martin, 1995). Among 5th and 6th graders, awareness of televised beer advertising was significantly associated with increased knowledge of beer brands and slogans and more positive beliefs about drinking as well as higher rates of intention to drink as an adult (Grube, 1995). This finding suggests that alcohol advertising may increase young people's favorable view of drinking, although data on actual subsequent drinking behavior are not yet available. The initiation of radio and TV advertising for distilled spirits after a 40-year self-imposed ban by the distilled spirits industry provides an opportunity to study the effects of the advertisements on both minors and adults in a naturalistic setting.

In sum, the research literature suggests that no single intervention approach is likely simultaneously to reduce underage drinking and its negative consequences for health, safety, and the justice system. Rather, a mix of "carrots and sticks" is needed to alter individual perceptions of the desirability of drinking by altering norms and expectations and to increase the deterrent effect of the law.

Similarly, a mix of prevention programs is needed with some targeted at the most vulnerable youth who often are involved in other problem behaviors and others designed to reach all adolescents. Particularly in focusing on high-risk youth, early interventions to address developmentally appropriate goals are needed. Whether targeted at a high-risk group or the general population, the most effective interventions appear to be multilevel (i.e., targeted to individuals and the larger environment), since efforts to address individual alcohol consumption without altering the socioenvironmental conditions that support underage drinking are likely to be of limited effectiveness. Similarly, programs that focus simultaneously on reducing risk (e.g., inconsistent parental discipline, easy alcohol availability) and promoting protective factors (e.g., strengthening bonds to family and school) have a greater likelihood of success.

DISCUSSION AND DIRECTIONS FOR RESEARCH

There are large bodies of research on the etiologies of juvenile delinquency and substance abuse and many evaluations of delinquency prevention and alcohol intervention programs. There also is clear awareness of the association between alcohol use and delinquency. Numerous epidemiological studies focused on alcohol use and abuse suggest that the early onset of alcohol consumption, binge drinking, and alcohol-related problems not only are risk factors for subsequent alcohol-related problems but are associated with deviant lifestyles including delinquency and drunk driving in adolescence. Nevertheless, few criminological inquiries have examined the contribution of alcohol prevention efforts to reducing youth crime (except the offenses of underage drinking and DUI).

One intervention to reduce alcohol-related risks and problems—increasing the MLDA to 21—has been shown to reduce underage drinking and driving after drinking; other programs based on interventions in families, schools, communities have resulted in more mixed findings regarding their impact on underage drinking. But virtually no studies have demonstrated their wider effects on other problem behaviors. Thus, a number of issues remain for further research related to underage alcohol use, its association with delinquency, and ways to reduce the latter by addressing the former.

Etiologic studies might expand understanding of why youth drink at various ages in different contexts and how these relate to crime. For example, very little of the ample literature on alcohol-related violence is age-specific, but contextual factors may impact differently on legal and underage drinkers and need further exploration. In addition, the contribution of alcohol to gang violence is unclear. Similarly, the effect of the MLDA on changing the setting of minors' drinking from more controlled locations such as bars to parks and cars on alcohol-related violence has received only limited attention.

Knowledge of the disposition of arrests related to underage drinking is very limited, leaving ample room for studies of case processing and outcomes. For instance, what are the differences between the dispositions of DUI cases that are handled by juvenile and by traffic courts? What are the characteristics of the youth who get petitioned and adjudicated for liquor offenses? How do they differ from those handled informally? What is the effect of various sanctions on subsequent alcohol-related and other delinquent behavior? How can the apparent racial difference in the outcomes in liquor law violation cases be explained?

Despite many studies examining the effects of intervention programs on underage alcohol use and abuse, much remains unknown about their longer-term effects on alcohol consumption patterns as well as their impact on the use of other illegal drugs and delinquent behaviors. Many interventions have not been evaluated; studies of others have encountered methodological shortcomings such as limited outcome measures, the absence of controls for confounding variables, and short follow-up periods (Wells-Parker, Bangert-Drowns, McMillen, & Williams, 1995; for other discussions of problems in evaluation, see Lipsey et al., 1997; Tolan & Guerra, 1994). These problems need to be better addressed in future studies. So do the complexities arising from expanding their scope to include measures of their impact on self-reported offenses or on arrests for violent crimes. Nevertheless, such an expansion would greatly enhance knowledge of their broader effect on youth. While the preliminary findings from the methodologically rigorous community trials are promising, these alcohol use reduction programs have been targeted to all adolescents; few programs have targeted specific high-risk groups. Further efforts are needed to expand the scope of intervention studies to include a wider range of etiologic factors (e.g., not only paternal history of alcoholism but of criminality and co-occurring disorders), to address misuse rather than use of alcohol per se, and to focus on specific risk groups. This approach simultaneously would focus on reducing risk factors, promoting protective factors, and designing prevention efforts that span the age spectrum from preadolescent to young adulthood, with different emphases at various ages.

REFERENCES

Bailey, S. L., & Rachal, J. V. (1993). Dimensions of adolescent problem drinking. *Journal of Studies on Alcohol, 54*, 555–565.

Baker, S. P., O'Neill, B., Ginsburg, M. J., & Li, G. (1992). *The injury fact book* (2nd ed.). New York: Oxford University Press.

Barnes, G. M., & Welte, J. W. (1986a). Patterns and predictors of alcohol use among 7–12th grade students in New York State. *Journal of Studies on Alcohol, 47*, 53–62.

Barnes, G. M., & Welte, J. W. (1986b). Adolescent alcohol abuse: Subgroup differences and relationships to other problem behaviors. *Journal of Adolescent Research, 1*, 79–94.

Beck, K. H., & Lockhart, S. J. (1992). A model of parental involvement in adolescent drinking and driving. *Journal of Youth and Adolescence, 21*, 35–51.

Berkowitz, A. D., & Perkins, H. W. (1986). Problem drinking among college students: A review of recent research. *Journal of American College Health, 35*, 21–28.

Blomberg, R. (1992). *Lower BAC limits for youth: Evaluation of the Maryland .02 law*. Washington, DC: US Department of Transportation.

Botvin, G. J. (1990). Substance abuse prevention: Theory, practice and effectiveness. In M. Tonry & J. Q. Wilson (Eds.), *Drugs and crime* (Vol. 13, pp. 461–520). Chicago: University of Chicago Press.

Botvin, G. J., Baker, E., Dusenbury, L., Tortu, S., & Botvin, E. M. (1990). Preventing adolescent drug abuse through a multimodel cognitive–behavioral approach: Results of a 3-year study. *Journal of Consulting and Clinical Psychology, 58*, 437–446.

Butts, J., Snyder, H. N., Finnegan, T., Aughenbaugh, A. L., & Poole, R. (1995). *Detailed supplement to juvenile court statistics 1993.* Pittsburgh, PA: National Center for Juvenile Justice.

Butts, J., Snyder, H. N., Finnegan, T., Aughenbaugh, A. L., & Poole, R. (1996). *Juvenile court statistics 1993.* Pittsburgh, PA: National Center for Juvenile Justice.

Campbell, K. E., Zobeck, T. S., & Bertollucci, D. (1995). *Trends in alcohol-related fatal traffic crashes, United States, 1977–1993: Surveillance Report #34.* Bethesda, MD: National Institute on Alcohol Abuse and Alcoholism.

Carpenter, C., Glassner, B., Johnson, B. D., & Loughlin, J. (1988). *Kids, drugs, and crime.* Lexington, MA: Lexington Books.

CASA Commission on Substance Abuse at Colleges and Universities. (1994). *Rethinking rites of passage: Substance abuse on America's campuses.* New York: Columbia University.

Chaloupka, F. J. (1993). Effects of price on alcohol-related problems. Prevention research to reduce alcohol-related problems. *Alcohol Health & Research World, 17,* 46–53.

Collins, J. J. (1986). The relationship of problem drinking to individual offending sequences. In A. Blumstein, J. Cohen, J. Roth, & C. A. Visher (Eds.), *Criminal careers and "career criminals"* (Vol., 2, pp. 89–120). Washington, DC: National Academy Press.

Collins, J. J. (1989). Alcohol and interpersonal violence: Less than meets the eye. In N. A. Weiner & M. E. Wolfgang (Eds.), *Pathways to criminal violence* (pp. 49–67). Newbury Park, CA: Sage.

Collins, J. J., & Messerschmidt, P. (1993). Epidemiology of alcohol-related violence. *Alcohol Health & Research World, 17,* 93–101.

Cook, P. J. (1981). The effects of liquor taxes on drinking, cirrhosis, and auto accidents. In M. H. Moore & D. R. Gerstein (Eds.), *Alcohol and public policy: Beyond the shadow of prohibition* (pp. 255–285). Washington, DC: National Academy of Sciences.

Cook, P., & Moore, M. (1994). This tax's for you: The case for higher beer taxes. *National Tax Journal, XLVII,* 559–573.

Dembo, R., Williams, L., Getreu, A., Schmeidler, J., & Wish, E. D. (1991). A longitudinal study of the relationships among marijuana/hashish use, cocaine use and delinquency in a cohort of high risk youth. *Journal of Drug Issues, 21,* 271–312.

Dielman, T. E. (1995). School-based research on the prevention of adolescent alcohol use and misuse: Methodological issues and advances. In G. Boyd, J. Howard, & R. A. Zucker (Eds.), *Alcohol problems among adolescents: Current directions in prevention research* (pp. 125–146). Hillsdale, NJ: Lawrence Erlbaum Associates.

Dielman, T. E., Kloska, D. D., Leech, S. L., Schulenberg, J. E., & Shope, J. T. (1992). Susceptibility to peer pressure as an explanatory variable for the differential effectiveness of an alcohol misuse prevention program in elementary schools. *Journal of School Health, 62*(6), 233–237.

Donovan, J. E. (1993). Young adult drinking-driving: Behavioral and psychosocial correlates. *Journal of Studies on Alcohol, 54,* 600–613.

Donovan, J. W., & Jessor, R. (1985). Structure of problem behavior in adolescence and young adulthood. *Journal of Consulting and Clinical Psychology, 53,* 890–904.

Ellickson, P. L., McGuigan, K. A., Adams, V., Bell, R. M., & Hays, R. D. (1996). Teenagers and alcohol misuse in the United States: By any definition, it's a big problem. *Addiction, 91,* 1489–1503.

Elliott, D. S. (1987). Self-reported drinking while under the influence of alcohol/drugs and the risk of alcohol/drug-related accidents. *Alcohol, Drugs and Driving, 3,* 31–43.

Elliott, D. S. (1993). Health-enhancing and health compromising lifestyles. In S. G. Millstein, A. C. Petersen, & E. O. Nightengale (Eds.), *Promoting the health of adolescents: New directions for the 21st century* (pp. 119–145). New York: Oxford University Press.

Elliott, D. S. (1994). Serious violent offenders: Onset, developmental course, and termination—The American Society of Criminology 1993 Presidential Address. *Criminology, 32,* 1–21.

Elliott, D. S., Huizinga, D., & Ageton, S. S. (1985). *Explaining delinquency and drug use.* Beverly Hills, CA: Sage.

Elliott, D. S., Huizinga, D., & Menard, S. (1989). *Multiple problem youth: Delinquency, substance use and mental health problems.* New York: Springer-Verlag.

Fagan, J. (1990). Intoxication and aggression. In M. Tonry & J. Q. Wilson (Eds.), *Drugs and crime* (Vol. 13, pp. 241–320). Chicago: University of Chicago Press.

Fagan, J., Weis, J. G., & Cheng, Y. T. (1988). Delinquency and substance use among inner city students. New York: York City Criminal Justice Agency.

Federal Bureau of Investigation. (1998). *Uniform crime reports: Crime in the United States 1997.* Washington, DC: US Department of Justice, Federal Bureau of Investigation, October 13.

Fergusson, D. M., Lynskey, M. T., & Horwood, L. J. (1995). The prevalence and risk factors associated with abusive or hazardous alcohol consumption in 16-year-olds. *Addiction, 90,* 935–946.

Fergusson, D. M., Lynskey, M. T., & Horwood, L. J. (1996). Alcohol misuse and juvenile offending in adolescence. *Addiction, 91*, 483–494.

Forster, J., Murray, D., Wolfson, M., & Wagenaar, A. C. (1995). Commercial availability of alcohol to young people: Results of alcohol purchase attempts. *Preventive Medicine, 24*, 342–347.

Giesbrecht, N., Krempulec, L., & West, P. (1993). Community-based prevention research to reduce alcohol-related problems. *Alcohol Health & Research World, 17*, 84–88.

Glicksman, L., McKenzie, D., Single, E., Douglas, R., Brunet, S., & Moffatt, K. (1993). The role of alcohol providers in prevention: An evaluation of a server intervention program. *Addiction, 88*, 1189–1997.

Gorman, D. M., & Speer, P. W. (1995). Preventing alcohol abuse and alcohol related problems through community interventions: A review of evaluation studies. *Psychology and Health, 10*, 1–38.

Grasmick, H. G., Bursik, R. J., Jr., & Arneklev, B. J. (1993). Reduction in drunk drinking as a response to increased threats of shame, embarrassment and legal sanctions. *Criminology, 31*, 41–67.

Grube, J. W. (1995). Television alcohol portrayals, alcohol advertising, and alcohol expectancies among children and adolescents. In S. E. Martin (Ed.), *The effects of the mass media on the use and abuse of alcohol* (pp. 105–122). NIAAA Research Monograph No. 28. Rockville, MD: US Department of Health and Human Services.

Grube, J. W., & Voas, R. (1996). Predicting underage drinking and driving behaviors. *Addiction, 91*, 1843–1857.

Hansen, W. B. (1992). School-based substance abuse prevention: A review of the state of the art in curriculum, 1980–1990. *Health Education Research, 7*, 403–430.

Hansen, W. B. (1993). School-based prevention research to reduce alcohol-related problems. *Alcohol Health & Research World, 17*, 54–60.

Harford, T. C., & Mills, G. S. (1978). Age-related trends in alcohol consumption. *Journal of Studies on Alcohol, 39*, 207–210.

Hartstone, E., & Hansen, K. V. (1984). The violent juvenile offender: An empirical portrait. In R. A. Mathias, P. Demur, & R. S. Allison (Eds.), *Violent juvenile offenders: An anthology* (pp. 83–112). San Francisco: National Council on Crime and Delinquency.

Hawkins, D., Catalano, R. F., & Kent, L. A. (1991). Combining broadcast media and parent education to prevent teenage drug abuse. In L. Donohew, H. E. Sypher, & W. Bukowski (Eds.), *Persuasive communication and drug abuse prevention* (pp. 283–293). Hillsdale, NJ: Lawrence Erlbaum Associates.

Hawkins, J. D., Catalano, R. F., & Miller, J. Y. (1992). Risk and protective factors for alcohol and other drug problems in adolescence and early adulthood: Implications for substance abuse prevention. *Psychological Bulletin, 112*, 64–105.

Hawkins, J. D., Arthur, M. W., & Catalano, R. F. (1995). Preventing substance abuse. In D. Farrington & M. Tonry (Eds.), *Building a safer society: Strategic approaches to crime prevention* (Vol. 19, pp. 343–427). Chicago: University of Chicago Press.

Haworth-Hoeppner, S., Globetti, G., Stern, J., & Morasco, F. (1989). The quantity and frequency of drinking among undergraduates at a southern university. *International Journal of the Addictions, 24*, 829–857.

Hingson, R., Heeren, T., Mangione, T., Morelock, S., & Mucatel, M. (1982). Teenage driving after using marijuana or drinking and traffic accident involvement. *Journal of Safety Research, 13*, 33–37.

Hingson, R., Howland, J., Heeren, T., & Winter, M. (1991). Reduced BAC limits for young people: Impact on night fatal crashes. *Alcohol, Drugs and Driving, 7*, 117–127.

Hingson, R., Heeren, T., & Winter, M. (1994). Lower legal blood alcohol limits for young drivers. *Public Health Reports, 109*, 738–744.

Hingson, R., McGovern, T., Howland, J., Heeren, T., Winter, M., & Zakocs, R. (1996). Reducing alcohol-impaired driving in Massachusetts: The Saving Lives Program. *American Journal of Public Health, 86*, 791–797.

Hirschi, T. (1969). *The causes of delinquency*. Berkeley: University of California Press.

Howard, J. (1993). Alcohol prevention research: Concepts, phases, and tasks at hand. *Alcohol Health & Research World, 17*, 5–9.

Howard, J., & Boyd, G. (1996). Community organizing, public policy, and the prevention of alcohol problems. *Alcoholism: Clinical and Experimental Research, 20*, 265A–269A.

Jessor, R. (1982, May). Problem behavior and developmental transition in adolescence. *Journal of School Health*, 295–300.

Jessor, R., & Jessor, S. L. (1975). Adolescent development and the onset of drinking. *Journal of Studies on Alcohol, 36*, 27–51.

Jessor, R., & Jessor, S. L. (1977). *Problem behavior and psychosocial development. A longitudinal study of youth*. San Diego, CA: Academic Press.

Johnston, L. D., O'Malley, P. M., & Bachman, J. G. (1999a). *National survey results on drug use from the Monitoring the Future Study, 1975–1995* (Vol. I). Rockville, MD: NIDA.

Johnston, L. D., O'Malley, P. M., & Bachman, J. G. (1999b). *National survey results on drug use from the Monitoring the Future Study, 1975–1992* (Vol. II). Rockville, MD: NIDA.

Johnston, L. D., O'Malley, P. M., & Bachman, J. G. (2000). *Monitoring the future: National results on adolescent drug use: Overview of key findings, 1999*. Bethesda, MD: NIDA.

Kandel, D. B. (1980). Drug and drinking behavior among youth. *Annual Review of Sociology*, *6*, 235–285.

Kandel, D. B., & Yamaguchi, F. (1985). Developmental patterns of the use of legal, illegal and medically prescribed psychotropic drugs from adolescence to young adulthood. In *Etiology of drug abuse implications for prevention* (pp. 193–235). NIDA Research Monograph 56. DHHS Publication No. (ADM) 85-1335. Washington, DC: US Government Printing Office.

Klepp, K. I., Perry, C. L., & Jacobs, D. R. (1991). Etiology of drinking and driving among adolescents: Implications for primary prevention. *Health Education Quarterly*, *18*, 415–427.

Klitzner, M., Vegega, M., & Gruenewald, P. (1988). An empirical examination of the assumptions underlying youth drinking/driving prevention programs. *Evaluation and Program Planning*, *11*, 219–235.

Klitzner, M., Bamberger, E., & Gruenewald, P. (1990a). The assessment of parent-led prevention programs: A national descriptive study. *Journal of Drug Education*, *20*, 111–125.

Klitzner, M., Bamberger, E., & Gruenewald, P. (1990b). The assessment of parent-led prevention programs: A preliminary assessment of impact. *Journal of Drug Education*, *20*, 77–94.

Klitzner, M., Stewart, K., & Fisher, D. (1993). Reducing underage drinking and its consequences. *Alcohol Health & Research World*, *17*, 12–18.

Klitzner, M., Gruenewald, P. J., Bamberger, E., & Rossiter, C. (1994). A quasi-experimental evaluation of Students Against Drunk Driving. *American Journal on Drug and Alcohol Abuse*, *20*, 57–74.

Laixuthai, A., & Chaloupka, F. J. (1993). Youth alcohol use and public policy. *Contemporary Policy Issues*, *XI*, 70–81.

Lipsey, M. W., Wilson, D. B., Cohen, M. A., & Derzon, J. H. (1997). Is there a causal relationship between alcohol use and violence? A synthesis of evidence. In M. Galanter (Ed.), *Recent trends in alcoholism* (Vol. 13, pp. 245–283). New York: Plenum Press.

Martin, C. S., Kaczynski, N. A., Maisto, S. A., Bukstein, O. M., & Moss, H. B. (1995). Patterns of DSM-IV alcohol abuse and dependence symptoms in adolescent drinkers. *Journal of Studies on Alcohol*, *56*, 672–680.

Martin, S. E. (1995). Alcohol and the mass media: Issues, approaches and research directions. In S. E. Martin (Ed.), *The effects of the mass media on the use and abuse of alcohol* (pp. 277–298). NIAAA Research Monograph No. 28. Rockville, MD: US Department of Health and Human Services.

Martin, S. E., & Andreasson, S. (1996). Zero tolerance laws: Effective public policy? *Alcoholism: Clinical and Experimental Research*, *20*(Suppl), 147A–150A.

Mayhew, D. R., Donelson, A. C., Beirness, D. J., & Simpson, H. M. (1986). Youth, alcohol and relative risk of crash involvement. *Accident Analysis and Prevention*, *18*, 273–287.

Miczek, K. A., Weerts, E. M., & DeBold, J. F. (1993). Alcohol aggression and violence: Biobehavioral determinants. In S. E. Martin (Ed.), *Alcohol and interpersonal violence: Fostering multidisciplinary perspectives* (pp. 83–120). NIAAA Research Monograph No. 24. Rockville, MD: US Department of Health and Human Services.

Mitic, W. R. (1989). Adolescent drinking problems: Urban vs. rural differences in Nova Scotia. *Canadian Journal of Community Mental Health*, *8*, 5–14.

McKnight, A. J. (1993). Server intervention: Accomplishments and needs. *Alcohol Health & Research World*, *17*, 76–83.

Moskowitz, J. M. (1989). The primary prevention of alcohol problems: A critical review of the research literature. *Journal of Studies on Alcohol*, *50*, 54–88.

Murdoch, D. D., Pihl, R. O., & Ross, D. (1990). Alcohol and crimes of violence: Present issues. *International Journal of the Addictions*, *25*, 1065–1081.

Newcomb, M. D., Maddahian, E., & Bentler, P. M. (1986). Risk factors for drug use among adolescents: Concurrent and longitudinal analyses. *American Journal of Public Health*, *76*, 525–531.

Office of the Inspector General. (1991). *Youth and alcohol: Laws and enforcement—Is the 21-year-old drinking age a myth?* Washington, DC: Office of the Inspector General, USDHHS.

O'Leary, D., Gorman, D. M., & Speer, P. W. (1994). The sale of alcoholic beverages to minors. *Public Health Reports*, *109*, 816–818.

O'Malley, P. M., & Wagenaar, A. C. (1991). Effects of minimum drinking age laws on alcohol use, related behaviors and traffic crash involvement among American youth: 1976–1987. *Journal of Studies on Alcohol*, *52*, 478–491.

Parker, R. N., & Rehbun, L. A. (1995). *Alcohol and homicide: A deadly combination of two American traditions*. Albany, NY: SUNY Press.

Pentz, M. A., Dwyer, J. H., MacKinnon, D. P., Flay, B. R., Hansen, W. B., Wang, E. Y. I., & Johnson, C. A. (1989). A multi-community trial for primary prevention of adolescent drug abuse: Effects on drug use prevalence. *Journal of the American Medical Association, 261*, 3259–3266.

Pernanen, K. (1991). *Alcohol in human violence*. New York: Guilford.

Perry, C. L., Williams, C. L., Forster, J. L., Wolfson, M., Wagenaar, A. C., Finnegan, J. R., McGovern, P. G., Veblen-Mortenson, S., Komro, K. A., & Anstine, P. S. (1993). Background, conceptualization, and design of a community-wide research program on adolescent alcohol use: Project Northland. *Health Education Research, 8*, 125–136.

Perry, C. L., Williams, C. L., Veblen-Mortenson, S., Toomey, T. L., Komro, K. A., Anstine, P. S., McGovern, P. G., Finnegan, J. R., Forster, J. L., Wagenaar, A. C., & Wolfson, M. (1996). Project Northland: Outcomes of a communitywide alcohol use prevention program during early adolescence. *American Journal of Public Health, 86*, 956–965.

Presley, C. A., Meilman, P. W., & Lyerla, R. (1993). *Alcohol and drugs on American college campuses: Use, consequences and perceptions of the campus environment*. Carbondale: Southern Illinois University.

Preusser, D. F., & Williams, A. (1992). Sales of alcohol to underage purchasers in three New York counties and Washington, D.C. *Journal of Public Health Policy, 13*, 306–317.

Preusser, D. F., Preusser, C., & Ulmer, R. (1992). *Obstacles to enforcement of youthful impaired driving*. Prepared for the National Highway Traffic Safety Administration, Washington, DC: US Department of Transportation.

Preusser, D. F., Williams, A. F., & Weinstein, H. B. (1993). *Policing underage alcohol sales*. Arlington, VA: Insurance Institute for Highway Safety.

Reiss, A. J., & Roth, J. A. (Eds.). (1993). *Understanding and preventing violence*. Washington, DC: National Academy Press.

Roizen, J. (1993). Issues in the epidemiology of alcohol and violence. In S. E. Martin (Ed.), *Alcohol and interpersonal violence: Fostering multidisciplinary perspectives* (pp. 3–36). NIAAA Research Monograph No. 24. Rockville, MD: US Department of Health and Human Services.

Ross, H. L. (1984). Social control through deterrence: Drinking-and-driving laws. *Annual Review of Sociology, 10*, 21–35.

Russ, N. W., & Geller, E. S. (1987). Training bar personnel to prevent drunken driving: A field evaluation. *American Journal of Public Health, 77*, 952–954.

Saffer, H., & Grossman, M. (1987). Beer taxes, the legal drinking age, and youth motor vehicle fatalities. *Journal of Legal Studies, 16*, 351–374.

Saltz, R., & Elandt, D. (1986, Spring). College student drinking studies: 1976–1985. *Contemporary Drug Problems*, 117–157.

Shope, J. T., Dielman, T. E., Butchart, A. T., Campanelli, P. C., & Klosta, D. D. (1992). An elementary school-based alcohol misuse prevention program: A follow-up evaluation. *Journal of Studies on Alcohol, 53*, 106–121.

Sickmund, M. (1991). *Juvenile court drug and alcohol cases: 1985–1988*. Juvenile Justice Bulletin NCJ 132073: OJJDP Update on Statistics. Washington, DC: Office of Juvenile Justice and Delinquency Prevention.

Snyder, H. N. (1997). *Juvenile arrests 1995*. Juvenile Justice Bulletin. Washington, DC: Office of Juvenile Justice and Delinquency Prevention.

Snyder, H. N. (1998). *Juvenile arrests 1997*. Juvenile Justice Bulletin. Washington, DC: Office of Juvenile Justice and Delinquency Prevention.

Snyder, H. N. (1999). *Juvenile arrests 1998*. Juvenile Justice Bulletin. Washington, DC: Office of Juvenile Justice and Delinquency Prevention.

Snyder, H. N., & Sickmund, M. (1995). *Juvenile offenders and victims: A national report*. Washington, DC: Office of Juvenile Justice and Delinquency Prevention.

Sutherland, E. H., & Cressey, D. R. (1978). *Criminology*. Philadelphia: Lippincott.

Tobler, N. S. (1992). Drug prevention programs can work: Research findings. *Journal of Addictive Diseases, 11*, 1–28.

Tolan, P., & Guerra, N. (1994). *What works in reducing adolescent violence: An empirical review of the field*. Boulder, CO: Center for the Study and Prevention of Violence.

Turrisi, R., Jaccard, J., Valera, E. M., & Kelly, S. Q. (1994). Parent and teen perceptions regarding parental efforts at controlling teen drunk driving. *Journal of Applied Social Psychology, 24*, 1387–1406.

US Department of Health and Human Services. (1991). *Healthy People 2000: National health promotion and disease prevention objectives*. NIH Pub. No. (PHS)91-50212. Washington, DC: US Government Printing Office.

Virkkunen, M. (1977). Arrests for drunkenness and recidivism in juvenile delinquents. *British Journal of the Addictions, 72*, 201–204.

Wagenaar, A. C. (1983). *Alcohol, young drivers and traffic accidents: Effects of minimum-age laws*. Lexington, MA: DC Heath Co.

Wagenaar, A. C., & Perry, C. L. (1994). Community strategies for the reduction of youth drinking: Theory and application. *Journal of Research on Adolescence, 4*, 319–345.

Wagenaar, A. C., & Wolfson, M. (1994). Enforcement of the legal minimum drinking age in the United States. *Journal of Public Health Policy, 15*, 37–53.

Wagenaar, A. C., & Wolfson, M. (1995). Deterring sales and provision of alcohol to minors: A study of enforcement in 295 counties in four states. *Public Health Report, 110*, 419–427.

Wagenaar, A. C., Finnegan, J. R., Wolfson, M., Anstine, P. S., Williams, C. L., & Perry, C. L. (1993). Youth alcohol access: Where and how adolescents obtain alcoholic beverages. *Public Health Reports, 108*, 459–464.

Wechsler, H., Davenport, A., Dowdall, G., Moeykens, B., & Castillo, S. (1994). Health and behavioral consequences of binge drinking in college: A national survey of students at 140 campuses. *Journal of the American Medical Association, 272*, 1672–1677.

Wells-Parker, E., Bangert-Drowns, R., McMillen, R., & Williams, M. (1995). Final results from a meta-analysis of remedial interventions with drink/drive offenders. *Addiction, 90*, 907–926.

Welte, J. W., & Barnes, G. M. (1985). Alcohol: The gateway to other drug use among secondary-school students. *Journal of Youth and Adolescence, 14*, 487–498.

White, H. R. (1997). Longitudinal perspective on alcohol use and aggression during adolescence. In M. Galanter (Ed.), *Recent developments in alcoholism* (Vol. 13, pp. 81–104). New York: Plenum Press.

White, H. R., & Labouvie, E. W. (1989). Toward an assessment of adolescent problem drinking. *Journal of Studies on Alcohol, 50*, 30–37.

White, H. R., Brick, J., & Hansell, S. (1993a). A longitudinal investigation of alcohol use and aggression in adolescence. *Journal of Studies on Alcohol, Suppl. 11*, 62–77.

White, H. R., Hansell, S., & Brick, J. (1993b). Alcohol use and aggression among youth. *Alcohol Health & Research World, 17*, 144–150.

Windle, M. (1991). Alcohol use and abuse: Some findings from the National Adolescent Student Health Survey. *Alcohol Health & Research World, 15*, 5–10.

Windle, M. (1994). Coexisting problems and alcoholic family risk among adolescents. In T. F. Babor, V. Hesselbrock, R. E. Meyer, & W. Shoemaker (Eds.), *Types of alcoholics: Evidence from clinical, experimental and genetic research* (pp. 157–164). New York: New York Academy of Sciences.

Windle, M., Shope, J. T., & Bukstein, O. (1996). Alcohol use. In R. J. DiClemente, W. B. Hansen, & L. E. Ponton (Eds.), *Handbook of adolescent health risk behavior* (pp. 115–159). New York: Plenum Press.

Wolfson, M., Wagenaar, A. C., & Hornseth, G. W. (1995). Law officers' views on enforcement of the minimum drinking age: A four-state study. *Public Health Reports, 110*, 428–438.

Wolfson, M., Toomey, T. I., Murray, D. M., Forster, J. L., Short, B. J., & Wagenaar, A. C. (1996a). Alcohol outlet policies and practices concerning sales to underage people. *Addiction, 91*, 589–602.

Wolfson, M., Toomey, T. L., Forster, J. L., Wagenaar, A. C., McGovern, P. G., & Perry, C. L. (1996b). Characteristics, policies, and practices of alcohol outlets and sales to underage people. *Journal of Studies on Alcohol, 57*, 670–674.

Yamaguchi, K., & Kandel, D. B. (1984a). Patterns of drug use from adolescence to young adulthood: II. Sequences of progression. *American Journal of Public Health, 74*, 668–672.

Yamaguchi, K., & Kandel, D. B. (1984b). Patterns of drug use from adolescence to young adulthood: III. Predictors of progression. *American Journal of Public Health, 74*, 673–681.

Yu, J., & Williford, W. R. (1992). The age of alcohol onset and alcohol, cigarette, and marijuana use patterns: An analysis of drug use progression of young adults in New York State. *International Journal of the Addictions, 27*, 1313–1323.

Zador, P. (1991). Alcohol-related relative risk of fatal driver injuries in relation to driver age and sex. *Journal of Studies on Alcohol, 52*, 302–310.

Part IV

Cross-Cultural Patterns of Delinquency

9

Two Worlds of Deviance

Russia and the United States

JAMES O. FINCKENAUER

As the year 1991 came to a close, the world witnessed the end of an historical era that had begun shortly after World War II. That era was dominated at the global level by two superpowers: the United States and the Soviet Union. Putting aside their resemblance in the capacity to make war, these two countries otherwise differed enormously on a number of important dimensions. Their cultural histories were different. Their economic, political, and legal systems were very dissimilar. Emanating from their individual histories and traditions, the two countries also had views about the societal roles and responsibilities of the individual and the community, and about raising and educating children, that were quite distinct. Of most relevance for our purposes, the United States and the Soviet Union also came at the task of resocializing troubled children from distinctly different directions.

Whatever comparative advantage one or the other country had in other spheres, in the area of juvenile delinquency (as with crime in general), the Soviet Union seemed to have the better of things. It is generally believed that the Soviet Union had far less delinquency than the United States. Establishing this belief as empirical fact, however, is impossible. Juvenile delinquency was defined differently; the age of criminal responsibility for children was different; and, because there was no uniform crime reporting system in the Soviet Union, the kind of crime statistics necessary for making comparisons was unavailable. Thus, we do not actually know that the Soviet Union had less delinquency than the United States.

Now of course, the Soviet Union is gone. It was dissolved at the end of 1991, becoming 15 separate and independent countries. The largest and most important of these is Russia. Since the breakup, Russia has undergone cataclysmic changes—economic, political, and social. Accompanying these enormous changes has been a considerable amount of crime and social disorder. The United States too has experienced changes over that period, but nothing remotely approaching the Russian experience. In this chapter, we will take a comparative look at Russian and American youth to see what have been the effects of some of these developments on the problem of juvenile delinquency. To some extent, the aforementioned problems with

JAMES O. FINCKENAUER • International Center, National Institute of Justice, Washington, DC 20531.

Handbook of Youth and Justice, edited by White. Kluwer Academic/Plenum Publishers, New York, 2001.

making comparisons remain. Nevertheless, as long as we are not sticklers for precision, we can form some impressions about the comparative nature and magnitude of delinquency.

COMPARATIVE OVERVIEW OF JUVENILE DELINQUENCY AND JUVENILE JUSTICE

Causes of Delinquency

In a number of respects the factors that are associated with juvenile delinquency in Russia are not that different from those in most other countries of the world, or at least not in the industrialized countries such as the United States. These factors include alcohol and drug abuse, dropping out of school, unemployment, having access to guns, joining street gangs, and coming from dysfunctional families. In the case of drugs and guns, however, the fact that these are presently less available means they are less of a problem in Russia than in the United States.

There is in Russia, however, a situation that if not unique is certainly atypical, and it is quite different from anything in the United States. In the years since the collapse of the Soviet Union, many Russians have fallen into a state of what might best be characterized as anomie or normlessness. They are suspended between what was and what will be. This is particularly so for young people. Many of their old Soviet-originated norms and values are gone, but new ones are not yet fully in place. A kind of amoral materialism and corruption permeates significant sectors of the country, creating a ripe environment for the sustenance of deviance (see Zinchuk & Karpukhin, 1995, for a discussion of this phenomenon). But before we move to a discussion of this latter circumstance, let us first examine the more typical factors to see how the two countries compare.

Universal Contexts

In 1990, there were 64.2 million persons under age 18 in the United States, a number that is projected to increase by 10 million in 2010 (Snyder & Sickmund, 1995, p. 2). The comparable figure for Russia (in 1992) was 39.9 million; but because of the increasing death rate and the declining birth rate, both the overall population and the youth population are dropping (Zinchuk & Karpukhin, 1995, p. 64). The increase in deaths is mainly due to alcoholism and poor health care. The decline in births reflects a combination of young couples' lack of confidence in the future, high numbers of abortions, and poor prenatal health care.

Russian young people are predominantly urban: 71% live in urban areas. There has been a dramatic shift of population from rural to urban Russia over the last generation. This shift has been accompanied by a breaking up of families, the decline in the birth rate, and the increased crime and delinquency. Because of the relatively low number of private cars in Russia, there has not been a suburban development there comparable to that in the United States. Approximately 30% of American youth live in central cities, but another 47% live in metropolitan suburbs surrounding cities. Thus, to the extent that juvenile delinquency (or at least serious juvenile crime) is mainly an urban phenomenon, both countries are vulnerable.

There are a number of indicators of family dysfunction, as well as other crime producing or criminogenic factors on which the two countries can be compared. Table 1 gives us an illustrative look at these factors. Given that the Russian youth population is roughly two thirds the size of the American youth population, we can project what the proportionate numbers for

Table 1. Comparative Criminogenic Factors

	Russia (actual)	Russia (expected)	United States
Children in substitute care	141,000[a]	280,667	421,000[b]
Runaways	70,000[c]	333,333	500,000[d]
Suicides	2,000[e]	1,443	2,165[f]
School dropouts	330,000[g]	244,333	383,000[h]
Alcohol abuse	33,139[i]	79,467	119,200[j]
Drug abuse	507[i]	57,133	85,700[j]
Public drunkenness	113,557[i]	12,600	18,900[j]

[a]41,400 orphans and approx. 100,000 in various state institutions in 1992 (Zinchuk & Karpukhin, 1995, p. 64).
[b]It is estimated that three fourths of these were in foster care (Snyder & Sickmund, 1995, p. 40).
[c]50,000 runaways from home, and 20,000 from orphanages and boarding schools (Zinchuk & Karpukhin, 1995, p. 40).
[d]Finkelhor et al (1990).
[e]Zinchuk & Karpukhin (1995, p. 65).
[f]Snyder & Sickmund (1995, p. 27).
[g]*The Current Digest* (1993, p. 31).
[h]Snyder & Sickmund (1995, p. 14).
[i]Zinchuk & Karpukhin (1995, pp. 67–68).
[j]Federal Bureau of Investigation (1993).

Russian youth could be expected to be, all other things being equal. Since we do not know what all those other things are, much less whether they are equal, these comparisons should be viewed only as suggestive. Beginning with children in substitute care (meaning placement outside the home), the number of Russian children is about half what might be expected. This is probably explained by two factors. First, foster care, which accounts for the vast majority of American children, is basically unknown in Russia. Second, the limited number of institutional beds in Russia puts a cap on the number of children who can be so placed. Related to the issue of families and child care, a Russian Interior Ministry researcher reported in 1994 that there were more than 3 million single-parent families in Russia, and that each year 500,000 children were being left without one of their parents (*The Current Digest*, 1994, Vol. XLVI, No. 1, p. 9).

Russian runaways are less than a quarter what might be expected given the relative sizes of the youth populations. It is difficult to conjecture what might account for this. Among the reasons might be that travel is less available and more difficult in Russia, and that Russian youth are less likely than American youth to have financial resources. The numbers also could reflect a reporting phenomenon, as witness the fact that the United States has heavily emphasized reporting runaway and missing children in recent years. For example, in addition to the runaways reported, the United States listed almost another 500,000 children as missing (Finkelhor, Hotaling, & Sedlak, 1990).

The estimated 2000 Russian youth suicides is more than would be expected, and that figure represents a 70% increase in the last decade. That rise could well be indicative of the personal and social turmoil presently going on in Russia. The US figures are from the US National Center for Health, and pertain to persons 19 or younger in 1991 (Snyder & Sickmund, 1995, p. 27). As in the United States, so in Russia, boys commit suicide about four to five times more than girls (*The Current Digest*, 1995, p. 15).

In 1995, the Russian Interior Ministry said that a third of the juvenile delinquents who had been "registered" in Russia in 1994 were 14 and 15, and that most of them were school dropouts. Registered means that the juvenile was officially recorded as being apprehended by the police. It is comparable to being arrested for recording purposes. An earlier report had indicated that more than 200,000 Russian children had been expelled from school in 1992, and that in addition, of the 400,000 children held back a grade in the 1991–1992 year, more than a third did not resume their education (*The Current Digest*, 1993, p. 31). This report is the basis for the Russian school dropout figure in Table 1. It is considerably larger than might be expected. The US school dropout figure is for 1992, and includes both youth that dropped out to avoid expulsion and those who were expelled.

A 1995 Russian Interior Ministry report indicated that "more and more young people committed crimes spurred up by drinking or drug abuse, and two thirds of the young criminals acted in gangs" (ITAR-TASS, August 22, 1995). Interior Ministry data for the years 1988–1992 reflect increases in the alcohol and drug problem among Russian youth, but also show that the nature of these problems appears to be different from that in the United States. For example, in Russia in 1988, the number of persons aged 18 and younger registered for crimes who were under the influence of alcohol or drugs was 18,649 and 291, respectively. By 1992, as shown in Table 1, these numbers had increased to 33,139 and 507. It was further reported that in 1993 there had been a "drastic increase in thefts, beatings and criminal acts associated with the making and selling of drugs" (*The Current Digest*, 1993, p. 18). It also was reported that 147,647 Russian youth received "administrative handling" for public drunkenness in 1988; but by 1992, this number had declined to 113,557 (see Table 1). Administrative handling means they were processed outside the criminal justice system and therefore are not counted in the criminal statistics. The decline from 1988 to 1992 probably had more to do with shifts in police policy than with any real reduction in the problem. In that same year in the United States (1992) there were 119,200 arrests of juveniles for liquor law violations and 85,700 for drug abuse. There were, however, "only" 18,900 arrests for public drunkenness. Again keeping in mind that the data are not precisely comparable because of differing definitions and reporting, it appears that the juvenile alcohol problem might be much greater in Russia but that drug abuse is a considerably smaller (albeit growing) problem. Neither of these conclusions would be surprising given the overall alcoholism problem in Russia and the relatively recent introduction of drugs.

Youth gangs are another growing problem in Russia. For example, the director of the Moscow City Internal Affairs Administration said that Moscow now has many local gangs, made up mostly of youth, who prey exclusively on people from outside the former Soviet Union. These gangs often are linked to organized crime, which differentiates them from most juvenile gangs in the United States. Although gangs are not uncommon in Russia, one report said that, "with their heavy emphasis on money-making they tend to resemble Prohibition-era packs of criminals rather than modern L.A.-style street fighters" (Goldberg, 1994a). Children's gangs made up of 9-, 10-, and 11-year-olds also are a new Russian problem. In neither country does the information available enable us to reach definitive conclusions about just how many gangs and gang members there are, nor on the volume of gang crime.

The Unique Russian Experience

Since 1991, Russian young people have experienced the crashing of practically every system that had acted to nurture and control them: family, schools, economy, health care, government, criminal justice system, and an array of youth services facilities. Juvenile delinquency is believed by some Russian authorities to be booming because it is "fueled by daily proof in this mob-ridden country that crime pays and [is] helped along by disorder in the courts, schools and city councils that used to help keep it under control" (Goldberg, 1994a).

Zinchuk and Karpukhin (1995, pp. 70–73) offered four "causes and conditions that foster the present situation with respect to juvenile crime":

- The decline in people's standard of living, the growth of inflation, and the growth in unemployment.
- A decline in the moral level of the society; "for a substantial portion of the population, the sole or principal goal is to satisfy material needs."
- The decline in the use of administrative prohibitions (regulations enforced outside the criminal law), and the weakening of law enforcement.
- The creation of "an atmosphere of legal nihilism" (by which they also seem to mean the undermining of law and law enforcement).

The Young People's Sociological Information Service (YPSIS) concluded that conditions such as the above had made Russian youth cynical, materialistic, and apolitical (*The Current Digest*, 1994, Vol. XLVI, No. 27). For example, in their 1994 survey of teenager's value orientations, they asked approximately 2000 Russian students what they did to earn pocket money. Among the third to a half (depending on their age) who earned money, the following means were used: selling newspapers, grooming dogs, working as messengers, but they also reported prostitution, extortion, racketeering, doing other's school assignments for money, buying and selling, and selling articles retrieved from the trash.

One Russian researcher described the current situation in respect to youth as exemplified by a lack of standards, by feelings of resentment, and by a disregard for the law (*The Current Digest*, 1994, Vol. XLVI, No. 1). It is thus perhaps not surprising that juvenile crime in Russia has increased substantially since 1991. The specifics are the subject of the next section.

Nature and Trends in Delinquency

Several caveats must be kept in mind in drawing any conclusions from the comparative data that will be presented here. First, as already indicated, the US youth population is a third again as large as the Russian youth population. Second, the US arrest figures include children under age 14. Since criminal culpability does not begin in Russia until age 14, recorded crime data do not include any children under that age. How much of a difference does this make in the magnitude of the problem? It was estimated by Russian police that in 1993, about 100,000 Russian children under 14 had committed crimes for which they could not be held responsible (Goldberg, 1994b).

A third factor has to do with the nature of the data themselves. It is known that there are reliability and validity concerns with the FBI's Uniform Crime Reports (UCR) juvenile arrest data, for example, the missing "dark figure" of crime. In Russia where there is no uniform crime reporting system, as flawed as it might be, the problems of accuracy and completeness are only compounded. The statistics presented thus should be taken only as rough indicators of the relative magnitude of the juvenile crime problem.

Table 2 shows data on registered youth for Russia and arrested youth for the United States. These data are for 1992, the latest year for which we have relatively comparable data. It is obvious at first glance that, even with the total population size differential, most of the numbers are vastly different.

As an indication of the cautions mentioned earlier, if we look only at the 16- to 17-year-olds, thus controlling for the truncating age effects, does it seem reasonable that there were eight times as many arrests in this age category in the United States as in Russia? Perhaps. But it is impossible to know how much of this difference is real and how much is a product of

Table 2. Juvenile Arrests in 1992

	Russia	United States
Total juveniles	188,186	2,296,000
Ages 16 and 17	128,870	1,056,160
Ages 15 and below (Russian data includes only 14- to 15-year-olds)	59,316	1,239,840
Females	12,910	528,080
Juvenile proportion of all arrests	16%	16%

differences in law enforcement practices and effectiveness and/or differences in reporting. Other data, in fact, point to a different conclusion about the relative prevalence of delinquency. The Russian Ministry of Internal Affairs reported in 1995 that juvenile delinquents accounted for 12% of the total number of young people in Russia (British Broadcasting Corporation [BBC], 1995). UCR data for the United States, on the other hand, show that only approximately 6% of all American juveniles were arrested in 1994 (Snyder, Sickmund & Poe Yamagata, 1996, p. 14).

In 1994, an interdepartmental commission reported that Russian teenagers between 14 and 18 had committed 225,000 crimes as of November of that year (BBC, 1994). Again assuming the figures can be compared, that would represent a considerable increase over the 1992 figures. This same commission indicated that juvenile delinquency in Russia had increased by 50% over the previous 5 years (1989–1993) and had roughly doubled since 1984. In the United States too there have been increases, but of a much lesser magnitude. Juvenile arrests increased 11% between 1988 and 1992 and 17% between 1983 and 1992 (Snyder & Sickmund, 1995, p. 109).

The Russian Interior Ministry released recorded crime data for juveniles for the first half of 1994 that showed that 100,862 arrests were made for serious crimes. This figure is only one fourth to one fifth the US arrest totals for more serious index crimes. One of the largest categories of arrests of Russian juveniles was for the crime of banditism (which refers generally to group commission of a variety of crimes, including what in the United States would be called muggings). As mentioned previously, Russian police report that youngsters often are involved with adult criminal gangs, and that in fact most (85%) of these gangs have teenage members. Their crimes include auto theft, drug dealing, extortion, and prostitution, but they also involve stealing and reselling weapons, rare metals, and even strategic raw materials. Contrary to past experience, firearms also are increasingly being used by such gangs.

The single-largest arrest category for Russian juveniles is theft. It accounts for more than half of all arrests for serious crimes. Theft also is by far the largest crime category for US juvenile arrests also accounting for more than half of the arrests for index crimes.

Responding to the Delinquency Problem

Despite the significant increase in juvenile delinquency in Russia in recent years, there has been no commensurate increase in resources and services to combat the problem. In fact, if anything, there are fewer facilities and programs available now than there were before the collapse of the Soviet Union. For example, some 5000 state-run summer youth camps have been closed. There also is not a single specialized treatment facility in the whole country for adolescent offenders who have mental health problems. Most importantly, the bulk of the commissions on juvenile affairs (CJA) (which were sort of a combination of youth service bureau, dispute resolution center, and lay court) have disappeared. The commissions provided counseling for juveniles and their families, supervised youth in a form of probation, and otherwise provided a range of support and services. These CJAs operated at every community level and were critical for keeping youngsters in community services and under local supervision. They have disappeared both because they were Soviet ideas and because no alternative support has been provided to fill the gap after the existing structure was dismantled.

The implications of the dismantling were described to a reporter by one juvenile officer in a Moscow police district (Goldberg, 1994b, p. 25): In the Soviet Union, there was a curfew that did not allow youngsters under 16 to be on the streets without their parents after 11 PM. This has been done away with, or is simply no longer enforced. Of the CJAs, this officer said, the "Commissions on Juvenile Affairs had the power to deprive abusive or neglectful parents of their children and send kids to orphanages or reform schools. Authorities could also fine parents for their children's crimes." Now, she said, "I can't even say we have a system" to deal with troubled children. "So much has been destroyed or made so complicated" (p. 25).

A March 31, 1993 article in the Russian newspaper *Nezavisimaya Gazeta* likewise illuminated many of the current difficulties facing Russia in dealing with juvenile delinquents. It was titled "Children Behind Bars—There is no System for Working with Troubled Children in Russia" (*The Current Digest*, 1993, p. 19):

> In the past few years, the whole system of work with difficult children and preventive measures against juvenile lawbreaking has broken down. Its basic weakness, one that has repeatedly been criticized, was the fact that decisions on the compulsory assignment of juveniles under the age of 14 to special educational institutions (in effect, deprivation of freedom) were made not by the courts but by public organizations—by the commissions on juvenile cases under the local bodies of power. [The law abolishing this procedure] also did away with the commissions on juvenile cases, which had about 500,000 teenagers on their books. The negative consequences of this soon became apparent: The curves of child neglect and juvenile crime started creeping upward right away....
>
> Paradoxically, despite a 50% to 250% increase in juvenile crime [a range that itself illustrates the difficulties with police crime statistics] ..., since 1987 the number of places in special educational institutions has been reduced by more than 25%.... This has led to a situation in which sometimes there isn't even any place to confine juveniles who have committed various crimes.

In order to begin to rectify the situation, Russian authorities have floated a number of new ideas. But because of the absence of resources, most remain just ideas. These include a program called the Interior Ministry and the Youth, in which law related education is to be offered in schools. Special training on working with juveniles is being proposed for the police. Also, there is something called the School Policeman program, which is intended to train "an experimental team of specialists in legal matters and to insure law and order at educational establishments" (ITAR-TASS, June 2, 1995).

The above are relatively low-budget items. The bigger problems, significantly more costly to correct, remain in restoring the commissions on juvenile affairs (or something like them) and giving these bodies adequate resources to provide alternative programming and aftercare.

The other major area needing reform concerns the institutional facilities. There now is no differentiation according to the seriousness of their crimes among those youth who are incarcerated. This means younger and/or minor offenders are confined with older and/or more serious ones. There also is no separate classification and handling of mentally retarded or mentally disturbed youngsters (it is estimated that upward of 70% of the children presently confined need at least some psychiatric or psychological services). There are staff psychologists in only 7 of 46 special educational institutions. In addition, the institutions complain that they receive only about half the medicines they need, that their food budgets are about one fourth what is requested, and that most lack such basic amenities as adequate bed space, sewage systems, running water, and steam heat.

The juvenile justice system in the United States is clearly in far better shape than it is in Russia. It may be dealing with many more clients, but there also are many more resources and programs of every kind. Most of the larger police departments in the United States have juvenile or youth aid bureaus that are staffed by specially trained officers and often by social workers or civilian counselors as well. American police have long recognized that juveniles require special handling. The same used to be true of Russian police agencies, which had special inspectorates on juvenile affairs to govern their work with juveniles, but these too have been abolished or are suffering from inadequate resources.

Juvenile institutions in the United States are in far better shape than their Russian counterparts. Although it is difficult to determine exactly what is the population of US juvenile correctional facilities, it seems clear that it is much larger than the 8500 reported for the Russian special schools and colonies. The latter are comparable to training schools in the United States. One estimate (for 1991) indicated 36,000 youth in long-term public facilities and 34,000 in privately operated long-term facilities in the United States (Snyder & Sickmund, 1995, p. 165). The conditions of confinement are definitely superior. Although detention facilities and training schools in the United States are often overcrowded and are lacking in some of the resources they need, they are not remotely close to the bad shape of the Russian institutions.

How effective are the juvenile justice systems of the two countries? Putting aside the difficulty (impossibility) of answering that question in all its complexity, we might look simply at reported recidivism rates for juveniles who have been released from incarceration. The Russian figure for 1993 was that 30 to 50% of previously incarcerated juvenile offenders commit crimes again. In 1995, the Russian Ministry of Internal Affairs reported a recidivism rate for "children and teenagers" of 22% (BBC, August 23, 1995). The latter means, said a Ministry spokesman, that one youngster in five commits another crime within 3 years of release. For neither year do we know how recidivism is being defined. Nor do we know, for the earlier report, what the follow-up period was. Thus we cannot conclude that recidivism is declining. Unfortunately, in the United States we have no nationwide comparable figures. A number of local or regional sample studies provide recidivism data that vary depending on the placement, the sample studied, the definition of recidivism, and the length of follow-up. There is some consensus that failure rates are generally high, on the order of 50 to 70%. There also is consensus that with respect to a variety of other possible indicators of system effectiveness, we still know relatively little about what really works to prevent and control juvenile delinquency.

ATTITUDES, NORMS, AND DEVIANT BEHAVIOR: A COMPARATIVE EMPIRICAL STUDY

The purpose of a 1992 collaborative study of legal socialization among Russian youth was to test links among legal reasoning, knowledge of the law, attitudes toward law enforcement, and delinquent behavior (Finckenauer, 1995). Legal socialization generally refers to the process whereby children learn about rules and laws, including the moral and legal obligations they have to obey the law. This socialization also involves learning about rule and law making and enforcement, about issues of fairness and justice, and about the sanctions for violations. Since sociolegal context and environment are believed to be important in shaping the legal socialization of children (See Tapp, 1987; Cohn & White, 1990), it was believed that post Soviet Russia, with all the chaos previously described, would provide a most efficacious context in which to get a picture of legal socialization. It also seemed to furnish fertile ground for capturing views about deviance.

At the time these data were collected in the fall of 1992, Russia was relatively newly embarked upon its transition from being an authoritarian Soviet state to being a more open and democratic society. This transition included new laws, new curricula (including legal education) in the schools, and generally new freedoms. Although things were in an anomic state, an optimistic glow about the future generally prevailed. Given the then recency of the revolutionary changes, it should be understood that all the Russian young people in the study had spent most of their lives in the Soviet system.

Among the Russian youth surveyed were 268 students at three Moscow city schools. Although these students are not special or atypical, it also cannot be claimed that they are representative of Russian youth. They are an availability sample. Despite this limitation, their behavior and views provide us with a useful snapshot of the Russian scene at that time.

Subjects were chosen equally from among the three schools. Weighted random samples were drawn to provide equal numbers of 10-to 12-year-olds, 13- to 15-year-olds, and 16- to 17-year-olds, and equal numbers of males and females.

The students completed a Russian-language version of a questionnaire called the Internalization of Legal Values Inventory (ILVI). Among the data produced from this inventory is information on age; socioeconomic status; living arrangement (with whom do you live); friends' perceptions of one's own law-abidingness; the wrongfulness of certain deviant acts; willingness to stick with friends in trouble; self-reported delinquency; and legal developmental level. It is with these variables that this particular discussion will deal. First, a word about how the variables were operationally defined. *Socioeconomic status* was dichotomized (higher or lower) based on the Rating Scale of Parental Occupations score for either mother's or father's occupation, whichever was higher. If the subject was not living with mother and/or father, other head of household was used. *Living arrangement* was defined as with whom you live. *Own law-abidingness* items asked, "How much would your friends agree that you (1) are a good kid; (2) break rules; (3) get into trouble; and (4) do things that are against the law?" *Wrongfulness* questions asked how wrong it would be for someone your age to do any of seven deviant acts (steal something worth less than $5, damage someone's property, smoke in school, cheat on school tests, drink alcohol, break into a building to steal something, and steal something worth more than $50). *Trouble* was defined by three questions: "If your friends were causing you to get into trouble, would you still spend time with them?" "If your friends were getting into trouble, would you try to stop what they were doing?" "If your friends were getting into trouble with the police, would you be willing to lie to protect them?" *Legal development level* was defined as preconventional (lower), conventional, and postconventional (higher) based on the mean of responses to 11 items measuring legal reasoning (see Finckenauer, 1995, for a discussion of the measurement of legal development). Finally, *delinquency* was measured by 28 self-report items taken from the US National Youth Survey (Elliott, 1988).

Subsequent to this Russian study, the same Internalization of Legal Values Inventory was administered in 1994–1995 to a sample of young males living in Monmouth County, New

Jersey (Jones-Brown, 1996). The special focus of that study was to investigate the role of race in legal socialization. It was designed to test the assumption that the US legal environment is perceived differently by black and white youth, and consequently produces different socialization effects.

The assumption of racial differences in how black versus white children experience the law and its enforcement has been well documented in the literature (e.g., Pope & Feyerherm, 1991; Mann, 1993). Our interest here is not so much in this black–white difference per se, but rather in ensuring that in the cross national comparison between Americans and Russians it is accounted for.

The Jones–Brown (1996) study included 125 black males and 25 white males, all aged 15 to 18. The subjects were drawn from two high schools, a boy's club, a summer basketball league, and a summer work program. As with the Russians, this sample too is neither representative or generalizable to the US youth population. Again, it is just a snapshot, but nevertheless one that is informative and enlightening.

Since Jones–Brown's (1996) US sample included only males aged 15 or over, the comparison here is likewise limited to Russian males 15 or over. There are 54 Russians in this age category. In order to avoid a large differential in the sizes of the samples, a weighted random sample of American youth was chosen from the original 150 cases. Weighting was necessary because the original sample included only 25 white males. Our US sample has 59 subjects, including 40 blacks and 19 whites. The mean age of the US sample was 16.5, and the Russian sample was 16.1.

Results

There are no statistically significant differences between the two samples in their living arrangements or in their socioeconomic status. There also is no significant difference in their perceptions of how their friends viewed their law abidingness. There are, however, some other differences between the US and Russian samples that are statistically significant.

The first area of difference is with regard to legal developmental level. With a possible range of 1 to 3 (from the lower preconventional to the higher postconventional), the legal developmental level of the Russian youth (mean = 2.03) is significantly higher than that of the US youth (mean = 1.84; $P < .001$). This means that the Russians are solidly in the middle—conventional—range of legal reasoning, whereas the Americans are slightly more toward the lower preconventional level. Conventional legal reasoning (which is the normal level for older teenagers such as these) is oriented toward law maintenance, law and order, and obeying the law because it is the law. Conventional legal reasoners believe in rules and that legitimate rules should be obeyed. Preconventional legal reasoning, on the other hand, is more oriented toward obeying the law simply because of a fear of sanctions. There is less of a feeling of moral obligation to obey the rules and less acceptance of rules as legitimate regulators of behavior. Associated with this, there also is a greater tendency to break the law if you do not believe you will be caught. This lower level of reasoning is more often associated with younger children. It should be stressed that the differences here are not large, and therefore should not be overemphasized.

On the wrongfulness of the seven deviant acts, a most revealing look at the comparative perceptions of deviance, there also is a significant difference between the two samples. On a range of 1 to 4 (from very wrong to not wrong), the American mean is 1.36, whereas the Russian mean is 2.31 ($P < .001$). The views of the US youth fall between very wrong and wrong on average, whereas the Russian youth are between wrong and only a little bit wrong. Most of this difference is accounted for by disagreement on the wrongfulness of smoking in school and drinking alcohol. There is not disagreement about breaking into buildings and stealing $50; both sets of youth regard these as very wrong. Since it is difficult to imagine that 16-year-old American males personally think smoking and drinking are seriously wrong, it might be that they are simply reflecting the fact that there are rules and laws about not doing these things, rather than expressing their own personal views of their harmfulness. They also could be showing the effects of the massive antismoking and antidrinking campaigns being waged in the United States. In the case of the Russian youth, they may be reflecting their personal views, an absence of comparable opposition campaigns, or some combination of both.

On another factor of special interest the results only approach statistical significance. The Russian youth are more inclined to still spend time with friends who are getting into trouble, to try to stop them from getting into trouble, and also to lie to protect them. The mean score is 1.57 for the Russians and 1.75 for the Americans ($P = .08$). This may say something about the peer connections being greater in Russia, as well as there being more of a tendency to reject adults and authority.

Finally, with regard to self-reported delinquent behavior, the difference again only approaches statistical significance. The delinquent acts were weighted by whether they were status offenses (e.g., running away from home), misdemeanors (e.g., being loud, rowdy, or unruly in public), or felonies (e.g., attacking someone with the idea of seriously hurting or killing them). Each of the 28 offenses reported was multiplied by its weight. Each subject was then scored on the proportion of the total possible harm he reported. That score is thus a combination of the number of offenses reported and the severity of those offenses. The average score for the US youth is 18.39, and for the Russian youth it is 24.32 ($P = .07$). The Russian youth are more deviant, committing both more and more serious offenses. Thinking back to our earlier comparisons based on official data, the results here could mean that the actual amount of juvenile deviance in Russia is considerably higher than that evidenced in the official data.

If we compare the two samples, it seems at first glance that contrary to the proposition that higher levels of legal reasoning are associated with less delinquent behavior, that might not be true here. The Russian youth overall both reasoned at a higher level and committed more delinquency. But let us return to this point momentarily. What is further suggested by the aggregate data is that seeing certain kinds of deviance as being less wrong or harmful and having a greater commitment to friends who are in trouble are associated with greater involvement in delinquency. A number of explanatory models were constructed for the two samples to see what factors best predicted the total amount of deviance they reported doing. For the Russian youth those factors are age, legal developmental level, friends' views of law abidingness, and normative judgments about wrongfulness. Those who are younger, have higher legal reasoning, think their friends see them as being law-abiding, and think the various behaviors are wrong report less deviance. Thus, although across the two samples the Russians were higher-level reasoners but also saw less harm in certain behaviors and were more delinquent, within their own sample these factors are nevertheless discriminating. How could the Russian youth have both higher legal reasoning and more delinquency than the American youth on the one hand, and yet have their reasoning still be predictive of their delinquency on the other? This occurred because those Russian youth below the mean reasoning level accounted for a substantially higher amount of the self-reported deviance, whereas among the American youth reported delinquency was more evenly distributed across the reasoning levels. This gives evidence that contrary to other research, for example, Morash (1978), legal reasoning may be associated with deviant behavior.

For the black US youth, the only significant factor predicting deviance is their friends'

Table 3. Explaining Cross-National Delinquency

Variables	B	SE B	Beta	T	Sig T
Russia/United States	−.88	3.62	−.26	−.24	.81
Legal developmental level	−13.26	5.12	−.20	−2.60	.01
Age	−3.45	2.10	−.12	−1.64	.10
Living arrangement	1.33	1.25	.78	1.07	.29
Socioeconomic status	4.97	2.95	.12	1.69	.10
Friends' perceptions	9.52	1.58	.47	6.03	.00
Wrongfulness of deviant acts	8.54	2.12	.39	4.03	.00
Sticking with friends in trouble	−.38	1.13	−.03	−.34	.73
Constant	59.35	37.73		1.57	.12

Multiple R .70
Adjusted R square .45
R square .49
Standard error 12.77

Analysis of variance:

	DF	Sum of square	Mean square
Regression	8	16256.62	2232.08
Residual	102	16635.41	163.09

F = 12.46
Sig F = .00

views of them. Those blacks who think their friends think well of them report less delinquent behavior. For the US whites, the only significant factor is living arrangement. Those in other than two-parent households tend to report more deviance.

Table 3 shows a predictive model for the combined samples, with nationality (Russian–American) included as a variable. Legal development, friends' perceptions, and wrongfulness are significant predictors of delinquency, but nationality clearly is not.

What should we conclude from this comparison? It seems that these particular Russian youth differ from these particular American youth in certain respects: their levels of legal reasoning, their views of the wrongfulness of certain deviant acts, and perhaps their commitment to delinquent peers. The first two of those factors, along with how your friends see you, also are most predictive of delinquency. Thus, there may be some interaction effect between those factors and nationality. By itself, however, simply knowing whether these youth are Americans or Russians does not help us to predict their involvement in deviance.

ISSUES FOR COMPARATIVE RESEARCH ON DEVIANCE

The research initiative described above represented an attempt to test the applicability in Russia of a theory (legal socialization) developed in the United States. This initiative is indicative of a genre of one-way theory testing. Most of the major delinquency theories have originated in the United States. American criminologists who have a comparative bent are very interested in testing these theories in other countries, including Russia. Russian criminologists, on the other hand, do not often share this same enthusiasm.

Russian criminology is quite different from American criminology. For a variety of reasons it is at a different stage of development and it has a different focus. Russian research on crime and delinquency was either suppressed or distorted for political purposes for many years, especially during the Stalinist period. Even after the death of Stalin, more than 30 years passed before there was a *glasnost* (openness) regarding crime data in the late 1980s. Previous to this, explanations and data concerning crime were politicized to support the propaganda about the success of the Soviet system in eliminating deviance. Russian scholars did not have access to Western criminological literature or even to their own crime data, except in very limited circumstances. In addition, what criminology there was in Russia was affiliated with governmental institutions and law faculties and institutes, such as the Institute of State and Law of the Soviet (now Russian) Academy of Sciences.

The latter circumstance is still true today. This means that research often is conducted in the interests of the sponsoring government agency, such as the Ministry of Internal Affairs. This would be comparable to a US situation in which most criminological research was being done at the behest of the Department of Justice. In addition, the traditional affiliation of criminology with the field of law means that its social science aspects may be downplayed or nonexistent. Consequently, deviance research in Russia may not be well-grounded in theory or use rigorous empirical research designs.

These issues aside, there also are other problems facing the foreign scholar wanting to study deviance in Russia. It should be stressed that change is taking place and that progress on many of these issues is being made. One difficulty is gaining entree if one wishes to do experimental research, field research, ethnography, and the like. There are cultural as well as language barriers operating here. The cultural barriers arise from the institutional control of research, as well as from a heavy survey research tradition. Many institutional researchers seem to believe that it is enough for them to simply talk with foreign scholars and to share their research reports. It is not necessary in their view for outsiders to actually do their own studies.

There also is the problem alluded to earlier of the availability of statistical data. There is no uniform crime reporting system. The data that are recorded are of suspect reliability and validity. Sample studies are usually cross-sectional surveys of nonrepresentative samples. The official data are not systematically augmented by victimization surveys and self-report studies. None of this should be taken to mean that all these problems have been solved in the United States, nor that there are no difficulties here. Nor should we conclude that Russian scholars are not cognizant of these issues. Instead, it simply illustrates the point about Russian criminology being at a different stage of development.

As in other aspects of Russian life today, social scientists have severely limited resources. They do not have anywhere near the computer and data-processing capabilities that researchers in many other countries have. Research budgets are practically nonexistent. Scholars in general are very poorly paid. This makes it impossible for them to work with Western colleagues in a truly parallel way. Western criminologists wanting to do work in Russia must have their own resources, and these must be substantial. They should be prepared to pay for all the costs of research, sometimes including reimbursing their Russian colleagues. This includes paying individuals for interviews and for data or other information that one would expect to freely get elsewhere. It should also be recognized that any reciprocity involving Russian scholars coming to the United States may well require the American side to foot all the bills. Absent any reciprocity, Russian scholars may resent the one-way nature of proposed research collaborations.

The challenges aside, and there are none that are unmanageable, the study of deviance among Russian children and youth can be tremendously rewarding for all parties. The same is true of comparative research on juvenile justice and delinquency. One suggested way to begin would be with a variety of applied research projects, that is, projects that are intended to actually have an impact on deviance as well as producing knowledge about it. The proposed law-related education initiative in the schools is one such possibility. This could be relatively easily designed as an action research project. Given the current situation in Russia, joint action research projects ought to receive the highest priority for Russian and US collaborative efforts in the field of youth and justice.

REFERENCES

British Broadcasting Corporation. (1994, November 28). *BBC summary of world broadcasts.* Downloaded from LEXIS-NEXIS.

British Broadcasting Corporation. (1995, August 23). *BBC summary of world broadcasts.* Downloaded from LEXIS-NEXIS.

Cohn, E. S., & White, S. O. (1990). *Legal socialization.* New York: Springer-Verlag.

The Current Digest. (1993). Vol. XLV, No. 18.

The Current Digest. (1994). Vol. XLVI, No. 1.

The Current Digest. (1994). Vol. XLVI, No. 27.

The Current Digest. (1995). Vol. XLVII, No. 21.

Eliott, D. (1988). *National youth survey [United States].* Boulder, CO: University of Colorado, Behavioral Research Institute.

Federal Bureau of Investigation. (1993). Uniform crime reports for 1992. Washington, DC: Superintendent of Documents, GPO.

Finckenauer, J. O. (1995). *Russian youth: Law, deviance, and the pursuit of freedom.* New Brunswick, NJ: Transaction Publishers.

Finkelhor, D., Hotaling, G., & Sedlak, A. (1990). *Missing, abducted, runaway, and thrownaway children in America.* Washington, DC: Office of Juvenile Justice and Delinquency Prevention.

Goldberg, C. (1994a). Moscow's brothers Yakovlev. *Los Angeles Times,* July 15.

Goldberg, C. (1994b). Social disorder lets young criminals run streets of Moscow. *The Houston Chronicle,* July 16.

ITAR-TASS. (1995, June 2). Juvenile delinquency growing in Russia. The Russian Information Agency.

ITAR-TASS. (1995, August 22). Russia worried by juvenile delinquency—Interior Ministry. The Russian Information Agency.

Jones-Brown, D. (1996). *Race and legal socialization.* Unpublished doctoral dissertation. New Brunswick, NJ: Rutgers.

Mann, C. R. (1993). *Unequal justice: A question of color.* Bloomington and Indianapolis: Indiana University Press.

Morash, M. (1978). *Implications of the theory of legal socialization for understanding the effect of juvenile justice procedures on youths.* Unpublished doctoral dissertation. College Park, MD: University of Maryland.

Pope, C., & Feyerherm, W. (1991). *Minorities and the juvenile justice system. Final report.* Washington, DC: Office of Juvenile Justice and Delinquency Prevention.

Snyder, H. N., & Sickmund, M. (1995). *Juvenile offenders and victims: A national report.* Washington, DC: Office of Juvenile Justice and Delinquency Prevention.

Snyder, H. N., Sickmund, M., & Poe-Yamagata, E. (1996). *Juvenile offenders and victims: 1996 update on violence.* Washington, DC: Office of Juvenile Justice and Delinquency Prevention.

Tapp, J. L. (1987). The jury as a socializing experience: A socio-cognitive view. In R. W. Rieber (Ed.), *Advances in forensic psychology and psychiatry* (Vol. 2, pp. 1–32)). Norwood, NJ: Ablex Publishing.

Zinchuk, E. G., & Karpukhin, I. G. (1995). Juvenile crimes of greed. *Russian Education and Society, 37,* 62–77.

10

Youth Crime in Western Europe

Will the Old World Imitate the New?

ROSEMARY BARBERET

INTRODUCTION

Although most of the discipline of criminology can be traced to European roots, now the trend in who looks to whom for crime modalities and trends, research avenues, and related public policy is reversed. Europeans often turn to the United States, despite the availability of local innovations in crime and criminal justice policy. Not only are certain criminal modalities in Europe either "imitations" of American ones or new variations on an old theme, but research and policy frequently are imported from the United States and adapted, for better or for worse, to the European context. A 1998 *New York Times* article (Cowell, 1988, pp. 1, 4) entitled "Europe Envies America: Now, Teenagers Turn to Crime" is emblematic of this trend. The article speaks of increases in juvenile crime in a "post-welfare state, post-cold war, post-industrial, post-baby boom" Europe, arguing that Europe is ill-equipped to cope with this phenomenon. According to the article, traditional European leftist solutions to the crime problem, more geared toward prevention and rehabilitation, are being reconsidered along with "get-tough" policies imported from America.

This chapter will examine juvenile crime and victimization trends in Western Europe and also the response to these at the policy level. The idea is to present a comparative chapter, although not an exhaustive review of the European literature, since few reviewers have the language skills to review all that exists on this topic in Europe, which will allow the reader to reflect on juvenile crime issues from an international perspective.

MEASUREMENT

It would be difficult to establish a data-driven European youth policy, or even adult criminal justice policy, on a comparison of the available official statistics in Europe. There is yet no central depository or coordinating agency for criminal justice statistics in Europe,

ROSEMARY BARBERET • Scarman Centre, University of Leicester, Leicester LE1 7QA, United Kingdom.

Handbook of Youth and Justice, edited by White. Kluwer Academic / Plenum Publishers, New York, 2001.

although Interpol, the United Nations, HEUNI (European Institute for Crime Prevention and Control, affiliated with the United Nations), Eurostat, and the Council of Europe have made periodic attempts to gather and compare international crime data. Usually, however, these compilations give few details regarding youth crime, and one must collect individual country-level statistics for a detailed view of those patterns. Pfeiffer (1998), in an excellent and recent review of violent youth crime in Europe, warns of the dangers of making even the slightest comparisons among nations on official statistics. Crime definitions vary per country, as do the bottom and upper age limits of juvenile status, police practices, the likelihood of victim reporting, and differences in the administration of justice. All these caveats lead Pfeiffer to conclude that it makes most sense to analyze official crime patterns on a country-by-country basis.

Given Pfeiffer's caveats, alternative measures of youth crime that rely on the survey method, a criminological staple, prove even more useful in the European context. These alternative ways of gathering crime data involve either interviewing possible offenders (the self-report method) or possible victims (victimization surveys). For many years these alternative measures were utilized mainly in North America, but in the last two decades they have been adapted to the European context, and now we have examples of both national and international self-report and victimization surveys in Europe. Such ventures as the International Victimization Survey, conducted in 1989, 1992, and 1997, which interviews persons aged 16 and over (see van Dijk, Mayhew, & Killias, 1990; Alvazzi del Frate, Zvekic, & van Dijk, 1993), and the International Self-Report Delinquency Study, conducted once so far in 1992–1993, which included youths between the ages of 14 and 21 (see Jünger-Tas, Terlouw, & Klein, 1994), although not without methodological problems, offer a comparative picture of youth crime and victimization to a greater degree than official police and court statistics. For both ventures, native criminologists adapted a core instrument in English to their own linguistic and cultural context and similar samples in similar time periods were secured. These two projects, coordinated by Europeans, represent a great contribution to a "European criminology" in that they demonstrate the enormous value of using the survey method to gain good indices of crime in an area of the world with so many legal, linguistic, and other cultural differences.

YOUTH CRIME PATTERNS

Despite researchers' misgivings about the value of official statistics, the Council of Europe periodically publishes compilations of national data on the number of young people involved in the criminal justice system. Table 1 lists the absolute numbers of persons under age 21 under detention in a series of European countries for 1993, 1994, 1995, and 1996 and the percentage this number represents of the total number of persons under detention. These data do not appear to show us a clear picture of a western European juvenile crime wave.

Police data from a selection of western European countries reveal that youthful offenders, in this case defined as those under age 18, reflected as a percentage of all offenders detained by the police, are more prone (relative to those over 18) to commit crimes such as robbery, theft, and burglary and least prone to homicide and drug trafficking. The countries listed show relative homogeneity in this aspect (see Table 2). Data roughly comparable from the United States, reflecting the proportion of juveniles under age 18 among all arrests in 1996, shows generally more involvement in property as opposed to violent crimes, with rates similar to those of England and Wales and greater than those for other countries in Table 2. For example,

Table 1. Persons under 21 under Detention on September 1, 1993, 1994, 1995, and 1996, as a Percentage of the Total Number of Persons Detained[a]

Country	1993		1994		1995		1996	
	Absolute number of persons detained under age 21	Percent of the total number of persons detained	Absolute number of persons detained under age 21	Percent of the total number of persons detained	Absolute number of persons detained under age 21	Percent of the total number of persons detained	Absolute number of persons detained under age 21	Percent of the total number of persons detained
Switzerland[b]	117	2.9	—	—	—	—	169	4.2
Luxembourg	39	9.2	21	4.8	29	6.2	23	5.6
Belgium	700	9.7	604	8.5	866	11.5	536	7
Greece[b]	—	—	246	3.6	—	—	387	7.3
Netherlands	969	12.4	1027	12	—	—	876	7.6
France	5190	10.1	5456	10.2	5507	10.4	5396	10
Sweden[b]	178	3.9	—	—	171	3.6	174	3.7
Italy	2529	5.0	—	—	2172	4.4	2165	4.5
Norway	151	5.8	148	5.5	154	6.4	155	6.8
Portugal	879	8.1	516	5.2	—	—	828	5.8
England and Wales[c]	8016	17.6	8451	17.1	8707	17.0	9763	17.8
Finland	161	5.1	136	4.6	140	4.6	106	3.6
Scotland	875	14.8	680	12.2	726	12.8	1112	18.8
Spain	1831	4.0	1019	2.5	—	—	—	—

[a]From Tournier (1994); Council of Europe (1994–1995, 1998).
[b]Data applies only to the convicted population.
[c]Includes those aged 21 whose sentence was executed when they were under 21 years of age.

Table 2. Police Data on Percentage of Suspected Offenders Aged Under 18, Selected Offenses, 1990

Country	Intentional homicide (all)	Intentional homicide (completed only)	Assault	Rape	Robbery	Theft	Burglary	Drug offenses	Drug trafficking
England and Wales	7	7	18	9	39	35	39	12	6
France	6	5	9	14	26	27	29	7	4
Germany	4	—	10	6	24	25	25	6	4
Hungary	9	10	10	18	26	20	25	27	—
Italy	7	10	13	10	16	33	—	7	3
Netherlands	5	3	11	9	23	23	23	2	2
Norway	5	8	11	13	7	30	—	5	—
Sweden	3	6	9	5	20	16	21	2	2
Switzerland	4	—	8	4	19	25	20	7	4

[a]From Council of Europe (1995).

juveniles were involved in 32% of arrests for robbery, 37% for burglary, and 34% for larceny/theft (Snyder, 1997, p. 3).

Data from the International Self-Report Delinquency Study (see Table 3) show that youth from 14 to 21 years old are most likely to be involved in property *and* violent offenses. It is important to keep in mind, however, that self-report surveys rarely reach very violent youths and tend to overinclude relatively trivial offenses. Again, drug use and sale is not an activity admitted by as many young people as the other categories, although the range is from 6% (three Italian cities) to 21% (Switzerland). Note the comparison of the European city and country samples to a city (school-based) sample from Omaha, Nebraska, where rates are generally equivalent or higher across the board.

Table 4 shows that among property offenses, graffiti, vandalism, and shoplifting are those behaviors admitted by larger numbers of youths in all countries.

Table 5 shows that among violent offenses carrying a weapon, though generally not a firearm, and participating in group fights, riots, or disorders are those behaviors admitted by larger numbers of youths participating in the survey. For all behaviors except group fights and riots, the Omaha, Nebraska sample shows the highest rates.

Table 6 highlights the fact that among drug offenses, alcohol and soft drugs (cannabis) are those admitted by higher numbers of youths in the age group studied (14–21).

It is important to remember that youths not only are offenders but also victims, and that there is overlap between the offender and victim population (Lauritsen, Sampson, & Laub, 1991; Finkelhor & Asdigian, 1996). There is less research on this topic in Europe (and elsewhere) because victimization and offending data are rarely gathered together: self-report studies do not usually include victimization data, and victimization surveys do not usually include a self-report component. While in the United States the National Youth Survey (see

Table 3. Selected Prevalence Rates of Participation in Delinquent Acts in a 12-Month Period, 1992

City/country	Property offenses[b]	Violence overall	Violence against persons[c]	Violence against objects[d]	Drugs[e]	Overall delinquency[f]
Helsinki, Finland	39	35	23	23	13	80
Belfast	26	24	12	17	20	47
Netherlands	30	29	22	14	15	61
Liège, Belgium	27	30	—	—	8	56
Mannheim, Germany	21	22	—	—	7	51
Switzerland	34	29	—	—	21	72
Portugal	21	30	—	—	11	57
Spain	20	34	22	23	15	58
Three Italian cities[g]	17	14	14	13	6	65
Omaha, Nebraska[g]	37	35	35	15	17	61

[a]From Jünger-Tas et al. (1994).
[b]Includes stealing from a telephone booth or vending machine; shoplifting; stealing at school; stealing at home; stealing at work; stealing bike/moped/motorcycle; stealing a car; stealing from/out of a car; pickpocketing; purse snatching; burglary; stealing anything else; buying stolen goods; selling stolen goods.
[c]Includes threatening someone; engaging in fights or riots; carrying a weapon; beating up nonfamily; beating up family; hurting with a weapon.
[d]Includes graffiti, vandalism, arson.
[e]Includes using or selling soft and hard drugs.
[f]Includes b–d and other "youth-related offenses": fare dodging on a bus, tram, metro, or train; and driving without a license or insurance.
[g]School-based samples.

Table 4. Selected Prevalence Rates of Participation in Property Offenses and Violent Offenses Against Objects in a 12-Month Period, 1992

City/country	Shoplifting	Stealing a bike/ moped/motorcycle	Purse-snatching	Burglary	Graffiti	Vandalism
Helsinki, Finland	13.5	2.7	0.7	4.8	7.0	19.6
Belfast	4.5	1.2	0.2	2.3	8.8	12.5
Netherlands	5.1	5.3	0.1	1.6	3.7	12.6
Liège, Belgium	11.6	1.7	0.4	5.8	15.5	13.6
Mannheim, Germany	4.7	1.3	0.0	1.0	3.3	4.7
Switzerland	11.4	1.5	0.2	0.6	3.7	17.0
Portugal	4.5	0.9	0.1	4.9	7.0	16.1
Spain	6.6	0.5	0.1	6.9	9.5	16.3
Three Italian cities[g]	6.5	0.7	0.0	0.0	9.3	7.6
Omaha, Nebraska[g]	11.3	0.0	0.4	5.2	3.0	13.7

[a]From Jünger-Tas et al. (1994).
[b]School-based samples.

Elliot, Huizinga, & Ageton, 1985) is perhaps the best known exception to this trend, European exceptions are the research of Anderson et al. (1991) in Edinburgh and Hartless, Ditton, Nair, and Phillips (1995) in Glasgow, Scotland, which suggests as does American research that delinquent behavior increases the risk of victimization.

Table 7 below highlights victimization rates for Western Europe by age. Here we see that, as the international literature on youth victimization generally shows, young people have higher rates of victimization in Europe as well. Those aged 16–19 have higher rates than any other age group for sex offenses, personal theft, and robbery. Their rates for assault and burglary are equal to the 20–24 age group. Higher rates for the 16–19 age group vis-à-vis other age groups are also a feature of victimization in the United States (see Bureau of Justice Statistics, 1997, p. 4).

Table 5. Selected Prevalence Rates of Participation in Violent Offenses Against Persons in a 12-Month Period, 1992

City/country	Carrying a weapon	Threatening someone	Group fights	Beating up nonfamily	Hurting with weapons
Helsinki, Finland	12.4	0.9	12.6	1.0	1.4
Belfast	6.5	0.1	6.1	2.4	1.1
Netherlands	15.4	0.2	10.1	2.5	0.7
Liège, Belgium	13.3	0.1	7.3	2.9	2.3
Mannheim, Germany	13.7	0.7	4.3	0.7	0.7
Switzerland	11.2	0.0	8.8	0.9	0.7
Portugal	10.8	0.3	11.1	2.5	0.8
Spain	8.4	0.4	17.2	2.3	1.1
Three Italian cities[g]	3.4	0.0	10.4	2.2	0.1
Omaha, Nebraska[g]	18.0	1.3	15.0	4.3	2.4

[a]From Jünger-Tas et al. (1994).
[b]School-based samples.

Table 6. Selected Prevalence Rates of Participation in Drug Use and Sales in a 12-Month Period, 1992

City/country	Alcohol use	Soft drug use	Soft drug sales	Hard drug use	Hard drug sales
Helsinki, Finland	70.2	12.9	—	0.8	—
Belfast	68.9	18.6	1.7	8.6	1.6
Netherlands	75.9	15.0	0.7	1.1	0.2
Liège, Belgium	73.4	7.9	1.6	0.9	0.0
Mannheim, Germany	—	6.7	0.7	0.7	0.0
Switzerland	—	20.7	3.4	1.8	0.2
Portugal	39.7	11.0	1.7	2.7	0.3
Spain	79.3	15.0	0.8	2.5	0.3
Three Italian cities[g]	—	6.2	0.4	0.3	0.0
Omaha, Nebraska[g]	58.8	14.8	3.0	5.9	1.7

[a]From Jünger-Tas et al. (1994).
[b]School based samples.

Pfeiffer's (1998) own review, a country-by-country analysis of youth violence in Europe over the past decade, merits a mention in its own right. According to an apparently thorough look at ten European countries (England and Wales, Sweden, Germany, the Netherlands, Italy, Austria, France, Denmark, Switzerland, and Poland) Pfeiffer concludes that while juvenile crime rates overall may not have risen in the last 10 years, there has been a trend in all the countries studied of an increase in violent crimes committed by young people and recorded by law enforcement authorities. These offenders tend to be juveniles more than young adults, are usually male, and commit offenses against other young males.

Table 7. Victimization Rates for Western Europe[b] for Selected Crimes by Age Category, 12-Month Period[a]

Age group	Assault	Sex offense[c]	Personal theft	Robbery	Burglary
16–19	7.5	8.6	11.6	2.5	2.2
20–24	7.5	8.2	8.0	1.7	2.2
25–29	4.7	4.2	5.4	0.6	1.8
30–34	3.7	3.9	5.4	0.5	1.9
35–39	3.8	2.1	4.6	0.6	1.9
40–44	3.2	1.9	4.2	1.1	1.6
45–49	3.5	1.8	2.3	0.9	1.8
50–54	2.3	1.1	3.4	0.7	1.3
55–59	1.8	0.5	2.3	0.8	1.7
60–64	1.7	0.5	2.6	0.6	1.1
65–69	1.1	0.4	2.3	0.3	1.2
70+	0.9	0.0	2.1	0.5	1.2

[a]From the International Crime Survey, Dutch Ministry of Justice, The Hague.
[b]"Western Europe" includes in this case England and Wales, Scotland, Northern Ireland, Netherlands, Germany, Switzerland, Sweden, Italy, Spain, Norway, Belgium, France, Austria, and Finland. The data reflect these countries' last participation in the three waves of the International Victimization Survey (1989, 1992, 1996).
[c]Question asked of women only.

CURRENT RESEARCH ON YOUTH CRIME: A EUROPEAN PERSPECTIVE

Apart from comparative statistics on the European crime problem, there are a series of youth crime "problems" that are currently on the European criminological research agenda, in part because they appear empirically to be serious problems, but also because they represent particularly "European" phenomena, and thus appear to violate commonly held values. Most of these phenomena are thought to be causes of current youth violence, which is a general research interest at this time in Europe. These include football (soccer) hooliganism, hate crime as perpetrated by youth subcultures, migrants and crime, vandalism and public disorders, and bullying (see Graham, 1997, p. 3, for an echo of these categories of youth offending).

Football hooliganism is of particular interest because of the massive popularity of this sport in Europe (and other areas of the world) vis-à-vis the United States and recent outbursts of violence at football games that have caused damage not only to people and property but to the name of the sport itself. The research in this area is extensive, and thus can be summarized only. Football hooliganism research is dominated by the British, is not always limited to that conducted by criminologists, and can be split roughly into two areas: etiologic (who are football hooligans, how are they organized, and why do they do it?) (Armstrong & Harris, 1991; Hobbs & Robbins, 1991; Horak, 1991; Williams & Taylor, 1994; Jünger-Tas, 1996) and preventive–situational (how does football violence emerge situationally and what can be done to prevent or control football hooliganism) (Stott & Reicher, 1998; Clarke, 1983). Although football hooligans are not necessarily all young, most of the research includes the concept of youth as an explanatory factor.

Competing and complementary views exist within the football hooliganism literature. For some (Jünger-Tas, 1996, pp. 33–35) football hooliganism is merely another manifestation of youth aggression and offending. Many of the psychosocial correlates of football hooliganism are those of ordinary juvenile delinquency, and many football hooligans have criminal records. Nevertheless, there must be something about the organization and image of the sport that attracts these sorts of fans and serves as a good place for violence to occur. Other researchers see football hooliganism as tied to male working-class subculture, with changes in the game—and the working classes—serving to polarize this subculture (Dunning, 1994; Williams & Taylor, 1994).

Situational research tries to explain why football violence may emerge at some matches and not at others. As an example of this line of research, Stott and Reicher (1998) argue that football violence emerges situationally among those who do and do not espouse it at matches through a process in which the police treat crowds in a negative, homogeneous fashion. Drawing from research on crowd conflict, Stott and Reicher's research has implications for policing football matches. More applied work from a true situational prevention model is that of criminologists Clarke (1983) and Felson (1998), who assume that football attracts some violent spectators and set about to dissuade that violence. Clarke (1983) notes that some football violence can be controlled by modifying bus schedules that bring the (largely carless) violence-prone fans to the stadiums, allowing them only a limited time before the game to access alcohol and become disorderly. Furthermore, club stewards can be given free train passes to accompany fans on rides to the games, thus reducing disorder. Felson (1998, pp. 172–173) explains that American sports events are less violent than European soccer games because an effort is made to sell tickets to families and businesses, who provide informal social control, private alcohol is not allowed in the stadiums, beer sales in the stadiums are controlled by security staff who monitor the behavior of fans, and after the game people are ushered out quickly so as to avoid lingering and fighting. European football clubs have adopted some of these mechanisms in an effort to ensure safer games.

Hate crime, as perpetrated by youthful right extremist groups (skinheads, neo-Nazis, and the like) is of particular interest in Europe because of its association with native Nazi and Fascist movements and current-day xenophobia and intolerance in Europe in general, topics that are high priority in the policies and activities of the Council of Europe and the European Commission. The research available is limited, as hate crimes are not always counted separately, and thus the victims of these crimes are often difficult to distinguish. Furthermore, forays into these subcultures on the part of criminologists are relatively rare. Hate crime is perpetrated in Europe against homosexuals, ethnic and racial minorities, the poor and homeless, and others. The research that does exist attempts to identify the particular makeup of the subcultures, the existence (or not) of an ideology, how the subcultures are created and expanded, and what state responses should be (Anti-Defamation League, 1995; Adán Revilla, 1996; Costa, Pérez Tornero, & Tropea, 1996; Aronowitz, 1994; Witte, 1994).

Crime as perpetrated by and against migrants in Europe is another current topic on the European research agenda. Increasingly, Europe is becoming host to migrants from former colonies, Eastern Europe and the former Soviet Union, and other nations, many of whom are young, although conventional research suggests that it is their children, the second-generation immigrants, who are most likely to engage in misbehavior. The debate on migrants and crime is heated, especially on the lack of agreement between official statistics and self-report data regarding crimes committed by young migrants (see, for example, Jünger, 1989; Bowling, 1990). Two comparative edited volumes (Marshall, 1997; Tonry, 1996) explore the evidence in this area. Although these volumes are not limited to only youthful migrants, they document the methodological difficulties of ascertaining the involvement of migrants in crime and victimization and the overrepresentation of migrants in official statistics. Possible reasons given are difficulties (including victimization) experienced in the country of origin; cultural differences between migrant groups that ease or impede assimilation, or that favor or disfavor delinquency, family disruption, or the socioeconomic disadvantage of migrants as a factor in crime causation; social conditions of the host country and policies that help migrants adjust (or not) and may feed into crime-causing mechanisms; and criminal justice practices that directly or indirectly cause or exacerbate migrant disadvantage (see, for example, Jünger, 1990a).

Vandalism and public disorders are another topic of concern in Europe, due in part to the participation of youths in political demonstrations and the character of youth leisure in southern Europe particularly, which thanks to a favorable climate tends to be public (outdoors) as opposed to private (indoors). In Europe and in southern Europe particularly, cities and towns are becoming increasingly concerned about youth congregating in public places on the weekends, drinking and behaving noisily, frequently disturbing neighbors and vandalizing public and private property. Although this is a problem of youth in other areas of the world (see Bell & Burke, 1992, for a similar phenomenon in Arlington, Texas), its effects are perhaps more discernible in Europe where private residences and entertainment areas coexist in the center of cities and towns and where the buildings prone to suffer vandalism often have incalculable historical value. Unfortunately, southern Europe also suffers from the continent's weakest criminology, and little is available to scientifically document this phenomenon. Most of the research in this area is situational and comes from England (Clarke, 1992) and the Netherlands (van Andel, 1992; Jünger-Tas, 1992), although Jünger-Tas mentions youth-centered antivandalism programs in the Netherlands ("HALT") that serve to make young people accountable for their actions by obliging them to repair the harm done.

School bullying also is of particular interest in Europe, and one of the first studies was conducted in Sweden (Olweus, 1973). Since that date there have been numerous studies in Europe on bullying (see, for example, Jünger, 1990b; Ortega, 1994; Mellor, 1990). Farrington's review of the bullying literature (Farrington, 1993) bases itself essentially on European studies. It is probably a "light" version of what in the United States would be termed "school violence," but Europeans are genuinely concerned about school bullying and its possible prevention. The bullying literature centers around the characteristics of bullies and their victims, the situations in which bullying occurs, the relationship of bullying to other aggressive and delinquent acts, and strategies towards prevention and control (Olweus, 1993).

What is perhaps most interesting about all the above topics is that they overlap. Rightist extremist groups have become attracted to football gathering in "radical" supporter groups and using matches as a venue for violent confrontations. Hate crime victims include migrants and minorities. Extremist groups and football hooligans engage in public disorders. Also, Jünger (1990b) found that ethnic minority victims of bullying in the Netherlands attributed their victimization to their ethnicity.

There are a series of American criminological research topics that are of very little interest in Europe. A good example is the American street gang, with its notions of territoriality, "cafeteria-style" or mixed varieties of offending, and moderate cohesion, as contrasted by Klein (1995, pp. 213–228) to European subcultural counterparts (football hooligans, extremist groups, immigrant gangs) that to date are still different from American gangs. However, Klein seems to think that immigrant groups in particular have the makings of becoming very similar to American street gangs; if immigrant groups in impoverished settings become increasingly marginalized, it is quite possible that they will turn into American-style gangs.

This discussion brings us to a discussion of the theoretical perspectives advanced in Europe to explain juvenile offending. In poorer or more unstable parts of Europe, these perspectives are generally related to strain theory and a "winner–loser" culture, giving great importance to youth unemployment and the lack of integration of youth into adult society as a result, which produces alienation (Pfeiffer, 1998). However, in wealthier parts of Europe, opportunities and the lack of social control over youths that are "too independent" have resonance (Friday, 1992; Graham, 1997; Jünger-Tas et al., 1994). Comparative European research still has not shown that juvenile offending can be explained similarly across countries.

YOUTH JUSTICE POLICY IN THE EUROPEAN UNION

Against a mainly American backdrop of punitive measures aimed at youthful offenders, European juvenile justice policy is at a crossroads. There has been some "importation" of American practices, such as curfews for young people in England and more stringent treatment of juvenile offenders by the justice system in Germany; however, many European countries still regard juvenile offenders as wayward children or victims of society, in need more of help than punishment. This situation may change with the "moral panic" that is rising in Europe about violent crime committed by young people.

Although the European Parliament has no authority over penal policy, the European Commission does handle matters of police cooperation and social affairs. This would allow the commission to influence European policy in areas related to the prevention of juvenile delinquency and victimization and the official reaction of police authorities to youth crime and victimization. An example of the latter is the recent interest of the commission in domestic violence and the trafficking of women and children, with consequent calls for proposals in the area of research and intervention.

Youth policy of the European Union, as reflected by the activities of the European Commission at General Directorate V (Social Affairs) and XXII (Youth, Education, and Training) only recently has addressed the topic of juvenile offending and only indirectly. To date, relevant European Union policy has consisted of fostering limited research and measures that help youth across Europe to gain a "sense of European citizenship" (which means, basically, tolerance for those who are different) and measures to help increase youth employment and generally reduce "social exclusion," a catchall phrase for social problems that include delinquency and antisocial behavior.

The Council of Europe, as part of its historical dedication to human rights, democracy, and the rule of law, also works to prevent social exclusion among youth, promote tolerance and democratic values, and harmonize European legal systems. In this respect the Council of Europe has played an important role in attempting to produce comparable statistics on crime and delinquency and in assembling researchers and policymakers to discuss different aspects of the crime problem.

CHALLENGES FOR YOUTH CRIME AND VICTIMIZATION RESEARCH IN EUROPE

The challenges for youth crime and victimization research in Europe rest heavily on the strength of the criminological community dedicated to these issues. It must be noted that in some countries criminology and criminological research is well-developed, well-funded, and respected. In others, it is underdeveloped, badly funded, and not consulted. This is evidenced by the lack of rigorous research in some countries in this area.

It seems imperative that any sort of "European" youth crime and victimization research is additionally dependent on the multilingual talents of researchers and the willingness to fund and participate in cooperative ventures such as the International Victimization Surveys and the International Self-Report Delinquency Study. Efforts by the Council of Europe to produce timely and comparable official statistics are encouraging and should be continued in an effort to harmonize definitions and counting rules.

Europe is in desperate need of more longitudinal studies of crime and victimization. Most of the research available is descriptive and cross-sectional. This makes it very difficult to ascertain whether youth crime is increasing or decreasing. The needs exist at the national level as well (see Farrington, 1992). As the European Union consolidates, it may be possible to centralize data collection efforts. Europe also is in need of more research that looks at both offending and victimization among youth and the overlap between the two phenomena. Too often our research paints a black and white picture of young people as villains, when a more blurry picture is appropriate.

Finally, program evaluation and policy research is of the utmost importance in Europe, where as I have mentioned there are contrasts of countries who have imported the US "get-tough" policies and others who tend more toward rehabilitative policies and alternative treatments of young offenders. A good example of this sort of research is the first European meta-analysis of the correctional treatment of offenders (Redondo, Garrido, & Sánchez-Meca,

1997) that highlights that younger offenders have higher success rates, juvenile centers provide better success rates than adult prisons, and psychosocial treatment is more effective than punishment.

CONCLUSION

This chapter has sought to provide a brief review of youth crime patterns in Europe. Recently, Tonry and Moore (1998) published a thematic volume in the *Crime and Justice* series devoted to youth violence. In their introduction, they speak of a decade-long epidemic of youth violence in the United States, but term its repercussions a "moral panic." What was empirically true at one point in its decline had become "larger than life." Whether Europe is experiencing as a whole something similar—an epidemic or a "moral panic"—is a conclusion that would reach beyond what data and research are available. At best we can say that if country-specific studies do indicate increases, although only in violent crime committed by youths, and if these increases are not due to recording and reporting practices, the rates are still lower than their US counterparts. What is perhaps more worrisome is the dearth of comparable longitudinal data and research on the causes, consequences, treatment, and prevention of juvenile crime in Europe compared to the United States and the lack of a centralized body to commission such research. It would seem that the first step toward addressing concerns about juvenile crime and victimization would be to organize such a research effort. If it were possible to do this profiting from the trials and errors of American research and practice, then perhaps the old world would not be so prone to imitate the new.

REFERENCES

Adán Revilla, T. (1996). *Ultras y skinheads: La juventud visible: Imágenes, estilos y conflictos de las subculturas juveniles en España.* Oviedo, Spain: Ediciones Nobel.

Alvazzi del Frate, A., Zvekic, U., & van Dijk, J. (1993). *Understanding experiences of crime and crime control.* Rome: UNICRI.

Anderson, S., Kinsey, R., Loader, J., & Smith, C. (1991). *"Cautionary tales": A study of young people and crime in Edinburgh.* Edinburgh: Centre for Criminology, Edinburgh University.

Anti-Defamation League. (1995). *The skinhead international: A worldwide survey of neo-Nazi skinheads.* New York: Anti-Defamation League.

Armstrong, G., & Harris, R. (1991). Football hooligans: Theory and practice. *Sociological Review, 3*, 427–458.

Aronowitz, A. (1994). Germany's xenophobic violence: Criminal justice and social responses. In M. Hamm (Ed.), *Hate crime: International perspectives on causes and control* (pp. 37–69). Cincinnati, OH: Anderson.

Bell, J., & Burke, B. (1992). Cruising Cooper Street. In R. V. Clarke (Ed.), *Situational crime prevention: Successful case studies* (pp. 108–123). Albany, NY: Harrow & Heston.

Bowling, B. (1990). Conceptual and methodological problems in measure "race" differences in delinquency. *British Journal of Criminology, 30*(4), 483–492.

Bureau of Justice Statistics. (1997). *Criminal victimization 1996.* Washington, DC: US Department of Justice, Office of Justice Programs, Bureau of Justice Statistics.

Clarke, R. V. (1983). Situational crime prevention: Its theoretical basis and practical scope. In M. Tonry & N. Morris (Eds.), *Crime and justice: An annual review of research* (Vol. 4). Chicago: University of Chicago Press.

Clarke, R. V. (1992). *Situational crime prevention: Successful case studies.* Albany, NY: Harrow & Heston.

Costa, P.-O., Pérez Tornero, J. M., & Tropea, F. (1996). *Tribus urbanas: El ansia de identidad juvenil: Entre el culto a la imagen y la autoafirmación a través de la violencia.* Barcelona: Paidós.

Council of Europe. (1994–1995). *Bulletin d'Information Pénologique*, 19–20.

Council of Europe. (1995). *Draft model of the European sourcebook of crime and criminal justice statistics.* Strasbourg: Council of Europe.

Council of Europe. (1998). *Bulletin d'Information Pénologique*, *21*.

Cowell, A. (1998). Europe envies America: Now, teenagers turn to crime. *New York Times*, February 1, pp. 1, 4.

Dunning, E. (1994). The social roots of football hooliganism: A reply to the critics of the "Leicester School." In R. Giulianotti, N. Bonney, & M. Hepworth (Eds.), *Football violence and social identity*. London: Routledge.

Elliot, D., Huizinga, D., & Ageton, S. (1985). *Explaining delinquency and drug use*. Beverly Hills, CA: Sage.

Farrington, D. P. (1992). Trends in English juvenile delinquency and their explanation. *International Journal of Comparative and Applied Criminal Justice*, *16*(2), 151–163.

Farrington, D. P. (1993). Understanding and preventing bullying. In M. Tonry (Ed.), *Crime and justice: A review of research* (Vol. 17, pp. 381–458). Chicago: University of Chicago Press.

Felson, M. (1998). *Crime and everyday life*. Thousand Oaks, CA: Pine Forge Press.

Finkelhor, D., & Asdigian, N. (1996). Risk factors for youth victimization: Beyond a lifestyles/routine activities theory approach. *Violence and Victims*, *11*, 3–19.

Friday, P. C. (1992). Delinquency in Sweden: Current trends and theoretical implications. *International Journal of Comparative and Applied Criminal Justice*, *16*, 231–246.

Graham. J. (1997). *Preventing youth violence*. Paper presented at Crime Prevention: Towards A European Level conference. May 11–14. Noordwijk, The Netherlands.

Hartless, J., Ditton, J., Nair, G., & Phillips, S. (1995). More sinned against than sinning. *British Journal of Criminology*, *35*, 114–133

Hobbs, D., & Robbins, D. (1991). The boy done good: Football violence, changes and continuities. *The Sociological Review*, *39*, 551–579.

Horak, R. (1991). Things change: Trends in Austrian football hooliganism from 1977–1990. *The Sociological Review*, *39*, 531–548.

International Crime Survey. (1989, 1992, 1996). The Hague, Netherlands: Dutch Ministry of Justice.

Jünger, M. (1989). Discrepancies between police and self-report data for Dutch racial minorities. *British Journal of Criminology*, *29*, 273–284.

Jünger, M. (1990a). *Delinquency and ethnicity: An investigation on social factors relating to delinquency among Moroccan, Turkish, Surinamese and Dutch boys*. Deventer and Boston: Kluwer Law & Taxation.

Jünger, M. (1990b). Intergroup bullying and racial harassment in the Netherlands. *Sociology and Social Research*, *74*, 65–72.

Jünger-Tas, J. (1992). La prevención de la delincuencia juvenil: Teoría y Práctica en Holanda. In Garrido Genovés & Montoro González (Eds.), *La reeducación del delincuente juvenil: Los programas de éxito*. Valencia, Spain: Tirant lo Blanch.

Jünger-Tas, J. (1996). Youth and violence in Europe. *Studies on Crime and Crime Prevention*, *5*(1), 31–58.

Jünger-Tas, J., Terlouw, G., & Klein, M. (Eds.). (1994). *Delinquent behavior among young people in the western world*. Amsterdam: Kugler.

Klein, M. W. (1995). *The American street gang: Its nature, prevalence and control*. New York: Oxford University Press.

Lauritsen, J., Sampson, R., & Laub, J. (1991). The link between offending and victimization among adolescents. *Criminology*, *29*, 265–292.

Marshall, I. H. (Ed.). (1997). *Minorities, migrants and crime: Diversity and similarity across Europe and the United States*. Thousand Oaks, CA: Sage.

Mellor, A. (1990). *Bullying in Scottish secondary schools*. Edinburgh: Scottish Council for Research in Education.

Olweus, D. (1973). *Hakkycklingar och översittare. Forskning om skolmobbning*. Stockholm: Almqvist & Wicksell.

Olweus, D. (1993). *Bullying at school: What we know and what we can do*. Oxford, England: Blackwell.

Ortega, R. (1994). Las malas relaciones interpersonales en la escuela: Estudio sobre la violencia y el maltrato entre compañeros en la segunda etapa de EGB. *Infancia y Sociedad*, *27–28*, 191–216.

Pfeiffer, C. (1998). Juvenile crime and violence in Europe. In M. Tonry (Ed.), *Crime and Justice: A review of research* (Vol. 23, pp. 255–328). Chicago: University of Chicago Press.

Redondo, S., Garrido, V., & Sánchez-Meca, J. (1997). What works in correctional rehabilitation in Europe: A meta-analytical review. In S. Redondo, V. Garrido, J. Pérez, & R. Barberet (Eds.), *Advances in psychology and law: International contribution* (pp. 499–523). Berlin: De Gruyter.

Snyder, H. (1997). Juvenile arrests 1996. *Juvenile Justice Bulletin*. Washington, DC: US Department of Justice, Office of Justice Programs, Office of Juvenile Justice and Delinquency Prevention.

Stott, C., & Reicher, S. (1998). How conflict escalates: The inter-group dynamics of collective football crowd "Violence." *Sociology*, *32*, 353–377.

Tonry, M. (Ed.). (1996). Ethnicity, crime and immigration. *Crime and justice: An annual review of research* (Vol. 21). Chicago: University of Chicago Press.

Tonry, M., & Moore, M. (1998). Youth violence. *Crime and justice: An annual review of research* (Vol. 24, pp. 1–26) Chicago: University of Chicago Press.

Tournier, P. (1994). *Statistique pénale annuelle du conseil de L'Europe (S.PACE), Enquête 1993*. Strasbourg, France: Conseil de L'Europe.

van Andel, H. (1992). The care of public transport in the Netherlands. In R. V. Clarke (Ed.), *Situational crime prevention: Successful case studies* (pp. 151–163). Albany, NY: Harrow & Heston.

van Dijk, J., Mayhew, P., & Killias, M. (1990). *Experiences of crime across the world: Key findings of the 1989 international crime survey*. Deventer, The Netherlands: Kluwer.

Williams, J., & Taylor, R. (1994). Boys keep swinging: Masculinity and football culture in England. In T. Newburn & E. Stanko (Eds.), *Just boys doing business? Men, masculinities and crime* (pp. 214–233). London: Routledge.

Witte, R. (1994). Comparing state responses to racist violence in Europe: A model for international comparative analysis. In M. Hamm (Ed.), *Hate crime: International perspectives on causes and control* (pp. 91–103). Cincinnati, OH: Anderson.

Part V

Environmental Influences

11

Forging Criminals in the Family

JOAN McCORD

Families contribute to criminality in at least three ways: by genetic transmission, through placement in physical and socioeconomic contexts, and by virtue of their child-rearing practices. I discuss each of these, noting some of the difficulties involved in their study and identifying some of the major results of research as well as some of the important issues remaining.

GENETIC TRANSMISSION

Crime tends to run in families. Because of this fact, many observers have assumed that a genetic contribution to criminality would be identified. A recently popular book on the subject (Herrnstein & Murray, 1994) played on this assumption, giving a high profile to questions about heritability. The book generated a series of arguments that confound scientific claims with political and social ones.

Before considering the scientific claims and their grounds, let me turn to some mistaken beliefs about what is involved in claiming a genetic contribution to criminality.

The first mistaken belief is that the only way genes could influence crime is by causing crime directly. This mistaken belief has led people to criticize genetic studies on the grounds that crime is socially defined. What has been rejected, however, is not a claim made by reputable scientists.

A different claim deserves serious consideration. That is the claim that, just as genetically determined characteristics increase or decrease dispositions favoring athletic or musical abilities, other genetically determined characteristics increase or decrease dispositions favoring criminality.

These might be rate of autonomic response, which could affect learning or risk taking. These might be activity level, which could influence the amount of trouble a child causes. Or these might be the abilities involved in social or academic learning, abilities that help children read the cues others convey regarding how they feel and what they want. The socially defined

---

JOAN McCORD • Criminal Justice Department, Temple University, Philadelphia, Pennsylvania 19104.

Handbook of Youth and Justice, edited by White. Kluwer Academic/Plenum Publishers, New York, 2001.

nature of sports, music, and crime would be consonant with heritability of activity level, autonomic response rates, and intelligence.

The second mistaken belief is that heredity and environment are independent of one another. Some researchers, for example, have attempted to apportion variance into hereditary and environmental contributions (e.g., Braungart, Plomin, Defries, & Fulker, 1992; Goldsmith & Gottesman, 1981; Goodman & Stevenson, 1989; Rowe, 1986). Such attempts necessarily are restricted by the nature of the samples, by how the measures are obtained (e.g., through observation or interviews), and by measurement properties of the scales being used.

Sorting out heredity and environment is like trying to decide whether nature or nurture is responsible for the bloom of an orchid. Although the color of an orchid is determined to a large extent biologically, whether an orchid will bloom at all depends on whether it receives sufficient sun, warmth, and water. If there is plenty of water and warmth but variable sunshine, the amount of sunshine will contribute all the variance to predictions about the heartiness of different colors of orchids.

Human height provides another example. Given relatively constant environments, height is largely genetically determined. But diet greatly influences height, so that among genetically similar people most of the variations in height come from diet.

In his summary of the issue for the National Academy of Sciences, Gregory Carey (1994) noted: "it must be recalled that heritability is a function of the amount of environmental variability for a trait" (p. 44). In short, genetic determination takes place within epigenetic contexts.

The third mistaken belief is that genetic contributions to crime require biological interventions. Prostheses can overcome even such "pure" biological handicaps as genetically missing limbs. Genetically influenced diseases such as diabetes and hypertension may be controlled through diet, exercise, and even meditation.

If there are specific genetic risks, the opportunities for discovering how to overcome them are surely greater if they are understood. Four types of evidence seem to show that there are genetic factors related to crime.

Family Resemblances and Intergenerational Transfer

Many studies show that parents who have criminal records have a relatively high probability of producing children who are criminals (e.g., Farrington, Gundry, & West, 1975; Glueck & Glueck, 1950; McCord, 1977, 1991a; Osborn, & West, 1979; Robins, 1966; Rowe & Farrington, 1997). Such studies show resemblance even when parental criminality took place only before the birth of a child and even when it is implausible to believe that parents directly taught their children to be criminals.

A genetic interpretation is in line with the fact that breeders are able to create animals with traits that could be related positively or negatively to crime. For example, the pit bull and some German shepherds have been bred to behave with aggression, a characteristic related to criminal behavior. Other dogs, like the Labrador retriever and cocker spaniel, have been bred to be affectionate and friendly, characteristics found rarely among criminals.

Physical attractiveness and athletic abilities, both of which include genetic components, have been shown to be related to general popularity and success (Webster & Driskell, 1983). Popularity and success, in turn, are negatively related to crime (Cairns & Cairns, 1994; Farrington, 1988).

Those dubious about a genetic interpretation point to collinear conditions based on the frequency with which families that produce criminals live in and produce criminogenic environments. Such families tend to quarrel, they typically live in depressed and congested areas, and they tend to use poor strategies for socialization of their children (Sampson & Laub, 1993; McCord, 1991a). Effects of these types of family environments are discussed below.

Continuities in Misbehavior

A second type of evidence rests on continuities from earliest childhood to adult criminality. As very young children, criminals were typically troublemakers (Ensminger, Kellam, & Rubin, 1983; Farrington, 1986; McCord, 1994; Sampson & Laub, 1993; Wolfgang, Figlio, & Sellin, 1972). In addition, the longitudinal studies carried out by Eron and Huesmann have tied aggression at age 8 to aggression in their offspring 22 years later (Huesmann & Eron, 1984; Eron, Huesmann, Dubow, Romanoff, & Yarmel, 1987). These continuities have been interpreted as evidence showing what some have referred to as a "bad seed."

As mentioned above, slow autonomic responses, neurological deficits, and propensities toward risk-taking behaviors mark the childhoods of many who later became criminals (Farrington, 1987, Hare, 1978; Mednick, 1977; Moffitt, 1994; Moffitt, & Silva, 1988; Satterfield, 1987; Siddle, 1977; Wadsworth, 1976). These characteristics appear to be heritable (Frick, Lahey, Christ, Loeber, & Green, 1991).

Against a genetic interpretation, one should note that prenatal and early childhood environments affect social responsiveness, desensitization, and activity level. Insufficient stimulation during infancy may also affect autonomic responsiveness, neurological development, and willingness to take risks (Kraemer, Ebert, Schmidt, & McKinney, 1991). Furthermore, harsh and inconsistent discipline seem to produce childhood misbehavior (Patterson, Debaryshe, & Ramsey, 1989).

Possibly, rejection leads an infant to feel bad, sad, or angry. These emotions have endocrine interpretations that affect heart rate and other factors associated with hyperactivity. Scientists may be measuring physiological effects of early environment rather than genetic factors when linking biological measures to criminality.

Twin Comparisons and Adoption Studies

Evidence more closely linked to genetic factors comes from comparisons between monozygotic and dizygotic pairs of twins. The monozygotic, genetically identical twins have been shown to be more similar with regard to extraversion, activity level, impulsivity, task-oriented behaviors, and desire for excitement (e.g., Goldsmith & Gottesman, 1981; Goodman & Stevenson, 1989; Pedersen, Plomin, McClearn, & Friberg, 1988; Tambs, Sundet, Eaves, Solaas, & Berg, 1991). These variables are related to crime.

Although the similarities of monozygotic twins persist even when they have been reared apart, critics note that separation does not necessarily imply relevant differences in environments. Furthermore, the physical similarities in appearance of monozygotic twins may lead to their receiving similar treatment. This would influence apparent genetic impact by increasing similarities in the environment.

Genetic studies rarely include direct measures of social conditions. Furthermore, the most commonly used measure of heritability, h^2, devised by Falconer (1960), assumes the equivalence of environmental variance for monozygotic and dizygotic twins and it assumes additive effects of heredity and environment. Both assumptions are questionable.

Studies of adopted children have been used to provide additional evidence regarding genetic factors. In such studies, adopted children are compared with both their biological and their adopting parents in what has come to be known as a cross-fostering design (Capron & Duyme, 1991; Mednick, Gabrielli, & Hutchings, 1987). In this type of analysis, if the sons were more likely to be criminal when only the biological parents were criminal than when only the adopting parents were criminal, the evidence has been interpreted as showing genetic effects (at least so long as adoption occurred prior to the criminality of the biological parents).

Results of such studies show greater association between sons and biological-parent criminality than with adopting-parent criminality (Bohman, Cloninger, Sigvardsson, & von Knorring, 1982; Crowe, 1975; Mednick, Gabrielli, & Hutchings, 1987; Schulsinger, 1977). Adoption agencies are unlikely to place children in families with criminal parents, however, so that there is little variance in criminality among the latter (Cadoret, Troughton, & O'Gorman, 1987; Carey, 1994). The cross-fostering results may, therefore, be merely a statistical artifact.

The approach builds its argument on the assumption that whether or not a parent is a criminal will be salient in both biological and adopting families. Yet socialization practices create the conditions in which biological potentialities for criminality develop, and these are not measured in cross-fostering studies.

Criminal parents who release children for adoption are likely to differ in many ways from noncriminal parents who release children for adoption. These differences may result in selective placement of the children, placements that could influence the children's criminality. Adopting parents may treat adopted children of criminal parents especially harshly or inconsistently, thereby increasing criminogenic environments.

Summary of Genetic Contributions to Criminality

Overall, then, studies that focus on genetics have shown suggestive evidence that something inherited has some influence on behavior.

The premise that resemblance between parent and child is either sufficient or necessary evidence for genetic transmission is a false premise from which much nonsense has followed. Even such a clearly genetically transmitted characteristic as sex would not appear to be so by this criterion: Mothers do not resemble their sons in terms of sex and stepfathers do resemble their sons despite absence of genetic transmission.

Genetic carriers may show no phenotypical marks of the characteristic they carry genetically. Until the mechanisms of genetic transmission are better understood, much of the literature about genetic contributions to character and to crime should be viewed as speculative.

In criminology, nevertheless, genetic explanations have largely rested on evidence regarding similarities with respect to criminality between biological fathers and sons. What has been missing from the genetic studies is consideration of the impact of social and physical environments on inherited potentialities.

Similar environments can be expected to produce different results, depending on the genetic makeup of those in their midst. A person who is easily bored, who almost constantly seeks high levels of stimulation for example, may misbehave in a classroom that provides security and comfort to classmates.

We need to use animal models as well as close observations in longitudinal studies of twins and adopted children in order to learn about the interaction of heredity and environment. Understanding the genetics of family transmission may help to create environments conducive to more healthful development for individuals as well as society.

PHYSICAL AND SOCIOECONOMIC ENVIRONMENTS

Families influence the development of their offspring through their social and physical placement. Parental education and occupation have far-reaching consequences for children. So too does the area in which they live (Rutter, 1978).

To perhaps a surprising extent, crime rates differ geographically. Within the United States, victimization rates for violent crimes tend to be higher in the South and West than in the Midwest or Northeast. Excluding murder and nonnegligent manslaughter, the Bureau of Justice Statistics (1992) estimated that for every 100,000 people in 1991 there were 3,420 victims of violent crimes in the West and 3,110 in the South. Comparable estimates for the Midwest and Northeast were 3,050 and 2,180. Arrest rates from 1970 through 1989 suggest that murder and nonnegligent manslaughter were most likely in the South, forcible rape and assault were most prevalent in the West, and robbery occurred most frequently in the Northeast (Brown, Flanagan, & McLeod, 1984; Maguire & Flanagan, 1991).

Differences among regions in terms of violence have given rise to several theories. Among them perhaps the most cogent suggests that some cultures promote the idea that defending a reputation requires willingness to fight if insulted or if a member of one's family is insulted. Such cultures, dubbed "cultures of honor," appear to be particularly dominant in the South (Butterfield, 1995; Nisbett, 1993). Similar cultures have been described within urban areas, where they are sometimes called "street cultures" (e.g., Anderson, 1997).

In recent years, crime rates have been higher in urban than in suburban or rural areas. In 1990, there were approximately 856 violent crimes per 100,000 people living in cities that had populations of at least 50,000. The violent crime rate for smaller cities in 1990 was approximately 458 per 100,000. In rural areas, the violent crime rate was 207 per 100,000 inhabitants (Flanagan & Maguire, 1992). Rates of violent crime in general are correlated with city size (US Department of Justice, 1991).

Of course there are variations in crime rates within regions and within cities (Bursik, 1988; Reiss & Roth, 1993; Sherman, Gartin, & Buerger, 1989). High rates of violence within cities have been shown to reflect income inequality, male unemployment, and high levels of single-parent families in the community (Sampson, 1985, 1987, 1992). The presence of delinquent peers, absence of supervision over adolescent activities, and general disorderliness of neighborhoods seem to promote crime (Elliott, Huizinga, & Ageton, 1985; Elliott, Huizinga, & Menard, 1989; Matsueda & Heimer, 1987; Simcha-Fagan & Schwartz, 1986). Reiss and Rhodes (1961) showed that the social status of a boy's residential community as well as that of his family influenced his risk of delinquency. Sampson and Wilson (1995) describe effects of concentrated poverty in terms of impact on family structure and resources through unemployment and mobility, effects that are equally strong among whites and blacks.

The degree to which families are able to select their residences is partially restricted by social policies (Bartelt, 1993; Jackson, 1985; McCord, 1997a; Sugrue, 1993). In the past, at least, appraisal practices leading to federal guarantees for mortgages encouraged segregation. "Gentlemen's agreements" added to the effects of "red-lining" of neighborhoods resulted in isolation of blacks in poor sections of cities. Local authorization policies encouraged the very poor to remain in congested areas by permitting public housing only as replacement for existing slum dwellings. Tax moneys that support transportation have been devoted to highway construction, leaving the poor to depend on impoverished mass transport. Whether housing is imposed or selected, the location of housing clearly influences the options children have (Wilson, 1991).

One common theory used to account for the distribution of criminal behavior is that lack of socially acceptable opportunities leads to frustration and a search for alternative, often illegal, means to success. Evidence available through official records of criminal justice systems shows an inverse relationship between social class and crime rates, thus supporting the theory. Self-report studies of behavior serious enough to result in arrest, and studies of multiple offenders, also generally show that crimes are more frequent among members of lower classes and among those who have failed in or dropped out of school.

Opportunities influence behavior in ways other than as pathways to success. The prevalence of youth gangs seems to account, for example, for disproportionate rates of gang violence in some communities (Curry & Spergel, 1988; Horowitz, 1987). Neighborhood standards and common behaviors convey information about forms of behavior that are accepted (Eron & Slaby, 1994; Goody, 1991; Sampson, 1992). Of course, standards are partly formed by those who live within the neighborhood, so that such standards are neither intractable nor universal. Too little is known about the development of neighborhood norms, their influence, and how these change.

CHILD-REARING PRACTICES

Throughout Western history, observers have reasoned that child-rearing practices influence development. Plato, Aristotle, Locke, and Rousseau wrote recommendations for training children to be good citizens. Yet, until recently, scant evidence supported the belief that socialization affects behavior.

Some supporting evidence has depended on information from adolescents who simultaneously reported their parents' behavior and their own delinquencies (e.g., Cernkovich & Giordano, 1987; Hagan, Gillis, & Simpson, 1985; Jensen, & Brownfield, 1983; van Voorhis, Cullen, Mathers, & Garner, 1988). Because these studies are based on data reporting delinquency and socialization variables at the same time, they are unable to disentangle causes from effects.

Longitudinal data have been used to address the sequencing issue. In several such studies, adolescents have been the sole source of information (e.g., Fletcher, Darling, & Steinberg, 1995; Liska & Reed, 1985; Thornberry, Lizotte, Krohn, Farnworth, & Jang, 1991; Wells & Rankin, 1988). Their results have been used to examine such theories about the causes of delinquency as control theory, differential association theory, and interaction theory. Results that rely on a single source for information about both child rearing and behavior, however, should be suspect. In addition to problems of collinearity and of measurement quality, when adolescents provide all the information, problems of validity arise. There are empirical grounds for doubting that adolescents correctly perceive, accurately recall, and honestly report the behavior of their parents (Henry, Moffitt, Caspi, Langley, & Silva, 1994).

Experimental studies show that experience can affect behavior even when those affected seem to be unaware of the experience (Kellogg, 1980), so powerful features of their socialization may not have been noticed by the adolescents. Routine events tend to be less easily recalled than those related to extraordinary events (Christianson & Safer, 1996). Furthermore, reports of family interaction tend to reflect what is seen as socially desirable (McCord & McCord, 1962; Robins, 1966; Weller & Luchterhand, 1983; Yarrow et al., 1970).

In addition, reports about child rearing are likely to be influenced by the very features under study as possible consequences of faulty child rearing. For example, abused children tend to perceive their parents as less punitive than revealed by objective evidence (Dean, Malik, Richards, & Stringer, 1986); aggressive children tend to perceive behavior justifying aggression (Dodge & Somberg, 1987); and painful current state tends to exaggerate recall of painful events (Eich, Rachman, & Lopatka, 1990). If adolescents seek to understand their own behavior, their memories of earlier experiences may be distorted to serve the end of consistency (Winograd, 1994).

Studies of the impact of child rearing suffer from special problems, too, when parents report on their own behavior. Parents are likely to have limited and biased perspectives and to misrepresent what they recall. One study that included home observations as well as mothers' reports showed that the child's compliance was related to observed, though not to reported, behavior of the mother (Forehand, Wells, & Sturgis, 1978). Another study indicated that fathers and mothers typically gave different reports of the same situations, and that even when they described events similarly, their descriptions correlated differently with their perceptions of other events (Eron, Banta, Walder, & Laulicht, 1961).

A handful of studies have overcome some of these problems of measurement by using multiple informants and observations to measure family interactions (Larzelere & Patterson, 1990; Laub & Sampson, 1988; McCord, 1991b; Sampson & Laub, 1993). These have shown that "family process and delinquency are related not just independent of traditional sociological controls, but of biosocial controls as well" (Laub & Sampson, 1988, p. 374).

Parents (or caregivers) forge criminals through child-rearing practices in three ways: (1) by conveying values through their own actions and by what they approve; (2) by developing or failing to develop ties with family members and the community; and (3) by establishing legitimacy through the methods they use to enforce their desires on their offspring.

Conveying Values

Children learn what to value in the family environment as their parents and siblings interact with them (McCord, 1997b). Studies of very young children have shown that kindness or concern for others is as natural as selfishness or aggression (Bergin, Bergin, & French, 1995; Caplan, 1993; Harris, 1994; Hay, 1994; Zahn-Waxler, Radke-Yarrow, 1982; Zahn-Waxler & Radke-Yarrow, Wagner, & Pyle, 1988). Between the ages of 1 and 2 years, children begin to show stable patterns of nurturance (Cummings, Hollenbeck, Iannotti, Radke-Yarrow, & Zahn-Waxler, 1986; Rheingold & Emery, 1986).

Children are taught to value helpfulness by exposure to nurturing, helpful adults who provide altruistic reasons for their actions (Miller & Eisenberg, 1988; Yarrow, Scott, & Waxler, 1973). Children are taught to value aggression by exposure to and encouragement for fighting and other self-interested acts (Bandura & Walters, 1959; McCord, 1991c).

A variety of studies suggest that children learn both aggression and altruism through imitation (Bandura, Ross, & Ross, 1961; Berkowitz, Parke, Leyens, West, & Sebastian, 1978; Bryan & London, 1970; Eisenberg, 1986; Eron & Huesmann, 1984, 1986; Farrington, 1978; Friedrich & Stein, 1973; Goldstein & Arms, 1971; McCord & McCord, 1958; Rosenhan & White, 1967; Rushton, 1979; Staub, 1979; White, 1972; Widom, 1989; Wilkens, Scharff, & Schlottman, 1974; Zahn-Waxler, Radke-Yarrow, & King, 1979). Parents who have criminal records also tend to be aggressive (McCord, 1991a). Such parents are likely to transmit values to suggest that aggression is an appropriate response to frustration.

Ties with Family Members and the Community

Social bonds between parents and their children are central to healthful child development. Indeed, one dominant theory of criminal behavior, control theory (Hirschi, 1969), is based on the fact that delinquents tend to lack close ties with their parents (Liska & Reed, 1985; McCord, 1986, 1996). In confirmation of this perspective, parental neglect appears to be among the most criminogenic conditions for child rearing (Loeber & Stouthamer-Loeber, 1986).

Social bonds between parents and their children seem to provide motives for accepting rules and obligations related to living peacefully in social surroundings. When the bonds are weak, children turn to peers for companionship and guidance (Kandel, Kessler, & Margulies, 1978; Steinberg, 1987). Peer companionship, especially during adolescence, has a tendency to produce delinquency (Dishion, McCord, & Poulin, 1999).

Establishing Legitimacy

Parents of delinquents tend to use harsh and often irrelevant discipline in the attempt to impose their wishes or demands (Farrington, 1991; Laub & Sampson, 1995; Patterson, 1982). By way of contrast, parents of well-socialized children have used little (if any) punishment. Such families seem to treat a child as a reasoning, though inexperienced, individual whose desires and beliefs ought to be taken into consideration.

The power of legitimizing mutual respect can be seen in an experimental study of preschoolers (Parpal & Maccoby, 1985). The experimenters randomly selected mothers for training to respond to their children's requests and to avoid directing them during a specified period of time each day for 1 week. After a week of "practice," their children complied with more of the mother's requests in the laboratory than did the comparison group whose mothers used praise and criticism to try to manipulate their children.

Outside the laboratory, similar results have been found. In one such study, 25 infants were observed at home throughout their first year, at 3-week intervals for 4 hours. Frequency of verbal commands, frequency of physical intervention, and extent of floor freedom permitted the child were unrelated to the infant's compliance. The authors concluded "that a disposition toward obedience emerges in a responsive, accommodating social environment without extensive training, discipline, or other massive attempts to shape the infant's course of development" (Stayton, Hogan, & Ainsworth, 1971, p. 1065).

Another study based on home observations of 16 infants initially either 15 or 20 months old over a period of 9 months showed that mothers who explained consequences to their child had children who were more altruistic, especially if the explanations included the importance of not hurting others. Neutral explanations, withdrawal of love, and physical punishments, however, were ineffective techniques for teaching children cooperative, helpful behavior (Zahn-Waxler et al., 1979).

On the other hand, parents who use physical punishments to enforce their demands appear to increase the probability that their offspring will view the use of force as legitimate (McCord, 1996, 1997c).

SUMMARY

Genetic transmission of characteristics that contribute to risk for misbehavior, social environments that encourage toughness and antisocial actions, and child-rearing practices that legitimize the use of force have been used to explain how families contribute to crime. Unfortunately, little is known about conditions in the environment that can ameliorate poor child rearing or which types of child rearing are most effective for different types of children. Yet integrated knowledge, crossing biological, sociological, and psychological components of development, would greatly increase the probability for understanding criminal behavior and perhaps for crime prevention.

REFERENCES

Anderson, E. (1997). Violence and the inner-city street code. In J. McCord (Ed.), *Violence and childhood in the inner-city* (pp. 1–30). New York: Cambridge Press.

Bandura, A., & Walters, R. H. (1959). *Adolescent aggression*. New York: Ronald.

Bandura, A., Ross, D., & Ross, S. A. (1961). Transmission of aggression through imitation of aggressive models. *Journal of Abnormal and Social Psychology*, *63*, 575–582.

Bartelt, D. W. (1993). Housing the "underclass." In M. B. Katz (Ed.), *The "underclass" debate* (pp. 118–160). Princeton, NJ: Princeton University Press.

Bergin, C. A. C., Bergin, D. A., & French, E. (1995). Preschoolers' prosocial repertoires: Parents' perspectives. *Early Childhood Research Quarterly*, *10*(1), 81–103.

Berkowitz, L., Parke, R. D., Leyens, J. P., West, S., & Sebastian, J. (1978). Experiments on the reactions of juvenile delinquents to filmed violence. In L. A. Hersov & M. Berger (Eds.), *Aggression and anti-social behaviour in childhood and adolescence* (pp. 59–71). Oxford, England: Pergamon Press.

Bohman, M., Cloninger, C. R., Sigvardsson, S., & von Knorring, A. (1982). Predisposition to petty criminality in Swedish adoptees. *Archives of General Psychiatry*, *39*, 1233–1241.

Braungart, J. M., Plomin, R., Defries, J. C., & Fulker, (1992). Genetic influence on tester-rated infant temperament as assessed by Bayley's infant behavior record-nonadoptive and adoptive siblings and twins. *Developmental Psychology*, *28*, 40–47.

Brown, E. J., Flanagan, T. J., & McLeod, M. (Eds.). (1984). *Sourcebook of criminal justice statistics 1983*. Washington, DC: US Government Printing Office, US Department of Justice, Bureau of Justice Statistics.

Bryan, J. H., & London, P. (1970). Altruistic behavior by children. *Psychological Bulletin*, *73*, 200–211.

Bureau of Justice Statistics. (1992). *Criminal victimization in the United States, 1990*. Washington, DC: US Department of Justice.

Bursik, R. J. (1988). Social disorganization and theories of crime and delinquency: Problems and prospects. *Criminology*, *26*, 519–551.

Butterfield, F. (1995). *All God's children*. New York: Alfred A. Knopf.

Cadoret, R., Troughton, E., & O'Gorman, T. W. (1987). Genetic and environmental factors in alcohol abuse and antisocial personality. *Journal of Studies on Alcohol*, *48*(1), 1–8.

Cairns, R. B., & Cairns, B. D. (1994). *Lifelines and risks: Pathways of youth in our time*. New York: Cambridge University Press.

Caplan, M. (1993). Inhibitory influences in development: The case of prosocial behavior. In D. F. Hay & A. Angold (Eds.), *Precursors and causes in development and psychopathology* (pp. 169–198). Chichester, England: Wiley.

Capron, C., & Duyme, M. (1991). Children's IQs and SES of biological and adoptive parents in a balanced cross-fostering study. *European Bulletin of Cognitive Psychology*, *11*(3), 323–348.

Carey, G. (1994). Genetics and violence. In A. J. Reiss, K. A. Miczek, & J. A. Roth (Eds.), *Understanding and preventing violence* (Vol. 2, pp. 21–58). Washington, DC: National Academy Press.

Cernkovich, S. A., & Giordano, P. C. (1987). Family relationships and delinquency. *Criminology*, *25*(2), 295–319.

Christianson, S.-A., & Safer, M. A. (1996). Emotional events and emotions in autobiographical memories. In D. C. Rubin (Ed.), *Remembering our past: Studies in autobiographical memory* (pp. 218–243). New York: Cambridge University Press.

Crowe, R. R. (1975). An adoptive study of psychopathy: Preliminary results from arrest records and psychiatric hospital records. In R. R. Fieve, D. Rosenthal, & H. Brill (Eds.), *Genetic research in psychiatry* (pp. 95–103). Baltimore: Johns Hopkins University Press.

Cummings, E. M., Hollenbeck, B., Iannotti, R., Radke-Yarrow, M., & Zahn-Waxler, C. (1986). Early organization of altruism and aggression: Developmental patterns and individual differences. In C. Zahn-Waxler, E. M. Cummings, & R. Iannotti (Eds.), *Altruism and aggression: Biological and social origins* (pp. 165–188). Cambridge, England: Cambridge University Press.

Curry, G. D., & Spergel, I. A. (1988). Gang homicide, delinquency, and community. *Criminology*, *26*, 381–405.

Dean, A. L., Malik, M. M., Richards, W., & Stringer, S. A. (1986). Effects of parental maltreatment on children's conceptions of interpersonal relationships. *Developmental Psychology*, *22*, 617–626.

Dishion, T. J., McCord, J., & Poulin, F. (1999). When interventions harm: Peer groups and problem behavior. *American Psychologist*, *54*, 1–10.

Dodge, K .Q., & Somberg, D. R. (1987). Hostile attributional biases among aggressive boys are exacerbated under conditions of threats to the self. *Child Development*, *58*, 213–224.

Eich, E., Rachman, S., & Lopatka, C. (1990). Affect, pain, and autobiographical memory. *Journal of Abnormal Psychology*, *99*, 174–178.

Eisenberg, N. (1986). *Altruistic emotion, cognition, and behavior*. Hillsdale, NJ: Lawrence Erlbaum.

Elliott, D. S., Huizinga, D., & Ageton, S. S. (1985). *Explaining delinquency and drug use*. Beverly Hills, CA: Sage.

Elliott, D. S., Huizinga, D., & Menard, S. (1989). *Multiple problem youth: Delinquency, substance use and mental health problems*. New York: Springer Verlag.

Ensminger, M. E., Kellam, S. G., & Rubin, B. R. (1983). School and family origins of delinquency: Comparisons by sex. In K. T. Van Dusen & S. A. Mednick (Eds.), *Prospective studies of crime and delinquency* (pp. 73–97). Boston: Kluwer-Nijhoff.

Eron, L. D., & Huesmann, L. R. (1984). The relation of prosocial behavior to the development of aggression and psychopathology. *Aggressive Behavior, 10*(3), 201–211.

Eron, L. D., & Huesmann, L. R. (1986). The role of television in the development of prosocial and antisocial behavior. In D. Olweus, J. Block, & M. R. Yarrow (Eds.), *Development of antisocial and prosocial behavior* (pp. 285–314). New York: Academic Press.

Eron, L. D., & Slaby, R. G. (1994). Introduction. In L. D. Eron, J. H. Gentry, & P. Schlegel (Eds.), *Reason to hope: A psychosocial perspective on violence and youth* (pp. 1–22). Washington, DC: American Psychological Association.

Eron, L. D., Banta, T. J., Walder, L. O., & Laulicht, J. H. (1961). Comparison of data obtained from mothers and fathers on child-rearing practices and their relation to child aggression. *Child Development, 32*, 455–472.

Eron, L. D., Huesmann, L. R., Dubow, E., Romanoff, R., & Yarmel, P. (1987). Aggression and its correlates over 22 years. In D. H. Crowell, I. M. Evans, & C. R. O'Donnell (Eds.), *Childhood aggression and violence: Sources of influence, prevention, and control* (pp. 249–262). New York: Plenum Press.

Falconer, D. S. (1960). *Introduction to quantitative genetics*. New York: Ronald Press.

Farrington, D. P. (1978). The family backgrounds of aggressive youths. In L. A. Hersov & M. Berger (Eds.), *Aggression and antisocial behaviour in childhood and adolescence* (pp. 73–93). Oxford: Pergamon.

Farrington, D. P. (1986). Stepping stones to adult criminal careers. In D. Olweus, J. Block, & M. Radke-Yarrow (Eds.), *Development of antisocial and prosocial behavior* (pp. 359–384). New York: Academic Press.

Farrington, D. P. (1987). Implications of biological findings for criminological research. In S. A. Mednick, T. E. Moffitt, & S. A. Stack (Eds.), *The causes of crime: New biological approaches* (pp. 42–64). Cambridge, England: Cambridge University Press.

Farrington, D. P. (1988). Social, psychological and biological influences on juvenile delinquency and adult crime. In W. Buikhuisen & S. A. Mednick (Eds.), *Explaining criminal behaviour: Interdisciplinary approaches* (pp. 68–89). New York: E.J. Brill.

Farrington, D. P. (1991). Childhood aggression and adult violence: Early precursors and later life outcomes. In D. J. Pepler & K. H. Rubin (Eds.), *The development and treatment of childhood aggression* (pp. 5–29). Hillsdale, NJ: Lawrence Erlbaum.

Farrington, D. P., Gundry, G., & West, D. J. (1975). The familial transmission of criminality. *Medical Science Law, 15*(3), 177–186.

Flanagan, T. J., & Maguire, K. (Eds.) (1992). *Sourcebook of criminal justice statistics 1991*. Washington, DC: US Government Printing Office, US Department of Justice, Bureau of Justice Statistics.

Fletcher, A. C., Darling, N., & Steinberg, L. (1995). Parental monitoring and peer influences on adolescent substance use. In J. McCord (Ed.), *Coercion and punishment in long-term perspectives* (pp. 259–271). New York: Cambridge University Press.

Forehand, R., Wells, K. C., & Sturgis, E. T. (1978). Predictors of child noncompliant behavior in the home. *Journal of Consulting and Clinical Psychology, 46*, 179.

Frick, P. J., Lahey, B. B., Christ, M. A. G., Loeber, R., & Green, S. (1991). History of childhood behavior problems in biological relatives of boys with attention-deficit disorder and conduct disorder. *Journal of Clinical Child Psychology, 20*, 445–451.

Friedrich, L. K., & Stein, A. H. (1973). Aggressive and prosocial television programs and the natural behavior of preschool children. *Monographs of the Society for Research in Child Development, 38*(4) (Serial No. 151), 1–64.

Glueck, S., & Glueck, E. T. (1950). *Unraveling juvenile delinquency*. New York: Commonwealth Fund.

Goldsmith, H. H., & Gottesman, I. I. (1981). Origins of variation in behavioral style: A longitudinal study of temperament in young twins. *Child Development, 52*, 91–103.

Goldstein, J. H., & Arms, R. L. (1971). Effects of observing athletic contests on hostility. *Sociometry, 34*(1), 83–90.

Goodman, R., & Stevenson, J. (1989). A twin study of hyperactivity. 2. The aetiological role of genes, family relationships and perinatal adversity. *Journal of Child Psychology and Psychiatry and Allied Disciplines, 30*, 691–710.

Goody, E. (1991). The learning of prosocial behaviour in small-scale egalitarian societies: An anthropological view. In R. A. Hinde & J. Groebel (Eds.), *Cooperation and prosocial behaviour* (pp. 106–127). New York: Cambridge University Press.

Hagan, J., Gillis, A. R., & Simpson, J. (1985). The class structure of gender and delinquency: Toward a power-control theory of common delinquent behavior. *American Journal of Sociology, 90*, 1151–1178.

Hare, R. D. (1978). Electrodermal and cardiovascular correlates of psychopathy. In R. D. Hare & D. Schalling (Eds.), *Psychopathic behavior* (pp. 107–143). Chichester: John Wiley & Sons.

Harris, P. L. (1994). The child's understanding of emotion: Developmental change and the family environment. *Journal of Child Psychology and Psychiatry and Allied Disciplines, 35*, 3–28.

Hay, D. F. (1994). Prosocial development. *Journal of Child Psychology and Psychiatry and Allied Disciplines, 35*, 29–71.

Henry, B., Moffitt, T. E., Caspi, A., Langley, J., & Silva, P. A. (1994). On the "remembrance of things past": A longitudinal evaluation of the retrospective method. *Psychological Assessment, 6*, 92–101.

Herrnstein, R. J., & Murray, C. (1994). *The bell curve: Intelligence and class structure in American life*. New York: The Free Press.

Hirschi, T. (1969). *Causes of delinquency*. Berkeley: University of California Press.

Horowitz, R. (1987). Community tolerance of gang violence. *Social Problems, 34*, 437–450.

Huesmann, L. R., & Eron, L. D. (1984). Cognitive processes and the persistence of aggressive behavior. *Aggressive Behavior, 10*, 243–251.

Jackson, K. T. (1985). *Crabgrass frontier: The suburbanization of the United States*. New York: Oxford University Press.

Jensen, G. F., & Brownfield, D. (1983). Parents and drugs. *Criminology, 21*(4), 543–555.

Kandel, D. B., Kessler, R. C., & Margulies, R. Z. (1978). Antecedents of adolescent initiation into stages of drug use: A developmental analysis. In D. B. Kandel (Ed.), *Longitudinal research on drug use* (pp. 73–99). New York: Wiley.

Kellogg, R. T. (1980). Is conscious attention necessary for long-term storage. *Journal of Experimental Psychology, 6*, 379–390.

Kraemer, G. W., Ebert, M. H., Schmidt, D. E., & McKinney, W. T. (1991). Strangers in a strange land: A psychobiological study of infant monkeys before and after separation from real or inanimate mothers. *Child Development, 62*, 548–566.

Larzelere, R. E., & Patterson, G. R. (1990). Parental management: Mediator of the effect of socioeconomic status on early delinquency. *Criminology, 28*, 301–323.

Laub, J. H., & Sampson, R. J. (1988). Unraveling families and delinquency: A reanalysis of the Gluecks' data. *Criminology, 26*, 355–380.

Laub, J. H., & Sampson R. J. (1995). The long-term effect of punitive discipline. In J. McCord (Ed.), *Coercion and punishment in long-term perspectives* (pp. 247–258). New York: Cambridge University Press.

Liska, A. E., & Reed, M. D. (1985, August). Ties to conventional institutions and delinquency: Estimating reciprocal effects. *American Sociological Review, 50*, 547–560.

Loeber, R., & Stouthamer-Loeber, M. (1986). Family factors as correlates and predictors of juvenile conduct problems and delinquency. In M. Tonry & N. Morris (Eds.), *Crime and justice* (Vol. 7, pp. 29–149). Chicago: University of Chicago Press.

Maguire, K., & Flanagan, T.J. (Eds.). (1991). *Sourcebook of criminal justice statistics 1990*. Washington, DC: US Government Printing Office, US Department of Justice, Bureau of Justice Statistics.

Matsueda, R. L., & Heimer, K. (1987, December). Race, family structure, and delinquency: A test of differential association and social control theories. *American Sociological Review, 52*, 826–840.

McCord, J. (1977). A comparative study of two generations of native Americans. In R. F. Meier (Ed.), *Theory in criminology: Contemporary views* (pp. 83–92). Beverly Hills, CA: Sage.

McCord, J. (1986). Instigation and insulation: How families affect antisocial aggression. In J. Block, D. Olweus, & M. R. Yarrow (Eds.), *Development of antisocial and prosocial behavior* (pp. 343–357). New York: Academic Press.

McCord, J. (1991a). The cycle of crime and socialization practices. *Journal of Criminal Law and Criminology, 82*(1), 211–228.

McCord, J. (1991b). Family relationships, juvenile delinquency, and adult criminality. *Criminology, 29*, 397–417.

McCord, J. (1991c). Questioning the value of punishment. *Social Problems, 38*(2), 167–179.

McCord, J. (1994). Family socialization and antisocial behavior: Searching for causal relationships in longitudinal research. In I. G. M. Weitekamp & H.-J. Kerner (Eds.), *Cross-national longitudinal research on human development and criminal behavior* (pp. 217–227). Dordrecht, Netherlands: Kluwer.

McCord, J. (1996). Family as crucible for violence. *Journal of Family Psychology, 10*, 147–152.

McCord, J. (1997a). Placing American urban violence in context. In J. McCord (Ed.), *Violence and childhood in the inner-city* (pp. 78–115). New York: Cambridge Press.

McCord, J. (1997b). He did it because he wanted to … In W. Osgood (Ed.), *Nebraska symposium on motivation* (pp. 1–43). Lincoln, NE.

McCord, J. (1997c). On discipline. *Psychological Inquiry, 6*, 215–217.

McCord, J., & McCord, W. (1958). The effects of parental role model on criminality. *Journal of Social Issues, 14*, 66–75.

McCord, J., & McCord, W. (1962). Cultural stereotypes and the validity of interviews for research in child development. *Child Development, 32*, 171–185.

Mednick, S. A. (1977). A bio-social theory of the learning of law-abiding behavior. In S. A. Mednick & K. O. Christiansen (Eds.), *Biosocial bases of criminal behavior* (pp. 1–8). New York: Gardner.

Mednick, S. A., Gabrielli, W. F., & Hutchings, B. (1987). Genetic factors in the etiology of criminal behavior. In S. A. Mednick, T. E. Moffitt, & S. A. Stack (Eds.), *The causes of crime: New biological approaches* (pp. 74–91). Cambridge, England: Cambridge University Press.

Miller, P. A., & Eisenberg, N. (1988). The relation of empathy to aggressive and externalizing/antisocial behavior. *Psychological Bulletin, 103*, 324–344.

Moffitt, T. E. (1994). Natural histories of delinquency. In E. G. M. Weitekamp & H.-J. Kerner (Eds.), *Cross-national longitudinal research on human development and criminal behavior* (pp. 3–61). Dordrecht, Netherlands: Kluwer.

Moffitt, T. E., & Silva, P. A. (1988). Self-reported delinquency, neuropsychological deficit, and history of attention deficit disorder. *Journal of Abnormal Child Psychology, 16*, 553–569.

Nisbett, R. E. (1993). Violence and U.S. regional culture. *American Psychologist, 48*, 441–449.

Osborn, S. G., & West, D. J. (1979). Conviction records of fathers and sons compared. *British Journal of Criminology, 19*(2), 120–133.

Parpal, M., & Maccoby, E. E. (1985). Maternal responsiveness and subsequent child compliance. *Child Development, 56*, 1326–1344.

Patterson, G. R. (1982). *A social learning approach*, Vol. 3: *Coercive family process*. Eugene, OR: Castalia Publishers.

Patterson, G. R., Debaryshe, B. D., & Ramsey, E. (1989). A developmental perspective on antisocial behavior. *American Psychologist, 44*, 329–335.

Pedersen, N. L., Plomin, R., McClearn, G. E., & Friberg, L. (1988). Neuroticism, extraversion, and related traits in adult twins reared apart and reared together. *Journal of Personality and Social Psychology, 55*, 950–957.

Reiss, A. J., Jr., & Rhodes, A. L. (1961). Delinquency and class structure. *American Sociological Review, 26*, 720–732.

Reiss, A. J., Jr., & Roth, J. A. (Eds.). (1993). *Understanding and preventing violence*. Washington, DC: National Academy Press.

Rheingold, H., & Emery, G. N. (1986). The nurturant acts of very young children. In D. Olweus, J. Block, & M. Radke-Yarrow (Eds.), *Development of antisocial and prosocial behavior* (pp. 75–96). New York: Academic Press.

Robins, L. N. (1966). *Deviant children grown up*. Baltimore: Williams & Wilkins.

Rosenhan, D., & White, G. M. (1967). Observation and rehearsal as determinants of prosocial behavior. *Journal of Personality and Social Psychology, 5*, 424–431.

Rowe, D. C. (1986). Genetic and environmental components of antisocial behavior: A study of 265 twin pairs. *Criminology, 24*, 513–532.

Rowe, D. C., & Farrington, D. P. (1997). The familial transmission of criminal convictions. *Criminology, 35*, 177–201.

Rushton, J. P. (1979). Effects of prosocial television and film material on the behavior of viewers. In L. Berkowitz (Ed.), *Advances in experimental social psychology* (Vol. 12, pp. 321–351). New York: Academic Press.

Rutter, M. (1978). Family, area and school influences in the genesis of conduct disorders. In L. A. Hersov & M. Berger (Eds.), *Aggression and anti-social behaviour in childhood and adolescence* (pp. 95–113). Oxford: Pergamon Press.

Sampson, R. J. (1985). Structural sources of variation in race- and age-specific rates of offending across major U.S. cities. *Criminology, 23*, 647–673.

Sampson, R. J. (1987). Urban black violence: The effect of male joblessness and family disruption. *American Journal of Sociology, 93*, 348–382.

Sampson, R. J. (1992) Family management and child development: Insights from social disorganization theory. In J. McCord (Ed.), *Facts, frameworks, and forecasts: Advances in criminological theory* (Vol. 3, pp. 63–93). New Brunswick: Transaction Press.

Sampson, R. J. & Laub, J. H. (1993). *Crime in the making: Pathways and turning points through life*. Cambridge, MA: Harvard University Press.

Sampson, R. J., & Wilson, W. J. (1995). Toward a theory of race, crime, and urban inequality. In J. Hagan & R. D. Peterson (Eds.), *Crime and inequality* (pp. 37–54). Stanford, CA: Stanford University Press.

Satterfield, J. H. (1987). Childhood diagnostic and neurophysiological predictors of teenage arrest rates: An eight-year prospective study. In S. A. Mednick, T. E. Moffitt, & S. A. Stack (Eds.), *The causes of crime: New biological approaches* (pp. 146–167). Cambridge, England: Cambridge University Press.

Schulsinger, F. (1977). Psychopathy: Heredity and environment. In S. A. Mednick & K. O. Christiansen (Eds.), *Biosocial bases of criminal behavior* (pp. 109–141). New York: Gardner.

Sherman, L. W., Gartin, P. R., & Buerger, M. E. (1989). Hot spots of predatory crime: Routine activities and the criminology of place. *Criminology*, *27*(29), 27–55.

Siddle, D. A. T. (1977). Electrodermal activity and psychopathy. In S. A. Mednick & K. O. Christiansen (Eds.), *Biosocial bases of criminal behavior* (pp. 199–211). New York: Gardner.

Simcha-Fagan, O., & Schwartz, J. E. (1986). Neighborhood and delinquency: An assessment of contextual effects. *Criminology*, *24*, 667–699.

Staub, E. (1979). *Positive social behavior and morality: Socialization and development* (Vol. 2). New York: Academic Press.

Stayton, D. J., Hogan, R., & Ainsworth, M. D. (1971). Infant obedience and maternal behavior: The origins of socialization reconsidered. *Child Development*, *42*, 1057–1069.

Steinberg, L. (1987). Single parents, stepparents, and the susceptibility of adolescents to antisocial peer pressure. *Child Development*, *58*, 269–275.

Sugrue, T. J. (1993). The structures of urban poverty: The reorganization of space and work in three periods of American history. In M. B. Katz (Ed.), *The "underclass" debate* (pp. 85–117). Princeton, NJ: Princeton University Press.

Tambs, K., Sundet, J. M., Eaves, L., Solaas, M. H., & Berg, K. (1991). Pedigree analysis of Eysenck Personality Questionnaire (EPQ) scores in monozygotic (MZ) twin families. *Behavior Genetics*, *21*, 369–383.

Thornberry, T. P., Lizotte, A. J., Krohn, M. D., Farnworth, M., & Jang, S. J. (1991). Testing interaction theory: An examination of reciprocal causal relationships among family, school, and delinquency. *Journal of Criminal Law and Criminology*, *82*, 3–35.

US Department of Justice. (1991). *Crime in the United States 1990*. Washington, DC: US Government Printing Office.

Van Voorhis, P., Cullen, F. T., Mathers, R. A., & Garner, C. C. (1988). The impact of family structure and quality on delinquency: A comparative assessment of structural and functional factors. *Criminology*, *26*, 235–261.

Wadsworth, M. E. J. (1976). Delinquency, pulse rates and early emotional deprivation. *The British Journal of Criminology*, *16*, 245–256.

Webster, M., & Driskell, J. E. (1983). Beauty as status. *American Journal of Sociology*, *89*, 140–165.

Weller, L., & Luchterhand, E. (1983). Family relationships of "problem" and "promising" youth. *Adolescence*, *18*(69), 43–100.

Wells, L. E., & Rankin, J. H. (1988). Direct parental controls and delinquency. *Criminology*, *26*, 263–285.

White, G. M. (1972). Immediate and deferred effects of model observation and guided and unguided rehearsal on donating and stealing. *Journal of Personality and Social Psychology*, *21*, 139–148.

Widom, C. S. (1989). Child abuse, neglect, and violent criminal behavior. *Criminology*, *27*(2), 251–271.

Wilkens, J. L., Scharff, W. H., & Schlottman, R. S. (1974). Personality type, reports of violence and aggressive behavior. *Journal of Personality and Social Psychology*, *30*, 243–247.

Wilson, W. J. (1991, February). Studying inner-city social dislocations: The challenge of public agenda research—1990 presidential address. *American Sociological Review*, *56*, 1–14.

Winograd, E. (1994). The authenticity and utility of memories. In R. Fivush (Ed.), *The remembering self: Construction and accuracy in the self-narrative* (pp. 243–252). New York: Cambridge University Press.

Wolfgang, M. E., Figlio, R. M., & Sellin, T. (1972). *Delinquency in a birth cohort*. Chicago: University of Chicago Press.

Yarrow, M. R., Campbell, J. D., & Burton, R. V. (1970). Recollections of childhood: A study of the retrospective method. *Monographs of the Society for Research in Child Development*, *35*(1), 1–83.

Yarrow, M. R., Scott, P. M., & Waxler, C. Z. (1973). Learning concern for others. *Developmental Psychology*, *8*(2), 240–260.

Zahn-Waxler, C., & Radke-Yarrow, M. (1982). The development of altruism: Alternative research strategies. In N. Eisenberg (Ed.), *The development of prosocial behavior* (pp. 109–137). New York: Academic Press.

Zahn-Waxler, C., Radke-Yarrow, M., & King, R. A. (1979). Child-rearing and children's pro-social initiations toward victims of distress. *Child Development*, *50*, 319–330.

Zahn-Waxler, C., Radke-Yarrow, M., Wagner, E., & Pyle, C. (1988, April). The early development of prosocial behavior. Presented at the ICIS meetings, Washington, DC.

12

Youth Collectivities and Adolescent Violence

JAMES F. SHORT, JR.

INTRODUCTION

Several problems confront anyone who has the audacity to tackle the topic of this chapter. The most daunting of these is the lack of a theoretically viable typology that situates gangs, or types of gangs, in a larger set of youth collectivities. If the variety of terms used by police to describe "gang groups and members" is "bewildering" and "dismaying" (Klein, 1995, pp. 102–103), definitions used by researchers and other scholars who study the phenomena loosely termed "gangs" are only slightly less so. Yet the scholarly literature on gangs continues to proliferate.

In part because of confusion regarding the definition of gangs, many who study youth collectivities do not use the term, referring instead to "co-offending" among young people (Reiss, 1986; Reiss & Farrington, 1991), "bands of teenagers congregating on street corners" (Skogan, 1990), "unsupervised peer groups" (Sampson & Groves, 1989), "networks" of juveniles who violate the law (Sarnecki, 1986), or simply "delinquent groups" (Warr, 1996). Shaw and McKay and their colleagues (McKay, 1969; Shaw & McKay, 1931, 1942; Shaw, 1930; Shaw, Zorbaugh, McKay, & Cottrell, 1929; Shaw & Moore, 1931), whose early work inspired much of the subsequent research and theory concerning gangs, did not have much to say about gangs, as such. Instead, they emphasized patterns of friendship, association of younger with older offenders, and the coexistence in "delinquency areas" of organized crime and other forms of adult criminality. Even Frederic Thrasher's (1927) brilliant and classic study presents a bewildering variety of descriptions of groups among his 1,313 gangs. For that matter, one doubts that Thrasher, or anyone else, ever really counted all those gangs.

Gangs themselves are not very good at specifying either definitions or numbers of

---

JAMES F. SHORT, JR. • Department of Sociology, Washington State University, Pullman, Washington 99164-4014.

Handbook of Youth and Justice, edited by White. Kluwer Academic / Plenum Publishers, New York, 2001.

members. A gang member's response to Malcolm Klein's (1995) inquiry as to what a gang is was typical: "We a defensive club, man" (p. 5). The black gangs we studied in Chicago in the late 1950s and early 1960s most often described themselves as clubs as well, despite the fact that they often took pride in their notoriety as gangs in Chicago media. Yet neither Klein's gangs nor ours bore much resemblance to the social and athletic clubs that were—and are—an important part of social life in many "old ethnic white" communities (Suttles, 1968; but see Sanchez-Jankowski, 1991).

Similar group processes, collective behaviors, and comparison processes characterize many youth collectivities. In the absence of a viable typology, these similarities confuse both empirical and theoretical understanding, as Sherif and Sherif (1964) noted more than 30 years ago.

If I seem preoccupied with such a first principle, consider the following. Based largely on data collected from police departments, Klein, Curry, and their associates, have documented the rapid spread of street gangs to many cities throughout the United States. Violence accompanies this phenomenon in virtually all reporting areas. Are these gangs all alike—an unlikely coincidence, surely? How, in fact, are they similar, and in what respects are they different? What criteria should be employed for purposes of classification? How do gangs relate to drug crews, "wilding" groups, milling crowds, networks involved in delinquency, "tagger crews," punks, soccer hooligans, skinheads, bikers, and so forth, seemingly ad infinitum? Diversity of gangs—their behavior, organization, inter- and intragang relationships, and relationships with others in their communities—is itself bewildering and dismaying for those who would generalize about them.

Moreover, gangs change. As long-time gang researcher, Joan Moore, observes, "What anybody 'knows' about a gang in any given year—even a gang member's knowledge—may ... be out of date the very next year" (quoted in Klein, 1995, p. 101). Importantly, surveys and ethnographic studies suggest, for example, that the age range of many gangs, especially among gangs in the inner city, has changed. Patterns of gang ethnicity have changed. Klein observes that white gangs are increasingly rare, except in smaller cities. Gangs are now mainly Hispanic or African American, but in several cities gangs composed of immigrants or the children of immigrants from several Asian countries have been observed (see Sanders, 1994; Chin, 1996a,b). To the extent that gang membership becomes a "master status" for law enforcement and others, as Miethe and McCorkle (1997) suggest, the suspicion grows that for some it also becomes a code word justifying prejudicial attitudes and discriminatory behavior toward minorities.

Studies document an increase in violence among some gangs and perhaps greater instrumental use of violence (as opposed to the largely expressive, gang status-related violence of traditional street gangs). In a few places, an increase in the involvement of females in gangs has occurred. We know that patterns of drug use and selling and of participation in other income-producing activities also vary greatly, but the extent of such variations remains unknown.

Despite a resurgence of gang research, many questions concerning youth collectivities and their behavior remain largely unanswered.[1] While it is clear that violence among adolescents is not always attributable to gangs, however they are defined, both macrolevel research and field observations in a variety of settings suggest that similar forces often are associated with the emergence and maintenance of gangs and of other violence-producing groups and crowds, and that they share certain group and collective behavior processes. These forces and processes help to account for both diversity and change, and for continuity in the forms taken by such collectivities.

DEFINING GANGS AS UNSUPERVISED YOUTH GROUPS

For purposes of this chapter, I use elements that are common to virtually all serious studies of gangs: gangs are groups whose members meet together with some regularity, over time, on the basis of group-defined criteria of membership and group-defined organizational characteristics; that is, gangs are non-adult-sponsored, self-determining groups that demonstrate continuity over time.

From the earliest studies of gang, conflict between youth groups has been observed as an important feature of gangs, often as a defining characteristic. Thrasher (1927), the first social scientist to study gangs more or less systematically, defined the gang as "an interstitial group originally formed spontaneously, and then integrated through conflict" (p. 57). Several more recent studies confirm the importance, if not the universality, of conflict for gang formation and identity, as well as the importance of conflict in the life histories of gang members (see, especially, Hagedorn, 1998; Sullivan, 1989; Sanchez Jankowski, 1991; Klein, 1995).

In these terms crowds of young people are not gangs, though gang members may be crowd participants and crowds may coalesce into gangs, should gangs be provoked in the course of ongoing interaction within crowds or from external provocation. Brymer (1967) observed such a transformation among a milling crowd of "200–300 teenagers" gathered at a neighborhood drive-in restaurant in a southwestern US city. Passing the drive-in, the adolescents in his car identified various neighborhood cliques. A short time later, however:

> ... something in the situation had changed so as to provoke an identification of the crowd ... as "El Circle" gang ... all of the persons in the crowd were facing the street in a tense, quiet atmosphere; this contrasted with an earlier loud, boisterous situation with all persons talking in their respective clique groups, with some "clique-hopping." Upon investigation, it was learned that a rival "gang" passed by in a car and shouted certain epithets about the mothers of the "Circle" boys, as well as challenges. Objectively, it was probably a clique that had passed by, but it had been identified by the persons in the crowd as a "gang." (Brymer, 1967, in Short, 1974, pp. 416–417)

While the criteria employed in my definition of gangs lack precision, they are intended to distinguish gangs from other groups that come together only briefly or on few occasions (see below, and Reiss, 1986; Sanders, 1994), as well as from larger collectivities of young people, such as milling crowds in which gang members may participate, but in which being a member of a gang is not salient to the behavior of interest. In this view, street gangs are to be distinguished also from certain other groups to be noted.

Note that this definition does not specify that gang members define themselves as a gang. Empirically, some do and some do not (see Short, 1968). Street groups that by this definition are gangs often define themselves by other terms, as previously note, for example, as clubs (see Suttles, 1968; Keiser, 1969).

Defining gangs in this way avoids the logical circularity of including in the definition the behavior that is to be explained.[2] There is a great deal of variation to be explained, within and between gangs and other collectivities. A variety of subspecies, as it were, have been distinguished (see, e.g., Miller, 1980; Fagan, 1989; Sanchez-Jankowski, 1991; Klein, 1995; Spergel, 1995). Most of these have not proven to be useful, empirically or theoretically. Gangs vary a great deal in organization, appearance, leadership structure, behavior, and viability and in characteristics that often are attributed to them or used to define them (such as affectations of clothing, names, and behaviors such as fighting, drug use, and property crime). A viable typology of youth collectivities, including gangs, would be extremely useful for understanding and controlling violence and other criminal behavior among such collectivities (see, especially, Klein, 1995; Moore, 1993).

Klein emphasizes the versatile behavior repertoire of "street gangs," but he includes "commitment to a criminal orientation" among his defining criteria. Klein attempts to finesse the logical problem by focusing attention on "the tipping point beyond which we say 'aha—that sure sounds like a street gang to me' " (Klein, 1995, p. 30). From this perspective, "play groups" are not gangs. Yet, as Klein acknowledges, quite ordinary play groups often become delinquent and so acquire the gang appellation (see Thrasher, 1927; Hagedorn, 1998). The gangs that my colleagues and I studied in Chicago (Short & Strodtbeck, 1965) evidenced little commitment to a criminal orientation, though they were heavily involved in a broad array of delinquent behaviors. To the extent that contemporary street gangs share a criminal orientation, that is a significant change from earlier periods (see, e.g., Fagan, 1996; Venkatesh, 1996).

In what follows, except as otherwise noted, "gangs" and "street gangs" are used interchangeably but without the definitional requirement of commitment to a criminal orientation. Most play groups of unsupervised youths are not so committed, though many engage in occasional delinquent episodes, individually and collectively, such as vandalism, fighting among themselves and with others, thefts of a minor nature, sexual predation, substance abuse, and drug selling. Gangs that become committed to a criminal orientation of course pose far more serious problems for the individuals, families, and communities that become their victims, as well as for gang members themselves. Note that the emphasis on "tipping points" and the definition of gangs employed here focus both on processes and circumstances that may result in criminal or otherwise seriously objectionable behavior by youth groups, and for some gangs a criminal orientation. What can we say about these processes and circumstances?

When John Moland and I followed up two of the African-American gangs that we had studied a decade earlier in Chicago, we found a revealing portrait of one gang that had passed the tipping point from play group to delinquent gang. Among the 16 gangs we studied most intensively, the "Nobles" (we first called them the "Chiefs") ranked in the top one third in their involvement in "conflict" behaviors. They were the most involved of all our gangs in sexual activities, and they were second highest in drug use and drug selling. They also were a very "social" gang, ranking third in sports involvement and other social activities (Short & Strodtbeck, 1965, p. 95). Excerpts from an extensive interview with a former member of the gang suggest how the transition from sports and other nondelinquent, "hanging" behavior occurred (adapted from Short & Moland, 1976, pp. 166–167):

> … the Nobles was originally a baseball team. I came into contact with them when I was in the seventh grade. I played softball pretty good. After the game we would hang out and have a little fun, you know. After awhile the group began to grow and gather in an area called Ellis Park. A lot of girls used to be around and we would go to parties. The Nobles used to hang around in little bunches and hit on people for money and if you got into it with one of them you would have to deal with a group of them. The thing about the Nobles was that a lot of people were not actually members, insofar as being in the club is concerned, but you wouldn't be able to distinguish between those who were members and those who were not. They were beginning to hang together. For example, if they would go into the (public housing) project for a party or something and they would get into a humbug, well then they would send somebody around to the hanging place for the whole area, the poolroom where they all hung out at. And there was a long open court way where a lot of people hung out over there for there was a lot of drugs over there and a lot of "slick" things happened over there. There were a lot of people over there who were not actual members of the club but they were under the group banner thing. So the group began to expand on that level.

> Actually when you would be dealing with Nobles as a club you would not be dealing with that mass. But when you got down to some action as an outsider you wouldn't be able to distinguish as to who (was a member and who was not).

Although they were heavily involved in delinquency, individually and as a group, the Nobles never developed a criminal orientation as a group. We classified them as a "conflict gang" because of their occasional involvement with other gangs in such fighting. However, the Nobles never got caught up in the (sometimes protracted) "gang wars" of so many Chicago gangs of the period. They remained essentially a play group, despite frequent run-ins with the law, a lot of fighting (group and individual), drug use (mainly alcohol and marijuana) and selling (mainly marijuana, though one core member was addicted to heroin and had been convicted of selling heroin), and a very high rate of illegitimate parenthood. A decade later, of the 19 core members of the original gang for whom we were able to obtain such information 13 were employed, 3 were dead, and 3 were unemployed and heavily involved with drugs. The Nobles grew less cohesive over the 2 years following our initial study, despite a brief and futile attempt by some members of the gang to reorganize formally. They virtually lost any group identity shortly thereafter (Short & Strodtbeck, 1965, p. 34).

In our terms of reference the Nobles was a street gang that was heavily involved in delinquent behavior, including a good deal of violence. Their turf was located in an area (Douglas, Chicago Community Area No. 35) long characterized by high rates of crime and delinquency, but in which population composition and community institutions were relatively stable, compared to other black communities in the city (McKay, 1969). Douglas in fact had experienced the largest decrease in rates of official delinquency of all Chicago communities over the period, 1958–1961, coinciding approximately with the period of our most intensive field studies. Together with their lack of a criminal orientation and the lack of cohesion of the gang, and despite the existence of heavy drug traffic in the area, we were convinced that community stability helped to explain the relatively successful adult adjustment of members of the Nobles street gang.

In contrast with the Nobles, the Vice Lords ("Vice Kings" in Short & Strodtbeck) were never a play group. Created out of alliances and conquests in the cauldron of gang conflict on Chicago's west side (see Keiser, 1969; Dawley, 1973), the Vice Lords became one of Chicago's "supergangs" during the late 1960s, primarily as a result of factors associated with street gang rivalries. Keiser (1969) lists these as: (1) the release from the Illinois State Training School for Boys of several Vice Lord leaders; (2) newspaper publicity portraying another gang (the Blackstone Rangers) as "the toughest, best organized gang" in Chicago, a serious challenge to the Vice Lords; (3) "hostile incidents" with other gangs; and (4) the perceived failure of nationalist groups to deliver on promises, compromising the appeal of black nationalism to the gang. Keiser's observations were confirmed by our chief Vice Lord informant, the gang's most powerful leader, with the additional note that the members of other gangs who were confined in the State Training School determined while confined to form the "toughest, best organized gang" in the city upon their release.

Like the Nobles, the Vice Lords had a versatile repertoire of behaviors—delinquent and nondelinquent—but they were a "conflict gang" above all. Among our gangs, they ranked first in conflict and third in sexual activities but only ninth in drug-related behaviors and involvement in sports and other social activities.

Importantly, the Vice Lords' turf was located in Lawndale, the Chicago community that experienced the largest increase in rates of official delinquency between 1958–1961 (see McKay, 1969). At this time, Lawndale was in the midst of rapid population turnover, from predominantly white residents to overwhelmingly black residents, with much attendant disruption of community institutions. In contrast to the Nobles, members of the Vice Lords continued to be heavily involved in the drug traffic and in drug use, as well as in other criminal activities.

Whatever the dynamics of supergang formation during the 1960s, large aggregations of gang "nations" have dominated public and to some extent law enforcement preoccupation with gangs in more recent years. Attention has focused particularly on gang nations in Chicago and Los Angeles and their alleged expansionist tendencies in pursuit of new drug markets. There is good evidence that gangs have proliferated in the United States and that they are found increasingly in cities where previously they did not exist, "from a few to many hundreds of American cities" (Klein, 1995, p. 31). Klein conducted personal phone interviews with a large number of police gang experts. Among cities with populations of 100,000 or more, 94% "reported a genuine gang presence" in their cities. For a random sample of 60 cities between 10,000 and 100,000 population this figure was 38%, confirming the general impression that gang problems are located primarily in large cities.[3] Klein notes, however, that his data suggest that as many as 800 to 900 of the approximately 2250 smaller cities also report having experienced gang problems.

Data collected by Klein and his colleagues suggest that the "gang problem" in the United States has escalated rapidly. About half of the cities report the emergence of gangs only since 1985. Gangs in "new gang" cities sometimes imitate gangs in other cities, especially Chicago and Los Angeles, often adopting similar names and other symbols. More direct influence also occurs when gang members from cities with well-established gangs move to other cities. The best research, however, suggests that most gangs are "homegrown," rather than initiated by outsiders (in addition to Klein, 1995, see Hagedorn, 1998).[4]

How, then, do these homegrown gangs develop? Some (we do not know how many or what proportion) form for entirely nondelinquent purposes. Evidence comes from several sources. Moore (1993) reports that the Chicano gangs she and her colleagues studied in Los Angeles "generally started out ... as adolescent friendship groups" (p. 35). Several of the Milwaukee gangs studied by Hagedorn (1998) began as "break-dancing" groups that were solidified by conflict with rival dancing groups. Others were "corner groups of friends" who became gangs after conflict with other corner groups. Still others had "direct roots in Chicago" after "former Chicago gang members moved to Milwaukee, where their children formed gangs named after their old Chicago gang" (Hagedorn, 1998, p. 59). Some gangs are simply "hanging groups" that become progressively involved in delinquent behavior [e.g., the Chiefs and Nobles that we studied in Chicago, or MacLeod's (1987) "hallway hangers"; see, also, Sullivan (1989)], while some engage in virtually no delinquent behavior (MacLeod's "Brothers").[5]

As many observers have noted, most male adolescent groups, including those that are adult-sponsored and supervised, engage in a good deal of rough-and-tumble play, much of which is intended as display for peers and others. Among unsupervised groups status often becomes associated with fighting prowess, particularly among lower- and working-class males. Miller and colleagues found that seven out of ten aggressive acts committed by members of the "Junior Outlaws" were directed within the gang. The vast majority of observed aggressive acts (94%) were verbal rather than physical, most of them reflecting gang-serving qualities and behaviors, for example, group solidarity and cohesion, facilitating and coordinating collective action, securing and maintaining relations of mutual equality among group members, reciprocity in intragroup relations, and personal qualities that served "as criteria of group acceptance" and "prestige conferral" (Miller, Geertz, & Cutter, 1961).

Graffiti has been shown to be important both in establishing gang identity and as a symbolic form of gang conflict (Klein, 1995). Some individual "taggers" and "tagger groups" have become conflict-oriented gangs as a result of conflict over graffiti. Hutchison (1993) has documented the many functions played by gang graffiti in the barrios of Los Angeles, San Diego, San Francisco, and Chicago, from merely identifying a particular gang or to demarcate its territory, to expanding the status and the reputation of the gang or its alliances with other gangs, and insulting or taunting opposing rival gangs by defacing their graffiti. While gang graffiti advertises gangs to the larger community, some, Hutchison observes, is so esoteric as to be accessible only to participants in the local gang subculture (see also Conquergood, 1993).

To summarize, street gangs (unsupervised youth groups) appear to become violent as a result of one or more of the following processes: (1) escalation of the natural rough-and-tumble punching and wrestling that occurs among most male groups and the association of status with fighting prowess that is related to such behavior; (2) competition with rival gangs, often leading to conflict over status-enhancing behaviors, such as graffiti, dancing, or athletic contests, or economic behaviors, such as control of drug markets; (3) definitions of others and behavior toward the gang that push a violent identity on the gang; and (4) group processes that create or reinforce group cohesion based on violent or otherwise delinquent behavior, which often involve individual and group status considerations (see Jansyn, 1966; Klein & Crawford, 1967; Short & Strodtbeck, 1965; Hagedorn, 1998).

Though precise distinctions are difficult to make, for heuristic purposes street gangs as here defined can be distinguished from several other forms of youth groups. Klein (1995) notes, for example, that neither "skinheads" nor "bikers" are street gangs. Skinheads are "inside, they're working on their written materials, or if outside they're looking for a target not just lounging" (p. 22). Bikers are "focused on their machines, or cruising, or dealing drugs in an organized manner.... Street gangs seem aimless; skinheads and bikers are focused, planful. Street gangs get into any and every kind of trouble" (p. 22).[6] Similarly, the large collectivities of British and other European football (soccer) "thugs" that journalist Bill Bufford (1991) and others have written about clearly are not street gangs. Nor, for the most part, are they groups, but rather floating crowds or mobs that coalesce at times into highly violent groupings with little structure (see, also, Van Limbergen, Colaers, & Walgrave, 1989). These collectivities are less likely than gangs to be composed entirely of adolescents, though as we shall see the age range of some gangs has expanded to include young adults as well as adolescents. The violence—real and potential—of each of these types of groups is undeniable but beyond the focus of this chapter.

THE COMMUNITY CONTEXT OF AGE AND GENDER RELATIONSHIPS

Several researchers have noted diversity in age grading and gender relationships among the gangs they have studied. Both Short and Strodtbeck and Schwartz observed differences in the age range of boys versus girls in large "party" gatherings: Short and Strodtbeck (1965) in an inner city African-American Chicago neighborhood and Schwartz (1987) in "Cambridge," a white suburban working-class community. Girls tended to be younger and boys to have a significantly larger age range, from mid to late teens and young adult. In the early 1960s, our detached worker was quite explicit in his explanation of this difference in a "quarter party" he attended with members of his gang:

> The age group in this party amazed me—must have been from about 11 to the 30s. There were girls there as young as 11, but no boys younger than about 15. The girls are there as a

> sex attraction, and with the older boys and men around, you know the younger boys aren't going to do any good. (Short & Strodtbeck, 1965, p. 110)

Schwartz's field observer described "400 or 500 kids," representing a broad spectrum of youth in Cambridge, partying in a forest preserve as:

> mainly 15-, 16-, 17-year-old girls, a few younger kids, and guys about 17, 18, 19, with a few older guys. Everybody is drinking beer, and every now and then a little fight breaks out. Kids are always coming up to you asking for some kind of dope—if you want to buy or sell it. (1987, p. 145)

Aggressive behavior was common to both parties. The Cambridge incident appears to be a case of crowd behavior. A confrontation with "guys from Newton" on the previous evening had left several people seriously injured, and on the succeeding evening, serious violence was narrowly averted when the police intervened. In the Chicago case, "quarter parties" had become institutionalized in the local community, attracting young people, including gang members, and older residents. Serious fighting between members of the gangs in attendance at this particular party was stopped only with the intervention of the detached worker.

Schwartz, whose major focus was on "authority relationships" between young people and adults, described youth culture in Cambridge as "fragmented." He attributed this and the rebelliousness of young people in Cambridge to "the tenuousness of the bridge between the generations." The "expressive significance" of the behavior on this occasion, his observer noted, "lies in being together with one's friends in a way that does not enable adults to place restrictions on one's freedom." (p. 146)[7] In contrast, social life in the Chicago community involved young and old alike in quasi-public and informal settings such as quarter parties, pool halls, and taverns in which licit and illicit activities often mixed and were the subject of everyday conversation (see also Valentine, 1978; Drake & Cayton, 1962; Hannerz, 1969; Liebow, 1967).

Communities and Social Capital

The community context of adult–adolescent relationships clearly is critical to the understanding of violent behavior perpetrated by all types of youth collectivities. Moreover, relationships between adults and adolescents are increasingly important, empirically because of the increased age range of gang membership, theoretically because of their importance for social as well as human capital, and other socialization- and labor market-related considerations. Note that in this context family relationships beyond the immediate family assume particular importance.

Sullivan's (1989) research illustrates the relationship between human and social capital and violence. As they grew older, the young men in Hamilton Park (his white group) were able to secure better-quality jobs than were the minority (Latino and black) youth he studied. Hamilton Park youth had "found jobs more plentiful at all ages," and they were better able to hold on to jobs because "they had become more familiar with the discipline of the workplace" (a type of human capital) (pp. 201–202). Acquisition of familiarity with, and acquiescence to, the discipline of the workplace was made possible by a type of social capital, however, namely, the superior personal networks that these boys shared with adults in Hamilton Park: "Personal networks, not human capital in the form of either education or work experience, accounted for most of the disparities between the neighborhood groups" (Sullivan, 1989, p. 103).

Personal networks separated local neighborhood groups in their ease of access to the same sets of jobs. During the mid-teens these personal networks were solely responsible for allocating jobs to some groups and not to others. With increasing age youths did begin to move outside the local neighborhood and to come into more open competition for jobs. Personal networks still maintained a great deal of importance in finding adult jobs, however, and those with effective personal job networks were likely to carry the added advantage of the more extensive work experience that those same networks had already given them. Thus, a type of social capital (interpersonal networks with the adult community) facilitated the acquisition of a type of human capital (work experience) for the young men from Hamilton Park, compared to their less favored minority counterparts in Projectville and La Barriada.[8]

Anderson (1990, 1999) and others have noted the impact on young people in underclass communities when "old heads"—respectable and respected middle- and working-class adults who make it a point to advise and look after young people—leave or are replaced by younger, flashier, and successful drug dealers.

But families, too, are important, and often neglected by gang researchers, so focused are we on what goes on the street. Anderson as well as Furstenberg (1993) shed new light on the nature of immediate family relationships in lower and underclass communities. Anderson notes the terrible cross-pressures faced by conventional parents in underclass communities in which the "code of the streets" competes with parents, whose disciplinary goals and practices also are compromised by that code (Anderson, 1990, 1999). Conventional families, when they exist, act as a buffer against teen pregnancy and single parenting, so important to the poverty–ethnicity–violence cycle. To quote Anderson (1999):

> Two parents, and extended networks of other relatives, can form a durable team, a viable supportive unit engaged to fight the various problems confronting so many inner-city teenagers.... Equipped with a survivor's mentality, it has weathered a good many storms, which have given it wisdom and strength. The parents are known in the community as "strict" with their children; they impose curfews and tight supervision, demanding to know their children's whereabouts at all times. Determined that their children not become casualties of the inner-city environment, these parents scrutinize their children's friends and associates carefully, rejecting those who seem to be "no good" and encouraging others who seem to be on their way to "amount to something." (p. 153)

We know all too little about precisely how different parenting practices influence violent and other disapproved types of behavior and how such behaviors influence parenting and parent-child interaction. The experience of child service agencies in underclass communities such as Robert Taylor Homes (Chicago) dramatically emphasizes the problems faced by even the most caring parents in communities in which "gang wars" have become "drug wars," with escalating violence (see Center for Successful Child Development, 1993; Venkatesh, 1996) Several studies suggest, however, that the most violent gang members, and the more delinquent in other ways, are those for whom deficits in both human and social capital are greatest (see, e.g., MacLeod, 1987; Sullivan, 1989; Decker, 1996). Some gang researchers, perhaps romanticizing gangs, seem to suggest that street gangs become a substitute source for intergenerational social capital formation (Padilla, 1993; Conquergood, 1992). While the social capital thus gained may be functional for survival on the street and in the street gang world, it is likely to be highly dysfunctional in conventional society.

ETHNICITY, ETHNIC CONFLICT, AND YOUTH VIOLENCE

Age grading is not uniform among gangs, nor is expansion of the age range that has been observed in some gangs. The latter importantly is much greater among those inner city minority gangs where it has been studied. In an appendix to Sanchez-Jankowski's *Islands in the Streets* (1990), the age ranges of his 37 gangs are noted by ethnicity of the gang members. Ages of his Latino gangs ranged from 12 to 42 years, averaging 12.5 years. These figures for his black gangs were 14 to 37 years, with a mean of 12.3 years, and for white gangs, 14 to 26 years, mean of 7.6 years.[9] The age ranges for four gangs classified as black/Latino and five as Latino/black was even greater, averaging 22.25 and 13.2 years, respectively. These data are consistent with other researchers' findings concerning the "stretching" of gang members' ages (see, e.g., Hagedorn, 1998). Researchers note that the tendency for minority gang members to stay with the gang rather than dropping out as they age and assume adult responsibilities primarily results from the economic disadvantage of minority populations, as it is played out among street gangs.

The significance of the greater age range of gang members for violence is not entirely clear, though it is likely that this too varies related *inter alia* to local community conditions. Among these conditions, poverty, race, and ethnicity always seem to be important, if not always consistent.

Ethnic, or at least racial, homogeneity appears to characterize most gangs. The reasons may have as much to do with ecological segregation as with ethnic identity and conflict, but conflict is too common to be dismissed. Classification of the race and ethnicity of gang members is a major and largely ignored problem. Sanchez-Jankowski (1991) notes that his "black gangs" included African-American and Jamaicans, and his "Latino gangs" included Chicanos (Mexican-Americans and Mexicans), Puerto Ricans, Dominicans, Salvadorans, and Nicaraguans. White gangs in this study consisted of "Irish and other whites"; but he notes that Italian gangs "remained steadfast in their decision not to participate" (1991, pp. 10, 11). So too did Asian and Samoan gangs in Los Angeles. Cooperation with researchers, of course, might reflect significant differences in both gangs and communities.

The significance of race and ethnicity for street gang violence is by no means clear, as demonstrated by widely varying patterns in different places and over time. Carolyn Block and Richard Block, using Chicago police data, report that the percentage of homicides in that city accounted for by youth gangs tripled between 1965 and 1981, and that the rate was much higher for Latino gangs than for either black or white gangs, though the black rate was higher than the white. Between 1982 and 1989, the gang-related homicide offending rate for young (ages 15–19) Latino males was 120 per 100,000 population. Comparative rates for young black and white males were, respectively, 50 and 14 per 100,000 population (Block, 1993; Block, Block, & Block, 1993; see also Curry & Spergel, 1988). More recently, Block and Christakos (1993) report that, for 1991–1993, gang-related homicide victimization for young men aged 15–24 was higher for black males (66 per 100,000) than for Latino males (47 per 100,000).

Los Angeles studies of official records indicate that the homicide offending rate for young black males increased more rapidly than and surpassed the rate for young Hispanic males between 1979–1981 and 1989–1991. Comparable rates for 15- to 19-year-old black males were 60 per 100,00 in 1979–1981, and 192 per 100,000 in 1989–1991, an increase of more than 300%, compared to rates of 70 per 100,000 Hispanic males in 1979–1981, and 94 per 100,000 in 1989–1991, an increase of 34%. (Hutson, Anglin, Kyriacou, Haart, & Spears, 1995).[10]

Varying and changing patterns of youth gang violence such as these are poorly understood. The Blocks emphasize the need for detailed, continuously updated information, and we might add more rigorous attention to even the most basic of classification criteria.

"Wilding" and Hate Crimes

Some of the most puzzling, if quantitatively not the most significant, youth collectivities associated with violence are so-called "wilding" groups and hate-motivated crowds. Most of the significant questions remain unanswered. The term was initially applied to an incident in New York City's Central Park. A white female jogger was brutally attacked and raped by a group of young black males. The boys were not identified nor did they identify themselves as a gang. Clearly the attack was a collective act, or set of acts, perpetrated by a small group of young men. In contrast, a Texas "wilding" group studied by Cummings' (1993) clearly seems to have been a gang, though a very unusual one. We know little of the full range of their activities except that they involved exceptionally brutal attacks on usually elderly whites by a group of young black males. Their brutality, Cummings notes, was accompanied by great excitement, escalating as group members competed among themselves. Cummings' interpretation of these incidents emphasizes both racial antagonisms and the social marginality and unstable personalities of the gang members. Though similar in the latter respect to an earlier study of gang violence in New York city (Yablonsky, 1962), pathological personality characteristics generally have not been found to characterize most gang members (see below).

Communal collective violence involving crowds of mostly young people has been a common feature of communities in this and many other countries. Recent examples in the United States have been documented by Pinderhughes (1993). While gang members may participate in such crowd behavior, gang membership is not the most salient feature. As we found in our Chicago study, and as others have reported, white gang members sometimes behave violently, or threaten to do so, as gangs with the support of community adults, whose values and interests they share (see Short & Strodtbeck, 1965; Suttles, 1968; Susser, 1982; Schwartz, 1987; Sanchez-Jankowski, 1991; Block, 1993).

EXPLAINING GANG VIOLENCE

With few exceptions, violent behavior among even the most violent gangs is relatively rare. Moreover, when violent episodes occur within or between gangs, or when gangs attack others or destroy property, some gang members typically do not participate. Studies, past and present and in many places, demonstrate great variability in levels of violence within as well as between gangs (see, e.g., Thrasher, 1927; Short & Strodtbeck, 1965; Moore, 1978; Klein, 1995).

What causes such variation? There are of course variations in the extent to which gang communities are characterized by poverty, physical deterioration, and institutional breakdown. Some of these differences vary by the race and ethnicity of community residents, though such variation is not as well documented as we might wish.[11] The macrolevel of explanation, however, sets the stage for consideration of both individual and microsocial levels of explanation of violent behavior.

Socialization into Violence

Socialization into violence begins early in the lives of young people in communities where gangs are most commonly found. The American Psychological Association Commission on Youth and Violence, for example, found that 45% of the first and second graders studied in Washington, DC, reported they had witnessed muggings, 31% had witnessed shootings, and 39% had seen dead bodies (Hechinger, 1992). Increasingly, such violence involves adolescents attacking other adolescents. Elliott's (1994) self-report study found that by the age of 17 more than a third of black males and a quarter of non-Hispanic white males had committed at least one serious violent offense. School-based surveys of students find a high incidence of physical fighting, especially among African-American and Hispanic males.

For many young people in the ghettos and barrios of the inner city, socialization into violence occurs primarily on the street, "away from home, school, and other traditional institutions" (Vigil, 1993, p. 99). This is where personal identity is established. As Vigil notes, "one of the first goals in the streets is to determine where one fits in the hierarchy of dominance and aggression that the street requires for survival" (Vigil, 1993, pp. 99–100).

By all accounts gang life is especially violent compared to life for those who do not belong to gangs, even in gang-ridden communities. Decker (1996), confirming what others have found elsewhere, reports that participation in violence, "especially expressive violence, is a central feature of gang life," in St. Louis. Sanchez-Jankowski (1991) concludes that "violence is the currency of life and becomes the currency of the economy of the gang" (p. 139). The fact that intragang fighting is more common than is either intergang fighting or other violent behavior directed outside the gang emphasizes the ubiquity of violence in the experience of gang members (see also Miller et al., 1961; Hagedorn, 1998).

Sullivan (1989), too, found that fighting with age peers, some with serious consequences, occurred at an early age among the cliques of white, Hispanic, and black youth he studied in Brooklyn. The experience gained in this way often was later "applied to the systematic pursuit of income" (p. 109). While most fighting among boys in their early and middle teens is about status (Decker, 1996; MacLeod, 1987; Horowitz, 1983; Short & Strodtbeck, 1965), for some the scarcity of resources, the symbolic significance of some property, and the lack of access to legitimate means of acquiring these symbols also translate into violence at an early age (Anderson, 1990).

The Individual Level of Explanation

Bandura (1986) notes that we humans possess certain distinctive human capabilities that enable us to be active agents in our own behavior. Among these are the capacity to use symbols, fundamental to the capability of forethought, as well as "self-regulatory" and "self-reflective" capabilities.

Self-regulation is especially difficult for gang members, however. Because they are unsupervised, constraints that operate in conventional institutional settings are absent, giving freer rein to individual obstreperousness and group processes. Members of the Chicago gangs we studied did not lack self-reflection, but pressures from within the gang often, even typically, prevented its expression. Individual gang members who approached detached workers or our field observers for advice concerning a variety of "growing up" problems, terminated such inquiries abruptly if other gang members came on the scene or sought to enter the conversation. Data systematically collected from gang members indicated their largely conventional values—data confirmed for most gang members by more recent data reported by Hagedorn (cf. Gordon, Short, Cartwright, & Strodtbeck, 1963; Hagedorn, 1998).

Yet, members of street gangs appear to be characterized by low self-concept, social disabilities or deficits, limited skills and interests, and poor impulse control.[12] Other individual characteristics relate to macrosocial deficits, as indicated by weak contacts with adults, defiance of parents, and perceptions of barriers to jobs and other opportunities. Early conduct disorder, early delinquency onset, and admitted violence involvement also predict gang membership (Klein, 1995).

Gang violence, in addition to being more prevalent and serious than violent behavior committed by nongang members, is different in other ways. Gang homicides are not as closely related to intimate personal relationships as are nongang homicides, for example, and membership in gangs often is implicated in both homicide perpetration and victimization (Maxson, Klein, & Cunningham, 1996). Fighting within and between gangs typically involves group processes that, while they may not be unique to gangs, are more likely to occur in gang settings because of the absence of constraining influences.

Violence is related to the "character matrix" of the gang members studied by Sanchez-Jankowski (1991), who emphasizes their "intense sense of competitiveness," "mistrust or wariness" of others, "self reliance," their sense of social isolation and survivalist worldview, and the "defiant air" they adopt in public appearance (pp. 23–26). Vigil (1988) attributes the necessity for fear management among Chicano gang members to similar emotions. The "wildness or quasi-controlled insanity" ("locura") that facilitates Chicano gang violence is a "mind-set" that aids "fear management" (pp. 231 ff).

The Role of Pathology in Gangs

Disagreements continue to exist among gang researchers and theorists concerning the interpretation of personal characteristics such as these. While most investigators report that some gang members suffer from individual pathology in various forms, few attribute major significance to the role of such pathology in gang behavior. Klein's observations in Los Angeles, and his conclusions are similar to ours in Chicago: "For most gang members ... therapy is far less important than provision of education skills, job skills, and a chance to break out of the reliance on their peer group for ego satisfaction.... Most members are surprisingly close to normalcy, given their pathogenic settings in the ghettoized areas of our cities" (Klein, 1995, p. 93).

Not surprisingly, disagreement concerning the "rationality," self-reflectiveness, and other individual characteristics of gang members, and the role of emotions in gang behavior, also exist. Rationality and rational choice—among individuals, groups, and organizations—is much debated, researched, and theorized about (see Cook & Levi, 1990). What may appear to be a gang member's irrational, impulsive, unmotivated behavior, or behavior made without much reflection, may be quite rational given available alternatives and the context within which choices are made. We know little about such matters with respect to gang behavior. Fear clearly is rational for those who live in homes and neighborhoods characterized by violence and among members of violent gangs. Not to be fearful in many circumstances would be irrational. Nevertheless, a quality of mental toughness that was not apparent in earlier gang studies comes through in much of the more recent research.

It is difficult to conceive of an environment that is as intensely competitive as Sanchez-Jankowski (1991) suggests, however, or of gang members who are as uniformly impulsive and sociopathic as once described by Yablonsky (1962). Alternatives to the pathologies that drive Sanchez-Jankowski and Yablonsky's gang members are offered in several studies, however. Sullivan (1989) notes that for his Brooklyn gangs criminal activities were not only economically rational, but rewarding in other ways:

> They call success in crime "getting paid" and "getting over," terms that convey a sense of triumph and irony which is not accounted for in the grim depiction of their acts as the economic strategies of the disadvantaged.... "Getting over" ... refers to success at any endeavor in which it seems that one is not expected to succeed. It is equivalent to "beating the system".... What they "get over on" is the system, a series of odds rigged against people like themselves. Both phrases are spoken in a tone of *defiant pride*. They are phrases in the shared language of youths who are out of school, out of work, and seriously involved in crime. (p. 245; emphasis added)

"Crime as work" also was a major theme of Padilla's (1993) research, and his gangs also participate in a very violent world.

Klein (1995) concludes that young people who join gangs "are not so much different from other young people as they are caricatures" of them (p. 76). Gang members rarely have been tested systematically or systematically compared with nongang members on standardized protocols. When we did so in our Chicago study, gang boys were found to be more self-critical and self-questioning than other boys and to be characterized by uncertainty and poor regard for self. They also tended to be less decisive, slower in making judgments, and more suggestible than other boys. They had poor immediate memory and were less effective in performance tests.[13] Evaluations of members of their own gangs were less positive than were evaluations made by both lower-class and middle-class nongang members of their friends. While no consistent gang member personality emerges from these relatively few studies, observational and laboratory research converge on a rather unflattering portrait of the average individual gang member. The matter is extraordinarily complex, however (see Short & Strodtbeck, 1965, chapter 7; also, Sullivan, 1989, chapter 10). We found that boys who exhibited "crazy" behavior were not accorded leadership status, and Sullivan reports that boys who were exceptionally active in high-risk criminal activities were regarded as "crazy" and irrational, even by those who took part in some of the same types of crimes.

The Microsocial Level of Explanation: Group Processes

Gangs have lives of their own quite apart from macroeconomic and demographic changes and the effectiveness of formal and informal social control institutions and mechanisms. The series of studies by the Blocks and their colleagues, noted above, documents a variety of patterns of gang violence, their dynamic character, and some of their underlying causes.

Virtually all gang researchers find that gangs engage in a broad spectrum of both criminal and noncriminal behavior (Cohen & Short, 1958; Cloward & Ohlin, 1960; Klein, 1995; Spergel, 1995). The Blocks regard as especially important the distinction between instrumental and expressive purposes of gang behavior. Violence that has as its object the acquisition of money or property is termed instrumental, while violence perpetrated, for example, in retaliation for another gang's attack or in support of group norms is classified as expressive. Most turf-related violence, for example, is primarily expressive, while robbery and other types of violence associated with drug marketing are most often instrumental in character.

Most of Chicago's street gang violence in recent years, the Blocks report, has been turf related, with the highest rates of assaults and homicides occurring over disputed and limited gang territories. Expressive violence by gangs, by the criteria in their study, tended to characterize poor but "relatively prospering neighborhoods with expanding populations" while instrumental violence was found most often "in disrupted and declining neighborhoods" (Block et al., 1993, p. 8). Confirming research conducted in other large cities, the connection between drug offenses and street gang homicides was found to be weak in Chicago (see, e.g., for Los Angeles, Klein, 1995; Meehan & O'Carroll, 1992; Hutson et al., 1995). Also confirming other research, street gang homicides were associated with the increasing lethality of weapons, especially high-caliber, automatic, or semiautomatic weapons.

An important finding from the Blocks' series of studies concerns the sporadic occurrence of street gang violence, again emphasizing its dynamic character. In Chicago, a cyclical pattern of "spurts" in gang-related homicide rates appears to characterize both Latino and black gangs. Block and Christakos observe that peaks in such cycles "are not citywide but occur in specific neighborhoods and involve specific street gangs. Each peak tends to correspond to a series of escalating confrontations, usually over control of territory (either traditional street gang turf or an entrepreneurial drug market) (Block & Christakos, 1993, p. 14).

Youth cultures associated with gatherings of young people in parks, malls, and drive-ins where violent episodes often occur also vary and change in response to a variety of factors. Differences between them and intra- and intergang fighting appear to lie principally in the fact that gang violence typically serves group purposes (see, e.g., Sanchez-Jankowski, 1991; Klein, 1971; Short & Strodtbeck, 1965; Miller et al., 1961). Violent behavior by individual gang members also is heavily influenced by group values and the perceived requirements of group membership or status within the group, as well as by the individual's sense of honor, self-respect, and self-esteem, which for many gang members also are closely tied to group norms (see, in addition to the above, Horowitz & Schwartz, 1974; Horowitz, 1983; Klein, 1995; Spergel, 1995).

The interpersonal and group dynamics of such behavior are not well understood. However, a small research literature suggests that such behavior should not be viewed as irrational. Almost certainly it is not predictable based solely on knowledge of personal characteristics of individuals. Group processes associated with particular gang roles, with status within or between gangs, are implicated in much individual and collective violent behavior by gang members (see Klein, 1995; Sanchez-Jankowski, 1991; Short, 1990; Farrington, Berkowitz, & West, 1981; Short & Strodtbeck, 1965).

Gang Fighting and Status

Microsocial analyses informed the nature of group processes, as well as how subcultural norms influenced behavior among the gangs we studied in Chicago. A detached worker's report of the behavior of members of his gang following a skirmish with a rival gang is illustrative:

> In the car, Commando and the other boys were extremely elated. There were expressions like: "Baby, did you see the way I swung on that kid"; "Man, did we tell them off"; "I really let that one kid have it"; "Did you see them take off when I leveled my gun on them"; "You were great, Baby. And did you see the way I ...," etc. It was just like we used to feel when we got back from a patrol where everything went just right. (The worker had been a paratrooper in the Korean conflict.) The tension was relieved, we had performed well and could be proud.
>
> Here, we observed, the status function of the conflict subculture is seen in bold relief. (Short and Strodtbeck, 1965, p. 202).

More than a year after this episode was reported, the same detached worker called me to report a conversation with a Vice Kings leader, concerning Big Jake, a leader of another gang. The worker "had better watch Big Jake," the boy said, because "he has to do something. He's got to build that rep again. He's been gone. Now he got to show everybody he's back!"

Much has changed since our Chicago research was conducted. While these types of status-serving group processes appear to occur among many street gangs, guns certainly have become more prevalent and far more lethal ("zip guns" were still prevalent in the 1960s). Moreover, even casual encounters on the street may result in serious injuries or death, when individuals feel they have been "dissed" by too long eye contact or a gesture that may or may not be intended. The "code of the streets," as Anderson (1999) notes, makes everyone vulnerable, even the innocent. Planned violence, such as drive-by shootings, also have become more common. Under such circumstances, gang conflict may become a deadly zero-sum game, not only for gang members, but for others, as well (see, especially, Sanders, 1994).

A Note on Gang Norms

Despite high excitement, mutual provocation, and sometimes deadly consequences, most gang incidents are short-lived and rather easily brought under control. Such incidents reinforce both individual and group status in the gang social world, and they perpetuate the investment of gang members in their "rep" and the popular image of gangs as street warriors, whose group norms require their participation in conflict with rival gangs. Were it not for detailed accounts of such incidents, such an interpretation would seem reasonable. It would then be necessary to discount the influence of the norms after the fights stopped, however. Why are fights so easily stopped, as most are? Why do some gang members not participate in particular violent events or in fighting generally? In nearly all cases we observed, some members never became involved.[14]

Careful review of such incidents finds that those most centrally involved are gang leaders and boys striving for leadership and other core group members. Variation in gang roles and personal investment in and identity with the gang influences individual involvement in the give and take of violent incidents.

Normative properties of groups doubtless influence the behavior of gang members, but that influence among the gangs we studied was tenuous and largely situational. Chicago gangs at the time of our studies were loosely structured, with flexible criteria for membership (see also Carney et al., 1969); so also were Los Angeles gangs (Klein, 1971). Membership, at least active membership, fluctuated and group cohesion was not very strong, except under special circumstances that drew members together. Members of the gangs we studied came and went for days or weeks at a time, and unless they occupied particularly strong leadership or other roles central to the group, most were hardly missed. More recently, Decker and Lauritsen (1996) report that leaving the gang similarly is not very difficult.

The Role of Group Cohesiveness

The role of group cohesiveness in promoting violent and other delinquent behavior, has been the subject of much debate. Klein (1971, 1995) and Klein and Crawford (1967) find strong support for the hypothesis that group cohesion among his Los Angeles gangs was positively related to delinquency among gang members (Klein, 1971, pp. 107 ff). Jansyn (1966), however, found that both delinquent and nondelinquent behavior by members of the gang he studied (in Chicago) increased following low points of group cohesion. His interpretation of this finding was that gang activity was a response to low cohesiveness. Similarly, Sanchez-Jankowski (1991) reports that "fear of organizational decline" sometimes is "crucial in the leadership's decision to launch an attack on a rival gang. They believe that such conflict will deter internal conflict, encourage group cohesion, and create more control over members" (p. 163).

It is possible that Klein's findings may be characteristic of street gangs that do not have a history of cohesiveness, in contrast to Jansyn's gang; that is, when gangs lacking cohesiveness become more cohesive, group activity (including delinquent behavior) may increase. The Chicago gangs that my colleagues and I studied were not as cohesive as Jansyn's gang. They appeared to become more cohesive in response to status threats to their leaders or to the gang, and on such occasions were often more delinquent. Klein's data are persuasive, and we regrettably did not measure cohesiveness among our gangs systematically nor did we measure changes in behavior over time. The role of cohesiveness in gang behavior is clearly important and in need of further research and theoretical development.

Field reports document the operation of group processes in the production of violent behavior, but systematic and sustained analysis at this level of explanation is lacking [but see Horowitz & Schwartz (1974) and Horowitz (1983), who stress the importance of "honor" among Chicano gangs in Chicago; also, Klein (1995), Hagedorn (1998), Sanders (1994), Short and Strodtbeck (1965)]. Regrettably, researchers often do not systematically collect data appropriate to this level of analysis or analyze such data in group process terms. Sanchez-Jankowski (1991), for example, attributes "both individual and collective gang violence" to "fear, ambition, frustration, and personal/group testing of skills" (p. 140). His observations and reported verbalizations by gang members suggest, however, that these factors often take the form of status seeking or enhancement or reactions to status threats. Members behave violently in order to "move up in the organization" (p. 144), for example, or because others have failed to grant respect (p. 152) or have challenged one's honor (p. 142). "In the course of this research," Sanchez-Jankowski reports, "267 cases were observed of one gang attacking others to gain control over a new territory for purposes of material improvement and/or growth in membership" (p. 344), suggesting status as well as economically motivated behavior.

Gangs, Gang Members, and Community Institutions

With few exceptions, studies consistently report that gang members are less closely tied to conventional institutions and therefore are less constrained by the social controls inherent in such institutions than are youth from the same communities who do not belong to gangs (Fagan, 1990; Short, 1990; MacLeod, 1987; Sullivan, 1989; Vigil, 1988; cf. Moore, 1989). The major exception is Joan Moore, who is careful to distinguish between different Hispanic groups and to note variations in their political and economic status and in the extent to which gangs are integrated into local community life.

Field research conducted in different communities portray extremely varied gang–community relationships. Hagedorn found that Milwaukee gangs were alienated from their local communities and isolated from the larger society, while Sanchez-Jankowski (1991) portrays gangs as "a formal element" operating "on an independent and equal basis with all the other organizations active in the low-income community" (p. 179). However, he acknowledges that the "social contract" between gangs and communities is "very delicate and capricious" and can be "quite fluid" (pp. 179–180). Again, much variation is evident (see, e.g., Skogan, 1990; Sullivan, 1989; Schwartz, 1987; Suttles, 1968).

Moore and Hagedorn find parallels between their findings in this respect and earlier studies of Chicano gangs in Los Angeles and Chicago (Moore, 1978, 1993; Horowitz, 1983). Because more stable residents often know gang members and their families, they are more likely to be more tolerant of them, even though they recognize the effects of drug dealing. More marginal residents are more anxious, viewing gang members simply as "dangerous strangers." However, most residents have negative views about the neighborhood and feel unsafe at home as well as in the streets (see, also, Bursik & Grasmick, 1993).

Recent discussions of this subject are to be found in work by Anderson (1998), Hagedorn (1998), Fagan (1998), Venkatesh (1996), and Chin (1996a,b). For 3 years, Venkatesh was a participant–observer of gangs and community institutions in Robert Taylor Homes, in Chicago. His study is a dramatic documentation of the local consequences of William Julius Wilson's thesis concerning the emergence of an underclass in this community (see Wilson, 1987, 1996). With this development, Venkatesh reports, illicit economic activity escalated and youth gangs in the housing project achieved a large measure of control of drug distribution and other illicit sources of income. Gang violence changed from "gang wars" to "drug wars," resulting in greater exposure to danger of bystanders, including children (see also Hagedorn, 1998). Although most residents do not participate in illicit activities and all resent and are fearful of gang violence, the failure of law enforcement (police and housing authority) to protect the community has further enhanced the role of gangs as "vigilante peer groups" who provide such security services as nightly escorts for young women (see also Suttles, 1968). The complex picture sketched by these researchers defies easy characterization or easy solution.

More recently, Venkatesh, together with economist Steven Levitt, documented a highly organized, "franchise" type of street-level drug dealing in which street gangs control drug traffic in local territories (see American Bar Foundation, 1999).[15] Although simple compared to legitimate firms of "comparable size," organization of the operation was steeply structured, with financial benefits flowing chiefly to the "top tier" of four to six leaders and about a dozen others who were responsible for "guiding the long-term strategies of the multistate organization, maintaining relationships with suppliers and affiliates in other regions of the country ... collecting dues, overseeing recruitment of new members, allocating punishments, and serving as liaisons to the community" (p. 4). Below this level were affiliated gangs whose responsibility it was to maintain control of drug traffic over particular areas that often were disputed and the object of episodic gang wars. Observations and records of one such constituent gang over a period of 4 years revealed that the "foot soldier" gang members who actually did the most dangerous work of selling drugs made on average "$200 per month or less" for "about 20 hours a week," while the gang leader "retained between $4,200 and $10,900—an annual wage of $50,000 to $130,000" and the leader's lieutenants ("an enforcer, a treasurer, and a runner") "earned only about $1,000 per month" for essentially full-time work (pp. 6–7). Levitt and Vankatesh estimate that most foot soldiers, unable to maintain their own residences, lived with other family members, and that "75 to 80%" of them held legitimate jobs in addition to dealing drugs. The enterprise involved terrible risks: "Gang members active for the entire four-year period had about a one in four chance of dying. On average, gang members suffered more than two non-fatal injuries (mostly gunshot wounds) per member, and almost six arrests" (p. 7).[16] This type of enterprise also is inherently vulnerable to law enforcement and gang rivalries; the gang operation under observation was abruptly terminated "when the gang leader and other officers were arrested," leading to division of its turf among other gangs (p. 5).

Chin (1996a,b) documents historical and contemporary connections between Chinese and Chinese immigrant communities in the United States, their relationships with host US cities, and the involvement of Chinese-American youth gangs in violent and predatory activities such as extortion. Here, too, the persistence of poverty has led to "enervated social institutions," and the presence of traditional adult criminal organizations in these communities has shaped the structure and the behavior of street gangs.

The picture of gangs and gang members that emerges from this literature is complex and at times contradictory. While some reported differences between gangs may be attributable to the research interests and methods of researchers, it is clear that there are real differences among gangs and gang members and between communities and changing macrolevel circumstances.

Local neighborhoods and communities are the most immediate social settings in the experience of young people. Sullivan (1989) notes that even the meaning of crime for the gangs he studied was shaped by "the local area in which they spend their time almost totally unsupervised and undirected by adults, and the consumerist youth culture promoted in the mass media" (p. 249). The relevance of this assessment for violence is that the gang context so often is an arena within which status threats and other group processes are played out, with violent consequences. Opportunities for violent behavior are greater in the gang context, especially for young people who have been socialized into violence or who may lack skills and supportive social bonds that might enable them to avoid conflict. Adding competition over drug markets—unregulated by conventional institutions—produces an extremely volatile and violent mix.

Despite growing consensus concerning the importance of underclass phenomena for gangs, much is unknown (Reiss & Roth, 1993). Similarly, while the street gangs–drugs connection has been exaggerated by law enforcement and the media, a growing body of evidence suggests that gangs, or in any case, gang members, have become more sophisticated and successful in drug marketing and that this is changing both the character of some gangs and their roles in local communities (American Bar Foundation, 1999; Huff, 1996; Fagan, 1996). When this happens, violence becomes less expressive and more instrumental (American Bar Foundation, 1999; Taylor, 1990; Chin, 1996a,b; Williams, 1989). The perception that this is happening, or has happened, together with largely minority population gang membership, leads to the conflation of gangs and minority youth among many in the general public and some in law enforcement. Gang membership then may become a "master status," the consequences of which are not altogether clear.

COMMUNITY AND LEGAL RESPONSES TO GANGS

Researchers studying public reactions to gangs report widely varying images and responses, from terrorist organizations to community protectors, from denial to moral panic (see discussions in Sanchez-Jankowski, 1991; Zatz, 1987; Hagedorn & Macon, 1988; Jackson & Rudman, 1993; Miethe & McCorkle, 1997). Hagedorn and Macon (1988) quote an official in Indianapolis to the effect that "we do not have a gang problem here. We do have a slight problem in the summer with groups of youths running around with shotguns. But we don't have a gang problem." Noting that Indianapolis was bidding for the 1992 Olympics, the official went on to say that the city "couldn't possibly have a gang problem until 1993" (pp. 21–22). Police in some cities have denied the existence of a gang problem because it makes the police look bad.

At the other extreme, gang problems may be exaggerated by officials in order to attract more public funds, by news media that feed on sensational events, or by a public that sees in gangs and gang members reflections of feared racial or ethnic stereotypes. The result may be, in Cohen's (1972) terminology, a "moral panic." Moral panics, in Cohen's analysis, arise when conditions, episodes, or groups "become defined as a threat to societal values and interests" (p. 9). Objects of moral panics are stereotyped and public concern escalates, often far beyond the objective realities. Zatz (1987), for example, noted that Phoenix police increased their estimates of gang activity in that city from only a few gangs to 100 or more virtually overnight. The department published a "Latin Gang Member Recognition Guide" that included disparaging cartoon representations of Hispanics. Hagedorn and Macon (1988) likewise characterized the rapid escalation of official and public recognition of Milwaukee's gang problem as a moral panic. Miethe and McCorkle (1997) draw a similar conclusion in their study of Las Vegas; that is, that a "moral panic" concerning gangs greatly exceeded the reality of gangs in that city.

Such public and official reactions are not inconsequential. Miethe and McCorkle (1997) note that legislation designed to curb gang violence and to increase police and prosecutorial options in dealing with gangs followed quickly in the wake of the moral panic in Las Vegas.

Investigation of prosecutions under the legislation discovered, however, that gang offenders were much more likely than nongang offenders to have their charges dismissed and that nongang cases were more likely than gang cases to receive prison sentences following conviction. These differences could not be accounted for statistically by controlling for such factors as the age or ethnicity of offenders, seriousness of offense, or prior arrests or convictions. For many in the public and in official circles it appears that gang membership may have become a "master status" (see Hughes, 1945). The very large minority overrepresentation of gang members in Las Vegas and elsewhere has the further consequence that, again for many people, "gang" has become a code word for "minority."

The seemingly paradoxical finding that laws designed to "get tough on gangs" result in more dismissals of charges and fewer convictions is less surprising than might at first appear. Police and prosecutors often are under pressure to respond to high-profile, especially violent, offenses. They may, therefore, arrest persons suspected of such offenses without sufficient evidence to convict, or simply to "clear" the offenses from the record of crimes outstanding. Political motives also may be involved, for example, elevated numbers of gang arrests may be offered as justification for enhanced police budgets when a police department wishes to create or expand a specialized "gang unit." Moreover, as several studies have found, arrests often serve purposes other than crime control per se, for example, "teaching a lesson" to suspects who fail to defer to police authority (see Hepburn, 1978). As suggested by conflict theorists, crimes that involve victimization of lower socioeconomic persons by lower socioeconomic offenders may be less threatening to the more affluent (and powerful), and therefore may be treated as less serious than crimes that victimize the more affluent (see Zimring, Eigen, & O'Malley, 1976). Miethe and McCorkle's (1997) findings lend support to this notion insofar as gang membership has become a master status for law enforcement.

In California, Jackson and Rudman (1993) also characterize the response to gangs as a moral panic based on an image of gangs as "vaguely defined youth street gangs whose overriding purpose was to make large amounts of money through the distribution and sale of crack and other drugs" (p. 258) an image quite at odds with reality (see Klein, 1995). Jackson and Rudman document the legal response to gangs as one that overwhelmingly emphasized gang suppression and incarceration.

Klein (1995) cites a Los Angeles Police Department antigang street sweep program called "Operation Hammer" as an extreme and spectacularly unsuccessful example of an attempt at gang suppression. Launched in 1988, the program featured a force of 1000 police officers who swept through the south central section of Los Angeles (by all accounts the most gang-ridden section of the city) on a spring weekend. The initial sweep resulted in 1453 arrests of likely gang members for a variety of offenses, only 60 of which were felonies. Charges were filed in only 32 cases, and most of those arrested were released without formal charges. Nearly half of the arrestees were not gang members. "This remarkably inefficient process," Klein notes, "was repeated many times, although with smaller forces—more typically one hundred or two hundred officers." (Klein, 1995, p. 162).

Howell (1998) has documented antigang strategies throughout the United States, including gang suppression statutes in more than a dozen states. A few states have focused on gang reduction by focusing on elementary and secondary school students (Washington), providing tax credits for employers who hire gang-involved or gang-affected youth (Oregon), or on efforts to prosecute career gang criminals while providing educational and recreational opportunities aimed at gang prevention (Hawaii) (see Chesney-Lind et al., 1992). Howell (1996) reviews a large number of such programs, some of which have been accompanied by evaluation efforts. He concludes that the most promising programs are "likely to contain multiple components, incorporating prevention, social intervention, treatment, suppression, and community mobilization approaches" (p. 28).

Howell's conclusion is based on both empirical findings and theoretical premises. While evaluation of complex programs such as those recommended is extraordinarily difficult, such evidence as exists strongly suggest that multiple components are likely to be necessary if the pernicious influences of gangs are to be countered and gangs effectively prevented or suppressed. These include sustained research, public education, family and community interventions, for example, community reconstruction, block watches, community policing, early school programs, public health measures, job training and job creation, and individual and peer-group counseling (see also Howell, 1996; Curtis, 1987; Center for Successful Child Development, 1993; Atkinson, 1996; Walker & Schmidt, 1996; Trump, 1996).

CONCLUSION

A bewildering variety of sometimes-violent youth collectivities confronts societies in many parts of the world. Klein's informal survey of youth collectivities in other countries is particularly instructive. Many of the same sorts of "youth culture types: sports fanatics, bikers, punks, heavy metal groups, and neo-Nazis," he reports are found in other countries; so, too, are street gangs, where conditions are similar to those associated with street gangs in the United States. Klein singles out several Russian cities, Berlin, Port Moresby, Brussels, Mexico City, "and perhaps Manila and South Africa as locations of American-style street gangs" (Klein, 1995, p. 222). Others, such as Stockholm and its suburbs, Zurich, Frankfurt and surrounding cities, Stuttgart, and Melbourne, evidence a "commuting to turf" pattern, the result of public housing projects that are located outside central cities, rather than in the inner cities, as in the United States. Here youths marginalized by poverty and ethnicity periodically converge via public transportation to central city areas to engage in carousing, "smash-and-grab" hits on stores, rolling drunks, and robberies before returning to their homes. The lack of territorial linkages with these loosely structured, ethnically mixed collectivities, Klein (1995) notes, "does not easily produce street gangs" (p. 224). In still other cities—Klein mentions London and Manchester, especially—gang problems appear to be primarily drug-oriented, and their violent behavior is directly associated principally with drug marketing.

Virtually all these patterns appear to have in common the existence of marginalized youth—by ethnic, economic, or lifestyle status—with poor prospects for integration in or social mobility within dominant majority societies. They are, in Klein's view, largely underclass phenomena, a common threat linking many adaptations of youth who are responsible for a very large proportion of violent behavior in many societies, including the United States.

As noted above, we are beginning to understand the nature of processes by which street gangs become violent: (1) escalation of the natural rough-and-tumble punching and wrestling that occurs among most male groups and the association of status with fighting prowess; (2) competition with rival gangs, often leading to conflict over status enhancing behaviors, such as graffiti, dancing, or athletic contests, and more recently drug trafficking; (3) definitions of others and behavior toward street gangs that push a violent identity on them; and (4) group processes that create or reinforce group cohesion based on violent or otherwise delinquent behavior; these often involve individual and group status considerations (see Jansyn, 1966; Klein & Crawford, 1967; Short & Strodtbeck, 1965; Brymer, 1967; Hagedorn and Macon, 1988; Short, 1996).

Important beginnings have been made also in identifying the nature of macrolevel forces that produce street gangs and that sometimes transform "garden variety" street gangs toward other adaptations. Among these, the spread of gang culture, a highly commercialized youth culture, and a growing underclass are paramount. At the community level, however, the particular forms taken by youth collectivities are shaped by local cultures and social structures that in turn both reflect and influence family patterns, opportunity structures, and social control (Schwartz, 1987; Furstenberg, 1993; Sullivan, 1989; Anderson, 1990).

Observers of youth groups everywhere note that status differences within and between them tend to be highly refined. The criteria for adolescent stratification—typically the basis for inclusiveness and exclusiveness—include economic affluence, skills in valued activities, public appearance, school performance, and perhaps most importantly, lifestyle differences. Observers also note that adolescent friendship and rejection involve especially intense relationships. Feelings of rejection and disrespect, as well as those of friendship and respect, also are especially intense among adolescents and often are the basis for group and subcultural formation.

Schools are perhaps the most important contexts for adolescent friendship, achievement, and recognition. School contexts, including the journey to and from school, are the settings for much adolescent behavior, including delinquent and criminal behavior. On occasion they also have been the setting for the most extreme forms of violence (e.g., mass killings by students or others alienated from their fellows or from mainstream institutions in general). Although the specific causes of such extreme alienation are complex, it is likely that schools have been especially targeted precisely because of their importance in the lives of adolescents. For some, school becomes a symbol of rejection, both by peers and an adult world that seems far removed from adolescent concerns. Additionally, the ready availability of guns at times transforms normal adolescent turmoil and conflict into deadly confrontation.

Young people are influenced by a variety of subcultures, among them street gang culture, which has diffused widely across the United States and in some other countries. Items of clothing, graffiti, and hand signals associated with gangs have become widely known via media portrayals. Youth who know little beyond such symbols may use them and affect behaviors associated with them. When they identify themselves as gangs and/or become identified as gangs by others, their gang status is enhanced.

A more general cultural phenomenon is also at work, however. Youth culture has been widely diffused throughout much of the world. Macrosocial and economic forces fail to provide meaningful roles for young people in the adult world, separating them from participation in that world. A vast gap between generations has occurred, bringing with it cultural differentiation among the young and between them and their elders. Youth subcultures influence and are influenced by a broader youth culture that contains elements common to many such varieties, such as youth-oriented preferences in music, interactive media, distinctive types of clothing, and differences in lifestyles. Media advertising caters to youthful appetites, fads, and currency. The seductions of commercial products provide yet another basis for inclusion and exclusion, for friendship and rejection, and among some young people for alienation.

More than ever before in history, young people, targeted for commercial exploitation and isolated from mainstream adult roles and institutions, confront economic conditions beyond their control. Economic decline, severe unemployment, and the unavailability of "good jobs" are associated not only with street gangs, but with their transformation into "economic gangs" (including drug gangs) and with ethnic, racial, and class-related identities and antagonisms that lead to other types of collective violence (Hagedorn, 1998). These same forces alter both intergang relationships and relationships between gangs and their communities. Relationships between adults and young people, shaped by generational backgrounds and community cultures, "translate" these and other macrolevel forces at the local community level. To the extent that conventional institutions fail to protect local residents and to provide other services, the violent, status- and economic-enhancing behaviors of gang members create opportunities for new accommodations between gangs and other community residents (Venkatesh, 1996). To the extent that gang membership confers "master status" among law enforcement personnel and in the general public, gangs and gang membership contribute to the deterioration of relationships between racial and ethnic groupings in the larger society.

ACKNOWLEDGMENTS

Portions of this chapter have been presented at various times in other places, including a much longer essay prepared for the Center for the Study and Prevention of Violence, University of Colorado (see Short, 1996), and a much shorter paper presented at meetings of the American Society of Criminology, in November 1995. I am grateful to Delbert Elliott for his comments on the Center for the Study and Prevention of Violence version.

ENDNOTES

1. I have suggested elsewhere that understanding gang diversity and change requires that we study unsupervised youth groups before they become involved in delinquency, at least serious delinquency, and before they become transformed into other types of organizations, such as "working gangs" (Padilla, 1993) or drug crews. I do not mean to suggest that more specialized gangs always or necessarily develop from "garden variety" street gangs, but I suspect that many do, and we need to know a great deal more about such changes (see Short, 1997, 1998).

   Second, I believe we must cease including the behavior we wish to explain in our definitions of gangs or types of youth collectivities. Only then can we encompass diversity in our theories, rather than excluding it, as most gang researchers do (see Short, 1996, 1997, 1998, for elaboration of these and related points; for an alternative view, see Klein, 1995).

   Third, it is imperative that formal criteria be developed for a typology of youth collectivities. Among candidates for inclusion in such a typology are the following: the degree to which groups meet with some regularity as opposed to transitory groupings; crowds, in the collective behavior sense versus groups; crowds to be distinguished further in terms of regularity of their gathering, for example, soccer hooligans who gather on a regular basis versus neighborhood crowds that gather on a somewhat regular basis with understood purposes (to have a good time, to keep unwanted persons out of the neighborhood) versus crowds that gather spontaneously or on a onetime basis, for example, those that gather under unique circumstances, such as occurred following the Rodney King verdict, a world series victory, an election defeat, or for a political convention (Chicago in 1968 is a good example), or rioting crowds that "erupt" in response to conditions, for example, in the mid-1960s. Groups can be classified according to similar criteria, for example, regularly meeting groups versus onetime only groups, for example, apparently, the Central Park "wilding" group. Cummings' (1993) "wilding gang," however, met regularly and carried out their depredations over an extended period of time.
2. This logical principle is often ignored by gang researchers and law enforcement agencies, most of whom include criminal behavior or "orientation" in their definitions of gangs. See discussions of this issue in Bursik and Grasmick (1993), and Ball and Curry (1995). The differences between my definition and Klein's are not so great as might appear. The chief consequence of the more restrictive definition in surveys of general populations of young people is that fewer gangs are identified and the beginnings of delinquent orientations are ignored.
3. Data collected by the National Youth Gang Center from law enforcement agencies confirm this relationship.
4. This is not to say that gangs are never "exported" from one city to another. Klein's survey found that police in a few cities reported the presence of drug gangs "initiated from outside cities, including Detroit" (Erie and Ft. Wayne; the latter claiming outside influences from Chicago and Indianapolis, as well; see Klein, 1995).
5. The objection that the definition of gangs here employed does not distinguish gangs from "hobby or personal interest groups," to quote one critic, misses this point. Note also that while adult sponsorship and/or adult

supervision distinguishes gangs from other youth groups, neither necessarily nor always is successful in preventing delinquency or violence. Hobby groups, even church-sponsored groups, can become gangs, to the extent that they become independent of adult sponsorship and supervision. Few would argue, however, that adult sponsorship and supervision is irrelevant to adolescent behavior, in that they are more likely to be successful in insulating groups from situations in which violence is likely to occur and to lessen the risk of delinquent behavior in other ways, for example, as role models, teachers.

6. Note, however, that a full typology of youth collectivities would have to include both skinheads and bikers. An explanation of behavioral differences between these groups and street gangs necessarily would include differentiation on the basis of ideology and specialization of interests (street gangs have neither, while skinheads are highly ideological and bikers are highly specialized interest groups). Both by the definition here employed are "subspecies" of gangs. So are the "surfer groups and doper groups" that San Diego police and William Sanders do not classify as gangs (see Sanders, 1994, p. 166).
7. Schwartz analyzes youth–adult relationships in terms of how local "cultures reflect different resolutions of similar issues" concerning young people. In Cambridge the issue was loyalty to local traditions versus social mobility. Other issues in other communities provided axes around which authority relationships and values influences youth cultures and behavior (see my more extended analysis in Short, 1990).
8. Coleman (1988) introduced the notion of social capital to sociologists. Several indicators of relationships between adults and the gang members we studied compared to boys from the same communities who did not belong to gangs—a major source of the boys' social capital—demonstrated the superior quality and quantity of such relationships among boys who did not belong to gangs. Middle-class boys clearly were advantaged when compared to lower-class boys, as were whites compared to blacks (Short, Rivera, & Marshall, 1964). When we asked boys in one African-American community to nominate adults they knew best, gang members were able to nominate fewer adults and they rarely saw them in conventional institutional settings, compared to nongang boys. Interviews with the adults nominated by boys who belonged to gangs and those who did not confirmed the weaker and less conventional contacts of gang members. This was especially true for adults in caretaker roles who are traditionally helpful to young people (Rivera & Short, 1967).

   Our gang members clearly engaged in more violent and other types of delinquent behavior than did the nongang boys. Sullivan (1989) comments that

   > the underlying similarity in the prevalence of adolescent street fighting establishes a baseline for comparing the extent to which youths from different neighborhoods then went on to apply violence to the pursuit of income. It appears that all these youths had an equal capacity for violence and that street fighting was equally common in all three neighborhoods but peaked well before the age of peak involvement in income-motivated crime. The fact that the youths from the two minority neighborhoods went on to participate in much more violent street crime must then be explained in the context of their *alternative legal and illegal opportunities for gaining income.* (pp. 201–202, emphasis added)

   The reciprocal nature of social capital, human capital, and crime also is suggested by longitudinal studies by Sampson and Laub (1993) and Hagan (1993). Hagan's analysis of data on London youth stresses the importance for later employment and criminality of

   > early embeddedness among delinquent friends and ... delinquent behavior ... further, that parental criminality plays a more salient role in the development of early adult unemployment than parental unemployment.... Criminal youths are embedded in contexts that isolate them from the likelihood of legitimate adult employment. (1993, pp. 486–487)

   Hagan cites Freeman and Holzer's (1991) analysis of US data demonstrating

   > that with increasing age, from one-sixth to one-third of 18- to 34-year-old US high school dropouts are under the supervision of the criminal justice system ... (and that) as many as three-quarters of 25- to 34-year-old black dropouts are under such supervision ... criminal involvement has become so concentrated among young, impoverished black American males that it must be considered a major determinant of their prospective employment. (Hagan, 1993, p. 487)

9. $N = 15$ Latino gangs, 7 white gangs, and 6 black gangs.
10. Note that even the terminology of ethnicity varies from study to study. Neither race nor ethnicity is rigorously or consistently defined or adhered to in official data sources, or for that matter in social science discourse. Classification of persons as Hispanic or Latino, Asian or Oriental, black or African-American, white, or Native American is largely based on social criteria. Persons so identified often identify themselves in very different ethnic terms that are not recognized in these broad categories.

11. Minorities continue to change with tides of immigration and related social changes. Additionally, not all gangs are located in the underclass or in inner-city areas. Some of the studies reviewed in this chapter are composed of working-class youth. Most of these, such as Sanchez-Jankowski's (1991) "Irish" gangs, are non-Hispanic whites. Padilla (1991) studied Puerto Rican gangs from working-class areas in Chicago. Studies of middle- and upper-class gangs are rare (Muehlbauer & Dodder, 1983; Chambliss, 1973; Greeley & Casey, 1963). Because middle- and upper-class youth are more likely to be channeled into adult-sponsored groups and activities, gangs among these youth are less prevalent than among youth in working- and lower-class areas (Schwartz, 1987; Schwendinger & Schwendinger, 1985).
12. Their limited social horizons, somewhat low intelligence scores, and lack of sophistication and skills in interpersonal relationships, work relationships and requirements, and sexual knowledge, despite being sexually active, led us to the hypothesis that gang members were characterized by "social disabilities" (see Short & Strodtbeck, 1965; Gordon et al., 1963).
13. Measurement of personality characteristics was designed and supervised by Desmond S. Cartwright (Cartwright, Howard, & Reuterman, 1980; also Gordon et al., 1963).
14. This is not to say that nonparticipation in events may not have consequences. Behavior that is considered cowardly may be punished, either physically or by diminished status within the gang. Gang members often tread a fine line between bravado and restraint when in the presence of other gang members (Sanders, 1994).
15. *Researching Law: An ABF Update* is a publication of the American Bar Foundation. The referenced article discusses collaborative research between ABF Research Fellow Steven Levitt and Sudhir Vankatesh.
16. A decade after our initial contact, 19% of Vice Lords and 16% of the Nobles were dead, the majority also by violent means (see Short & Moland, 1976).

REFERENCES

American Bar Foundation. (1999). Financial accounting, risk taking, and wage gaps in a drug-dealing street gang. *Researching Law: An ABF Update*, *10*(1), 4–5.

Anderson, E. (1990). *Streetwise: Race, class and change in an urban community*. Chicago: University of Chicago Press.

Anderson, E. (1999). *The code of the streets*. New York: W.W. Norton.

Atkinson, W. K., II. (1996). Organizing the community response in Aurora, Colorado. In C. R. Huff (Ed.), *Gangs in America* (2nd ed., pp. 257–262). Thousand Oaks, CA: Sage.

Ball, R. A., & Curry, G. D. (1995). The logic of definition in criminology: Purposes and methods for defining "tangs." *Criminology*, *33*, 225–245.

Bandura, A. (1986). *Social foundations of thought and action: A social cognitive theory*. Englewood Cliffs, NJ: Prentice-Hall.

Block, C. B. (1993). Lethal violence in the Chicago Latino community. In A. V. Wilson (Ed.), *Homicide: The victim–offender connection*. Cincinnati, OH: Anderson.

Block, C. B., Block, R., & Block, R. (1993). Street gang crime in Chicago. In *Research in Brief*. Washington, DC: National Institute of Justice, US Department of Justice.

Block, R., & Christakos, A. (1993). Major trends in Chicago homicide: 1965–1994. Illinois: Report of the Illinois Criminal Justice Information Authority.

Brymer, R. A. (1967). Toward a definition and theory of conflict gangs. Presented at the annual meeting of the Society for the Study of Social Problems, San Francisco.

Bufford, B. (1991). *Among the thugs*. New York: Vintage Books.

Bursik, R. J., & Grasmick, H. G. (1993). *Neighborhoods and crime: The dimensions of effective community control*. Lexington, MA: Lexington Books.

Carney, F., Mattick, H. W., & Callaway, J. N. (1969). *Action on the streets*. New York: Association Press.

Cartwright, D. S., Howard, K. I., & Reuterman, N. A. (1980). Multivariate analysis of gang delinquency: IV. Personality factors in gangs and clubs. *Multivariate Behavioral Research*, *15*, 3–22.

Center for Successful Child Development. (1993). *Beethoven's Fifth: The first five years of the Center for Successful Child Development; Executive summary*. Chicago: The Ounce of Prevention Fund.

Chambliss, W. (1973, November–December). The Saints and the roughnecks. *Society*, pp. 24–31.

Chesney-Lind, M., Marker, N., Rodriguez-Stern, I., Yap, A., Song, V., Reyes, H., Reyes, Y., Stern, J., & Taira, J. (1992). *An evaluation of Act 189: Hawaii's response to youth gangs*. Honolulu, HI: Center for Youth Research, Social Science Research Institute, University of Hawaii, Manoa.

Chin, K.-L. (1996a). *Chinatown gangs: Extortion, enterprise, and ethnicity*. New York: Oxford University Press.

Chin, K.-L. (1996b). Gang violence in Chinatown. In C. R. Huff (Ed.), *Gangs in America* (pp. 157–184). Thousand Oaks, CA: Sage.

Cloward, R. A., & Ohlin, L. E. (1960). *Delinquency and opportunity*. New York: Free Press.

Cohen, A. K., & Short, J. F., Jr. (1958). Research in delinquent subcultures. *Journal of Social Issues, 14*(3), 20–37.

Cohen, S. (1972). *Folk devils and moral panics: The creation of the Mods and Rockers*. London: MacGibbon and Kee.

Coleman, J. S. (1988). Social capital in the creation of human capital. *American Journal of Sociology, 94*(suppl), S95–S120.

Conquergood, D. (1992). *On reppin' and rhetoric: Gang representations*. Evanston, IL: Center for Urban Affairs and Policy Research, Northwestern University.

Cook, K. S., & Levy, M. (Eds.). (1990). *The limits of rationality*. Chicago: University of Chicago Press.

Cummings, S. (1993). Anatomy of a wilding gang. In S. Cummings & D. J. Monti (Eds.), *Gangs: The origin and impact of contemporary youth gangs in the United States* (pp. 49–73). Albany, NY: SUNY Press.

Curry, G. D., & Spergel, I. (1988). Gang homicide, delinquency, and community. *Criminology, 26*, 381–405.

Curtis, L. A. (Ed.). (1987). Preface. *Annals of the American Academy of Political and Social Science, 494*, 9–18.

Dawley, D. (1973). *A nation of lords*. New York: Anchor.

Decker, S. (1996). Collective and normative features of gang violence. *Justice Quarterly, 13*, 243–264.

Decker, S. H., & Lauritsen, J. L. (1996). Breaking the bonds of membership: Leaving the gang. In C. R. Huff (Ed.), *Gangs in America* (pp. 103–122). Thousand Oaks, CA: Sage.

Drake, St. C., & Clayton, H. R. (1962). *Black metropolis: A study of Negro life in a northern city*. New York: Harper.

Elliott, D. S. (1994). Serious violent offenders: Onset, developmental course, and termination. *Criminology, 32*, 1–21.

Fagan, J. (1990). Social processes of drug use and delinquency among gang and non-gang youths. In C. R. Huff (Ed.), *Gangs in America* (pp. 183–219). Thousand Oaks, CA: Sage.

Fagan, J. (1989). The social organization of drug use and drug dealing among urban gangs. *Criminology, 27*, 633–669.

Fagan, J. (1996). Gangs, drugs, and community change. In C. R. Huff (Ed.), *Gangs in America* (2nd ed., pp. 39–74). Thousand Oaks, CA: Sage.

Farrington, D. P., Berkowitz, L., & West, D. J. (1981). Differences between individual and group fights. *British Journal of Social Psychology, 20*, 163–171.

Freeman, R., & Holzer, H. (1991). The deterioration of unemployment and earnings opportunities for less educated young Americans: A review of evidence. Paper presented at National Academy of Sciences Panel on High Risk Youth.

Furstenberg, F. (1993). How families manage risk and opportunity in dangerous neighborhoods. In W. J. Wilson (Ed.), *Sociology and the public agenda* (pp. 231–258). Newbury Park, CA: Sage.

Gordon, R. A., Short, J. F., Jr., Cartwright, D., & Strodtbeck, F. L. (1963). Values and gang delinquency: A study of street-corner groups. *American Journal of Sociology, 69*(6), 927–944.

Greeley, A., & Casey, J. (1963, Spring). An upper middle class deviant gang. *American Catholic Sociological Review*, pp. 33–41.

Hagan, J. (1993). The social embeddedness of crime and unemployment. *Criminology, 32*, 465–491.

Hagedorn, J. (1998). Gang violence in the postindustrial era. In M. Tonry & M. Moore (Eds.), *Youth violence. Crime and justice* (Vol. 24, pp. 365–419). Chicago: University of Chicago Press.

Hagedorn, J. M. (with Macon, P.). (1988). *People and folks: Gangs, crime, and the underclass in a rustbelt city*. Chicago: Lake View Press.

Hannerz, U. (1969). *Soulside: Inquiries in ghetto culture and community*. New York: Columbia University Press.

Hechinger, F. M. (1992). *Fateful choices: Healthy youth for the 21st century*. New York: Hill and Wang.

Hepburn, J. R. (1978). Race and the decision to arrest: An analysis of warrants issued. *Journal of Research in Crime and Delinquency, 15*, 54–73.

Horowitz, R. (1983). *Honor and the American dream*. New Brunswick, NJ: Rutgers University Press.

Horowitz, R., & Schwartz, G. (1974). Honor, normative ambiguity and gang violence. *American Sociological Review, 39*(2), 238–251.

Howell, J. C. (1996). Youth gangs, homicides, drugs, and guns. Paper prepared for the National Youth Gang Center, Institute for Intergovernmental Research, Tallahassee, FL.

Howell, J. C. (1998). Prevention of youth violence. In M. Tonry & M. Moore (Eds.), *Youth violence. Crime and justice* (Vol. 24, pp. 263–315). Chicago: University of Chicago Press.

Huff, C. R. (1996). The criminal behavior of gang members and nongang at-risk youth. In C. R. Huff (Ed.), *Gangs in America* (2nd ed., pp. 75–102). Thousand Oaks, CA: Sage.

Hughes, E. C. (1945). Dilemmas and contradictions of status. *American Journal of Sociology, 50*, 353–359.

Hutchison, R. (1993). Blazon nouveau: Gang graffiti in the barrios of Los Angeles and Chicago. In S. Cummings & D. Monti (Eds.), *Gangs: The origins and impact of contemporary youth gangs in the United States* (pp. 137–171). Albany: SUNY Press.

Hutson, H. R., Anglin, D., Kyriacou, D. N., Haart, J., & Spears, K. (1995). The epidemic of gang-related homicides in Los Angeles County from 1979 through 1994. *Journal of the American Medical Association, 274*, 1031–1036.

Jackson, P. (with Rudman, C.). (1993). Moral panic and the response to gangs in California. In S. Cummings & D. Monti (Eds.), *Gangs: The origins and impact of contemporary youth gangs in the United States* (pp. 257–275). Albany: SUNY Press.

Jansyn, L. R. (1966). Solidarity and delinquency in a street corner group. *American Sociological Review, 31*, 600–614.

Keiser, R. L. (1969). *The Vice Lords: Warriors of the streets.* New York: Holt, Rinehart and Winston.

Klein, M. (1971). *Street gangs and street workers.* Englewood Cliffs, NJ: Prentice-Hall.

Klein, M. (1995). *The American street gang.* New York: Oxford.

Klein, M. W., & Crawford, L. Y. (1967). Groups, gangs, and cohesiveness. *Journal of Research in Crime and Delinquency, 4*, 63–75.

Liebow, E. (1967). *Tally's corner: A study of Negro streetcorner men.* Boston: Little Brown.

MacLeod, J. (1987). *Ain't no makin' it: Leveled aspirations in a low-income neighborhood.* Boulder, CO: Westview Press.

Maxson, C., Klein, M., & Cunningham, L. (1996). Defining gang homicide: An updated look at member and motive approaches. In C. R. Huff (Ed.), *Gangs in America* (2nd ed., pp. 3–20). Thousand Oaks, CA: Sage.

McKay, H. D. (1969). Rates of delinquents and commitments: Discussion and conclusions. In C. R. Shaw & H. D. McKay (Eds.), *Juvenile delinquency and urban areas* (rev. ed.). Chicago: University of Chicago Press.

Meehan, P. J., & O'Carroll, P. W. (1992). Gangs, drugs, and homicide in Los Angeles. *American Journal of the Disabled Child, 146*, 683–687.

Miethe, T. D., & McCorkle, R. C. (1997). Gang membership and criminal processing: A test of the "master status" concept. *Justice Quarterly, 14*(3), 407–428.

Miller, W. B. (1980). Gangs, groups, and serious youth crime. In D. Schichor & D. Kelly (Eds.), *Critical issues in juvenile delinquency* (pp. 115–138). Lexington, MA: D.C. Heath.

Miller, W. B., Geertz, H., & Cutter, S. G. (1961). Aggression in a boys' street-corner group. *Psychiatry, 24*, 283–298.

Moore, J. W. (with Garcia, R., Garcia, C., Cerda, L., & Valencia, F.). (1978). *Homeboys.* Philadelphia: Temple University Press.

Moore, J. W. (1989). Is there a Hispanic underclass? *Social Science Quarterly, 70*(2), 265–284.

Moore, J. W. (1993). Gangs, drugs, and violence. In S. Cummings & D. Monti (Eds.), *Gangs: The origins and impact of contemporary youth gangs in the United States* (pp. 27–46). Albany: SUNY Press.

Muchlbauer, G., & Doder, L. (1983). *The losers: Gang delinquency in an American suburb.* New York: Praeger.

Padilla, F. (1993). The working gang. In S. Cummings & D. Monti (Eds.), *Gangs: The origins and impact of contemporary youth gangs in the United States* (pp. 173–192). Albany: SUNY Press.

Pinderhughes, H. (1993). "Down with the program": Racial attitudes and group violence among youth in Bensonhurst and Gravesend. In S. Cummings & D. Monti (Eds.), *Gangs: The origins and impact of contemporary youth gangs in the United States* (pp. 75–94). Albany: SUNY Press.

Reiss, A. J., Jr. (1986). Co-offender influences on criminal careers. In A. Blumstein, J. Cohen, J. A. Roth, & C. A. Visher (Eds.), *Criminal careers and career criminals* (Vol. II, pp. 121–160). Washington, DC: National Academy Press.

Reiss, A. J., Jr., & Farrington, D. (1991). Advancing knowledge about co-offending: Results from a prospective longitudinal survey of London males. *Journal of Criminal Law and Criminology, 82*(2), 360–395.

Reiss, A. J., Jr., & Roth, J. S. (Eds.). (1993). *Understanding and preventing violence.* Washington, DC: National Academy Press.

Rivera, R. J., & Short, J. F., Jr. (1967). Significant adults, caretakers, and structures of opportunity: An exploratory study. *Journal of Research in Crime and Delinquency, 4*, 76–97.

Sampson, R. J., & Laub, J. H. (1993). *Crime in the making: Pathways and turning points through life.* Cambridge, MA: Harvard University Press.

Sampson, R. J., & Groves, W. (1989). Community structure and crime: Testing social-disorganization theory. *American Journal of Sociology, 94*(4), 774–802.

Sanchez-Jankowski, M. (1991). *Islands in the street: Gangs in American urban society.* Berkeley: University of California Press.

Sanders, W. (1994). *Gangbangs and drive-bys: Grounded culture and juvenile gang violence.* New York: Aldine de Gruyter.

Sarnecki, J. (1986). *Delinquent networks.* Report No. 1986:1. Stockholm: National Swedish Council for Crime Prevention, Research Division.

Schwartz, G. (1987). *Beyond conformity or rebellion: Youth and authority in America.* Chicago: University of Chicago Press.

Schwendinger, H., & Schwendinger, J. (1985). *Adolescent subcultures and delinquency*. New York: Praeger.
Shaw, C. R. (1930). *The jack-roller*. Chicago: University of Chicago Press.
Shaw, C. R., Zorbaugh, F., McKay, H. D., & Cottrell, L. S. (1929). *Delinquency areas*. Chicago: University of Chicago Press.
Shaw, C. R., & Moore, M. E. (1931). *The natural history of a delinquent career*. Chicago: University of Chicago Press.
Shaw, S. R., & McKay, H. (1931). *Social factors in juvenile delinquency*. Washington, DC: US Government Printing Office.
Shaw, C. R., & McKay, H. (1942). *Juvenile delinquency and urban areas*. Chicago: University of Chicago Press. (rev. ed. 1969).
Sherif, M., & Sheriff, C. (1964). *Reference groups: Exploration into conformity and deviation of adolescents*. New York: Harper and Row.
Short, J. F., Jr. (1968). Comment on Lerman's "Gangs, networks, and subcultural delinquency." *American Journal of Sociology, 73*, 513–525.
Short, J. F., Jr. (1974). Collective behavior, crime, and delinquency. In D. Glaser (Ed.), *Handbook of criminology* (pp. 403–449). Chicago: Rand McNally.
Short, J. F., Jr. (1990). Gangs, neighborhoods, and youth crime. *Criminal Justice Research Bulletin, 5*(4), 1–11.
Short, J. F., Jr. (1996). *Gangs and adolescent violence*. Boulder, CO: Center for the Study and Prevention of Violence.
Short, J. F., Jr. (1997). *Poverty, ethnicity, and violent crime*. Boulder, CO: Westview.
Short, J. F., Jr. (1998) The level of explanation problem revisited. *Criminology, 36*, 3–36.
Short, J. F., Jr., & Moland, J. (1976). Politics and youth gangs. *Sociological Quarterly, 17*, 162–179.
Short, J. F., Jr., & Strodtbeck, F. L. (1965). *Group process and gang delinquency*. Chicago: University of Chicago Press.
Short, J. F., Jr., Rivera, R., & Marshall, H. (1964). Adult–adolescent relations and gang delinquency. *Pacific Sociological Review, 7*, 56–65.
Skogan, W. G. (1990). *Disorder and decline: Crime and the spiral of decay in American neighborhoods*. New York: Free Press.
Spergel, I. A. (1995). *The youth gang problem: A community approach*. New York: Oxford University Press.
Sullivan, M. (1989). *"Getting paid": Youth crime and work in the inner city*. Ithaca, NY: Cornell University Press.
Susser, I. (1982). *Norman Street: Poverty and politics in an urban neighborhood*. New York: Oxford University Press.
Suttles, G. D. (1968). *The social order of the slum: Ethnicity and territory in the inner city*. Chicago: University of Chicago Press.
Taylor, C. S. (1990). *Dangerous society*. East Lansing: Michigan State University Press.
Thrasher, F. M. (1927). *The gang: A study of 1,313 gangs in Chicago*. Chicago: University of Chicago Press. (rev. ed., 1936; abridged ed., 1963)
Trump, K. S. (1996). Gang development and strategies in schools and suburban communities. In C. R. Huff (Ed.), *Gangs in America* (2nd ed., pp. 270–280). Thousand Oaks, CA: Sage.
Valentine, B. (1978). *Hustling and other hard work: Life styles in the ghetto*. New York: Free Press.
Van Limbergen, K., Colaers, C., & Walgrave, L. (1989). The societal and psycho-sociological background of football hooliganism. *Current Psychology Research and Reviews, 9*, 4–14.
Venkatesh, S. A. (1996). The gang and the community. In C. R. Huff (Ed.), *Gangs in America* (2nd ed., pp. 241–255). Thousand Oaks, CA: Sage.
Vigil, J. D. (1988). *Barrio gangs*. Austin, TX: University of Texas Press.
Vigil, J. D. (1993). The established gang. In S. Cummings & D. Monti (Eds.), *Gangs: The origins and impact of contemporary youth gangs in the United States*. Albany: SUNY Press.
Walker, M. L., & Schmidt, L. M. (1996). Gang reduction efforts by the Task Force on Violent Crime in Cleveland, Ohio. In C. R. Huff (Ed.), *Gangs in America* (2nd ed., pp. 263–269). Thousand Oaks, CA: Sage.
Warr, M. (1996). Organization and instigation in delinquent groups. *Criminology, 34*, 11–37.
Williams, T. (1989). *The cocaine kids: The inside story of a teenage drug ring*. Menlo Park, CA: Addison-Wesley.
Wilson, W. J. (1987). *The truly disadvantaged: The inner city, the underclass, and public policy*. Chicago: University of Chicago Press.
Wilson, W. J. (1996). *When work disappears: The world of the new urban poor*. New York: Knopf.
Yablonsky, L. (1962). *The violent gang*. New York: Macmillan.
Zatz, M. (1987). Chicano youth gangs and crime: The creation of a moral panic. *Contemporary Crises, 11*, 129–158.
Zimring, F. E., Eigen, J., & O'Malley, S. (1976). Punishing homicide in Philadelphia: Perspectives on the death penalty. *University of Chicago Law Review, 43*, 227–252.

13

Community

ROBERT J. BURSIK, JR.

INTRODUCTION

As Henry McKay (1949) observed over 50 years ago, "neighborhoods are the most meaningful part of the child's social world" (pp. 32–33). As such, it is difficult to overstate their effects on child and adolescent development. Recent research, for example, has shown that the nature of the residential environment significantly shapes a youth's sense of well-being and has an effect on the formation of other psychological characteristics (see, for example, Hill & Madhere, 1996; Pretty, Conroy, Dugay, Fowler, & Williams, 1996; Sampson, 1997). Therefore, given the well-established observation that rates of delinquency increase dramatically in early adolescence, it is not surprising that a great deal of research has focused on how the likelihood of such behavior is affected by community factors.

Neighborhoods, of course, are found in urban areas throughout the world and delinquency is a nearly universal phenomenon. However, the development of neighborhood-based theories of delinquent behavior has been a particularly American enterprise. In fact, a strong community orientation can be found in two of the earliest formal attempts to study youthful illegal activities in the United States (Blackman & Burgess, 1917; Breckenridge & Abbott, 1912). While it is extremely dangerous to impute the motivations that led to this emphasis, it is safe to assume that at least one reason is that public opinion in the United States traditionally has associated crime with the activities of particular ethnic and racial groups (see Simon, 1985), and, as Abrahamson (1996) has clearly shown, neighborhood dynamics have played a central role in the assimilation (or lack of same) of those groups into local social, economic and political institutions. As will be illustrated later in this chapter, the focus on the association between race–ethnicity and delinquency continues to be an important theme in contemporary neighborhood research, which has shown that the nature of that relationship is extremely complicated.

The first section of this chapter presents an overview of the social disorganization model developed by Clifford Shaw, Henry McKay, and their associates (Shaw, Zorbaugh, McKay, & Cottrell, 1929; Shaw & McKay, 1931, 1942, 1969) in an attempt to account for

ROBERT J. BURSIK, JR. • Department of Criminology and Criminal Justice, University of Missouri at St. Louis, St. Louis, Missouri 63121.

Handbook of Youth and Justice, edited by White. Kluwer Academic / Plenum Publishers, New York, 2001.

neighborhood variation in delinquency rates. Although this framework was first proposed 70 years ago, it provides the intellectual context that is essential to appreciate contemporary work in this area. Then, the extensions and revisions of this theory that have led to the recent revitalization of modern local community approaches will be presented. The final section of the chapter will focus on what arguably has been the most complicated issue in this theoretical tradition: the relationship between the level of a community's economic deprivation and its delinquency rates.

THE TRADITIONAL SOCIAL DISORGANIZATION MODEL

In 1921, Clifford Shaw and his colleagues began compiling a record of the home addresses of all male juveniles referred to the Cook County (Illinois) Juvenile Court that eventually spanned the years 1900 to 1965 (for a full description of this project, see Bursik, 1988; Bursik & Grasmick, 1993a). The data were aggregated into a series of discrete periods, and the residential locations of each of these individuals were plotted on a map of Chicago for each of these temporal groupings. On the basis of visual inspections of these maps, as well as through the use of some rudimentary statistical models, Shaw and McKay (1942) reached two very important conclusions. First, the relative distribution of delinquency rates remained fairly stable over time among Chicago's neighborhoods despite dramatic changes in the ethnic and racial composition of these neighborhoods. This led them to conclude that "[I]n the face of these facts, it is difficult to sustain the contention that, by themselves, the factors of race, nativity, and nationality are vitally related to the problem of juvenile delinquency" (1942, p. 162). That is, they argued that the observed local community variation in delinquency rates was primarily a function of certain features of the neighborhoods in which adolescents resided and not due to differences in the racial and ethnic composition of the juvenile population.

The second pattern suggested by these data was equally important: Delinquency rates were negatively correlated with the distance of the neighborhood from the central business district of Chicago. Since Burgess's (1925) earlier Chicago research had documented the existence of a strong positive correlation between the economic status of residential areas and distance from the center of the city, this finding indicated that delinquency rates were negatively correlated with the economic composition of local communities. However, Shaw and McKay did not propose that there was a simple direct relationship between such economic processes and the likelihood of delinquency. Rather, drawing from with the theory of human ecology developed by Burgess (1925) and Park and Burgess (1924), they argued that areas characterized by economic deprivation tended to have high rates of population turnover because they were undesirable residential communities and people abandoned them as soon as it became economically feasible. In addition, since poor neighborhoods were more likely to serve as the locations of initial settlement for new immigrant groups, economically depressed areas also tended to be characterized by racial and ethnic heterogeneity. Shaw and McKay argued that in turn, rapid population change and heterogeneity were likely to result in *social disorganization*, a concept they adopted from the seminal work of Thomas and Znaniecki (1920, p. 1131), which referred to the declining influence of existing social rules of behavior (such as those pertaining to criminal activity) on individual members of the community. This declining influence of rules was seen by Shaw and McKay as the primary cause of high neighborhood delinquency rates.

Although the social disorganization framework was a central component of American criminology for many years, a number of important shortcomings led to its demise (see Bursik, 1988; Bursik & Grasmick, 1993a). Two are of particular importance for the purposes of this chapter. First, the influence of economic deprivation on delinquency is assumed to be exclusively indirect, that is, it has an effect on the rates of illegal juvenile behavior only to the extent that it affects residential turnover and heterogeneity, which in turn affect the likelihood of social disorganization. Therefore, once the effects of these mediating factors have been taken into account, the correlation between the economic composition of an area and its level of juvenile crime should fall to zero (see Bursik & Grasmick, 1993b). However, studies have documented the existence of relatively impoverished communities that are stable, well-organized neighborhoods yet nevertheless have long traditions of high rates of delinquency (see, for example, Gans, 1962; Whyte, 1981).

Second, Shaw and McKay did not provide an extensively developed discussion of the social disorganization concept itself, of the mechanisms through which it might be expected to arise in high turnover, heterogeneous neighborhoods, nor of why delinquency might be an expected outcome. This problem was further compounded by the fact that due to their reliance on census and published agency statistics, they were not able to incorporate any direct empirical indicators of disorganization into their model and therefore could only infer its effects. In addition, the language of Shaw and McKay sometimes did not clearly differentiate between the presumed outcome of disorganization (i.e., delinquency) and disorganization itself. This led a number of criminologists to mistakenly (but understandably) equate social disorganization with the phenomenon it was intended to explain (see Lander, 1954). As a result, the concept of social disorganization increasingly came to be viewed as tautological and of little theoretical relevance.

Because of these and other problems, the social disorganization perspective eventually was seen by many as a framework of only historical interest with little relevance for contemporary criminology. However, the model experienced a dramatic revival during the 1980s when a number of criminologists recognized that some of these theoretical shortcomings could be resolved by reformulating the concept of social disorganization within the context of recent developments in urban and structural sociology.

THE CONTEMPORARY SOCIAL DISORGANIZATION APPROACH

The Systemic Reformulation[1]

One of the hallmarks of the modern reformulation of the social disorganization framework has been a focus on the regulatory capacity of a neighborhood that is embedded in the structure of that community's affiliational, interactional, and communication ties among the residents. Bursik and Grasmick (1993a,b), for example, define disorganization as the inability of a neighborhood to exercise the kinds of social control through these networks that are necessary to achieve the shared goal of the residents to live in an area relatively free from the threat of serious crime. Sampson, Raudenbush, and Earls' (1997, p. 919) closely related concept of "collective efficacy" broadens the assumption of local consensus to include not only a desire to control crime, but also the effective supervision of children and the maintenance of public order.[2] Since the development of this approach has been influenced strongly by models of human ecology that assume that local communities are "complex systems of friendship and kinship networks, and formal and informal associational ties rooted in family life and personal socialization requirements" (Berry & Kasarda, 1977, p. 56), the contemporary version of Shaw and McKay's theory often is referred to as the *systemic* social disorganization model of community crime rates (see Taylor, 1997).

The systemic approach to delinquency has made it much easier to conceptually differentiate social disorganization from the ecological processes that make the regulation of neighborhood activities difficult and from the rates of delinquency that may be a result. For example, since relational networks are difficult to establish and maintain when a community is characterized by rapid population turnover, high levels of residential instability are assumed to lead to low capacities for neighborhood regulation (see Bursik & Grasmick, 1993a, p. 33). Likewise, the work of Merry (1981) suggests that racial and ethnic heterogeneity can significantly decrease the degree to which relational networks span the various subgroups living in a community, since mutual distrust often exists among these groups. Thus, the regulatory capacity of an area's network structure is expected to be relatively low in areas characterized by high levels of racial and ethnic heterogeneity.

Two characteristics of these networks are especially relevant to the control of delinquent behavior. The first represents the kind of networks that are found in a community. Drawing from the work of Hunter (1985), Bursik and Grasmick (1993a, 1995) have delineated three basic network levels, each associated with a different potential for social control (see the extensive discussion of Taylor, 1997). The *private* level of control focuses on networks that integrate juveniles into the intimate informal primary groups of a neighborhood; especially relevant for the control of delinquency are those groups with multigenerational memberships. It is through these associations that information is transmitted concerning expectations of appropriate behavior, and if those expectations are violated, the networks are used to impose various informal sanctions on the offending member. The second, or *parochial* level of control represents networks in which the relationships among the members of the system do not have the same degree of intimacy as at the private level. For example, a resident may informally keep an eye on the public activities of local children with whom she or he is familiar, or may alert fellow neighbors to the presence of outsiders who might be considered threatening.

Sullivan (1989) has used rich ethnographic material to illustrate how such factors can account in part for the differences in delinquency that he observed in three New York neighborhoods. Unfortunately, the quantitative evidence concerning the private and parochial control of delinquency is at best mixed. The work of Sampson and Groves (1989) and Sampson et al. (1997) provides strong support for the relevance of these two considerations for local community crime control. On the other hand, Elliott et al. (1996) present evidence that while the degree to which juveniles are integrated into local networks is negatively related to the likelihood of problem behavior in Denver, this is not the case in Chicago. Likewise, the research of Simcha-Fagan and Schwartz (1986) provides only limited support for the systemic model of delinquency. However, the findings of both studies should be viewed with some caution, for the observed between-neighborhood variation in these systemic factors was relatively modest in the Elliott et al. study, and the data analyzed by Simcha-Fagan and Schwartz were collected in a very limited number of neighborhoods. Nevertheless, such contrary evidence suggests that we are far from fully understanding the systemic dynamics associated with the control of delinquency.

A third type of systemic network that has been proposed by Hunter as well as Bursik and Grasmick departs significantly from the traditional orientation of Shaw and McKay. A large body of work (such as Spergel & Korbelik, 1979) has shown that externally determined contingencies can mitigate the ability of local networks and institutions to control the threat of crime. The important role of such external factors has been documented consistently in the resource mobilization literature, where it has been found that for a social movement to be successful, it is necessary to develop effective linkages between the social movement and other groups outside the collectivity (McCarthy & Zald, 1987). Contemporary systemic approaches refer to the regulatory capacities that may develop as a result of such external as the *public* level of control. This component of the systemic model will be discussed more fully in the final section of this chapter.

In addition to the focus on the kinds of local networks, systemic theories of delinquency also focus on variation in the structure of local networks. In part, this represents a response to the criticism that Shaw and McKay failed to recognize that social organization can take many forms. For example, although two communities may have strong networks of private control, these networks can differ significantly along a number of dimensions. The most basic source of such variation pertains to the size of the networks that are found in a community, that is, the number of people who are bound together through formal or informal ties. Sampson and Groves, for example, found that British neighborhoods in which respondents report relatively high average numbers of friends within a 15-minute walk of their homes have significantly lower rates of property crime.

A second commonly discussed dimension of systemic variation represents the degree to which the networks span the various groups residing in the area or what has been referred to as closure (see the discussion of Sampson, 1995). Greenberg, Rohe, and Williams (1985), for example, report that residents are not likely to intercede in illegal events that involve strangers and are reluctant to assume responsibility for the welfare of property that belongs to people whom they barely know. Therefore, the social boundaries that may exist between groups in heterogeneous neighborhoods can decrease the breadth of supervisory activities because of mutual distrust among groups in such areas. For the purposes of delinquency control, the suspiciousness with which older residents of a neighborhood may regard the young is especially important in this regard.

Although criminological research has yet to fully explore the implications of network closure, the potential importance of this structural characteristic of the neighborhood was apparent to Shaw over 50 years ago and was one of his central emphases when he created the Chicago Area Project (CAP), one of the oldest (and still ongoing) delinquency control–prevention projects in the United States (see Finestone, 1976, pp. 127–128). Shaw felt that for delinquency prevention activities to be effective, they first had to become the activities of the adults that constituted the natural social world of the neighborhood youth. Although there was not a standard program that was instituted in every community targeted by CAP, all activities were designed to bring community adults into meaningful contact with local youths, thereby creating linkages that spanned these two neighborhood constituencies. For example, many areas created "detached worker" programs, in which young adults were hired to develop informal but intimate relationships with local juveniles. He or she was expected to spend as much time as possible with adolescents during afterschool and evening hours and to be alert for the presence of youths with serious emotional or mental problems. Most importantly, he or she was to "embody for emulation by local youth a model of 'conventional' moral and social values" (Schlossman & Sedlak, 1983, p. 42).

Although there are many other structural characteristics of neighborhood networks that are potentially relevant to our understanding of the community context of delinquent behavior, the difficulty and expense entailed in collecting such data on a large scale has led to the typical focus on size and closure noted in the preceding section. However, it has become increasingly apparent that while all multigenerational networks have the potential to act as agencies of social control, such structures facilitate a wide range of expressive and instrumental exchanges, not all of which are directly related to the control of delinquency. For example,

Anderson (1993) has shown that some inner-city parents with very strong bonds of attachment to and conventional aspirations for their children do not always socialize them fully in accordance with standard middle-class expectations for fear that it may foster the likelihood of victimization "on the streets." Therefore, while the existence of large and spanning network linkages may be necessary conditions for the prevention and control, they certainly are not sufficient.

Social Capital

It has been increasingly recognized that the failure to account for the content of the interchanges that occur among network members has been an important shortcoming of the systemic model. In response, a growing number of researchers have begun to examine the degree to which systemic network linkages are used to transfer the kinds of social capital to the youth of a community that make it less likely that they become involved in crime.

Although the term "social capital" was introduced into the social sciences by Loury (1977), it has received its fullest attention in the work of Coleman (1990) and refers to the capability of achieving shared goals that is created through resources that are transmitted through socially structured relationships among individuals in groups (see Hagan, Merkens, & Boehuke, 1995). Coleman (1990, pp. 310–311) explicitly notes that one of the most important of these goals is the achievement of social control. That is, social capital refers not only to the transmission of group norms and expectations pertaining to appropriate behavior for neighborhood youth, but also to the imposition of a wide variety of informal negative sanctions if those expectations are violated (see Taylor, 1997; Bursik, 1999).

While it is generally uncontested that a sensitivity to the opinion and potential reactions of significant others acts as a powerful constraint on criminal behavior, the critical question for the systemic model is the degree to which this form of social capital is transmitted through neighborhood-based association structures (see Sampson, 1997). This is an especially important consideration because, as Coleman observes (1990, p. 302), social capital is not fungible, that is, it is function-specific and not relevant to all outcomes. For example, some forms of nonconforming behavior may be tolerated by the members of a group as long as they do not interfere with the attainment of some other goal (Janowitz, 1976, pp. 9–10). That is, the social capital imbedded in neighborhood relational networks will serve as an effective source of delinquency control to the extent that adolescents perceive that these linkages are likely to be used to administer negative sanctions in response to illegal behavior. Such perceptions are not assured, for a youth may have strong linkages to a set of neighbors, both adult and adolescent, but those ties may be based on considerations unrelated to crime.

Although social capital (especially that which accrues from intergenerational relationships) has received a growing amount of attention in criminology (see, for example, Hagan, 1993; Hagan et al., 1995; Sullivan, 1989), only recently have attempts been made to formally integrate its dynamics into systemic theories of local community crime (see Sampson, 1997). As a result, few large-scale quantitative neighborhood studies have incorporated direct measures of this concept into their study designs, and some, such as Bursik (1999), have focused on criminal rather than delinquent behavior.

A major exception is the Project on Human Development in Chicago Neighborhoods (PHDCN), directed by Felton Earls of Harvard University. Although this project still is ongoing at the time of this writing, an initial report (Sampson et al., 1997) provides strong support for the viability of such an approach. The residents of 343 "neighborhood clusters" were asked to report the likelihood that their fellow neighbors would intervene if children were skipping school and hanging out on a street corner, if children were spray painting graffiti on a local building, if children were showing disrespect to an adult, if a fight broke out in front of their house, and if the fire station closest to their home was threatened with budget cuts. The "collective efficacy" scale based in part on these items was strongly and negatively associated with community levels of violence, victimization, and homicide.

In closing this section, it must be noted that despite the important theoretical and analytic advances that have been made in community studies of delinquency since the early 1980s, significant measurement problems continue to plague social capital–systemic neighborhood research. Until richer network data become available, any conclusions that are drawn concerning this model must be considered preliminary. Nevertheless, initial findings such as those noted in this section are very promising.

NEIGHBORHOOD ECONOMIC DEPRIVATION AND DELINQUENCY

As noted above, one of the central theoretical assumptions of the Shaw and McKay model of social disorganization was that the effect of economic deprivation on delinquency was strictly indirect, mediated by the effects of residential turnover, population heterogeneity, and social disorganization. Therefore, the logical underpinnings of the framework would be called into serious question if the economic composition of a neighborhood continued to have a significant direct effect on delinquency after controlling for these factors. Unfortunately, this appeared to be the case when evidence was presented by urban sociologists indicating that many cities had highly stable, organized neighborhoods that nevertheless had long traditions of poverty and crime.

The documentation of such exceptions to the Shaw and McKay predictions in itself does not call the entire framework into question, for such neighborhoods might simply be random anomalies. However, Bursik and Grasmick (1993b) recently reexamined this issue using more sophisticated statistical tools than were available to Shaw and McKay. As expected by the social disorganization model, the strongest predictors of delinquency rates in Chicago's neighborhoods were indicators of the regulatory capacities of these communities. Nevertheless, the direct effect of economic deprivation remained persistent and significant. Similar results have been presented by Peterson and Krivo (1993), Sampson et al. (1997), and others.

The theoretical implications of these findings are not trivial. As noted by Bursik (1988), the traditional social disorganization (and, by extension, systemic) model is a group-level formulation of control theory (see Hirschi, 1969). This framework assumes that since delinquency is a "rational" means of obtaining desirable resources with a minimum of time and effort, everyone is motivated to engage in such behavior. Therefore, the critical question is not what causes someone to engage in delinquency, but rather what holds someone back from engaging in delinquency. These controls are represented in the systemic model by the degree to which network structures conducive to the transmission of social capital are present in a neighborhood. That is, the more social capital that a juvenile has obtained from within the neighborhood, the greater the costs of illegal behavior. However, the persistence of the economic deprivation effect suggests certain motivation processes may be operating.

Shaw and McKay attempted to resolve this dilemma by introducing the notion of "delinquency traditions" that were transmitted from generation to generation of residents in some communities (see Bursik & Grasmick, 1993b). Such traditions were assumed to arise because children from lower-class communities were exposed to a diverse set of norms and standards of behavior. These included those held by residents whose moral values were in "direct opposition to conventionality as symbolized by the family, the church, and other institutions common to our general society ... (even) within the same community, theft may be defined as right and proper in some groups" (Shaw & McKay, 1942, p. 171). The tautological and logical problems with this solution have been discussed extensively elsewhere (Kornhauser, 1978). For the purposes of this chapter, it is sufficient to note that it contradicts the basic systemic assumption that all neighborhood residents desire an existence relatively free from the threat of serious crime. Without such an underlying consensual premise, the rationale of the systemic model disappears. Therefore, it is no exaggeration to state that the successful explanation of the economic deprivation effect in a manner that is logically consistent with the other elements of the model is the most critical challenge faced by contemporary systemic theorists.

Recent developments suggest that such a resolution indeed is possible. As has been widely discussed, the ecological structures of many cities are very different from what they were during the time of Shaw and McKay. In the traditional human ecology framework that had such a great influence on their approach, the availability of unskilled jobs in manufacturing industries provided relatively open access to the occupational structure of urban areas. Unfortunately, as industries moved into suburban and rural areas, those jobs that fostered the eventual ability of the urban poor to be occupationally mobile have become decreasingly available to the residents of central city neighborhoods. In addition, as noted by Wilson (1987, p. 101), the 33 largest central cities in the United States experienced dramatic increases in the size of their African-American populations between 1950 and 1980. When coupled with the concomitant decreases in the white populations during the same period, "underclass" neighborhoods predominantly populated by extremely poor, minority-status residents were a common feature of most urban areas.

Such neighborhoods certainly existed during the time of Shaw and McKay. The major difference is that the economic changes noted above have eliminated many of the unskilled jobs that traditionally provided the initial entry for disadvantaged groups into the occupational system (Wilson, 1987, p. 102). In addition, such dynamics have led to the increased disengagement of these neighborhoods from the economic, social, and political environments in which they are embedded, further exacerbating the problematic nature of daily life. Wilson has referred to the outcome of these processes as the "concentration effects" of poverty in which the residents are "overwhelmingly socially disadvantaged" (p. 144).

Such dynamics have been shown to be closely related not only to the transmission of the kinds of social capital relevant to delinquency control, but also those relevant to conventional economic achievement (Coleman, 1990). Recent research has indicated that these two forms of social capital can be mutually reinforcing in their effects on illegal adolescent behavior. Sullivan (1989), for example, presents convincing evidence that the differences in the kinds of delinquent behavior engaged in by the juvenile residents of his three study communities reflected the degree to which the adults in those communities were integrated into the broader institutions of the metropolitan area and the social capital that such embeddedness enabled them to transmit to the younger generation. This was especially the case in terms of the "alternative legal and illegal opportunities for gaining income" that existed in these areas (Sullivan, 1989, p. 202). Similarly, Anderson (1990, p. 57) has shown that the limited employment opportunities for poor blacks in the Northton community that he studied not only made the underground economy of drugs and vice seem attractive to young residents, but it also undermined "the interpersonal trust and moral cohesion that once prevailed." As Anderson later observes:

> Northton is thought to embody a "little tradition" and has the reputation of being economically depressed and beset by classic urban ills: drugs, crime, illiteracy, poverty, and a

> high proportion of female-headed families on welfare, as well as one of the highest infant mortality rates in the country. (p. 239)

In light of such evidence, the critical questions for the systemic social disorganization theory is whether the economic disengagement of neighborhoods in itself fosters the motivation to engage in crime and whether the persistence of such a tradition represents the existence of an alternative cultural system.

Years ago, Whyte (1981) observed that "Cornerville's problem is not lack of organization but failure of its organization to mesh with the structure of the society around it" (p. 273). Drawing from this observation, Bursik and Grasmick (1993a,b) suggested that a full consideration of the public level of systemic control described above can account for the residual effects of economic deprivation on criminal behavior.[3] That is, public systemic networks that link neighborhoods to the broader urban milieu also are sources of social capital. If these linkages do not exist or are very weak, that capital related to local social control is not forthcoming, resulting in few constraints on illegal behavior. Likewise, the lack of public networks can undermine the perceived legitimacy of the social capital embodied in private and parochial networks, especially if the members of these networks are viewed as representatives of an irrelevant external conventional order.[4] Therefore, it is possible to account for the findings of Sullivan and Anderson from a control theoretic perspective.

Relatedly, the existence of a "tradition" of crime in a neighborhood does not necessarily entail the existence of a cultural system that endorses such behavior, as suggested by Shaw and McKay. In fact, Kornhauser (1978) and others have presented very strong evidence that such subcultures do not exist in the United States. Rather, drawing from the classic work of Matza and Sykes (1961), the recent research of Hagan, Hefler, Classen, Boehnke, and Merkens (1998) suggests that such traditions might more profitably be viewed as a system of "subterranean values" that are not strongly opposed to the dominant norms and values of American society. That is, the fact that one has been raised in a society that emphasizes economic success, competition, and individualism yet lives in a residential area that is so marginalized that it is impossible to pursue these goals makes it likely that norms against criminal behavior may be "neutralized," that is, not rejected and replaced by alternatives, but simply made temporarily inoperative. Therefore, what is passed from generation to generation in such neighborhoods is not an alternative cultural system, but a set of situations in which it is considered appropriate to violate beliefs concerning proper behavior. If a neighborhood eventually is able to reengage itself with the broader economic and political system, it is expected that the level of such neutralization would decrease dramatically. Thus, the patterns observed by researchers such as Anderson and Sullivan can be accounted for purely in terms of the structure of public networks without resorting to a cultural explanation.

Obviously, many of the propositions made in this section will remain in the realm of conjecture until large-scale studies have been designed to test these hypotheses. However, the fact that it is possible to offer an explanation for the patterns found in contemporary research without violating the core assumptions of the systemic model indicates that the promise of this model has just begun to be realized.

CONCLUSION

This chapter has attempted to provide a general sense of the contemporary criminological understanding of the link between delinquent behavior and the community context in which it unfolds. There is no question that despite the fact that neighborhood delinquency research has one of the longest traditions in American criminology, our understanding of these relationships still is very rudimentary. Nevertheless, the numerous consistent findings that have emerged over many decades of study indicate that theories of delinquency that fail to take these considerations into account are at best incomplete, and at worst misleading.

ENDNOTES

1. Although a large body of research has been conducted within the systemic framework, most of this work has focused on adult crime. In this review the discussion has been restricted to those studies which have focused specifically on delinquency, unless otherwise noted.
2. The "collective efficacy" model of Sampson et al. (1997) is nearly identical to the systemic theory of social disorganization described in this section. However, the use of this alternative terminology has the advantage of avoiding much of the intellectual baggage associated with the traditional social disorganization framework.
3. The direct effect of economic deprivation that persists after controls for residential turnover, population heterogeneity, and social disorganization have been made.
4. See Anderson's (1990) discussion of the "old heads" in Northton.

REFERENCES

Abrahamson, M. (1996). *Urban enclaves: Identity and place in America*. New York: St. Martin's Press.

Anderson, E. (1990). *Streetwise: Race, class, and change in an urban community*. Chicago: University of Chicago Press.

Anderson, E. (1993, May). Violence and the inner-city poor. *Atlantic*, pp. 81–94.

Berry, B. J. L., & Kasarda, J. D. (1977). *Contemporary urban ecology*. New York: Macmillan.

Blackman, F. W., & Burgess, E. W. (1917). *Lawrence social survey*. Lawrence, KA: University of Kansas, Department of Sociology.

Breckenridge, S. P., & Abbott, E. (1912). *The delinquent child and the home*. New York: Charities Publication Committee.

Burgess, E. W. (1925). The growth of the city. In R. E. Park, E. W. Burgess, & R. D. McKenzie (Eds.), *The city* (pp. 47–62). Chicago: University of Chicago Press.

Bursik, R. J., Jr. (1988). Social disorganization and theories of crime and delinquency: Problems and prospects. *Criminology*, *26*, 519–551.

Bursik, R. J., Jr. (1998). The informal control of crime through neighborhood networks. *Sociological Focus*, *32*, 85–97.

Bursik, R. J., Jr., & Grasmick, H. G. (1993a). *Neighborhoods and crime. The dimensions of effective community control*. New York: Lexington.

Bursik, R. J., Jr., & Grasmick, H. G. (1993b). Economic deprivation and neighborhood crime rates, 1960–1980. *Law and Society Review*, *27*, 263–283.

Bursik, R. J., Jr., & Grasmick, H. G. (1995). Neighborhood-based networks and the control of crime and delinquency. In H. D. Barlow (Ed.), *Crime and public policy* (pp. 107–130). Boulder, CO: Westview Press.

Coleman, J. S. (1990). *Foundations of social theory*. Cambridge, MA: Harvard University Press.

Elliott, D. S., Wilson, W. J., Huizinga, D., Sampson, R. J., Elliott, A., & Rankin, B. (1996). The effects of neighborhood disadvantage on adolescent development. *Journal of Research in Crime and Delinquency*, *33*, 389–426.

Finestone, H. (1976). *Victims of change: Juvenile delinquents in American society*. Westport, CT: Greenwood Press.

Gans, H. J. (1962). *The urban villagers*. New York: Free Press.

Greenberg, S. W., Rohe, W. M., & Williams, J. R. (1985). *Informal citizen action and crime prevention at the neighborhood level*. Washington, DC: National Institute of Justice.

Hagan, J. (1993). The social embeddedness of crime and unemployment. *Criminology*, *31*, 465–491.

Hagan, J., Merkens, H., & Boehuke, K. (1995). Delinquency and disdain: Social capital and the control of right-wing extremism among East and West Berlin youth. *American Journal of Sociology*, *100*, 1028–1052.

Hagan, J., Hefler, G., Classen, G., Boehnke, K., & Merkens, H. (1998). Subterranean sources of subcultural delinquency beyond the American dream. *Criminology*, *36*, 309–342.

Hill, H. M., & Madhere, S. (1996). Exposure to community violence and African-American children: A multidimensional model of risks and resources. *Journal of Community Psychology*, *24*, 26–43.

Hirschi, T. (1969). *Causes of delinquency*. Berkeley: University of California Press.

Hunter, A. J. (1985). Private, parochial and public orders: The problem of crime and incivility in urban communities. In G. D. Suttles & M. H. Zald (Eds.), *The challenge of social control: Citizenship and institution building in modern society* (pp. 230–242). Norwood, NJ: Ablex.

Janowitz, M. (1976). *Social control of the welfare state*. New York: Elsevier.

Kornhauser, R. R. (1978). *Social sources of delinquency*. Chicago: University of Chicago Press.

Lander, B. (1954). *Toward an understanding of juvenile delinquency*. New York: Columbia University Press.

Loury, G. (1977). A dynamic theory of racial income differences. In P. A. Wallace & A. Le Mund (Eds.), *Women, minorities, and employment discrimination* (pp. 153–186). Lexington, MA: Lexington.

Matza, D., & Sykes, G. (1961). Juvenile delinquency and subterranean values. *American Sociological Review*, *28*, 712–720.

McCarthy, J. D., & Zald, M. N. (1987). Resource mobilization and social movements: A partial theory. In M. N. Zald & J. D. McCarthy (Eds.), *Social movements in an organizational society* (pp. 15–42). New Brunswick, NJ: Transaction.

McKay, H. D. (1949). The neighborhood and child conduct. *Annals of the American Academy of Political and Social Science*, *262*, 32–41.

Merry, S. E. (1981). *Urban danger: Life in a neighborhood of strangers*. Philadelphia: Temple University Press.

Park, R. E., & Burgess, E. W. (1924). *Introduction to the science of sociology*, 2nd ed. Chicago: University of Chicago Press.

Peterson, R. D., & Krivo, L. J. (1993). Racial segregation and black urban homicide. *Social Forces*, *71*, 1001–1026.

Pretty, G. M., Conroy, C., Dugay, J., Fowler, K., & Williams, D. (1996). Sense of community and its relevance to adolescents of all ages. *Journal of Community Psychology*, *24*, 365–379.

Sampson, R. J. (1995). Communities. In J. Q. Wilson & J. Petersilia (Eds.), *Crime* (pp. 40–67). San Francisco: ICS Press, Institute for Contemporary Studies.

Sampson, R. J. (1997). The embeddedness of child and adolescent development: A community-level perspective on urban violence. In J. McCord (Ed.), *Violence and childhood in the inner city* (pp. 31–77). Cambridge: Cambridge University Press.

Sampson, R. J., & Groves, W. B. (1989). Community structure and crime: Testing social-disorganization theory. *American Journal of Sociology*, *53*, 766–779.

Sampson, R. J., Raudenbush, S. W., & Earls, F. (1997). Neighborhoods and violent crime: A multilevel study of collective efficacy. *Science*, *277*, 918–924.

Schlossman, S., & Sedlak, M. (1983). *The Chicago area project revisited*. Santa Monica, CA: Rand Corporation.

Shaw, C. R., & McKay, H. D. (1931). *Social factors in juvenile delinquency. National Commission on Law Observation and Enforcement*. Washington, DC: US Government Printing Office.

Shaw, C. R., & McKay, H. D. (1942). *Juvenile delinquency and urban areas*. Chicago: University of Chicago Press.

Shaw, C. R., & McKay, H. D. (1969). *Juvenile delinquency and urban areas*, 2nd ed. Chicago: University of Chicago Press.

Shaw, C. R., Zorbaugh, F. M., McKay, H. D., & Cottrell, L. S. (1929). *Delinquency areas*. Chicago: University of Chicago Press.

Simcha-Fagan, O., & Schwartz, J. E. (1986). Neighborhood and delinquency: An assessment of contextual effects. *Criminology*, *24*, 667–703.

Simon, R. J. (1985). *Public opinion and the immigrant: Print media coverage, 1880–1980*. Lexington, MA: Lexington.

Spergel, I. A., & Korbelik, J. (1979). *The local community service system and ISOS: An interorganizational analysis*. Chicago: Executive Report to the Illinois Law Enforcement Commission.

Sullivan, M. L. (1989). *Getting paid: Youth crime and work in the inner city*. Ithaca, NY: Cornell University Press.

Taylor, R. B. (1997). Social order and disorder of street blocks and neighborhoods: Ecology, microecology, and the systemic model of social disorganization. *Journal of Research in Crime and Delinquency 34*, 113–155.

Thomas, W. I., & Znaniecki, F. (1920). *The Polish peasant in Europe and America*, Vol. IV. Boston: Gorham Press.

Whyte, W. F. (1981). *Street corner society*, 3rd ed. Chicago: University of Chicago Press. (Originally published 1955)

Wilson, W. J. (1987). *The truly disadvantaged: The inner city, the underclass, and public policy*. Chicago: University of Chicago Press.

14

Segregation and Youth Criminal Violence

A Review and Agenda

RUTH D. PETERSON, LAUREN J. KRIVO, and MARIA B. VÉLEZ

It is widely known that youth, as both offenders and victims, are disproportionately involved in serious and violent crime in the United States. Youth offenders, aged 10 to 19, accounted for 28% of all arrests for violent crime but composed only 14% of the total US population in 1995 (Federal Bureau of Investigation, 1996; US Bureau of the Census, 1995). Youth aged 12 to 19 are victimized at higher rates than persons in any other age category; in particular, their rate is at least twice that of any group 25 and older. In 1993, the personal crime victimization rate of persons aged 12 to 15 was 125 per 1000 while that for persons aged 16 to 19 was 121 per 1000 (US Department of Justice, 1995). This victimization rate drops precipitously to 61 per 1000 by age 25 to 34. Clearly, relative to other age groups youth are at a substantially greater risk of criminal behavior and victimization.

Further, the gap between youth and adult crime levels has widened in recent years as criminal risks for the young have increased more rapidly than for other age groups. From 1989 to 1993, arrests for violent crimes increased by 9% for adults, in contrast to an alarming 36% for juveniles (Federal Bureau of Investigation, 1994). And since the early 1990s, overall violent index crimes actually have decreased slightly each year while youth violence has continued to climb (Snyder & Sickmund, 1995). These trends clearly indicate that violent crime among youth is a major and growing problem in the United States. Indeed, such patterns have prompted Federal Bureau of Investigation (FBI) Director, Louis J. Freeh to remark on the "ominous increase in juvenile crime," which when "coupled with population trends portend future crime and violence at nearly unprecedented levels" (Federal Bureau of Investigation, 1995, p. 1).

However, these trends do not affect all groups equally nor are they evenly distributed

RUTH D. PETERSON, LAUREN J. KRIVO, and MARIA B. VÉLEZ • Department of Sociology, Ohio State University, Columbus, Ohio 43210.

Handbook of Youth and Justice, edited by White. Kluwer Academic / Plenum Publishers, New York, 2001.

across geographic areas. Most notably, African Americans account for a disproportionately large share of arrests for violent crime (44%) (Federal Bureau of Investigation, 1996) and as such have dramatically higher rates than whites; arrest rates for violent crimes are five to six times higher for blacks than whites (US Department of Justice, 1995). Crime also is more of a problem for urban communities. Violent crime rates are notably higher in cities (920 per 100,000 persons) than in suburban or rural areas (428 and 253 per 100,000 persons, respectively) (Federal Bureau of Investigation, 1996). In combination, these patterns suggest that criminal violence affects black urban youth more severely than other populations.

EXPLAINING THE PATTERNS

Scholars have sought to understand why crime is so prevalent among urban African Americans, especially those who are young. Increasingly, racial residential segregation is seen as a possible explanation. There are two mechanisms that might link segregation to higher levels of violent crime among youth in predominantly black urban neighborhoods: ascriptive inequality and social isolation.

Segregation and Ascriptive Inequality

First, segregation is a central expression of racial inequality and such inequality has long been linked to heightened violence. For example, among contemporary scholars, a major perspective on black violence emphasizes the criminogenic consequences of social and economic inequality experienced by African-Americans in the United States (Balkwell, 1990; Blau & Blau, 1982; Braithwaite, 1979). This explanation is partly grounded in Merton's (1968) social structure and anomie thesis as well as Coser's (1968) analysis of deprivation, discrimination, and diffuse aggression. In general, inequality perspectives link criminal and deviant behavior as a response to the deprivation experienced by certain segments of the population when there is a disjuncture between cultural goals (economic success) and structural arrangements (socioeconomic resources). This disjuncture results in feelings of frustration and alienation that are reflected in criminal and deviant patterns.

Blau and Blau (1982) argue that the expression of such frustration in the form of violent crime is particularly pronounced when economic inequality is based on ascriptive characteristics like race. This frustration occurs because such inequality is viewed as illegitimate in democratic societies such as the United States where access to resources should not be based upon ascribed criteria. When ascriptive inequality occurs, ethnic and class differences are reinforced and pervasive conflict is engendered. Due to the weak political power of "have-nots," which accompanies ascriptive inequality, racially and ethnically disadvantaged groups are unable to organize successful collective action (e.g., strikes, boycotts). Instead, the conflict and hostilities engendered by ascriptive inequality find expression in diffuse aggression, including criminal violence.

How does segregation fit into this framework? Black–white residential segregation is one of the most central and enduring dimensions of racial inequality in the United States (Alba & Logan, 1993; Farley & Frey, 1994; Frey & Farley, 1996; Massey & Denton, 1987, 1988). In 1990, residential separation between blacks and whites was so high that an average of 69.4% of metropolitan blacks (or whites) would have had to change their neighborhood of residence to achieve an even racial distribution (Harrison & Weinberg, 1992). In many places, black–white residential segregation is so high that it has been characterized as a pattern of hypersegregation, whereby blacks have virtually no contact with whites in their own or neighboring communities (Denton, 1994; Massey & Denton, 1989, 1993). Such segregation is heavily ascriptive as demonstrated in the large number of studies showing that black–white income differentials do not explain the high levels of residential segregation within US cities (Denton & Massey, 1988; Farley, 1977; Kain, 1986; Massey, 1979; Simkus, 1978; Zubrinsky, 1996). Further, considerable research makes clear that prejudice and discrimination in the housing market are the major mechanisms producing residential environments that are separated along racial lines (Bobo & Zubrinsky, 1996; Galster, 1987; Pearce, 1979; Schuman & Bobo, 1988; Turner, Struyk, & Yinger, 1991; Wienk, Reid, Simonson, & Eggers, 1979; Yinger, 1995; Zubrinsky & Bobo, 1996). Such pronounced segregation is associated with a number of negative social conditions in black neighborhoods, including heightened poverty, more physical deterioration, poorer schools, and higher crime rates (e.g., Galster & Keeney, 1988; Massey, 1990; Massey, Condron, & Denton, 1987).

Logan and Messner (1987) specify how racial residential segregation, as a form of ascriptive inequality, would be linked with increased levels of violent crime. They note:

> racial segregation imposes a significant barrier to black upward mobility and quality of life. Place of residence locates people not only in geographical space but also in networks of social opportunities—it influences prospects for employment, for public services, for educational advancement, for appreciation in home values, and more. Residential segregation by race accordingly implies that opportunities for achievement are limited for certain groups, and it conflicts with basic American value commitments which encourage members of all groups to strive for socioeconomic success. Such a "disjuncture" between structural arrangements and fundamental cultural values, Merton argued, tends to undermine the legitimacy of social norms and thereby promotes deviant behavior. (1987, p. 510).

Thus, Logan and Messner (1987) argue that high levels of racial segregation should result in feelings of greater resentment, frustration, hopelessness, and alienation among African-Americans. This, in turn, would be reflected in diffuse forms of aggression, including high rates of criminal violence.

Segregation and Social Isolation

The social isolation of disadvantaged segregated communities is a second mechanism that might link residential segregation to violent crime, as is suggested by the works of Wilson (1987, 1996) and Massey and Denton (1993). Segregation, however, would not directly produce violent crime, but rather is a macrosocial force that concentrates group disadvantage and increases social isolation. It is this concentration of disadvantage with its associated heightened isolation that links to violence. In particular, segregation creates a structural context in which group disadvantage is concentrated in geographically limited areas of the city (Massey, 1990; Massey & Eggers, 1990; Massey, Gross, & Eggers, 1991). Racial residential segregation means that levels of disadvantage for groups (e.g., high rates of poverty, male joblessness, and female-headed families) are confined to separate portions of the urban area. As Massey (1990) notes, when segregation is high, high or rising levels of poverty must be concentrated in the small number of areas where the segregated group lives. In other words, because group members themselves are not spread evenly across the urban area, their poverty cannot be distributed evenly across space. Rather, their poverty is "concentrated" in the neighborhoods where they live.

The concentration of disadvantage, in turn, is the structural condition that directly increases violence. As Krivo and Peterson (1996) argue, higher levels of violence in disadvantaged communities are promoted through the simultaneous effects of two forces: (1) the presence of conditions that encourage individuals to behave violently, and (2) the absence of mechanisms to discourage violence. A variety of conditions (socialization, role modeling, and adaptive behavior) encourage violence and facilitate its more common occurrence in areas in which disadvantage is highly concentrated. In these neighborhoods, residents observe that violence is a common response to conflict and stress. People witness more violent acts and learn to model this behavior from individuals who do not restrain their own violent impulses (Sampson & Wilson, 1995). Also among youth, ethnographic evidence suggests that peer pressure to engage in crime and violence is especially strong in such disadvantaged areas (e.g., Anderson, 1990; Bourgois, 1995). At the same time, Anderson (1990) notes that there are fewer "old heads" who teach the lesson that staying out of trouble and refraining from violence pays off. Moreover, this message has little credibility in contexts in which employment and other opportunities are relatively restricted.

Disadvantage that is highly concentrated also encourages an escalation of violent behavior as an adaptive response (Massey, 1996). As Wilson (1996) notes, drug trafficking and weapons have become more widespread in disadvantaged inner-city neighborhoods. In this setting, the use of threatening postures and violent behaviors become necessary defensive mechanisms for protecting one's life or helping to ensure economic and personal well-being. These behaviors can breed a cycle of violence in which one set of aggressive actions produces a violent response, which in turn fuels additional violence. In the context in which employment and other "legitimate" opportunities for advancement are severely limited, the potential gains in safety from violence outweigh the costs (social stigma and/or criminal punishment) of harming others.

In addition to crime-generating factors, violence is more prevalent in disadvantaged segregated communities because social control is undermined. This occurs at many levels. There are fewer informal networks among families, neighbors, and friends, making it more difficult for residents to identify strangers and monitor each other's property and safety as well as supervise peer groups (Sampson & Groves, 1989). Similarly, a relative lack of social and economic resources decreases the ability of residents to organize formally to fight crime, for example, neighborhood watches (Greenberg, Rohe, & Williams, 1982). Social control is further diminished by the relative absence of local organizations (churches, banks, schools, libraries, stores, recreation facilities) that provide jobs and services, keep people occupied, and foster mainstream values and conventional norms. Finally, highly disadvantaged neighborhoods may suffer from inadequate police protection. Such communities are subject to "benign neglect" in that there is insufficient deployment of police (Wacquant, 1993), and available police are less likely to respond at all or to respond immediately to calls from residents (Smith, 1986). Due to such limited informal and formal social control, the perceived costs associated with crime and violence are lessened and any possible deterrent effects are diminished.

Another way that segregation might impact crime and violence is through its direct effect on social control. (This deviates from the previous argument that segregation's effect on social control and violence might be mediated by the concentration of disadvantage.) For instance, segregated black communities have long suffered from direct disinvestment by business and government in ways that destabilize communities. Studies indicate that there is discrimination in the allotment of business and mortgage loans and property insurance to predominantly black neighborhoods (Bradbury, Case, & Dunham, 1989; Guy, Pol, & Ryker, 1982; Shlay, 1988, 1989; Yinger, 1995, Chapter 5). These actions lower homeownership rates in such areas, thereby decreasing the number of residents who are most invested in the community and its members. Businesses also have explicitly avoided locating in such areas (Cole & Deskins,

1989; Squires, 1994). Consequently, there are fewer businesses to provide jobs and to provide a sense of ongoing conventional activity and community viability (Skogan, 1990). Destabilization also occurs as a by-product of broader trends of deindustrialization that have decreased employment more in central city and minority areas than in other localities (Wilson, 1987, 1996; Squires, 1994). As manufacturing plants and other industries in these neighborhoods close, they often leave behind empty decrepit buildings and surrounding parking lots. As a whole, these structural forces undermine basic institutional structures that stabilize neighborhoods and foster mainstream values and conventional norms, and hence, increase violence.[1]

PREVIOUS RESEARCH

In brief, both inequality and social isolation perspectives provide theoretical reasons for expecting racial residential segregation to be linked with criminal violence in urban communities. Both explanations also suggest that racial minorities would be the groups most impacted by residential segregation. However, there is relatively little research evaluating these arguments, and therefore, our understanding of the relative validity of theoretical explanations described above is quite limited.

Among the few existing crime studies including segregation, some do not treat this variable as a central theoretical construct. In this line of research, segregation is just one of several indicators of macrostructural conditions included in multivariate models attempting to explain different type of crime rates (Rosenfeld, 1986; Sampson, 1985) or race differences in homicide (Potter, 1991). Rosenfeld (1986) and Sampson (1985) demonstrated that higher residential segregation is associated with higher levels of at least some types of violence. In particular, Rosenfeld (1986) found that residential segregation had a significant positive effect on murder and robbery (but not assault) rates in Standard Metropolitan Statistical Areas in 1970. Using race-specific homicide arrest rates for cities in that same year, Sampson (1985) also showed that residential segregation significantly increased white but not black homicides. Last, Potter (1991) demonstrated that residential isolation had a sizable and significant positive effect on the difference in homicide between blacks and whites in metropolitan areas. The lack of theoretical focus and the inconsistency in findings of these studies leave considerable room for more focused analyses of segregation's effect on violence.

Some other works, however, have begun to investigate segregation in order to evaluate the types of theoretical arguments previously described. Drawing on the inequality framework, Logan and Messner (1987) argue that residential segregation affects crime through its independent influence on hindering social and economic mobility for blacks. Thus they examine the effects of segregation on rates of suburban violent crime controlling for a variety of other macrosocial factors. They find mixed support for the segregation–inequality argument across different types of crime. For 1970, segregation had a significant effect on robbery and aggravated assault but not on homicide and rape. For 1980, segregation was related significantly to criminal homicide and robbery but not to rape and assault.

Most recently, Peterson and Krivo (1993) and Shihadeh and Flynn (1996) build on this work but also draw on social isolation arguments. Both studies demonstrate that there are strong effects of racial residential segregation on levels of black urban violence, and that these effects are not due solely to inequality. Peterson and Krivo (1993) assessed whether racial residential segregation and other race-specific ecological conditions affect black urban homicide victimization rates for 1980. They also sought to distinguish whether the effect of segregation was due to ascriptive inequality or social isolation. Peterson and Krivo (1993) found that black–white residential segregation has a stronger impact on homicide rates than any other structural predictor, including inter- and intraracial economic inequality. However, only the more public stranger and acquaintance killings (and not the more personal and private family homicides) are affected by segregation. They argue that this suggests that social isolation and its associated elements of diminished public social control are the mechanisms by which segregation leads to higher levels of homicide. Shihadeh and Flynn (1996) reinforce this conclusion in their analysis of the effects of varying measures of segregation on black urban violence. When they measure segregation in terms of black–white spatial isolation, they find that this factor is second only to population size in the strength of its influence on black urban robbery and homicide for 1990.

Peterson and Krivo (1999) explored further whether social isolation is the mechanism linking segregation to criminal homicide in a more recent paper. This paper tested the argument that segregation has an indirect effect on homicide through the way it spatially concentrates disadvantage and thereby socially isolates some groups (i.e., blacks). Their analysis of black compared to white homicides confirms this hypothesis. Segregation has an indirect effect on black killings that is mediated by the concentration of black disadvantage. There is no parallel effect of segregation on white homicide. The lack of a significant effect of segregation on white killings is expected, since disadvantaged whites tend not to be spatially separated from more affluent whites.[2]

A BETTER UNDERSTANDING OF SEGREGATION AND YOUTH VIOLENCE?

The above investigations indicate the importance of residential segregation for some aspects of violent crime. However, they do not give us a complete understanding of segregation's impact. In particular, studies have not explored the influence of segregation across the variety of different groups. As the above review indicates, existing research has considered crime within racial groups, with particular attention to African-American violence. These studies indicate that the influence of segregation is not the same for blacks and whites. However, other populations that may be particularly affected by the conditions associated with segregation have not been studied. For example, age distinctions are especially important and these have gone fully unexamined in this literature. In particular, the high levels of youth violence noted above with their overconcentration among inner-city blacks suggest the possibility that the isolating effects of segregation may be particularly important for African-American youth.

Why would this be the case? The answer is that the forces encouraging violent actions and discouraging the control of violent behavior may be more consequential for youth. First, the role modeling and socialization consequences of social isolation are particularly pertinent for persons who have not yet taken on more permanent adult roles and statuses, that is, young persons. Given this, the consequences of segregation and concentrated disadvantage would be most pronounced for this group. Second, these socialization consequences may take on even greater importance for youth in structurally disadvantaged contexts where adult supervision by parents, neighbors, and other community members is less prevalent. If informal observation and supervising networks in communities are directed disproportionately at overseeing youth activities, their relative absence will have especially pronounced consequences for crime among this age group. Third, we also noted that institutional resources may be a key to stabilizing areas and controlling crime. To the degree that local institutions such as recreation centers, libraries, churches, stores, other businesses and the like provide activities and jobs that occupy the time of young people and connect them to conventional activities during the many hours when they are not in school, institutional breakdown will heighten youth crime even more than that of other populations. Put simply, the absence of adult supervision and alternative institutional control mechanisms means that nonemployed young people have a great deal of time to "hang out" in settings like street corners. In such places, nonconventional role modeling and defensive posturing, including carrying weapons, may be more widespread, thereby leading to higher levels of youth crime. However, areas with a strong institutional base should provide many mainstream alternatives to such activities.

Unfortunately, prior research has not compared the sources of youth and adult crime in neighborhoods. Therefore, we do not know if these arguments are valid. Given the high levels of youth crime, it is imperative that scholars begin to address these issues empirically . Several types of studies should be on the research agenda. First, to assess whether segregation's impact is indeed greater for youth than adult crime, quantitative analyses of age disaggregated crime rates should be conducted. To do so, we should draw on the research models described above and compare the relative explanatory power of segregation, disadvantage, and other factors on crime for youth versus older age groups. Second, scholars should examine city-level effects of aggregate segregation and conduct refined analyses of neighborhoods classified by racial composition (e.g., predominantly African American, predominantly white, versus mixed neighborhoods). It also is important that these basic models be extended to examine a variety of additional questions such as: Are the relationships applicable to both youth offending and victimization rates? Are rates of youth violence similarly impacted across race, class, and sex backgrounds?

To date, analysts have not been able to address these questions due to a lack of available data. The only age-specific crime data available on a national level are unpublished arrest data provided by the FBI for aggregate units like cities. While these data give a broad picture, they are limited in that reported crimes do not always result in arrests, and all arrested persons are not associated unequivocally with the crimes in question (up to 47% of arrests are rejected for prosecution) (see Boland, Conly, Mahanna, Warner, & Sones, 1990; Zawitz, Gaskins, Koppel, Greenfeld, & Greenwood, 1988). One additional national source of data is the Supplementary Homicide Reports (SHR), which provide victims' and offenders' age, race, and other individual characteristics for homicide incidents. With these data, the types of analyses proposed here could be performed on homicide for cities or other police reporting units.

To perform more detailed analyses of crime incidents (rather than arrests) by age, researchers currently must obtain data directly from police departments. Therefore, they are dependent on the cooperation of police officials in providing relevant data. Given the difficulty of acquiring such cooperation, analyses of only a few selected jurisdictions are likely to result. Still, such case studies should be conducted, for they will provide important initial insights and set the stage for examining a wider range of units when appropriate data are available. For example, the FBI is currently in the process of switching from reporting only aggregated counts of crimes to incident-based reporting of crime similar to that available for homicide in the SHR. These data will allow for the age, race, and other disaggregated analyses suggested here and will take us a long way toward a more refined understanding of the influence of segregation on crime.

The quantitative analyses described above should be supplemented with two additional lines of research. One line would involve qualitative analyses of selected black and white neighborhoods with varying levels of disadvantage. Specifically, residents should be interviewed and neighborhoods observed with an eye to gathering information about community structures that are unavailable from existing secondary sources. In particular, such comparative case studies of communities will capture more in-depth pictures of the relationships among residents, their neighbors, and local institutional structures as well as how these affect criminal victimization and offending especially among youth.

These in-depth case studies could in turn provide sound insights on which to base more extensive quantitative analyses of the intervening mechanisms connecting segregation with youth crime. Having established which conditions may be important to measure and examine, we could then proceed to collect and analyze in quantitative fashion the most important direct measures of the availability and usage of local resources for a fuller range of communities, including black, white, and mixed communities of varying class compositions. This type of in-depth analysis of segregation, disadvantage, community structure, relationships among residents, and crime will further our understanding of the circumstances under which segregation is a source of youth and adult criminal violence.

ENDNOTES

1. An alternative perspective on how segregation affects violent crime would focus on the way in which segregation reinforces violent cultures, especially within minority communities. The cultural perspective emphasizes that criminal violence is the outcome of a value system that prescribes violence as an appropriate way to deal with conflict. This perspective has been challenged by proponents of structural explanations (Blau & Blau, 1982; Braithwaite, 1979; Hawkins, 1986; Krivo & Peterson, 1996; Sampson & Wilson, 1995). As we have noted elsewhere, "cultural differences are themselves adaptations to structural inequity" (Krivo & Peterson, 1996, p. 639) (see also Sampson & Wilson, 1995).
2. Two other papers incorporate segregation as central to the theoretical and empirical understanding of the causes of violent crime. However, these do not focus on explaining heightened levels of violent crime overall. Rather, they explore the implications of segregation for the distribution of interracial versus intraracial criminal violence. Messner and South (1986) and South and Felson (1990) take this approach and evaluate Blau and Blau's (1982) contention that under conditions of high racial residential segregation, "contacts, including those of a criminal nature, are largely confined to members of the same racial group" (Messner & South, 1986, p. 981). Accordingly, residential segregation should be associated negatively with interracial and positively with intraracial victimization. These studies found the expected pattern for robbery (Messner & South, 1986) and rape (South & Felson, 1990).

REFERENCES

Alba, R. D., & Logan, J. R. (1993). Minority proximity to whites in suburbs: An individual-level analysis of segregation. *American Journal of Sociology*, *98*, 1388–1427.

Anderson, E. (1990). *Streetwise: Race, class, and change in an urban community*. Chicago: University of Chicago Press.

Balkwell, J. W. (1990). Ethnic inequality and the rate of homicide. *Social Forces*, *69*, 53–70.

Blau, J. R., & Blau, P. M. (1982). The cost of inequality: Metropolitan structure and violent crime. *American Sociological Review*, *47*, 114–129.

Bobo, L., & Zubrinsky, C. L. (1996). Attitudes on residential integration: Perceived stats differences, mere in-group preference, or racial prejudice? *Social Forces*, *74*, 883–909.

Boland, B., Conly, C. H., Mahanna, P., Warner, L., & Sones, R. (1990). *The prosecution of felony arrests, 1987*. Washington DC: Bureau of Justice Statistics.

Bourgois, P. I. (1995). *In search of respect: Selling crack in El Barrio*. New York: Cambridge University Press.

Bradbury, K., Case, K. E., & Dunham, C. R. (1989, September/October). Geographic patterns of mortgage lending in Boston, 1982–1987. *New England Economic Review*, pp. 3–30.

Braithwaite, J. (1979). *Inequality, crime and public policy*. London: Routledge and Kegan Paul.

Cole, R. E., & Deskins, D. R., Jr. (1989). Racial factors in site location and employment patterns of Japanese auto firms. *California Management Review*, *31*, 9–22.

Coser, L. A. (1968). Conflict: Social aspects. In D. L. Sills (Ed.), *International encyclopedia of the social sciences* (Vol. 3, pp. 232–236). New York: Macmillan.

Denton, N. A. (1994). Are African-Americans still hypersegregated in 1990? In R. D. Bullard, J. E. Grigsby, III, & C. Lee (Eds.), *Residential apartheid: The American legacy* (pp. 49–81). Los Angeles: CAAS Publications.

Denton, N. A., & Massey, D. S. (1988). Residential segregation of blacks, Hispanics, and Asians by socioeconomic status and generation. *Social Science Quarterly, 69*, 797–817.

Farley, R. (1977). Residential segregation in urbanized areas of the United States in 1970: An analysis of social class and racial differences. *Demography, 14*, 497–518.

Farley, R., & Frey, W. H. (1994). Changes in the segregation of whites from blacks during the 1980s: Small steps toward a more integrated society. *American Sociological Review, 59*, 23–45.

Federal Bureau of Investigation. (1994). *Crime in the United States, 1993: Uniform crime reports*. Washington DC: US Government Printing Office.

Federal Bureau of Investigation. (1995). *Crime statistics press release, 1994*. Washington, DC: US Government Printing Office.

Federal Bureau of Investigation. (1996). *Crime in the United States, 1995: Uniform crime reports*. Washington DC: US Government Printing Office.

Frey, W. H., & Farley, R. (1996). Latino, Asian, and black segregation in U.S. metropolitan areas: Are multiethnic metros different? *Demography, 33*, 35–50.

Galster, G. C. (1987). The ecology of racial discrimination in housing: An exploratory model. *Urban Affairs Quarterly, 23*, 84–107.

Galster, G. C., & Keeney, W. M. (1988). Race, residence, discrimination, and economic opportunity: Modelling the nexus of urban racial phenomena. *Urban Affairs Quarterly, 24*, 87–117.

Greenberg, S., Rohe, W. M., & Williams, J. R. (1982). *Safe and secure neighborhoods: Physical characteristics and informal territorial control in high and low crime neighborhoods*. Washington, DC: National Institute of Justice.

Guy, R. F., Pol, L. G., & Ryker, R. E. (1982). Discrimination in mortgage lending: The Home Mortgage Disclosure Act. *Population Research and Policy Review, 1*, 283–296.

Harrison, R. J., & Weinberg, D. H. (1992). Changes in racial and ethnic residential segregation, 1980–1990. Paper Presented at the Annual Meetings of the American Statistical Association.

Hawkins, D. F. (1986). Black and white homicide differentials: Alternatives to an inadequate theory. In D. F. Hawkins (Ed.), *Homicide among black Americans* (pp. 109–134). Lanham, MD: University Press of America.

Kain, J. F. (1986). The influence of race and income on racial segregation and housing policy. In J. M. Goering (Ed.), *Housing discrimination and federal policy* (pp. 99–118). Chapel Hill, NC: University of North Carolina Press.

Krivo, L. J., & Peterson, R. D. (1996). Extremely disadvantaged neighborhoods and urban crime. *Social Forces, 75*, 619–650.

Logan, J. R., & Messner, S. F. (1987). Racial residential segregation and suburban violent crime. *Social Science Quarterly, 68*, 510–527.

Massey, D. S. (1979). Effects of socioeconomic factors on the residential segregation of blacks and Spanish Americans in U.S. urbanized areas. *American Sociological Review, 44*, 1015–1022.

Massey, D. S. (1990). American apartheid: Segregation and the making of the underclass. *American Journal of Sociology, 96*, 329–357.

Massey, D. S. (1996). The age of extremes: Concentrated affluence and poverty in the twenty-first century. *Demography, 33*, 395–412.

Massey, D. S., & Denton, N. A. (1987). Trends in the residential segregation of blacks, Hispanics, and Asians: 1970–1980. *American Sociological Review, 52*, 802–825.

Massey, D. S., & Denton, N. A. (1988). The dimensions of residential segregation. *Social Forces, 67*, 281–315.

Massey, D. S., & Denton, N. A. (1989). Hypersegregation in U.S. metropolitan areas: Black and Hispanic segregation along five dimensions. *Demography, 26*, 373–391.

Massey, D. S., & Denton, N. A. (1993). *American apartheid: Segregation and the making of the underclass*. Cambridge, MA: Harvard University Press.

Massey, D. S., & Eggers, M. L. (1990). The ecology of inequality: Minorities and the concentration of poverty, 1970–1980. *American Journal of Sociology, 95*, 1153–1188.

Massey, D. S., Condran, G. A., & Denton, N. A. (1987). The effect of residential segregation on black social and economic well-being. *Social Forces, 66*, 29–56.

Massey, D. S., Gross, A. B., & Eggers, M. L. (1991). Segregation, the concentration of poverty, and the life chances of individuals. *Social Science Research, 20*, 397–420.

Merton, R. K. (1968). *Social theory and social structure*. New York: Free Press.

Messner, S., & South, S. J.. (1986). Economic deprivation, opportunity, structure and robbery victimization: A test of routine activities/lifestyle theories. *Social Forces, 64*, 975–991.

Pearce, D. M. (1979). Gatekeepers and homeseekers: Institutional patterns in racial steering. *Social Problems, 26,* 325–342.

Peterson, R. D., & Krivo, L. J. (1993). Racial segregation and urban black homicide. *Social Forces, 71,* 1001–1026.

Peterson, R. D., & Krivo, L. J. (1999). Racial segregation, the concentration of disadvantage, and black and white homicide victimization. *Sociological Forum, 14,* 465–493.

Potter, L. B. (1991). Socioeconomic determinants of white and black males' life expectancy differentials, 1980. *Demography, 28,* 303–321.

Rosenfeld, R. (1986). Urban crime rates: Effects of inequality, welfare dependency, region, and race. In J. M. Byrne & R. J. Sampson (Eds.), *The social ecology of crime* (pp. 116–130). New York: Springer-Verlag.

Sampson, R. J. (1985). Race and criminal violence: A demographically disaggregated analysis of urban homicide. *Crime and Delinquency, 31,* 47–82.

Sampson, R. J., & Groves, W. B. (1989). Community structure and crime: Testing social-disorganization theory. *American Journal of Sociology, 94,* 774–802.

Sampson, R. J., & Wilson, W. J. (1995). Race, crime, and urban inequality. In J. Hagan & R. D. Peterson (Eds.), *Crime and inequality* (pp. 37–54). Stanford, CA: Stanford University Press.

Schuman, H., & Bobo, L. (1988). Survey-based experiments on white racial attitudes towards residential integration. *American Journal of Sociology, 94,* 273–299.

Shihadeh, E. S., & Flynn, N. (1996). Segregation and crime: The effect of black social isolation on the rates of black urban violence. *Social Forces, 74,* 1325–1352.

Shlay, A. B. (1988). Not in that neighborhood: The effects of population and housing on the distribution of mortgage finance within the Chicago SMSA. *Social Science Research, 17,* 137–163.

Shlay, A. B. (1989). Financing community: Methods for assessing residential credit disparities, market barriers, and institutional reinvestment performance in the metropolis. *Journal of Urban Affairs, 11,* 201–223.

Simkus, A. A. (1978). Residential segregation by occupation and race in ten urbanized areas, 1950–1970. *American Sociological Review, 43,* 81–93.

Skogan, W. G. (1990). *Disorder and decline: Crime and the spiral of decay in American neighborhoods.* Berkeley: University of California Press.

Smith, D. A. (1986). The neighborhood context of police behavior. In A. J. Reiss, Jr., & M. Tonry (Eds.), *Communities and crime* (pp. 313–341). Chicago: University of Chicago Press.

Snyder, H. N., & Sickmund, M. (1995). *Juvenile offenders and victims: A focus on violence.* Pittsburgh, PA: National Center for Juvenile Justice.

South, S. J., & Felson, R. B. (1990). The racial patterning of rape. *Social Forces, 69,* 71–93.

Squires, G. D. (1994). *Capital and communities in black and white: The intersections of race, class, and uneven development.* Albany: State University of New York Press.

Turner, M. A., Struyk, R. J., & Yinger, J. (1991). *Housing discrimination study: A synthesis.* Washington, DC: Office of Policy Development and Research, US Department of Housing and Urban Development.

US Bureau of the Census. (1995). *National and state population estimates: 1990 to 1994.* Current Population Reports, P25-1127. Washington, DC: US Government Printing Office.

US Department of Justice. (1995). *Sourcebook of criminal justice statistics—1994.* Bureau of Justice Statistics. Washington, DC: US Government Printing Office.

Wacquant, L. J. D. (1993). Urban outcasts: Stigma and division in black America ghetto and the French urban periphery. *International Journal of Urban and Regional Research, 17,* 366–383.

Wienk, R. E., Reid, C. W., Simonson, J. C., & Eggers, F. J. (1979). *Measuring racial discrimination in American housing markets: The housing market practices survey.* Washington, DC: US Department of Housing and Urban Development.

Wilson, W. J. (1987). *The truly disadvantaged: The inner city, the underclass, and public policy.* Chicago: The University of Chicago Press.

Wilson, W. J. 1996. *When work disappears: The world of the new urban poor.* New York: Alfred A. Knopf.

Yinger, J. (1995). *Closed doors, opportunities lost: The continuing costs of housing discrimination.* New York: Russell Sage Foundation.

Zawitz, M. W., Gaskins, C. K., Koppel, H., Greenfeld, L. A., & Greenwood, P. (The RAND Corporation). (1988). The response to crime. In M. W. Zawitz (Ed.), *Report to the nation on crime and justice* (pp. 55–112). Washington, DC: Bureau of Justice Statistics.

Zubrinsky, C. L. (1996). "I have always wanted to have neighbor just like you": Race and residential segregation in the city of angels. Ph.D. dissertation, Department of Sociology, University of California at Los Angeles.

Zubrinsky, C. L., & Bobo, L. (1996). Prismatic metropolis: Race and residential segregation in the city of angels. *Social Science Research, 25,* 335–374.

Part VI

Behavioral Questions

15

The Development of Delinquency

An Interactional Perspective

TERENCE P. THORNBERRY and MARVIN D. KROHN

INTRODUCTION

One of the most intriguing issues confronting criminology today is that of continuity and change in delinquent careers. Prior research has demonstrated substantial levels of continuity in antisocial behavior across the life course. Indeed, Lee Robins (1978) has commented that: "... adult antisocial behavior virtually requires childhood antisocial behavior ..." (p. 611). If the empirical story ended there, the theoretical task of criminological theory would be much less challenging and interesting than it in fact is. But the story does not end there. For in addition to continuity, there is substantial change in delinquent careers. That is, many offenders, even those with an early onset of antisocial behavior, do not persist in their offending; hence, the second part of what has come to be called Robins' (1978) paradox: "... yet most antisocial children do not become antisocial adults" (p. 611). How can we account for this twin observation: that childhood antisocial behavior is almost a prerequisite for later antisocial behavior, yet most children who are antisocial outgrow that behavior, avoiding later involvement in delinquency and crime?

Several recent theoretical models have attempted to account for this observation, for example, the work of Thornberry (1987), Patterson, Reid, and Dishion (1992), Moffitt (1993, 1997), and Sampson and Laub (1993, 1997). In this chapter we focus on one of them—Thornberry's interactional theory—to present a systematic explanation of both continuity and change in antisocial careers.[1]

Continuity and Change

In the criminological literature, the twin concepts of continuity and change often are discussed solely in terms of antisocial behavior. That is, continuity is primarily portrayed as the continuation of antisocial behavior across the life course. As suggested by Robins' quote,

TERENCE P. THORNBERRY • School of Criminal Justice, University at Albany, Albany, New York 12222.
MARVIN D. KROHN • Department of Sociology, University at Albany, Albany, New York 12222.

Handbook of Youth and Justice, edited by White. Kluwer Academic/Plenum Publishers, New York, 2001.

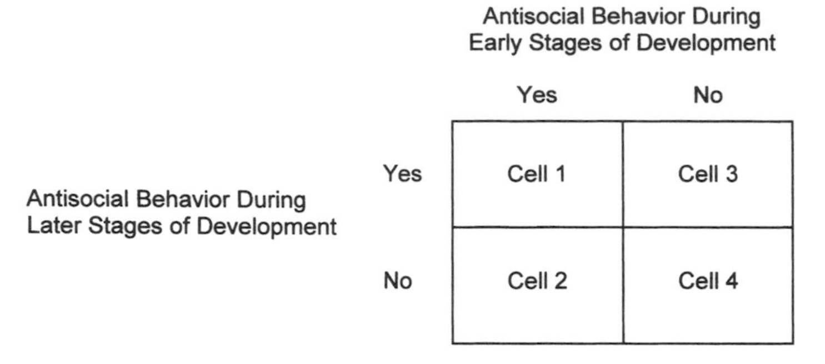

Figure 1. A simplified view of continuity and change in delinquent careers.

the central issue is: Why do children who begin offending early continue offending? Similarly, change is primarily portrayed as the termination of offending. Here the central issue is what Rutter (1988) has called "escape from the risk process" (p. 3). While understanding the causal processes associated both with the continuity and termination of offending is of fundamental importance, a full understanding of continuity and change involves more than an examination of early-onset offenders and why some of them continue offending while others stop. It also requires an understanding of the continuity and change that is initiated with prosocial behaviors. Why do some prosocial children continue to avoid antisocial behavior throughout their lives, while others initiate antisocial behavior only at later ages?

Figure 1 presents a very simplified model of this process. It dichotomizes the life course into early and later stages and antisocial behavior as either present or absent. Perhaps the most interesting aspect of this simple table is that all four cells are populated. Because of that, a full theoretical understanding of continuity and change in antisocial behavior over the life course should consider all four possible processes.

Continuity is represented in cells 1 and 4. Cell 1 contains individuals who begin offending at early stages and continue offending at later stages; it is the cell that has received most of our attention. Cell 4 represents continuity in prosocial behaviors or at least in nonoffending. Less theoretical or empirical attention has been paid to the causal processes associated with this type of continuity. Understanding these processes may have great practical and theoretical significance, however, since the whole purpose of our trade is to convert people from those in cells 1, 2, and 3 to those in cell 4.

Cells 2 and 3 represent change in offending over the life course. Cell 2 contains individuals who begin offending at earlier stages and change is represented by the termination of offending. Cell 3 contains "late-bloomers," individuals who avoid offending early and change is represented by a later onset of offending careers.

The complexity of continuity and change is far greater than that suggested by the simplified model portrayed in Fig. 1. The life course obviously cannot be dichotomized into early and late periods; it unfolds continuously as the person ages. Similarly, antisocial behavior is not dichotomous, either present or absent. Antisocial careers can begin at almost any age and can have widely varying durations and patterns of escalation, intermittence, and severity (Loeber & LeBlanc, 1990). Since age of onset has played a critical role in discussions of delinquent careers, we briefly discuss the importance of the age of onset as a backdrop to our explanation of the continuity and change in antisocial careers.

Age of Onset and Duration of Antisocial Careers

Recently, Patterson (Patterson, Capaldi, & Bank, 1991; Patterson et al., 1992) and Moffitt (1993, 1997) have presented typological theories of delinquency that use age of onset as the key defining attribute for the different types of delinquents. Both theories argue that the delinquent population really consists of two fundamentally different types of offenders with different etiologies. For Moffitt, they are life-course-persistent and adolescence-limited offenders; for Patterson et al., they are early starters and late starters. Life-course-persistent offenders and early starters begin offending in early childhood; adolescence-limited offenders and late starters wait until adolescence to begin their offending careers.

While having great heuristic value, these stark types do not comport very well with data on age of onset. Figure 2 describes the age of onset of serious offending in the three projects of the Program of Research on the Causes and Correlates of Delinquency. Analysis is limited to male respondents who report offending in at least two assessments (Stouthamer-Loeber, Loeber, Huizinga, & Porter, 1997). Although there is some left- and right-hand censoring, the onset curves have a smooth, continuous form. Very early onset is less common, about 10% by age 9, but then onset increases in a smooth function from age 9 through age 16. Figure 3 presents onset curves for general delinquency for the total Rochester sample and for respondents who reported offending in at least two assessments. Again, the onset of delinquency is seen to be continuously distributed. While rarer in early childhood and more common in midadolescence, delinquent careers can begin at all ages.

While some offenders do start early and some do start late, these data do not suggest that there are only two types of offenders—early and late starters. Onset is earlier or later, continuously distributed over childhood and adolescence. If so, then the empirical validity of these types and the concomitant need for separate etiological explanations may be question-

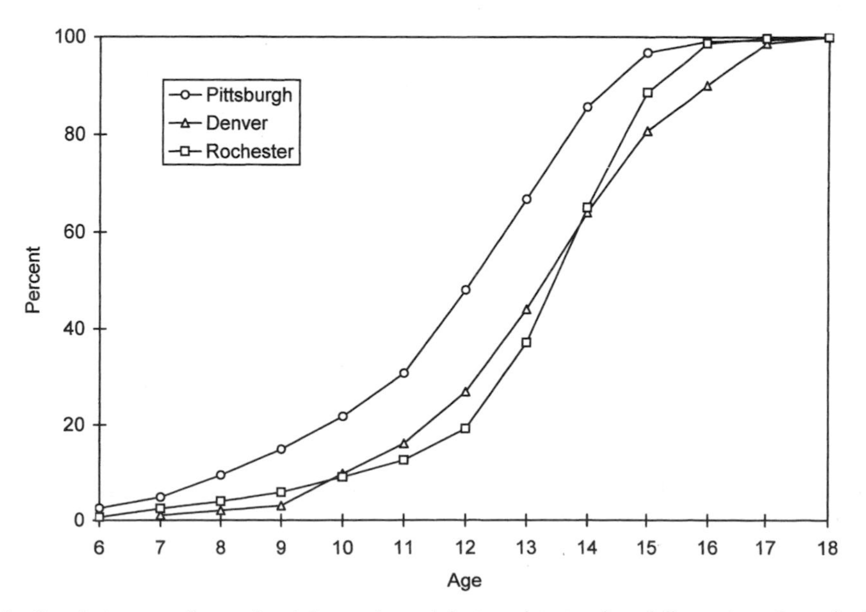

Figure 2. Cumulative age of onset for violent and nonviolent persistent serious delinquents, males only. Source: Stouthamer-Loeber, Loeber, Huizinga, and Porter, 1997.

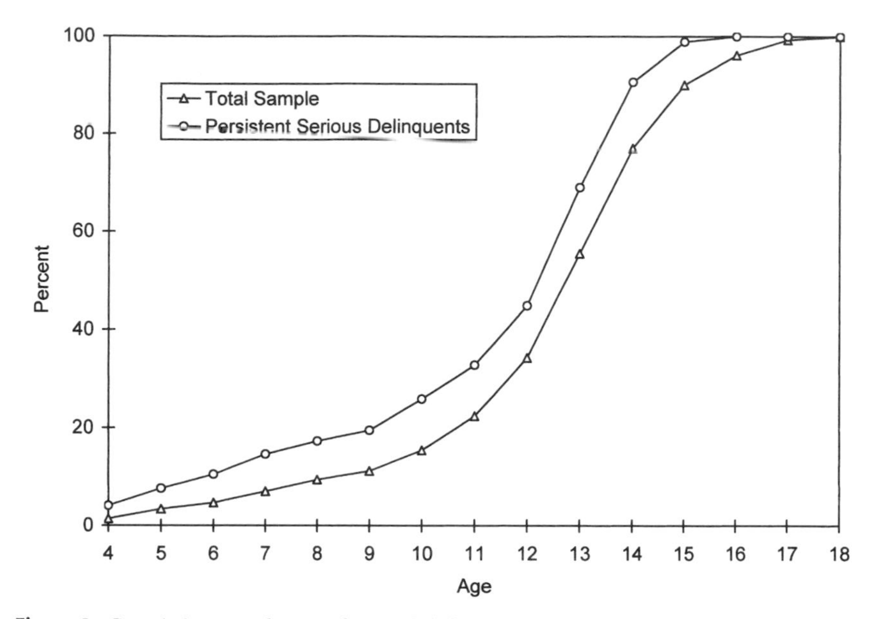

Figure 3. Cumulative age of onset of general delinquency, Rochester Youth Development Study.

able. Instead, we may need a unified theory that accounts first for the timing of onset. Since antisocial and delinquent behavior violates conventional norms and is injurious, the precocious or early onset of this behavior pattern can be viewed as one indicator of its underlying severity. Early or precocious onset may require more powerful but not necessarily different causal influences than later onset. A unified theory would then have to explain the relationship between the timing of onset and varying duration of criminal careers. As we shall see, while there is a consistent positive relationship between earlier onset and longer careers, there also is a substantial degree of independence between these two parameters of delinquent careers.

In sum, a full theory of continuity and change in delinquent and criminal careers not only has to consider all four processes presented in Fig. 1, it also needs to recognize that these behaviors unfold and change in a continuous process over the life course. This is a difficult challenge and one that will not be quickly solved. In this chapter, we begin examining these issues from the perspective of interactional theory.

INTERACTIONAL THEORY

There are three fundamental premises to an interactional theory of delinquency that in combination can be used to explain continuity and change in delinquent behavior. First, interactional theory adopts a developmental or life course perspective. Second, it emphasizes behavioral interactions and bidirectional causality. Third, it incorporates the impact of social structural influences in explaining the development of individual delinquent careers.

Life Course Influences

Elder and colleagues define the life course as the "sequence of culturally defined age-graded roles and social transitions that are enacted over time" (Caspi, Elder, & Herbener,

1990, p. 15; see also, Elder, 1997). These sequences are described in terms of trajectories—long-term patterns of development—and transitions—events or short-term changes in these trajectories.

Delinquency itself can be considered a behavioral trajectory that unfolds over time; for most people it has an onset, duration, and, for most offenders, a termination. Movement along this behavioral trajectory can be explained at least in part by movement along other life course trajectories that are related to major social institutions, such as family and work (Thornberry, 1997).

An interactional perspective implies that delinquency is not caused by a static underlying trait that is stable across developmental stages and heterogeneously distributed in the population (for an example of this type of theory, see Gottfredson & Hirschi, 1990). In contrast, interactional theory assumes that the causes of delinquency vary systematically with stages of the life course and with the success or failure with which the life course has been traversed. As such, it takes into account the opportunities that are opened and closed to individuals by the effect that their behavior has on others and on their life chances. In brief, interactional theory is a dynamic model in the sense that all "state-dependent" models are dynamic (see Nagin & Paternoster, 1991). It implies that prior states and behavior, including antisocial behavior, have important developmental consequences and in fact are causally related to later states and behaviors. This leads to the second fundamental premise of interactional theory.

Bidirectional Causality

A second cornerstone of interactional theory is its emphasis on bidirectional or reciprocal causation. To understand the causal dynamics behind delinquent careers, it is not adequate or accurate to simply identify the causes of delinquency. It is also necessary to examine how delinquency and these other factors interact and to consider how involvement in delinquency can produce changes in those other factors over time. This emphasis on bidirectionality stems from interactional theory's fundamental assertion that behavior patterns emerge from *interactions* between the person and his or her environment and not simply from the environment acting upon the individual. Prosocial behavior patterns also are brought about by interactions between the person and the environment. This approach is similar to transactional theories in psychology (see, e.g., Cairns & Cairns, 1994; Magnusson, 1988).

Social Structure

The third premise of interactional theory is that life course trajectories are embedded in the social structure. To understand how these trajectories develop, it is imperative to understand how they are produced by and related to social structural factors such as social class, race, and neighborhood. Several dimensions need to be considered.

First, the individual's structural position influences and to some extent determines the initial values of process variables at early stages of the life course. For example, children born to severely disadvantaged families are more likely to start life with deficits on a host of important explanatory variables, including family, school, peer, and individual attributes, as compared to children born to more advantaged families.

Second, the children of severely disadvantaged families are likely to have multiple and cumulating deficits. Children born to more advantaged families, while they may experience difficulties in some behavioral areas, are less likely to experience deficits in many areas and, therefore, are less likely to experience the cascading impact of multiple, interacting deficits.

Third, children from severely disadvantaged backgrounds are likely to have fewer buffering or protective factors available in their environments to short-circuit burgeoning antisocial careers. For example, family and neighborhood relationships that function as social capital (Coleman, 1988) and that facilitate the achievement of ends are likely to be substantially less for disadvantaged youth than they are for more advantaged youth.

With this brief introduction to interactional theory as a backdrop we begin our examination of continuity and change in antisocial behavior. We first discuss individuals who initiate antisocial behavior at the youngest ages *and* who persist in offending across long portions of their lives; these individuals epitomize continuity in antisocial behavior. We then discuss individuals whose onset of offending occurs at later ages and whose careers are marked by varying patterns of continuity and change.

PRECOCIOUS OFFENDERS

Some individuals initiate antisocial behavior during toddlerhood and the preschool years (Shaw, Keenan, & Vondra, 1994) and continue their antisocial behavior through to adulthood (Moffitt, 1993). These individuals epitomize continuity in antisocial behavior and are most consistent with Moffitt's concept of the life-course-persistent offender. While proportionately small, the criminal careers of these individuals are marked by persistence and seriousness.[2] What accounts for this pattern of both precociousness and persistent antisocial behavior?

Their very early onset can be explained by the combination of individual deficits, ineffective parenting, and position in the social structure. Children who exhibit very early manifestations of antisocial behavior are likely to have a variety of negative temperamental qualities and neuropsychological deficits; they often are irritable and impulsive, with low levels of self-control and emotion regulation (Grolnick, Bridger, & Connell, 1996; Kopp, 1989; Moffitt, 1993, 1997). Children with very-early-onset antisocial behavior also are likely to have parents who exhibit a variety of parenting deficits. These deficits reflect the parent's inability to monitor and reward prosocial behaviors, to provide guidance in the development of problem-solving skills, and to monitor and effectively punish antisocial behavior. Parenting deficits include low affective ties and involvement with the child, explosive physical disciplinary styles, frequent irritable exchanges, poor teaching and problem-solving strategies, and inconsistent standard setting.

In children whose antisocial careers are marked by both very early onset and long-term duration, these individual characteristics and inept parenting styles are likely to become causally interwoven over time. Bidirectional influences between the child's temperamental qualities and the parent's child management style can be observed as early as toddlerhood. Young children with negative temperamental qualities are more subject to parental hostility, criticism, irritability, and coercive responses (Lee & Bates, 1985; Rutter & Quinton, 1984; Zahn-Waxler, Iannotti, Cummings, & Denham, 1990). In turn, ineffective parenting creates maladaptive, coercive, and uncontrolled responses in the child (Belsky, Woodworth, & Crnic, 1996; Moffitt, 1993; Shaw & Bell, 1993). This mismatch between negative child characteristics and an adverse family context increases the odds that parent and child will develop a coercive style of interaction (Patterson et al., 1992) and that the child will develop persistent patterns of oppositional and aggressive behavior.

The onset of offending for these individuals is not caused entirely by individual and familial influences, however. While important, they exist in a broader social context and to a substantial degree are brought about by that context. These offenders are likely to be born to families experiencing structural adversity that we define as a position in the social structure that leads to accumulated disadvantage for the individual and his or her family. Among its attributes are chronic poverty, unemployment, welfare dependence, residence in areas of concentrated poverty, and especially the co-occurrence of these attributes. The impact of structural adversity may be particularly salient for minority youth who face additional barriers to successful development because of societal discrimination and stigmatization (Jones, 1989; McLoyd, 1990; Spencer & Dornbusch, 1990). Structural adversity increases parental stress and reduces social capital, all of which increase poor family management skills and ineffective parenting (Belsky et al., 1996; Conger, Ge, Elder, Lorenz, & Simons, 1994; Patterson et al., 1992). Structural adversity also accompanies elevated rates of negative temperamental qualities (Moffitt, 1996, 1997; Stott, 1978).

In brief, very-early-onset offending is brought about by the *combination and interaction* of structural, individual, and parental influences. Extreme social adversity contributes to both parenting deficits and negative temperamental qualities in the child; in turn, both attributes, and especially their interaction, greatly increase the likelihood of early onset offending.

Why, for some youth, does this very-early-onset offending persist throughout long portions of the life course? There are two processes that account for long-term continuity. The first is produced by continuity in these basic causal processes across the life course. Families experiencing extreme levels of structural adversity do not often escape that adversity and the development of children raised in those families is constantly threatened by its consequences. Similarly, there is continuity to ineffective parenting styles, in part caused by the constancy of the social environment in which these families find themselves (Patterson et al., 1992). Finally, there is continuity in negative temperamental traits and neuropsychological deficits from childhood through the adult years (Caspi, Bem, & Elder, 1989; Moffitt, Lynam, & Silva, 1994).

The second process concerns the consequences of behavior, including early manifestations of antisocial behavior. This process is at the core of interactional theory. Prolonged involvement in antisocial behavior, especially more serious forms of antisocial behavior, can have severe negative consequences for many aspects of the child's development. Persistent antisocial behavior will continue to elicit coercive responses from the parent as the child ages (Lee & Bates, 1985). In addition, children who have learned coercive behavioral styles in the family are apt to extend them to external settings such as peer relationships and school behavior. "There is now substantial evidence that aggressive children are likely to be rejected by their peers" (Coie & Dodge, 1988, p. 828) (see also, Coie, Dodge, & Kupersmidt, 1990) and that rejected children lose the positive influence of prosocial peers in acquiring social and behavioral competencies (Coie, Lochman, Terry, & Hyman, 1992; Ladd, 1990). Aggressive children also are at risk for school failure (Patterson et al., 1992). The coercive training they received in the family and the rejection by peers increase the chances of early academic adjustment problems, even controlling for prior academic competence (Ladd, 1990).

As these youth age, they are ill-prepared to meet the developmental challenges of adolescence and to prepare themselves for adult life. In a series of papers, we and our colleagues have shown that delinquent behavior reduces social bonds (Jang & Smith, 1997; Krohn, Thornberry, Collins-Hall, & Lizotte, 1995; Thornberry, Lizotte, Krohn, Farnworth, & Jang, 1991), increases affiliation with deviant peers and fosters deviant belief systems (Krohn, Lizotte, Thornberry, Smith, & McDowall, 1996; Thornberry, Lizotte, Krohn, Farnworth, & Jang, 1994), and disrupts orderly and timely transitions to adult roles (Krohn, Lizotte, & Perez, 1997; Thornberry, Smith, & Howard, 1997). Moreover, these papers also have demonstrated that maladjustment in family, school, peer relations, and beliefs themselves become interwoven over the life course.

In brief, early, persistent involvement in antisocial behavior and delinquency generates cumulative and cascading consequences in the person's life course. It reduces the formation of social bonds and social capital and increases embeddedness in deviant networks and belief systems, all of which serve to foreclose conventional lifestyles and entrap the individual in deviant lifestyles.

EARLY ONSET OFFENDERS

For a sizable portion of the population involvement in antisocial behavior and delinquency begins during the elementary school years, from about ages 6 through 13. Onset is less common at the younger ages and becomes more common as the individual approaches adolescence. Thus, after a period of generally prosocial development during early childhood these children change and begin some period of involvement in antisocial behavior and delinquency. What triggers this change in behavior?

It is unlikely that their antisocial behavior is characterized by the intense coupling of difficult temperament, ineffective parenting, and structural adversity that characterize precocious offenders. If those attributes are indeed intensely coupled, there would be little to inhibit the onset of antisocial behavior until the school-age years. In other words, it is not clear what would buffer or protect a youngster from initiating antisocial behavior if they in fact have negative temperamental qualities in combination with ineffective parenting and structural adversity.

If these attributes are uncoupled, however, sources of protection become available and the onset of antisocial behavior may be delayed. Clearly not all children with negative temperamental qualities are born into distressed families living in disorganized neighborhoods. The resources available to these more advantaged families may reduce the behavioral consequences of the child's difficult temperament, at least until they start school and expand their peer relationships. Once the child reaches school and broadened social networks, however, the consequences of difficult temperament, for example, peer rejection, may increase the likelihood of antisocial behavior.

Thus, one source of antisocial behavior initiated during the school-age years may be individual temperamental qualities. This seems to us a less important pathway at these ages though, in light of the biological and neuropsychological underpinnings of temperament and the likelihood that these temperamental qualities will be expressed at very young ages. Indeed, rather than looking to individual differences to account for this behavior pattern, interactional theory looks to the external social environment as the more likely point of origin.

Growing up in families and neighborhoods characterized by poverty and disorganization increases a variety of deficits that lead to more serious antisocial careers, here represented by a relatively early onset of these behaviors. Structural adversity increases a variety of stressors, for example, parental depression, stressful life events, and financial worries, that impede effective parenting and increase poor family management styles. In turn, these reduce the formation of strong bonds of attachment between parent and child. At these ages preparation for and success in school become increasingly important. Structural adversity both directly and indirectly through its impact on the family forecloses opportunities and reduces the child's ability to succeed in school, leading to weakened bonds of commitment to school and attachment to teachers (Polk & Schafer, 1972). Overall, structural adversity reduces the social bonds that control behavior, as well as the human and social capital that enable the pursuit of prosocial adaptations.

Structural adversity increases access to deviant opportunity structures. Delinquent peers, gangs, drug markets, and "deviance service centers" are embedded in the social fabric of many of these communities (Hagan, 1992). While unimportant in explaining the extremely early onset of antisocial behavior for the precocious offender, deviant opportunities become increasingly important for explaining the onset of offending as the child ages.

Overall, the absence of strong bonds and social capital to control behavior becomes coupled with abundant deviant opportunities to produce antisocial behavior. Based on this, we predict a strong negative association between both the strength and number of these deficits and age of onset. As these deficits diminish, however (that is, as bonding increases and deviant opportunities decrease), age of onset will increase and move toward the modal age of onset that occurs during early adolescence. Note that this is not a typological theory with different etiologies for the different types of offenders. Instead, it argues that as the potency of the causal forces increase, both in their intensity and coupling, the age of onset will decrease. In contrast, as the causal forces diminish the age of onset increases.

Continuity

Early onset offending is characterized by a substantial degree of continuity in offending over time. Moreover, the *earlier* the onset, the *greater* the continuity. For example, using National Youth Survey data, Elliott (1994) reports that of the serious violent offenders who initiated offending prior to age 11, 45% continued offending into their 20s. Of those who started at ages 11–12, only one fourth continued offending, and "the probability was lower and relatively constant for those who initiated at ages 13–17" (Elliott, 1994, p. 14). Two processes help account for continuity, especially the higher level of continuity for offenders with younger ages of onset.

First, according to interactional theory, early-onset offending is caused by exposure to multiple deficits that cause delinquency (structural adversity, weak bonds, and deviant influences) and more extreme levels of these deficits. As argued above, the stronger these deficits are, the earlier the onset is likely to be; the weaker they are, the more likely delinquency will be delayed until it is more age-normative. Furthermore, it is reasonable to assume that the stronger these deficits are, the more stable they are likely to be over time. For example, extremely distressed families are more likely to remain distressed than are less distressed families. This observation helps explain the relationship between the age of onset and the continuity of offending. Since more extreme deficits are needed to bring about early-onset offending and since more extreme deficits are themselves more likely to be stable, these deficits will remain in place to continue causing antisocial behavior over time. Since the strongest deficits are associated with the earliest ages of onset, this source of continuity is likely to be greatest for offenders with earlier rather than later onsets. Thus, stable causal influences are one source of continuity in antisocial behavior and the stability of these causal influences is likely to be greater for earlier onset offenders.

The second process concerns the interlocking nature of these deficits. Weak bonds and strong delinquent associations and beliefs cause delinquency, but delinquency has feedback effects to further erode social bonds and to isolate the youth in more and more deviant social networks. Also, the weakening bonds and developing deviant influences themselves become interrelated over time. Thus, the well-known empirical finding that serious delinquency is associated with multiple risk factors is not simply a function of the co-occurrence of these deficits; it is more fundamentally a function of mutual causality. Position in the social structure creates a variety of deficits that intersect in the life course for the individual. These deficits then become causally interrelated to create distinct life course trajectories toward continuity in antisocial behavior.

Change

Although there is a substantial degree of continuity in offending for these offenders, especially those who begin offending at younger ages, there also is a substantial degree of change. Indeed, that is the whole point of Robins' (1978) paradox: "most antisocial children do *not* become antisocial adults" (p. 611, emphasis added). Recall the data from the National Youth Survey reported by Elliott (1994): among those who initiate prior to age 11, over half, 55%, stop offending at some point before they reach the age of 20. Of those who start at ages 11 or 12, approximately 75% stop. Why is that?

At least three general processes can help account for desistance. First, while there is substantial stability in the social forces that bring about antisocial behavior, they are not entirely unchanging. For example, families do experience upward mobility and move to new neighborhoods and better schools; parental stressors such as family conflict, depression, and drug use can be ameliorated; and bonds between parents and children can improve. These environmental changes provide for turning points in the child's life course trajectory and in their antisocial careers, especially if antisocial behavior has not yet become an ingrained part of their behavioral repertoire.

A second explanation for desistance is that the causal factors that give rise to the initial antisocial behavior are not intensely coupled. For example, there are many youth with deficits in some areas, such as a distressed family, who have compensating assets in other areas, such as intelligence and school performance. The deficits they do experience put them at risk for delinquency, but the fact that they are offset by competing assets reduces the chances that they will have long, persistent antisocial careers. More generally, these youngsters have a richer set of protective factors, in part brought about by the somewhat less tenuous social position of their families (see Rutter, 1987; Smith & Carlson, 1997; Smith, Lizotte, Thornberry, & Krohn, 1995; Werner & Smith, 1992).

Relatedly, these youth are less likely to experience the tight interweaving of deficits brought about by feedback effects from delinquent behavior. While the negative consequences of delinquency will find fertile soil in the areas in which deficits already exist (the distressed family in our example), they will find resistance in the areas of resilience (school performance in our example). Thus, it is less likely that the various life course trajectories will become interwoven to create an amplifying loop toward increased involvement in antisocial careers.

Finally, we should not lose sight of the impact of systematic efforts at planned change in accounting for desistance. Some prevention and treatment programs work (see, for example, Howell, Krisberg, Hawkins, & Wilson, 1995; Lipsey & Wilson, 1998, for reviews), and youth exposed to those programs will have earlier desistance. Services, especially those not provided by the juvenile justice system, are more apt to be utilized by youth from more advantaged backgrounds and that may help account for their shorter careers.

Overall, these processes—improved social environments, loosely coupled causal forces, and effective treatments—provide for both reduced antisocial behavior and enhanced prosocial competencies. As a result, these adolescents are better prepared to make smoother transitions to adult roles and to embark on more conventional adult lives. The earlier the antisocial career begins, the more difficult it is for these transitions to occur; but regardless of age of onset, the processes outlined in this section can engender desistance from antisocial careers.

LATER ONSET OFFENDERS

This brings us to offenders who begin their delinquent careers later in life; those referred to by Patterson et al. (1991) as late starters and by Moffitt (1993, 1997) as adolescence-limited offenders. This proportionately large group epitomizes change: after a relatively long period of prosocial adjustment, they begin offending during the early adolescent years and, for most, terminate their involvement in delinquency before the end of adolescence.

Interactional theory hypothesizes that these youngsters are unlikely to have been exposed to the more extreme and interwoven causal forces described up to this point. That is, they are less likely to be drawn from positions in the social structure characterized by structural adversity, they are more likely to have adequate prosocial bonds, and they are likely to have relatively low access to deviant opportunity structures. They also are likely to have compensating mechanisms in their backgrounds to offset the consequences of exposure to any major risk factors that may exist. For example, some youngsters growing up under conditions of structural adversity postpone initiation into delinquency in part because of strong parental relationships and controls that buffer them from the effects of limited prosocial opportunities. Overall, these characteristics produce generally conforming outcomes during childhood. What generates their break from conformity to involvement, albeit short-term involvement, in antisocial behavior?

Prior to adolescence their behavior is largely controlled by parents and teachers, they are embedded in conventional networks, and they are largely dependent on those networks for resources. By the end of adolescence, however, they are expected to be independent of their parents and prepared to enter and succeed in the adult world. Thus, one of the major developmental tasks of adolescence is establishing what Conger (1991, p. 208) labels "age-appropriate autonomy." Adolescents are expected to make more of their own decisions and to be more responsible for those decisions. With this added responsibility comes the expectation of more "adultlike behavior." Conger suggests that the development of such autonomy relies on the processes of both separation and continued connectedness. Whereas adolescents must have sufficient freedom from parental authority to make decisions about their lives, they still need guidance and support from parents. Balancing the need for adolescent autonomy with the concern for parental monitoring of attitudes, behaviors, and decisions creates the tension between parents and children that often is evident during adolescence.

In the process of establishing age-appropriate autonomy, young adolescents seek distance from parents, teachers, and more generally adult authority. Their emerging physical, sexual, and social maturity provides the human capital needed for increased independence at these ages. Benson, Williams, and Johnson (1987, p. 36) report that "the importance of making one's own decisions, grows more dramatically than any other value area" during the adolescent years. The attainment of autonomy, however, does not increase at the same rate. The effort to forge their own identities creates tension in the relationship between parents and their children. For adolescents, this tension is often manifested in feelings of anger toward parents who continue to exert control over their lives (Benson et al., 1987). For parents, the concern is for their loss of control and as a result their worry over the safety and welfare of their child (Gecas & Seff, 1990). The conflict with and alienation from parents reduce the impact of parental bonds and parental control on the behavior of their adolescent children. Similar processes unfold with teachers and other adult authority figures. While these young adolescents are never entirely alienated from parents and teachers, distance is created in these relationships.

Cut free from the strict bonds of parental and adult supervision, adolescents gravitate toward each other—toward adolescent peer groups as their dominant social networks. In large part, peers replace parents, or at least are added to parents, as major sources of rewards and approval of behavior (Gecas & Seff, 1990). But since age-graded peers are all going through the same process of autonomy at roughly the same time, adolescent peer groups are closed to adult authority while valuing behaviors that demonstrate rebellion from adult authority (Cohen, 1955; Stinchecomb, 1964).

One consequence, of course, is to encourage and reinforce deviant behaviors—deviant lifestyles, experimentation with alcohol and drug use, and involvement in minor forms of delinquency. Much of this behavior involves precocious behavior typically reserved for adults, for example, smoking and drinking, and much of it is, in Albert Cohen's (1955) felicitous phrase, "nonutilitarian, malicious, and negativistic" (p. 25). While clearly delinquent, this behavior typically involves less serious forms of delinquency and involvement in the most serious forms, for example, armed robbery, burglary, and heroin use, is uncommon.

Those youngsters who were buffered from the consequences of structural adversity by strong prosocial bonds are in a particularly precarious position during this stage of their lives. For them, the realization of limitations on their conventional opportunities is more salient and access to deviant opportunities more abundant. Increased responsibility for decisions about short-term behavior often leads to choosing the increasingly attractive alternative of deviant behavior.

As delinquent behavior persists, it has feedback effects, albeit minor ones, on social bonds. While adolescence may not be the period of "storm and stress" it once was characterized to be, it still is a stressful period for many parents and adolescents (Gecas & Seff, 1990). Parents often have a difficult time "understanding" their children and the rebelliousness of the adolescent drives down shared involvement and time. In turn, this allows for greater immersion in adolescent peer networks and more involvement in delinquent activity on the part of the adolescent.

While desistance is quite likely for these adolescents, involvement in persistent antisocial careers is not impossible. Some actions can have profound consequences for altering behavioral trajectories in unexpected directions. For example, teenage parenthood, especially teenage motherhood, can foreclose prosocial opportunities and lead to unexpected levels of structural adversity and antisocial behavior (Kellam, Ensminger, & Turner, 1977; Morash & Rucker, 1989). Youngsters from disadvantaged backgrounds may be enticed by the immediate economic payoff of some deviant activities. Involvement in alcohol and substance abuse also can prolong involvement in antisocial careers. Sampson and Laub (1993) found heavy alcohol use to be a strong thread running through the lives of men in the Glueck sample (Glueck & Glueck, 1943) who had higher than expected levels of adult antisocial behavior.

Although persistent deviant behavior is a distinct possibility, more typically involvement in delinquency is relatively short. Two processes account for this. First, the motivating force for delinquency is developmentally specific. As the need for autonomy is met, the benefits derived from rebelliousness wither. Second, unlike more persistent offenders, these youth have substantial levels of human and social capital to draw on to extricate them from whatever trouble their involvement in deviance produced. The very forces that lead to their generally prosocial child development—for example, family, success in school—are still available to assist in desistance. Although conflicts arise over appropriate short-term behaviors, these adolescents continue to recognize the importance of parents' opinions on long-term goals. Moreover, the tensions that are produced between parents and children during adolescence do not generally undermine the overall quality of the affective relationship (Gecas & Seff, 1990). Because of the availability of these resources, these adolescents also are prepared to make relatively smooth transitions to conventional adult roles and social networks. Once these transitions are made, opportunities for the continuation of delinquent behavior become more and more foreclosed.

PROSOCIAL CAREERS

Just as there is a relatively small proportion of the population who persist in offending across the life course, there are those who manage to avoid involvement in delinquency entirely. For example, in the Rochester Youth Development Study, 12% of the respondents (9% of the males and 14% of the females) did not self-report involvement in delinquency or substance use prior to the end of high school. What accounts for their persistent prosocial orientation?

To establish a persistent pattern of prosocial behavior, conditions in early childhood either must prevent the development of predispositions to antisocial behavior or be able to compensate for those predispositions so that they do not lead to antisocial behavior. Social and economic circumstances well above those characterized as indicative of structural adversity therefore play a key role in generating conforming behavior early in the life course. Although having the economic means to provide for one's family does not preclude the possibility of having children who exhibit antisocial behavior, it does reduce the risk. A secure financial position reduces parental levels of stress and antisocial behavior, thereby increasing the probability that they will exhibit more appropriate parenting behaviors. They also are likely to have the human and social capital to ameliorate or correct the developmental consequences of early temperamental difficulties such as oppositional behavior.

The strong bond to the family and the absence or control of negative temperamental qualities set the stage for continuity of prosocial behavior. Antisocial behavior is not part of the behavioral repertoire of these children and therefore such behavior does not have an adverse effect on family life, peer relationships, and school success. Indeed, the prosocial behavior exhibited by these children serves to increase the strength of the child's ties to conventionality. Parents respond to the good behavior of their children by rewarding them, exhibiting more affection and greater involvement (Gecas & Seff, 1990). Teachers favor children who are attentive and interested in their schoolwork. Children tend to establish friendship ties with peers who behave in similar ways (Kandel, 1978), thus establishing a social network that constrains behavior toward conformity (Krohn, 1986).

Not only does the pattern of relationships established in the early years increase ties to conventionality, but as these children age they are more likely to have limited access to deviant social networks and learning environments. The boundaries of social groupings that are formed in adolescence often are difficult to penetrate (Schwendinger & Schwendinger, 1985). Thus, prosocial youth are encapsulated in a prosocial cocoon facilitating their continued conformity. The increased demand for autonomy results in decisions about alternative prosocial activities rather than between prosocial and antisocial behavior.

These youth also are more likely to have developed the necessary human and social capital to successfully meet the challenges of the transition to adulthood. Not burdened with structural adversity, poor school records, or deviant labels that beset the youth who are involved in antisocial behavior, prosocial adolescents are more likely to experience smooth, on-time transitions to adulthood.

CONCLUSION

In its initial statement by Thornberry (1987), interactional theory presented a theoretical explanation for delinquent behavior, especially as it is exhibited during the adolescent years. In the decade since interactional theory was first proposed, longitudinal data increasingly have pointed to the importance of extending our understanding of antisocial careers across the full life course, from infancy through adulthood. This view has been heavily influenced by life course theory (see Elder, 1997, for an excellent overview) and the adoption of this perspective by recent theories of crime (Moffitt, 1993, 1997; Sampson & Laub, 1993, 1997). In this chapter we have examined these same issues from the perspective of interactional theory.

Our starting point stems from an understanding that the age of onset of antisocial behavior is continuously distributed across the age structure, at least from toddlerhood through early adolescence. Rather than viewing antisocial behavior as starting early *or* late as implied by typological theories, the data suggest that it starts *earlier* or *later*. Moreover, it appears that desistance too is continuously distributed. While there is a clear correlation between early onset and the length of careers, it also is clear that these two dimensions of antisocial careers are to a substantial degree independent.

The issue of continuity and change is quite complex. There is long-term life course continuity in both antisocial behavior and in prosocial behavior. There also are substantial degrees of change, with somewhat intricate patterns interweaving age of onset and age of desistance. For example, while early onset is correlated with greater persistence, it is quite clear that some offenders with an early onset persist for many years while others desist fairly quickly. To explain these patterns is a daunting challenge. In this chapter we have made an initial attempt to do so; one that no doubt leaves many unanswered questions. It is an intriguing and important issue though, and one that warrants careful consideration in future theoretical and empirical works.

Acknowledgments

This chapter was prepared under Grant 96-MU-FX-0014 from the Office of Juvenile Justice and Delinquency Prevention, Office of Justice Programs, US Department of Justice, and Grant 5 R01 DA05512-07 from the National Institute on Drug Abuse. Points of view or opinions in this chapter are those of the authors and do not necessarily represent the official position or policies of the funding agencies. The authors would like to thank Drs. Carolyn Smith and Rolf Loeber for helpful comments on earlier drafts of this chapter.

ENDNOTES

1. Following Tolan, Guerra, and Kendall (1995), we adopt a broad definition of antisocial behavior as

> a spectrum of behavior usually marked by aggression but representing transgressions against societal norms. In many cases, such behavior represents illegal acts, but not always. Antisocial behavior can range from relatively innocuous but obnoxious behavior such as tantrums and oppositional behavior to the most socially and criminally offensive acts. (p. 515)

We use the terms antisocial behavior, delinquency, and criminal offending somewhat interchangeably in this chapter but with concern for the developmental- or age-appropriateness of these various manifestations of antisocial behavior.

2. Although we focus on continuity of antisocial behavior in this section, we recognize that not all offenders who initiate antisocial behavior at these very young ages continue to misbehave through adulthood. The explanation for their desistance is similar to the reasons why early onset offenders desist and it is discussed in the next section.

REFERENCES

Belsky, J., Woodworth, S., & Crnic, K. (1996). Troubled family interaction during toddlerhood. *Development and Psychopathology*, *8*, 477–495.

Benson, P., Williams, D., & Johnson, A. (1987). *The quicksilver years: The hopes and fears of early adolescence.* San Francisco: Harper & Row Publishers.

Cairns, R. B., & Cairns, B. D. (1994). *Lifelines and risks: Pathways of youth in our time.* New York: Cambridge University Press.

Caspi, A., Bem, D. J., & Elder, G. H. Jr. (1989). Continuities and consequences of interactional styles across the life course. *Journal of Personality, 57,* 375–406.

Caspi, A., Elder, G. H. Jr., & Herbener, E. S. (1990). Childhood personality and the prediction of life-course patterns. In L. Robins & M. Rutter (Eds.), *Straight and devious pathways from childhood to adulthood* (pp. 13–35). New York: Cambridge University Press.

Cohen, A. (1955). *Delinquent boys.* New York: Free Press.

Coie, J. D., & Dodge, K. A. (1998). Aggression and antisocial behavior. In W. Damon (Ed.), *Handbook of child psychology* (Vol. 3, pp. 779–862). New York: Wiley.

Coie, J. D., Dodge, K. A., & Kupersmidt, J. (1990). Peer group behavior and social status. In S. R. Asher & J. D. Coie (Eds.), *Peer rejection in childhood* (pp. 17–59). New York: Cambridge University Press.

Coie, J. D., Lochman, J. E., Terry, R., & Hyman, C. (1992). Predicting early adolescent disorder from childhood aggression and peer rejection. *Journal of Consulting and Clinical Psychology, 60,* 783–792.

Coleman, J. S. (1988). Social capital in the creation of human capital. *American Journal of Sociology, 94*(Suppl), S95–S120.

Conger, J. J. (1991). *Adolescence and youth: Psychological development in a changing world,* 4th ed. New York: HarperCollins Publishers.

Conger, R. D., Ge, X., Elder, G. H. Jr., Lorenz, F. O., & Simons, R. L. (1994). Economic stress, coercive family process and developmental problems of adolescents. *Child Development, 65,* 541–561.

Elder, G. H. Jr. (1997). The life course and human development. In R. M. Lerner (Ed.), *Handbook of child psychology* (Vol. 1, pp. 939–991). New York: Wiley.

Elliott, D. S. (1994). Serious violent offenders: Onset, developmental course, and termination. *Criminology, 32,* 1–21.

Gecas, V., & Seff, M. A. (1990). Social class and self-esteem: Psychological centrality, compensation, and the relative effects of work and home. *Social Psychology Quarterly, 53,* 165–173.

Glueck, S., & Glueck, E. (1943). *Criminal careers in retrospect.* New York: The Commonwealth Fund.

Gottfredson, M. R., & Hirschi, T. (1990). *A general theory of crime.* Stanford, CA: Stanford University Press.

Grolnick, W. S., Bridger, L. J., & Connell, J. P. (1996). Emotion regulation in 2-year-olds: Strategies and emotional expression in 4 contexts. *Child Development, 67,* 928–942.

Hagan, J. (1992). The poverty of a classless criminology—The American Society of Criminology 1991 Presidential Address. *Criminology, 30,* 1–19.

Howell, J. C., Krisberg, B., Hawkins, J. D., & Wilson, J. J. (Eds.). (1995). *Sourcebook on serious, violent and chronic juvenile offenders.* Thousand Oaks, CA: Sage.

Jang, S. J., & Smith, C. A. (1997). A test of reciprocal causal relationships among parental supervision, affective ties, and delinquency. *Journal of Research in Crime and Delinquency, 34,* 307–336.

Jones, R. L. (Ed.). (1989). *Black adolescents.* Berkeley, CA: Cobb & Henry.

Kandel, D. B. (1978). Similarity in real life adolescent friendship pairs. *Journal of Personality and Social Psychology, 36,* 306–312.

Kellam, S. G., Ensminger, S. E., & Turner, R. J. (1977). Family structure and the mental health of children. *Archives of General Psychiatry, 34,* 1012–1022.

Kopp, C. B. (1989). Regulation of distress and negative emotions: A developmental view. *Developmental Psychology, 25,* 343–354.

Krohn, M. D. (1986). The web of conformity: A network approach to the explanation of delinquent behavior. *Social Problems, 33,* 581–593.

Krohn, M. D., Thornberry, T. P., Collins-Hall, L., & Lizotte, A. J. (1995). School dropout, delinquent behavior, and drug use: An examination of the causes and consequences of dropping out of school. In H. B. Kaplan (Ed.), *Drugs, crime, and other deviant adaptations: Longitudinal studies* (pp. 163–183). New York: Plenum Press.

Krohn, M. D., Lizotte, A. J., Thornberry, T. P., Smith, C. A., & McDowall, D. (1996). Reciprocal causal relationships among drug use, peers, and beliefs: A five-wave panel model. *Journal of Drug Issues, 26,* 405–428.

Krohn, M. D., Lizotte, A. J., & Perez, C. M. (1997). The interrelationship between substance use and precocious transitions to adult statuses. *Journal of Health and Social Behavior, 38,* 87–103.

Ladd, G. W. (1990). Having friends, keeping friends, making friends, and being liked by peers in the classroom: Predictors of children's early school adjustment. *Child Development, 61,* 312–331.

Lee, C. L., & Bates, J. E. (1985). Mother–child interaction at two years and perceived difficult temperament. *Child Development, 56,* 1314–1325.

Lipsey, M. W., & Wilson, D. B. (1998). Effective intervention for serious juvenile offenders: A synthesis of research.

In R. Loeber & D. P. Farrington (Eds.), *Serious and violent juvenile offenders: Risk factors and successful interventions* (pp. 313–345). Thousand Oaks, CA: Sage.
Loeber, R., & LeBlanc, M. (1990). Toward a developmental criminology. In M. Tonry & N. Morris (Eds.), *Crime and justice: An annual review of research* (Vol. 11, pp. 375–473). Chicago: University of Chicago Press.
Magnusson, D. (1988). *Individual developments from an interactional perspective: A longitudinal study*. Hillsdale, NJ: Lawrence.
McLoyd, V. (1990). The impact of economic hardship on black families and children: Psychological distress, parenting, and socioemotional development. *Child Development, 61*, 311–346.
Moffitt, T. E. (1993). "Life-course-persistent" and "adolescence-limited" antisocial behavior: A developmental taxonomy. *Psychological Review, 100*, 674–701.
Moffitt, T. E. (1996). The neuropsychology of conduct disorder. In P. Cordella & L. J. Siegel (Eds.), *Readings in contemporary criminological theory* (pp. 85–106). Boston, MA: Northeastern University Press.
Moffitt, T. E. (1997). Adolescence-limited and life-course-persistent offending: A complementary pair of developmental theories. In T. P. Thornberry (Ed.), *Developmental theories of crime and delinquency* (Vol. 7, pp. 11–54). New Brunswick, NJ: Transaction Publishers.
Moffitt, T. E., Lynam, D. R., & Silva, P. A. (1994). Neuropsychological tests predict persistent male delinquency. *Criminology, 32*, 101–124.
Morash, M., & Rucker, L. (1989). An exploratory study of the connection of mother's age at childbearing to her children's delinquency in four data sets. *Crime and Delinquency, 35*, 45–93.
Patterson, G. R., Capaldi, D., & Bank, L. (1991). An early starter model for predicting delinquency. In D. J. Pepler & K. H. Rubin (Eds.), *The development and treatment of childhood aggression* (pp. 139–168). Hillsdale, NJ: Erlbaum.
Patterson, G. R., Reid, J. B., & Dishion, T. J. (1992). *Antisocial boys*. Eugene, OR: Castalia.
Polk, K., & Schafer, W. E. (1972). *Schools and delinquency*. Englewood Cliffs, NJ: Prentice-Hall.
Robins, L. N. (1978). Sturdy childhood predictors of adult antisocial behavior: Replications from longitudinal studies. *Psychological Medicine, 8*, 611–622.
Rutter, M. (1987). Psychological resilience and protective mechanisms. *American Journal of Orthopsychiatry, 47*, 316–331.
Rutter, M. (1988). Longitudinal data in the study of causal processes: Some uses and some pitfalls. In M. Rutter (Ed.), *Studies of psychosocial risk: The power of longitudinal data* (pp. 1–28). Cambridge, England: Cambridge University Press.
Rutter, M., & Quinton, D. (1984). Parental psychiatric disorder: Effects on children. *Psychological Medicine, 14*, 853–880.
Sampson, R. J., & Laub, J. (1993). *Crime in the making: Pathways and turning points through life*. Cambridge, MA: Harvard University Press.
Sampson, R. J., & Laub, J. (1997). A life-course theory of cumulative disadvantage and the stability of delinquency. In T. P. Thornberry (Ed.), *Developmental theories of crime and delinquency* (Vol. 7, pp. 133–161). New Brunswick, NJ: Transaction Publishers.
Schwendinger, H., & Schwendinger, J. S. (1985). *Adolescent subcultures and delinquency*. Westport, CT: Praeger.
Shaw, D. S., & Bell, R. Q. (1993). Developmental theories of parental contributors to antisocial behavior. *Journal of Abnormal Child Psychology, 21*, 35–49.
Shaw, D. S., Keenan, K., & Vondra, J. I. (1994). Developmental precursors of antisocial behaviors ages 1 to 3. *Developmental Psychology, 30*, 355–364.
Smith, C. A., & Carlson, B. (1997). Stress, coping, and resilience in children and youth. *Social Service Review, 71*, 231–256.
Smith, C. A., Lizotte, A. J., Thornberry, T. P., & Krohn, M. D. (1995). Resilient youth: Identifying factors that prevent high-risk youth from engaging in delinquency and drug use. In J. Hagan (Ed.), *Delinquency and disrepute in the life course* (pp. 217–247). Greenwich, CT: JAI Press.
Spencer, M. B., & Dornbusch, S. M. (1990). Challenges in studying minority youth. In S. S. Feldman & G. R. Elliott (Eds.), *At the threshold: The developing adolescent* (pp. 123–146). Cambridge, MA: Harvard University Press.
Stinchecomb, A. L. (1964). *Rebellion in a high school*. Chicago: Quadrangle Press.
Stott, D. H. (1978). Epidemiological indicators of the origins of behavior disturbance as measured by the Bristol Social Adjustment Guides. *Genetic Psychology Monographs, 97*, 127–159.
Stouthamer-Loeber, M., Loeber, R., Huizinga, D., & Porter, P. (1997). *The early onset of persistent serious offending*. Unpublished report to the Office of Juvenile Justice and Delinquency Prevention, Washington, DC.
Thornberry, T. P. (1987). Toward an interactional theory of delinquency. *Criminology, 25*, 863–891.
Thornberry, T. P. (Ed.). (1997). Introduction: Some advantages of developmental and life-course perspectives for the

study of crime and delinquency. In *Developmental theories of crime and delinquency* (Vol. 7, pp. 1–10). New Brunswick, NJ: Transaction Publishers.

Thornberry, T. P., Lizotte, A. J., Krohn, M. D., Farnworth, M., & Jang, S. J. (1991). Testing interactional theory: An examination of reciprocal causal relationships among family, school, and delinquency. *Journal of Quantitative Criminology*, *82*, 3–35.

Thornberry, T. P., Lizotte, A. J., Krohn, M. D., Farnworth, M., & Jang, S. J. (1994). Delinquent peers, beliefs, and delinquent behavior: A longitudinal test of interactional theory. *Criminology*, *32*, 47–83.

Thornberry, T. P., Smith, C. A., & Howard, G. J. (1997). Risk factors for teenage fatherhood. *Journal of Marriage and the Family*, *59*, 505–522.

Tolan, P. H., Guerra, N. G., & Kendall, P. C. (1995). Introduction to special section: Prediction and prevention of antisocial behavior in children and adolescents. *Journal of Consulting and Clinical Psychology*, *63*, 515–517.

Werner, E. E., & Smith, R. S. (1992). *Overcoming the odds: High risk children from birth to adulthood.* Ithaca, NY: Cornell University Press.

Zahn-Waxler, C., Iannotti, R. J., Cummings, E. M., & Denham, S. (1990). Antecedents of problem behaviors in children of depressed mothers. *Development and Psychopathology*, *2*, 271–291.

16

Reasoning and Justice

SUSAN O. WHITE

A large part of law-in-action involves a process of reasoning in which people consider whether a behavior is right or wrong, legal or illegal, and weigh the fairness of law enforcement and the justice of legal outcomes. For the most part, social science has ignored this process of reasoning when examining the nexus between youth and justice, choosing instead to focus on explaining juvenile delinquent behavior or describing the operation of the justice system or measuring system outcomes. That reasoning is part of the nexus between youth and justice has not been denied. The challenge has been to design quality research with which to test the hypothesis.

Social science has not been entirely silent about legal reasoning, however. This chapter describes and critiques several lines of research that suggest a significant role for the process of reasoning in the nexus between youth and justice. Key questions are: Is there a causal connection between reasoning and behavior? Is reasoning a person variable (internal to the individual) or is it a product of the social environment? Is moral reasoning connected to particular contexts? What basic psychological processes underlie the use and effects of moral reasoning? What basic social processes underlie the use and effects of moral reasoning?

Several theoretical approaches have been used to address these general questions, among them cognitive developmental theory, differential association theory, social relations theory, attribution theory, and theories about the connections between beliefs/values and behaviors. Only the first two have been applied to youth in particular. Cognitive developmental theory was initiated by an interest in how children and youth develop the capacity to reason about moral problems, although this literature is no longer entirely age specific. Differential association, a version of social learning theory, focuses on explaining juvenile delinquency, that is, why some youth deviate from social norms, often to the extent of breaking the law. These two theoretical approaches are discussed and critiqued in the first two sections below. A third approach, which analyzes the social processes that affect moral reasoning, is proposed in the third section.

SUSAN O. WHITE • Department of Political Science, University of New Hampshire, Durham, New Hampshire 03824.

Handbook of Youth and Justice, edited by White. Kluwer Academic / Plenum Publishers, New York, 2001.

THE COGNITIVE MODEL OF MORAL REASONING

On the face of it, a developmental approach would seem to offer considerable insight into youth behaviors and attitudes, since a large proportion of the social scientific work that is focused on youth is based on theories that purport to explain physical, emotional, and cognitive development from childhood through adolescence to adulthood. Of these, only cognitive developmentalists claim to address the nexus between youth and justice directly, however. From Piaget (1932) to Kohlberg (1969, 1984, 1986) to Tapp and Levine (1970, 1974), cognitive development theory created a debate about how youths form and change their conceptions of justice and fairness.

Kohlberg's (1969) influential "stage theory" of cognitive development asserted that children move through three levels (and six stages) in invariant sequence, from an egocentric preconventional level to a community or peer-determined conventional level toward a post-conventional level of "principled" reasoning. Theoretically, the postconventional stages produced moral reasoning that was independent of the social influences that defined conventional reasoning. Much research has shown that relatively few individuals, and perhaps even whole cultures, ever reach stage six; both preconventional and conventional reasoning are common in all cultures (Kohlberg, 1984).

Reasoning and Behavior

Much of the social science research community took a somewhat "so what?" attitude toward the cognitive claims, however, because the cognitive model simply assumed that behavior was related to the reasoning process and then proceeded to concentrate almost solely on reasoning. Some research, especially with delinquents, did attempt to demonstrate the relationship between moral reasoning and behavior empirically. Blasi (1980) reviewed a number of these studies and found some evidence that adjudged delinquents were more likely to use the lowest level of moral reasoning (preconventional), as defined by Kohlberg (1969), than nondelinquents. He also found, however, that both groups exhibited considerable inconsistency across Kohlberg's three levels of moral reasoning: preconventional, conventional, postconventional. In addition, methodological defects in the studies Blasi reviewed (such as a lack of matching nondelinquent samples in some cases and noncomparability across definitions of delinquency) made it difficult to draw useful conclusions.

A different kind of attempt to demonstrate the empirical relationship between reasoning and behavior produced some rather startling results, however. In a field experiment, Cohn and White (1990) tested competing hypotheses from cognitive developmental and social learning theory. They found that legal reasoning (Levine & Tapp, 1977; Tapp & Levine, 1970, 1974) was a better predictor (than the legal environment) of legal socialization effects, such as changes in attitudes toward rules and their enforcement, changes in legal reasoning, and changes in rule-violating behaviors over time. This study challenged the "so what?" attitude toward the cognitive model and prompted further investigation into the relationship between reasoning and behavior.

Challenging the "So What"

The cognitive model assumes that reasoning and behavior are related because the model defines cognitive structures in terms of a dynamic of social interaction in which developing individuals shape their environment while adapting to it:

> The fundamental mechanism in the learning process is the cognitive structure which is a representation of the environment through which people receive and organize information. Incoming information is "assimilated" into an existing cognitive structure which in turn acts on the information in order to "accommodate" to changes signalled by the new information. (Cohn & White, 1992, p. 98)

In this interactional learning process, the individual maintains autonomy while responding to environmental influences.

The finding that reasoning was a better predictor of legal socialization effects prompted meticulous investigation of the social interaction data involved. The study (Cohn & White, 1990) was a quasi-experiment that varied the style and extent of rule enforcement in two college dormitories; the data were surveys of residents' attitudes in the two experimental and control settings at the beginning of the fall semester and at the end of the spring semester. What did these data reveal about reasoning and the cognitive learning process during legal socialization? First, there was little evidence of a direct relationship between reasoning and behavior; rather, the relationship was mediated by norms of behavior and rule enforcement. The research design measured four variables over time: (1) legal reasoning "level" or type (Levine & Tapp, 1977; Tapp & Levine, 1970, 1974); (2) approval–disapproval of 24 rule-violating behaviors; (3) approval–disapproval of enforcing rules against the same behaviors; and (4) reported frequency of engaging in the behaviors. Variables 2 and 3, understood as norms of behavior and enforcement, mediated between reasoning and behavior (Cohn & White, 1990, pp. 99ff).

The mediating model illustrates how social action underlies the cognitive learning process. Cognitive development measures of legal reasoning represent general concepts or organizing principles, for example, "what is a rule," "what is a law," "why should people follow rules," "what is a fair rule." The mediating variables in question—norms of behavior and norms of rule enforcement—are specific and situational, for example, "to what extent do you approve or disapprove of underage drinking"; "to what extent do you approve or disapprove of enforcing rules against kegs in dorm rooms?" According to the authors of the study, "the mediating model suggests that these norms provide the linkage between the general conceptual structure and the particular situation" (Cohn & White, 1992, p. 102). They also provide the basis for interpreting information about a social situation in moral–legal terms. In this way, the reasoning process creates moral meaning.

A second conclusion about reasoning and the cognitive learning process that can be drawn from these data resulted from a path analysis (Blalock, 1964; Duncan, 1985). This analysis used the mediating model as the basis for tracing the causal path between reasoning and behavior. In one version the path ran from reasoning through the mediating norms to behavior; in the other version, the direction of the path was reversed. It was found that the latter direction occurred most frequently, suggesting that moral–legal reasoning often follows instead of preceding the behavior to which it is linked. The authors speculated that this finding illustrated a critical concept in cognitive development theory, namely, the effects of "disequilibrium" in a new social environment.

Kohlberg (1969) argued that cognitive learning derives from "discrepancies between the child's action system or expectancies and the experienced events" and suggested "some moderate or optimal degree of discrepancy as constituting the most effective experience for structural change" (p. 356). In short, the concept of "equilibration" in cognitive development theory anticipates that the causal arrow between reasoning and behavior will move in both directions during the learning process. Periods of "disequilibrium" define adolescence, when both creativity and experiential pressures combine to produce new cognitive structures, new moral meanings. According to Cohn and White (1992), "sometimes the cognitive structures determine the moral meaning of a behavior and sometimes disequilibration reverses the process, allowing the behavioral experience to define the cognitive structure." The mediating norms "can either help the cognitive structure to interpret the behavior or can facilitate the formation of new cognitive structures" (1992, p. 103).

While this conclusion does not wholly answer the "so what?" complaint against cognitive theory, it does provide a plausible explanation for some prominent findings in the delinquency literature about the use of reasoning in justifying or excusing behavior (Hartung, 1965; Scott & Lyman, 1968; Sykes & Matza, 1957). These findings are discussed in more detail below, but it should be noted here that the use of excusing or justifying locutions does not entail a causal relationship with the behaviors they are referencing. The processes of equilibration and disequilibration defined by the cognitive model suggest that the purposes served by these locutions need not be motivational in character. But what do these processes have to do with reasoning about justice?

In short, the primary "so what?" question with respect to the claims of the cognitive model cannot be answered solely by reference to the processes of cognition. We still have to ask: If there is a relationship between reasoning and behavior in a justice context, how does the cognitive model account for it? Another finding from the field experiment is suggestive. The data included both attitudinal and behavioral measures concerning rule enforcement: approval–disapproval of enforcing rules against 24 rule-violating behaviors and reported frequency of engaging in these same behaviors. One might argue that situations of rule enforcement are *prima facie* instances of moral–legal content. If the cognitive model is correct that there is a relationship between reasoning and behavior, such situations should induce that connection and these data should provide two ways of detecting it. That is, one can ask whether an individual agrees or disagrees with the rule and whether the individual has followed or violated it.

Is a connection between reasoning and behavior more likely to occur when the individual agrees with the rule or disagrees with the rule? According to the study, "neither agreement or disagreement with the rule had any systematic effect on the likelihood of a connection between reasoning and action" (Cohn & White, 1992, p. 107). When the question was asked about the effects of being a follower or violator, the answer was the same: "A connection between reasoning and action was as likely to occur for rule-followers as for rule-violators" (p. 107). In other words, the mere existence of moral–legal content per se in these rule enforcement situations did not appear to induce a connection between reasoning and behavior, nor did this moral–legal content differentiate between positive and negative experiences with rule enforcement.

Cognitive developmental theory goes beyond the mere existence of moral–legal situational content, however, to require a particular mode of interaction with the social environment, namely, role-taking. The field experiment provided the basis for exploring whether this aspect of cognitive development finally revealed an empirical connection between reasoning and behavior. Role-taking experiences are meaningful for cognitive development because, according to the theory, they place the individual in a context of different points of view. In this way, the individual has opportunities to develop the capacity for seeing other points of view and for the sense of reciprocity that underlies the concept of fairness. Role-taking, as defined in this way, is a fundamental cornerstone of cognitive developmental theory (Cohn & White, 1990; Kohlberg, 1969, 1976; Levine & Tapp, 1977).

The field experiment was designed to provide role-taking experiences for subjects in one condition but not for the subjects in the other condition (Cohn & White, 1990). In one dormitory, a "peer authority" condition was established in which the residents decided all cases of rule violation through their internal conduct board; in another dormitory, all cases of rule violation were referred to a university conduct board. As part of this "external authority" condition, staff were required to enforce all rules strictly. By contrast, enforcement in the peer authority condition was controlled by the residents. The cases that were considered by the internal peer authority board were debated extensively within the resident population, affording many opportunities for role-taking in a moral–legal context. The external authority condition provided no opportunities for role-taking, but did result in retaliation against enforcers and extensive vandalism.

Once again, path analysis was used to determine the relationship between legal reasoning and rule-violating behavior, as mediated by the norms of behavior and rule enforcement. The authors conducted separate path analyses for each of the experimental conditions to compare the frequency with which the path models successfully predicted a mediated relationship between reasoning and behavior in each of the two conditions. Significant predictive path models were found to be more frequent in the peer authority condition than in the external authority condition. The authors concluded that this differential in connections between reasoning and behavior in the two experimental conditions resulted from the extensive opportunities for role-taking in the peer authority condition and the lack of such opportunities in the external authority condition (Cohn & White, 1990, 1992).

In summary, the "so what" complaint against the cognitive model is a response to the lack of concern about demonstrating rather than assuming a relationship between reasoning and behavior. The complaint was successfully challenged by the Cohn and White field experiment, which not only demonstrated a relationship between reasoning and behavior but did so within the framework of cognitive developmental theory. Even if the reader does not find the theory itself persuasive, however, this study strongly suggests that those interested in the nexus of youth and justice should take reasoning seriously (Cohn & White, 1992).

From Development to Difference?

Another, and probably more problematic, complaint against cognitive developmental theory has to do with its conceptual foundation in developmentalism. The theory's intellectual grandfather, Piaget (1932), and father, Kohlberg (1969), both thought that a child's reasoning passed through "stages" or "levels" of development, from the concrete and egocentric concerns of the young child to greater social awareness. Kohlberg specified three levels (encompassing six stages) of cognitive development: preconventional, conventional, and postconventional, occurring in invariant sequence. Children at level one are egocentric and largely closed to social convention; at level two, a child is open to group influence and social expectations; a child at level three can make principled judgments regardless of societal expectations and pressures. This description of the complex Kohlbergian scheme, although brief and oversimplified, should suffice for the purpose of discussing the argument that developmentalism is an unacceptable basis for a scientific understanding or account of reasoning.

The principal complaint that has been directed both at Kohlberg's analysis of moral reasoning (1969, 1976, 1984) and at Tapp and Levine's (Tapp & Levine, 1970, 1974; Levine & Tapp, 1977) analysis of legal reasoning is fourfold. Critics contend that a "levels" analysis is (1) mistaken with respect to invariant sequence; (2) inaccurate across gender, class, and culture; (3) elitist; and (4) biased toward Western values.

Kohlberg argued that the developmental process through the six stages (three levels) of moral reasoning occurs in invariant sequence. He also argued that the stages were related to each other logically, in a "hierarchy" of moral thought. A number of studies have produced findings that are contrary to the invariant sequence assumption. Blasi's (1980) review of empirical studies of moral reasoning indicates that subjects often gave inconsistent responses, that is, over a series of questions, individual subjects gave responses representing different Kohlbergian stages. Levine and Tapp (1977) reported various inconsistencies among different age groups and opted to reject a strict interpretation of stage theory (i.e., with rigid invariant sequence) in their own theory of legal development. Cohn and White (1990), using the Tapp and Levine Rule/Law Interview scales (Levine & Tapp, 1977; Tapp, 1970; Tapp & Levine, 1974) to measure legal reasoning in college students, also found within-person inconsistencies. Even Kohlberg (1984) and his students eventually hedged their strict position on invariant sequence. They interpreted incongruous findings by introducing the concept of a "soft" stage that acknowledges within-person inconsistencies while adhering to the principle of invariant sequence. Clearly, empirical testing provided little support for this aspect of Kohlberg's theory.

While invariant sequence has been vulnerable to empirical attack, its concomitant "hierarchy" of moral thought created more of an ideological controversy. Many critics pointed out that the "hierarchy" reflected a view of moral reasoning that fit the ideal of Kantian–Rawlsian liberalism but ignored gender, class, and culture differences. The gender problem was first delineated by Gilligan (1982) who noted that female subjects were less likely than males to reason at the highest level. Third-level reasoning, according to Kohlberg's theory, is based on principles of justice rather than the morality or conventional ethos of the community. Gilligan argued that Kohlberg's signature dilemmas were designed to elicit certain kinds of specifically male concerns, especially with respect to rights claims and fairness across individuals, and to exclude specifically female concerns about caring and relationships. She proposed a dual theory in which both views of morality received equal weight.

Gilligan's theory challenges Kohlberg's "hierarchy" in two ways: (1) by replacing the hierarchical structure of reasoning with alternative modes of moral thinking, and (2) by focusing more on the circumstances of the respondents' social environment than on cognitive processes. That is, males tend to be drawn to competitive situations, in which fairness and the delineations of rights and responsibilities prevail, whereas females tend to be drawn to situations in which relationships are at stake. It is not that females reason at a lower level, Gilligan argued, but rather that the gendered circumstances of life lead females to reason differently about morality than do males. She further argued that Kohlberg's methodology, tied as it was to dilemmas about rights and fairness across individuals, was as faulty as his theory.

Other critics followed a similar line of attack with respect to class and culture (e.g., Broughton, 1986; Emler, 1983; Locke, 1986; Miller, 1984; Miller & Bersoff, 1992; Shweder, 1991; Vine, 1986). It was argued, for example, that the so-called punishment orientation of level one, or preconventional, reasoning is as much a function of socialization into working-class attitudes toward authority as it is of the egocentric perspectives exhibited in young children. Ethnic groups also vary in attitudes toward authority. Consequently, adults from some class and/or ethnic backgrounds will often exhibit level one, or preconventional, reasoning by Kohlbergian criteria. This kind of bias, it was argued, smacks of elitism masked as science.

In response to these criticisms of the hierarchy assumption, some of Kohlberg's students have attempted comparative studies to demonstrate the cultural universality of his theory's definition of moral judgment (Kohlberg & Nisan, 1984; Snarey & Reimer, 1984). The Israeli study, whose population was a kibbutz, not surprisingly found considerable commitment to communal (and therefore "conventional," according to Kohlberg's scoring scheme) values. This finding tends to support the thrust of Gilligan's critique that cultural learning and situational variation undercuts the hierarchy assumption. Snarey and Reimer (1984, p. 618) insisted, however, that commitment to communal values simply masked postconventional principles as conventional responses. Kohlberg and Nisan (1984) finally backed off from that claim when discussing their study in Turkey. A traditional culture, they admitted, may result in socialization that produces a *different* kind of moral development, one that is not compatible with the hierarchical structures found in the West: "It is possible that in other cultures, principles are held which are distinct from ours, and moral reasoning is used that does not fit the structures I have described" (p. 593).

Kohlberg's elaboration of the moral content to be found in reasoning goes well beyond the fundamentals of cognitive development. His attempt to stretch cognitive stage theory into a universal model of moral reasoning ultimately fails, as Shweder (1991) demonstrates elegantly in his book *Thinking Through Cultures*. Shweder argues (with particular reference to the use of symbolism in Hindu narratives of morality) that meaning, including moral meaning, is constructed differently in different cultures (Chapter 5; see also Miller, 1984). Therefore, moral reasoning by members of these other cultures will make use of their cultural narrative models.

Other students of narrative have shown that the construction of meaning varies situationally as well as culturally. This is ultimately the message of Gilligan's work on the differences in moral reasoning produced by the gendered circumstances of social life. A similar line of argument was developed by Conley and O'Barr (1990) in their study of the use of language in courts, finding that the talk of legal practitioners was oriented to rules, while laypersons in the same court context were more concerned with social relationships. These kinds of differences in the construction of moral meaning cannot be resolved into a philosophical hierarchy of values, a logical structure of rights and responsibilities, as was envisioned by the Kohlbergians.

On the basis of all of these counterexamples, it must be concluded that the strength of the cognitive model of moral reasoning cannot be found in "invariant sequence" and "hierarchy," but rather in the incorporation of different cultural and situational norms. In the end, the cognitive model defines and illuminates *difference* perhaps more than development. And since differences in norms are not dependent on any rigid sequence of developmental stages, they are not exclusively relevant to the nexus between youth and justice.

A SOCIAL LEARNING MODEL

Are we left, then, with the conclusion that moral reasoning is simply the product of cultural, class, gendered, or situational influences? Leaving aside the Kohlbergians' commitment to developmentalism, such a conclusion is problematic because it suggests that moral reasoning is neither principled nor autonomous (Vine, 1986, p. 439), but simply another form of (perhaps coerced?) behavior. Certainly, some social scientists have taken a social learning position with respect to moral reasoning (Aronfreed, 1976; Garbarino & Bronfenbrenner, 1976; Mischel & Mischel, 1976) and to the role of language ("verbalizations") in deviant behavior (Akers, 1985; Cressey, 1953; Hartung, 1965; Scott & Lyman, 1968; Sykes & Matza, 1957). What are the implications of such a position?

First, the literature that takes a social learning approach to the use of moral or legal language has been written with specific (although not exclusive) reference to the nexus between youth and justice. Some of it (e.g., Aronfreed, 1976; Garbarino & Bronfenbrenner, 1976; Mischel & Mischel, 1976) were rejoinders to Kohlberg's cognitive development model, taking issue in one way or another with his Kantian characterization of the developing autonomous moral individual. On the other hand, Akers (1985), Cressey (1953), Hartung (1965), Scott and Lyman (1968), Radosevich and Krohn (1981), and Sykes and Matza (1957) were focusing in particular on the role of language ("neutralizing definitions," "vocabularies of motive," "excuses," "accounts") in the etiology of delinquent behavior. While otherwise quite diverse in perspective, these social scientists were primarily concerned with socialization to virtue–vice, that is, with how children learn moral reasoning and behavior from the social environment.

Second, the focus on social context and socialization processes places reasoning in a role as one factor in a series of related events. The term "motivation," which has both technical and commonsense meanings, often has been used to convey this sense of a (perhaps predictable) chain of events (McCord, 1997). The implications of "neutralizing techniques" and "excuses" have been debated over the years, especially in the criminology literature, to no clear resolution. Some have argued that these excusing verbalizations may represent important motivators or "reasons for" engaging in certain acts (McCord, 1992, 1997), while others have dismissed them as mere after-the-fact rationalizations that do not operate as "imperatives for social action" (Hamlin, 1988). A longitudinal analysis of attitudes toward violence, using data from the National Youth Survey, suggests that both arguments may be correct, although for different populations (Agnew, 1994). Further, this study raises the intriguing possibility that "neutralization is most strongly related to violence among those who disapprove of violence (p. 572)."

A third implication of the social learning approach is that moral reasoning among youth populations often may be a function of the peer culture (White, 1993) and in a much stronger sense than was envisioned by Kohlberg's concept of "equilibration." Although the potential for understanding the nexus between youth and justice is obvious, it is clear from the thin and scattered literature that we have much to learn about the complexities and extent of peer influence on moral reasoning. The methodological difficulties in specifying relationships between the instrumental use of language and the social environment are severe, however, and appear to have deterred many from engaging in such research. The next section examines one attempt to explore the effects of peer influence on moral reasoning.

A SOCIAL PROCESS EXPLANATION OF MORAL REASONING

This section summarizes research into the effects of peer influence on moral reasoning. The study to be discussed was based on the premise that motivation is not, or not only, a factor internal to the individual. It is argued that motivation is a social phenomenon, derived from and defined by the basic social processes that provide meaning to all human interaction. Motivation in social contexts that give rise to questions of justice is given expression through the language of moral reasoning. The language itself is held in common within peer groups and is learned through peer interaction. The theoretical bases for this premise are familiar in works from the social scientist Sutherland (1955) to the philosopher Wittgenstein (1953). Even if motivation is a social phenomenon, however, it is obvious that variation occurs. Understanding this variation depends on understanding how peer influence operates to legitimate or devalue behavior in social contexts that give rise to questions of justice.

A Methodology

In order to clarify this process, Cohn and White (1991) showed mock hearing vignettes to small groups of university students in an experimental design. The intent was to elicit group discussion of the events portrayed in the vignettes, the accusations that resulted, and both group and individual judgments of blame or exoneration. Although these were mock hearings, each was based on a real case. Many of the subjects thought they were actually deciding the cases even though they were told that the videos were mock hearings.

The cases were designed to tap into normative responses from the subjects, who were members of the community. An earlier phase of the research had measured community norms in the following way: Members of the community were asked whether (1) they approved or disapproved of a number of rule-violating behaviors, and (2) they approved or disapproved of enforcing the rule against each of these behaviors (Cohn & White, 1990). Drawing on these data, three vignettes were created for use in the reasoning study (Cohn & White, 1991), each illustrating a particular configuration of norms on the campus. One represented a *normal prosecution*, in which a student who had engaged in behavior that was disapproved by the community was charged with assault. Specifically, this student "beat up" another student who had flirted with his girlfriend. A second vignette was termed a *deviant prosecution* because the behavior, although against the rules, did not meet with community disapproval. In the third case, the community was divided about the behavior being prosecuted, which was therefore termed a *conflict prosecution*.

More specifically, the normal prosecution case was designed so that the norm and the rule coincided, that is, the community in general disapproved of the behavior in question and approved of enforcing the rule against members who violated it. In the deviant prosecution case, the norm and the rule did not coincide. The case involved throwing beer bottles out of a dormitory window, breaking (accidentally) the windshield of a parked car. The behavior was a well-known "game" (called "hit the dumpster") that was commonly engaged in throughout the campus. The community in general neither disapproved of the behavior nor approved of enforcing the rule against it. The conflict prosecution case involved an accusation of sexual harrassment and assault in a dormitory setting. The specific facts of this case were such that the community was split, with some members disapproving the behavior and approving enforcing the rule against it, and others refusing to take the behavior seriously and disapproving enforcing the rules against it.

The study found that, in accordance with the prior measures of approval–disapproval, members of the community had little difficulty deciding that the defendant in the normal prosecution case was guilty. They had more difficulty with the deviant prosecution case because the bottle throwing had resulted in serious damage. But finally, arguing that "everybody does it" and suggesting that dormitory staff did not have 100% proof that the defendant threw the bottle that damaged the car, most members of the community found the defendant not guilty. The reasoning in both cases clearly reflected community norms. It should be noted that the verdicts in each case could have been different in a different peer culture, that is, the assault in the normal prosecution could have been perceived as a fight and therefore not serious enough to warrant blame or punishment; the bottle-throwing incident could have been perceived as serious vandalism with the potential for bodily harm. But the reasoning in these cases followed the norms of this community.

The results of the conflict prosecution case revealed what happens to peer influence and its effects on reasoning about justice when the community is divided. Once again, the reasoning followed norms, but in this case the community was divided and there were conflicting norms. The subjects reflected this normative conflict and reasoned accordingly. As in the other two cases, the reasoning itself took the form of debates over how to interpret the facts. The process of interpretation through group discussion followed a decision-making model that has become familiar to students of jury behavior: creating stories to make sense of the evidence (Pennington & Hastie, 1983, 1986, 1991, 1992). The stories incorporate what the juror hears in trial testimony into the juror's personal understanding of the situation, thereby bringing the juror's experiences to bear on interpreting the facts. The resulting story also is the product of group discussion in which the several members of the group negotiate the meaning of this or that aspect of the testimony to arrive at the final version of the story.

An Illustrative Case

To understand how this process developed in the conflict prosecution case, it will be important to consider some factual detail. The defendant, Kevin, was accused of sexually harassing over a period of months Linda, the Resident Assistant (RA) in his dormitory. Linda complained informally to the Hall Director who discussed Kevin's behavior with him and also warned him to stop. Kevin continued to harass Linda, however, and eventually trapped her in her room, closed the door, and pushed her to the floor. Another student heard the commotion and interrupted Kevin's advances.

The prosecution facts were related in testimony to the hearing board by Linda and the Hall Director; Kevin's version of the facts also was related to the hearing board as testimony. This testimony, plus a witness for each side and questioning of all witnesses by the board members, was presented by videotape to the subjects. Linda testified that over a period of months, Kevin had continually put his arm around her, touched her breasts, made remarks about her body, pinched her bottom, and snapped her bra, all in front of other students. Linda felt Kevin was trying to humiliate her because she was an RA. She felt she had to "laugh it off" in front of the other residents, so as not to lose her authority, but she told Kevin privately several times to stop. Kevin testified that he was "just joking around," which was his normal behavior. Hiding in Linda's room and closing the door was "a practical joke," as was his statement, "I'm stronger than you are," when she asked him to open the door. He admitted that he fell on top of her in the closed room but only "accidentally." His witness (female) testified that Kevin was "always joking around with girls" but was "a nice guy," and the things he did and said "did not offend" her.

The 14 group deliberations in the conflict prosecution case were similar in both structure and content. As in the other cases, the discussion proceeded within a general framework of story construction (Bennett & Feldman, 1981; Gergen & Gergen, 1984; Pennington & Hastie, 1983, 1986, 1991, 1992) wherein the members of the groups, in the course of their deliberations, try to decide who is right and who is wrong by creating a story that makes sense of the testimony. In creating the story, the members of the group interpret the facts to fit a picture of blame when they think the defendant acted wrongly or of vindication when they think the defendant acted rightly or was justified in what he did. Unlike the other two cases, however, competing stories began to emerge in each deliberation group as they discussed the conflict prosecution. One story vindicated Kevin while the other blamed him.

The *vindication story* accepted Kevin's "just joking around" defense and emphasized Linda's incapacity to cope with Kevin's "jokester" nature. The *blame story* acknowledged Linda's feelings of pain and frustration over Kevin's continuing conduct toward her, accepted her fear of his actions in her room, and emphasized that both she and the Hall Director had told him to stop. In short, the competition was over how to interpret the actions. The moral meaning of the actions was different in each story, leading the adherents of one to find Kevin innocent and of the other to find him guilty. Detailed examples of the reasoning process are presented and discussed below.

Constructing a story within a group from testimonial evidence entailed several distinct techniques. First, members of the group engaged in a process of normative definition, focusing on the personalities of the two parties and the nature of the acts. A second technique involved making reference to personal experiences within the community as benchmarks or models for interpreting events and behaviors portrayed in the testimony. Third, the discussions included many appeals to group members to validate or invalidate interpretations that were being put forward. Fourth, the members of the group contested among themselves. Eventually two subgroups emerged that constructed contrasting stories, each based on different normative definitions and their accompanying interpretations. The four techniques are illustrated below.

The Stories

In the case of Linda and Kevin, a critical element in each story was how each party could be characterized as a person. The personal characterizations would form the basis for blame or vindication. Those who favored Linda's interpretation focused on why Kevin would say and do these things. For example:

> "It seemed real immature when he was—his reaction to the whole thing."
>
> "Part of the reason I went for, uhm ... I have the feeling he was in the wrong was —I just felt like he was ... was the kind of person who said uhm, 'Well, women like this kind of thing.'"
>
> "That's his personality. That's the way he is. And ... it's just kind of sad, I mean, if that's the way a person is."
>
> "If she came up to him and told him to cut it out—to stop it ... he may try to do it more so she doesn't get the better of him. And he's gotta keep up his reputation in the dorm."
>
> "He could be the type of person who could, you know, just blow off this whole hearing, blow off everything."

But those who favored Kevin's interpretation talked about Linda as an RA, characterizing her as weak and even incompetent:

> "Yeah, it doesn't seem as if she is right for that type of floor."
>
> "I mean we all saw Linda was very serious and very emotional."
>
> "And she cannot handle a guy's floor. It's obvious that she can't. That she does not have the tolerance and the ... and just even the understanding in relating to the guys. That's something that an RA has to be able to do."
>
> "She struck me as a person who is very—I don't want to say rigid—but very serious."
>
> "Uptight."
>
> "And she's proper."
>
> "I think she was quick to jump the gun about being ..."
>
> "She wasn't very confident about herself either."
>
> "But also like he said that it wasn't as if he did this every day. He did it every once in a while and I think she just, where she is such a serious person, she just kept—every time he did it, it was another jab, and she just let it hang there."
>
> "I think she'd overreact."

It was important for the blame story that Kevin be characterized as the sort of person who would do bad things or who would behave outside the mainstream. It was important for the vindication story that Linda be characterized as the sort of person who could not cope with ordinary interactions. The blame story did not have a particular characterization of Linda, because the focus was on Kevin's actions, on what Kevin himself had admitted that he did. The vindication story, however, had to portray Linda in such a way that her credibility and authority would be undermined.

Portraying Linda as incompetent and therefore at fault was not sufficient to support vindication, however, because Kevin had admitted to the factual allegations against him (although not to their interpretation). In order to vindicate Kevin, this behavior and Kevin himself had to be characterized as harmless. In the vindication story, Kevin became a "jokester":

> "(the witness) she said that he acts that way all the time, and even toward an RA. Now maybe the other guys were hesitant about including Linda in their little festivities or whatever but, uhm, it seemed to me that Kevin was the type who it just didn't matter. I mean a jokester or a flirt."
>
> "I think that is the only way that he knows how to kind of like break the ice or something. He does it to joke around. And when they were saying how they thought that she didn't like him, the only way he knows how to deal with that is joke around and get her to like him."
>
> "It seemed as though, on that floor, the way that Linda was talking, the way that (the witness) was talking, Kevin was this big jokester. And a lot of times, jokesters get a lot of attention. They build this big image for themselves. They become kind of popular on the floor."
>
> "It's like he does it to all the girls on his floor, but it's just this one individual who's bothered by it."
>
> "I think that's what he was trying to do, though, with his joking. With his continuous joking he was trying to make it better."

The normative definitions of the parties were thus complete. There was no characterization of Linda in the blame story, but Kevin was portrayed as immature and insensitive. In contrast, the vindication story portrayed Kevin as a harmless jokester and Linda as an incompetent RA who was unable to cope with normal social interactions. This initial phase of normative definition was crucial to the process of constructing the stories because it provided the point of departure for a direction toward blame or vindication.

As the personal portrayals of the parties were developing through the group discussion, participants buttressed their characterizations with references to personal experiences. These references contributed to the direction the story was taking (toward blame or vindication) and allowed the participants to locate themselves in the context of the story. The references also were exchanges among the participants through which they developed a common ground of shared or similar experiences as a basis for their interaction in the deliberation process. In the other two cases, where there was little normative disagreement, the stories developed rather easily from the characterization of the parties toward consensus on characterizing the situation. But as disagreement arose in the sexual harassment case and the stories began to diverge, the comparing of experiences turned more toward contrasts. First, participants explored ambiguity:

> "I have two best friends here who are both males. And when they hug me or push me or choke me or ... I ... I'm just like, 'You guys, get away from me.'"
>
> "Yeah. That's fine. Great."

"But when somebody else went to do that ..."

"A stranger."

"... I'd be like ..."

"That's the general impression I was getting and I'm ... I mean, I felt like, I'm sorry, but I mean ... I mean, I don't mind it myself."

"But there are a lot of women that do."

"Because I'm used to it, because my best friend is like that. He's very ... he's very open, and he's very ... You know, like he's always fooling around. But there's a lot of women out ... my sister for one. She does not like people doing stuff like that to her."

"I wonder what the RAs are like in that building. Our RA on the floor, she's not there all the time, but the people respect her. And people have hall sports and stuff, but if she says 'stop,' they'll stop. And then we have the other floors where the RAs aren't as respected and then they say 'stop,' and they leave and it starts up again. No one listens to them."

"And that's hard because I know that RAs have a great deal of responsibility and that they, uhm, have a lot of pressure on them; a lot of people are depending on them. But what it comes down to is that if you can't handle it, then it's no good for the students and it's no good ..."

"Well, I don't know. 'Cause I know these guys down my hall in my dorm drive me nuts and I just ignore it. I still think they shouldn't do it, but I just don't say anything. I know it's not me 'cause I don't do anything. I just ignore them."

"I know people who have been brought up on sexual assault charges once for ... it was around Halloween time and they put masks on and went into a girl's room and woke her up and they were, like, just standing over her bed and she was so disoriented when she woke up that she didn't know what was going on. And they didn't say anything or touch her and she interpreted it as sexual harassment."

Then they made clear contrasts:

"Yeah. I agree. Because I have two friends that I'm really close with, and they're guys. And they hug me, you know. And I don't think anything of it. But if somebody else who walked into the room that I know that they don't know ..."

"I remember first week, my freshman year. Oh, it was my first 3 weeks. I was in this guy's room, and his roommate came in. And like, you know, it was one of the weekends and his roommate was kind of tipsy and he was a little bit tipsy and he came in laughing and knocked me on the floor and started tickling me. You know, and I didn't take it badly."

"There's a guy in my dorm—it bothers me. He's come up to the girls in my dorm, put his arms around them and put his tongue in their ear. Well, he thinks he looks real cool. He thinks the girls all like that. You tell him it bothers them and he say, "nah, nah."

"Someone in my dorm called an RA blondie and she took it as sexual harassment. He didn't jump her. It was just a few little things and he was trying to help her out. She never gave him a chance ... They just took him to Jud Board."

"One ... if there's going to be a case ... He's my RA. I have on the first floor. And the things he does to us, other people might consider assault. Like she would consider it assault. 'Cause he's the type of guy ... you've probably seen him around a lot ... You know, he ... He'll come around ... he'll put his arm around you and he knows ... And you know. I feel real uncomfortable and stuff lots of time. He's pissed me off a lot. And it's just something like *that*. You know? I couldn't take it. Like the first couple weeks I was like 'I'm not walking by this guy's door.' You know."

"I think that guys do that a lot though. Like, in my hall like guys like they say things and like I just ignore it. I don't even pay attention when they do it or say anything. Uhm, I don't know. Everybody does it ... Do you know what I mean? If everyone, I mean if everyone went to Jud Board every time."

Finally, the discussion began to turn toward interpreting "what happened." The blame story focused on Kevin's lack of response to complaints and warnings from Linda and the Hall Director. For example:

"And she warned him repeatedly, and the Hall Director warned him, so he should have known that it was maybe in some other woman's eyes it wouldn't be sexual harassment for them, but for her, it was."

"I think that the harassment charges are so true. Especially because they're not really even friends or anything. Like they're just RA and stuff like that. I also think that it would bother me if someone was coming into my room without me having them ... especially someone I didn't really ... I don't mind my friends coming into the room, but somebody else, it'd really bother me."

"On this assault thing, I just can't see him going into her room knowing that she doesn't appreciate him ... knowing that the Hall Director had to call him in. And him going in there to scare her."

"I thought Kevin was guilty of harassment, and that he's innocent on sexual assault. I couldn't imagine that he couldn't even comprehend if what Linda was saying was true. If someone was talking to me like that, I would be extremely mad about it, because I don't think that's a proper way to act toward another person, and I don't think he should be able to think that's an appropriate way to act."

"He shouldn't have said anything like that, but it should have been known that it was affecting her authority. Because that's part of her, you know, and that's part of what's really damaging about this harassment."

Many were torn, however. For example:

"You know, one thing that is true about, you know, as, you know, the guys on my floor a lot of the times will say things that I could take them as degrading, or whatever, but I just take them in stride, because it always happens. You know, everyone always gets spoken to that way, and it's kind of sad that it works out that way because it really is sexist. You know what I mean? And maybe that is what she is saying, 'It's not fair. Why are you treating me differently because I'm a woman?' You know what I mean? And I think it is sexist and I really disagree with it, but it's almost the norm. You know, to be treated that way, and—I mean not to an extreme, if I was treated extremely or really harassed, then I, you know, would really have a problem with it, but just basic stuff."

In short, the participants who constructed the blame story found that Kevin's lack of response was inexplicable in the context of normal social relations. The last comment also reflects some concern over the effects on Linda of Kevin's actions. And there also was a hint of a feminist reaction in several comments. For example:

"Uhm, yeah, I mean, when he was saying that he does that to the girls all the time, that's saying that he has no respect for girls."

"With the male as the dominating force and he feels that he can get away with that kind of stuff."

For the most part, however, there was little discussion of the sexual assault charge among those who constructed the blame story. The vindication story was dominated by the discussion of that charge. Comments on the sexual assault charge from the vindication story focused primarily on Linda's lack of understanding of social norms of behavior and the socially accepted definitions of sexual conduct. For example:

> "I thought he was innocent on both cases because I've heard the same thing on ... I live in Hubbard and I hear that stuff every day on the same subjects. Maybe the environment, the two different environments they grew up in. In Kevin's, that's just an everyday, you know, occurrence of life; it's joking around. And I know a lot of people ... myself when I see someone who seems upset or anything, I joke around with them to try to cheer them up."
>
> "I think ... I do believe that she was reading into it more than what was really happening."
>
> "If she didn't have to deal with ... well ... look out you're on a floor with all males, there may be some harassment going on that you'll need to look out for. There may be ..."
>
> "Maybe she needs a lesson too on ..."
>
> "Yep. She may have been really quick to jump the gun because that may have been one of her fears as an RA."
>
> "I think assault, like he said, is more, you know, doing something more extreme and physical than what he did."
>
> "Yeah, and plus the fact that he was going into the thing thinking it was a joke."

It was clear from a number of comments that the normative definition of sexual assault in that community did not include threats or physical contact unless a completed "rape" occurred. For example:

> "Like assault, when I think of assault, I think of like rape."
>
> "Uhm, so I don't think he was really guilty. 'Cause assault really means assault, you know, if you get raped or something, then obviously it is assault."

The fact that Kevin admitted that he had hidden in Linda's room, had closed the door when she returned to her room and then made a sexually suggestive remark, had grabbed her when she tried to open the door to leave, and had fallen on top of her and then made a sexually suggestive remark did not fit the community's expectations of what would count as sexual assault. In short, the interpretation of that factual situation was socially mediated to exclude any factors that might fit a characterization of sexual violence.

So many of the participants changed their initial judgment on sexual assault as the deliberations unfolded (62% down to 29%) that it is important to identify what kinds of social influences contributed to the transition from one normative definition to another. One typical exchange is instructive:

> "He was part of the social norm. It doesn't mean that he was right or wrong, but ..."
>
> "Who says what the punishment should be? That's tough. He thought he was right."
>
> "He has to be shown that he ... in some cases that type of thinking is wrong, in that, you know ..."
>
> 'But he was led to believe that it'd all right to do it that way, you know? So it should be ..."
>
> "That's not true, because she told him for her, it wasn't right."

This exchange demonstrates how the normative process is influenced by basic social understandings of what is blameworthy and what is not. While it led to vindication for Kevin, it did not actually endorse his behavior. Rather, since it is understandable that Kevin would think what he did was socially acceptable, he could not be blamed.

Furthermore, it was not difficult to find socially understandable bases for undermining Linda's right to complain. For example:

> "I think that's why she interpreted what happened in the room the way she did. I think, just because the way she felt about him. That had a lot to do with it."
>
> "He wasn't viewing Linda as a stranger. He was viewing her as ... another person on the floor, and he was being friendly with her. But she was viewing him as ..."
>
> "A stranger."

After all, Linda's interpretation did not have much standing because it was merely a subjective judgment that was not ratified by social interpretation. For example:

> "It's also how she interprets it. If he says something just kidding and in that tone of voice, but she takes it as an advance, then ..."
>
> "Especially if he gets on her nerves to begin with, then everything else that he does or says she's gonna interpret it the wrong way."
>
> "Like I said, if she doesn't like him to begin with, then, you know, she's going to interpret things accordingly."

In short, the vindication story discredited Linda's interpretation of the incident and allowed participants to discount a number of her factual claims. For example, a number of adherents to the vindication story asserted that Linda should have told Kevin to stop, when it had been admitted in testimony by Kevin that he had been told to stop more than once by Linda and was officially warned by the Hall Director. Adherents of the vindication story also discounted Linda's fear at finding Kevin in her room and at his subsequent behavior. They also discounted her version of being grabbed as she reached for the door and her description of what occurred with Kevin on top of her on the floor.

In fact, the vindication story not only discredited Linda's interpretation but resulted in sympathy for Kevin. For example:

> "Yeah, I like when he said that he's afraid that he's not going to go and touch people any more. See he's ... now he's ... he's got ... he's kind of being denied his rights, too, because he can't act the way he thinks he's been ... acted all his life, because one person said, "Wait ..."
>
> "I think he might resent her even if he does get relocated because he's got his friends on the floor already, and just because she feels that, uhm, snapping her bra is offensive, he has to move to a whole different dorm and find new friends."
>
> "And in a way that's not fair."

The blame story did prevail on the issue of sexual harassment. But 12 of the 14 groups changed from an initial finding of guilty on sexual assault to vindication on that charge. The discussion of a penalty for Kevin also followed the vindication story. In fact, some thought that Linda should be relocated and even receive a penalty. For example:

> "I would say guilty, but I'd also say that Linda's guilty."
>
> "Yeah. I would say both."
>
> "I would make a very light penalty."
>
> "Yeah. Very light penalty for him."
>
> "I suggest that she be moved. That she get out of there."
>
> "When you think about it, he was so shocked to be there and ... he seemed so stressed out."
>
> "It was kind of good for him to know that people may react like that."

"Yeah. Exactly. He's aware of it now. I really don't believe that he did anything vicious."

"The only thing I disagree with now is ... the dislocation on his part ... he's got a lot of friends there now, and if she ..."

"Well, obviously she wasn't too comfortable to be there to begin with."

"I think she should be the one relocated."

"Yeah. She ought to be relocated to an all girls' dorm."

"And he just have some disciplinary action taken, you know?"

"Maybe he can work with a group this semester. Like, don't they have groups about sexual harassment?"

"Yeah. Just something for 6 weeks, 4 weeks."

"He's had the experience now. He's been accused of this and ..."

"And she can be relocated."

"So, do we all agree that there was no sexual assault, and they're both guilty?"

"Of misinterpreting each other. Misinterpretation."

"They're both guilty of miscommunication."

"We can't, you know, we can't exactly say that because she's not on trial for anything."

"But I think that he should be marked down as guilty."

"Yeah."

"With the punishment already done."

"I don't think discipline would even be necessary."

"Yeah. I think this is enough for him."

"But she should be relocated."

"Yeah."

The effects of these interpretations on normative judgments were striking. Prior to the deliberation, 62% of the respondents found Kevin guilty of sexual assault. After the deliberation, only 29% were willing to say that Kevin was guilty of sexual assault. All 14 groups "hung," that is, they remained split, each with a distinct blame story and a distinct vindication story. Since the prosecution facts were unambiguous and not disputed as facts by the defense, it seems clear that there was deep normative support for a vindication story within the community. The deliberation process revealed pressure toward accepting these acts as something other than, less than, sexual violence. The effects of this pressure resulted in a willingness among many to redefine the acts as harmless, thus legitimizing them. The blame story was supported by many others, however, who accepted the prosecution facts at face value.

Reasoning about Questions of Justice

The group discussions or deliberations represent the process of reasoning to a conclusion about questions of justice. It takes place through the creation of stories, based on the statements of the parties and the norms of the community, that make sense of the testimonial evidence to those who sit in judgment. As was mentioned above, the deliberations exhibit four techniques of how stories are constructed under these circumstances. First, the deliberators focused on the personalities of the two parties and the nature of the acts, in a process of normative definition. Second, the deliberators made references to their personal experiences within the community and used these references as benchmarks or models for interpreting events and behaviors that were described in the testimony. Third, the deliberators continually appealed to each other to validate or invalidate the various interpretations that were being discussed. Fourth, the deliberators debated and contested these interpretations among themselves until one story emerged as the truth (a blame story in the normal prosecution case and a vindication story in the deviant prosecution case), or until two competing stories emerged when the community norms were in conflict: a blame story and a vindication story. Each of the two competing stories was well formulated, although they provided completely different interpretations of the same set of facts.

What do the stories reveal about motivation as a social phenomenon? It is clear that the subjects were interpreting facts, but they were dong so in the context of a higher-order interpretation of the motivations involved. The community was divided normatively with respect to Kevin's behavior, that is, some found it blameworthy, whereas others found it acceptable. Those who found the behavior blameworthy concluded that Kevin intended to harass and assault Linda. Those who were not willing to blame Kevin found another interpretation of his motivation, one that was innocuous and that removed any taint of malice from his behavior. Kevin's behavior, in this interpretation, had not even harmed Linda; or, if she felt injured, that harm was only accidental. By contrast to this vindication story, the blame story accepted Linda's inferences about Kevin's motivation.

Therefore, in addition to the four techniques of story construction discussed above, this analysis reveals that the interpretation of facts in story construction concerning questions of justice is primarily an interpretation of motive, from which the fact interpretation then follows. The interpretation of motive is governed by norms concerning the social dynamics of certain situations. In the assault case, which was termed a normal prosecution, the norms of the community coincided with the prosecution's interpretation of motive. The bottle-throwing case exemplified a prosecution that conflicted with community norms because the community attached an innocuous motive to certain actions when they occurred in a particular behavioral context. When the community was divided, as in the sexual harrassment–assault case, it was because competing norms led to differing interpretations of motive and therefore to the construction of both a blame story and a vindication story.

In terms of moral reasoning, it is clear that the members of this community were very concerned to do justice, even though no one mentioned the word. The process of attributing blame (Shaver, 1985) puts a spotlight on questions of justice. This process also reveals how motivation is often a social phenomenon, formed and interpreted on the basis of community norms. As such, it becomes an important ingredient in moral reasoning. Other methodological approaches that assume the importance of a social process, such as an interactional model (Carpendale & Krebs, 1995) or information integration strategies (Miller & Bersoff, 1992), also have contributed to a better understanding of social and cultural influences on moral reasoning. The value of the social process explanation of moral reasoning, however, is that it reveals how the normative structure of the community leads to a particular definition of a moral problem and to the social dynamics involved in any situation that give rise to questions of justice. In short, it goes beyond accounting for the (perhaps multiple) sources of moral reasoning to delineate the very social process by which moral meaning is created.

CONCLUSION

This chapter has summarized several lines of research into the sources and effects of moral reasoning in children and youth, and has presented an alternative explanation based on the social processes that underlie the creation of moral meaning. The limitations of the cognitive and social learning models were identified in the first two sections. While the early literature on the cognitive model was specifically directed at the nexus between youth and justice (Kohlberg, 1969, 1976, 1984; Levine & Tapp, 1977; Tapp & Levine, 1970, 1977), Kohlberg's claims of universality and invariant sequence have not survived extensive rebuttals by new research focusing on gender, class, and cultural differences. Cross-cultural research in particular has undermined Kohlberg's claims (Miller, 1984; Miller & Bersoff, 1992; Shweder, 1991; Snarey, 1985). Despite its commendable rigor, the Kohlbergian cognitive developmental model cannot withstand its critics.

The social learning model seems at least a step in the right direction, because it appears to shore up the weaknesses of the cognitive model. As a learning theory, however, it tends to ignore reasoning in favor of its underlying behavior, that is, verbalizations. In this regard, Akers' (1985) analyses do not extend much beyond Sutherland's (1955) original formulation of differential association theory. Sykes and Matza's (1957) concept of neutralization is intriguing, but further research has been minimal. The importance of the social context and role taking in formulating moral reasoning was underscored again by the findings of Cohn and White (1990, 1991, 1992).

Finally, a study of group deliberations on questions of justice (Cohn & White, 1991) and of motivation as a social phenomenon (White, 1993) demonstrates the value of a social process explanation of moral reasoning. The potential of this approach argues for further research on the actual interchanges that occur within group deliberation processes in order to develop a better theoretical understanding of peer influence on the formation and use of moral reasoning.

REFERENCES

Agnew, R. (1994). The techniques of neutralization and violence. *Criminology, 32*(4), 555–580.

Akers, R. L. (1985). *Deviant behavior: A social learning approach.* Belmont, CA: Wadsworth.

Aronfreed, J. (1976). Moral development from the standpoint of a general psychological theory. In T. Lickona (Ed.), *Moral development and behavior* (pp. 54–69). New York: Holt, Rinehart and Winston.

Bennett, W. L., & Feldman, M. (1981). *Reconstructing reality in the courtroom.* New Brunswick, NJ: Rutgers University Press.

Blalock, H. M. (1964). *Causal inferences in non-experimental research.* Chapel Hill: University of North Carolina Press.

Blasi, A. (1980). Bridging moral cognition and moral action: A critical review of the literature. *Psychological Bulletin, 88*(1), 1–45.

Broughton, J. M. (1986). The genesis of moral domination. In S. Modgil & C. Modgil (Eds.), *Lawrence Kohlberg: Consensus and controversy* (pp. 363–385). London: The Falmer Press.

Carpendale, J., & Krebs, D. L. (1995). Variations in level of moral judgment as a function of type of dilemma and moral choice. *Journal of Personality, 63*(2), 289–313.

Cohn, E. S., & White, S. O. (1990). *Legal socialization: A study of norms and rules.* New York: Springer-Verlag.

Cohn, E. S., & White, S. O. (1991). The relationship between legal reasoning and behavioral context. *Droit et Societe, 19,* 389–408.

Cohn, E. S., & White, S. O. (1992). Taking reasoning seriously. In J. McCord (Ed.), *Facts, frameworks, and forecasts. Advances in criminological theory* (Vol. 3, pp. 95–114). New Brunswick, NJ: Transaction Publishers.

Conley, J. M., & O'Barr, W. M. (1990). *Rules versus relationships: The ethnography of legal discourse.* Chicago: The University of Chicago Press.

Cressey, D. R. (1953). *Other people's money.* Glencoe, IL: Free Press.

Duncan, D. D. (1985). Path analysis: Sociological examples. In H. M. Blalock (Ed.), *Causal models in the social sciences* (pp. 55–79). New York: Aldine.

Emler, N. P. (1983). Morality and politics: The ideological dimension in the theory of moral development. In H. Weinreich-Hastie & D. Locke (Eds.), *Morality in the making: Judgment, action and social context* (pp. 47–71). New York: Wiley.

Garbarino, J., & Bronfenbrenner, U. (1976). The socialization of moral judgment and behavior in cross-cultural perspective. In T. Lickona (Ed.), *Moral development and behavior* (pp. 70–83). New York: Holt, Rinehart and Winston.

Gergen, K. J., & Gergen, M. M. (1984). The social construction of narrative accounts. In K. J. Gergen & M. M. Gergen (Eds.), *Historical social psychology*. Hillsdale, NJ. Lawrence Erlbaum.

Gilligan, C. (1982). *In a different voice: Psychological theory and women's development*. Cambridge, MA. Harvard University Press.

Hamlin, J. E. (1988). The misplaced role of rational choice in neutralization theory. *Criminology, 26*(3), 425–438.

Hartung, F. E. (1965). *Crime, law and society*. Detroit, MI: Wayne State University Press.

Kohlberg, L. (1969). Stage and sequence: The cognitive–developmental approach to socialization. In D. A. Goslin (Ed.), *Handbook of socialization theory and research* (pp. 347–480). Chicago: Rand McNally.

Kohlberg, L. (1976). Moral stages and moralization: The cognitive–developmental approach. In T. Lickona (Ed.), *Moral development and behavior* (pp. 31–53). New York: Holt, Rinehart and Winston.

Kohlberg, L. (Ed.). (1984). *The psychology of moral development*. Vol. 2. *Essays on moral development*. San Francisco: Harper and Row Publishers.

Kohlberg, L. (1986). A current statement on some theoretical issues. In S. Modgil & C. Modgil (Eds.), *Lawrence Kohlberg: Consensus and controversy* (pp. 485–546). London: Falmer Press.

Kohlberg, L., & Nisan, M. (1984). Cultural universality of moral judgment stages: A longitudinal study in Turkey. In L. Kohlberg (Ed.), *The psychology of moral development*. Vol. 2. *Essays on moral development* (pp. 582–593). San Francisco: Harper and Row Publishers.

Levine, F. J., & Tapp, J. L. (1977). The dialectic of legal socialization in community and school. In J. L. Tapp & F. J. Levine (Eds.), *Law, justice and the individual in society: Psychological and legal issues* (pp. 163–182). New York: Holt, Rinehart and Winston.

Locke, D. (1986). A psychologist among philosophers: Philosophical aspects of Kohlberg's theories. In S. Mogdil & C. Mogdil (Eds.), *Lawrence Kohlberg: Consensus and Controversy* (pp. 21–38). London: The Falmer Press.

McCord, J. (1992). Understanding motivations: Considering altruism and aggression. In J. McCord (Ed.), *Facts, frameworks, and forecasts* (pp. 115–135). New Brunswick, NJ: Transaction Publishers.

McCord, J. (1997). "He did it because he wanted to ..." In D. W. Osgood (Ed.), *Motivation and delinquency*. Vol. 44. *Nebraska Symposium on Motivation* (pp. 1–43). Lincoln: University of Nebraska Press.

Miller, J. G. (1984). Culture and the development of everyday social explanation. *Journal of Personality and Social Psychology, 46*(5), 961–978.

Miller, J. G., & Bersoff, D. M. (1992). Culture and moral judgment: How are conflicts between justice and interpersonal responsibilities resolved? *Journal of Personality and Social Psychology, 62*(4), 541–554.

Mischel, W., and Mischel, H. N. (1976). A cognitive social-learning approach to morality and self-regulation. In T. Lickona (Ed.), *Moral development and behavior* (pp. 84–107). New York: Holt, Rinehart and Winston.

Pennington, N., & Hastie, R. (1983). The story model for juror decision making. In R. Hastie (Ed.), *Inside the juror: The psychology of juror decision making* (pp. 192–221). New York: Cambridge University Press.

Pennington, N., & Hastie, R. (1986). Evidence evaluation in complex decision making. *Journal of Personality and Social Psychology, 51*, 242–258.

Pennington, N., & Hastie, R. (1991). A cognitive theory of juror decision making: The story model. *Cardozo Law Review, 13*, 5001–5039.

Pennington, N., & Hastie, R. (1992). Explaining the evidence: Tests of the story model for juror decision making. *Journal of Personality and Social Psychology, 62*, 189–206.

Piaget, J. (1932). *The moral judgment of the child*. New York: Harcourt, Brace & World.

Radosevich, M. J., & Krohn, M. (1981). Cognitive moral development and legal socialization. *Criminal Justice and Behavior, 8*(4), 401–424.

Scott, M. B., & Lyman, S. M. (1968). Accounts. *American Sociological Review, 33*, 46–62.

Shweder, R. A. (1991). *Thinking through cultures*. Cambridge, MA: Harvard University Press.

Shaver, K. G. (1985). *The attribution of blame*. New York: Springer-Verlag.

Snarey, J. R. (1985). Cross-cultural universality of social–moral development: A critical review of Kohlbergian research. *Psychological Bulletin, 97*(2), 202–232.

Snarey, J. R., & Reimer, J. (1984). Cultural universality of moral judgment stages: A longitudinal study in Israel. In L. Kohlberg (Ed.), *The psychology of moral development*. Vol. 2. *Essays on moral development* (pp. 594–620). San Francisco: Harper & Row.

Sutherland, E. H. (1955). *Principles of criminology* (rev. by D. R. Cressey). Chicago: Lippincott.

Sykes, G. M., & Matza, D. (1957). Techniques of neutralization: A theory of delinquency. *American Sociological Review, 22*, 664–670.

Tapp, J. L. (1970). Methodology. In L. Minturn & J. L. Tapp (Eds.), *Authority, rules and aggression: A cross-national study of children's judgments of the justice of aggressive confrontations: Part II*, Washington DC: Department of Health, Education and Welfare.

Tapp, J. L., & Levine, F. J. (1970). Persuasion to virtue: A preliminary statement. *Law and Society Review, 4*, 565–582.

Tapp, J. L., & Levine, F. J. (1974). Legal socialization: Strategies for an ethical legality. *Stanford Law Review, 27*, 1–72.

Tapp, J. L., & Levine, F. J. (Eds.). (1977). *Law, justice and the individual in society: Psychological and legal issues*. New York: Holt, Rinehart and Winston.

Vine, I. (1986). Moral maturity in socio-cultural perspective. In S. Mogdil & C. Mogdil (Eds.), *Lawrence Kohlberg: Consensus and controversy* (pp. 431–450). London: The Falmer Press.

White, S. O. (1993). *A social process explanation of motivation*. Paper delivered at the llth International Congress of Criminology, Budapest.

Wittgenstein, L. (1953). *Philosophical investigations*. New York: Macmillan.

17

How Reliable Are Children's Memories?

STEPHEN J. CECI, MARY LYN HUFFMAN, ANGELA CROSSMAN, MATTHEW SCULLIN, and LIVIA GILSTRAP

In this chapter we examine the role of behavioral scientists as reporters of research findings that may be contrary to public knowledge and expectations. The research to be examined relates to the suggestibility of children's memory and was prompted in part by the recent flood of highly publicized and horrifying accusations of child sexual abuse in this country and abroad. Specifically, the discussion focuses on the contrast between public perceptions of children's testimonial competence versus actual research findings about children's vulnerability to suggestion.

Behavioral scientists have a long and distinguished history of informing society on matters of general and personal interest, dating back to the turn of the century when Harvard's Otto Münsterberg advocated for psychologists to apply their knowledge in court cases (Ceci & Bruck, 1993a). Since that time, American courts have looked to those who study human behavior for answers to a great variety of psychological questions. However, social scientists have not always been able to provide the sorts of absolute answers sought by society. In fact, some commentators have cogently argued that social science is by its nature "contested truth," with consensual agreements about theory and facts being far from the norm (Rein & Winship, 1999).

Despite the fact that social scientists frequently do not agree on the "truth" about human behavior, the public continues to seek "expert" opinion on various matters of public and personal interest. Given the limitations inherent in research in the social and behavioral sciences, researchers often emphasize the fact that consensus is still lacking and/or that findings from the laboratory need to be qualified by important caveats.

STEPHEN J. CECI, ANGELA CROSSMAN, MATTHEW SCULLIN, and LIVIA GILSTRAP • Department of Human Development, Cornell University, Ithaca, New York 14853. **MARY LYN HUFFMAN** • Department of Psychology, Rhodes College, Memphis, Tennessee 38112.

Handbook of Youth and Justice, edited by White. Kluwer Academic / Plenum Publishers, New York, 2001.

In the area of children's testimonial competence, there is no caveat more important than informing the court about the various reliability risks that are inherent in research, pointing out the manifold qualifications that may limit the application of a set of findings to a particular case at bar. Throughout this chapter we shall review social science evidence and insert the caveats that may limit its wholesale application in court cases. One repeated concern is that while research findings are applicable to samples at the aggregate level, they may not be applicable to specific individuals. For example, if most teenage mothers were sexually abused as children, should a parent whose daughter becomes pregnant assume she had been sexually abused as a child? Obviously not, because the group trends are always accompanied by within-group variability. The particularities present in any individual case makes it difficult to know.

Although this caveat is well known to social scientists, it often is lacking among participants in the arena where our work gets considered; namely, juvenile and criminal justice proceedings. The difficulty inherent in attempts to predict an individual child's behavior from information about the behavior of a group of children is frequently lost when an expert witness testifies about age-related differences in memory, suggestibility, and testimonial competence. Researchers are capable of providing courts with useful information *if* they are allowed to report *all* of what they have learned, including the shortcomings, exceptions, and potential confounds of their findings. But the exigencies inherent in the highly adversarial system we labor under makes this kind of scholarly discourse difficult and even unlikely.

Existing research on the topic of children's suggestibility has established that, under the following conditions, young children *can* be highly suggestible: when they are questioned by a biased interviewer (White, Leichtman, & Ceci, 1997); when they experience repeated erroneous suggestions and hold preexisting stereotypes (Leichtman & Ceci, 1995); when they are asked to use anatomical dolls to reenact an alleged event (Bruck, Ceci, Francoeur, & Renick, 1995); when they are repeatedly asked to visualize events (Ceci, Loftus, Leichtman, & Bruck, 1994b); and when they are subjected to repeated interviews (Ceci, Huffman, Smith, & Loftus, 1994a). We underscore the word "can" because these same studies also demonstrate that not all children succumb to the baleful effects of the above conditions; some children are quite resistant to suggestive interviews and as yet we have not been successful at identifying who these children are, at least not with any confidence. Hence, when social science research gets introduced in court, it needs to be accompanied with the caveat that not all children are equally vulnerable and we have no sound and sure method of knowing whether the children involved in the particular case at bar are the rule or the exceptions.

In order to explore the relationship between research on children's memory and testimony and its policy applications, this chapter also will discuss strengths and weaknesses of children's memories, counterintuitive findings in the current research, and individual differences between children's suggestibility.

SITUATIONAL EFFECTS ON SUGGESTIBILITY

Experiment I: Children's Memories for Events about Others

Early researchers studying child witnesses expressed profound skepticism regarding their capacities as witnesses to various sorts of criminal activity. For example, Brown (1926) stated: "Create, if you will, an idea of what the child is to hear or see, and the child is very likely to see or hear what you desire" (p. 133). This skepticism was based on experiments in which children observed some casual act and then were asked leading questions about peripheral aspects of the act such as the color of a man's beard or what he was wearing. Hence, the data that were gathered were more relevant to "bystander" conditions than to participant conditions. With respect to nonsexual, nonparticipant events, the perception of children as unreliable reporters of such "objective" information has continued to the present. Hence, the conventional wisdom with regard to children is that they are highly suggestible witnesses of events centering on other people, events for which they were bystanders rather than participants.

In the past decade, there has been a movement to reject the view that the child witness is unconditionally suggestible and to replace it with a view that is more complicated. According to this new view, young children are able to report events from their distant past with a high degree of accuracy, provided that the events were understood by the child at the time of their occurrence and no attempt had been made to usurp the children's report accuracy through the use of highly suggestive procedures (see Ceci & Bruck, 1993b, for review).

One highly suggestive procedure that has been a continuing concern to many researchers is the potential impact of repeated interviews on the accuracy of children's memory reports, particularly when the interviews are suggestive and accompanied by a stereotyped belief (Ceci & Bruck, 1995). This is especially important, given the clinical and forensic reality that during some juvenile and criminal investigations, child witnesses are repeatedly interviewed over extended periods of time by adults who inadvertently inculcate a negative stereotype about the defendant. It was against this backdrop that Leichtman and Ceci (1995) attempted to understand the impact of both sets of circumstances when they co-occur. These researchers designed a situation in which a child witness was repeatedly suggestively interviewed, with or without an accompanying stereotype.

In the Leichtman and Ceci study, a stranger named "Sam Stone" made a 2-minute visit to preschoolers (ages 3–6 years) in their day care center. The children were asked to describe his visit on four separate occasions over a 10-week period. Children in the control condition received no stereotyping information about Sam Stone prior to his visit, and during the four subsequent interviews they were asked nonleading, nonsuggestive questions about what Sam Stone had done during his visit. One month later, children were interviewed a fifth time by a new interviewer who elicited free recall about the visit and then, using probes, asked about two "nonevents" that involved Sam Stone doing something to a teddy bear and a book. In reality, he never touched either item.

Consistent with general expectations, none of the children in the control group made false reports during the free narrative, and in response to the question about the nonevents, "Did Sam Stone do anything to a book or a teddy bear," most of the children in the control group accurately replied "No." Only 10% of the youngest (3- to 4-year-old) children's claims asserted that Sam Stone did anything to a teddy bear or book. And when asked if they actually saw the misdeeds (as opposed to thinking or hearing he did something), only 5% of their answers continued to contain claims that anything occurred. Finally, when gently challenged ("You didn't really see him do anything to the book/the teddy bear, did you?"), only 2.5% of the youngest children still insisted that the fictitious misdeeds had occurred. None of the older (5- to 6-year-old) children claimed that they had seen Sam Stone do anything with either object. Thus, when not misled or supplied with negative stereotypes about Sam Stone, even the youngest children were quite accurate in their reports, despite being subjected to repeated interviews.

Another group of children did receive stereotypical information about Sam Stone's personality prior to his visit. They were told a total of 12 stories, 3 per week for 1 month, depicting Sam Stone as a kind but very clumsy person. For example, the children were told this story:

> You'll never guess who visited me last night. [pause] That's right. Sam Stone! And guess what he did this time? He asked to borrow my Barbie and when he was carrying her down the stairs, he tripped and fell and broke her arm. That Sam Stone is always getting into accidents and breaking things!

Following Sam Stone's visit, these children also were interviewed four times over a 10-week period. However, each interview contained erroneous suggestions, such as "When Sam Stone ripped that book, was he being silly or was he angry?" During the fifth interview (which was identical to the interview the control group underwent), 46% of the youngest and 30% of the oldest preschoolers spontaneously reported that Sam Stone had committed one or both misdeeds during their free narratives. Further, in response to specific questions, 72% of the youngest children claimed that Sam Stone did one or both of the misdeeds. Nearly half, 44%, stated that they actually saw him do these things, while 21% continued to insist that he did them, despite gentle challenges. Although they were more accurate, a full 11% of older preschoolers also insisted that they had seen Sam Stone perform the misdeeds.

Obviously, then, even the youngest of child witnesses are capable of accurately reporting the behaviors of others when they are allowed to deliver their reports with little interference or misguidance from adult interviewers. Yet, when faced with both suggestive questioning and an existing, negative stereotype about an individual, preschoolers were less resistant to misleading information regarding the behavior and appearance of other people. Whether or not this degree of suggestibility is seen with personally salient events, however, awaited further research that we report below.

Experiment IIa: Children's Reports of Real and Imagined Personal Experiences

The conventional wisdom in recent decades has been that, while children may be suggestible about other people's actions, their own personal experiences are too salient to be susceptible to suggestion. In addition, there has been resistance to the proposition that children could come to believe things that they had only been asked to imagine (e.g., by a therapist). In order to test these assumptions, Ceci et al. (1994a,b) asked preschoolers to think about a number of events repeatedly. Events were both actual events that they had experienced (e.g., an accident that resulted in stitches) and fictitious events that they had not experienced (e.g., getting a finger caught in a mousetrap and having to go to the hospital to have it removed).

For 10 consecutive weeks, preschoolers were individually interviewed by a trained adult. They were asked if each of the real and fictitious events had ever happened to them. For example, the interviewer asked: "Think real hard, and tell me if this ever happened to you. Can you remember going to the hospital with the mousetrap on your finger?" The interviewer asked the children to think real hard about all of the events each week.

After 10 weeks of thinking about both real and fictitious personal experiences, 58% of the children produced false narrative accounts to one or more fictitious events, with 25% of the children producing false accounts to the majority of the false events. Thus, the mere act of repeatedly imagining participation in an event caused these preschoolers to falsely report that they had engaged in the events when they had not. In fact, it seemed as though many of the children firmly believed that these fictitious events had actually occurred, with 27% of them initially refusing to accept debriefing. Many insisted, to both researchers and their parents, that they remembered the events happening.

An important correlate to this finding relates to a manipulation of the types of events imagined (Ceci et al., 1994b). Under very similar circumstances, children in this study were shown to have the highest false assent rates to neutral, nonparticipant events (an increase from

42% to 68% mean assent rate between the 1st and 11th interviews) and the lowest to negative events (from 13% to 30%), with positive and neutral participant events falling in the middle (these are average values, with younger children assenting more often on each trial and older children less often).

This supplies some evidence for the claim that negative, personal events (as in abusive or threatening experiences) are more resistant to false suggestions than neutral ones, which is generally consistent with popular opinion. However, it also shows that "although abusive events may be more resistant to suggestive interviewing methods than other types of events, [they] are by no means immune to the deleterious effects of suggestive interviewing techniques" (Ceci et al., 1994b, p. 316).

Experiment IIb: The Persistence of Children's False Beliefs

Given many children's initial insistence that the fictitious events they imagined in the studies above actually occurred, Huffman, Crossman, and Ceci (1996) decided to follow up on as many of the children as possible 2 years later to see whether or not they recalled their former reports. After interviewing 22 of the original children they found that although the children remembered 91% of the true events, they only assented to 13% of the false events (as opposed to 34% found originally by Ceci et al., 1994a). Their high rate of remembering true events makes it unlikely that their "recanting" of false events is due to forgetting. In combination with previous research, this finding raises important yet unanswered questions about the fate of children's false beliefs and the potential social ramifications of their existence.

What, then, are we to conclude about the longevity of false beliefs? Will false beliefs dissipate through time? We would contend that false beliefs contain fewer perceptual and reality-based cues than memories for true events, leaving them more vulnerable to fading through time.

Experiment III: Children's Reports about a Visit to Their Pediatrician

The studies above detailed ways in which children seemingly can come to believe that they witnessed events that never occurred. However, it has been argued that the acts the children were questioned about were minor, peripheral events that lacked relevance to issues raised by claims of sexual abuse and that more salient and personally significant events would be resistant to the suggestibility effect (Goodman, Aman, & Hirschman, 1987a).

In order to examine memory for a more forensically relevant situation, one in which the child plays a key role in an event involving his or her body, Bruck et al. (1995) examined children's memories for details about a visit to a pediatrician's office. We looked at the effects of postevent suggestions on children's memories for an inoculation, an event that involves some degree of stress as well as pain and discomfort. We were interested in the vulnerability to suggestion of children's perceptions about how they had felt during the event, as well as their memory for the roles of key participants, as these are often central issues in child abuse allegations. Intuitively, one would expect that the children's memories for such a painful, personally salient event would be highly resistant to postevent suggestions, despite the degree of stress involved.

The study was conducted in two phases, both of which involved a group of 5-year-old children visiting their pediatrician for an annual checkup. In the first phase, children were given a routine examination by their pediatrician and then led to an "inoculation room" where a research assistant discussed a poster on the wall. Five minutes later, the pediatrician entered the room and administered an oral polio vaccine and a diphtheria–pertussis–tetanus (DPT) shot. The research assistant remained present and coded the child's level of distress and how long it took the child to stop crying and become ready for the next part of the study. The child was then taken to another room by the research assistant and randomly assigned to one of three feedback conditions in which the child was told how he or she had acted while receiving the inoculation.

Children in the pain-denying group were told that the shot did not seem to hurt them at all and that it does not hurt big kids to get a shot (no-hurt condition). Other children were given pain-affirming feedback and told that the shot seemed to have hurt them a lot, but that children generally hurt when they get a shot (hurt condition). The final group was simply told that the shot was over and that many children get shots (neutral condition).

After giving the child feedback, the research assistant gave the child a treat and read the child a story about a child who gets injured after falling from a tree. The mother in the story gave the fictional child the same feedback that the child subject had received from the research assistant.

One week later, a second research assistant interviewed the children in their homes. From these interviews, we learned that children's reports of how much they had cried and hurt during the inoculation procedure were positively correlated with distress ratings made by the research assistant during the inoculation, but they did not differ on the basis of feedback condition. Hence, in the first interview, children's reports about a personally relevant, stressful experience were not rendered less accurate by suggestive feedback given immediately following the event, a finding consistent with public expectations for children's performance.

In the second phase of the study, children were suggestively interviewed three additional times approximately 1 year later. They were repeatedly given either no-hurt feedback (i.e., told that they had been brave and had not cried at the time of the inoculation) or neutral feedback (i.e., not told how they acted). For ethical reasons, the pain-affirming hurt condition was discontinued to avoid inducing a phobia of doctors in the children. During a fourth interview, the children again were asked to rate how much the shot had hurt and how much they cried. This time there were large suggestibility effects, with children in the no-hurt condition reporting significantly less hurt and crying than children who were not given feedback.

The results of this study are consistent with those of the Sam Stone study, despite the fact that the events and experiences about which the children were misled were different. In the Sam Stone study, repeated suggestions and stereotypes led to convincing claims of witnessing nonevents. In the inoculation study, misleading information given in repeated interviews after a long delay influenced children's memories of personally experienced, salient, and scripted events that involved pain and discomfort. These findings are at odds with the conventional wisdom regarding children's resistance to suggestion about such personally salient events. It is important to note, however, that even when given misleading information, the children were fairly accurate during initial questioning 1 week after the inoculation. Unfortunately, it is common for child witnesses to be questioned repeatedly over extended periods of time, and our results indicate that caution is necessary to avoid biasing children's memories for an event over the course of multiple interviews.

Study IV: Using Anatomical Dolls to Symbolically Represent Actions

While we have just discussed how children can be influenced in their recollections of events involving painful and personally salient bodily touching, investigations of potential child sexual abuse often focus on issues such as where and in what manner a child was touched in a situation where abuse is suspected. However, it is commonly assumed that children may either be embarrassed about events that involve sexual bodily touching or lack the vocabulary for describing what happened to them, especially when the touching may have involved the anal or genital area.

In order to facilitate discussion with young children about these issues, many investigators and clinicians make use of anatomically detailed dolls. The belief of many investigators is that the use of the dolls with young children, along with skillfully worded interview questions, can bring about more accurate recollections about personally experienced bodily events, such as sexual abuse (Boat & Everson, 1993). However, many began to use the dolls in forensic investigations before they had been tested and normed on groups of abused and nonabused children. This is problematic, because if nonabused children can be led to use the dolls in a manner suggesting physical or sexual abuse, then use of dolls in the interviewing process could potentially cause investigators to mistakenly conclude in some cases that abuse had occurred when it had not. In fact, recent empirical research on the use of the dolls during questioning has failed to demonstrate the dolls' benefits as interview aids (Bruck et al., 1995).

Whether elicited with or without the aid of dolls, children's testimony about events involving anal or genital touching can have very serious legal ramifications. Consequently, Bruck and colleagues (1995) sought to examine whether the errors in reporting that had been observed in earlier studies would also arise from a naturally occurring event involving genital touching, which presumably would cause embarrassment rather than pain and discomfort.

In order to approach this matter in an ethically acceptable manner, visits by 40 3-year-old children to a professor of pediatrics for a routine physical examination were studied. The children were assigned to either a genital examination condition, in which they received a genital examination before being interviewed, or to a no-genital examination condition, in which they received a general physical examination before their interview and their genital examination after the interview.

Five minutes after the initial pediatric examination, in an interview with the children's mothers present, the children were asked to describe in their own words where the doctor touched them. The children were then presented with anatomical dolls and asked to tell and demonstrate where the pediatrician had touched them.

One significant finding was that 3-year-olds were generally confused by questions about their bodies and about symbolically representing them with anatomical dolls. Approximately 50% of the children who were touched in the genital region did not indicate that they were touched there when questioned either with or without dolls. Thus, they made errors of omission. Most importantly, however, a sizable number of children in both groups made errors of commission when questioned with the dolls. In all, nearly 60% of the total sample indicated genital insertions, used the props in a sexualized manner, or committed other aggressive acts that would otherwise be cause for concern. This is contrary to a commonly held belief that children who have not been sexually touched will not indicate sexual events with dolls (Goodman & Aman, 1990). Hence, on the basis of this research, it would seem best not to use anatomical dolls when interviewing 3-year-olds unless the dolls' incremental validity as a forensic tool can be demonstrated.

The possibility of reaching a misleading conclusion from a doll-aided interview is illustrated by what happened when we gave a 3-year-old child in a pilot study an anatomically correct doll after she had undergone a physical examination. The exam did not involve any anal or genital touching or even the removal of her underpants, either before or after the initial questioning.

Immediately following her examination, the child made two mistakes with the doll, inserting her fingers into the doll's vagina and incorrectly using a measuring tape on her own head and the doll's ankle. She responded correctly to all other questions about where the doctor touched her and correctly demonstrated the use of other props, such as a stethoscope, light, and reflex hammer, both on herself and on the doll.

Three days later the same child was again shown the anatomically detailed doll. This time the child inserted a stick the pediatrician had used to tickle her foot into the doll's vagina, although upon further questioning she denied that this had happened. Most remarkably, when shown the doll for a third time 3 days later, she hammered the stick violently into the doll's vagina with a reflex hammer. She then inserted a toy ear scope into the doll's anus. When repeatedly asked by the interviewer whether the doctor had really done this to her, she tenaciously clung to her claim that these events had actually occurred. When her father mentioned that her mother had been in the room and did not notice anything like that occurring, she explained that it had happened while her mother was out of the room.

While this only represents the behavior of a single child in a pilot study, her interactions with the doll are reminiscent of those obtained by counselors in the Margaret Kelly Michaels case. In this case, children were given anatomically detailed dolls and asked to use them to describe what Michaels had done to them. The children were given kitchen utensils and asked how they had been used against them through the use of leading questions such as, "Did Kelly ever do anything to you with a knife that hurt you or bad things to you with a knife?" or, "Why don't you show me what Kelly did with the big wooden spoon?" While the children often denied that they had been abused with utensils, after repeated proddings, many eventually placed a utensil into a doll's vagina or anus. The investigators concluded that the children had been sadistically sexually abused by Michaels with a variety of utensils, for which she was later convicted. While this conviction was overturned, due in large part to the suggestive manner in which the child witnesses had been initially and repeatedly questioned, it was not before Michaels had served 5 years in prison.

In sum, the studies discussed thus far have shown that, contrary to widely held public opinion, young children can have difficulty accurately reporting events that involve their bodies, when questioned either with or without anatomically correct dolls. The use of dolls as a tool to aid accurate testimony is especially problematic, as young children appear to have difficulty using dolls to symbolically represent their bodies, and hence may inaccurately manipulate the dolls in a manner that suggests that physical or sexual abuse occurred, given only a minimal degree of suggestion.

Experiment V: Source Errors and Metacognition

Thus far, we have provided evidence that contradicts a number of popular beliefs about children's memories. However, each study discussed did support what may be considered to be one of the most widely accepted findings in the area, namely that younger children are more suggestible than older children. Even this statement, however, is not completely accurate, as still more evidence suggests that we do not yet fully understand the relationship between age and suggestibility. For instance, while researchers have attributed younger children's higher suggestibility to poorer source attribution and metacognitive abilities, the following experiment suggests that in some instances, older children's superior metacognitive abilities may make them more susceptible to source errors than younger, less cognitively sophisticated children.

In this experiment, Ceci, Masnick, and Hembrooke (in preparation) examined children's source misattributions in a group activity. The activity was a game that involved stating or acting out examples of a category. Each child had to generate a response that had not yet been used by another child. For example, if the category was "animals" and other children had said "zebra" and "tiger," the next child would have to choose a new animal such as "bear."

Two weeks after the activity, we asked children to recall as many of their responses as possible. Next, children listed as many unused responses as they could remember (i.e., those that were not made by any of the children). Finally, we presented the children with a list of responses and asked them to discriminate between the responses they had made and those that were made by other children.

Surprisingly, older children (5- to 6-year olds) plagiarized more of their peers' responses than younger children (3- to 4-year olds), with the older children more often claiming that they had made responses that their peers had made. From our observations of the children playing, we realized that older children had visibly rehearsed the responses they were going to make while they were waiting for their turn. Younger children, on the other hand, waited until their turn and then spontaneously chose a response; that is, they did not engage in advance encoding. We interpreted this observation to mean that during the discrimination task, older children were more often deciding whether they had merely thought about the response or had verbalized it, while younger children, who had not made any attempt at rehearsal prior to their turn, had only been discriminating between their and other's verbalizations. Possibly, discriminating between two events that involve the same child (e.g., saying vs. thinking) is a more difficult cognitive task than discriminating between two events that involve different children (e.g., saying vs. another child saying).

Based on this logic, we hypothesized that the advance encoding used by the older children might actually be interfering with their later recall. We sought to test this interpretation by repeating the experiment with one important modification. The experimenter whispered in each child's ear an item that they should say, provided that no one had said it before them. This assured that the younger children would engage in advance encoding just like their older counterparts.

As we expected, younger children now plagiarized significantly more of their peers' contributions than did older children. Presumably, this reversal occurred because whispering in the children's ears was tantamount to making them engage in advance encoding. If correct, then this implies that younger children, although deficient in the spontaneous use of advance encoding, exhibit greater difficulties than older children in discriminating between such encoding, their own vocalized responses, and the responses of others.

Interestingly, an unexpected piece of evidence from the second experiment additionally supported our interpretation of the first experiment. The evidence was that children's plagiarisms came disproportionately from the children who went immediately before them. Only the children before them could have preempted their advance encoding due to the experimental design. Thus, children were not making random errors but specifically failing to recall whether they had been thinking about a response when another child made it or had actually made the response themselves.

In the first version of this experiment, older children's metacognitive superiority worked to their disadvantage. Advance encoding of a response led to more errors in the later discrimination task. Contrary to the expected age effect, younger children actually made fewer memory errors because they did not plan ahead by rehearsing options before their actual turn.

When both groups attempted advance encoding, the expected age difference resurfaced, with older children making fewer source errors than younger children. In addition to incorporating others' responses as their own, younger children now made the additional implicit memory error of naming the responses of others as ones that were not made at all. Perhaps they had been so busy encoding the whispered option while others were responding that it interfered with their later recall.

INDIVIDUAL DIFFERENCES IN SUGGESTIBILITY

Study VI: Moral Development and Cognition

What would lead one child to be highly suggestible and another to be resistant to misleading information? Although the previously cited research has established a developmental pattern in the suggestibility of preschool children on the aggregate level, researchers have just begun tapping the cognitive and social differences that may lead some individuals to be highly suggestible and other individuals to be highly resistant to suggestions. For example, Huffman (1997) recently related children's degree of resistance to suggestion to their individual metamemory abilities, the use of intentions in making moral judgments, and the moral salience of the events in question.

Conceptually, a child's metamemory ability refers to his or her ability to understand how memory works and the limitations of memory. For instance, whether or not a child understands that it is necessary to study a set of numbers in order to recall them later reflects his or her metamemory ability. A child's use of intentionality cues is the ability to take into account internal motives when making moral judgments about an actor's behavior (e.g., deciding a child should not be punished for his or her actions if someone is accidentally hurt) instead of focusing solely on the consequences of the action (e.g., deciding that the child should be punished for hurting someone, regardless of intent).

In order to examine these individual variables in relation to suggestibility, a methodology similar to Leichtman and Ceci (1995) was implemented. The stimulus event for this study included a visit by Sam Stone to preschool and first-grade classrooms. During his 10-minute visit, he read a story to the children and either colored with the children (in the first-grade classrooms) or played blocks with the children (in the preschool classrooms). Before leaving, Sam Stone either knocked over a box of crayons or a tower made out of blocks. He did not pick up the blocks or crayons before leaving the room.

After Sam's visit, each child was suggestively interviewed three times about what Sam did and did not do during his visit. The interviewers asked the children about six false events, two of which were morally positive (e.g., picking up the blocks/crayons), two that were neutral (e.g., sneezing a lot), and two negative events (e.g., pushing or tripping a child) and about three true events.

To assess children's use of intentionality cues, children were asked to make moral judgments about story characters pictured in different situations that varied both the actor's intentions and the consequences of the actors' actions (e.g., child A wants to share a toy with child B and accidentally trips child B as he approaches to play; children would be asked whether child A was good or bad). By providing stories with either positive intentions and negative consequences or negative intentions and positive consequences, the interviewer was able to determine whether a child focused on an individual's intentions or on the consequences when making moral judgments.

Other interviews assessed children's use of metamemory ability by asking them basic questions about memory and its limitations, including foundational subscales written by Kreutzer, Leonard, and Flavell (1975) to other subscales dealing directly with suggestibility (i.e., the effect of repeated and leading questions and visual imagery on memory accuracy). A total of 22 subscales were used.

After the third interview, first-graders' accuracy for the true events was 99% and their accuracy for false events was 76%. Preschool children's accuracy for the true events was 94% and their accuracy for the false events was 30%.

As predicted, children's memories for morally positive and morally negative events were less suggestible than morally neutral events. Although children consented to 40% of the morally positive events and 40% of the morally negative events, they consented to 57% of the neutral events. Why were children less likely to consent to the positive and negative events than the neutral events? Perhaps it is because neutral events do not carry the same consequences as morally positive events (i.e., rewards) or morally negative events (i.e., punishment). Thus, these events are not likely to be as morally salient to children, making the children's memories more easily manipulated by suggestion.

With respect to age differences, on 19 of the 22 metamemory subscales, preschoolers scored significantly lower than first-graders, indicating an overall lower level awareness of their memories and how they function in younger children. In addition, preschool children used fewer intentionality cues than first-grade children. Younger children were more likely to focus on the consequences of an action and not the actor's intentions. Most significantly, children at both ages who focused on consequence cues (instead of intentionality cues) were less suggestible for negative events. Perhaps morally charged events raise red flags in these children's minds causing them to think, "If Same Stone tripped a child, I would remember because we get punished for tripping or pushing someone else." Though thought narratives were not provided by the children, this may help to explain why morally positive and negative events were less suggestible than neutral ones.

In addition, after a delay of 4.5 months, children's suggestibility for the negative events related significantly to their metamemory ability. Thus, both preschool and first-grade children who understood the limitations of memory were less suggestible for these events, even after a lengthy delay.

This research is important for two reasons. First, it establishes that there are individual differences in suggestibility, which supports the common view that some individuals are simply more "gullible" than others. Second, it is the first link between any aspect of moral development and suggestibility. Suggestibility is not only related to the meaning of an event (i.e., morally positive, neutral, or negative), but also to the child's perspective of right and wrong (i.e., the role of intentions in making moral judgments). This will further aid research on individual differences in suggestibility, since the child's perspective on morality may be related to his or her suggestibility.

POLICY APPLICATIONS

Study VII: Interviewers' Confirmatory Biases

The research we have presented and a good deal more that has gone unmentioned have greatly increased our knowledge and understanding of children's individual susceptibility to suggestion. However, the child's role is only half of the story, since there cannot be suggestibility without suggestion. Hence, researchers also have looked at the role of adult interviewers in children's vulnerability to suggestion.

The ways in which child witnesses are initially questioned and, hence, the role of interviewers in this process are important policy considerations. For instance, the fact that Kelly Michaels' conviction for child sexual abuse was overturned, in large part because of the suggestive manner in which the child witnesses had been initially and repeatedly questioned, is one good example of the importance of the interviewer role. It highlights the policy implications of having (or not having) a thorough understanding of the impact of interviewers and the biases they bring into an interview with child witnesses.

In the experiments discussed thus far, interviewers intentionally asked questions that they knew were misleading. However, in many forensic interviews, the interviewer suspects that some event has happened and probes for information about that event, often using misleading questions without realizing it and perhaps unaware of the risks associated with use of such a strategy. In the following experiment, White et al. (1997) decided to simulate a forensic situation by leading an experienced interviewer to form inaccurate hypotheses about an event and then asking this interviewer to question child witnesses about the event.

As a part of the experiment, children aged 3 to 6 years played a game of Simon Says and were interviewed about the game 1 month later. The interviewer, a trained social worker, received a one-page sheet containing events that might have occurred during the game. The report contained both factual and erroneous information. For example, if child A had touched child B's nose and patted her own head, the interviewer might have been told that child A had touched child B's toe (inaccurate) and patted her own head (accurate). We instructed the interviewer to determine what information about the event the child was still able to remember. We asked the interviewer to begin by asking the child for a description of the event, avoiding suggestions and leading questions. After the free recall, the interviewer could use any strategies that she felt prudent to elicit the most factually accurate recall from the children.

When we had accurately informed the interviewer, she elicited the correct information from the children nearly 100% of the time. However, when we had misinformed the interviewer, 34% of the 3- to 4-year-olds and 18% of the 5- to 6-year-olds corroborated one or more of the false events. In addition, as the interview progressed, children who had accommodated false information became more credible in their affect and speech patterns when describing the false event. As a result, we became interested in determining what would happen if we repeated the entire process a second time with a new interviewer.

One month later, we gave the first interviewer's notes to a second interviewer and asked her to reinterview the children. Just as the first interviewer had used our information to form biases about the event, the second interviewer imitated the biases of the first. Not only did the children's confidence levels about the false claims increase, but the number of false events that they accepted as true also increased. Thus, we find that another extremely important source of potential variability in children's susceptibility to suggestion is the potential bias of the adult interviewing the child, bias that can have far-reaching and even devastating practical implications.

THE ULTIMATE GOAL: CONVINCING THE JURY

Of course, given perfectly untainted testimony by any witness, adult or child, the next obvious obstacle in the path of achieving justice is the jury. They are the individuals responsible for deciding the truth of what each witness says. Whether a misled and inaccurate child witness is believed or an accurate one is not, the consequences are equally disastrous for those involved. The obvious question, then, is how credible are child witnesses to jurors? What are the parameters guiding jurors' assessments of these young witnesses and are they parameters that lead the way to justice?

Research by psychologists using written case summaries, trial transcripts, and videotaped testimony as the primary stimuli indicates that mock jurors possess influential negative stereotypes and biases of child witnesses and their memory abilities (Ross, Dunning, Toglia, & Ceci, 1990). However, these stereotypes do not seem to have a uniform impact on jurors' perceptions of witness credibility, with some finding a bias against child witnesses (Goodman, Golding, Helgeson, Haith, & Michelli, 1987b; Leippe & Romanczyk, 1987), others finding children more credible than adult and older child witnesses (Duggan et al., 1984; Goodman, Bottoms, Herscovici, & Shaver, 1989; Leippe & Romanczyk, 1989; Nightingale, 1993), and still others finding no age-related differences in witness credibility (Wells, Turtle, & Luus, 1989).

This lack of consistency has led to the search for those factors that impact a child (or adult) witness' credibility. Nightingale (1993), for example, examined the impact of corroboration of testimony and type of case. She found that mock jurors were more willing to decide in favor of the child witness in a civil case (wrongful injury) than in a criminal (sexual abuse) case. In addition, she found that corroboration increased the likelihood of conviction and decreased the amount of blame ascribed to the child witness. Paradoxically, it also resulted in less severe penalties for the defendants.

These and other similar findings must be taken with caution, however, as the primary stimulus material was a trial transcript. Other evidence indicates that observing a child testifying, as opposed to reading about it, influences juror decision making differently, overcoming jurors' initial biases and stereotypes about child witnesses, in addition to being more reflective of reality (Luus, Wells, & Turtle, 1995). Why this is found is currently the subject of debate. One possible explanation is that the child witnesses are disconfirming negative stereotypes about their abilities through their behaviors and communication, thereby increasing their credibility, whereas trial summaries offer no such opportunity for disconfirming the readers' stereotypes (Ross et al., 1990).

Whatever the true cause for the difference, the next important question is, given actual testimony, how do mock jurors assess accuracy and do they do it well? In a study of mock jurors' use of an adult's eyewitness testimony, Cutler, Penrod, and Stuve (1988) found that, of ten factors that impact and predict eyewitness identification accuracy, only eyewitness confidence had a statistically significant impact on jurors' assessment of the accuracy of the identification and on their verdicts. Lindsay, Wells and O'Connor (1989) also found that adult eyewitness confidence predicted credibility, despite the fact that confidence did not predict accuracy. With child witnesses, mock jurors seem similarly ill-equipped to assess accuracy.

Leippe and Romanczyk (1989) found that mock jurors' ratings of both adult and child witness' confidence and consistency predicted their assessments of credibility. However, neither variable was much related to actual witness accuracy. In fact, young children (5–6 years old) with shorter narrative reports were more accurate than those with longer narratives (the relationship was reversed for adults and 9- to 10-year-olds). Younger children who said "I don't know" more frequently were more accurate than those who did not, with the relationship again reversed for adults and older children. Finally, for older children and adults, powerfulness of speech was positively correlated with greater accuracy levels. Hence, given these results, it would seem that jurors are in need of guidance regarding which factors best relate to a witness' accuracy. The sort of guidance sought may be available through the testimony of social scientists, or experts, in the courtroom.

THE ROLES OF SCIENCE AND SOCIAL SCIENTISTS IN SOCIETY

Social scientists are regularly brought into the courtroom to testify as expert witnesses, in order to inform jurors about a variety of scientific questions. These experts provide data about the nature and causes of human behavior and thought processes. But, what does it mean to be an "expert" and what kind of data are "experts" presenting?

An expert is someone who has read virtually everything on a particular subject, thought about the material, and come to a conclusion based on their understanding of the facts. In other domains of knowledge, expert witnesses are called in to provide facts that are well-established, albeit obscure (e.g., information about a bank security system). However, the ambiguous nature of social scientific data makes it difficult to find results that are so well-established as to be considered fact.

If social scientist expert witnesses were simply asked by the legal system to present the state of knowledge in their particular fields, then expert opinions would never differ. Unfortunately, knowledge of the field is not the typical social science information that is useful in a court of law. Hence, courts often elicit contradictory testimony from the different experts called in to testify because they ask social scientists to present their interpretations of the data, in addition to reporting the state of knowledge in their fields.

Interpretations necessarily involve the assumptions, theories, and personal biases of the interpreter. Still, the subjective nature of the interpretation is minimized when the query requires a simple demonstration. For example, if the question was, "Can children be made to bear false witness," then one would only need to show that one child has borne false witness in order to answer the question in the affirmative. In this example, the question requires a minimum of subjectivity in the response. However, when the questions asked become more specific, such as, "What is the likelihood that this child is bearing false witness," the answers become much more subjective and a matter of professional opinion, not fact.

It is here, when scientists are asked to directly apply general data to specific cases, that the application of social science to society becomes the most problematic and even dangerous. There are no formulas or telltale psychological signs of sexual abuse, for example. There currently is no reliable method for assessing children's narratives to find which are true and which were suggested. This can be especially problematic when a particular child's behavior conforms to public stereotypes but is otherwise inconclusive. For example, one child in Oklahoma City, Lua, who was at the center of a child abuse case, was highly knowledgeable about particular sexual acts and paraphernalia, supposedly an indication of abuse. However, it was discovered that there was a supply of pornographic material openly available in the child's home, supplying the type of exposure the child needed to gain her information (Terr, 1994).

This is not to say that experienced and well-trained scientists are incapable of accurately informing a jury of the likelihood that a particular child is "bearing false witness." However, it does mean that experts must be aware that their opinions are just that—opinions—based in fact, but by no means facts themselves. This distinction must not be lost by those in the legal community as well, where expert witnesses are often treated as the keepers of the "truth." Although the expert adds information to the lay knowledge that the judge and jury already possess and corrects some common misconceptions, one must not lose sight of the problems associated with making subjective predictions about individuals.

Guidelines for Clinical Practitioners

While our studies have uncovered some important findings about children's suggestibility, it is important to consider the practical implications of our work for anyone who is called on to interview or provide therapy for a potential child witness. Diagnosing and confirming sexual abuse can be a very difficult task, as there often are no witnesses to the abuse and there frequently is no unambiguous medical evidence that abuse occurred. There also is no definite group of signs or symptoms that indicate sexual abuse and there is a good deal of overlap in the behavior of children who have been sexually abused with those who have not, with about a third of abused children showing no symptoms at all (Kendall-Tackett, Williams, & Finkelhor, 1993). Therefore, investigators must conduct fact-finding interviews in a careful, nonbiased manner in order to avoid pressuring children to behave in a manner consistent with a preconceived profile of an abused child.

Thus, it is especially important not to mislead children because of the likelihood that they will be believed, accurate or not, as discussed above. Our studies have shown that the amount of detail and emotional expressiveness shown by a child when telling a narrative may enhance the child's believability, even though the account may have resulted from suggestions from investigators. As an illustration of this fact, we showed videotapes of children who participated in the Sam Stone study to hundreds of professionals who specialize in interviewing children. They performed no better than chance at divining which children were providing accurate accounts of what happened when Sam Stone visited the classroom. Nonetheless, we would like to stress that children can provide highly accurate information when they are interviewed in a proper manner. Consequently, below are a number of recommendations for those who are giving forensic interviews:

- Minimize the number of interviews the child is given, as our studies have shown that repeated interviews with a biased interviewer or interviewers can have a detrimental effect on memory. An interview consists of any conversation between adults and children about an event, not just those that occur in a forensic setting.
- In an interview, ask nonleading questions and avoid having a confirmatory bias where a "yes" answer is expected for every question.
- Do not repeat closed-end questions as this creates the impression that the child initially has answered the question incorrectly.
- Avoid creating a negative stereotype of a person the child is being questioned about.
- Be patient and nonjudgmental with the child and do not provide rewards or encouragement for responding with particular answers.
- When a child chooses to remain silent, respect that silence and do not attempt to entice or force the child to speak.
- Be conscious of and open to alternative explanations and hypotheses, as single-minded pursuit of evidence supporting one hypothesis all too easily can lead to an inaccurate, tainted report by a misled child.

It is important to remember that the use of one or more of these suggestive techniques in a single interview may not cause irreparable harm to a child's credibility, especially if they are done by an unbiased interviewer. It is when these techniques are used repeatedly over a lengthy period of time that they can have a detrimental effect on a child's memory for an event. Bear in mind also that there are substantial age differences in suggestibility, with preschoolers generally being more suggestible than older children. Preschoolers are more likely to make mistakes about salient events involving actions upon their own bodies and are less likely than older children to understand what is being asked for when called upon to symbolically represent their bodies with anatomical dolls.

While we have been critical of suggestive therapeutic techniques, we would like to stress that therapy can play an important role in helping a child client who may be called upon to testify about matters related to the subject of therapy, such as sexual abuse. Given the slow pace of our criminal justice system, withholding therapy from the child until after the criminal proceedings in order to avoid biasing the child's testimony clearly would be a grave injustice.

For therapists dealing with child abuse victims, there are a number of additional considerations to protect both the potential child witness and the defendant. First, the child's therapist should not be playing the role of a forensic fact finder, but instead should focus on addressing the child's current issues and concerns. Also, it is important to avoid therapeutic techniques, such as guided imagery, where a child is asked to visualize past events or imagine certain scenarios. If a defendant is innocent, these techniques could promote and reinforce false allegations. If a defendant is guilty, these techniques can be challenged by the defense and used to discredit the child's testimony. Ideally, therapy should consist of helping the child develop everyday coping strategies that will not be challenged by the defendant's attorney as being a source of false memories, while helping the child obtain a positive mental health outcome. In an amicus brief for the Kelly Michaels case, which was signed by 45 respected scientists in cognitive, developmental, and clinical psychology, this position was further elucidated:

> The authors of this brief also wish to convey their deep concern over the children in this case. Our concern is that if there were incidents of sexual abuse, the faulty interviewing procedures make it impossible to ever know who the perpetrators were and how the abuse occurred. Thus, poor interviewing procedures make it difficult to detect real abuse. But we have further concerns. And these involve the interviewing techniques which we view as abusive in themselves. After reading a number of these interviews, it is difficult to believe that adults charged with the care and protection of young children would be allowed to use the vocabulary that they used in these interviews, that they would be allowed to interact with the children in such sexually explicit ways, or that they would be allowed to bully and frighten their child witnesses in such a shocking manner. No amount of evidence that sexual abuse had actually occurred could ever justify the use of these techniques especially with three- and four-year-old children. Above and beyond the great stress, intimidation, and embarrassment that many of the children so obviously suffered during the interviews, we are deeply concerned about the long-lasting harmful effects of persuading children that they have been horribly sexually and physically abused, when in fact there may have been no abuse until the interviews began. The authors of this brief will be permanently disturbed that children were interviewed in such abusive circumstances regardless of the ultimate innocence or guilt of the accused (Bruck & Ceci, 1995, pp. 310–311).

With knowledge comes responsibility, and since our studies have helped illuminate some of the ways in which children can be affected by suggestion, we hope that they will be of aid to those of us who are responsible for protecting the welfare of our children by helping ensure that children's testimony is as accurate and as fact based as possible.

REFERENCES

Boat, B. W., & Everson, M. D. (1993). The use of anatomical dolls in sexual abuse evaluations: Current research and practice. In G. S. Goodman & B. L. Bottoms (Eds.), *Child victims, child witnesses* (pp. 47–69). Chicago: University of Chicago Press.

Brown, M. R. (1926). *Legal psychology*. Indianapolis, IN: Bobbs-Merrill.

Bruck, M., & Ceci, S. J. (1995). Amicus brief for the case of *State of New Jersey v. Margaret Kelly Michaels* presented by committee of concerned social scientists. *Psychology, Public Policy and the Law*, *1*, 272–322.

Bruck, M., Ceci, S. J., Francoeur, E., & Renick, R. (1995). "I hardly cried when I got my shot!" Influencing children's reports about a visit to their pediatrician. *Child Development*, *66*, 193–208.

Ceci, S. J., & Bruck, M. (1993a). Child witnesses: Translating research into policy. *SRCD Social Policy Report*, *7*(3), 1–30.

Ceci, S. J., & Bruck, M. (1993b). The suggestibility of children's recollections: A historical review and synthesis. *Psychological Bulletin, 113*, 403–439.

Ceci, S. J., & Bruck, M. (1995). *Jeopardy in the courtroom: A scientific analysis of children's testimony*. Washington, DC: American Psychological Association Books.

Ceci, S. J., Huffman, M. L. C., Smith, E., & Loftus, E. (1994a). Repeatedly thinking about a non-event: Source misattributions among preschoolers. *Consciousness and Cognition, 3*, 388–407.

Ceci, S. J., Loftus, E. F., Leichtman, M. D., & Bruck, M. (1994b). The possible role of source misattributions in the creation of false beliefs among preschoolers. *International Journal of Clinical and Experimental Hypnosis, 42*(4), 304–320.

Ceci, S., Hembrooke, H., & Masnick, A. (in preparation). Cryptoplagiarism: Oppositely valenced developmental processes.

Cutler, B. L., Penrod, S. D., & Stuve, T. E. (1988). Juror decision making in eyewitness identification cases. *Law and Human Behavior, 12*(1), 41–55.

Duggan, L. M., Aubrey, M., Doherty, E., Isquith, P., Levine, M., & Scheiner, J. (1989). The credibility of children as witnesses in a simulated child sex abuse trial. In S. J. Ceci, D. F. Ross, & M. P. Toglia (Eds.), *Perspectives on the child witness* (pp. 71–79). New York: Springer-Verlag.

Goodman, G. S., & Aman, C. (1990). Children's use of anatomically detailed dolls to recount an event. *Child Development, 61*, 1859–1871.

Goodman, G. S., Aman, C., & Hirschman, J. E. (1987a). Child sexual and physical abuse: Children's testimony. In S. J. Ceci, M. P. Toglia, & D. F. Ross (Eds.), *Children's eyewitness memory* (pp. 1–23). New York: Springer-Verlag.

Goodman, G. S., Golding, J. M., Helgeson, V. S., Haith, M. M., & Michelli, J. (1987b). When a child takes the stand: Jurors' perceptions of children's eyewitness testimony. *Law and Human Behavior, 11*(1), 27–40.

Goodman, G. S., Bottoms, B. L., Herscovici, B. B., & Shaver, P. (1989). Determinants of the child victim's perceived credibility. In S. J. Ceci, D. F. Ross, & M. P. Toglia (Eds.), *Perspectives on the child witness* (pp. 1–22). New York: Springer-Verlag.

Huffman, M. L. C. (1997). Individual differences in children's suggestibility for morally charged events. (Doctoral dissertation, Cornell University, 1997). *Dissertation Abstracts International, 58*(4-B), 2154.

Huffman, M. L. C., Crossman, A. M., & Ceci, S. J. (1996). An investigation of the long-term effects of source misattribution error: Are false memories permanent? Presentation at the Biennial meeting of the American Psychology-Law Society. Hilton Head, SC.

Kendall-Tackett, K. A., Williams, L. M., & Finkelhor, D. (1993). Impact of sexual abuse on children: A review and synthesis of recent empirical studies. *Psychological Bulletin, 113*, 164–180.

Kreutzer, M. A., Leonard, S. C., & Flavell, J. H. (1975). An interview study of children's knowledge about memory. *Monographs of the Society for Research in Child Development, 40*(1), 1–57.

Leichtman, M. D., & Ceci, S. J. (1995). The effect of stereotypes and suggestions on preschoolers' reports. *Developmental Psychology, 31*(4), 568–596.

Leippe, M. R., & Romanczyk, A. (1987). Children on the witness stand: A communication/persuasion analysis of jurors' reactions to child witnesses. In S. J. Ceci, M. P. Toglia, & D. F. Ross (Eds.), *Children's eyewitness memory* (pp. 155–177). New York: Springer-Verlag.

Leippe, M. R., & Romanczyk, A. (1989). Reactions to child (versus adult) eyewitnesses: The Influence of jurors' preconceptions and witness behavior. *Law and Human Behavior, 13*(2), 103–132.

Lindsay, R. C. L., Wells, G. L., & O'Connor, F. J. (1989). Mock-juror belief of accurate and inaccurate eyewitnesses: A replication and extension. *Law and Human Behavior, 13*(3), 333–339.

Luus, C. A. E., Wells, G. L., & Turtle, J. W. (1995). Child eyewitnesses: Seeing is believing. *Journal of Applied Psychology, 80*(2), 317–326.

Nightingale, N. N. (1993). Juror reactions to child victim witnesses: Factors affecting trial outcome. *Law and Human Behavior, 17*(6), 679–694.

Rein, M., & Winship, C. (1999). The dangers of "strong" causal reasoning in social policy. *Society, 36*, 38–46.

Ross, D. F., Dunning, D., Toglia, M. P., & Ceci, S. J. (1990). The child in the eyes of the jury: Assessing mock jurors' perceptions of the child witness. *Law and Human Behavior, 14*(1), 5–23.

Terr, L. (1994). *Unchained memories: True stories of traumatic memories lost and found*. New York: Basic Books.

Wells, G. L., Turtle, J. W., & Luus, C. A. E. (1989). The perceived credibility of child eyewitnesses: What happens when they use their own words? In S. J. Ceci, D. F. Ross, & M. P. Toglia (Eds.), *Perspectives on children's testimony* (pp. 23–46). New York: Springer-Verlag.

White, T. L., Leichtman, M. D., & Ceci, S. J. (1997). The good, the bad, and the ugly: Accuracy, inaccuracy, and elaboration in preschoolers' reports about a past event. *Applied Cognitive Psychology, 11*, S37–S54.

Part VII

Administration of Justice

18

Juvenile Court and Its Systems of Juvenile Justice

SIMON I. SINGER

The history of juvenile justice reforms in the United States and many other parts of the Western world is an uneven one (Sutton, 1988). Reforms that brought about juvenile justice are a consequence of modern-day efforts to deal with the most stubborn and defiant juveniles. Although troubled juveniles and juvenile crime have always existed, what has changed is the manner in which officials are able to deal with misbehaving juveniles. The intractable problem of what to do with the delinquent has produced solutions that go beyond the child, the family, or the community. Modern-day responses draw on ever more complex institutional responses that stretch considerably beyond the political and organizational limits of a traditional juvenile court and its system of justice.

In an earlier time, it would have been appropriate to review juvenile justice strictly in terms of the juvenile court. That no longer is the case because the juvenile court is not the only center of juvenile justice. Other legal avenues have emerged that have produced other less obvious ways of pursuing the best interests of the child and the state in places located both inside and outside the juvenile court, such as the offices of probation and diversion intake officials. It is only a small part of juvenile justice that we can say is now actually located in the courtroom of juvenile court.

Why modern-day juvenile justice has relegated the juvenile court to just one of many centers within the spectrum of juvenile justice is a complex question that requires detailed intimate knowledge of the reasons for treating and punishing juveniles. Such reasons are not easily observable from the stated reforms or from official sources of data. To understand the real reasons for juvenile justice reforms and their implementation, a considerable amount of localized knowledge is required: knowledge not only of the stated legal rules but also knowledge of the political and organizational interests that lead to various legal decisions.

To review the intimate details of a particular system of juvenile justice would require a detailed description of a specific state and its juvenile justice system that might be of little interest to a general audience. What seems more appropriate is to speak in broad general terms:

SIMON I. SINGER • Department of Sociology, SUNY at Buffalo, Buffalo, New York 14260.

Handbook of Youth and Justice, edited by White. Kluwer Academic / Plenum Publishers, New York, 2001.

to see how juvenile justice might be different today than it was in previous generations and how variation in juvenile justice may produce opportunities for comparative forms of research.

I begin by first reviewing several ways of thinking about juvenile justice. Essentially, I argue that a sociological vision of juvenile justice is an organizational one that takes into account the unstated as well as stated reasons for the creation and implementation of juvenile justice reforms. To adhere to a textbook description of how the juvenile justice system operates would be to neglect a whole strand of sociological theory that stresses the need to look under the surface of any organizational rule or setting. I draw in particular on the work of Stanley Cohen (1985), who has emphasized the importance of looking at the diverse ways in which modern-day forms of criminal justice, as well as juvenile justice, distribute power and control, to make the case for systems of juvenile justice.

I then move into some specifics that list the various legal avenues for dealing with juveniles in complex systems of juvenile justice. These legal avenues follow the theoretical argument that modern-day societies have a deep-seated need to classify juveniles with a diverse set of labels; that the traditional labeling approach of thinking about delinquents and nondelinquents into either/or categories makes little sense today. My argument is not unique to juvenile justice for it follows other broader developments in modern society. Juvenile justice continues to expand because of societal needs to create new legal avenues for labeling juveniles. In the final part of this chapter, I conclude with a call for looking at the less visible legal avenues of juvenile justice.

PERSPECTIVES ON JUVENILE JUSTICE

Ideological

The literature on juvenile justice is replete with numerous examples that often expound the virtues of either taking the words of reformers seriously or not considering them at all. The take-it-seriously view may be considered overly naive for it presents too literal an interpretation of the reformers' words. In textbook fashion, the take-it-seriously view might cite the actual statements of reformers to show a singular vision of juvenile justice. This may often take the form of an ideology of treatment, in that the juvenile court is believed to have separated itself from the criminal court based on its stated rehabilitative objectives. The stated purposes of the juvenile court are considered important relevant sources for future sets of reform. This point is stressed by John Sutton (1988) in his historically sensitive analysis of juvenile justice when he notes that the assumptions of prior generations of reformers were regularly modified and refitted to deal with the local concerns and interests of each successive generation of reformers (Sutton, 1988, p. 5).

Indeed, most reviews of juvenile justice tend to start with the words of reformers, such as those of the frequently cited Judge Julian Mack (1909) who developed Chicago's first juvenile court. A simple interpretation of Judge Mack's words suggests that the juvenile court was created solely for the "best interests of the child":

> Why is it not just and proper to treat these juvenile offenders, as we deal with the neglected children, as a wise and merciful father handles his own child whose errors are not discovered by the authorities? Why is it not the duty of the state, instead of asking merely whether a boy or a girl has committed a specific offense, to find out what he is physically, mentally, morally, and then if he learns that he is treading the path that leads to criminality, to take him in charge, not so much as to punish as to reform, not to degrade but to uplift, not to crush but to develop, not to make him a criminal but a worthy citizen. (1909, p. 107)

But a close reading of Judge Mack's words makes apparent a vision of more than one narrowly defined place for dealing with the juvenile as a delinquent. The juvenile court was only for those kids "treading the path that leads to criminality," because criminal court was already there to deal with those juveniles whose offenses and prior history already placed them in the adult world of crime. In the past, as is the case today, the criminal court was there not as a first resort, but as a last resort option when the sanctions in juvenile court no longer appeared appropriate.

In their establishment of juvenile courts, turn-of-the-century reformers did not confine their vision of juvenile justice to just a juvenile court. They also saw probation as an integral part of the juvenile court. For instance, Mack also wrote that "taking a child away from its parents and sending it even to an industrial school is, as far as possible, to be avoided" (Mack, 1909, p. 116). Similarly, Judge Ben Lindsey (1925), who is credited with Denver's first juvenile court, wrote:

> When the juvenile court is considered in its larger aspect, I believe it will be admitted that it is made up of certain principles now recognized in the movement for human betterment. I would say that one of the most important is the principle of probation (p. 275)

The ideology of helping children produced all the justification that was needed to create a diverse set of legal avenues. The juvenile court coupled with a preexisting criminal court made it possible for a subsystem of probation to operate in ways that further allowed officials to identify juveniles as delinquents at the first sign of their deviance.

Whether or not the reformers really believed in the best interests of juveniles is not the question. Taking the words of reformers seriously allows us to see how an idea could go beyond a singular institutional reform, such as the juvenile court, into other legal avenues, such as probation. The ideas that led to the creation of juvenile court is one of many deposits of power. As Stanley Cohen (1985) argues, each ideological deposit of power created new sources of power that could later be drawn on to further create new sets of reform. The idea behind modern criminal justice with its newly created penitentiaries at the turn of the century inevitably laid the groundwork for the idea of juvenile justice with its houses of refuge and the juvenile court. The house of refuge and the juvenile court are institutional steps along the way to something larger in the sense of a contemporary juvenile justice system with its diverse and varying avenues of social control.

Organizational Convenience

Ideology is not the only aspect of law. There are other reasons for law. These reasons may be considered sources of power related to particular organizational concerns and interests that go beyond the stated legal reforms. These deposits are less visible than the codified reasons for a reform. They relate to the administrative reasons for carrying out a stated reform. Frequently the high cost of justice or treatment is cited as the reason for compromising the stated reform. That is why David Rothman (1980), in his book *Conscience and Convenience*, first gives us the ideology that goes into the creation of the reform and then details how the reform was compromised to suit the needs of the state in maintaining their administrative convenience. In Rothman's analysis of juvenile justice, the best interests of the child quickly merged with the best interests of the state to maintain a familiar story of the high cost of treatment being compromised by the organizational needs of the state.

Coupled with an organizational convenience model in modern-day attempts to understand juvenile justice is an element that goes beyond the observable to include a grander vision of control. A certain political economy is at work, but it is not the radicalism of the old that sees juvenile justice strictly in terms of class. Other factors are at work in the child-saving activities that produce juvenile justice, and these factors can best be summarized in terms of analyses that go beyond the power of class and look at the power of professionals operating "little theatres of punishment." These theatres are to be found in various systems of governmental control (Foucault, 1977). This is the deposits of power metaphor again, but as Cohen draws on Foucault, it is one that emphasizes the point that juvenile justice, like criminal justice, consists of a diverse set of avenues of treatment and control. Some of these are visible and some are not in the same sense that Foucault talks about the carceral function of the penitentiary. The nature and extent of punishment in the modern state as directed by the state may be visible only to a segment of officials but not to the general population.

In taking the words of reformers too seriously we may be too quick to neglect the hidden interests that drive juvenile justice. Those interests go beyond the best interests of the child so that what you see is not always what you get. There is more to juvenile justice than just pursuing the best interests of the child; there is the other end of juvenile justice that attempts to pursue not only the best interests of the state, but also the best interests of professionals located in varying parts of the juvenile justice system. The cost of reform is just one of those interests. Other interests may be related to avoiding a crisis in a delinquent's repeated offensive behavior. The risk assessment that officials make at various stages of the juvenile justice process may have little to do with the actual risk of repeated delinquency and more to do with the risk of creating an organizational crisis.

Organizational interests in avoiding crisis are visible to officials in the decision making that goes into first and last resort sanctions. Words are used to justify less visible legal avenues and their negotiated orders of justice. There is a need to justify at various levels of decision making what is being done to the juvenile, not just to pursue the best interests of the child, but to seek the needed documentation that makes it possible to justify the best interests of the state. This comes back in the form of a case file in which the characteristics and prior history of the juvenile is documented for the purpose of justifying later decisions (Emerson, 1981). How those avenues were created are related not only to the reformers words, but also to additional deposits of power that the reformers helped to stimulate.

Platt (1977) often is cited as presenting the straightforward Marxian version of elite class interests as the reason for Chicago's first juvenile court: class determines the creation and implementation of juvenile justice. But a close reading of Platt suggests a more complicated image of class and the child savers responsible for the juvenile court. The child savers motivations and actions varied not only to reflect their upper-class status but also their particular concerns and interests. For Platt there were some important differences worth noting and repeating. For example, he is careful to note that Louise Bowen differed from Jane Addams. Louise Bowen was typical of a conventional philanthropist, while Jane Addams personified a professional child saver. Jane Addams was committed to juvenile justice in ways that Louise Bowen could not possibly understand. Addams was in the trenches of settlement houses and juvenile justice, while Bowen was still within her elite circle of upper-class friends and rarely went out to meet the kids, except for, say, Christmas dinners. Both had a place in the creation of the juvenile court. But Jane Addams in her writings and actions would perpetuate a particular kind of bureaucratic interest. Professional interests along with class interests produced in Jane Addams a new pocket of professional power that could not be duplicated by a Louise Bowen.

Pockets of power, or specific bureaucratic interests, are highlighted in Hagan and Leon's (1977) contrasting description of Toronto's juvenile court. The debates that existed at the time between journalistic reformers and police commissioners on the emerging juvenile court suggest that there was more bureaucratic conflict, or struggle, between various officials and legal agencies than what might be assumed from a simple class analysis of juvenile justice. The exchange between journalists, judges, and police chiefs suggests how the advantages and disadvantages of juvenile court were assessed from several different standpoints (Hagan & Leon, 1977, p. 595). These are differences that are worth highlighting, because by presenting the unique stories of emerging systems of juvenile justice in different places and in different periods of time, we can learn that there is not just one singular juvenile justice system but many systems of juvenile justice.

The deposits of power that produced systems of juvenile justice also can be understood as an important part of the negotiated order of juvenile justice (Sutton, 1988). Political and organizational concerns and interests recreate a particular kind of convenience that often compromises the conscience of reformers. There is the "conscience" of it all in the form of a set of beliefs about what ought and could happen to help children who develop into law-abiding adults. But at the same time, there also is the convenience of juvenile justice in making it an easier legal avenue to arrest, charge, and convict juveniles. It was and still is less difficult to deal with juveniles in juvenile court. In criminal court, officials are more hesitant to see juveniles as adult offenders in an adult legal process. Officials look to the juvenile court to produce a less formal and less severe set of sanctions. Juvenile justice makes a milder set of adjudications and dispositions possible through a variety of institutional settings, ranging from police officers in the juvenile division to divisions of youth with community kinds of placements.

Another way to view the cycle of juvenile justice is one in which treatment and punishment models of convenience come and go, because there is a constant search for ways to do something about juvenile crime and juvenile justice. That need to do something produces what Bernard (1992) notes as a cycle of reform that is finely fitted to ideological and political convenience. In the cyclical view of reform, organizational concerns and interests are generalized to produce the internal as well as external demands that lead officials to alternate their calls for reform between those that emphasize treatment if punishment is "in," and conversely, punishment if treatment happens to be "in."

This functional perspective that sees juvenile justice as a closed system neglects its social organization. Juvenile justice is not a closed system but an open system in which there are various organizational interests and concerns to do something about juvenile crime and justice. The juvenile court emerged not just because it provided an alternative response to juvenile crime in the form of treatment but because it provided an alternative legal route to the criminal court that fit modern-day organizational concerns. The route to juvenile court extended the traditional category of offenses into the less severe status offenses, such as truancy and running away. The idea of a juvenile court sold because it was to be a legal setting that could begin to track misbehaving youth at the first sign of serious deviance with its ability to use more benign official labels of deviance. Calling the offender a delinquent instead of a criminal worked to justify the larger theater of juvenile justice.

The newly emerging juvenile court could deal with those minor offenses that the criminal justice system's prosecutors, judges, and jurors were becoming too hesitant to deal with in a formal criminal court. By making it easier to charge, adjudicate, and place juveniles in a separate legal track, officials could go beyond the formal boundaries of criminal court. The organizational convenience model of juvenile justice is one that stresses the importance of avoiding crisis, the crisis that emerges through the high cost of crime and justice.

Yet the organizational convenience model poses several difficulties for scholars attempting to understand the past and future course of juvenile justice. For instance, it does not take into consideration the unique characteristics of some systems of juvenile justice. Social structure and good intentions are always placed in the background. What is of greater relevance is how to avoid crisis. The system operates in too rational, coherent a manner, always in the best interests of the state. This clearly is not the case, in that juvenile justice is repeatedly described as a failure, not a success. The organizational convenience model also neglects to tell us why, in some jurisdictions, one particular brand of reforms are more convenient that in other jurisdictions. This is the uneven development of juvenile justice that Sutton (1988) notes, in which the juvenile courts first developed in densely populated urban areas of America and then spread to other US jurisdictions.

Why it became more convenient to have juvenile justice in certain places during particular times is a difficult question to address with an organizational convenience model of reform. It requires us to move beyond the ideal and the singular system view of juvenile justice and to consider its varying legal avenues in their full complexity. Localized concerns often do make a difference in the actions of one set of reformers in contrast to another set. Similarly, decision making by one set of officials is related to organizational interests and concerns that go beyond what might be seen merely in terms of convenience. Often what appears convenient to one set of officials is inconvenient to another. For example, at times the police may figure it is more convenient to charge juveniles in the juvenile court than to warn or to divert to a social service agency. At such times, the decision to charge is not a decision driven by absolute dollar costs, assuming that it is cheaper to divert than to charge in the juvenile court. Such decision making considers elements not only of law but of organizational costs that go beyond monetary costs.

Although costs are part of the convenience package, it is not the only determinant of convenience and juvenile justice. Juvenile and criminal justice are part of a vast network of governmental control, but it is not the type of control that is really that good at controlling crime. A lot of reforms and legal decision making really are not that convenient or that cost-efficient. The system does not operate in a coherent, rational way to deal with juvenile crime. No one has yet to figure out a solution to delinquency.

What makes one aspect of juvenile justice more convenient than another, however, must be addressed in any perspective that considers the organizational convenience model to explain the gap between the stated and unstated reasons for pursuing the best interests of the child and the state. Here we are back to a political economy model that goes beyond specific class interests; it is a model that stresses the tiny theatres of punishment argument of Foucault. It is an image of social control that sees class and convenience as just one aspect of the more general and less visible forms of power that exist outside most tiny theatres of punishment.

Systems of Juvenile Justice

A good part of what is cycled into the juvenile justice system is just recycled into the criminal justice system. The more inclusionary aspects of control that extend into the family and school in the name of "community treatment" are not necessarily more effective than the older exclusionary forms of control that existed prior to modern-day forms of juvenile justice. Rather than making governmental social control in the form of juvenile justice more visible, the opposite has occurred. The less visible avenues have emerged. In the name of preventing and controlling, there is a blurring that previously did not exist between private and public avenues of control. That blurring has produced a modern state in which it is difficult to know exactly who is in control of whom.

In the name of effectiveness, both the hard and soft ends of juvenile justice have expanded at a rate that is too difficult to measure or even observe. The more visible hard end of juvenile justice always has been there to make the soft end work. It is not without some threat of further sanctions that officials can get parents and their children to agree to the kinds of contractual arrangements that previously would not have entered their minds. Community treatment has widened the net but has not necessarily made the net any more effective or for that matter efficient. It is as if there is a net but the net is not evenly distributed with the same-sized holes. In the less efficient and effective view of juvenile justice, the holes in the governmental net of social control are unevenly distributed, catching some delinquents while letting others go.

The modern-day net-widening view of juvenile justice is the perspective that best captures contemporary systems of juvenile justice. It does so for it suggests how the "soft end" of the legal process has produced a variety of intake, adjustment, and mediation services. The soft end is inclusionary. The object of inclusionary programs is a simple one, as Cohen (1985) tells us, and that is to retain delinquents "as long as possible within conventional social boundaries and institutions, there to be absorbed" (p. 219). They not only give juveniles a second and third chance, but they also provide officials with the documentation they need to justify more and more forms of control.

But for those juveniles who resist the repeated warnings of officials in group and individual counseling, or through drug rehabilitation, first-offender programs, and even probation, the "hard end" of the juvenile justice process has become even harder. It is difficult to see how the hard end can get any harder with the closed system model of juvenile justice. But with the open system perspective, both the hard and soft ends in today's juvenile justice become more visible in that they direct us to looking for juvenile justice in a variety of legal settings.

Waiver to criminal court, or what I have called elsewhere the "recriminalization of delinquency" (Singer, 1996), is one legal avenue that is a significant aspect of contemporary juvenile justice. By taking a closed system view of juvenile justice, the effects of waiver are minimum because they are outside the juvenile justice system. But an open system view allows us to see that waiver is very much a part of juvenile justice for it allows us to understand how legal threats are both increasing and decreasing in their severity. Waiver allows us to see how the hard end of juvenile justice is expanding, while inclusionary forms of punishment allow us to see how the soft end of juvenile justice also is expanding at an even more rapid rate.

Inclusionary and exclusionary techniques of control work together to redefine the nature of crime and punishment by creating and recreating new and old legal avenues of control. The evidence for this is the diversity of labels that have accumulated over the last several decades. No longer is it the case, as it was the case, that juveniles entering the juvenile court were considered either delinquent or not. Today the number of available labels has increased to the point where officials have at their disposal the ability to refer to some delinquents as PINS (person in need of supervision), delinquent, restrictive delinquent, juvenile offender, and youthful offender.

Garland (1985) shows that in England a history of delinquency legislation produced a complex system of welfare that created the necessary backup system that made inclusionary treatment programs work:

> This segregative sector, then, operated as the coercive terminus for the whole penal network, in just the same way that the penal complex as a whole supplied the coercive backup for the institutions of the social realm. It formed the "deep end" of the complex, which functioned as a sanction of last resort, supporting the others by its threatening presence. (p. 243)

Deep and shallow ends are guided by a normalizing function that is all too invisible to those outside the system. It makes the process all too loose and negligent of the organizational rationale that is expressed in the words of the creators of the juvenile court. Ideologies often are not there, and when they are, they conflict with each other at varying stages of the process. The system is made up of officials who are not of one mind set but of multiple minds. As a consequence, contemporary systems of juvenile justice are loose, very loose, by definition.

TIGHTLY AND LOOSELY COUPLED SYSTEMS OF JUVENILE JUSTICE

It is possible to envision a tightly coupled system as having surfaced in some jurisdictions during some periods of time. For example, in Denver's first juvenile court, Judge Ben Lindsey appeared to take a proactive interest in the juveniles who came before him by trying to understand the social context of adolescence and delinquency. Lindsey is reported to have scolded police officers about their attempt to get delinquents to testify against each other, because it violated their cultural norms. He allegedly developed the kind of trust and rapport among youth that allowed Lindsey to place delinquents in a reformatory without official escort. He also is described as having regularly visited the juveniles he placed in the local reformatory and as an early proponent of "family court," with integrated jurisdiction over divorce as well as delinquency (Levine & Levine, 1992).

Although a part of the Ben Lindsey story may be more myth than reality, it fitted an idealized vision of what a wise and kind juvenile court judge could do in the role of a "superparent." While the juvenile court could be duplicated, Lindsey's unique style could not be easily reproduced. In the process of institutionalizing the juvenile court, positions are often filled "by those who lack the appropriate human qualities, or the positions themselves are so bureaucratized that initiative and flexibility are lost" (Levine & Levine, 1992, p. 140). Judge Mack was aware of Judge Lindsey's work and produced a different kind of juvenile court. He acted as a mover and shaker for reform in a different way from that of a Judge Lindsey (Colomy & Kretzmann, 1995). Mack argued that Lindsey's work could not be replicated:

> Judge Lindsey cannot be imitated, because his work depends upon his personality.... His real greatness is his work as his own chief probation officer. Now, if a judge happens to be fitted by nature to be the chief probation officer in his community, and if his community is of a size that he can combine the work of the judge and chief probation officer, that community is fortunate. But the lines of our work should not be laid out on the basis that we are going to find that unique personality in any of our communities. (Mennel, 1973, pp. 138–139)

The fact that there were too few "personalities" to fill the role of a superparent produced a juvenile court that was more loosely coupled in some jurisdictions than in others. In the more densely populated city of Chicago, juvenile court judges did not have the time to be both probation officers and judges. Other progressive reformers also recognized that the "cult of judicial personality" could not be replicated in emerging systems of juvenile justice (Rothman, 1980, p. 242). They believed in a juvenile justice system in which there would be a staff of probation officers, psychologists, and other experts to guide the judges' decision making. A complex division of labor was envisioned for juvenile justice systems located in large urban areas where the juvenile court judge would be just one part of the decision-making process. In smaller towns and rural areas, there was less of a need for the work of a professional staff of probation officers and the emergence of complex systems of juvenile justice (Rothman, 1980, p. 243).

The difference between Chicago and Denver's juvenile courts is described as one in which the Chicago juvenile court followed a more bureaucratic legal route. In contrast, Denver's juvenile court was led by a charismatic figure in the shape of Ben Lindsey who was able to produce personal attachment to the juveniles, motivating them to become involved in his reelection campaigns. But Lindsey's court had considerable trouble duplicating itself. It was not a court, according to Mack, that could easily produce the professional competencies that would make it possible to easily duplicate itself. It required a set of professionals in place of the charismatic characteristics of a single juvenile court judge. Recall my earlier point about the influence of probation as the singular most important institutional development that made juvenile court feasible.

With this background in mind it is not too difficult to predict what would happen next. Probation moved from being a voluntary agency to a professional one with its own unique set of professional interests and concerns. One general interest was to expand, and it did so at a rapid rate, not because of any proof that it was really that cheap to do so (as the organizational convenience camp would suggest), but because it could satisfy a diverse set of organizational and political concerns and interests. Probation could help satisfy deep pockets of power that previously did not exist prior to the emergence of juvenile justice.

The diverse legal avenues in which juvenile justice is able to develop differs sharply from a tightly coupled system view. In the simple and too often summary presentation of juvenile justice, an image of a tightly coupled system is presented with a singular set of goals and means of accomplishing them. Such descriptions mistakenly lead us to assume that juvenile justice decision making centers exclusively on what juvenile court judges do when in reality other decision makers are just as important. It is not just the juvenile court judge who determines the ultimate legal status of the delinquent or juvenile offender, but also school, mental health, police, probation, division for youth, and criminal justice officials. And each set of officials involved in the legal decision making of juveniles is touched by its own set of organizational concerns and interests in pursuit of the stated best interests of juveniles and justice.

Thus the negotiated order of juvenile justice and its subsystems like criminal justice may be viewed as producing loosely coupled systems of justice. The "glue" that holds loosely coupled systems of juvenile justice together is "impermanence, dissolvability, and tacitness" (Weick, 1976, p. 3). Applying Weick's (1976) list of the organizational elements to juvenile justice suggests the following: first, minimal regulations and confidentiality act to insulate and buffer loosely coupled systems from their external environment so that juvenile justice is less subject to public criticism; second, loosely coupled systems in the short run appear cheaper to operate. It takes time and money to coordinate officials and services, particularly in large jurisdictions where there are numerous agencies in the business of treating juveniles with a multitude of organizational concerns and interests.

Meyer and Rowan (1977) characterize loosely coupled educational systems as operating with rules and decisions that are often violated, unimplemented, and with uncertain consequences. Decision making appears vague and involves little coordination. Modern-day educational systems help to perpetuate rationalized myths about the proper techniques of learning to meet their organizational interests. In other words, there is much to be gained not only for students but also for officials in the stated objectives and techniques of modern educational settings.

The objectives and techniques of juvenile justice, however, differ sharply from that of formal education. Bruce Jackson (1984) reminds us that bureaucracies dealing with offenders or deviants are different from other governmental agencies, such as hospitals, schools, and departments of defense. Criminal justice agencies attempt "to get rid of something," while "those other agencies are all deeded to doing something (teaching the kids, curing the sick, making a war)" (Jackson, 1984, p. 299).

Jackson's insight is further reflected in his less than complimentary metaphor:

> The workers in criminal justice are probably closer to the workers in a city's garbage department than anything else: they take off the streets stuff no one else wants or has use for. The portions that are useful are set loose or recycled, and the portions that are considered too contaminated for further use are destroyed or housed in places of extreme isolation—a dump for radioactive or poisonous chemicals for one agency, a dump for long-term convicts on the other. (p. 299)

As Jackson observes, legal decision making requires picking out delinquents for either recycling or isolation. It requires what organizational theorists have called "a garbage can model" of decision making in which a considerable amount of time is spent avoiding and delaying decisions, hoping that by recycling or throwing it away the problem will somehow also go away (Mohr, 1976).

The various organizational goals within and between systems of juvenile and criminal justice can perhaps best be visualized on the playing field of a very large football stadium where there are several teams looking toward a multitude of organizational goals. A few goal posts are facing the direction of treatment and several others toward just desserts, retribution, and deterrence. Moreover, there are sets of players on each team striving to reach their particular administrative objectives. It is in the interest of the police to go off in one direction, while probation officers pursue another. Unlike a normal football team, players begin to shift their positions based on the prevailing winds of local public and official opinion. Public prosecutors might enter the field as quarterbacks based on the campaign of one district attorney, while being called to sit on the sidelines for another district attorney. Very large football stadiums need only be situated near densely populated urban centers. A different game would of course emerge in a much smaller stadium where fewer politicians, reporters, and citizens are in the stands to tell the players exactly what to do.

The analogy to football is really off base when we consider the fact that no one in juvenile justice is really keeping score. By not keeping score, officials appear to care less about rates of treatment or punishment and more about maintaining the appearance of a game. This is because success is not measured by the number of delinquents that are rehabilitated after treatment or deterred after punishment. The salaries or promotion of juvenile justice officials are not contingent on rates of recidivism. For legal officials it is how the game is played that counts most in producing success or failure.

Juvenile court, and its various subsystems, is just another direction in which modern-day forms of governmental control have maintained and enhanced their legal legitimacy. They are part of other subsystems that loosen the administration of justice. In formulating the concept of loose coupling as it applies to a variety of social and biological systems, Glassman (1973, p. 91) notes that "one method by which a system maintains loose coupling is by having a subsystem which is more tightly coupled." Diversion from and to the juvenile court is such a subsystem; it allows juvenile justice to persist and to maintain itself as a loosely coupled system.

But simply to argue that juvenile justice is a product of loosely coupled systems and of the system's need to reinvent itself does not really explain the timing and shape of reforms. It does not explain why there is simultaneously an effort to get both hard and soft on juvenile crime. The particular direction in which recriminalization develops can be best understood by returning to notions of power and bureaucratic interests. Bureaucratic interests are pursued in avenues that are organizationally convenient. In the cycling and recycling of deviants, a wider net has emerged in which definitions of criminal and noncriminal are constantly revised and consequently blurred. These need to be illustrated with some specific examples.

Soft-End Diversion

The juvenile court started as a court to which juveniles should be diverted to, not a court from which juveniles are to be diverted. Recall that prior to the creation of juvenile courts, the only jurisdiction for juveniles who committed offenses was the criminal court. Criminal court was not eliminated. Criminal courts still existed for those juveniles who were not seen as amenable to the juvenile court. More sweeping juvenile justice reforms later reduced the proportion of juveniles eligible for the juvenile court but did not eliminate the possibility of criminal court completely. It is only now that a new cycle of reforms has produced a juvenile justice process in which the criminal court is seen less as a last resort and more as a first resort for those juveniles charged with serious offenses.

Today the juvenile court exists in between the very soft and the very hard ends of juvenile justice. In relation to the criminal court, it is the soft end of the legal process for an increasing proportion of eligible juveniles. But there is an even softer end in the form of intake diversion prior to a juvenile's entrance into the juvenile court. Before a juvenile is even considered eligible for a hearing in criminal court with the presence of counsel, there are stages in juvenile justice in which juveniles can be diverted to the soft end of the system. Perhaps between the arrest and charging stages of decision making, it is best to think in terms of steps. These steps are not always taken in that in a proportion of cases officials leap from one stage to the next.

Leaping would occur for those cases in which the offender committed an offense that was too serious for officials to consider except with formal charges in the juvenile court. The seriousness of a case also may be defined in terms of prior offenses. The thicker a juvenile's case file is with offenses, the more likely officials are to leap into a formal court. Steps instead of leaps are taken, however, for the huge number of cases in which the juvenile's offense is not considered sufficiently serious to warrant charging in the juvenile court. This can occur at the police stage of decision making where a juvenile may be informally warned instead of charged. Many police agencies have procedures for formally warning juveniles, and in England this can involve what is known as a "formal caution."

Warnings are not made without some kind of agreement or explicit threat of a formal or more severe sanction if the juvenile repeats his or her infraction. Moreover, agreement may be reached to avoid the juvenile court on the condition that the juvenile participates in some program of treatment. How this agreement is reached and which program is selected are not necessarily determined by the best interests of the child. In some locations, the mere availability of space in a program may dictate whether or not the juvenile is diverted. The cost of diversion may be minimized by merely releasing the juvenile with a warning. In either case, within the various stages of juvenile justice there often are very small and less visible steps in which officials may decide that formal charging is inappropriate.

In some states, an intake officer may decide whether or not it is appropriate to charge the juvenile in the juvenile court. This frequently occurs for those cases in which the juvenile is charged with a minor offense or what might be considered a status offense. Decisions are made to consider the various options at that point, usually in the presence of a parent and without the presence of counsel. These nonadversarial procedures may appear closest to the initial juvenile court with its emphasis on finding out who the child is along with, taking into account his or her best interests.

It is soft and inclusionary because diversion attempts to track and retain eligible juveniles in the community as long as possible. It goes under the guise of not labeling the juvenile as a delinquent, but the term "delinquent" was coined on the assumption that it did not label the delinquent as a criminal. In the process of tracking and making the soft end with all its inclusionary forms of control work, there is an element of formal control. Names with offenses are kept. A file is produced for each child that touches the varying parts of juvenile justice. Such information is technically confidential and supposedly cannot be publicly released. But for officials it is a source of knowledge and, of course, power.

We know little about the effects of diversion at the soft end. Such cases are difficult to follow and are often of little concern to the public. They are difficult to follow because there is a proportion of juveniles who are not formally diverted. Such juveniles are not identified as being part of the juvenile justice process. Much of their identification depends on the exclusive and intimate knowledge that officials have of their cases as they enter into and out of systems of juvenile justice. When the case reaches a distinct stage, such as intake, the knowledge that officials have is still confidential; but it is important to bear in mind that it also is kept a secret to insulate officials as well as juveniles from public review.

The nonadversarial, discretionary forms of decision making that take place at early stages in juvenile justice can lead to disparities that further divide juveniles into deserving and undeserving categories of delinquents. Miller (1979) makes this point in emphasizing the bureaucratic nature of contemporary forms of juvenile justice. It is one that takes the conflict perspective a step further by suggesting that it is not a question of delinquents or nondelinquents at the soft end; it is a question instead of the relative degree of delinquency that produces the kinds of soft-end decisions that might appear to those who are subject to the labels as arbitrary and unfair. So for those at the soft end there is a degree of decision making that discriminates between juveniles who are perceived as deserving and those who are seen as undeserving of treatment or diversion.

The reasons for discrimination at the soft end may be similar to those that take place at the hard end. Matza (1964) has written that the decision to incarcerate a delinquent is related to the principle of parental sponsorship and residential availability. The doctrine of "parental sponsorship" guides the principle of individualized justice. At the point of sentencing, for example, the severity of the offense and parental sponsorship interact so that

> whether a juvenile goes to some manner of prison or is put on some manner of probation ... depends first, on a traditional rule-of-thumb assessment of the total risk of danger and thus scandal evident in the juvenile's current offense and prior record of offenses; this initial reckoning is then importantly qualified by an assessment of the potentialities of "out-patient supervision" and the guarantee against scandal inherent in the willingness and ability of parents or surrogates to sponsor the child. (1964, p. 125)

That is, all things being equal, "those with adequate [parental] sponsorship will be rendered unto probation, and those inadequately sponsored to prison" (Matza, 1964, p. 125).

In other words, juveniles who have someone to say to the judge, "I will take this child and watch him like a hawk," are more likely to avoid conviction and incarceration than juveniles without parental sponsorship. But other officials at earlier stages in the legal process also may be exposed to evidence of sponsorship. The police officer may see parental concern and interest in a mother's assurance that her child will not repeat the offense. A concerned school teacher might call the prosecutor before the first court appearance to tell of the charged juvenile's excellent school performance. And the list goes on of the many ways in which sponsorship can be invoked at various stages of the legal process to protect juveniles from a criminal label.

Those principles that Matza (1964) saw as operating in a traditional juvenile court still may persist in the routine decisions that officials must make early on in the juvenile justice process. Of course, the stated reasons are the best interests of the child or the need to protect the community, but the real reason, as we learn from Matza's observation of a traditional juvenile court, is more closely related to the organizational characteristics of the jurisdiction as well as the characteristics of the juvenile.

But at the soft end, the potential impact of individualized justice is a principle that contains "many more items in its framework of relevance" (Matza, 1964, pp. 114–115). It requires officials to consider "a full understanding of the client's personal and social character" (Matza, 1964, p. 115). That determination is not possible given the routine kinds of decisions that officials must make at early stages in the juvenile justice process.

Hard-End Diversion

The hard end of juvenile justice is different today than it was in previous generations. It was always there just as the soft end was always there. But the hard end today includes new legal avenues, more exclusionary forms of control. Although it is difficult to imagine the operation of any system of social control without its last-resort sanctions (Emerson, 1981), juvenile justice today has expanded its available maximum forms of punishment to be more inclusive of decision making in criminal court. The language of exclusion has taken on an added dimension for juveniles with the threat of prosecution in criminal court. That threat always existed for a small segment of delinquents, mainly those charged with acts of murder. But of late it has expanded to include a wider range of offenses than what was previously the case.

Some states bought into the child welfare model so thoroughly that they eventually dropped any provisions for bringing juveniles into the adult legal process, even for murder offenses. New York was one such state. In 1978, it moved from a state without any waiver legislation to one with automatic waiver. In effect, New York's juvenile offender law lowered the age of criminal responsibility for eligible juveniles to 13 for murder and 14 for a wide range of other violent offenses. The court of initial jurisdiction became the criminal court for a large segment of juveniles who were previously only eligible for juvenile court.

Like other "get tough" forms of criminal justice legislation, waiver reform in practice appears to have bark rather than bite. There is little that is automatic about legislative waiver or any other type of waiver that attempts to control juvenile crime by creating another form of diversion. It is a misnomer to refer to automatic waiver as automatic when discretion is merely shifted from juvenile justice officials to that of criminal justice officials. Transfer to criminal court via the more traditional form of waiver, commonly referred to as "judicial waiver," begins in the juvenile court through a waiver hearing as mandated by the Supreme Court in its Kent decision.

Although the Kent decision listed a set of criteria that might be used in any waiver hearing, the list of possible reasons for waiver are by definition vague. They include such terms as "amenability to treatment." Under New York's juvenile offender law, additional terms are used to guide officials to justify a reverse waiver process in which eligible juvenile offenders are sent to juvenile court instead of criminal court. For instance, the juvenile offender law (Singer, 1996) lists among its many criteria: "the history, character and condition of the defendant," and "the purpose and effect of imposing upon the defendant a sentence authorized for the offense" (p. 58).

Waiver and other attempts to criminalize juvenile justice (Feld, 1984) is a product of newly emerging demands to do something to control delinquency and serious delinquents. The last-resort options of the juvenile court no longer are seen as adequate to deal with rising rates of violent juvenile crime. How those last-resort options were adjusted to deal with repeated crises over juvenile crime and justice, I have argued, relates to the recriminalization of delinquency (Singer, 1996). The juvenile court has been recriminalized so that the last resort options are expanded to a point where more and more juveniles are seen as eligible for the criminal court.

Still, recriminalization has not eliminated the need for juvenile justice. It has accomplished what Cressey and McDermott (1973) predicted several decades ago when they stated:

> there will be a polarization of attitudes and programs: lawbreaking juveniles are likely to be processed along the lines of the adult model and hence will receive more due process and less humanistic consideration—after all, are they not merely small criminals? Juveniles who have been called "predelinquents," because they can't get along at home or in school, will be diverted. (p. 61)

Criminalization or recriminalization has widened the net by expanding the soft and hard ends of diversion. All the same rules that apply in that waiver may be seen as just as arbitrary and unfair as decision making in juvenile court. There is some empirical evidence to support that. Despite the formal judicial waiver hearing mandated in the Supreme Court's 1966 Kent decision, systems of judicial waiver that originate in juvenile court have been criticized as arbitrary because nonserious delinquents too often are brought into criminal court. Hamparian et al. (1982, p. 130) found that only 32% of judicial waivers in 1978 were for violent offenses. Osbun and Rode (1984, p. 199) found that transferred juveniles in Minnesota included many "juveniles whose records do not appear to be very serious." They argued that juvenile court judges failed "to identify many juveniles whose records are characterized by violent, frequent, and persistent delinquent activity" (p. 199). In Minnesota, Feld (1990, p. 40) found that offense seriousness and prior arrests explained very little (3%) of the variance in judicial waiver decisions. Drawing on a sample of violent juvenile offenders in cities with judicial waiver statutes, Fagan and Deschenes (1990, p. 348) noted that "judicial waiver statutes empower the juvenile court judge to make a transfer decision without applying objective criteria." Based on his extensive review of waiver legislation, Feld (1987, p. 494) suggested that "judicial waiver statutes reveal all of the defects characteristic of individualized, discretionary sentencing schema."

The empirical research literature on judicial waiver has led Feld (1987, p. 511) to conclude further that the punishment-oriented objectives of waiver are best met in states that have adopted legislative waiver reforms. Bishop and Frazier (1991, p. 300) also suggest that one way to introduce "greater equity and predictability to the transfer process would be to look to the legislature to bring more offenses (or offense/prior record combinations) within the ambit of the legislative exclusion statute." But the conclusion that legislative waiver eliminates and reduces nonobjective sources of judicial discretion is based largely on research in states with judicial waiver procedures.

To conclude, diversion into the hard end of the system has allowed juvenile justice to become more bureaucratic. Diversion to the juvenile court from the criminal court at the turn of the century made it possible to have not one but two legal settings for eligible juveniles. Diversion from the juvenile court today makes it possible to produce tiny theatres of punishment that go beyond the initial image of a juvenile court. Although diversion may be implemented in the name of treatment, it is still a system that operates through the threat of more severe forms of punishment.

In a more bureaucratic juvenile court, juveniles are still receiving the worst of both worlds: neither treatment nor justice. The more bureaucratic layers of juvenile justice make treatment difficult because of a diverse set of organizational concerns and interests. For example, some of these bureaucratic conflicts are highlighted by Jacobs (1990) in his excellent ethnography of a contemporary juvenile court. Jacobs relates the conflict that emerges between juvenile court and school officials when they battle over financial responsibility for the placement of delinquents who are in need of special education. He states that the school system retained "a high-priced legal firm billing hundreds of thousands of dollars each year to represent them." Litigation was the preferred avenue in negotiating juvenile justice rather than settling "issues of casework responsibility and authority solely through the exercise of their good offices" (Jacobs, 1990, p. 75).

What Jacobs was able to observe in a juvenile court located in an affluent suburb, where resources were not in short supply and where juvenile justice officials were well paid, was a loosely coupled system of justice. The looseness in juvenile justice today, as it plays out with soft and hard forms of diversion, goes beyond the convenience or cost of administering justice. Clearly it is not cost-efficient to go through litigation to figure out who is responsible for servicing the juvenile. But officials often find themselves with little choice but to stick to their particular organizational concerns and interests; there is an expanding set of administrative rules along with legal rules that need to be followed in the more bureaucratic contemporary juvenile court.

But what are the effects of the looseness that appear in systems of juvenile justice? The first effect may be seen on an institutional level of reform. One reform leads to another and, as I have argued up to this point, the system in juvenile justice has expanded beyond how the initial reformers envisioned the juvenile court. One form of diversion has not been without its unintended consequence of producing another form of diversion. Diversion at the soft end has led to diversion at the hard end. One reform has led to another reform; each reform might be initially envisioned as the ultimate reform but actually it is just temporary, until the next set of reforms moves into place. This is part of the cycle of juvenile justice reforms (Bernard, 1992). But the effects of loosely coupled systems are not confined to an abstract bureaucracy of officials. There are the children to consider as well.

THE CONTEMPORARY SENSE OF INJUSTICE REVISITED

Within the loose structure of the juvenile justice process, a message is being sent to officials as well as to juveniles. It is a message that is not too far removed from the message of justice as Matza observed to be the case with a traditional juvenile court. The message is one that emphasizes the inconsistency of justice. It is a message that appears in more diverse places than in the juvenile court that Matza observed in the early part of the 1960s. The inconsistency of justice comes through when juveniles see not only disparities in their adjudication and disposition in juvenile court, but also when they see disparities in systems of juvenile justice.

Recall my point that, unlike juvenile justice in an earlier period of time, contemporary forms of juvenile justice contain more than one legal avenue producing many systems of juvenile justice. The decision making that takes place among intake officials independent of the judicial decision making by juvenile court judges provides not only an additional legal avenue for diversion but also an additional legal avenue for discrimination and disparity. Systems of juvenile justice emerge because the organizational concerns and interests of intake officials often are independent of other juvenile justice agencies.

The same ground rules that Matza argued existed in the traditional juvenile court also operate in each subsystem of juvenile justice. But those ground rules are not the same for delinquents as they are for officials. Delinquents require officials to maintain a higher standard and are able to distinguish between officials. A great deal of differentiation is going on. Some officials are more just than others. The Coney Island mirror effect takes place, setting a higher standard for officials than is required for that of delinquents (Matza, 1964, p. 140). When juveniles observe officials and bureaucratic forms of conflict, it may be no different than the message they get on the street. It is a tough and bureaucratic world. Juveniles who enter juvenile justice systems learn that not everything needs to be told; lawyers have to hold things back to make the case for their clients, and similarly, delinquents need to hold things back as well.

RECONSIDERING TRUST AND ABSTRACT SYSTEMS OF JUSTICE

The importance of trust in contemporary social systems is emphasized in the work of Giddens (1991). In his book *Modernity and Self-Identity*, he writes that

> The protective cocoon is the mantle of trust that makes possible the sustaining of a viable Umwelt.... That substratum of trust is the condition and the outcome of the routinised nature of an "uneventful" world—a universe of actual and possible events surrounding the individual's current activities and projects for the future, in which the bulk of what goes on is "non-consequential" so far as that person is concerned. (p. 129).

When a child's developing sense of trust is shattered because of physical or psychological abuse within the household, on the street, or inside the school, then it is difficult to imagine how that child can be accepting of the abstract system of juvenile justice. As I have repeatedly argued, it is increasingly abstract with an increasing number of services and programs.

Giddens makes two other essential points that are worth considering in terms of the newly created trust that is demanded of those being processed in systems of juvenile justice. First, abstract systems of trust "deskill" individuals. They are in the business of putting things into compartments. This is one of many aspects of a bureaucracy. No one person has the full picture, and it seems no individual is in charge. There is no official that the juvenile is accountable to in all respects, the way that was initially suggested at the turn of the century in the form of a superparent juvenile court judge. Similarly, officials in abstract systems of juvenile justice are not accountable to a singular administrative objective. There are too many objectives and too many theories guiding decision making as to what to do with the juvenile as a dependent, delinquent, or offender.

Matza's delinquents clearly can be seen in the context of juveniles who have sensed legal injustice because they expected treatment and received punishment. A sentence of incarceration instead of probation merely because of the availability of institutional space or the absence of parents who care for delinquents is justification for or rationalizes repeating their delinquency. They have discovered that officials must make routine decisions and are not really that interested in all the things there are to know about the juvenile and the particular reasons for his or her offense. Moreover, our juvenile justice systems seem more often guided by the principles of avoidance of crisis and savings of costs. There are still few resources available to officials who are interested in imparting and developing a sense of personal trust, the kind of personalized trust that can provide the moral rewards that can produce a real change of behavior. Officials know too well that they might risk a charge of getting too involved if they were to try to provide the love that so many delinquents need.

What Is To Be Done?

We need to consider the diverse sources of juvenile justice in its varying forms. There is a need to be honest not only with juveniles but with ourselves; that not only do we know little about how to treat but also how to punish. Moreover, we need to go beyond thinking about juvenile justice as a singular tightly coupled system of justice. We need to recognize it for what it is: a loosely coupled system with many different legal avenues of control.

To present juvenile justice as a "system" in which decision making is tightly coupled to treatment or punishment-oriented objectives is to return us to a pass that no longer can exist. For example, in their book *Reinventing Juvenile Justice*, Krisberg and Austin (1993), as do many others, make the case for a treatment-oriented "juvenile justice *system*." They argue that part of the problem with juvenile justice is that political concerns over juvenile crime has led to the system moving away from the initial purpose of the juvenile court. For example, they state that "... the juvenile justice system lacks a coherent and consistent perspective on how to define those children who should be handled in special juvenile courts and those who require adult court referrals" (p. 6). But at the same time, in the next sentence they recognize that "The handling of special cases based on maturity levels or age is determined by laws and by localized and informal court cultures" (p. 6). Moreover, they make the important point that "the juvenile justice system contains a diversity of programs and services designed to treat and rehabilitate wayward youngsters" (p. 7).

Krisberg and Austin (1993) are well aware of the complexity of juvenile justice. They are sensitive to the political and legal cultures that produce a diversity of juvenile justice legal rules and agencies to enforce and implement them. They state, for instance, that "The juvenile justice system receives referrals from a range of institutions and agencies, including law enforcement, school, social services, community based, and parental" (p. 110). The juvenile court is of course central to a juvenile justice system for Krisberg and Austin. The juvenile court could be substituted in the above sentence for the phrase "juvenile justice system." But such a system is not without cost. They require what Krisberg and Austin note as important to the juvenile justice system and that is "diversion" from the formal adjudication of juveniles as delinquents. The juvenile court of course is not the system in the sense that "diversionary reforms" often exist outside of the juvenile court. Diversion at the police or even at the intake end of juvenile justice is made without the necessary knowledge or approval of a juvenile court.

In speaking about a juvenile justice system, Krisberg and Austin are reinventing the American image of a juvenile court at the center of juvenile justice. It is an important point because it emphasizes the need to make one agency responsible for maintaining the best interests of the child and the state. Waiver policies neglect that policy for they loosen the process as Krisberg and Austin put it, though not in exactly the same terms.

Krisberg and Austin are right in their idealized image of a juvenile justice system, but we have yet to arrive there. It is important to also bear in mind that textbooks do differ. Take for example a textbook on English juvenile justice, such as that by Morris and Giller (1987). They refer right from the beginning to systems of juvenile justice. In the second paragraph of their introductory chapter they state that "Systems of juvenile justice do not, of course, exist in a social policy vacuum. They co-exist alongside other systems or networks of social control which also seek to regulate the lives of juveniles" (p. 1).

Why would some American and English texts speak specifically about a juvenile justice system on the one hand, while others refer to systems of juvenile justice? The answer rests perhaps on the central image of a juvenile court. We need more talk about what that image is. In the meantime, there is a research direction that can be pursued that continues to highlight both the soft and hard ends of juvenile justice. This research asks not just what happens in the more visible juvenile court or with the more visible acts of delinquency, but also in the less visible offices of intake and probation officers. In this way we can further understand the real as well as the stated reasons for juvenile court and its systems of juvenile justice.

REFERENCES

Benard, T. J. (1992). *The cycle of juvenile justice*. New York: Oxford University Press.

Bishop, D. M., & Frazier, C. E. (1991). Transfer of juveniles to criminal court: A case study and analysis of prosecutorial waiver. *Notre Dale Journal of Law, Ethics and Public Policy, 5*, 281–302.

Cohen, S. (1985). *Visions of social control*. Oxford, England: Blackwell.

Colomy, P., & Kretzmann, M. (1995). Projects and institution building: Judge Ben B. Lindsey and the juvenile court movement. *Social Problems, 42*, 191–215.

Cressey, D., & McDermott, R. A. (1973). *Diversion from the juvenile justice system*. Ann Arbor: National Assessment of Juvenile Corrections, University of Michigan.

Emerson, R. (1981). On last resorts, *American Journal of Sociology, 87*, 1–22.

Fagan, J., & Deschenes, E. P. (1990). Determinants of judicial waiver decisions for violent juvenile offenders. *Journal of Criminal Law and Criminology, 81*, 314–347.

Feld, B. C. (1984). Criminalizing juvenile justice: Rules of procedure for the juvenile court. *Minnesota Law Review, 69*, 141–276.

Feld, B. C. (1987). Criminal law: The juvenile court meets the principle of the offense: Legislative change in juvenile waiver statutes. *Journal of Criminal Law and Criminology, 78*, 471–533.

Feld, B. C. (1990). Bad law makes hard cases: Reflections on teen-aged axe-murderers, judicial activism, and legislative default. *Law and Inequality: A Journal of Theory and Practice, 8*, 1–101.

Foucault, M. (1977). *Discipline and punish: The birth of the prison*. New York: Pantheon Books.

Garland, D. (1985). *Punishment and welfare: A history of penal strategies*. VT: Gower.

Giddens, A. (1991). *Modernity and self-identity*. Cambridge, England: Polity Press.

Glassman, R. B. (1973). Persistence and loose coupling in living systems. *Behavioral Science, 18*, 83–98.

Hagan, J., & Leon, J. (1977). Rediscovering delinquency: Social history, political ideology and the sociology of law. *American Sociological Review, 42*, 587–598.

Hamparian, D., Estep, L. K., Muntean, S. M., Priestino, R. R., Swisher, R. G., Wallace, P. L., & White, J. L. (1982). *Major issues in juvenile justice information and training youth in adult courts: Between two worlds*. Washington, DC: US Department of Justice.

Jackson, B. (1984). *Law and disorder: Criminal justice in America*. Urbana: University of Illinois Press.

Jacobs, M. D. (1990). *Screwing the system and making it work*. Chicago: University of Chicago Press.

Kent v. United States, 383 U.S. 541, 555 (1966).

Krisberg, B., and Austin, J. (1993). *Reinventing juvenile justice*. Thousand Oaks, CA: Sage.

Levine, M., & Levine, A. (1992). *Helping children: A social history*. New York: Oxford University Press.

Lindsey, B. B. (1925). Colorado's contribution to the juvenile court. In J. Addams (Ed.), *The child, the clinic, the court* (pp. 274–290). New York: Johnson Reprint Corp. (Reprinted 1970).

Mack, J. (1909). The juvenile court. *The Harvard Law Review, 23*, 105–126.

Matza, D. (1964). *Delinquency and drift*. New York: John Wiley.

Mennel, R. B. (1973). *Thorns and thistles: Juvenile delinquents in the United States, 1825–1940*. Hanover: The University of New Hampshire Press.

Meyer, J. W., & Rowan, B. (1977). *Institutionalized organizations: formal structure as myth and ceremony. American Journal of Sociology, 83*, 340–363.

Miller, J. G. (1979). The revolution in juvenile justice: From rhetoric to rhetoric. In L. T. Empey (Ed.), *Future of childhood and juvenile justice* (pp. 66–111). Charlottesville: University Press of Virginia.

Mohr, L. B. (1976). Organizations, decisions, and courts. *Law and Society Review, 10*, 621–642.

Morris, A., & Giller, H. (1987). *Understanding juvenile justice*. London: Croom Helm.

Osbun, L. A., & Rode, P. A. (1984). Prosecuting juveniles as adults: The quest for "objective" decisions. *Criminology, 22*, 187–202.

Platt, A. M. (1977). *The child savers: The invention of delinquency*, 2nd ed. Chicago: University of Chicago Press.

Rothman, D. J. (1980). *Conscience and convenience: The asylum and its alternatives in progressive America*. Boston: Little Brown.

Singer, S. I. (1996). *Recriminalizing delinquency: Violent juvenile crime and juvenile justice reform*. New York: Cambridge University Press.

Sutton, J. R. (1988). *Stubborn children: Controlling delinquency in the United States, 1640–1981*. Berkeley: University of California Press.

Weick, K. E. (1976). Educational Organizations as Loosely Coupled Systems. *Administrative Science Quarterly, 21*, 1–19.

19

Family Preservation and Reunification

How Effective a Social Policy?

RICHARD J. GELLES

Family preservation programs are not new. They go back at least to the turn of the 20th century with the settlement house movement, Hull House, and Jane Addams. Family preservation programs are designed to help children and families, including extended and adoptive families, that are at risk of abuse or delinquency, or are in crisis.

While family preservation programs have been a key component of the child welfare system for nearly a century, the rediscovery of child abuse and neglect in the early 1960s and the conceptualization of the problem as one arising out of the psychopathology of the parents or caretakers changed child welfare emphasis from one of preserving families to one of protecting children. Intensive family preservation programs emerged in the mid-1970s in response to an exponential increase in child abuse and neglect reporting and a similar exponential increase in foster care placements and the cost to public child welfare agencies of such placements. Also, the conceptual model that explained child maltreatment shifted in the 1970s away from a medical, psychopathological model to a more social model that emphasized stress, poverty, social isolation, and a lack of understanding of proper parenting behaviors and skills. It was assumed that family preservation programs, both traditional child welfare efforts at family reunification and the newer "intensive" family preservation programs, would be effective, based on assumptions about the causes of child abuse and neglect, the cost-effectiveness of the programs, and that children fare better with their birth parents.

This chapter examines the policy and practice of family preservation and reunification. There are a number of important problems with both the traditional and newer "intensive" family preservation programs. First, the policy and the programs are based on an inadequate understanding of the causes of abuse and neglect and the process and amenability to change of caretakers who maltreat their children. Second, although intensive family preservation pro-

---

RICHARD J. GELLES • Center for the Study of Youth Policy, School of Social Work, University of Pennsylvania, Philadelphia, Pennsylvania 19104-6214.

Handbook of Youth and Justice, edited by White. Kluwer Academic / Plenum Publishers, New York, 2001.

grams have been (and continue to be) touted as effective, cost-effective, and able to balance child safety with the goal of family preservation, rigorous empirical research has yet to support any of these claims of effectiveness.

The chapter concludes by proposing that the current debate between preservation and safety resembles the swing of a pendulum. The forces behind the pushes of the pendulum from one side (preservation) to the other (safety) tend to be high-profile cases of child abuse fatalities or inappropriate intrusions of state child welfare agencies into families who have not placed their children at risk. A more constructive discussion is to examine under what conditions family preservation might be effective if such services were better targeted to the families where there is a low risk of abuse and a high likelihood of change.

FAMILY PRESERVATION AND THE DOCTRINE OF REASONABLE EFFORTS

As noted in the introduction of this chapter, family preservation has been the traditional preferred intervention in cases of child abuse and neglect. For more than a century, child abuse and neglect have been conceptualized as a child welfare problem that is best responded to by the social service or child welfare system. As a result, the criminal justice system has operated on the periphery of child maltreatment. Even when the medical community spearheaded the rediscovery of child abuse in the early 1960s, the prescribed social policy response was to enact mandatory reporting laws that required physicians and other professionals to report suspected cases of child abuse and neglect to a designated child welfare agency, not to the police.

Because child maltreatment has been viewed as a child welfare matter, the basic assumption that guides intervention is that social and clinical interventions are more effective in protecting children and preventing the reoccurrence of abuse and neglect than arrest, prosecution, or other legal interventions. Because the essential philosophy of the child welfare system is compassion and not control (Rosenfeld & Newberger, 1977), the preferred response is to provide support for families as a means of protecting children.

At the core of the compassionate approach is the belief that children do best when cared for and raised by their biological caretakers. The theoretical and empirical work on attachment (see for example, Bowlby, 1958, 1969; Harlow, 1958, 1961; Lindsey, 1994) has been used to support this assumption, but even professionals and policymakers who are unfamiliar with research on attachment endorse the assumption that the preferred method of intervening in cases of child maltreatment is to preserve the family, so long as the safety of the child can be assured.

The main exception to the practice of family preservation occurred in the wake of the rediscovery of child abuse in the 1960s. When Kempe, Silverman, Steele, Droegemueller and Silver published their seminal paper, "The Battered Child Syndrome" (1962), they focused almost exclusively on serious and life-threatening acts of physical violence directed at young and mostly defenseless children. Kempe and the medical community advocated the enactment of mandatory reporting laws for child abuse so that serious injuries to children were not deliberately or inadvertently overlooked and untreated by professionals.

Mandatory reporting, combined with public awareness campaigns and technological developments, such as toll free-lines (800 numbers), resulted in extraordinary increases in reports of child abuse and neglect. At the same time, because the medical and psychiatric communities were at the forefront of the campaign to identify child abuse as a serious social problem, the prevailing causal model was a medical–psychiatric–psychopathology model that explained abuse as a function of the psychopathology of the caretaker.

Because the cause of abuse was thought to be some character or personality defect of the parents or caretakers, for almost a decade separating children from abusive parents became an important initial and long-term intervention. However, even during this period, it was rare that more than half of validated cases of abuse and neglect resulted in an out-of-home placement.

By 1978, there were a little less than a million reports of child maltreatment in the United States each year and some 500,000 children in foster care in the United States (Pelton, 1989; Tatara, 1993). The combination of increased reports, increased numbers of child in out-of-home placements, and the cost of such placements raised concerns across the child welfare system. At the same time as these concerns were raised, there was a shift in the explanation of child abuse and neglect. The causal model changed from a medical–psychiatric model that focused on character disorders, personality disorders, and psychiatric problems to a social and social psychological model that focused on poverty, social isolation, and social learning that resulted in the intergenerational transmission of violence and abuse and cultural attitudes about children and physical punishment (Gelles, 1973; Gil, 1970; Parke & Collmer, 1975).

The shift had a gradual but major impact on child welfare interventions and policy. Abusive parents, rather than being thought of as characterologically disordered and different, were now viewed as being at one end of a continuum of parenting. Their abusive and neglectful behavior was not considered the sole result of a personality or psychiatric disorder, but rather the result of a surplus of stressors and a deficit of resources. Anyone, this model proposed, could abuse or neglect a child given certain social and economic circumstances. Even if there were clinical signs of psychiatric disorder, these too were thought to arise from social and environment conditions (see, for example, Gelles, 1973; Lindsey, 1994). This being the case, the major task of child welfare agencies became case management that assisted families in coping with stressors and providing personal, social, and economic assistance.

By the late 1970s, the new model explaining child abuse and neglect was well integrated in the scholarly and professional literature. At the same time, as noted above, out-of-home placements had reached 500,000 (Pelton, 1989; Tatara, 1993). In addition, news reports more frequently described situations where children were harmed or even killed in foster care placements. In Rhode Island, for example, a youngster named Keith Chisolm was removed from his mother by the Department of Social and Rehabilitative Services. The boy had not been physically or sexually abused; rather, he was the victim of neglect. Keith was later beaten to death by his foster father, a man who previously had been arrested for assault and battery. Cases like this made child protective workers in Rhode Island reluctant to remove any but the most grievously injured children from their biological parents. Cases such as this cause what Lindsey (1994) refers to as the "child welfare pendulum" to swing from the side of focusing on child protection to the other side that focuses on family preservation.

The Adoption Assistance and Child Welfare Act of 1980

The new child protection–family preservation policy that emerged in the late 1970s was crystallized by the federal Adoption Assistance and Child Welfare Act of 1980 (PL 96-272), which experts and advocates generally consider the most significant legislation in the history of child welfare. The two major child welfare provisions of the act were on permanency planning and "reasonable efforts." Permanency planning was a response to concerns over what child welfare experts had labeled "foster care drift." Although data on foster care were scarce and often incomplete at that time, researchers and practitioners generally believed that too many children were lingering in the foster care system. Permanency planning mandated that states develop permanency plans for children: either that they be returned to their birth parents or placed for adoption within 18 months of entrance into the child welfare system. The second child welfare provision of the legislation was embodied in the two words: "reasonable efforts." Again, aimed at reducing foster care drift and inappropriate out-of-home placement, the policy of "reasonable efforts" was stated in a brief but important section of the legislation:

> ... in each case, reasonable efforts will be made (A) prior to the placement of a child in foster care, to prevent or eliminate the need for removal of a child from his home, and (B) to make it possible for the child to return to his home. (42 USC, 67[a] [15] [1988 Supp I].)

States had to demonstrate that they made reasonable efforts and that they were in compliance with the permanency planning provision of the law in order to qualify for federal funding for adoption and foster care.

It appeared that the Adoption Assistance and Child Welfare Act of 1980 had the desired effect. Data on foster care placements indicated that out-of-home placements declined to under 300,000 per year by the mid-1980s (Pelton, 1989; Tatara, 1993). The reduction, however, did not continue, and by the mid-1990s, foster care placements approached 600,000 per year (Tatara, 1993).

Despite the good intentions behind the law and likely initial success in reducing foster care placements, the Adoption Assistance and Child Welfare Act of 1980s had some unintended consequences. One problem was the ambiguity around the very concept of "reasonable efforts." Nowhere in the federal legislation or ensuing legal decisions in state courts was the concept "reasonable efforts" ever clearly defined. As a result, child protection workers, administrators, legal staff, and judges had no guidelines for how much or how long they had to make efforts at reunification before moving to permanent out-of-home placement for abused and neglected children. A second problem was the actual implementation of the law. Because there were no specific definitions or guidelines for what constituted "reasonable" and because family preservation was a long-held bedrock value of the child welfare system, child welfare workers and administrators often interpreted "reasonable efforts" to mean that they should make "every possible effort" to keep children with or reunite them with the birth parents.

Intensive Family Preservation Services

Intensive family preservation services are an alternative to the "business-as-usual" family preservation–family reunification child welfare casework used by child welfare agencies. The intensive family preservation services movement began in Tacoma, Washington, in 1974. Child psychologists David Haapala and Jill Kinney developed a program they called "Homebuilders" with a grant from the National Institute of Mental Health. The goal of the program was to work intensively with families *before* a child is removed. There are now many variations of intensive family preservation services in use across the country. The core goal of such programs is to maintain children safely in the home or to facilitate a safe and lasting reunification. Intensive family preservation services programs were designed for families that have a serious crisis threatening the stability of the family and the safety of the family members.

Although, as noted above, there are many variations of intensive family preservation services programs, the essential feature is that such programs are short-term, crisis intervention. Services are meant to be provided in the client's home. The length of the sessions can be variable. Unlike traditional family preservation services, intensive family preservation services are available 7 days a week, 24 hours a day. Perhaps the most important feature of intensive family preservation services is that caseloads are small—caseworkers may have only two or three cases. In addition, the length of time is brief and fixed at a specific number of weeks. Both hard and soft services are provided. Hard services include food stamps, housing, homemaker services; soft services include parent education classes and individual and/or family counseling.

ARE INTENSIVE FAMILY PRESERVATION SERVICES EFFECTIVE?

The initial evaluations of intensive family preservation services were uniformly enthusiastic. The programs were claimed to have reduced the placement of children, reduced the cost of out-of-home placement, and at the same time assured the safety of children. Foundation program officers and program administrators claimed that families involved in intensive family preservation services had low rates of placement and "100% safety records" (Barthel, 1991; Forsythe, 1992). Program administrators also claimed success in reducing placement and assuring safety. Susan Kelley, Director of the Division of Family Preservation Services, Office of Children and Youth Services for the state of Michigan, testified before Congress that of 2505 families who participated in Michigan's Families First program in the first year, one incident of abuse was reported (Barthel, 1991).

There were, however, major methodological and design limitations of the early evaluations of intensive family preservation services. The vast majority of the evaluations of intensive family preservation services either employed no control group or used a comparison group that was not an appropriate match for the group receiving treatment. Moreover, there were questions raised about whether "placement avoidance" was the appropriate outcome measure for the evaluations. Peter Rossi (1992) cautioned that "placement avoidance" was not a proper outcome variable, since placement avoidance was itself the treatment. In his 1992 review, Rossi concluded that the evaluation studies did not convincingly demonstrate that intensive family preservation services reduced placement or reduced child welfare costs. The claim that children were safe was not actually evaluated in these early studies.

There have been at least 46 evaluations of intensive family preservation services of one form or another (Heneghan, Horwitz, & Leventhal, 1996; Lindsey, 1994). Of these 46 evaluations and of nearly 850 published articles on intensive family preservation, only 10 studies actually evaluated intensive family preservation services, included outcome data in the report, and used a control group of some kind. In California, New Jersey, and Illinois, the evaluations used randomly assigned control groups, included outcome data, and had large enough samples to allow for rigorous evaluation. In all three studies, there were either small or insignificant differences between the group receiving intensive family preservation services and the control group receiving traditional casework services. Even in terms of placement avoidance, there was no difference between the two groups, thus suggesting that earlier claims that intensive family preservation services were successful in reducing placement obtained those results because of the low overall rate of placement in child welfare agencies. These results also point to how difficult it is for child welfare caseworkers to accurately classify a family as "high risk" for being placed, since 80 to 90% of the children in the control group were not placed, even though these children theoretically were selected for the study because they were at high risk of being placed.

As noted above, the outcome measures of most evaluations do not include data specifically designed to measure child outcomes. Thus, it also is impossible to verify the claim of the safety record of intensive family preservation services. Critics of intensive family preservation services programs argue that children are injured or even killed when they are inappropriately returned to their abusive caretakers (Gelles, 1996). Indeed, there is considerable anecdotal evidence that such children are injured and killed when left with or returned to abusive parents. However, there are no data yet on whether children involved in intensive family preservation services have higher rates of reinjury or fatalities compared to children served by traditional child welfare casework.

Thus, the empirical case for intensive family preservation has yet to be made. Amid the claims and counterclaims on intensive family preservation and following the funding of the Family Preservation and Support Act of 1993, the Department of Health and Human Services funded a national evaluation of family preservation and support services. This evaluation, conducted by Westat, The Chapin Hall Center for Children, and James Bell Associates, is examining a full range of family preservation and support programs at a number of sites across the country. The study is using a randomized trial design with a variety of outcome measures, including placement, cost, and family functioning.

Given that the claims for the effectiveness of intensive family preservation have not been supported to date by scientific evidence, there is concern for the widespread adoption of intensive family preservation services. Peter Rossi, for one, criticized the states and the federal government for running "... pell mell into family preservation without considering the evidence for it" (MacDonald, 1994, p. 53).

WHY FAMILY PRESERVATION AND REUNIFICATION POLICIES ARE INEFFECTIVE

There are a number of reasons why intensive family preservation services specifically and the broader policy of family reunification are not effective. First, it is possible that intensive family preservation services, in and of themselves, are simply not effective. The theory behind the program may be faulty and the programs themselves therefore may not be addressing the key causal mechanisms that cause child abuse. Second, the programs may be effective, but they may not be implemented properly by the agencies and workers that are using the programs. When the evaluation data for the Illinois Family First program were made public (Schuerman, Rzepnicki & Littell, 1994), an initial reaction was that there was considerable variation in how intensive family preservation was being implemented at the different sites in Illinois and the overall implementation was not true to the "Homebuilders" model of intensive family preservation. Thus, the lack of support for the effectiveness was blamed on the programs not being properly implemented. Third, the theory behind the program may be accurate and the program itself may be appropriate, but the "dose" may be too small. It may be that more services are necessary or the length of the intervention should be increased. If this were true, however, it would partially negate the cost-effective claims for intensive family preservation services.

With regard to theory, there are other plausible explanations for the apparent ineffectiveness of intensive family preservation services. As noted earlier in this chapter, current child welfare programs, including intensive family preservation, assume that abuse and maltreatment are one end of a continuum of parenting behavior. However, it is possible that this model of abusive behavior is inaccurate. It may be that there are distinct types of abusers and maltreators (Gelles, 1991, 1996). Abuse may not arise out of a surplus of risk factors and a deficit of resources, but rather there may be distinct psychological and social attributes of those caretakers who inflict serious and/or fatal injuries compared to caretakers who commit less injurious acts of maltreatment. If there are different types of maltreaters and different underlying causes for different types of abuse, it is reasonable to assume that a "one-size-fits-all" intervention or policy would not be effective across the board.

Another problem with the child welfare system and with intensive family preservation and family reunification is the crude way behavior change is conceptualized and measured. Behavior change is thought to be a one-step process: one simply changes from one form of behavior to another. For example, if one is an alcohol or substance abuser, then change involves stopping using alcohol or drugs. If one stops but then begins again, then the change has not successfully occurred. A second assumption is that maltreating parents or caretakers all want to change, either to avoid legal and social sanctions or because they have an intrinsic motivation to be caring parents. As a result, those who design and implement child abuse and neglect interventions assume that all, or at least most, parents, caretakers and families are ready and able to change their maltreating behavior. However, research on behavior change clearly demonstrates that change is not a one-step process. Rather, changing behavior is a dynamic process and that one progresses through a number of stages in trying to modify behavior. It also assumes that there are cognitive aspects to behavior change that can be measured (Prochaska & DiClemente, 1982, 1983, 1984; Prochaska, Norcross & DiClemente, 1994).

One of the reasons why child welfare interventions in general and intensive family preservation programs in particular may have such modest success rates is that most interventions are "action" programs often provided to individuals and families in what Prochaska and his colleagues call the precontemplator or contemplation stage of change. This is what others may refer to as denial or ambivalence about the need for change.

TOWARD A SAFER AND MORE EFFECTIVE CHILD WELFARE POLICY

In response to criticisms leveled at intensive family preservation services interventions, as well as widespread media coverage of cases of children who were killed by caretakers after being left with or reunited with abusive caretakers, proponents of intensive family preservation have modified their unqualified support for the effectiveness and safety of programs like Homebuilders. Susan Notkin (1996) Director of the Program for Children of the Edna McConnell Clark Foundation, said in a letter to the *Wall Street Journal* that

> even the staunchest proponents of such an approach (intensive family preservation) do not believe that every family can or should be "preserved." On the contrary, a balanced and well-functioning child welfare system needs a full toolbox of services—from early prevention to intensive family preservation to foster care and adoption. (A, p. 15)

The Edna McConnell Clark Foundation has been one of the strongest supporters of the Homebuilders model and intensive family preservation. An earlier report by the Edna McConnell Clark Foundation was a glowing testimony to the effectiveness of intensive family preservation that claimed few risks with such programs (Barthel, 1991). Susan Kelly, Director of Michigan's Family First program, is now quoted as saying that

> Family preservation efforts were never intended to be a stand alone program or a program that is expected to fill all the needs of every at risk family. It's a false dichotomy to say we should have foster care or family preservation. (Lawton, 1996).

The problem with these arguments is that the same individuals also continue to promote family preservation programs by stating that they are effective. Moreover, preserving families is still the preferred approach to dealing with child welfare. Thus, although there appears to be an effort to find a balance between preservation and safety, preservation remains the child welfare system's central goal. Taking Susan Notkin's toolbox metaphor one step further, the best-promoted and most widely used tool in the box is still preservation and reunification. As the homily goes, "if the only tool you have is a hammer, the whole world tends to become a nail." The argument that we need a full tool box notwithstanding, the child welfare system still tends to reach for one tool first and foremost—preservation and reunification.

An additional problem that continues to plague the child welfare system is that the system tends to swing back and forth between child protection and family preservation in what Lindsey (1994) refers to as a pendulum. Public outcry over sensational cases—children killed by biological caretakers—pushes the pendulum toward child protection; children injured or killed in foster care or false accusations of abuse, push the pendulum toward family preservation. Theory, informed research, and rigorous evaluations of interventions exert much less force on the movement of the pendulum.

One thing that is clear is that there is no "one-size-fits-all" explanation for child maltreatment and no "one-size-fits-all" intervention or treatment. No side of the pendulum can or will be effective all the time. Nonetheless, striking an appropriate balance is extremely difficult. The most constructive approach is to examine under what conditions family preservation might or might not be effective and to better target services or intervention to families and children.

Schuerman and his colleagues (1994) identified "targeting" as a key issue in their examination of Families First in Illinois. One reason why Families First was not found to be effective was that it was delivered to many families for whom it was not intended or appropriate, families in which there was not an "imminent risk of placement." A second targeting problem is when services are delivered to families or individuals who may not be ready or able to change and are the least likely to benefit from efforts to help. One means of improving targeting and matching interventions is to develop better risk assessment for use by the child welfare system. Child abuse investigators and assessment workers all engage in risk assessment. Some agencies and investigators use formal, written risk assessment devices; others rely on clinical judgment, clinical intuition, or just accumulated experience. A survey conducted in 1991 found that 42 of the 50 states have experimented with or implemented some form of systematic formal risk assessment (Berkowitz, 1991). The reliability and validity of risk assessment instruments are variable. Some risk assessment is merely formalized clinical judgment, while other risk assessment is what I have called "olfactory risk assessment"—homes that smell of urine or feces, homes that are filthy, with trash and garbage not disposed of, and disorganized homes are typically rated as high risk; while homes that smell of "Lestoil," that are neat as a pin and structurally sound, are regarded as low risk, irrespective of the presence of other important risk factors. Some instruments are well grounded in the scientific study of the causes and correlates of maltreatment; one such instrument is the Child at Risk Field System (CARF) (Doueck, English, DePanfilis, & Moore, 1993). But even this risk assessment instrument only assesses proximate risk factors for maltreatment; it does not measure whether parents or caretakers are ready or willing to change their behavior.

A more sensitive and appropriate risk assessment model would assess recognized risk factors such as income, substance abuse, an so forth as well as "stage of readiness to change," so that action-oriented interventions will be targeted for families ready to use them. More importantly, child welfare agencies will be able to move to protect children at high risk by

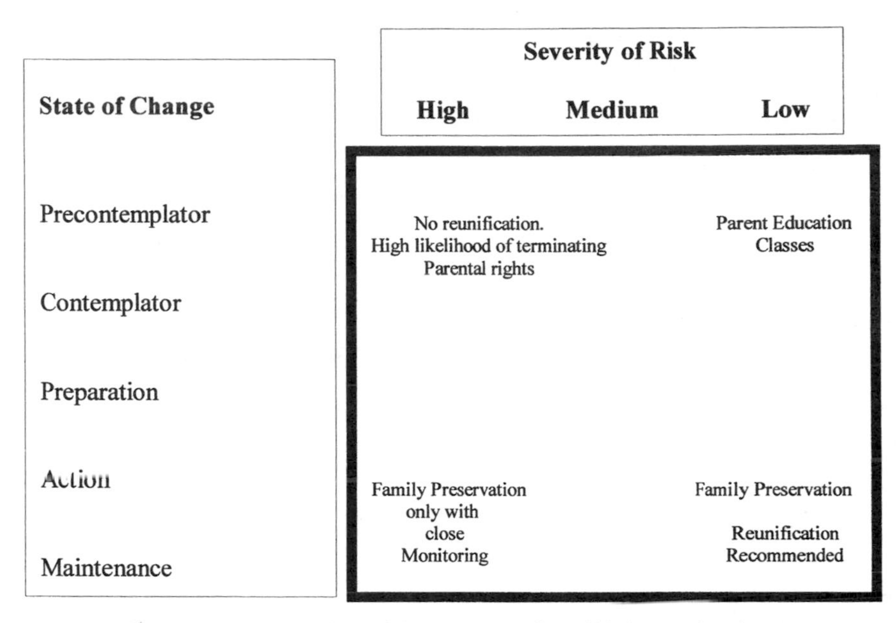

Figure 1. Two dimensions of risk assessment for child abuse and neglect.

identifying risk in terms of presence of risk factors *and* reluctance, unwillingness, or inability to change. Agencies will not have to wait for a child to be seriously or permanently injured to suspend "reasonable efforts," because they will have the ability to identify families where "reasonable efforts" are unlikely to work, for example, high-risk parents not ready to change (precontemplators). The grid in Figure 1 illustrates this kind of risk assessment.

Risk assessment, however, is not the entire solution to the problems that plague the child welfare system. The system still considers the preservation of families its highest priority. Thus, for the system to truly change and *meet the needs of children*, it should replace "reunification and preservation" with "child safety and the best interests of the child" as its main goals. Although it is admirable to try to balance the goals of preservation with child safety, social scientists who are familiar with statistics and the problem of type I and type II error know that one cannot simultaneously reduce both type I and type II error. A choice must be made: families can be preserved, but at the cost of injuries and harm to children; or children can be protected at the cost of inappropriate intrusion into some families. The child welfare system needs to give up the notion that it can have both preservation and protection all the time. A child-centered system using appropriate risk assessment, which matches interventions to stage of change, is the best promise for an effective and safe child welfare system.

REFERENCES

Barthel, J. (1991). *For children's sake: The promise of family preservation*. New York: Edna McConnell Clark Foundation.

Berkowitz, S. (1991). *Findings from the state survey component of the study of high risk child abuse and neglect groups*. Rockville, MD: Westat.

Bowlby. J. (1958). The nature of the child's tie to his mother. *International Journal of Psychoanalysis*, *39*, 350–373.

Bowlby, J. (1969). *Attachment and loss. Vol. 1 Attachment*. New York: Basic Books.

Doueck, H. J., English, D. J., DePanfilis, D., & Moore, G.T. (1993). Decision-making in child protective services: A comparison of selected risk-assessment systems. *Child Welfare, 72*, 441–452.

Forsythe, P. (1992). Homebuilders and family preservation. *Children and Youth Services Review, 14*, 37–47.

Gelles, R. (1973). Child abuse as psychopathology: A sociological critique and reformulation. *American Journal of Orthopsychiatry, 43*, 611–621.

Gelles, R. J. (1991). Physical violence, child abuse, and child homicide: A continuum of violence, or distinct behaviors? *Human Nature, 2*, 59–72.

Gelles, R. J. (1996). *The book of David: How preserving families can cost children's lives*. New York: Basic Books.

Gil, D. (1970). *Violence against children: Physical child abuse in the United States*. Cambridge, MA: Harvard University.

Harlow, H. (1958). The nature of love. *American Psychologist, 13*, 673–685.

Harlow, H. (1961). The development of affection patterns in infant monkeys. In B. M. Foss (ed.), *Determinants of infant behavior* (vol. 1, pp. 75–88). London: Metheun.

Heneghan, A. M., Horwitz, S. M., & Leventhal, J. M. (1996). Evaluating intensive family preservation programs: A methodological review. *Pediatrics, 97*, 535–542.

Kempe, C. H., Silverman, F. N., Steele, B. F., Droegemueller, W., & Silver, H. K. (1962). The battered child syndrome. *Journal of the American Medical Association, 181*, 107–112.

Lawton, K. A. (1996). Controversial program tries to keep endangered kids out of foster homes. *The American News Service*, Release number 1996–09–06.

Lindsey, D. (1994). *The welfare of children*. New York: Oxford University Press.

MacDonald, H. (1994). The ideology of "family preservation." *The Public Interest, 115*, 45–60.

Notkin, Susan. (1996). Letter to the editor. *Wall Street Journal*, 6 June: 1, p. 15.

Parke, R. D., & Collmer, C. W. (1975). Child abuse: an interdisciplinary analysis. In M. Hetherington (Ed.), *Review of child development research* (vol. 5, pp. 1–102). Chicago: University of Chicago Press.

Pelton, L. (1989). *For reasons of poverty: A critical analysis of the public child welfare system in the United States*. New York: Praeger.

Prochaska, J. O. & DiClemente, C.C.. (1982). Toward a more integrative model of change. *Psychotherapy: Theory, Research and Practice, 19*, 276–288.

Prochaska, J. O., & DiClemente, C.C. (1983). Stages and processes of self-change in smoking: Toward an integrative model of change. *Journal of Consulting and Clinical Psychology, 5*, 390–395.

Prochaska, J. O., & DiClemente, C.C. (1984). *The transtheoretical approach: Crossing traditional boundaries of change*. Homewood, IL: Dow Jones/Irwin.

Prochaska, J. O, Norcross, J. C., & DiClemente, C. C. (1994). *Changing for good*. New York: Morrow.

Rosenfeld, A., & Newberger, E. H. (1977). Compassion vs. control: Conceptual and practical pitfalls in the broadened definition of child abuse. *Journal of the American Medical Association, 237*, 2086–2088.

Rossi, J.S. (1992, March). *Stages of change for 15 health risk behaviors in an HMO population*. Paper presented at the meeting of the Society of Behavioral Medicine, New York.

Schuerman, J., Rzepnicki, T. L., & Littell, J. H. (1994). *Putting families first: An experiment in family preservation*. New York: Aldine de Gruyter.

Tatara, T. (1993). *Characteristics of children in substitute and adoptive care*. Washington, DC: Voluntary Cooperative Information System, American Public Welfare Association.

United States Congress. (1980). *Adoption Assistance and Child Welfare Act* (PL 96-272). 42 USC, 620–628, 670–679(a) (1988, Supp I).

20

Children's Rights

BARBARA BENNETT WOODHOUSE

INTRODUCTION

"Children's rights" is one of the hot button phrases of our times. Operating as an ideological Rorschach, the notion of rights for children divides people along deep cultural and religious as well as political fissures. From the Right, influenced by the hierarchical model of the patriarchal family, religious fundamentalists and conservatives attack the idea as destructive of parental authority and corrosive of traditional family values.[1] From the Left, radically egalitarian thinkers agitate in favor of children's liberation from adult control, as part of the unfinished business of raising all oppressed minorities to full and equal citizenship.[2] Most Americans sit uncomfortably on the fence, admiring the libertarian ring of the phrase "children's rights" but wondering what such an idea might mean in practice.

Our skepticism is justified. The very term "children's rights" sounds like an oxymoron. In the American system of laws, the notion of "rights" seems to presuppose an autonomous party capable of exercising his or her powers through informed and independent choice. But children are born into dependency, and the infant's helplessness is a fact of life in every human society. Adding to children's essential dependency, modern Americans have set aside the life stage called "childhood" as a special time of innocence coupled with incapacity, during which the young are to be protected from their own immaturity and sheltered from adult experiences and adult responsibilities. The legal distinction between childhood and adulthood, reflected in concepts like "minority status" and "the age of majority," is grounded in beliefs about children's lack of capacity to act rationally and their need to be under some responsible adult's control and care.

Many would ask, how can dependent persons, lacking the capacity for autonomous choice, possess and exercise "rights?" While recognizing this dilemma, proponents of children's rights have insisted that children are persons, equally entitled with all others to be treated *justly* by the law, even if they are treated differently.[3] Advocates for children also question the empirical bases for some of our judgments about children's incapacity and suggest a closer examination of how laws and policies might avoid reifying imagined differ-

BARBARA BENNETT WOODHOUSE • University of Pennsylvania Law School, Philadelphia, Pennsylvania 19104.

Handbook of Youth and Justice, edited by White. Kluwer Academic / Plenum Publishers, New York, 2001.

ences without ignoring real differences.[4] They point to past episodes in our history, when other groups have been classified as lacking the capacity to figure as complete "persons" in our system of justice, and they remind us that our shared certainty about the inferiority or disability of these excluded groups—Africans, women, Irish, Jews, Native Americans, Asians—rested on stereotypes that crumbled once they were subjected to rigorous scrutiny. Nevertheless, all but the most ardent liberationists concede that children are different. The difficulty of integrating children into our theories about justice and into our legal system exposes underlying tensions between the child's initial helplessness and his or her emerging capacities, between children as individuals, as family members, and as citizens of states and nations. The struggle to articulate a theory of children's rights has pushed thoughtful people, in America and internationally, to stretch for a more nuanced rights discourse and a more child-centered perspective on rights.

In the discussion that follows, I will explore the language and the history in America of rights for children, highlighting the dual roles of children's needs and children's capacities in defining their emerging rights. I will then suggest certain key principles, shared with human rights initiatives generally, that have driven modern movements for children's rights. I will conclude by discussing the international movement to articulate children's specific human rights, which resulted in the 1989 United Nations Convention on the Rights of the Child, and its implications for children's rights in America.

DEVELOPING A SPECIAL LANGUAGE OF CHILDREN'S RIGHTS: NEEDS-BASED AND CAPACITY-BASED RIGHTS

Any interdisciplinary discussion must begin by choosing a vocabulary and defining terms. I will adopt the vocabulary of legal scholars (rather than the equally valid languages of anthropology, religion, sociology, psychology, or moral philosophy) because law is the dominant language of "rights talk" in America. Modern Americans, more than most societies, look to the courts for answers they used to find in religion and custom. They use the language of law to discuss social questions like what defines a family, what separates the child from the adult, and what do parents and children owe each other, the community, and themselves—all questions that go to the root of defining a scheme of rights and responsibilities.

Legal scholars tend to divide the universe of rights into categories that seem distinct and separate but often overlap in practice. One such division is the line between "positive" and "negative" rights.[5] A negative right is the right to be free from state intervention, a right to be "let alone" by the government. A positive right is a right requiring active state intervention, such as the right on the part of an individual to receive a positive good or benefit. We can divide rights along a different axis into categories of civil and political rights which empower the rights-holder to participate in public life; economic or welfare rights which entitle the rights holder to economic justice and to basic necessities such as food, health care, or shelter; and social or cultural rights which focus on protection of individual and communal values. It is easy to see how these categories might blend and overlap. For example, protecting citizens' negative right to be free from unlawful deprivations of liberty may involve conferring a positive right on poor defendants to be provided with an attorney at public expense. Here, the positive right is derived implicitly from the negative right. Or political rights such as the right to participation in civil life through voting and citizen action may appear meaningless when segments of society lack basic economic and welfare rights. In international law it is now generally accepted that these categories are inevitably interrelated: positive rights may be necessary to the exercise of negative rights, and such economic and welfare rights as education and income security may be a necessary ingredient in the realization of political and civil rights.[6]

Even a cursory description of a typical framework for discussing rights exposes the difficulty of fitting children, especially very young children, into what seems an alien adult world bearing little relation to their needs and experiences. Most of the categories of rights described above require choices by the rights holder, who must decide whether and when to invoke them. The scheme of rights seems to imagine that the rights holder is capable of administering the right or entitlement for him or herself. Negative rights especially presuppose a zone of personal privacy and a state of independence that do not fit with children's experience. Children are not born autonomous. From the infant's perspective, a right to be "left alone" would constitute a death sentence. But children are still people, with claims to human dignity that can be asserted on their behalf by those who are entrusted with their care and custody. Children's special situation exposes the emptiness for children of any rights discourse that ignores the interdependency of individuals, families, and communities. It also exposes the inadequacy of framing "rights talk" primarily in terms of the individual's freedom to exercise her or his powers when dealing with a category of persons who begin in a state of almost complete powerlessness.

Many scholars have pointed out these dilemmas and have proposed various means of overcoming them, from focusing on children's empowerment to focusing on the empowerment of parents and guardians. Given the complex nature of children's situation, in constructing a scheme of children's rights, it seems important not to lose sight of either their dependency or their evolving capacities. Children's essential dependency provides the basis for arguing that children's rights include the right to have their basic needs met by parents and by society. The early progressives, who were the first to argue for children's rights, understood that they must harness the moral force of dependence and interdependence. We have learned that claims based on children's needs resonate far more powerfully for the average American than claims based on adults' needs. While Americans tend to idealize rugged individualism and demand at least the appearance of self-sufficiency from adults, we do not blame young children for their dependency on external sources of support.

Early progressives argued that adults must bear responsibility, both within the child's family and in the larger political community. Children's rights could not be contingent on autonomy but must exist in service of children's nature, defined as a capacity for growth to autonomy.[7] Children's needs-based rights reflect children's essential dependency at birth but also leave room to honor their inherent capacity for growth to maturity. Children's needs-based rights would include rights to nurture, education, food, medical care, shelter, and other positive goods without which children cannot grow into autonomous adults and productive citizens. Children's needs-based rights would also reflect their need to grow and to test the wings of their increasing autonomy.

The notion of children's dignity rights acts as a necessary complement to the notion of needs-based rights because it acknowledges that children are individual persons with the same claims to dignity as autonomous adults. As infants, they rely on others to articulate and protect their rights, but the framework of decision making must evolve as the child's capacities for autonomy evolve. It is important to understand that capacity for autonomous action is not a necessary attribute for asserting or vindicating dignity rights. For example, a patient in a hospital has what we usually think of as a negative right to refuse a medical procedure. Should that patient fall into a coma and be unable to object or consent to medical procedures, she or he does not lose his or her right to protection from state intrusion. The patient still retains the right to be treated as an individual with claims to dignity, but her or his rights are exercised on her or his behalf by a family member or a court-appointed guardian. The fact that these are still the *patient's* rights is clear in the legal standards requiring the guardian to be faithful to the patient's wishes, if known, and to place her or his interests before the guardian's if the patient's wishes are not known.

Recognizing children's dignity rights and assigning the protection of these rights to parents is one route to acknowledging that childhood is a journey to autonomy. While a child's ability to reason and understand evolves over time, the child's dignity rights are fully present at birth. Dignity rights call on the legal system to respect that the child, despite his or her lack of autonomy, does have rights based on present humanity as well as potential for autonomy. In making these rights operational, the law must reflect the child's dependency but also emerging capacity for participation and ultimately control. This analysis requires that we work harder to integrate children's needs with their capacities, acknowledging that dependency and autonomy are two sides of the same coin. A scheme of rights that focuses exclusively on one or the other will be incomplete, whether applied to adults or to children.

The questions remain: Who is responsible for meeting the needs of children? Who is responsible for speaking for the child and vindicating her or his rights? I will argue that parents, society and children themselves all play important roles in this endeavor and all must share responsibility according to their means and abilities.

Conflicts will arise not only in balancing children's "needs" for external support and direction against their "capacities" for autonomy, but also in balancing the competing claims of children against those of parents and government. No right is absolute and children's rights must be weighed in the balance with other competing claims of rights and authority. However, the power adults exercise over children—as parents, legislators, and judges—should not be taken for granted, but must be justified as furthering children's interests and meeting their special needs.

This scheme for analyzing family relationships and for thinking about children's relationships with adult authority shifts the focus from adults' rights to adults' responsibilities. In this scheme, parents exercise the fiduciary powers of a guardian or a trustee, with special authority to make decisions about the needs and interests of the beneficiary, their child. Parenthood is seen not as a form of ownership of children, but as a form of trusteeship. Parents are given the broad authority and freedom from state interference that they must have in order to nurture and protect their children in their journey to autonomous adulthood.[8]

Representatives of the state—judges, teachers, police—also exercise sweeping authority over children. Sometimes the state acts to reinforce parental authority (as when a teacher insists the child wear her mittens or a police officer returns a runaway child to her parents' home). Sometimes the state displaces parental authority (as when a school assigns a text the parent would not have chosen or a police officer removes a child at risk of abuse from her parents' home). But the state's relations with children are often frankly "paternalistic" in ways that would be inappropriate in the state's relationship with adult citizens. However, the model for state intervention in children's lives should not be one of absolute power justified by children's lack of power. The state's authority, like that of parents, should be grounded in children's combined dependency and emerging capacities for autonomy, giving rise to children's rights to have their essential needs met and their dignity respected, by the community as well as by their families.

PLACING CHILDREN'S RIGHTS IN HISTORICAL AND LEGAL CONTEXT

Having painted a picture of what a theory of children's rights ideally might look like, let me trace the actual development of a jurisprudence of children in American law.[9] The "black letter law"—the actual law on the books—tended to reflect long-standing traditions which took little notice of children or their rights. Historically, children's rights were simply the mirror image of their parents' responsibilities. Parents had a duty to educate and nurture the child, and they could expect the child's labor and obedience in return. Generally, children lacked independent status under law and often were treated more like family assets than like persons. Much of children's law, contained in laws and cases about domestic relations, apprenticeships, and indenture, was organized around children's labor value and the responsibility of training them for work. Well into the 19th century, a vagrant child, or one whose parents were too poor to meet their duties of support, would be removed involuntarily and placed in indentured servitude by the local poor authorities, usually until age 21.[10] The duty to care for the child and the right to exploit his labor value would shift from the parent to the child's new master.

The first line responsibility for meeting children's needs in American society still lies with the private family. A child has a "right" to support from his or her "legal" parents, usually the biological parent or parents but sometimes an adoptive parent or stepparent unrelated by blood. Traditionally, the rights and responsibilities of family members and the creation and dissolution of family relationships have been defined at the state as opposed to federal level. State statutes and cases about children, in contexts ranging from marriage, divorce, and child custody, to property, contract, and criminal responsibility, provide the building materials for children's law and operate sometimes to maintain old patterns of social organization and sometimes to construct new rights and new roles for children.

Traditionally, state laws have attempted to mark a clear break between dependence and independence. Most legal systems draw a sharp line based on chronological age between minors, whose affairs are entrusted to adults, and all other citizens, who may speak and act for themselves unless shown to be legally incompetent—a difficult task. They generally denied autonomy rights to all minors[11] but accorded full autonomy to persons who had reached the age of "majority." In legal jargon, minors lacked "capacity"; they were presumed to lack the rational powers necessary to sign a binding contract or bring a legal action on their own. Children could not testify under oath or initiate court cases. In all legal interactions with other persons and with the state, parents or guardians exercised authority and control.

In the past century, the concept of parents' absolute authority as a God-given right seems to be evolving gradually into the concept that parents are entitled to speak and act for the child because of their special relationship (protected by parental rights), and are presumed (absent clear and convincing evidence to the contrary) to be acting in the child's interests. We also have seen a relaxation of the bars to children's participation as witnesses in court cases.[12] Presently, we see increasing recognition of children's rights to a voice and often a choice in court proceedings and a general belief that they may require some special accommodations to their needs, including protection from their own immaturity.

In contrast with its attention to negative and procedural rights, American law provides scant recognition or protection of any positive rights to social supports from government. Attempts to argue that welfare rights are inherent in various provisions of the United States Constitution have failed completely when made on behalf of adults and have had only limited success on behalf of poor children.[13] In the absence of such rights, the federal government is under no affirmative obligation to provide social welfare programs or income transfers to raise children out of poverty. However, once Congress has created statutory entitlements like Supplemental Security Income (SSI) or Medicaid, the Constitution does step in to prohibit discrimination in distribution and it does offer some protection against unfair procedures in administration or termination of benefits. While federal constitutional law is silent regarding positive rights, many state constitutions, drafted or amended during the Progressive Era, explicitly recognize a responsibility on the part of states and localities to meet people's basic needs by providing goods such as public education or emergency shelter.[14]

In family and children's law, diversity reigns from state to state. Each state has its own rules on custody, adoption, children's courts, and child support. Restatements and uniform acts aim to increase coherence, but in the highly charged area of family law they often stir up more controversy than they resolve.[15] But this legal diversity is no accident; the framers of the Constitution purposefully circumscribed the power of the central federal government to override local values, requiring that Congress act only within its enumerated powers, such as the power to regulate commerce or to provide for the national defense. All other powers are reserved to the states. For the first 150 years of the nation's history, federal laws on children's issues simply did not exist outside narrow areas such as immigration and Indian law. In the period between the New Deal and the 1990s, however, the Supreme Court shifted to construing Congress' enumerated powers broadly and we have seen a proliferation of federal public law affecting children and families. Most such laws rely on Congress' commerce powers or its power to spend to promote the general welfare. Such "welfare" legislation especially has provided a rich source of federal entitlements for children with special needs or whose parents are unable to meet their needs—with an alphabet soup of programs for children from AFDC to WIC. Because of the many federal programs involving children, federal courts play a central role in interpreting children's statutory rights as well.[16] But such statutory entitlements, when compared to constitutional rights, are an ephemeral form of "rights" because they depend entirely on the will of Congress. What Congress gives, it can also take away.

Recently, we have seen the pendulum swing back in the direction of decentralization and localization of laws relating to children. Other chapters in this volume describe recent welfare reforms, which reduced or eliminated many of children's federal entitlements and shifted responsibility for children's welfare to state and local government. This trend toward decentralization also is reflected in recent pronouncements from the Supreme Court that reinforce the principle, often honored in the breach by earlier Courts, that Congress may not supplant the states in matters of local law making.

In 1996, the Court issued a wake up call in *United States v. Lopez,* overturning the Gun Free Schools Act because Congress had failed to articulate any nexus between the law and the federal government's enumerated powers.[17] The Gun Free Schools Act made possession of guns within 1000 feet of a school a federal criminal offense, punishable in federal courts under federal law. Schools, children, crime in schools—these are presumptively local matters, and absent a clear showing of authority under the commerce clause or some other federal power, said the Court, these matters must be left to the states.

Ironically, given the imbalance between children's dependency and their capacity for autonomy, children's negative rights are more fully reflected in American law and more plainly a matter of constitutional concern than are children's positive welfare, economic, and social rights. However, even these negative rights have had a checkered history, as the courts have struggled to apply concepts designed for autonomous adults to children of all ages. The primary source of such rights is the United States Constitution. This short document, which never mentions the words "family" or "children," increasingly has been interpreted in ways that limit both state and federal governments in their interactions with families and children. The first ten amendments to the United States Constitution, often called The Bill of Rights, articulate various constraints on the powers of government.

In the words of one eminent judge: "The Constitution is a charter of negative rather than positive liberties.... The men who wrote the Bill of Rights were not concerned that government might do too little for the people but that it might do too much to them."[18] Consciousness of these negative rights and the contrast with positive rights is deeply ingrained in American society. We learn quite early the civics lesson that government is not obligated to give the would-be speaker a platform but it cannot silence her or him. Government is not obligated to provide every person with a roof over his or her head, but it cannot enter any person's home without a search warrant. Steeped in the culture of the Bill of Rights, most Americans understand their rights primarily in terms of freedom from government interference: Government may not establish religion, force a person to testify against himself, or force a believer to forswear her God; police may not seize a person's body without a warrant, and courts may not convict a defendant of a serious crime without a trial by jury.

The process, begun in 1791, of articulating such negative rights through amendments to the Constitution, has continued over the years. Initially, the Bill of Rights applied to limit only federal not state or local powers. The Fourteenth Amendment, ratified in the aftermath of the Civil War, extended protections to citizens interactions with state as well as federal authorities.[19] The Fourteenth Amendment reads: "No state shall ... deprive any person of life, liberty, or property without due process of law; nor deny to any person within its jurisdiction the equal protection of the laws." This amendment, designed to protect former slaves from white tyranny and racial discrimination, has become a rich source of children's rights through the process of judicial interpretation. In a few cases, the Constitution directly addresses issues of justice for youth. Amendment XXVI, ratified in 1972, prohibits the denial of the vote in federal elections to citizens 18 and over on account of their age. Like prior amendments, it was a product of its moment in history. The nation was responding to public feeling over the injustice of drafting young men at age 18 to fight in the Vietnam War while denying them the privileges of citizenship necessary to shaping the country's policies. But the amendment also reflected the growing power of youth, who had fought and died in every war since the Revolution without the right to vote, but were now playing a decisive foreign policy role through their political activism on campuses and at conventions, which could not be ignored.

THE SUPREME COURT AS REFEREE OF FAMILY RIGHTS

I have noted some of the constitutional provisions that have been important to children, but much of the story is written not in the Constitution itself but in the decisions of the United States Supreme Court. In Chief Justice John Marshall's famous words, it is emphatically the province of the judiciary to "say what the law is."[20] As the highest court in the land, the Supreme Court has the duty to construe and interpret constitutional language to resolve specific cases and controversies. Since children and families are never mentioned in the Constitution, the process of applying the language to children's claims is especially problematic. Every word of our constitutional jurisprudence of families and children rests on the justices' powers of interpretation. The Court has had to read between the lines of the Constitution, finding protections of children's rights and family rights in the document's general statements about the values of life, liberty, property, and equality and in the historical events that motivated the drafting of our Constitution and its amendments. The energy created by these broad concepts has fueled the constitutionalization of the family and has driven the process by which "family rights" emerged as a major aspect of American law.

Substantive Due Process: The Peculiar Constitutional Pedigree of Family Rights

The first Supreme Court case to explicitly articulate a general theory of family rights was *Meyer v. Nebraska*, decided in 1923.[21] In *Meyer* the Court held that a state could not forbid the study of the German language in private schools. *Meyer*, was followed two years later by *Pierce v. Society of Sisters*, which held that a state may not require all students to attend public schools.[22] Part of the basis for these holdings was the notion that a parent's right to control the upbringing of his child and to educate the child in his own language, culture, and traditions was so fundamental to the "scheme of ordered liberty" that it could not be infringed by law. In the view of the Court, parenthood occupied a critical zone of freedom from governmental interference. *Meyer* and *Pierce* were part of a line of cases relying on a controversial doctrine that has been labeled "substantive due process." This doctrine empowers the courts to find various substantive limitations implicit in the due process clause of the Fourteenth Amendment, despite the fact that they are not specifically mentioned in the substantive language of the document.[23]

One popular aphorism describes sociology irreverently as "the pursuit of the obvious through obscure methods." The same could be said of law, and substantive due process theory would serve as exhibit A. The very idea of a "substantive" aspect of "due process" seems inherently illogical. Lawyers use the term "due process" to describe fair procedures, such as prior notice of a government action, an opportunity to be heard, and the right to counsel. We use the term "substantive" to refer to the actual substance of what the law says and does, not how the law is applied. In many contexts, legal theory places great weight on distinctions between substantive laws giving (or denying) legal rights and procedural rules governing how the substantive laws are administered. The doctrine of substantive due process seems to collapse the two categories, by saying that certain relationships or activities, although not expressly protected by the language of the Constitution, are so fundamental and involve such basic aspects of human liberty that protection of them is implicit in the ideal of justice which undergirds "due process." These rights, although not explicitly enumerated in the Constitution, are so important that any law that places burdens on them is cause for alarm, no matter how "fair" the process of enacting and enforcing the law may be. This doctrine stands as a judicially created second line of defense, a backup to the Bill of Rights. Like the Bill of Rights, it plays a role in preventing the tyranny of the majority by marking out zones that even democratically elected legislatures and officials using the fairest of procedures cannot invade, unless they can show a compelling reason for enacting the law and demonstrate that no less invasive means exists to serve the state's legitimate goals.

Critics of substantive due process theory charge that it gives the courts too much freedom and discretion to veto decisions of democratically elected legislators and officials. They point with disapproval to the judicial activism of cases such as *Roe v. Wade* that identified a novel "reproductive privacy right" lurking in the penumbra of various clauses of the Constitution and held that restrictions on abortion invaded this newly discovered right.[24] Defenders of substantive due process argue that, without such a theory, courts would be powerless to prevent abuses of human rights by the majority unless they were expressly prohibited by the language of the Constitution. They point with alarm to cases like *Buck v. Bell* which in 1927 upheld as rational and proper a government policy of surgically sterilizing persons with low I.Qs.[25] They praise cases like *Skinner v. Oklahoma* and *Moore v. City of East Cleveland* in which substantive due process theory was used to strike down laws requiring sterilization of repeat felony offenders and to invalidate zoning laws that would infringe on the rights of extended family members to live together.[26] Law professors love to ridicule substantive due process for its convoluted illogic. Yet when presented with the question of whether family privacy should be a specially protected value, by a large majority the public believes that it should.[27] Perhaps substantive due process theory can be excused as an extraordinarily obscure method the Court has adopted for arriving at an obvious truth.

While we agree that the family ought to receive special constitutional protection, problems arise in deciding how to balance the rights of family members. In family cases involving interlocking relationships, it often is difficult to untangle whose rights are being vindicated and whose rights are being burdened. Modern courts have interpreted *Meyer* and *Pierce* as acknowledging the intellectual liberty not only of parents to raise their children, but of children to be treated as individuals by the state and not "standardized" to a single model of citizenship. Viewed in this light, they may have been the first children's rights precedents. Viewed in historical context, these cases are actually far more complex and reflect the economic and social politics of their time.[28] They were not only about liberty; they also were about property. During the Progressive Era, government had reared its head as an agent of social change, redistributing wealth through revolutionary income taxes and social programs. Immigration from Eastern Europe, Ireland, and the Mediterranean threatened the social fabric of an Anglo-Saxon America. In the first decades of the 20th century, a strong block of conservative Supreme Court justices saw their role as one of protecting vested rights against assault by radical populist and progressive forces. Parents' rights to control of children were among the vested rights the Court sought to protect. Between the lines of cases like *Pierce* and *Meyer*, one can see the struggle then in progress to exert some measure of public control and public interest in children as a community resource and as future citizens, through mandatory education laws, child labor laws, and other child welfare initiatives.[29]

Substantive due process doctrine played a central role in allowing the Court to block economic reforms passed by state and federal governments. When confronted with Franklin Roosevelt's New Deal legislation, the Court at first fought against changes in the status quo, striking down legislation regulating farming and labor. Ultimately, the Court was forced by the tide of public opinion and by changing economic realities to abandon its role as referee of economic policies. However, the concept that made its debut in *Meyer* and *Pierce*, that the Court is the protector of a realm of personal liberties implicit in the constitutional scheme, has survived intact, and it is reflected in countless modern cases. It is no accident that so many of the modern cases relying on substantive due process theory involve children and families and protect family values such as marriage, reproduction, parental rights, and family relationships, since these aspects of human life have come to occupy such a critical place in our conception of personal liberty.

The Court had stated, in *Meyer* and *Pierce*, that parents rights were not without limits. In 1946, in a case called *Prince v. Massachusetts*, the justices illustrated how this principle worked in practice.[30] *Prince* involved a challenge to child labor regulations by a woman who had been charged with a misdemeanor for sending her niece to distribute Jehovah's Witness pamphlets on the streets at night. The Court found that the right of a parent or guardian to control a child's upbringing and religious activities did not override the state's interest in protecting its children from the evils of child labor. *Meyer*, *Pierce*, and *Prince* establish the basic framework that still prevails for evaluating the constitutionality of child protective laws and other forms of state intervention in the family.

In deciding whether a given intervention impermissibly intrudes on parents' protected privacy rights or their constitutional rights to control and custody, the Court asks whether the state's interest in protecting the child is so compelling and the intervention so carefully tailored to avoid necessary intrusion that it justifies the impairment of the parent's fundamental liberty interest in raising his child without government interference. The Court's traditional analysis is striking in its silence on the issue of children's rights. While parents have rights, which must be protected but may sometimes be overriden by the state, the concept of rights for children is conspicuously missing from this formulation. The child figures only indirectly in the formula, and children's concerns are not articulated as a right of the child but as legitimate interests of the state to be balanced against the parent's claims of freedom from state control.

Children Emerge as Constitutional Persons: The Equal Protection and Procedural Due Process Cases

Meyer, *Pierce*, and *Prince* were followed by a 20-year lull in articulating the relationship between the Constitution, the family, and its members. During this period, attention shifted to issues of racial equality, and children's rights to be protected from race-based discrimination in public schooling took center stage. In a series of school desegregation cases following *Brown v. Board of Education*, decided in 1954, children played a pivotal role in shaping the law and in expanding the public perception of the role of law.[31] The concept of children as a special class entitled to special protections and the concept of a public stake in children's future permeated the rhetoric of civil rights and was presented daily to television audiences viewing images of children on the front lines of the struggle to achieve racial equality.

Then, in the 1960s and 1970s, the Supreme Court, under Chief Justice Earl Warren and his successor Warren E. Burger, embarked on a series of rulings expanding the constitutional rights of individuals to privacy, equality, and due process. These decisions affected all areas of life, including marriage, family, and reproductive choice. These decisions also extended a measure of civil liberties to children, albeit more limited in scope than the protections afforded to adults.[32] The following list of landmark cases and their dates gives some idea of the many contexts in which the Warren and Burger Courts were called on to balance competing interests of child, parent, and state. Even though the Court often managed to avoid directly addressing children's rights-based arguments and opted in favor of deciding the case on more traditional grounds, these cases provide the foundation for our jurisprudence of children's constitutional rights:

- *In re Gault*, 387 U.S. 1 (1967) (establishing a minor's right to counsel in criminal and juvenile justice proceedings).
- *Levy v. Louisiana*, 391 U.S. 68 (1968) (striking down, under equal protection analysis, a state law discriminating against illegitimate children).
- *Tinker v. Des Moines Independent School District*, 393 U.S. 503 (1969) (recognizing limited free speech rights of youth in schools).
- *Wisconsin v. Yoder*, 406 U.S. 205 (1972) (requiring a religious exemption from mandatory schooling laws for Amish teenagers and discussing but not resolving the tension between children's interests and parents' assertions of religious freedom).
- *Goss v. Lopez*, 419 U.S. 565 (1975) (acknowledging due process rights of students subjected to disciplinary suspensions to present their case to school authorities within a reasonable time after being suspended).
- *Planned Parenthood v. Danforth*, 428 U.S. 52 (1976) (recognizing rights of mature minors to reproductive choice and striking down law that gave parent the power to veto a minor child's abortion decision).

- *Moore v. City of East Cleveland*, 431 U.S. 494 (1977) (overturning a zoning law that prevented children from living with extended family members).
- *Smith v. Organization of Foster Families*, 431 U.S. 816 (1977) (balancing children's interests in stability in foster care placements with the rights to reunification of their biological families).
- *Parham v. J.R.*, 442 U.S. 584 (1979) (acknowledging children's due process rights in civil commitment to mental institutions but deferring to parents' and doctors' decisions for the child).
- *Santosky v. Kramer*, 455 U.S. 745 (1982) (balancing children's rights to protection from physical abuse with the shared family interest in avoiding unnecessary terminations of family relationships).

Children did not always emerge victorious from these cases and arguments about children's rights have not always prevailed or even received an adequate hearing. But children, formerly all but invisible, increasingly play a significant role in constitutional law. Nevertheless, the Supreme Court's decisions reflect profound ambivalence about children's rights. Many of the landmark cases listed above have been limited by subsequent cases from the Rehnquist Court, cutting back on earlier more expansive precedents.[33] As one student of the Supreme Court has observed, the Court's decisions have "yielded incoherent results at times: with the Court protecting children from the dangers of inappropriate speech, yet failing to protect them from abusive parents; allowing states to limit the reproductive decision-making of minors on the grounds of immaturity, yet, at the same time, permitting states to subject minors to the death penalty."[34]

SUMMARY OF CHILDREN'S STATUS IN THE AMERICAN LEGAL SYSTEM

Here, in broad strokes, is a review of the picture I have painted of children in the American legal landscape. The landscape of American law has certain dominant features that characterize its approach to children. More than most other systems, it tends to localize responsibility for children, concentrating family lawmaking at the state and local level. It tends to privatize the raising of children through policies that concentrate responsibility in the nuclear family and deemphasize the roles of wider communities. This privatization produces a split between our sense of what we owe to our children and to other people's children. The American system of law, except in the context of criminal cases, tends to treat children as objects of lawmaking rather than participants, speaking of children's interests rather than their rights. In the legal system, again with the exception of child criminals, children have figured primarily as passive observers in the tussle between parents and the state (or between parent and parent) over who will have the power to articulate and defend the child's interests.

Although American children lack positive or needs-based rights, they do have various entitlements to food, shelter, medical care, education, and protection conferred by various local, state, and federal laws. Children's parents and child advocates can assert the child's constitutional rights to fairness and equality, within the frameworks of rules and benefits created by these government programs. But the entitlements themselves are not guaranteed by any system of positive constitutional rights and they can be taken away as the political mood of the country changes.

Finally, American youths enjoy a fairly highly developed scheme of negative rights and certain positive procedural rights that derive from these negative rights, such as the right to counsel in a juvenile proceeding, modified rights of speech and religion, the right to a disciplinary hearing at school, and so forth. But the rules developed for measuring and implementing children's rights often seem to fit children poorly: The rights seem either to hanging loosely on the child's small shoulders when he is treated like an autonomous adult or to pinch paternalistically when the mature child attempts to flex his muscles in defiance of unwanted adult interference.

To sum up the accomplishments of the children's rights movement, it is fair to say that that children's advocates in America have won a number of modified rights for minors that are variations on the Bill of Rights as it applies to adults. They have won various battles to extend to children the same protections as adults enjoy to be free of invidious discrimination based on race, religion, illegitimacy, sex, and other immutable characteristics. They have extended the due process protections afforded to adults so they aply to children's claims of entitlements. But children's rights advocates have failed to win any specific articulated scheme of special positive rights for children as children, such as the rights recognized in other legal systems to have their most basic economic and welfare needs met by society. And they have failed to win any significant protection from discrimination based on rules disabling minors because of stereotypes about age-based lack of capacity.

While the Supreme Court has responded to child advocates' attempts to put children's cases on the federal agenda, it has remained highly deferential to state authorities, has stopped far short of giving children full-blown autonomy rights and consistently has failed to provide children with effective rights to protection from harm.

IN SEARCH OF UNIFYING PRINCIPLES: FIVE PRINCIPLES THAT GUIDE HUMAN RIGHTS INITIATIVES IN GENERAL AND HAVE SPECIFIC IMPLICATIONS FOR CHILDREN

No system of laws remains static in the face of social change. The American legal tradition I describe above, however halting in its movements, is under constant pressure to respond to changing beliefs about children and their place in the social order. Professor Martha Minow, an astute observer of family law and social history, has noted that the children's rights movement has failed to keep pace with its own aspirations and has been less successful than rights movements by other constituencies. In examining why this is so, she has identified five legal frameworks children's advocates used in thinking and talking about children: child protection, child liberation, children as potential adults, children in need of traditional authority, and children as recipients of social resource redistribution.[35] She shows that arguments from within these frameworks often have seemed to work at cross purposes, impeding progress and blocking the formation of critical political coalitions in the American children's rights movement. Minow is clearly correct that the rhetoric of children's rights has drawn liberally on these themes without coming to terms with their inner contradictions. Advocates for children too often failed to integrate these themes in a coherent way, exacerbating the inherent tensions between them and between political groups that all support children's rights but advocate from within one or another framework.

Perhaps the difficulties encountered by the children's rights movement are not unique but intrinsic to rights movements generally. The five frameworks identified by Minow might be seen as a children's rights variation on a number of pervasive themes that bedevil all movements for perfecting our systems of justice. The segment of the children's rights movement that emphasizes child liberation reflects the high value Americans place on individual freedom but also exposes the limitations of such a principle when it encounters the reality of human interdependence. Those who argue for child protection must accept many of the same bargains with the devils of dependency and Big Brotherism as those who advocate special protections for other vulnerable groups such as women and elders. The tendency to focus on children as potential adults in order to advocate for equal opportunity obscures the importance of valuing children for themselves, much as our focus on equality in other contexts risks obscuring the dignity and importance of difference. Empowerment of the formerly disempowered and promotion of economic justice will always arouse strong resistance from forces that, quite rightly, place a high value on order and stability. This will be true whether the group agitating for redistributions of power and wealth is composed of men, women or children. The tensions among these basic values of protection, empowerment, individual dignity, maintenance of order, and economic justice are universal to all discussions about rights in a just society. Sometimes experienced as destructive, and sometimes as creative, the struggle to resolve these tensions is the stuff of which all human rights movements are made. Our ways of thinking about children's rights and strategies for advancing justice for children are integrally related to our ways of thinking about the rights and responsibilities of other members of families and of society.

It would be impossible to describe in this short space how radically the changing discourse of human rights has altered the face of the law relating to families or to show all the interconnections between changes in the status of children and changes in the status of men and women. A number of principles, however, tie these changes together and tie the children's rights movement to developments in family rights and human rights generally. While it is true they can operate at cross purposes, the friction created when the values embodied in these principles collide can be an energizing and motivating force rather than an obstructive force in building a balanced system of rights. Let me offer for examination five such "principles" that are different from but bear a strong relation to the five frameworks articulated by Martha Minow: (1) the equality principle, (2) the individual dignity principle, (3) the privacy principle, (4) the protection principle, and (5) the empowerment principle. Each principle represents a basic value that ordinary people as well as judges would agree ought to be reflected in the scheme of human rights. A sixth factor, the ever-present tension between individual liberty and the maintenance of social order, is seldom articulated as a "right," yet it operates as a moderating force that works to keep competing values in equilibrium. These principles provide a lens for examining past developments in children's rights and exploring how to shape an agenda for the future. These principles have developed in an adult-centric world. Each principle, I would argue, must be reexamined through the child-centered lens that dissolves the paradox of children's rights by seeing clearly both children's dependency and their capacities—honoring both their needs-based rights and their capacity-based rights in a scheme that recognizes their human dignity. The hardest tasks for children's advocates are the tasks of integrating these principles into a coherent scheme, working to reconceptualize them to fit children's unique needs and capacities, and deploying the persuasive power of these principles in courts and legislatures to advance the cause of children's rights.

The Equality Principle: The Right to Equal Opportunity

The notion that all men were created equal and endowed with rights was revolutionary in 1776. This equality principle, articulated in the Declaration of Independence and given teeth in the Civil War amendments, has provided the major vehicle for discerning rights in previously ignored segments of society. The meaning of equality has evolved over time. Quite clearly, the framers of the Constitution were committed to the equality of propertied white men, but they also were committed to preserving inequalities of class, sex, and color. The Jacksonian Era saw the arrival of popular democracy, as the vote was extended to all free white male citizens, regardless of income or class. The Civil War amendments required government to give equal treatment to all persons regardless of race, creed, or color. It was a small but painful step from racial equality to gender equality. Much of the old structure of law was predicated on the hierarchy of a father ruling his family like a king rules his subjects. As women gained political and economic power, the concept of marriage as an equal partnership emerged and pressures grew to acknowledge women's status as citizens and individuals.

In 1920, women won the constitutionally protected right to vote with the ratification of Amendment XIX. Women used their votes to enact new laws, and where the status quo remained obstinately in place, advocates like Ruth Bader Ginsburg, now an Associate Justice on the Supreme Court, used the equality principle articulated in the XIV Amendment and the power of the Courts to force an end to de jure sex discrimination. Beginning in 1971, with *Reed v. Reed*, the United States Supreme Court extended the principles of the Fourteenth Amendment to reach discrimination based on sex.[36] Prodded by United States Supreme Court decisions of the past few decades, states discarded many laws that treated girls and boys, as well as men and women, differently.[37] Meanwhile, family hierarchies and sharply defined gender roles are gradually dissolving because necessity as well as feminist theory has sent the majority of women into the wage economy.

Riding on the coattails of women's equality, children's claims for equal treatment have emerged as a new force. As we have seen, cases challenging discrimination against illegitimate children, against children of color, and against disabled children used the equality principle to secure rights for children and often to insist that children might be treated differently, but only based on real differences. Children's advocates can learn from women's advocates. Feminists have struggled with mixed success to articulate an equality principle that reflects biological and social realities without reifying women's difference or reenforcing stereotypes of women as essentially different from the dominant male paradigm and therefore less competent and less able. The equality principle encounters even more serious challenges when it is applied to children. At the core of the equality principle is the belief that distinctions between persons on account of race or sex are simply spurious. Hierarchies of race and gender, civil rights advocates have argued, are socially constructed and have no real basis in fact.[38] The Constitution, as interpreted by the current Supreme Court, virtually prohibits classifications of persons according to their race or color and permits very small latitude for classifications based on supposed differences between the sexes.[39]

But children, everyone acknowledges, are different and age is not an entirely spurious measure of children's capacity for equality or right to equal treatment. Few would argue against the proposition that persons under, say, 5 years of age as a class are incapable of taking care of themselves. The notion that children must be treated the same as adults would leave children to fend for themselves, unprotected by special rights to care and supervision. The tension between children's claims to "equal justice under law"[40] and the fact of children's essential dependency has pushed advocates for children's rights to construct more nuanced descriptions of equality. Equality for children must mean both more and less than the formal equality provided by rules that treat all persons the same. One facet that makes up a more complex idea of equality is the notion of equality of opportunity. This principle seems especially important in the lives of children, who inherit as their unequal legacies the inequalities that shaped their parents' lives. Professor Jane Maslow Cohen, noting the sad condition of children in America, examines the potential of various arguments to force recognition of children's rights to support. She finds powerful arguments in children's dependency, both natural and socially enforced, as well as in an equality norm that "promotes the equal regard in which we need to hold every child and the energy we ought to invest in each child's future productive worth."[41] Applying the twin measures of children's needs and capacities for autonomy to the notion of equality would suggest an emphasis on creating an environment for the individual child and for children as a class that supports their capacities for growth. Equality for children in society, as in family life, begins with meeting their basic needs and continues by recognizing and supporting their individual capacities.

The Individualism Principle: The Right to be Treated as a Unique Person, not a Fungible Object

The individualism principle provides a second major theme that ties children's rights to other changes in family law and laws on human rights. This principle requires government to treat all persons as individuals with claims to human dignity. Respect for children as individuals has worked a fundamental alteration in our thinking about family law and policy. Many critics blame family law reform for the erosion of traditional two-parent families. But they forget that children paid dearly to maintain the hierarchical family's stability. Restrictions against unmarried sex and divorce often penalized children, leaving them without legal rights or adequate remedies. We are acutely aware of the costs to children of living in divorced and single parent families. Yet few of us would return to a time when the punishment for an adult's violation of sexual norms was inflicted on the "bastard" child. In many ways, respect for children's rights has transformed the normative framework for thinking about family law and policy, making us ask whether it is "just" to use children instrumentally as a means of controlling the conduct of adults.[42]

A doctrine known as "best interest of the child," which emerged during the 19th century to displace absolutist protections of fathers' rights, provided the thin edge of the legal wedge that opened the door to acknowledging children as individuals in the family circle, with rights and interests of their own. While the principle has been criticized for its indeterminacy in resolving custody disputes, few now question the underlying assumption that decisions about children ought to take into account the well-being of the individual child whose case is under adjudication. Gone are the bright line rules that assigned control of children to their fathers in all but the most egregious and outrageous cases. In the mid-19th century, the rule of paternal sovereignty was modified to give precedence to mothers in all cases involving young children, based on the notion that children need the tender care of a mother. This doctrine opened the door to an evolution of consciousness. Now it is commonly accepted that children, unlike chattels, have legally cognizable interests in court cases affecting them, even if law places limits on children's standing to assert individual rights.[43]

Examining this principle through the lens of children's needs-based rights and dignity rights suggests that children's individuality must be honored in the context of children's dependency as well as in light of children's capacity for eventual autonomy. Treating children with the dignity owed to individual persons requires an assessment of the child's needs, even if the child has no autonomous views to articulate. It also suggests a careful listening to discern the child's perspective even before the child is capable of articulating it, and to consider that perspective seriously once the child is capable of articulating it.

The Empowerment Principle: The Right to a Voice and Sometimes a Choice

Empowerment is a modern sounding term for an old idea: the notion that members of a society ought to have the right to participate in collective decision-making and especially the right to a voice in critical decisions affecting one's own life. As we have seen, traditional rules on children assumed that children lacked the capacity to exercise power and also recognized the fact of children's relative powerlessness. The legal system empowered the parent but rarely the child. Viewing the world through children's eyes, as a place populated by large strangers whose ways are both frightening and mystifying, empowering parents is obviously the most effective way to empower children. In relations with the state and its agents whom children encounter in schools and hospitals and in the justice and social welfare system parents are usually the best advocates for children's interests. The law has empowered children in relations with the state by conferring special rights on parents to act and speak on children's behalf and to make decisions about their welfare that children lack the knowledge and maturity to make.

Sometimes, however, empowering parents has the effect of defeating rather than promoting children's empowerment. One such situation involves the child who is nearing the age of majority and has developed the actual if not legal capacity to make key life decisions for herself. The clash between claims of parental rights and children's rights has been especially sharp in cases pitting the abortion rights of a pregnant minor against the parents' traditional right to make decisions about children's medical care. These cases have forced the Supreme Court to acknowledge that persons cannot be classed as outside the protection of the Constitution merely because of their age, and therefore children must be treated as rights-bearing individuals, regardless of their "capacity"or developmental stage. The abortion cases also have pushed the Court to articulate how children are different, and when such differences may justify restricting children's autonomy in ways not inconsistent with their claims to dignity. Justice Powell's opinion in *Bellotti v. Baird*, identifies children's vulnerability, their lack of judgment, and societal respect for parent–child relationships as reasons for treating children differently, in contexts ranging from criminal justice to access to pornography. But the Court's opinions make clear that when a right as significant as reproductive choice is at stake, the state may not give to parents the power of an absolute veto, simply because of the child's status as a minor. This analysis marked a significant step toward conceptualizing children as individual entitled to be treated with dignity, but it represents the highwater mark in the movement to give minors a right to a voice in matters concerning them. State laws and judges routinely deny children standing in custody, juvenile detention, foster care, and adoption cases, despite the magnitude of the interests at stake.[44]

Critics sensitive to issues of civil liberties have questioned whether it is just to deny a voice to individual children based solely on their chronological age rather than their developmental stage or the nature of the interests at stake.[45] Most of us would agree that, for the sake of efficiency and predictability, even a very just system of laws must sometimes classify persons by generalizations such as date of birth (minimum ages for driving, for example, or minimum ages for leaving school). But there also is general agreement that a just system should not deprive an individual citizen of a voice in decisions that affect him or her based on group stereotypes of inferiority or disability. This is especially true when a court already is engaged in a judicial proceeding calling for individualized adjudication of other issues. We may decide, for example, that efficiency requires an age-based rule to determine eligibility for a driver's license, but should we use chronological age to deprive a child of the right to a voice in court when that child is developmentally capable of contributing to the fact-finding process? Increasingly, we have seen a relaxation of the bars to children's participation as witnesses in court cases.

An emphasis on children's empowerment, however, is a two-edged sword. Some argue that children's advocates cannot have it both ways. How can we argue with one breath that children are entitled to recognition of their autonomy and with the next breath that they are entitled to special rules and special protections? How can we defend a child's right to participate in decisions about his or her custody or education and then object to trying the child who breaks the law by the same rules we apply to adult lawbreakers? Here is where the concepts of needs and capacities are useful counterpoints. A very basic need, one that is essential to children's integration into society and their education for citizenship, is the need for a sheltered setting in which to try out one's emerging capacities, a place where youthful mistakes need not have cataclysmic consequences. Children's inclusion in decisionmaking, perhaps before they are entirely "competent," plays a crucial role in educating them for independence.[46] A just system of laws would allow the young to learn from their mistakes, but it would stop short of holding an immature youth equally accountable with an adult for the harms caused by wrong decisions. We recognize that lack of mature judgment makes young people less able to appreciate the consequences of their acts but also more capable of learning and changing.

The Protection Principle: The Right of the Weak to be Protected from the Strong

The right of the weak to be protected from the strong is such a basic element of a society ruled by law that we take it for granted. The very essence of "law and order" is the understanding that rights and responsibilities must replace raw power as the means of ordering social interactions. A basic premise of the American legal system inherited by the framers of the Constitution was the principle that an individual's liberty stops at the point when his fist contacts someone else's body, unless, of course, the actor was a husband or a father and the body was that of a wife or a child.

One of the most striking developments of the past decades has been the extension of the protection principle to violence within the family. This revolution reflects a growing belief that family members should be protected by the state from harms inflicted not only by strangers but also by family members. Shifts in the public consciousness about rights to protection are integrally related to changing notions about equality and privacy. Previously, the acceptance of gender hierarchy within families made male violence toward women and children appear an appropriate means for maintaining male domination and keeping order within the family.[47] Partners or spouses who previously had no recourse against violent mates can now seek orders of protection and evict the abusive individual from the home. Child protective laws have been enacted requiring reporting and intervention to prevent violence toward children. Intrafamily crimes of violence are grounds for arrest and incarceration, and domestic violence, whether against spouses, elders, or children, can no longer be considered a "private" matter. With the piercing of the veil of family privacy, molestation and physical abuse have come out of the closet.[48] Sex crimes and crimes of violence against children that once were ignored or hushed up are now prosecuted, bringing children into court as victims and witnesses.

However, two cases illustrate the limitations still imposed on effective protections for children by the traditional dichotomies between public and private and local and federal matters. In one major case, the public–private dichotomy was used to explain why children have no positive rights under the Constitution to protection from harm while they are in their parents' custody. The other case illustrates how the divisions of powers in our federal system hamper children advocates' attempts to use federal powers to establish uniform rights for children in all states to protection from abuse.

The argument that government authorities, once they know of a child at risk, have an affirmative duty to protect that child, was rejected by the Supreme Court in a 1989 case called *DeShaney v. Winnebago County Department of Social Services*.[49] The case involved a child named Joshua DeShaney who was permanently brain damaged from beatings inflicted by his father. The mother, on her child's behalf, sued the county for its gross negligence in failing to follow up on signs that he was at risk of serious harm. Three-year-old Joshua had been released to his father's custody after hospitalization for injuries that raised suspicions of physical abuse. The family remained under observation by a county social worker, who ignored clear signs of danger. The Court held that the state had no duty to intervene. Writing for the majority, Chief Justice Rehnquist reasoned that "the harm was inflicted not by the State of Wisconsin, but by Joshua's father. The most that can be said of the state functionaries in this case is that they stood by and did nothing when suspicious circumstances dictated a more active role for them." A powerful dissent authored by Justice Blackmun, exposed the fallacy of attempting to draw sharp lines between public and private spheres. Blackmun highlighted the active role of the state in drawing a circle of privacy around the home and setting the basic framework of laws authorizing adults to control children's bodies. Yes, Joshua was in his father's and not the state's "custody," Blackmun agreed, but within a legal framework that the state itself had created. Neighbors and citizens who reported their suspicions that Joshua was in danger had no power to intervene and relied on the Department of Social Services to do so once it had reason to know the child was being battered. "If DSS ignores or dismisses these suspicions [of a parent's brutality] no one will step in to fill the gap. Wisconsin's child protection program thus effectively confined Joshua DeShaney within the walls of Randy DeShaney's violent home until such time as DSS took action to remove him."

A second case, *Suter v. Artist M.*, illustrates the Court's reluctance to federalize areas of law that have been traditionally consigned to local authorities.[50] The case involved an attempt by advocates for children to establish a right under the federal Adoption Assistance and Child Welfare Act (AACWA) to effective services for children at risk. The Court refused to interpret AACWA as creating a governmental duty, enforceable by children and their representatives, to make "reasonable efforts" to avoid foster care placements and to speed family reunification. The advocates relied on the state's obligations to provide preventive services outlined in the statute. In contrast to other cases finding that a federal scheme of laws covering a certain area creates "entitlements" for children, the Court found that AACWA merely established policies on child abuse prevention under the "spending clause" and its provisions did not translate into enforceable rights for children. Instead, they created conditions that state and local authorities must meet in order to claim federal funds. While the federal government might withhold moneys from the states to penalize them for their failure to provide appropriate services to children, the children themselves had no right to obtain court orders forcing the authorities to make the "reasonable efforts" required by AACWA.

Viewed as cases about balancing the risk of removal against the risks of reunification, these cases seem to come from opposing camps. But they bear one striking similarity. While advocates in *DeShaney* argued that the state had a duty to remove the child who is clearly at severe and immediate risk and advocates in *Suter* argued that the state had a duty to provide those in-home services necessary to prevent child abuse and avoid removal, together these cases stood for the proposition that children have rights, enforceable at the federal level, to be protected from abuse in their own homes. Placing children in protective custody should be a last resort, not a first response. Translated into adult terms, children have the right to "law and order" in the places where they live, within their own homes, families, schools, streets, and neighborhoods. These cases illustrate the continuing power of a privatized and localized image of responsibility toward children and its effects on defeating children's claims of rights to protection from lawless violence in their own homes. Examining these cases through the lens of children's needs-based and capacity-based rights suggests that society cannot hide from violence toward children behind the public–private distinction. Given the comparative weakness of children, society bears a responsibility even greater than its responsibility toward women who are victimized by domestic violence and have at least some options for escape. At the same time, children caught in child protective proceedings cannot be treated with blind paternalism but must be given due process rights that recognize their individual capacity and allow them to participate as "heroes of their own lives."

The Privacy Principle: The Right to Protection of Intimate Relationships

Finally, a major force in shaping family law in general is the privacy principle. This principle has applied to protect an individual's most intimate personal choices from state regulation and intrusion. In the context of abortion, the most famous arena of privacy rights, the Court describes privacy rights primarily as individual rights of choice. But many family cases imply that privacy may be something that is shared, mutual, or collective and is essential to the functioning of family systems, not just to the rights of individual family members.

Once again, children present special challenges forcing us to articulate the privacy principle in more nuanced ways. Privacy, when seen as an aspect of personal choice, arguably means very little to a nursing infant. The notion of an infant's right to choose to nurse or not to nurse, to be diapered or not to be diapered, borders on the ridiculous. In a more serious vein, the rhetorical battle between those who advocate a right to life for the fetus and those who advocate a right to choice for the pregnant woman illustrates how difficult it is to factor children's choices into the battle about choice.

Privacy, however, means a great deal to the helpless infant when the zone of privacy is drawn around a concrete relationship with a caring adult rather than around the abstract notion of personal choice. Nurturing relationships, such as the mother–child dyad or nuclear or extended family, provide the environments within which bonded adults make choices (a source of empowerment) for children and ultimately teach children how to make choices for themselves. These intimate relationships shelter the growing child from the tender mercies of the bureaucratic state. We saw in cases like *Meyer* and *Pierce* how substantive due process theory was used both to establish the supremacy of the patriarch and to shield the family as a system from state intervention. In this second function, the privacy principle acts to protect children from being used as instrumental tools of state policy. Placing a high value on children's rights to family privacy suggests a preference for assigning the power to make choices for children—even life and death choices—to an adult who is attached to the child by deep personal bonds. Even persons who cannot make their own decisions must have the right to have those decisions made privately, within the family, rather than publicly, by a bureaucracy of strangers. Most of us would be horrified at the thought that the state should take over decision-making authority for every elder who could not make choices for him or herself. We trust families to make the most painful and conflicted of intimate decisions precisely because they are not neutral. Like the preference for family systems of decision making at the end of life, trusting families with decisions at the beginning of life maintains that crucial buffer zone between the individual and the cold and impersonal state.[51]

Family privacy, however, holds serious risks for the less powerful members of the family system—children, elders, and women—even as it protects important values for individuals and society. As one scholar of changes in modern family law has remarked, "Stamped on the reverse side of the coinage of individual liberty, family privacy, and sex equality, are alienation, powerlessness, and dependency."[52] Clearly, there are inherent tensions between principles of equality and dignity, protection and privacy. The current debates about "family values" are evidence of this tension between the needs of society, the needs of the family as a group, and the freedom of each family member. We are constantly forced to choose between competing and often inconsistent values. When does the protection principle favoring an obligation on the part of the state to intervene on behalf of children at risk outweigh the privacy principle favoring wide latitude in intimate decision making and child rearing? When does the equality principle behind equal treatment of men and women in custody disputes collide with the child's claim based in the dignity principle to be treated like an individual, and not parceled out fifty–fifty between competing claimants? Children are inevitably caught in the middle and our usual fallbacks—personal "choice" and individual "autonomy"—which provide the default settings for adults' rights provide no easy escape from the task of articulating a scheme of children's rights that reflects their dependency as well as their capacity. One of the critical challenges for American law and policy in the next century will be articulating a more delicate balance between the principles of equality, protection, privacy, empowerment, and dignity; one that avoids giving any one value primacy over all the others but acknowledges the importance of each to the other and examines the special interplay of these values in the special context of children's lives.

APPLYING A CHILD-CENTERED ANALYSIS OF RIGHTS PRINCIPLES TO ONE SET OF CUTTING EDGE ISSUES OF CHILDREN'S RIGHTS

American law is feeling the impact of thses principles, as advocates bring them to bear on defining children's rights in a number of different doctrinal contexts. These include children's rights in reproductive technology, transracial adoption, schooling, media, the courtroom, and many other arenas. In the following section, I will focus attention on a set of emerging rights claims that has important implications across a broad range of legal contexts, civil as well as criminal: the child's rights to standing and a voice, as elements of procedural due process, and the child's right to a determination grounded in the child's best interests, as an element of substantive due process.

Children's Due Process Rights in Civil Cases: The Right to Standing and a Voice

With *In re Gault* leading the way, children's rights to procedural due process in criminal and juvenile justice proceedings were among the first rights for children explicitly recognized by the Supreme Court. The justices have been much more reluctant to recognize due process rights for children in other contexts. The Court has long recognized the rights of adults to fair procedures in any judicial proceeding that threatens to deprive them of physical liberty (examples include involuntary commitment to a mental institution), of property interests (examples include eviction, termination of public benefits, mortgage foreclosure), of constitutionally enumerated rights (examples include the rights of free speech and assembly), and of other fundamental rights and liberty interests (examples include the right to marry, the right to pursue a profession, the right to travel, rights of procreation). Just what process is "due" depends on the type of case, but the Court has developed formulations or tests that it applies to analyze due process claims in a variety of contexts.[53]

The mysterious phrase "due process" (described earlier in connection with substantive due process theory) means nothing more or less than the right to procedures that are fundamentally fair. The bedrock elements of due process in our system always have been "notice and an opportunity to be heard," that is, the person whose life, liberty, or property is at risk must receive notification of an adverse action by a court or government entity and must have an opportunity to speak to the decisionmaker or have a representative speak on her behalf, either before or soon after the deprivation occurs. Depending on the complexity of the case and the weight of the interests at stake, due process may be satisfied by fairly simple, informal hearings or it may require the full range of elaborate procedures we all learned to expect from Perry Mason and Court TV: a court reporter to make a record of the proceedings so they can be reviewed by a higher tribunal, stringent application of the rules of evidence, appointed counsel and waiver of fees for indigent persons, the right of trial by jury, adjudication by an impartial tribunal, and the opportunity to call witnesses and present expert testimony.

Lawyers and judges often dismiss or overlook children's due process concerns in civil cases because the law has for so long been accustomed to treating children as parental property, lacking not only "capacity" but personhood. The same judge who would instantly appoint a guardian ad litem for an infirm elderly person may have difficulty seeing a child in an analogous case as a party who has "standing" (an interest sufficiently concrete to justify a right of participation in the proceedings). The judge may conclude that the child has no distinct and separate interests from her parents, or that the child's interests are sufficiently protected by giving due process to her parents. Or she may reason that the child is not entitled to procedural protections because there is no protected "liberty or property interest" at stake; for example, if all children must by law be under an adult's custody (usually a parent's), how can they claim a liberty interest in connection with decisions about which of several persons will be awarded custody? Or a judge may conclude that a custody dispute or adoption is a private matter that does not involve state action, a necessary component of a due process claim.

We already have seen one such case in the story of Joshua DeShaney. Another example of such reasoning is Justice Scalia's opinion for the majority in *Reno v. Flores*, a case challenging Immigration and Naturalization Services (INS) rules on detention of illegal alien juveniles.[54] Advocates for the children argued that they had a right to be released to their parents or guardians if continued custody in a detention center was not in their best interests. In order to protect against deprivation of this right to liberty, the INS had to use fair procedures in deciding whether to release a juvenile to a person nominated by her parent as a guardian. Justice Scalia reasoned that all children might be viewed as "in custody" regardless of whether they were in the custody of their parents, an institution like a school or orphanage, or detained by the INS. If the Court were to find that the Constitution conferred a right on children to have the justice of their detention in custody measured by whether it is in their best interest, it would radically extend the reach of constitutional law into all judgments about children, from court proceedings relating to abandoned children to custody adjudications in divorce disputes. Justice Scalia's analysis reflects an underlying acceptance of restraints on children's liberty as natural or inherent.

By pointing to the fact that children's custody normally goes unquestioned, Justice Scalia attempts to maintain a theoretical divide between public and private spheres, making government accountable only for state actions that create new restraints. He treats as invisible or private a large realm of government actions that reinforce existing restraints. This move frees government and the courts from any constitutional obligation to examine whether rules that apply to children are fair or just. By contrast, to question these assumptions would be to venture onto a "slippery slope" of legal reasoning, with no logical stopping point in view.

Inspired by past civil rights movements and by current feminists and critical legal theorists, who proclaim that "the public is the private," many scholars have begun to question the baselines we apply in delimiting the operative field of rights. Why do courts say there has been state intervention calling for due process protections when the police remove an abused child from his or her home, but the same courts would say the return of a runaway child to her parents' custody does not involve state intervention, even though she is taken from a place of refuge by a police officer and forced to return against her will?[55] Both acts have a profound effect on the child's liberty and property interests, and both forcible removal and forcible return potentially have life and death consequences. The importance to the child of due process protections is masked by the assumption that the parents' power over children is merely a private arrangement.

Similar challenges have been made to deprivation of due process for children in divorce, foster care, or adoption. From the child's perspective, any custody order is a government action invoking the coercive powers of the state. Most children's rights advocates would agree that in the garden variety uncontested divorce or adoption, the fact that the adults are in agreement indicates that the child's interests are not sufficiently at risk to warrant appointment of counsel or separate standing for the child. Here, the adults fulfill their role of empowering the child through their advocacy on behalf of the child's interests, in negotiations with each other and with the courts. However, when a court orders a change of custody or visitation in a sharply contested case, perhaps one involving a large imbalance of power between the parents, or when it orders a foster care placement or family reunification after a long period of separation or a serious incident of abuse, or when it enters or dissolves a decree in a contested adoption, these acts affect the child's liberty and property interests every bit as much as an eviction or an involuntary commitment affects an adult's interests. We cannot rely on the adults who usually speak for the child to fulfill their roles, because of conflicts of interest or because of doubts about their fitness.

Building on the arguments made in the criminal law context, advocates for children have questioned the lack of due process accorded to children in civil cases compared with the elaborate procedures available to adults in analogous situations. While often unsuccessful in arguing for constitutional rights, children's advocates have made astonishing progress in reforming state laws and the legal culture to expand due process protections. Few changes in our legal consciousness have been as rapid or widely accepted as the reforms giving children the right to representation and to a voice in cases in which the government is a party. Fifteen years ago, those who argued in favor of treating a child as a party represented by a child advocate were considered a radical fringe, whose ideas damaged the legal profession's credibility. Today, most states and key professional associations have adopted policies or legislation requiring that children who are the subject of involuntary foster care placements or termination of parental rights be assigned attorneys of their own.[56]

Are these protections constitutionally required? The Court has never decided this precise question, but neither Justice Scalia in *Flores* nor Chief Justice Rehnquist in *DeShaney* speak for all members of the Court in dismissing the notion of children's due process protections of the liberty interest involved in decisions about their custody. Several justices who concurred in the opinion in *Flores* specifically noted that children do have a liberty interest in being free from government restraints that are not rationally related to government's interests in promoting the welfare of the child.[57] As the discussion within the Court and the legal community evolves, I expect the Supreme Court eventually will recognize that children do have a liberty interests at stake in many custodial decisions. While ordinarily protected by giving standing to her parents, the child's interest is distinct from that of parents and state and requires extra protections whenever the parent or other person seeking custody has an obvious conflict of interest with the child. The Court will have to look beyond past traditions denying children a voice in civil proceedings and rely on present evidence of evolving standards of justice for children to acknowledge that a court's entry of a custody decree does affect a child's liberty. Although debate continues over precisely how to give children a voice in court proceedings, the idea that children must be provided with advocates whose role is to represent the child, not the parent or the state, is becoming firmly established.

Change has come more slowly in cases where government is not a party, such as garden variety custody and adoption cases. In the coming decades, we are sure to see continued pressure to examine the legal fictions we apply to families and children and test them against the yardstick of "fundamental fairness." Many of the cases that have fueled intense media controversy, including those of Baby Jessica, Baby Richard, Gregory K., and Kimberley Mays, involved challenges to legal rules that denied children an opportunity to be heard.[58] The outcome in these cases—being taken from a familiar home and family, losing one's identity and being made to take on another identity, or continuing to drift forever in foster care waiting for a parent who would never come—seemed so stark and cataclysmic that denying the child and his advocate a hearing on the merits struck the public as fundamentally unfair. Traditional rules that denied children standing to bring a claim, treated the decisions of biological parents who had never had custody as dispositive of the child's interests, denied children the right to independent representation, and foreclosed the child and his advocate from filing motions or presenting evidence. The lay observer was not persuaded and legislators responded with reformed laws. Here again, we may see public perceptions of children's rights to dignity, protection, and a voice outstripping existing precedents and potentially reshaping the law.

The implication of according children a right commensurate with their capacities to participate in any proceeding concerning them extends far beyond the traditional courtroom to a host of administrative law contexts. Many laws that give children statutory rights, such as the right of a disabled child under federal special education laws to a free appropriate public education, actually empower only parents and provide children themselves with no standing and little or no voice. These special education cases, like the famous case of *Wisconsin v. Yoder*, raise serious questions about when the state ought to begin listening to children's own views on their education rather than presuming that the parent knows best.

Setting the Substantive Foundation: The Right to a Determination Grounded in the Child's Best Interest

The best interest standard is a rule that lays a substantive foundation for an entire class of cases. Like the requirement in criminal law that the jury find guilt beyond a reasonable doubt, the best interest standard states a foundational premise and makes a judgment about priorities. A fundamental premise of criminal law in America is that justice is better served by erring on the side of acquitting the accused, because as a society we believe that it is more unjust to send an innocent person to jail than it is to free a guilty one. The best interest standard is a statement about the moral basis for exercising power over children and the respective weights we will give to protecting adults and to protecting children. It says that in cases about custody, adoption, foster care, and the like children's welfare should be given priority when the courts are forced to decide between the interests of children and conflicting interests of adults.

The best interest standard has come under attack for its indeterminacy—the difficulty of deciding what is actually in children's interests. Recently, a number of scholars have come to its defense, arguing that few legal standards are objective or self-explanatory, from the reasonable person standard applied in tort law to the business judgment rule that prevails in corporate law.[59] Currently, the best interest standard applies in most custody cases, often interpreted via intermediate principles intended to give more guidance to courts where there is some identifiable consensus about what arrangements are in children's best interests. The presumption in favor of the primary care giver is one such intermediate principle, standing for the proposition that children are better off in general staying with the parent who has played the central role in raising them.[60] The rule that custody will only be modified on a showing that circumstances have changed embodies the principle that children need stability and are not well served by rules that encourage endless battles over custody. In certain cases where children's interests are inextricably bound up with those of their parents, such as the termination of parental rights or the removal of a child from his or her home, courts and legislatures sometimes modify the best interest standard to tip the balance in favor of preserving the child's family relationships, that is, requiring a showing that termination or removal will not merely serve a child's "best interests" but is necessary to avoid a serious detriment to the child. A few states still treat parental rights as dispositive and refuse to consider the child's interests at all, unless the parents are proven unfit.

The Supreme Court has never decided when or whether applying the best interest standard might invade parents' constitutional rights, although it has said hypothetically that the state could not destroy an intact natural family merely on a showing that it would promote the child's best interests.[61] In my writing, I have argued for a child-centered perspective on parents' rights which would shift the emphasis from parents' rights of ownership in children to parents' role as advocates and trustees. When we peel away the layers of substantive due process doctrine and property-based tradition that have accrued around the notion of parents' rights, one key principle remains intact: one person may not have rights in another person. If children are persons, not property, are innocent of any crime, and have not "consented" to adult custody, I would argue that the strongest and perhaps only "just" basis for adult "rights" in children is in the rightful powers we give to a fiduciary, whose responsibility it is to protect the interests of a dependent person. Thus the guiding standard in decisions involving children must be the child's best interest, whether the decisionmaker is the parent or the state. Obviously, a child's interests are integrally related to those of family members and must be considered in context of the family as a whole. Advocates of a best interest standard do not imagine it applied in a vacuum, without reference to the child's history and experiences, or her biological and community ties.[62] It is a gross oversimplification to suppose that the best interest standard, applied in a child-centered framework, would simply take poor children and reassign them to affluent families. The standard must be applied with sensitivity to the complex of goods and entitlements—family relationships, identity, culture, and language, and the like—that together, taken in the context of children's social and cultural environments, form the fabric of a child's best interests.

We can and must protect the privacy of parents and the integrity of families, but it can be done without undermining the personhood of children, by refocusing our attention away from parents' possessory rights and toward the critical importance to children of family privacy and intimate family relationships. This may seem like a purely theoretical shift, but it is one that draws on the power of the dignity, equality, and protection principles and has important implications for how we view children and our responsibilities to children. It is a shift away from an instrumentalist tradition of rights *in* children. It also is a shift that the international law community has already made, in the Convention on the Rights of the Child.

THE ROLE OF INTERNATIONAL LAW AND THE PHENOMENON OF AMERICAN RESISTANCE: THE 1989 UNITED NATIONS CONVENTION ON THE RIGHTS OF THE CHILD

One striking feature of American law is its reluctance to look outside its own borders to sources of comparative or international law. During the same postwar period that saw a revolution in individual rights in America, international legal bodies were recognizing and formalizing basic human rights. The sufferings of children under the Nazi regime, along with others considered too weak to be of use to the Fascist state, forcefully illustrated how human rights abuses often fall most heavily on the young. A recent visit to the Anne Frank house in Amsterdam drove home to this writer the brutal fact of discrimination against children, simply because of their status as children. The Nazis singled out children as a class for extermination. When Anne Frank arrived at the concentration camps, she narrowly escaped being sent directly to the ovens. On arrival, all children under 15 were separated from their mothers and exterminated. Having celebrated her 15th birthday the month before, in her attic hideout, Anne was no longer classified as a child. She was spared, only to die of typhoid shortly before the concentration camp was liberated.

In response to the Holocaust and its perversion of the state's protective function toward the vulnerable, children were made a special object of concern in the wave of human rights activity by the newly established United Nations. In 1959, the United Nations Declaration of the Rights of the Child focused primarily on duties to children and government's obligation to meet their needs.[63] Today, treaties and conventions play a growing role in defining and reconceptualizing children's rights. We can expect to find more and more cases in state and federal courts citing the various new and revised Hague Conventions and United Nations Treaties.

Undoubtedly, the most important children's rights document in history is the 1989 United Nations Convention on the Rights of the Child (the Children's Convention) which has been ratified by virtually every nation in good standing in the world community, and as of this writing still awaits action by our Congress.[64] The Children's Convention has stirred up heated controversies in the United States precisely because it addresses the unresolved tension described above between public recognition of children's rights and the tradition of allocating power over children to the private realm of family life, under the complete authority of parents. Sadly, the prospects for a speedy ratification in the United States seem dim. At present, progress toward ratification of the Children's Convention is blocked by powerful coalitions of religious and political conservatives, who view it as undermining parents' constitutionally protected rights and fear it will compromise the autonomy of the United States.

The Children's Convention draws on a wide spectrum of international human rights traditions to focus on the special situation of children. It incorporates children's needs-based and capacity-based rights as well as their dignity rights. Its most important role is not in articulating claims to be asserted by children in courts of law, but in proposing norms of justice to guide those engaged in developing laws and social policies. By defining an underlying theory of adult power over children and of limitations on that power it creates benchmarks for adults who act on children's behalf to assess the rightness of their behavior. The convention's provisions combine recognition of children's essential dependency and their capacity for autonomy, treating children as interdependent members of families and communities but also as individuals with unique personalities. Children are seen as persons with emerging moral and cultural lives that parents and government are explicitly charged with respecting.

According to the scheme of the convention, children have the capacity for growth to autonomy and deserve the right to be treated in a manner consistent with this capacity. The convention identifies the right of children who are capable of forming their own views to express these views in matters affecting them either directly or through a representative. While children have rights to freedom of thought and religion, it is the duty of parents (not the state) to guide their children's development in these spheres, in a manner consistent with the child's evolving capacities. Entitlement to support and guidance from both parents, who will make the child's interest their basic concern, is articulated as a child's right, not as the parent's right. Children also have the right to know and be cared for by their parents and not to be separated from them except in the best interest of the child. Children share in the same basic human rights as their elders, including rights against racial, religious, and gender discrimination and against arbitrary state intrusion in the form of attacks on their privacy, family, home, ethnicity, or religion. The Children's Convention also recognizes certain rights that are especially important to children such as the right to recreation and to protection from physical abuse and sexual or economic exploitation and the entitlement to care within a family and the right to a family identity. Finally, the Children's Convention makes explicit the obligation of states to meet the basic economic needs of the young. It includes the right to an adequate standard of living, to education, to health care, and to social insurance. Government entities must seek to meet these economic obligations to the maximum extent of their available resources. Comparison with the 1959 UN Declaration of the Rights of the Child indicates that concern for children's material and developmental needs remains strong and is joined by an increased respect for children's voices, their personal dignity, and their membership in family and community.

As the approach of both the UN Declaration and the UN Convention illustrates, the attitude toward positive or economic rights has been far more liberal internationally than in the United States. The economic rights of families, an important component of what I term children's needs-based rights, are explicitly acknowledged by the constitutions of many nations and by major international treaties and conventions. Like the convention, such documents usually contain limitations clauses that try to place government's obligations to provide health care, food, shelter, and education in economic context, judging whether a country is living up to its duties toward its children by looking at whether its efforts are reasonable in light of the available resources and the country's stage of economic development.[65] Judged by international standards, the United States falls far short of meeting its obligations to provide for poor children.[66]

Most mainstream United States institutions, from the American Bar Association, American Academy of Pediatrics, and National Council of Churches to civic and women's groups such as the Soroptimists, have endorsed the convention and urged its ratification. Yet, as of this writing, the prospects for US ratification, even with significant reservations, seem seriously in doubt. Other nations have managed to craft reservations and declarations meeting concerns about preservation of local traditions and cultures, as well as concerns about restrictions on government policies toward juvenile justice, capital punishment, and age limits for military service. In the United States, by far the most vehement opposition comes from private citizens and nongovernmental sources. The Bush Administration did not sign the document in 1989, due to a ground swell of opposition from conservative constituents. After 2 more years of "study," the Clinton Administration finally signed the document on February 23, 1995, and stated its intention of referring it for Senate approval.

The United States Constitution, however, requires that treaties be approved by a two thirds vote of the Senate. Even before the convention was signed, opponents claimed to be only two votes short of blocking ratification, and former Senate Majority Leader Bob Dole reported calls and letters running a thousand to nothing against the convention. Senator Jesse Helms, the powerful Chair of the Senate Foreign Relations Committee, has publicly stated his opposition to the convention and has vowed to block any attempts to bring it before the committee for hearings. Why is the convention in such deep trouble in the United States of America, one of the countries most actively involved in its creation?

The answer lies in the peculiar history and dynamics of the American culture and politics of the family. As we have seen, American traditions reflect a culture of individualism and a belief in privatization that extends not only to economic policy, evident in the privatization movements of the past decades, but also to education and welfare policy and to family and children's policy. Many Americans fear that the convention would redefine the family, removing children from parental control and placing control of their upbringing in national and international governing bodies. These Platonic concepts are anathema to a large constituency of cultural and religious conservatives who seek to preserve what they perceive to be God-given rights, family values, and the American way.

Since Colonial times, citizens' groups and grass roots movements have played a key role in US political life. As noted earlier, mainstream professional, civic, and religious organizations generally endorse the convention. However, a large number of organizations often self-described as on the right wing, have mobilized their membership to write and telephone their Senators, urging rejection of the convention.[67] Some of these, such as the Family Research Council and the Heritage Foundation, are think tanks established through fund raising or foundations, with a general mission of educating citizens on policy issues and raising support for conservative causes. Others, like the National Center for Home Education or Human Life International, are citizen groups focusing on specific issues such as home schooling or abortion. Perhaps best known among the religiously based opposition is the Christian Coalition. The Christian Coalition is neither a church nor a coalition of churches, like the National Council of Churches, but rather a coalition of individual citizens, many of them fundamentalist Christians, who seek to influence government policies because they believe Christian values are threatened by them. In the mid-1990s, they were extremely successful in gathering political support for a "Contract with the American Family," which included opposition to the convention and advocated passage of a Parental Rights and Responsibilities Act to protect parents rights.[68]

While grass roots citizen activism is a hallowed American tradition, contemporary groups opposing as well as those favoring the convention have a powerful new tool for coalition building and citizen education: the world wide web. While many opposition writings appear in traditional print media or in newsletters, increasingly the opposition organizations named above are establishing web pages accessible to the average citizen via the home computer, now almost as ubiquitous as the television set in middle American homes. This new technology allows ordinary citizens to band together, recruit new members, and share information, albeit sometimes inaccurate or misleading information.[69]

Many examples of opponents' interpretations of the convention would amaze the individuals who participated in its drafting but appear repeatedly in the opposition literature and web sites. These include, for example, that Article 3 shifts the responsibility for parental decision making from parents to the state and ultimately the UN; that Article 13 subjects parents to prosecution for restricting children's access to pornography, rock music, and television; that Article 14 allows children to desert family religions for "Muslim or Buddhist" worship or for participation in "the occult" (i.e., witchcraft); that Article 15 gives children the right to join gangs, cults, and racist organizations; that Article 16 gives the child the right to abortion and contraception, without parental involvement or notification; that Article 18 encourages two-income families and enlists the state as a coparent, undermining traditional family values; that Article 27 requires parents to provide a state-determined minimum standard of living for their children, regardless of parents' own judgments about the children's needs; that Article 28 prohibits all corporal punishment, including parentally administered spanking, and requires compulsory public schooling, endangering the "home schooling" movement and violating parents' rights to raise their children according to Biblical commands; that Article 29 imposes inappropriate "New World Order" principles of equality of the sexes and requires equal treatment of all religious beliefs and ethnic groups, prohibiting parents from inculcating their own moral and religious beliefs in their children; that Article 32 prohibits children from performing labor, even under parental supervision, empowering children to refuse to do household chores; and finally, that Article 37 gives any child deprived of the foregoing rights and liberties the right to free legal counsel and access to the courts, to sue his or her parents. One critic concludes, expressing the general tenor of the opposition: "The implicit goal of the treaty is to create the ultimate child: the creature of the state, a member of the global community who looks to the state as provider, protector and even spiritual leader."[70]

For those who applaud the convention, these fears seem ridiculous. Most of us, even if we have doubts about certain provisions, greet this document as a positive step in encouraging governments around the world to reduce the suffering of children by placing a high priority on combating their exploitation, improving their living conditions, and providing them with education and medical care. However, proponents must make a concerted effort to revisualize the convention through the eyes of its critics, if they are to understand and meet their concerns. Opposition to the convention is rooted in our common law traditions,[71] which include a certain skepticism, dating back to cases like *Meyer* and *Pierce*, that sees government as the enemy of the family. As we have seen, it is heir to a strong tradition of rugged individualism, antifederalism, and distrust of big government which tends to assume that localized or privatized control is superior to centralized regulation. From this perspective, federal support of children's health, nutrition, and education programs is not a boon but a threat to traditional values, which emphasize individual rights and responsibilities and place governance of the family outside the zone of state powers. It is no wonder, given this legacy, that cultural conservatives see the establishment of universal basic welfare and education rights for children as leading inexorably to a totalitarian society that would destroy individual initiative and intellectual liberty.

These arguments have a familiar ring to historians of American culture and politics. It is no accident that some of the strongest opposition comes from the home schooling movement. Parents in America are currently educating as many as 1 million children at home, because the parents reject public schooling as a form of state usurpation of their right to control their children's intellectual and moral development. Early proponents of compulsory education encountered similar distrust, and despite the fact that all 50 states provide free public education, American children, as we saw earlier, still have no federal or constitutional rights to public schooling. Education policy has remained strongly localized, and attempts to set federal standards invariably arouse sharp debate.

Even Americans who do not embrace this distrust of government and of public services and public education tend to respond negatively to talk of children's rights. This helps to explain why cultural conservatives are so alarmed over the convention's articulation of rights to intellectual freedom, expression, religious freedom, and the like, even when tempered by language acknowledging the centrality of the family and of parental guidance and explicitly linking the exercise of such rights by the child to the child's capacity and maturity. Rather than viewing these rights as protections against governments that abuse the rights of families and children—a perspective that might come naturally to a survivor of the Holocaust or the Cambodian Khmer Rouge—or as offering protection against an abusive parent, many Americans across the spectrum of political thought see children's rights as opening a wedge for government to second guess the decisions of good and caring parents. To American critics, the notion of children as having rights seems to strike at the heart of the authoritative family structure, in which benevolent parents occupy the role of judges, teachers, and guardians of family morality and children are expected to obey and honor their parents.

Perhaps the very popularity of "rights rhetoric" in America contributes to opponents' misconception of the Children's Convention. As we have seen, ours is an intensely litigious society, and Americans have trouble imagining a right without a judicial remedy. Many citizens assume that a child's right to free expression, for example, must provide a basis for a lawsuit by the child or by some government interloper against a parent who attempts to control the child's reading matter or use of profanity. Opposition to the convention reflects a widespread uneasiness with the empowerment of children, also deeply rooted in American culture and history and exacerbated by contemporary anxiety about the breakdown of family authority structures.[72]

Finally, American critics tend to see the convention as a far more powerful instrument than its drafters imagined. They are unpersuaded by assurances that the convention's articles merely articulate principles that are to guide national and local legislative reforms. They find the Committee on the Rights of the Child established by Article 43 especially alarming. They see it as creating a panel of alien experts with the authority to force US legislatures, courts, and families to cater to its demands. Again, as strange as these concerns may appear to the world community, they are rooted in our own history. They reflect the same grass roots and religious opposition that defeated a Child Labor Amendment to the Constitution in the 1930s out of fear that education, chores, homework, and family life could all be brought under centralized federal control as involving some form of child labor.

Very few legal experts would agree with the opponents' sweeping interpretations of the convention. While many children's rights advocates might be delighted to see the provisions of the convention instantly become the supreme law of the land, most of us agree that neither the convention nor the committee created by Article 43 has the power to alter internal laws without additional legislative action. Cultural conservatives along with all other American voters would maintain the right to participate, step by step, in any debates about the reception of the convention's principles into US law, at federal, state, and local levels. Yet the fact remains the fears expressed above stand as a formidable roadblock to American ratification.

It remains to be seen whether the mainstream organizations and advocates for children's rights that endorse the convention will be able to mobilize sufficient support to offset these barriers to ratification. A cautious President Clinton, intent on seeking consensus, has been reluctant to push forward a convention that may enjoy unanimous support in the community of nations but which is certain to be politically divisive at home. Given the deeply entrenched beliefs animating the opposition and the necessity of a supermajority to ensure its ratification, the United States may well remain the lone holdout refusing to endorse what some have called the most rapidly and unanimously accepted international convention in the history of international law. Regardless of whether the convention wins ratification in the United States Senate, its rapid and enthusiastic global acceptance already has made it the international standard.

As the world shrinks to the proverbial global village, whether we will it or not, international law takes on a powerful role in setting norms for family behavior, for control of children, and for state intervention in the family. In the coming century, American constitutional law, which played a leading role in shaping concepts of "rights" in emerging democracies, is likely to shrink in influence and importance as new nations and transnational organizations begin to dominate the field of defining standards for human rights. An example of this is the process of constitution building that resulted in the 1996 Constitution of the Republic of South Africa. While the United States Bill of Rights influenced the drafters, they drew even more heavily on schemes like those of India and Canada that recognized cultural and group rights and on international conventions that explicitly articulate rights for children. The South African

Constitution is perhaps the most modern of children's rights documents and actually contains an extensive section on children, giving every child the right to a name and nationality; to family or parental care; to basic nutrition, shelter, health and social services; to protection from maltreatment, neglect, abuse, and degradation; to protection from exploitive labor practices; to protection against inappropriate work that places health, development, or education at risk; to special protections in detention; to have a lawyer in civil cases as necessary to avoid substantial injustice; not to be used in armed conflict; and to recognition that "the child's best interests are of paramount importance in every matter concerning the child."[73] The contrast between this document, with its comprehensive provisions, and the Constitution of the United States, which makes no mention of children, is striking evidence of the success of the movement for children's rights. Despite formidable barriers presented by the American legal tradition and American political systems, the notion that children have rights, as articulated in the Children's Convention, is rapidly becoming the new world standard. The laws of the United States will either evolve to meet this new standard or become increasingly isolated from the human rights norms of the rest of the world community.

Such reconstructions of legal relationships are inevitably necessary when a new and previously unprotected class of persons lays claims to rights. A revisioning of law and society in a less hierarchical, more complex model has been accomplished before when working people, blacks, and women, disabled persons, and ethnic minorities fought to be included as rights-bearers entitled to equality, dignity, participation, protection, and privacy. Contemporary policymakers and judges must find ways to open the door of rights to the class of persons defined by childhood, even if the transition involves reexamining constitutional precedents and American traditions once again, this time to recognize children's unique needs and capacities.

ENDNOTES

1. See *Christian Coalition, A contract with the American family* (Ralph Reed, Ed., Nashville, TN: Mooring, 1994).
2. See John Holt, *Escape from childhood* (New York: E. P. Dutton, 1974).
3. For a comprehensive international review of arguments in favor of rights for children, see The Ideologies of Children's Rights 4 (Michael Freeman & Philip Veerman, Eds. Norwell, MA: Kluwer Academic, 1992). In the United States, various legal scholars have proposed theories of children's rights, including Katherine Hunt Federle, Looking Ahead: An Empowerment Perspective on the Rights of Children, 68 Temple L. Rev. 1585 (1995); Wendy Anton Fitzgerald, Maturity, Difference, and Mystery: Children's Perspectives and the Law, 36 Ariz. L. Rev. 11 (1994); Martha Minow, Rights for the Next Generation: A Feminist Approach to Children's Rights, 9 Harv. Women's L. J. 1 (1986); Melinda A. Roberts, Parent and Child Conflict: Between Liberty and Responsibility, 10 N.D. J. L. Ethics & Pub Pol'y 485 (1996); Lee E. Teitelbaum, Foreword: The Meaning of Rights of Children, 10 N.M. L. Rev. 235 (1980); Barbara Bennett Woodhouse, "Out of Children's Needs, Children's Rights:" The Child's Voice in Defining the Family, 8 B.Y.U. J. Pub. L. 321 (1994); and many others.
4. See, for example, Randy Frances Kandel, Just Ask the Kid! Towards a Rule of Children's Choice in Custody Determinations, 49 U. Miami L. Rev. 299 (1994); Peter Margulies, The Lawyer as Caregiver: Child Competence in Context, 64 Fordham L. Rev. 1473 (1996); Gary B. Melton, *Reforming the law: The impact of child development research* (New York: Guilford Press, 1987); Catherine J. Ross, From Vulnerability to Voice: Appointing Counsel for Children in Civil Litigation, 64 Fordham L. Rev. 1571 (1996); Barbara Bennett Woodhouse, Hatching the Egg: A Child-Centered Perspective on Parents' Rights, 14 Cardozo L. Rev. 1747 (1993).
5. See the classic description provided by philosopher Isaiah Berlin, *Two concepts of liberty: An inaugural lecture delivered before the University of Oxford on 31 October 1958* (Oxford, England: Clarendon Press, 1958). See also Jeremy Waldron, *Introduction to Theories of Rights*, 1, 11 (Jeremy Waldron, Ed. New York: New York University Press, 1984).
6. See Indivisibility and Interdependence of Economic, Social, Cultural, Civil and Political Rights, G.A. Res. 44/130, U.N. GAOR, 44th Sess., Supp. No. 49, at 209, U.N. Doc. A/Res/44/130 (1989) (accepted Dec. 15, 1989);

Barbara Stark, Economic Rights in the United States and International Human Rights Law: Toward an "Entirely New Strategy," 44 Hastings L. J. 79 (1992).

7. See Lee E. Teitelbaum, Foreword: The Meanings of Rights of Children, 10 New Mexico L. Rev. 235 (1980), differentiating between an integrative view of rights, which emphasizes a progressive theory focusing on children's needs for integration into the community of persons, and the autonomous view of rights, which emphasizes a libertarian theory focusing on individual choice. Dean Teitelbaum sees both elements reflected in the developing jurisprudence of children's rights.
8. See Barbara Bennett Woodhouse, Of Bonding Babies, and Burning Buildings: Discerning Parenthood in Irrational Action, 81 Va. L. Rev. 2493 (1995), commenting on Robert Scott & Elizabeth Scott, Parents as Fiduciaries, 81 Va. L. Rev. 2401 (1995).
9. For comprehensive discussions of the historical development of children's law in America, see Mary Ann Mason, *From father's property to children's rights: The history of child custody in the United States* (New York: Columbia University Press, 1994); Michael Grossberg, *Governing the hearth: Law and family in nineteenth-century America* (Chapel Hill: University of North Carolina Press, 1985).
10. See Janet L. Dolgin, Transforming Childhood: Apprenticeship in American Law, 31 New Eng. L. Rev. 1113, 1116 (1997).
11. In modern times, many subrules developed on issues like the minimum age of marriageability or for purchasing alcohol, often setting different benchmarks for males and females. See Craig v. Boren, 429 U.S. 190 (1976) (invalidating a state law that unconstitutionally discriminated based on sex, allowing females 18 and over to purchase beer but prohibiting males under 21 from doing so).
12. See generally, Special Issue: Ethical Issues in the Legal Representation of Children, 64 Fordham L. Rev. (March 1966) (symposium issue devoted to children in the court system).
13. *Plyler v. Doe*, 457 U.S. 202 (1982), in which the Court struck down a Texas law prohibiting schools from enrolling illegal alien children, is often cited as the one chink in the armor of Supreme Court opinions denying that the Constitution confers positive rights on children because of their needs and vulnerability. Other cases, such as *San Antonio Independent School District v. Rodriguez*, 411 U.S. 1 (1973), refuse to recognize claims that poor children are constitutionally entitled to some basic level of education, or other such government programs.
14. See, for example, *Edgewood Independent Schoool District v. Kirby*, 777 S.W.2 391 (Supreme Court of Texas 1989), interpreting the Texas Constitution as conferring a right to an efficient system of free public education and holding that large differences in per capita expenditures between wealthy and poor districts violated children's rights. The Texas court noted similar rulings in at least nine other states.
15. The National Council of Commissioners on Uniform State Laws has promulgated a number of model laws, ranging from the 1994 Uniform Adoption Act to the 1988 Uniform Status of Children of Assisted Conception Act, many of which have been enacted into law by a number of states. The American Law Institute issues "restatements" of various areas of state law such as contract or tort, which attempt to enhance consistency and uniformity from state to state. Recognizing the diversity of family law rules, it has titled its recent effort in the area of family law not a "restatement" but rather "Principles Governing the Dissolution of Marriage."
16. See Susan Gluck Mezey, *Children in Court: Public policymaking and federal court decisions* (Albany, NY: SUNY Press, 1996), for a careful study of the impact of federal judicial decisions on children's law. She analyzes decisions involving Aid to Families with Dependent Children (AFDC), Women, Infants, and Children Program (WIC), Head Start, and other federally funded programs.
17. 115 S.Ct. 1624 (1995).
18. The words are those of former University of Chicago law professor and now Judge Richard Posner, from his opinion in *Jackson v. City of Joliet*, 715 F.2d 1200, 1204-04 (7th Cir. 1983).
19. See *Adamson v. California*, 332 U.S. 46 (1947) for a discussion of the doctrine we now call "incorporation," which holds that the due process clause of the Fourteenth Amendment was intended to incorporate in its prohibitions against state violations of due process all or at least some of the protections enumerated in the Bill of Rights.
20. *Marbury v. Madison*, 5 U.S. 137(1803).
21. 262 U.S. 390 (1923).
22. 268 U.S. 510 (1925)
23. Many scholars point to the Ninth Amendment, which states that "The enumeration in the Constitution, of certain rights, shall not be construed to deny or disparage others retained by the people," as authority that the framers recognized the existence of unenumerated rights.
24. Perhaps the most famous such critic is Robert H. Bork, whose nomination to the Supreme Court was defeated largely because of his critique of substantive due process theory. See Robert H. Bork, *The tempting of America: The political seduction of the law* (New York: Touchstone, 1990). Several members of the current Court

have voiced pointed criticisms of substantive due process, most notably Justices Antonin Scalia and Clarence Thomas.

25. See Daniel A. Farber, William N. Eskridge, Jr., Philip P. Frickey, *Constitutional law: Themes for the constitution's third century*, 404 (St. Paul, MN: West, 1993). *Buck v. Bell*, 274 U.S. 200 (1927) was the low watermark of Justice Oliver Wendell Holmes, Jr.'s career, and illustrates how, without some theory of unenumerated rights, legislatures would be free to enact laws that violate basic norms of humanity.
26. *Skinner v. Oklahoma*, 316 U.S. 535 (1942), overruled *Buck v. Bell*. *Moore v. City of East Cleveland*, 431 U.S. 494 (1976), struck down a local zoning ordinance that prevented a grandmother from sharing her home with an orphaned grandson, finding that extended family relationships were protected by the Constitution.
27. The strong public reaction to Robert Bork's rejection of privacy rights was evident in the statements of senators opposing his nomination. See "Taking a Stand on Confirmation: Senatorial Votes for and against Bork," *New York Times*, Sec. B, p. 6, col. 1, October 6, 1987. See also results of polls on abortion rights, for example, "Poll majority of Americans back abortion rights," Reuters North American Wire, Jan. 22, 1995; Mark Clements, "Results from national survey: Should Abortion Remain Legal?," *The Houston Chronicle*, *Parade*, p. 4, May 17, 1992 (71% favor continuing right to legal abortion).
28. See Barbara Bennett Woodhouse, "Who Owns the Child? Meyer and Pierce and the Child as Property, 33 Wm. & Mary L. Rev. 995 (1992), in which I review the origins of constitutional doctrines of parental rights in historical and social context.
29. See also Peggy Cooper Davis, *Neglected stories: The Constitution and family values* (New York: Hill and Wang, 1997).
30. 321 U.S. 158 (1944).
31. 347 U.S. 483 (1954).
32. Susan Gluck Mezey has identified 53 children's rights cases grounded on constitutional principles during the period from 1953 to 1993. Mezey, Children in court, at 17-27 (see note 16).
33. *Hazelwood School District v. Kuhlmeier*, 484 U.S. 260 (1988), appeared to narrow the holding of *Tinker*, and cases like *H.L. v. Matheson*, 450 U.S. 398 (1981), and *Hodgson v. Minnesota*, 497 U.S. 417 (1990), qualified abortion rights by permitting states to enact parental notification requirements.
34. Mezey, Children in court, at 26 (see note 16).
35. Martha Minow, in this perceptive essay, explores the failure of children's rights advocates to mobilize Americans behind their movement, and advocates (with reservations) a more unifying focus on human rights as opposed to the fragmentary agendas for liberation, protection and redistribution pursued in the past. Martha Minow, *What Ever Happened to Children's Rights?* 80 Minn. L. Rev. 267 (1995).
36. 404 U.S. 71 (1971) (striking down a law giving preference to male relatives as trustees of a decedent's estates).
37. The most recent Supreme Court case addressing gender discrimination against girls is *United States v. Virginia*, 518 U.S. 515 (1996), which held that Virginia Military Institute's policy against admitting girls violated their equal protection clause rights.
38. For an assault on gender stereotypes, see Justice Ruth Bader Ginsburg's cogent arguments in *U.S. v. Virginia* (see note 37).
39. See *U.S. v. Virginia* (see note 37), holding that any classification based on gender must be supported by an "exceedingly persuasive" justification, and *Palmore v. Sidotti*, 466 U.S. 429 (1984), holding that law may not give effect, directly or indirectly, to racial biases.
40. This motto is carved in the pediment of the United States Supreme Court in Washington, DC. Its emphasis is not on equal treatment but on equal justice.
41. Jane Maslow Cohen, Competitive and Cooperative Dependencies: The Case for Children, 81 Va. L. Rev. 2217 (1995).
42. See Barbara Bennett Woodhouse, Children's Rights: The Destruction and Promise of Family, 1993 B.Y.U. L. Rev. 497 (1993).
43. See Michael Grossberg, *A judgment for Solomon: The D'Hauteville case and legal experience in America* (New York: Cambridge University Press, 1996) for a fascinating look at the emergence of the child's best interest as a key determinant in custody cases. As Jean Koh Peters remarks, the question of the child's best interest remains the ultimate legal standard governing most children's cases, and it is incumbent on lawyers to develop a sophisticated and nuanced understanding of how to evaulaute children's interests in a variety of contexts. See Jean Koh Peters, The Roles and Content of Best Interest in Client-Directed Lawyering for Children in Child-Protective Proceedings, 64 Fordham L. Rev. 1505, 1513 (1996).
44. See Ross, From Vulnerability to Voice, at 1579 (see note 4), which notes the many contexts in which children have no right to counsel or to file motions and present evidence in proceedings concerning them.

45. Hillary Rodham Clinton was one of the earliest to articulate this position. See Hillary Rodham, Children's Rights: A Legal Perspctive, in *Children's rights: Contemporary perspectives*, 21 (Patricia A. Vardin & Ilene N. Brody, Eds., New York: Teachers College Press, 1979).
46. See Franklin Zimring, *The changing legal world of adolescence*, 89–96 (New York: Free Press, 1982) (arguing that the period of adolescence should be seen as a "learner's permit" for the transition to adulthood).
47. See Naomi R. Cahn, Civil Images of Battered Women: The Impact of Domestic Violence on Child Custody Decisions, 44 Vand. L. Rev. 1041 (1991); Reva B. Siegel, The Rule of Love: Wife Beating as Prerogative and Privacy, 105 Yale L. J. 2117 (1996).
48. See Michael R. Petit & Patrick A. Curtis, *Child abuse and neglect: A look at the states*, 1997 CWLA Stat Book, Tables 1.6 & 1.10 (Washington, DC: CWLA Press, 1997) (showing hundreds of thousands of verified reports annually of abuse).
49. 489 U.S. 189 (1989).
50. 503 U.S. 347 (1992).
51. See Scott & Scott, Parents as Fiduciaries, and Woodhouse, Of Babies, Bonding and Burning Buildings: Discerning Parenthood in Irrational Action (see note 4) for the crucial importance to children of a bonded parent.
52. Mary Ann Glendon, *The transformation of family law: State, law and family in Western Europe and the United States*, 147 (Chicago: University of Chicago Press, 1989).
53. See *Mathews v. Eldridge*, 424 U.S. 319 (1976), outlining a process of balancing the private interest affected by the action, the risk of erroneous deprivation from lack of a particular procedural protection, and the government's interests in efficient procedures.
54. See *Reno v. Flores*, 113 S.Ct. 1439 (1993).
55. See Woodhouse, Hatching the Egg (see note 4); Akhil R. Amar & Daniel Widawsky, Child Abuse as Slavery: A Thirteenth Amendment Response to DeShaney, 105 Harv. L. Rev. 1359 (1992); Frances Olsen, The Myth of State Intervention in the Family, in *Family matters: Readings in family lives and the law (M. Minow, Ed., New York: New Press, 1993).*
56. *See generally Fordham Symposium (see note 12).*
57. *See Flores v. Reno*, 507 U.S. 292 (1993).
58. For discussions of these cases see Woodhouse, Out of Children's Needs, Children's Rights (see note 3); Woodhouse, Of Bonding, Babies and Burning Buildings (see note 8).
59. See Jean Koh Peters, Best Interest (see note 43).
60. See Woodhouse, Hatching the Egg, at 1826 (see note 4).
61. This statement appears in *Smith v. Organization of Foster Families*, 431 U.S. 816, 842–847 (1977).
62. See Susan A. Wolfson, Children's Rights: The Theoretical Underpinning of the 'Best Interest of the Child'," and Joachim Wolf, The Concept of "Best Interest" in *Ideologies of children's rights* (M. Freeman & P. Veerman, Eds., Norwell, MA: Kluwer Academic, 1992).
63. See Ideologies of Children's Rights 4 (M. Freeman & P. Veerman, Eds., Norwell, MA: Kluwer Academic, 1992).
64. See United Nations Convention on the Rights of the Child, 20 Nov 89, G.A. Res. 44/25, 44 U.N. GAOR Supp. No. 49, U.N. Doc. A/44/736 (1989).
65. Children's Convention, Article 4.
66. See Children's rights in America: U.N. Convention on the Rights of the Child compared with United States law 95-95, 337 (Cynthia P. Cohen & Howard A. Davidson, Eds., Chicago: American Bar Association Center on Children and the Law, 1990).
67. See also Susan Kilbourne, U.S. Failure to Ratify the U.N. Convention on the Rights of the Child: Playing Politics with Children's Right, 6 Transnat'l & Contemp. Probs. 437 (1996).
68. For a discussion of the PRRA, see Barbara Bennett Woodhouse, A Public Role in the Private Family: The Parental Rights and Responsibilities Act and the Politics of Child Protection and Education, 57 Ohio St. L. J. 393 (1996).
69. An article by article analysis of the convention appeared, as of June 23, 1997, on a home schooling web page at http://www.learnathome.com/specrpts1.html. A user who locates the learnathome page, for example, will find quick "links" to an extensive array of web pages also publishing similar opposition materials, including the Family Research Council, http://www.frc.org/faq/faq25.html. A web search for references to the United Nations Convention on the Rights of the Child connects the searcher to sources as diverse as a network for information on organizations supporting the convention at http://193.156.14/webpub/crhome/crc.htm and a network called the Citizen Internet Empowerment Coalition advocating "Death to the New World Odor"(sic) and pointing the searcher to the web page of The New American at http://www.jbs.org/vo12no14.htn#child. The New American, typical of opposition websites, asks "Does the State Own Your Child?" and describes the convention as an assault on federalism and parents rights.

70. This statement is taken from Douglas Phillips, "The Legal Impact of the United Nations Convention on the Rights of the Child," published by The National Center for Home Education (on file with the author).
71. Barbara J. Nauck, Implications of the United States Ratification of the United Nations Convention on the Rights of the Child: Civil Rights, the Constitution, and the Family, 42 Cle. St. L. Rev. 675 (1994) (expressing doubts as to compatibility with US legal traditions).
72. See Barbara Bennett Woodhouse, "Who Owns the Child?" Meyer and Pierce and the Child as Property, 33 Wm. & Mary L. Rev 995 (1992) (reviewing history of opposition to children's rights).
73. Constitution of the Republic of South Africa 1996, Art. 28.

21

The Child Custody Standard

What Do Twenty Years of Research Teach Us?

DANIEL A. KRAUSS and BRUCE D. SALES

Although divorce rates in the United States appear to be on the decline, the legal process of divorce and the psychological, social, and economic problems associated with it are still a common experience for many children. Estimates predict that over 40% of all children will be confronted with and will have to adjust to the legal divorce of their parents (Bahr, Howe, Mann, & Bahr, 1994). Yet, contrary to public perception, a substantially smaller percentage of these children will have the structure of their future custodial relationship with their parents resolved through adversarial litigation in the court system (Bahr et al., 1994). Exact projections of custody disputes determined by court litigation are difficult to calculate, but large-scale empirical studies completed in different jurisdictions have found that 6–20% of all child custody cases are eventually decided in the courtroom (Bahr et al., 1994; Maccoby & Mnookin, 1992; Melton, Petrilia, Poythress, & Slobogin, 1997; Santilla & Roberts, 1990). While contested custody disputes are thought to have the greatest negative psychological impact on the children involved, it is widely believed that the process of divorce itself is likely to generate substantial, long-term, negative psychological sequelae in children. Empirical support for this belief is substantial; empirical studies have estimated that approximately 16% of children of divorce report clinical levels of maladjustment (Fiddler & Saunders, 1988) and that children of divorce are two to three times more likely to experience emotional problems than children from intact families (Akre, 1992).[1] In order to ameliorate at least some of the problems experienced by children of divorce and to maximize these children's potential to lead a successful life, courts have constructed and adopted the best interest of the child standard (BICS) to legally determine the custodial placement of children involved in divorce proceedings.[2]

The BICS has come under attack from both legal and psychological commentators. Legal scholars have argued that the ambiguity of this standard places too much discretion in the hands of the judge, creates more custody disputes and litigation, has negative psychological effects on the children and parents embroiled in custody disputes, and offers no real guidelines

DANIEL A. KRAUSS • Department of Psychology, Claremont McKenna College, Claremont, California 91711-6420. **BRUCE D. SALES** • Department of Psychology, University of Arizona, Tucson, Arizona 85721.

Handbook of Youth and Justice, edited by White. Kluwer Academic/Plenum Publishers, New York, 2001.

for judicial decision making (Elster, 1987; Fineman, 1988; Mnookin, 1975; Schneider, 1991; Scott, 1992). Feminist legal scholars also have attacked the BICS because they believe that the BICS and the judicial implementation of the BICS place female parents at a considerable disadvantage in the child custody dispute resolution process (Fineman, 1988; Scott, 1992). In addition to lamenting the ambiguity of the BICS, many psychologists have criticized the role mental health professionals currently play in custody determinations. They argue that their profession has no expertise to offer the court in the resolution of custody disputes (Faust & Ziskin, 1988), and that the presented "expert" clinical opinion testimony in these proceedings far overreaches the existing psychological research. Some scholars have gone so far as to suggest that many of the conclusions offered by mental health practitioners to the courts in child custody disputes are unethical (Lavin & Sales, 1998; Melton et al., 1997; Shuman, Sales, & O'Connor, 1994).

While many critiques detailing the inadequacies of the BICS exist, perhaps the most prominent was that by Mnookin (1975) who advanced an alternative standard that can best be described as the least detrimental alternative standard (LDAS). This chapter revisits the BICS, critically reviewing both the legal and empirical literatures. It concludes that the BICS should be abandoned and replaced with the still unused LDAS. To accomplish our goal, the chapter: (1) highlights the importance of competing concerns inherent in fashioning any child custody standard; (2) summarizes the history of adopted legal standards for the resolution of custody disputes; (3) details legal criticism of the most widely used standard today, the BICS; (4) considers the existing empirical research relevant to understanding the ability of courts and mental health professional experts to apply the BICS, or any other custody standard, and the likely outcome of applying the BICS; (5) reconsiders the role the primary experts (i.e., mental health professionals) play in BICS determinations; (6) advances a conceptual and empirical rationale for the long overdue adoption of the LDAS; and (7) and offers a critical discussion of the need for further empirical research that is still essential to fully justify any child custody standard.

COMPETING INTERESTS IN FASHIONING A CHILD CUSTODY STANDARD

The determination of an appropriate child custody arrangement for divorcing parents represents an unusual and extremely difficult problem for our legal system (Elster, 1987; Fineman, 1988; Mnookin, 1975; Schneider, 1991; Scott 1992). Twentieth-century American society and our legal system recognizes and advocates normative pluralism—the idea that no shared ideal dictates or defines proper work roles, family structure, or family values (Elster, 1987; Scott, 1992). This ideal is exemplified in the United States Constitution and in constitutional decisions that offer special protection to family and child-raising values, and guards these values from intrusion by the state or government (Farber, Eskridge, & Frickey, 1993). Generally, the state is not allowed to intrude into the practices of a family in the absence of a compelling state interest for its involvement (e.g., strong evidence of danger to a child from physical, sexual, or emotional abuse and/or neglect). In addition, significant legal barriers prevent the state from upsetting or rearranging the relationship between a biological parent and his or her child.[3] Yet, in direct contrast to these legal barriers, the resolution of child custody disputes forces the legal system to investigate the inner working of the family and oversee a restructuring of the family unit, without the level of heightened interest that is usually necessary for the court's involvement in these matters. Furthermore, because the determination of child custody requires that the court create or approve the creation of a custodial arrangement, the court must engage to some extent in judging the parents in a way that is antithetical to many legal and societal values (see *Palmore v. Sidotti*, 1984).

Recognizing the need for court intervention in disputed custody cases, what should the legal standard be to guide judicial decision making? Because society and our legal system both strongly value[4] the idea that like individuals should be treated similarly by the state under the law (Farber et al., 1993), a custody standard should offer criteria that will allow judges to decide similar cases similarly, without extralegal factors significantly affecting final dispositions,[5] while accommodating the need for appropriate judicial discretion to respond to individual case characteristics. Additionally, the standard should attempt to realistically achieve positive psychological outcomes for the children, while minimizing state intrusions into the workings of the family. The difficult task of balancing these disparate interests has led policymakers to experiment with a number of different standards (Melton et al., 1997; Rohman, Sales, & Lou, 1990; Sales, Manber, & Rohman, 1992).

HISTORY OF CHILD CUSTODY STANDARDS

Prior to the 19th century, the legal doctrine of *parental famillus* controlled the disposition of child custody (Bahr et al., 1994; Grisso, 1986; Fineman, 1988; Melton et al., 1997; Rohman et al., 1990; Sales et al., 1992). Under this doctrine, children were considered the property of their father, and when divorce occurred the children's placement was left solely to the discretion of their father. Late 19th-century and early 20th-century case law esaw the first appearance of child custody dispute resolution based on the interests of the children (Grisso, 1986; Rohman et al., 1990; Sales et al., 1992). Recognizing the importance of the child's interest in child custody determinations was a substantial departure from earlier custody rules that emphasized the importance of parental rather than children's rights.

The Tender Years Doctrine

The BICS was originally conceptualized as the tenders years doctrine. Under this early variant of the BICS, it was assumed that the mother was better suited and trained to care for the needs of children. Accordingly, the mother was deemed the appropriate caretaker for all children under the age of 7 and for female children of any age. The tender years doctrine was a rebuttable legal presumption, a standard that determines the legal decision unless the opposing side can offer sufficient evidence to overcome the presumption. If the opposing side offers no evidence or limited evidence against the presumptive rule, then the presumptive standard automatically becomes the legally appropriate decision (Strong, 1995). Under the tender years conceptualization, a father could successfully refute the legal presumption in favor of the mother and gain custody of his children only if he could provide in court sufficient evidence that the mother was an unfit parent.

The tender years standard remained in place until the 1970s, when a number of court decisions held that solely gender based rules were an unconstitutional violation of the equal protection clause of the XIVth Amendment of the United States Constitution (see *Reed v. Reed*, 1971; *Weinberg v. Wisenfeld*, 1975; *Frontiero v. Richardson*, 1973; *Stanley v. Illinois*, 1972; *Schlesinger v. Ballard*, 1975; *Craig v. Boren*, 1976; *Orr v. Orr*, 1979). The United States Supreme Court reasoned that it was discriminatory for the state or the government to make important decisions completely on the basis of the gender of the participants. Contributing to the demise of the tender years doctrine was a growing societal awareness that parenting capacity was not exclusively a product of gender (Sales et al., 1992). By 1990, all but five states had abolished their maternal custody preference (Bahr et al., 1994).

Since the widespread abolition of the tender years presumption, legal scholars have suggested and courts have used a number of other rebuttable legal presumptions to aid judges in making custody decisions. The primary caretaker doctrine, which states that presumptive custody should remain with the parent who performs the greatest amount of basic caretaking responsibilities, was advocated by many as a non-gender-based criterion that would effectuate the child's best interest (Fineman, 1988; Grisso, 1986; Scott, 1992). This doctrine's rationale was the belief that the placement with the primary caretaker would lessen the environmental and emotional instability associated with divorce, would maintain the children's most important parent–child relationship, and would place the children with the parent who had shown the most predivorce interest and ability to care for them (Fineman, 1988; Grisso, 1986). While this standard has not enjoyed large-scale acceptance as a presumptive doctrine, it is an important factor in custody considerations in most states.

The Psychological Parent Rule

During the years following the removal of the tender years doctrine, a group of psychoanalytic psychologists strongly argued for a new child custody standard, the psychological parent rule (Goldstein, Freud, & Solnit, 1979). Goldstein and colleagues' psychological parent standard proposed determining child custody solely on the basis of the level of psychological attachment the children had to each of their parents. The parent or parents who provided for the child's environmental stability, emotional needs, and affection needs was considered to be the psychological parent deserving exclusive custody. Based largely on unempirically supported psychoanalytic theory, Goldstein et al. further posited that contact with the nonpsychological parent should be minimized and that the psychological parent should be allowed to determine or completely prohibit the nonpsychological parent's visitation (Batt, 1992). As Goldstein et al. stated in their book

> children have difficulty relating positively to, profiting from, and maintaining contact with two psychological parents who are not in positive contact with each other. Loyalty conflicts are normal under such conditions and may have devastating consequences by destroying positive relationships with both parents. (p. 38)

According to their theory, contact with the nonpsychological parent would disrupt the child's relationship with their psychological parent and lead to poor future adjustment for the child. This psychological theory, cloaked as empirically validated science,[6] has not been widely accepted by the courts as a determinative standard. Nonetheless, it is still a factor in some court decisions and an element of the child custody assessments performed by many psychologists.

The UMDA Criteria

The most influential post-tender years development in the BICS was the promulgation of child custody determination criteria in the Uniform Marriage and Divorce Act (UMDA). This model law suggests that custody decisions should take into account:

1. The wishes of the child's parent or parents with respect to custody.
2. The wishes of the child as to his or her custody.
3. The interaction and interrelationship of the child with his or her parents, his or her siblings, and any other person who may significantly affect the child's best interest.

4. The child's adjustment to home, school, and community.
5. The mental and physical health of all individuals involved (Uniform Marriage and Divorce Act 402 amended 1975).

The UMDA also allows for consideration of any other criterion that might be important in discerning the child's best interest. The factors explicitly mentioned in the UMDA were conceptualized as important informative elements that should be used by judges in performing the mental calculus that leads to a determination of a child's best interest. The UMDA factors were not intended to be used as predictive criteria or as a legal presumption that would explicitly or readily determine the appropriate child custody arrangement in a particular case (Melton et al., 1997; Rohman et al., 1990; Sales et al., 1992). Consequently, the UMDA does not specify how much weight should be accorded each proposed criterion nor how each criterion should be balanced by judges in making final custody decisions. Although the UMDA has not been adopted by most jurisdictions in unaltered form (Schneider, 1991), its factors are used by a majority of jurisdictions explicitly in their child custody statutes and implicitly in their judicial determinations (Melton et al., 1997; Rohman et al., 1990).

Additional Statutory Criteria for Determining Custody

In creating their own child custody statutes, many jurisdictions have added a number of other factors to some or all the UMDA requirements. Included in these statutes have been considerations such as the identification of the primary caretaker or the psychological parent, the moral fitness of the parents, and the parent's ability to provide food and clothing (Miller, 1993). It should be expressly noted that as a consequence of the widespread variations in BIC standards from jurisdiction to jurisdiction there is not one BICS but rather a multitude of different standards. Furthermore, in each jurisdiction, final custody decisions are made by some implicit, unspecified judicial weighing and balancing of that jurisdiction's particular statutory criteria. This inexact judicial balancing between and within jurisdictions has led to wide variance in the factors that judges use to make child custody decisions and has led to wide variance in final adjudications (Grisso, 1986; Melton et al., 1997; Reidy, Silver, & Carson, 1989, Rohman et al., 1990; Sales et al., 1992).

Joint Legal Custody & Mediation Presumptions

In addition to the use of UMDA and the above-noted criteria to guide judges in making contested child custody decisions, more recent trends in the resolution of child custody disputes have been the adoption of (1) a rebuttable legal presumption of joint legal custody, and (2) policies requiring mediation designed to facilitate parental cooperation toward a pretrial settlement. It is assumed that both innovations help achieve a result that is in the best interests of the child (Bricklin, 1995; Dillion & Emery, 1996; Emery, Matthews, & Wyer, 1991; Emery, Matthews, & Kitzmann, 1994; Emery & Wyer, 1987; Kelly, 1993). Joint legal custody is a custodial arrangement in which both parents share the ability to make important legal decisions for their children[7] and generally assumes visitation and contact with both parents, but does not legally presume a specific amount of custody time sharing between the parents. Most jurisdictions will overturn the presumption of joint legal custody and award sole legal custody if one of the parents is shown to be unfit (Bricklin, 1995).

In contrast to joint legal custody, a mediation presumption specifies that, barring unusual circumstances, a couple in a contested child custody case must meet with a professional mediator in a settlement conference before the parents are permitted use of the courtroom to resolve their dispute. As of 1992, 33 states have adopted mandatory mediation as a requirement in child custody dispute resolution (Evans & Havercamp, 1994). Courts that recognize the rebuttable mediation presumption generally only allow parties to proceed directly to court litigation in child custody cases when there is a history of domestic violence, child abuse, or sexual abuse by one of the parents (see Arizona Rule of Civil Procedure 8.7). Jurisdictions that have adopted mandatory mediation have done so because mediation is assumed to be in the child's best interest by limiting court involvement in family life, decreasing hostility between parents, and increasing parental cooperation with regard to their children during and post-divorce. In addition, it is argued that mediation decreases court costs, while increasing the parties' procedural satisfaction (Emery et al., 1994; Emery & Wyer, 1987; Evans & Havercamp, 1994; Kitzmann & Emery, 1993; Hester, 1992).

LEGAL CRITICISMS OF THE BICS

Legal scholars have attacked the current conceptualization of the BICS on a number of grounds. Mnookin, perhaps the most outspoken of critics opposing the BICS, has suggested that the vast judicial discretion granted by the standard allows judicial biases to influence custody decisions (Coons, Mnookin, & Sugarman, 1993; Mnookin, 1975). Mnookin argues that there are no societal or psychologically accepted normative definitions of BICS, and consequently judges are forced to make decisions based on their own personal beliefs (Schneider, 1991). Some empirical support for this criticism has developed. For example, although the tender years doctrine has been abolished in all jurisdictions, judges (especially older judges) have been shown to make their custodial decision based on the prohibited tender years conceptualization of BICS (Lowery, 1981; Pearson & Ring, 1982; but see Weitzman, 1985, for an alternative explanation of these results).

Mnookin also contends that child custody decisions are unlike any other legal decisions in that judges are not trained to adjudicate them. In contrast to more routine legal decisions, child custody decisions involve the prediction of future parental and child behavior, require the appraisal of future child–parent relationships, focus on the placement of an individual who has a limited right to participation, have no precedential value, and involve the balancing of a number of inexact and possibly unquantifiable nonlegal interests (Mnookin, 1975; Schneider, 1991). For instance, under the UMDA criteria, it is not clear how a judge, in making a custody decision, should weigh one parent's more supportive school environment against the other parent's greater mental stability. Based on these arguments, Mnookin contends that judges have no expertise in making these decisions, and therefore should not be allowed to make these important determinations. Responses to Mnookin's criticism have pointed out that judges are trained to make difficult decisions, that custody decisions are not in actuality that different from other complex legal decisions (e.g., civil commitment),[8] and that no better system currently exists for deciding child custody (Schneider, 1991).

Consequences of the BICS's Ambiguity

In addition to challenging the extreme judicial discretion implicit in the present conceptualization of the BICS, other legal scholars have proposed that the standard's ambiguity leads to detrimental outcomes for the legal world, the parents, and the children involved in the child custody process. The use of such an inexact standard, legal scholars argue, ensures that more custody cases will be brought to litigation. Without a presumption or an idea of how the court is likely to decide, there is less benefit in attempting to settle cases prior to litigation because neither party has an accurate perception of the strengths or weaknesses of his or her case. As a result, it is contended, more parents with "weak" cases are likely willing to forego a custody settlement in the hopes that the judge may arbitrarily decide to give them custody of their children (Burt, 1983; Elster, 1987).[9] To date, however, no empirical research has directly examined whether the ambiguity of the BICS leads to greater litigation.

Additionally, the inexact BICS has been criticized for promoting various strategic behaviors by the parties that increase the costs of bargaining both pretrial and during the litigation (Becker, 1993; Elster, 1987, Hester, 1992; Scott, 1992),[10] and that are antithetical to honest negotiation, including dishonestly pretending to desire certain custodial arrangements so that they can receive concessions from the other party, threatening to move away or out of state with the child, inventing stories of sexual and physical abuse and neglect, and creating stories of moral unfitness of the other party. These behavior are likely to occur in any bargaining context, but are likely to be especially prominent and effective when it is not clear what will occur if a negotiated settlement is unreachable (Scott, 1992).

Feminist Critiques of the BICS

Along these lines, Elizabeth Scott (1992) argues that the indeterminate BICS may be especially detrimental to women in child custody negotiations. Using bargaining theory, she proposes that the maternal parent's greater interest in obtaining child custody[11] makes female parents particularly averse to losing custody. Bargaining theory suggests that losses tend to loom larger than gains in decisions similar to the child custody dispute resolution. Consequently, females are disadvantaged in negotiating because they are willing to make great concessions (i.e., agreeing to receive less child support, agreeing to joint legal or physical custody) to prevent the possible custodial loss of their children (Scott, 1992).

Fineman (1988) also contends that the current BICS may be especially biased against female parents seeking custody. Fineman argues that while the BICS may promote a marginal amount of gender equality because gender roles and stereotypes do not determine custody decision making, the BICS accomplishes this goal unfairly by not recognizing the reality of the female biological parent's likely greater predivorce investment in her offspring (Fineman, 1988). Fineman suggests that replacement of BICS with the primary caretaker rule is the only fair means of protecting the rights and the investments of female parents' in their children because the primary caretaker rule determines custody based on individuals' predivorce investment in the needs of their children. Furthermore, she contends that the mandatory mediation procedures explicit in many conceptualizations of the BICS disadvantage female parents by subjecting them to negotiating and bargaining without any of the procedural protections of litigation (Fineman, 1988). Court litigation of child custody disputes, on the other hand, ensure a wide variety of procedural protections, including the right to hire lawyers to protect participant's rights, the right to call witnesses, the right to cross-examine witnesses, the right to appeal decisions if legal errors were made, and the right to have the proceedings overseen by an impartial judge.[12] In contrast to litigation, the procedural rights of mediation participants differ in number and scope from jurisdiction to jurisdiction.

Additionally, Fineman proposes that the current conceptualization of BICS allows mental health professionals (MHPs) to co-opt the child custody dispute resolution process. She claims that MHPs have transmogrified a legal issue into an emotional and therapeutic crisis in which their services are necessary on a continuing basis to meet the needs of the participants

(Fineman, 1988). The MHP's self-serving interest, however, has not led to more productive and efficient resolution of disputes. According to Fineman, MHPs have limited ability and expertise in addressing the important legal issues of custody, and all the participants' interests (especially those of women) would be better served if child custody disputes were treated similarly to other legal decisions.

Conclusion

In sum, the current conceptualization of the BICS has been criticized for its ambiguity and promotion of significant judicial discretion, which allows judges to make child custody decisions based more on personal biases than on the factors suggested by child custody statutes. These decisions also have been characterized for requiring judges to balance and weigh unfamiliar factors that are outside a judge's area of expertise. Furthermore, the ambiguity of the standard has been hypothesized to increase litigation and to work against the interests of the legal system, the parents, and the children involved in divorce. Finally, the current conceptualization of BICS has been criticized by feminist scholars for placing female parents at a negotiating disadvantage, for removing the procedural protections of the litigation system, for devaluing the female parent's predivorce investment in her children, and for allowing MHPs to unfairly transform a legal concern into a therapeutic issue.

EMPIRICAL RESEARCH AND CRITICISMS RELATING TO CHILD CUSTODY STANDARDS

Child custody standards also can be evaluated by comparing their criteria and application to empirical research findings. Indeed, this approach makes sense because empirical research examining child custody dispute resolution has increased greatly over the past 10 years (see Dillion & Emery, 1996; Bricklin & Elliot, 1995; Johnston, 1996; Kelly, 1993; Maccoby, Buchanan, Mnookin, & Dornsbusch, 1993; Sales et al., 1992, for recent reviews of the literature). A complete review of all the literature is well beyond the scope of this chapter, but an attempt will be made to highlight and summarize the most important findings in each of several areas. In 1987, Melton, Petrila, Poythress, and Slobogin commented that

> Although there has recently been a significant albeit still very limited expansion of knowledge about the effects of divorce on children, there has been virtually no research meeting minimal standards of methodological rigor about the effects of custody arrangements on children and families of different characteristics. (p. 330)

Ten years after this comment was made, many more methodologically sound studies have been completed.[13] The findings of this work will be presented in a format suggested by Sales et al. (1992) and Kelly (1993). The research will be presented in terms of child characteristics (age, gender), parental characteristics (adjustment, parenting skills), family process characteristics (parental conflict, quality of the parent–child relationship), and legal characteristics (joint custody vs. sole custody, mediation vs. litigation). Additionally, an assessment of the influence these findings should exert on the choice of a child custody standard will be offered.

Empirical Research Findings

Ultimately, any legal standard for determining child custody disputes should attempt to secure beneficial psychological effects for the child. If such benefits cannot be achieved or reasonably be predicted to occur, then the chosen standard at least should attempt to minimize potential harmful effects to the child. The empirical research offers insight into the appropriateness of the existing and proposed child custody standards. As will be shown, the research findings expressly contradict many of the assumptions underlying past and present conceptualizations of the BICS,[14] and thus have important implications for current court procedures in child custody decisionmaking and for the standard used in these cases.

Child Characteristics

The child's characteristics at the time of divorce have been shown to have a relationship to his or her postdivorce adjustment. The most studied of the children's characteristics in the child custody dispute resolution research are age and gender. No direct, linear relationship between these characteristics and postdivorce adjustment has been found nor has a direct relationship between these child characteristics and the most suitable custody arrangement been demonstrated (Bricklin & Elliot, 1995; Kelly, 1993; Rohman et al., 1990; Sales et al., 1992). Younger children generally show greater short-term maladjustment to divorce and child custody arrangement, while adolescents have poorer long-term adjustment to divorce and child custody arrangements (Akre, 1992; Sales et al., 1992; Rohman et al., 1990). More recent reviews of the literature have suggested that developmental stage rather than age per se, may be a better predictor of postdivorce adjustment (Kelly, 1993; Sales et al., 1992). Finally, there exists no convincing empirical support for the assumption underlying the tender years doctrine; that young children will be better adjusted if they are placed in the sole custody of their mother rather than in joint custody or in father sole custody.

Empirical research examining the relationship between a child's gender and postdivorce adjustment presents a confusing picture. Early studies of the postdivorce adjustment of children seemed to indicate that boys experience considerably more problems than girls (Camera & Resnick, 1988; Sales et al., 1992). These early research findings, however, have been called into question by later work. These early studies have been questioned because they failed to follow children for suitably long periods of time and focused on more external measures of maladjustment (i.e., behavior problems, school problems, aggression, and acting out) rather than more internal measures of maladjustment (i.e., anxiety, depression, social withdrawal). Later research has shown that girls may experience more internalized problems, and that these difficulties may not manifest themselves until several year postdivorce (Amato & Keith, 1991; Bricklin & Elliot, 1995; Kelly, 1993; Zaslow, 1988). Presently, it is still not clear if a child's gender has significant effects on postdivorce adjustment.

Some empirical evidence suggests that the type of custodial relationship and the gender of child interactively influence postdivorce adjustment. Female children seem to show more signs of maladjustment when they are placed in sole father custody arrangements than in joint custody or sole mother custody arrangements (Buchanan, Maccoby, & Dornsbusch, 1991; Johnston, 1996; Maccoby et al., 1993). This relationship between gender, custody, and maladjustment has been attributed by some to be caused by the fact that especially troublesome children are commonly placed solely with the father (Buchanan et al., 1991; Johnston, 1996). When this proposed relationship was statistically controlled, however, a significant adjustment problem remained (Maccoby et al., 1993). No empirically supported explanation has been offered for this other than that a woman's presence as a role model may be particularly important to good adjustment of a female child. Further empirical research will be needed to explore the veracity of this hypothesis. Moreover, these limited findings should not be used to justify the adoption of the *tender years* doctrine or a maternal preference for all female children. Without understanding why this interaction between gender, custody, and maladjustment exists, it is impossible to exclude the possibility that father sole custody of female children could be equally as good as mother sole custody or joint custody of female children if fathers were made aware of factors that mitigated or exacerbated maladjustment.[15]

Parental Characteristics

In addition to child characteristics, a number of different parental characteristics have been linked by the empirical literature to children's postdivorce adjustment. A number of studies have demonstrated that emotional problems in the custodial parent (anxiety, depression, and personality disorders) are often correlated with the poor postdivorce adjustment of their children (Johnston, 1996; Kalter, Kloner, Schreier, & Okla, 1989; Kline, Tschann, Johnston, & Wallerstein, 1989; Schaefer, 1989, reported in Johnston, 1996). However, a few studies have found no relationship between a custodial parent's emotional problems and their children's adjustment (Bricklin & Elliot, 1995; Kline et al., 1989). Given that the contradictory studies are of similar methodological rigor, the weight of evidence seems to indicate that a parent's emotional problems should have some role in determining custody. This consideration should not play the primary role in determining custody, however, but should be a factor used in making custodial determinations.

Parenting skills also have been empirically shown to affect child adjustment (Maccoby et al., 1993; Stolberg & Walsh, 1989). Maccoby et al. (1993) found a positive, direct relationship between a custodial parent's parenting skills and his or her child's superior postdivorce adjustment. Maccoby and co-workers's (1993) research demonstrated that appropriate monitoring of their children by the custodial parent, joint decision making between the custodial parent and child, and an organized custodial household led to better school performance for the child. Other investigators studying poor parenting skills have found that deficient parenting skills were correlated with poorer childhood adjustment subsequent to divorce (Stolberg & Walsh, 1989). In sum, the weight of evidence suggests that poor parenting practices are linked with poor outcomes for divorced children. It is plausible that good parenting practices lead to better adjustment outcomes for divorced children, but these findings need to be replicated since Macobby and colleagues's (1993) study was the only one to address this issue.

Family Process Characteristics

Characteristics of family interactions also have been shown to affect the postdivorce adjustment of children. Perhaps the most consistent finding from this research is that parents that engaged in physically violent or abusive behavior toward their partner have children with particularly poor postdivorce adjustment (Buchanan et al., 1991; Camera & Resnick, 1988; Johnston, 1996; Johnston, Kline, & Tschann, 1989; Peterson & Zill, 1986). Lower levels of parental hostility and conflict also have been demonstrated to have a negative impact on children's postdivorce adjustment (Amato & Keith, 1991; Buchanan et al., 1991; Bricklin & Elliot, 1995; Johnston, 1996; Kelly, 1993; Maccoby et al., 1993; Rohman et al., 1990; Sales et al., 1992). This lower level of parental conflict has been estimated to occur in approximately 10% of child custody disputes (Maccoby & Mnookin, 1992). Yet, some empirical studies examining parental postdivorce conflict and child adjustment have failed to demonstrate statistically significant effects if the parents were able to cooperate and compromise in making postdivorce decisions concerning their children (Camera & Resnick, 1989). Thus, the exact relationship between parental hostility–conflict and children's postdivorce adjustment remains the topic of considerable dispute within the field. It is not known what level of conflict is necessary to produce a negative outcome for the children, nor is it known what specific components of the parental conflict cause the poor adjustment of their children. Some researchers advocate a direct link between parental hostility and poor child postdivorce adjustment,[16] while others propose that the negative effect of parental conflict occurs indirectly through poorer parenting behavior postdivorce (Kelly, 1993). The most recent reviews of the empirical literature have suggested that parental conflict, by itself, is not a direct determinant of children's postdivorce adjustment, but rather it is the extent to which the child feels caught in the middle between the two conflicting parents that more accurately predicts the children's maladjustment (Bricklin & Elliot, 1995; Johnston, 1996; Kelly, 1993). Future empirical research will be necessary to determine whether a child's "caught in the middle" feeling is a better predictor of adjustment than more general indicators of parental conflict.

Parental conflict may have especially deleterious effects on children's post-divorce adjustment when joint custody is awarded. A number of different studies have reported that the continued contact between parents, necessitated by joint legal custody arrangements, exacerbates adjustment problems for children with high-conflict parents (Buchanan et al., 1991; Johnston, 1996; Johnston et al., 1989; Maccoby et al, 1993).[17] This evidence argues strongly against states adopting presumptions of joint legal custody, unless they are willing to overturn this presumption on a evidentiary showing of parental conflict and hostility.

The quality of the parent–child relationship also has been hypothesized to be an important indicator of children's postdivorce adjustment. A warm, supportive relationship with the custodial parent, consistent expectations from the custodial parent, and stable monitoring by the custodial parent have been correlated with positive child postdivorce adjustment (Buchanan et al., 1991; Johnston, 1996; Johnston et al., 1989). Other empirically demonstrated factors relating the quality of the parent–child relationship to children's post-divorce adjustment are the child's perceived closeness to the custodial parent, the level of joint decision making between the child and the custodial parent, the level of conflict with the custodial parent, and the organization level of the custodial parent's household (Maccoby et al., 1993).

Legal Characteristics

Lastly, the legal interventions of the court (custodial arrangements and mediation) have been shown to have a significant impact on children's postdivorce outcomes. They also affect participant satisfaction and child support compliance. Yet, recent empirical studies of joint custody have not been able to demonstrate a substantial positive effect on postdivorce child adjustment when joint custody is compared with other custodial arrangements (Bricklin & Elliot, 1995; Buchanan et al., 1991; Kline et al., 1989; Maccoby et al., 1993; Sales et al., 1992). Children who are placed in joint custody arrangements are more satisfied with the arrangement than children in either sole father or sole mother custody (Maccoby et al., 1993). Further, there is some evidence that fathers are more compliant in paying child support when their children are in a joint custodial arrangement (Bahr et al., 1994; but see Sales et al., 1992, review for an alternative view). At the present time there is no compelling or substantial evidence that joint custody arrangements are correlated with better postdivorce outcomes for children.[18]

Psychological empirical research has examined the relationship between mediation and a number of different outcome measures. To date, no studies comparing mediation to litigation have indicated a more favorable postdivorce adjustment for children whose custodial arrangement was determined through mediation (Dillion & Emery, 1996; Emery et al., 1991, 1994; Emery & Wyer, 1987; Kitzmann & Emery, 1993; Pearson & Thoennes, 1989). Mediation has been shown, however, to decrease the number of custody hearings, to lead to more rapid resolution of disputes, to achieve similar results, and to have similar or lower rates of relitigation, when compared to litigation (Emery & Wyer, 1987; Emery et al., 1994; but see Beck & Sales, in press, for a much more cautious interpretation of this research). Mediation also has been demonstrated to lead to more compliance with child support and to greater cooperation between the parents (Emery et al., 1991; Pearson & Thoennes, 1989). Additionally, some research has indicated that participants are more satisfied with the process of mediation than they are with the litigation (Kelly, 1990). Yet, a number of other studies have determined that women are more satisfied with child custody dispute resolution through litigation rather than through mediation (Dillion & Emery, 1996; Emery et al., 1994).[19] Many explanations have been offered to account for these divergent results, but no study as yet has produced substantiated empirical support for a particular theory.[20] The wide variance in mediation studies results is likely caused by jurisdictional differences in the voluntariness of mediation programs, the length of mediation programs, the qualification and style of mediators, and the characteristics of the participants.[21] Taken as a whole, mediation research seems to indicate that considerable efficiency in child custody dispute resolution may be achieved by presumptive mediation rules. Yet, positive postdivorce child adjustment has not been linked to mediation and mediation may result in unsatisfying outcomes for some women participants.

Conclusion

In sum, the empirical research does not support the superiority of one custodial arrangement, presumptive custody standard, or legal procedure to resolve custody disputes, all of which makes the appropriateness of the BICS' application speculative. The assumptions underlying different conceptualizations of the BICS, including the tender years doctrine, the psychological parent rule,[22] the joint custody presumption, and the mandatory mediation presumption, have received little (if any) empirical support from the existing psychological research. At best, the research has shown that mediation may be more efficient than other forms of child custody dispute resolution and that joint custody may be particularly inappropriate when certain family process variables are present.

THE ROLE OF MENTAL HEALTH PROFESSIONALS IN CHILD CUSTODY DISPUTES

Despite the few empirical data supporting the BICS and the superiority of one custody arrangement over another, MHPs[23] are frequently used to offer expert opinions in the resolution of child custody disputes (Melton et al., 1997). Many scholars and critics have argued that MHPs are used as experts in these case because child custody decisions are difficult for judges to adjudicate. This problem is exacerbated under the indeterminate BICS, which offers so little guidance for judicial decision making (Davis & Dudley, 1985; Coons et al., 1993). Indeed, one court has even expressly noted that rational child custody decisions by judges based on the BICS are not possible (*Garska v. McCoy*, 1979). A prominent reason for this judicial deference to MHPs is offered by Davis and Dudley (1985): "It is hoped that mental health professionals will have what judges lack. The means to determine objectively what is the best interest of the child" (p. 506).[24]

MHPs usually are asked by the court to evaluate and assess one or more of the parents and their children[25] and provide expert clinical opinions detailing which parental placement or child custody arrangement will be in a specific child's best interest (Ackerman, 1996; Akre,

1992; Clark, 1995; Gindes, 1995. These evaluations have been a cause of intense debate within the field of psychology. Some commentators have argued that psychologists and other MHPs have no expertise in assessing a child's best interest, and consequently it is unethical for psychologists to offer "expert" opinions that have no real scientific basis (Lavin & Sales, 1998; Melton et al., 1987; Faust & Ziskin, 1988), while others have contended that psychologists should participate in child custody proceedings and should present expert testimony concerning an appropriate child custody placement because this psychological information can incrementally increase the validity of judicial opinions (Ackerman, 1996; Akre, 1992; Clark, 1995; Gindes, 1995; Roseby, 1995). But how so?

The BICS offers very little guidance in defining the child's best interest. In other words, the BICS does not have and is unlikely in the future to have an adequate operational definition.[26] It is not clear whether the standard is referring to a child's short-term or long-term psychological adjustment, a child's emotional adjustment, a child's school performance, a child's self-report of happiness, the stability of the child's family, the quality of a child's interaction with his parents or other significant individuals, all of these things, or some combination of these factors. As a result of the indeterminacy of the definition, it is impossible for psychologists to offer an "expert" opinion without a clear idea of what outcome or outcomes their "expert" opinion is intended to address.

Furthermore, the adoption of the UMDA criteria by many states and the adoption by others of additional factors (i.e., primary caretaker, psychological parent, moral fitness of the parents) have done little to clarify what the BICS truly means and what role psychologists should play in the decision-making process (Krauss & Sales, in press). Some commentators have noted that explicit statutory child custody criteria have at least made clear that there exist some factors that a psychologist has no expertise in evaluating. For example, in a state that includes the moral fitness of the parents or financial capability in its child custody statutes, it is argued that psychologists should not offer expert opinions regarding these factors (Grisso, 1986; Otto & Butcher, 1995). Yet, the majority of statutory child custody criteria (i.e., the mental health of the parents and child, the child's wishes, the child's adjustment to home, school, and community, and the relationship between the child and his parents and siblings) all seem to highlight areas where psychological assessment might be useful (Clark, 1995; Gindes, 1995; Oberlander, 1995). Unfortunately, the various child custody statutes, courts, MHPs, and psychological science have not been able to specify how these different factors should be assessed and weighed by psychologists or on which of these specific factors psychologists have expertise to offer opinions (Krauss & Sales, in press).

Even if a more explicit BICS could be formulated, it is not clear that psychologists would be able to overcome a number of technical assessment problems associated with child custody evaluations and expert clinical opinion testimony and subsequently present more useful information to the court. One of the primary problems with child custody evaluations is that the assessment of a child's best interest necessarily involves a future prediction by a psychologist. A psychologist must somehow forecast how a particular child is likely to be psychologically adjusted[27] several years postdivorce based on a myriad of complex factors and interactions. It is well noted that psychologists as a group are particularly inaccurate in making future behavioral predictions and may even be more inaccurate than laypersons (Grisso, 1986; Melton et al., 1997).

Moreover, even if an appropriate or several appropriate outcome variables were identified, current research in the child custody context has been unable to adequately specify which independent variables (e.g., parental conflict, parental adjustment, etc.) might accurately predict such an outcome criterion or criteria. To date, most research has focused on the psychological adjustment of children of divorced parents, and as previously mentioned substantial disagreement exists within the research field concerning which variables are the most important in determining a child's future adjustment (Bricklin & Elliot, 1995; Johnston, 1996; Kelly, 1993; Rohman et al., 1990; Sales et al., 1992). Recent reviews also have noted that psychological research is just beginning to identify important variables and has yet to develop a clear picture of the complexity of these variables' interaction with each other in determining postdivorce outcomes (Bricklin & Elliot, 1995). In addition, the majority of research has been pathology based, that is, investigating what factors lead to poor adjustment for children of divorce rather than exploring the elements leading to improved psychological adjustment for children of divorce.

Legal Standards for the Admissibility of Expert Testimony

Given the lack of science present in much "scientific expert" testimony presented in child custody dispute resolution cases, recent development in the law's evidentiary standards may offer a means to prohibit the admissibility of this testimony. The United States Supreme Court, in *Daubert v. Merrell Dow Pharmaceuticals Inc.* (1993), adopted an interpretation of federal rules of evidence, section 702, in regard to the admissibility of scientific evidence based on the evidentiary reliability of the information presented. In determining the reliability of the proferred scientific information,[28] *Daubert* offers the following pragmatic considerations for federal judges to use, but does not limit the judges to them: (1) whether the proferred information is testable and has been tested, (2) whether it has been published and subject to peer review, (3) whether there is general acceptance of the scientific information in the appropriate scientific community, (4) whether there is a known error rate to the proferred information and what is the probability that using the information will result in an error, and (5) whether the court should include any other factors in its assessment that might indicate the evidentiary reliability of the scientific information.

Based on the present conceptualization of the BICS, MHPs currently are not capable of offering scientifically derived opinions detailing an appropriate custodial placement for a child. An "expert" opinion based exclusively on their clinical experience is not likely to convey any predictive accuracy beyond that of a normal individual.[29] Additionally, assessments based on existing research and standardized assessment instruments are unlikely to improve court decision making in this area.[30]

On the other hand, MHPs could improve child custody decision making by summarizing pertinent empirical research for the court rather than presenting definitive expert opinions on the what would be in the child's best interest. There is ample precedent for courts accepting such context testimony by social scientists on other topics (for eyewitness testimony, see for example, *Arizona v. Chapple*, 1983). Indeed, psychological research may not yet or ever be able to predict what custodial arrangement will be in a specific child's best interest, but on a more general level the empirical research is presently capable of educating the court about what kinds of custodial arrangements are unlikely to be effective. In other words, the strength of psychological research and assessment in the child custody context may be in its ability to advise the court regarding which custodial arrangements do not usually work for different groups of people. For example, empirical psychological research has demonstrated that the children of parents who exhibit an extreme degree of hostility predivorce and during the divorce process do not usually benefit from continued contact between their parents post-divorce (Bricklin, 1995; Kelly, 1993; Sales et al., 1992). A court could use this psychological research as one element in its determination that an award of joint legal custody would be inappropriate in a situation in which there is a high degree of anger and hostility between the parents (see Krauss & Sales, in press, for a detailed discussion of the types of information psychologists can legitimately offer the courts in these types of cases).

LEAST DETRIMENTAL ALTERNATIVE STANDARD

Ultimately, the discussion above will not be particularly helpful until the legislatures and courts resolve the debate over what should be the legal standard for custody decision making. Although the BICS is the legal standard in child custody disputes, in reality judges determine child custody based on a negative standard: which custodial arrangement will do the least harm to the child, rather than which custodial arrangement will be in the child's best interest (Grisso, 1986; Mnookin, 1975; Schultz, Dixon, Lindeberger, & Ruther, 1989). Not surprisingly, given judicial behavior, this so-called LDAS appears to be a more useful standard to resolve contested child custody cases for a number of reasons. At first glance, this distinction between child custody standards may seem merely semantic, but the LDAS more effectively suggests what both the legal and psychological worlds are practically capable of achieving in this context.

First, and perhaps most importantly, a least-detrimental conceptualization most accurately represents what judges and society can realistically hope to accomplish in making child custody determinations. It would be ideal if judges were able to discern which custodial arrangement would result in a better outcome for children involved in contested child custody cases, but currently this is simply not the case. Societal norms and moral theory offer neither a consensual definition of a child's best interest nor an effective means for the courts to determine a child's best interest in a child custody dispute. Therefore, it is hypocritical of our legal system to pretend that the courts are appropriately using this standard when it is abundantly clear that judges are unable to effectively determine a child's best interest. At best, the current conceptualization of the BICS allows for a state-sponsored intrusion into the family structure and an inexact, implicit judicial weighing of parental fitness. At worse, the BICS allows for extralegal judicial biases to mandate a restructuring of the family system through a specific custodial decree.

In contrast to the BICS, the LDAS offers more realistic goals in determining postdivorce custodial arrangements. Divorce, litigation, and custody decisions cause emotional, mental, and physical difficulties for children. Children of divorce are subject to emotional strife between their parents, to less frequent contact with their parents, to different and unfamiliar home environments, and to an abundance of other problems. Custodial arrangements are not intended to improve a child's adjustment; rather, they are intended to minimize harm caused by the dissolution of the family. By focusing on minimizing these difficulties, judges can more appropriately seek to create custodial placements that will effectively ameliorate some of the harm caused by divorce.

Second, psychological research has more to offer a legal standard based on the least-detrimental alternative. As previously mentioned, empirical research in the area of divorce and child custody has been pathology centered, focusing on which variables and factors lead to poor or negative outcomes for divorced children, not on determining which factors lead to a more successful postdivorce adjustment (Bricklin, 1995). Consequently, the existing psychological research is more relevant to highlighting which parental factors (i.e., parental psychopathology and poor parenting skills), family process factors (i.e., parental hostility–conflict), legal factors (i.e., mediation vs. litigation and joint custody vs. sole custody), and individual factors (i.e., age, gender, and developmental stage) will likely contribute to a detrimental outcome for a child. As a result of this research bias, psychologists have greater scientific accuracy and expertise in evaluating which custodial arrangements are likely to do the most harm to children involved in a contested custody case. Psychological research currently has little or no ability to inform a legal standard or court decision that is seeking to maximize a specific child's postdivorce adjustment. This is particularly a concern because positive adjustment can be manifested in multiple ways and can be evaluated by multiple criteria reflecting diverse values in a hetergenous society.

Third, psychological evaluations based on the LDAS more effectively represent the expertise of MHPs in child custody assessment. Much like the empirical research, standardized psychological assessment instruments used in clinical evaluations are pathology focused. These instruments are not designed or intended to assess an individual's positive attributes; they were largely created to measure an individual's deficits in a particular area. As a result, psychological assessments based on these instruments do little to inform the evaluator or the court about which personality characteristics, abilities, or capacities are likely to improve outcomes for children in a child custody dispute. Rather, the assessment instruments are capable of pointing out deficits in the parents or child, which clinicians and judges may interpret as forecasting negative effects of certain custody arrangements (Krauss & Sales, in press). No Minnesota Multiphasic Personality Inventory-II profile, Rorschach score, or any other instrument can suggest that a parent is especially well-suited to care for the needs of his or her children.

Ironically, even under the LDAS, the courts must cautiously evaluate MHP proferred testimony. Although psychologists have greater scientific expertise in evaluating and researching harmful custody arrangements, MHPs have demonstrated limited scientific expertise, as both researchers and clinical evaluators, in recommending a custodial arrangement that will minimize postdivorce maladjustment for a specific child (Krauss & Sales, in press). The problems associated with generalizing to individual cases from group or nomothetic data used to develop the psychological assessment instruments and the dearth of methodologically sound empirical findings on postdivorce child adjustment serve to limit the ability of MHPs to accurately forecast postdivorce maladjustment. Consequently, MHPs should still refrain from offering expert testimony advocating a particular custodial arrangement for a specific child. By limiting their testimony to potential unfavorable custodial arrangements and expressing the limitations of their knowledge in individual cases, psychologists will be presenting more accurate and scientific information.

METHODOLOGICAL PROBLEMS AND EMPIRICAL RESEARCH NEEDS

Although the LDAS may more accurately reflect the law's approach in these cases and psychologists' capabilities as experts, the LDAS still suffers. For example, the circumspect testimony recommended above will leave the court with the problem of deciding which of a number of "not harmful" custodial arrangements will be an appropriate custodial placement for a particular child. In addition, many of the same criticisms associated with the present conceptualization of the BICS apply to the adoption of the LDAS: (1) the problem of judicial discretion in custody decision making; (2) the problem of between- and within-jurisdiction variability in custody decision making; (3) the problems associated with an indeterminate standard and effective bargaining and negotiation; (4) the problem associated with the rebuttable legal presumptions of joint custody and mediation; (5) the problems espoused by feminist critics of child custody decision making; and (6) the problem of MHPs overreaching their scientific basis in presenting expert clinical opinion testimony to the court. These issues will need to be addressed in formulating child custody decisions, as well as be the focus of future writings.

More broadly, research is needed to address the paucity and inconsistency of child custody research findings. Such research should focus on developing methodologically sufficient research designs, including: (1) concrete and explicit operational definitions of variables; (2) recognition and control of important confounding variables (i.e., age of the children, developmental stage, predivorce level of conflict, socioeconomic status of the parents, etc.); (3) longer follow-up periods; (4) assessment and follow-up of dropouts; (4) baseline or predivorce measures of parent and child adjustment; (5) more explicit descriptions of custody arrangements; and (6) more focus on positive adjustment.

The myriad difficulties inherent in this research can be best classified into three distinct categories of problems: operational definition problems often referred to as construct validation problems, internal validity problems, and external validity problems. As previously mentioned, operational definition refers to a uniform conceptualization of a construct (in this case BICS) that allows the idea to be broken down into an easily identifiable and assessable component or series of components. Without this definitional specificity, it is not possible to effectively measure and study the construct using social science techniques. In other words, social scientists need to know exactly what they are studying in order to determine which factors are likely to affect it. The lack of an operational definition prevents researchers from developing valid measurement techniques and valid standardized assessment instruments, comparing different studies that use divergent outcome measures, and summarizing the existing research in the field.

In contrast to operational definition problems, internal validity concerns inhibit researchers from interpreting direct causal relationships between changes in the independent variable or variables and changes in the dependent or outcome variable. In other words, internal validity problems detract from the researcher's ability to show that the outcome variable is only being affected by the experimentally manipulated variable. For example, researchers would like to be able control all other variables except gender to determine whether there is a direct relationship between gender and postdivorce adjustment. On the other hand, external validity concerns limit the generalizability of research findings beyond their subjects and conditions. For instance, because of external validity problems, research studies performed on children of divorce in California may not be scientifically applicable to children of divorce in New York.

Operational Definition Problem

Perhaps the greatest methodological problem with child custody and divorce research is the lack of a well-defined outcome variable or outcome measures. Child adjustment and child quality of life would seem to be important outcome variables, but no adequate means of operationalizing these constructs have been uniformly adopted by researchers. Some researchers simply use a child's self-report measures of adjustment to assess postdivorce adjustment, while others investigators rely on the opinion of parents, the observations of school teachers, or the child's grades to gauge postdivorce adjustment. The vast majority of studies fail to use multiple measures of outcomes, and as a consequence convergent validity of outcome measures cannot be established (i.e., evidence that the outcome measures are assessing the important construct—child adjustment—rather than their findings simply reflecting the researchers measurement techniques—measurement bias). For example, many parental self-reports of child adjustment postdivorce have been found to be poorly correlated with other outcome measures (Bricklin & Elliot, 1995). Comparing and synthesizing research that uses widely disparate means of operationalizing children's postdivorce adjustment are difficult if not impossible. Future research should focus on developing and using consistent outcome variables and measuring these variables through a variety of methods.

Internal Validity Problems

The primary internal validity problem faced by child custody and divorce empirical research is the inability of investigators to conduct true experiments. Consequently, researchers examining child custody issues have limited power to control a variety of outside factors while they attempt to establish a relationship between any one factor and the specified outcome variable. Any one of these concomitant factors or a combination of these factors could be confounding results by causing, exacerbating, or weakening the obtained relationship between the intended, independent variable and the outcome variable. For example, while factors such as the age of the children, the developmental stage of the children, the social support afforded to the custodial parent, the financial resources of the parents, the predivorce functioning of the parents, and the voluntariness of the custodial arrangement have been linked to eventual outcome measures, rarely are attempts made to control the influence of more than a few of these factors in any given study.[31] Moreover, all these factors are likely to interact with each other in unpredictable and nonlinear ways, making accurate descriptions of their interrelationship difficult, if not impossible, to explain by the methods currently available to social science research. Further research should make better attempts to recognize and statistically control empirical demonstrated variables that have been shown to affect research results but are not the main focus on the research project.

Further, internal validity also is limited by child custody researchers' inability to randomly assign different children to different custody arrangements and follow these children for several years to determine which arrangement produces the best outcome for the majority of children.[32] Without random assignment, observed effects could be the result of the preexisting characteristics that made the participants choose a specific custody arrangement rather than a characteristic of the custody arrangement.[33] Future research should make efforts to determine when preexisting group differences exist between selection of different custodial arrangements, what factors lead to this selection bias, and how these preexisting factors might affect eventual outcomes.

Additionally, internal validity of child custody empirical research is confounded by a time frame problem (Bricklin, 1995). It is unclear how long child custody participants should be followed to adequately assess outcome measures. Some commentators have discerned effects of divorce that continue to be present for 10 years following the formalization of a child custody arrangement and have found effects of child custody placement and divorce that do not appear until several years post-divorce[34] (Bricklin & Elliot, 1995; Kelly, 1993; Sales et al., 1992). Obviously, following participants for ten years postdivorce is extremely expensive and time consuming, complicated further by data interpretation problems produced by sample attrition over time. Nonetheless, researchers recognizing the advantages of longitudinal designs have been following subjects for longer periods of time. As of now, however, few research studies have been able to examine participants for a course of 10 years. Future research should follow participants for longer periods of time to determine how parental and child adjustment to divorce changes over more extended time frames.

Unfortunately, although long-term studies have generated more accurate participant outcome data, these studies' high dropout rates cause both external validity and internal validity difficulties. From an internal validity perspective, the results of long-term longitudinal studies may be biased toward individuals and characteristics of individuals who are capable of remaining in a longer study, instead of accurately describing the relationship between all subjects and subject characteristics and the outcome variable.[35] This bias occurs because dropout subjects are rarely (if ever) assessed to determine whether they differ significantly from those individuals who remain in the study (Dillion & Emery, 1996). Additionally, external validity concerns prevent or should prevent researchers from generalizing or interpreting research findings to apply to all experimental subjects unless assessments of dropout were completed and included in the results of the study. Future research should make greater attempts to assess dropout participants in order to more accurately limit the overgeneralization and overinterpreting that occurs with most studies in this area.

Researchers investigating the effects of child custody and divorce often have completed methodologically flawed research because they have failed to use necessary baseline measures or adequate control groups. Without initial measurements of the difficulties participants in child custody dispute resolution are experiencing, it is impossible to determine the degree to which the divorce and child custody process further affects their adjustment. Consequently, the internal validity of these studies is suspect because the research is unable to discern whether divorce and child custody arrangements directly contribute to changes in children's adjustment or whether many of the children's adjustment problems existed before divorce and child custody occurred. For example, it is plausible that, as a group, people who experience divorce and child custody disputes are more maladjusted prior to divorce and that the divorce proceedings have little or no effect on their later problems.[36] Similarly, the lack of control groups in most empirical research in this area makes it difficult to establish that children of divorce are significantly different from children in intact families or children in intact families with high degrees of conflict. As a result of this problem, it is not clear whether postdivorce child maladjustment is a direct consequence of the child custody process or a result of living in a family with a high degree of conflict.[37] To combat this problem, researchers should utilize intact high-conflict families as control groups or comparison groups for divorced families in their research designs.

External Validity Problems

The greatest external validity problem associated with child custody research was created by researchers who have been largely remiss in adequately defining their variables and their relationship to legal concepts. For example, while many studies compare joint custody to sole custody, almost all fail to mention whether they are investigating joint legal custody or joint physical custody. Investigators also commonly fail to mention the controlling legal standard or the controlling presumptions in the jurisdiction in which their study was completed. Given that different jurisdictions have different statutory criteria for determining custody and different standards concerning mediation and joint legal custody, comparing outcomes from studies across different jurisdictions is problematic.[38] These external validity problems result in empirical findings from one jurisdiction not being generalizable to another jurisdiction. More importantly, the failure of researchers to adequately specify the legal constraints of their study makes it impossible to determine the representativeness and generalizability of their research conclusions. Additional research should more explicitly define independent and dependent variables and more adequately express the limitations of their findings.

Finally in regard to methodological concerns, an external validity concern common in child custody research relates to the focus of child custody and divorce research. Child custody outcome research by and large has examined negative outcomes (i.e., maladjustment) rather than investigating variables that lead to positive outcomes (Bricklin & Elliot, 1995). This bias toward the pathological may eventually lead researchers to what is not in a child's best interest, but offers little in the way of answering the question of what is in a child's best interest. Also, in summarizing their data or that of other researchers, social scientists often commit the logical fallacy of the inverse and as a result overgeneralize their research conclusions. They incorrectly assume that the opposite of a variable that is correlated with maladjustment should be correlated with positive adjustment. For instance, a number of studies have found that inadequate parenting skills lead to maladjustment for children of divorce. All too often, these investigators have argued that their results imply that superior parenting skills lead to superior outcomes for divorced children. Before this claim can be made, empirical research must directly examine the link between superior parenting skills and better postdivorce child adjustment.[39] Future research needs to more effectively focus on what factors improve postdivorce adjustment instead of focusing exclusively on what factors cause poor postdivorce adjustment.

Substantive Research Needs

More substantatively, while research examining child characteristics, parental characteristics, family process characteristics, and legal characteristics is beginning to demonstrate significant results, empirical research is still far from explaining why certain characteristics cause poor postdivorce adjustment or understanding the complex manner in which these variables interact. Future psychological research should focus on examining the causal mechanisms that lead to postdivorce child maladjustment, as well as developing and testing theories of postdivorce adjustment that incorporate more complex interactions of child, parental, family process, and legal characteristics. By understanding these complex interaction, policymakers will be better able to construct custody arrangements that benefit children and develop postdivorce custody plans and treatments that benefit all the parties involved.

ACKNOWLEDGMENTS

Part of this chapter draws on an article by the authors that appeared in the journal *Psychology, Public Policy, and Law*. We thank the publisher of that journal, the American Psychological Association, for the right to use the material herein.

ENDNOTES

1. Some reviews of the psychological literature, however, indicate that the effects of divorce on children may not be as severe as social scientists and the general public originally believed (Amato & Keith, 1991; Bricklin, 1995; Kelly, 1993).
2. The BICS is only used by courts in contested child custody disputes between two previously married biological parents. Other legal standards are used by the court to determine child custody cases between other interested parties. This chapter only considers the former situation.
3. For instance, the termination of parental rights requires a higher evidentiary showing (clear and convincing evidence) by the state than the normal evidentiary standard of preponderance of the evidence that is most commonly used by the court to decide civil litigation issues.

4. This idea is legally embodied in the equal protection clause and the procedural due process concerns of the XIVth Amendment of the United States Constitution.
5. The importance of explicit factors and consistent judicial decision making will be explored further in the section presenting legal criticism of the BICS.
6. In fact, this theory has been expressly contradicted by empirical research. Although interaction with the noncustodial parent has not always been shown to increase postdivorce child adjustment (Amato & Keith, 1991; Kline et al., 1989; Buchanan et al., 1991; Pearson & Thoennes, 1989), many early studies have shown that this is often the case (Wallerstein & Kelly, 1980). Furthermore, children of divorce have uniformly expressed a desire to have more contact with the noncustodial parent (Johnston, 1996; Kelly, 1993; Maccoby et al., 1993). Moreover, children of divorce have not described loyalty conflicts as playing a significant role in most joint custody arrangements (Johnston, 1996; Maccoby et al., 1993).
7. In contrast to joint legal custody, joint physical custody presumes an equal time-sharing arrangement between the two parents.
8. In civil commitment proceedings, judges also must make assessments of future behavior (i.e., the future dangerousness of an individual); a decision that has limited or no precedential value; a decision concerning an individual, the proposed ward, who may have limited participation; and a decision based on inexact statutory criteria that may involve the restriction of significant individual rights.
9. This hypothesized increase in child custody litigation could affect the legal system, the parents, and the present and future adjustment of the children (Burt, 1983; Elster, 1987). Increased litigation leads to greater judicial backlog and longer time periods before child custody issues are resolved. Most importantly, more litigation means that greater numbers of children will have to adjust to prolonged court proceedings, temporary custody arrangements, and an increase in parental hostility (Emery et al., 1994; Emery & Wyer, 1987; Kelly, 1993; Kitzmann & Emery 1993). In addition, there seems to be some empirical support for the conclusion that longer more adversarial child custody adjudications will lead to negative outcomes for the children involved in them. Both parental hostility and environmental instability have been empirically linked to worse postdivorce adjustment for children (Bricklin & Elliot 1995; Sales et al., 1992).
10. A full discussion of bargaining theory and its relationship to child custody dispute resolution is beyond the scope of this chapter. For a more comprehensive review of this issue, see Mnookin and Kornhauser (1979) and Scott (1992).
11. This theory assumes that women have a greater preference than men for the custody of their children. The empirical research seems to offer some support for this idea, because the vast majority of uncontested child custody agreements are sole maternal custody (Bahr et al., 1994).
12. This is not an exhaustive list of the procedural protections inherent in courtroom resolutions of contested child custody disputes, but rather a list of some of the more important legal rights.
13. The literature as a whole still suffers from a myriad of conceptual and methodological problems that make a large portion of the findings subject to question. In fact, Amato and Keith (1991) in their meta-analytic review of child custody investigations described an inverse relationship between the methodological sophistication of studies and the strength of variable effects: the better the methodology, the weaker the variable effects. The final section of this chapter will address these issues.
14. This section organizes the empirical research by different variables types. This was done for convenience rather than to imply that these variable types do not have significant interaction with each other. As discussed in the last section, it is likely that independent variable interactions have a more significant influence on the outcome variable than any one variable has by itself.
15. One study has demonstrated that fathers having sole custody equal mothers having sole custody and parents having joint custody on a number of different parenting characteristics. This research found, however, that sole-custody fathers fail to monitor the children as consistently as parents in the other two custodial arrangements (Maccoby et al., 1993). Further research will be necessary to replicate this finding and explore the possibility that the lack of monitoring leads to poor adjustment for female children.
16. Some of these researchers have posited that the negative effects of parental conflict occur before the legal processes of divorce and child custody, and that this predivorce hostility is the best predictor of child maladjustment (Tschann, Kline, & Wallerstein, 1990).
17. Maccoby et al. (1993) has highlighted specific characteristics that lead to greater parental hostility and conflict postdivorce. These factors include larger family sizes, legal conflict (even when parental hostility is statistically controlled), discrepant parental views concerning each parent's role in predivorce parenting, and parental concern about the other parent's competence to parent.
18. This is especially true for parents who exhibit a significant degree of conflict. As previously mentioned, in these cases, joint custody will likely result in worse outcome for the children who are placed in them.

19. This would not surprise the opponents of mandatory mediation, who have argued that mediation does not mitigate power imbalances between the parties. Rather, they say, mediation allows men to strategically trade unwanted child custody for lower levels of child support, and that mediation leaves the parties without the adversarial and procedural protections of the court (Fineman, 1988; Hester, 1992).
20. For example, Dillion and Emery (1996) have suggested that the differential finding was a result of the different legal presumption operating in the jurisdiction in which the studies were conducted. They proposed that the maternal preference in operation in their jurisdiction made it more likely that the women could have received a more advantageous custodial arrangement if they proceeded to court (sole maternal custody was assumed by the researcher to be the most satisfying arrangement for the women). Consequently, the women who mediated settlements and agreed to more cooperative custody arrangements felt less satisfied. They also proposed that the significant dropout rates in their studies (50%) may have resulted in biased findings. Their follow-up results indicated that the more satisfied women participants had higher dropout rates (Dillion & Emery, 1996).
21. For a comprehensive analysis of mediation's assumptions, research support, and effectiveness, in child custody and divorce proceedings, see Beck and& Sales (in press).
22. See note 6 for empirical research expressly contradicting the psychological parent rule.
23. Rarely do child custody researchers offer expert testimony to the court in the resolution of contested child custody disputes. The vast majority of testimony in these cases is given by clinical psychologist and psychiatrists rather than researchers.
24. Ironically, some recent empirical studies estimate that MHPs offer expert testimony to the court less frequently than most individuals imagine. Psychologists testify in only 2–10% of all child custody cases (Melton et al., 1997).
25. A recent informal survey of psychologists who perform child custody evaluations has suggested that in 10–42% of evaluations, the MHP does not have access to all the relevant participants in the child custody dispute (Bricklin, 1995).
26. Operational definition refers to a uniform conceptualization of a construct (in this case BICS) that allows the idea to be broken down into an easily identifiable and assessable component or series of components. Without this definitional specificity, it is not possible to effectively measure and study the construct using social science techniques. In other words, social scientists need to know exactly what they are studying in order to determine the factors that are likely to affect it.
27. It is assumed for purposes of this hypothetical discussion that the child's long-term psychological adjustment is an important factor in determining the child's best interest.
28. Daubert applies to scientific knowledge, and "... the adjective scientific implies a grounding in the methods and procedures of science.... But in order to qualify as 'scientific knowledge' and inference or assertion must be derived by the scientific method" (*Daubert*, 1993, p. 2788).
29. The lack of accuracy in expert clinical opinions and their potential for misuse by the court does suggest the compelling argument that, even under a broad relevancy approach (see note 30), these expert opinions should not be admissible in the courtroom. Unfortunately, courts have focused almost exclusively on the credentials and training of the expert rather than on the quality of information the expert will be presenting when making admissibility decisions. As a result, the courts have not barred inaccurate and unscientific expert clinical opinion testimony from being offered by well-trained practitioners (Shuman & Sales, 1999).
30. While some state courts use *Daubert* criteria to determine the admissibility of scientific evidence, the majority of states have not changed their admissibility rules for this type of information. In addition, expert clinical opinion testimony generally has not been treated as scientific evidence by the courts and has not been subject to scientific evidentiary admissibility standards (Shuman & Sales, 1999). This testimony has been admitted under a broad relevancy approach to evidence (e.g., whether the information is relevant, and whether the probative value of the evidence is not substantially outweighed by the danger of unfair prejudice or confusion). It should be expressly highlighted that the mere acceptance of information or testimony by the court does not indicate that it is ethical or appropriate for MHPs to offer such testimony. Even if admitted, Lavin and Sales (1998) suggest that this type of testimony may still violate one's moral responsbilities as a mental health professional.
31. For example, consider the research discussed earlier on predivorce family characteristics. This work has demonstrated that predivorce characteristics of the family may be more important than postdivorce characteristics for predicting postdivorce child maladjustment. When predivorce hostility was statistically controlled, none of the most robust prior predictors of postdivorce child adjustment (i.e., parental conflict, parenting skills, and quality of parent–child relationship) were found to be statistically significant (Kelly, 1993; Kline et al., 1989). These results indicate that prior findings of significance for these variables may have been specious.
32. The only exception to the randomization problem is the mediation experiments performed by Emery and others in which they were actually able to randomly assign couples to mediation or litigation. This research, however, had

exceedingly high dropout rates (close to 50%), which make the representativeness of the sample highly suspect. The study also suffered from a number of other methodological problems (Dillion & Emery, 1996).

33. This problem may be best illustrated by a number of early studies that seemed to indicate that joint legal custodial arrangements led to better child adjustment than other custodial arrangements. However, many later studies found no such positive relationship between joint custody and child adjustment. As it turns out, the participants in the early studies all chose joint custody arrangements rather than having the court system mandate a joint arrangement, and the early joint custody participants had significantly higher socioeconomic status, educational attainment, and parental cooperation than the participants in the other custody arrangements to which they were compared (Maccoby et al., 1993).
34. The most notable of these effects may be the empirical findings that young children often have an extremely difficult time with divorce in the short term, but adolescents and girls in particular may have greater maladjustment several years postdivorce (Bricklin & Elliot, 1995; Sales et al., 1992).
35. It is likely that dropouts have more maladjustment, and consequently long-term studies may be biased toward more positive outcomes. However, without accurate follow-up there is no way to know if this is indeed the case.
36. It should be noted, however, that studies that have used adequate baseline measures have found significant negative consequences associated with the postdivorce custodial process (Amato & Keith, 1991; Johnston; 1996; Kelly, 1993; Rohman et al., 1990).
37. Some empirical research has found no difference between children of divorce maladjustment and the maladjustment of children who have lived in intact highly conflictual families (Kelly, 1993).
38. Likewise, sample population characteristics also may play an important role in limiting the generalizability of research conclusions. The sample population's socioeconomic status, educational level, racial composition, size, and religious beliefs may affect the studies generalizability to other populations.
39. This is by no means an exhaustive list of the methodological difficulties inherent in much child custody research, but rather highlights of areas of special concern for researchers.

REFERENCES

Ackerman, M. (1996). APA guidelines for child custody. *Fairshare*, *16*, 6–15.

Akre, L. (1992). Struggling with indeterminacy: For an interdisciplinary collaboration in redefining the best interest standard. *Marquette Law Review*, *75*, 628–640.

Amato, P., & Keith., P. (1991). Parental divorce and the well-being of children: A meta-analysis. *Psychological Bulletin*, *110*, 26–46.

Arizona Rules of Civil Procedure, Rules 8.7., Mediation.

Arizona v. Chapple, 135 Ariz. 281, 660 P.2d 1208 (1983).

Bahr, S., Howe, J., Mann, M., & Bahr, M. (1994.) Trends in child custody awards: has the removal of the maternal preference made a difference. *Family Law Quarterly*, *28*, 247–260.

Barefoote v. Estelle, 463 U.S. 880 (1983).

Batt, J. (1992.) Child custody disputes and beyond the best interest standard. *Nova Law Review*, *16*, 621–640.

Beck, C., & Sales, B. (in press). A critical reappraisal of family mediation. *Psychology, Public Policy, and Law*.

Becker, M. (1993). Judicial discretion in child custody: The wisdom of Solomon. *Illinois Bar Journal*, *81*, 650–660.

Bricklin, B. (Ed.). (1995). *The child custody evaluation handbook: Research-based solutions and applications*. New York: Brunner/Mazel.

Bricklin, B., & Elliot, G. (1995). Postdivorce issues and relevant research. In B. Bricklin (Ed.), *The custody evaluation handbook: Research-based solutions and applications*. New York: Brunner/Mazel.

Buchanan, C., Maccoby, E., & Dornsbusch, S. (1991). Caught between parents: Adolescents' experience in divorced homes. *Child Development*, *62*, 1008–1029.

Burt, R. (1983). Experts, custody disputes, and legal fantasy. *Psychiatric Hospitals*, *14*, 140.

Camera, K., & Resnick, G. (1988). Intraparental conflict and cooperation: Factors moderating children's post-divorce adjustment. In E. M. Hetherington & J. D. Arasteh (Eds.), *Impact of divorce, single parenting, and stepparenting on children*. Hillsdale, NJ: Lawrence Erlbaum.

Camera, K., & Resnick, G. (1989). Styles of conflict resolution and cooperation between divorce parents: Effects on child behavior and adjustment. *American Journal of Orthipsychiatry*, *59*, 560–574.

Clark, B. (1995). Acting in the best interest of the child: Essential components of a child custody evaluation. *Family Law Quarterly*, *29*, 19–37.

Coons, J., Mnookin., R., & Sugarman, S. (1993). Deciding what's best for children. *Notre Dame Journal of Law and Public Policy, 7*, 465–490.

Craig v. Boren, 429 U.S. 190 (1976).

Daubert v. Merrell Dow Pharmaceuticals Inc., 113 S.Ct. 2786 (1993).

Davis, P., & Dudley, R. (1985). Family evaluations and the development of standards for child custody determination. *Columbia Journal of Law and Social Problems, 19*, 505–515.

Dillon, P., & Emery, R. (1996). Divorce mediation and resolution of child custody disputes: Long-term effects. *American Journal of Orthopsychiatry, 66*, 131–140.

Elster, J. (1987). Solomonic judgements: Against the best interest of the child. *University of Chicago Law Review, 54*, 1–40.

Emery, R., & Wyer, R. (1987). Child custody mediation and litigation: An experimental evaluation of the experience of parents. *Journal of Consulting and Clinical Psychology, 55*, 139–186.

Emery, R., Matthews, S., & Kitzmann, R. (1994). Child custody mediation and litigation: Parents' satisfaction 1 year after settlement. *Journal of Consulting and Clinical Psychology, 62*, 124–129.

Emery, R., Matthews, S., & Wyer, M. (1991). Child custody mediation and litigation: An experimental evaluation of the experience of parents. *Journal of Consulting and Clinical Psychology, 59*, 410–418.

Evans, P., & Havercamp, S. (1994). Analysis of mediatiion assumptions: Strategies to help mediators in child custody disputes. *Mediation Quarterly, 11*, 229–245.

Farber, D., Eskridge, W., & Frickey, P. (1993) *Constitutional law: Themes for the constitution's third century*. St. Paul, MN: West.

Faust, D., & Ziskin, J. (1988). The expert witness in psychology and psychiatry. *Science, 241*, 31–35.

Fiddler, B., & Saunders, B. (1988). Children's adjustment during custody disputes: Relation to custody arrangement, gender, and age of the children. *Canadian Journal of Psychiatry, 33*, 517–523.

Fineman, M. (1988). Dominant discourse, professional language, and legal change in in child custody decision-making. *Harvard Law Review, 101*, 727–774.

Frontiero v. Richardson, 411 U.S. 677 (1973).

Garska v. McCoy, 278 SE2d 357 (1979).

Gindes, M. (1995). Guidelines for child custody evaluations for psychologists: An overview and commentary. *Family Law Quarterly, 29*, 37–62.

Goldstein, J., Freud, A., & Solnit, A. (1979). *Beyond the best interest of the child*. New York: Macmillan.

Grisso, T. (1986). *Evaluating competencies: Forensic assessments and instruments*. New York: Plenum Press.

Hester, T. (1992). The mental health professional in child custody determinations incident to divorce. *Women's Rights Law Reporter, 14*, 109–137.

Johnston, J. (1996). Children's adjustment in sole custody compared to joint custody families and principles for custody decision making. *Family and Concilliation Courts Review, 33*, 415–425.

Johnston, J., Kline, M., & Tschann, J. (1989). Ongoing post-divorce conflict: Effects on children of joint custody and frequent access. *American Journal of Orthopsychiatry, 59*, 576–592.

Kalter, N., Kloner, A., Schreiser, S., & Okla, K. (1989). Predictions of children's post-divorce adjustment. *American Journal of Orthopsychiatry, 59*, 605–618.

Kelly, J. (1990). *Mediated and adversarial divorce resolution process: An analysis of post-divorce outcomes*. San Francisco: Final Report prepared for the Fund for Research in Dispute Resolution.

Kelly, J. (1993). Current research on children's post-divorce adjustment: No simple answers. *Family and Conciliation Court Review, 31*, 29–49.

Kline, M., Tschann, J., Johnston, J., & Wallerstein, J. (1989). Children's adjustment in joint and sole physical custody families. *Developmental Psychology, 25*, 430–438.

Kitzmann, R., & Emery, R. (1993). Procedural justice and parent's satisfaction in a field study of child custody dispute resolution. *Law and Human Behavior, 17*, 553–567.

Krauss, D., & Sales, B. (in press). Legal standards, expertise, and experts in child custody decision-making. *Psychology, Public Policy, and Law.*

Lavin, M., & Sales, B. D. (1998). Moral justifications for limits on expert testimony. In Stephen J. Ceci & Helene Hembrooke (Eds.), *Expert witnesses in child abuse cases* (pp. 59–81). Washington, DC: American Psychological Association.

Lowery, C. (1981). Child custody decision in divorce proceeding: A survey of judges. *Professional Psychology, 12*, 492–498.

Maccoby, E., & Mnookin, R. (1992). *Dividing the child social and legal implications of custody*. Cambridge, MA: Harvard University Press.

Maccoby, E., Buchanan, C., Mnookin, R., & Dornsbusch, S. (1993). Postdivorce roles of mother and father in the lives of their children. *Journal of Family Psychology, 1*, 24–38.

Melton, G., Petrilia, J., Poythress, N., & Slobogin, C. (1987). *Psychological evaluations for the courts*. New York: Guilford Press.

Melton, G., Petrilia, J., Poythress, N., & Slobogin, C. (1997). *Psychological evaluations for the courts*, 2nd ed. New York: Guilford Press.

Miller, G. (1993). The psychological best interest of the child. *Journal of Divorce and Remarriage*, *19*, 21–35.

Mnookin, R. (1975). Child custody adjudication and judicial function in the face of indeterminacy. *Law and Contemporary Problems*, *39*, 226–293.

Mnookin, R., & Kornhauser, A. (1979). Bargaining in the shadows of law: The case of divorce. *Yale Law Journal*, *88*, 950–988.

Oberlander, L. (1995). Ethical responsibilities in child custody evaluations: Implications for evaluation methodology. *Ethics and Behavior*, *5*, 311–332.

Orr v. Orr, 440 U.S. 268 (1979).

Otto, R., & Butcher, J. (1995). Computer assisted psychological assessment in child custody evaluations. *Family Law Quarterly*, *29*, 79–96.

Palmore v. Sidotti, 466 U.S. 435 (1984).

Pearson, J., & Ring, M. (1982). Judicial decision making in contested custody cases. *Journal of Family Law*, *21*, 703–724.

Pearson, J., & Thoennes, N. (1989). Custody after divorce: Demographic and attitudinal patterns. *American Journal of Orthiopsychiatry*, *60*, 233–249.

Peterson, J., & Zill, N. (1986). Marital disruptions, parent–child relationships, and behavior problems in children. *Journal of Marriage and Family*, *48*, 295–307.

Reed v. Reed, 404 U.S. 71 (1971).

Reidy, C., Silver, L., & Carson, R. (1989). Child custody decisions: a survey of judges. *Family Law Quarterly*, *23*, 75–90.

Rice, M. (1997). Violent offender research implications for the criminal justice system. *American Psychologist*, *52*, 414–423.

Rohman, L., Sales, B., & Lou, M. (1990). The best interest standard in child custody decisions. In D. Weisstub (Ed.), *Law and mental health: International perspectives* (Vol. 5, pp. 40–90). New York: Pergamon.

Roseby, V. (1995). The use of psychological testing in a child focused approach to child custody evaluations. *Family Law Quarterly*, *29*, 97–110.

Sales, B., Manber, R., & Rohman, L. (1992). Social science research and child custody decision-making. *Applied and Preventive Psychology*, *1*, 23–40.

Santilla, L. & Roberts, M. (1990). Custody decisions in Alabama before and after the abolition of the tender years doctrine. *Law and Human Behavior*, *14*, 23–40.

Schlesinger v. Ballard, 419 U.S. 498 (1975).

Schneider, C. (1991). Discretion, rules, and law: Child custody and the UMDA best interest standard. *Michigan Law Review*, *89*, 215–246.

Schultz, B., Dixon, E., Lindeberger, J., Ruther, N. (1989). *Solomon's sword.* San Francisco: Jossey-Bass.

Scott, E. (1992). Pluralism, parental preference, and child custody. *California Law Review*, *80*, 615–672.

Shuman, D., & Sales, B. (1999). The admissibility of expert testimony based upon clinical judgment and scientific research. *Psychology, Public Policy and Law*, *5*, 3–15.

Shuman, D., Sales, B., & O'Connor, M. (1994). In a dim light: Admissibility of child sexual abuse memories in court. *Applied Cognitive Psychology*, *8*, 399–406.

Stanley v. Illinois, 405 U.S. 645 (1972).

Stolberg, A., & Walsh, P. (1989). Parental and environmental determinants of children's behavioral, affective and cognitive adjustment to divorce. *Journal of Divorce and Remarriage*, *12*, 265–282.

Strong, J. (1995). *Evidence law: Cases and materials*, 5th ed. St Paul, MN: West.

Tschann, J., Kline, M., & Wallerstein, J. (1990). Conflict, loss, change and parent–child relationships: Predicting children's adjustment during divorce. *Journal of Divorce*, *13*, 1–22.

Uniform Marriage and Divorce Act. (1975). 402 9A UCA, 197–198.

Wall, J. (1994). An integrated approach to child custody. *Journal of Divorce and Remarriage*, *21*, 39–57.

Wallerstein, J., & Kelly, J. (1980). *Surviving the break-up: How children and parents cope with divorce*. New York: Basic Books.

Weinberg v. Wiesenfeld, 420 U.S. 636 (1975).

Weitzman, L. (1985). *The divorce revolution: The unexpected social and economic consequences for women and children in America*. New York: Free Press.

Zaslow, M. (1988). Sex differences in children's response to parental divorce: Research methodology and postdivorce family norms. *American Journal of Orthopsychiatry*, *58*, 355–378.

Index

ISBN 0-306-46339-3
90000
9 780306 463396